Culture / Power / History

A READER IN CONTEMPORARY

SOCIAL THEORY

NICHOLAS B. DIRKS, GEOFF ELEY, AND
SHERRY B. ORTNER, EDITORS

PRINCETON UNIVERSITY PRESS

PRINCETON, NEW JERSEY

Library of Congress Cataloging-in-Publication Data

Culture / power / history : a reader in contemporary social theory
Nicholas B. Dirks, Geoff Eley, and Sherry B. Ortner, editors.
p. cm. — (Princeton studies in culture / power / history)
Includes bibliographical references and index.
ISBN 0-691-03220-3. — ISBN 0-691-02102-3 (pbk.)
1. Culture.   2. Power (Social sciences)   3. Social sciences.
I. Dirks, Nicholas B., 1950– .   II. Eley, Geoff, 1949–
III. Ortner, Sherry B., 1941– .   IV. Series.
HM101.C937   1993   93-1795

Publication of this book has been aided by a grant from Rackham School of Graduate Studies,
University of Michigan

This book has been composed in Adobe Times Roman

Princeton University Press books are printed on acid-free paper and meet the guidelines for
permanence and durability of the Committee on Production Guidelines for Book
Longevity of the Council on Library Resources

Printed in the United States of America

1   3   5   7   9   10   8   6   4   2

(Pbk.)
1   3   5   7   9   10   8   6   4   2

• CONTENTS •

THIS ANTHOLOGY was originally conceived to announce and introduce our book series, *Culture / Power / History*. In the meantime, the series itself has been launched, and in the intervening three years much has happened to clarify our understanding of what we are trying to achieve. With that element of exploratory clarification in mind, we would like this volume to serve as a kind of provisional manifesto. We believe that it possesses an evident interest on its own terms, both as a coherent whole and in the excellence of its individual parts. But it also has a purpose in relation to the series, and on those terms, it should be seen as a self-conscious declaration of intent, a carefully assembled presentation of the kind of work we would like the series to contain.

By our own formal affiliations, we are historians and anthropologists. But in practice our interests have become much more eclectic, and the intellectual context for this volume is a much richer transdisciplinary conversation—which includes feminist theory, a variety of sociologies, literary studies, and the un-disciplined range of contemporary analysis that goes by the name of cultural studies. Here, our project would probably not be thinkable without a particular institutional setting at the University of Michigan, namely the Program for the Comparative Study of Social Transformations (CSST), which originally allowed the three of us to come together. Without being an official mouthpiece of CSST, the idea for the series and the conception of this reader could not have cohered without the broader cross-disciplinary collaboration that has occurred through the seminars, conferences, and working groups of CSST.

In common with similar initiatives elsewhere, CSST has described a new and distinctive intellectual space, which is not so much "interdisciplinary" in the established meanings of university-based cross-departmental negotiation, as adisciplinary, in the sense that the preserving of secure disciplinary foundations has receded further and further behind the exploring of common problems, and the ground of current innovation—as, for example, in work on race and gender or, in a different sense, on film and other popular media—lies across and beyond the established boundaries of disciplinary discussion. We see ourselves as contributing to an emerging politics of knowledge in this respect, in a time of exciting and contentious intellectual flux. We would like to be seen as both the beneficiaries and the culprits of that flux. In one sense, this is a continuation of the agendas opened by the late 1960s. But in another it reconstitutes the latter in an environment that has become profoundly changed. We would like our anthology to open a window onto one part of this process, to show how the transcending of the disciplines—a kind of creative disobedience—is taking place.

We should stress that this particular selection of writings represents only one possible cut through the relevant intellectual history of the present. As a selection, it crystallizes from our own particular configuration of interests, and reflects our respective temporal and national formations, in ways—culturally, intellectually, politically—that the Introduction should make clear. We have paid no attention to disciplinary "balance," and in fact most of the readings are unrepentantly indifferent to disciplinary identities of the traditional kind. We have tried to avoid an overly "classical" appearance, of either authors or readings—with several exceptions—preferring to indicate such deeper intellectual histories in the Introduction. There are large areas of contemporary theory—from political economy, class formation, and the state to critical theory, psychoanalysis, and the larger domain of literary studies—that go relatively unrepresented. But this implies no hostility on our part, and no single volume can hope to cover all the ground, even of the ideas and work the three of us find most exciting. Sherpas, German radical nationalists, and little Indian kingdoms are also (mainly) unrepresented.

Having said that, we certainly have our own agenda. Each of the essays and selections reprinted here has been included for a very deliberate purpose. This is not a completely idiosyncratic assemblage of "interesting" pieces in some whimsical sense. The volume is organized by a set of definite and strongly held commitments—to the indivisibility of knowledge, in the sense of the complex and subtle interconnectedness of matters that intellectual and political conservatives would sooner keep apart; to historical contingency, cultural specificity, and the changeability of things; to the constructedness of the world and its categories; to feminism and its challenges to the given ways of knowing; to theory; to the transgression of disciplinary boundaries; to the critique of all reductionisms; and to the axiom that a better understanding of the world is indispensable to the chances of changing it. Running through the volume as a whole are two recurring motifs: showing the pervasiveness of the inequalities of the power relations through which the world is ordered; and thinking about how the order can be upset.

Thus this collection has no claims to being "comprehensive," for there is no "ground" to be covered in the usual sense, no clearly delimited field to survey. The book brings together some influences and exemplifications, drawn mainly from the haphazardly accumulating literatures of cultural studies, generously extended toward a range of further influences from social history, social theory, and cultural anthropology. It is meant to suggest some good ways of asking the questions. We hope it will be a good book with which to think.

We first sat down to plan the volume in the spring of 1989, when we first pooled our individual proposals for inclusion (in effect, our personal "top tens"), and then discussed intensively the range of purposes that different selections could be expected to perform. We began with some working notion of what bases needed to be touched, and added further texts as important spaces gradually became defined. The particular contents changed markedly during this lengthy process of clarification. We began from very different starting points, in disciplinary, theoretical, and area terms, it is fair to say, and the experience of working together, through all the drafting, discussion, and redrafting, has been immensely pleasurable and rewarding.

To describe accurately our range of indebtedness, innumerable people would have to be acknowledged. Most recently, careful readings by John Bowen and Tom Laqueur were extremely helpful in bringing the process to closure. Lorna Altstetter has been wonderful in helping us organize the editorial mechanics.

We are also grateful to the Rackham School of Graduate Studies at the University of Michigan for financial help toward offsetting the prohibitive costs of permission fees. Finally, we wish to express our great appreciation to Mary Murrell of Princeton University Press for her faith in this book and the series, for ongoing support and assistance of all kinds, and for her fine critical eye and ear. More generally, we need to acknowledge two enormous debts, where mentioning individual names would be invidious. One would be to successive cohorts of graduate students from all around the disciplinary map in the annual CSST course on "Culture, Practice, and Social Change," as well as to our immediate students in history and anthropology. The other would be to our colleagues in the CSST Faculty Seminar, who have provided a rare and precious context for intellectual exchange and discovery.

Linda Alcoff, "Cultural Feminism versus Post-Structuralism: The Identity Crisis in
Feminist Theory." Reprinted from *Signs: Journal of Women in Culture and Society*
13, no. 3 (1988): 405–36, by permission of the University of Chicago Press.

Sally Alexander, "Women, Class and Sexual Differences in the 1830s and 1840s:
Some Reflections on the Writing of a Feminist History." Reprinted from *History
Workshop* 17 (1983): 125–49, by permission of Oxford University Press.

Tony Bennett, "The Exhibitionary Complex." Reprinted from *New Formations* 4
(1988): 73-102, by permission of the author.

Pierre Bourdieu, "Structures, Habitus, Power: Basis for a Theory of Symbolic Power."
Reprinted from Bourdieu, *Outline of a Theory of Practice* (Cambridge: Cambridge
University Press, 1977), 159–97, with the permission of Cambridge University
Press.

Nicholas B. Dirks, "Ritual and Resistance: Subversion as a Social Fact." Reprinted,
with changes, from Douglas Haynes and Gyan Prakash, eds., *Contesting Power:
Resistance and Everyday Social Relations in South Asia* (New York: Oxford University Press, 1992), with permission of the University of California Press.

Geoff Eley, "Nations, Publics, and Political Cultures: Placing Habermas in the Nine-
teenth Century." Reprinted from Craig Calhoun, ed., *Habermas and the Public
Sphere* (Cambridge, Mass.: MIT Press, 1992), by permission of the author and the
MIT Press.

Michel Foucault, "Two Lectures." Reprinted from *Power/Knowledge* by Michel Foucault, copyright 1972, 1975, 1976, 1980 by Michel Foucault. Reprinted by permission of Pantheon Books, a division of Random House, Inc.

Henry Louis Gates, Jr., "Authority, (White) Power and the (Black) Critic; It's All
Greek to Me." Reprinted from *Cultural Critique*, no. 7 (Fall 1987): 19–46. Copy
right 1987 *Cultural Critique*, Oxford University Press. Used with permission.

Stephen Greenblatt, "The Circulation of Social Energy." Chapter 1 of *Shakespearean
Negotiations: The Circulation of Social Energy in Renaissance England* (Berkeley,
Calif.: University of California Press, 1988), 1–20. Reprinted, with changes, by permission of the Regents of the University of California and the University of California Press.

Ranajit Guha, "The Prose of Counter-Insurgency." Reprinted, with changes, from
Guha, ed., *Subaltern Studies II* (New Delhi: Oxford University Press, 1983), 1–42,
by permission of Oxford University Press.

Stuart Hall, "Cultural Studies: Two Paradigms." Reprinted from *Media, Culture, and
Society*, vol. 2 (Newbury Park, Calif.: Sage Publications, 1980), 57–82, by permission of Sage Publications, Inc.

Donna Haraway, "Teddy Bear Patriarchy: Taxidermy in the Garden of Eden, New
York City, 1908–1936." Reprinted from *Social Text*, 1983, 20–64, by permission of
the author and *Social Text*.

Susan Harding, "The Born-Again Telescandals." Reprinted, with changes, from "The
World of the Born-Again Telescandals," *Michigan Quarterly Review* 27, no. 4
(1988): 525–40, by permission of the University of Michigan and the author.

Dick Hebdige, "After the Masses." Reprinted from S. Hall and M. Jacques, eds., *New
Times: The Changing Face of Politics in the 1990's* (London and New York: Verso/

New Left Books, 1991), 76–93, by permission of the author and Verso/New Left Books.

Susan McClary, "Living to Tell: Madonna's Resurrection of the Fleshly." Reprinted from *Genders*, no. 7 (1990): 1–21, by permission of the author and the University of Texas Press.

Sherry B. Ortner, "Theory in Anthropology since the Sixties." Reprinted from *Comparative Studies in Society and History* 26, no. 1 (1984): 126–66, with the permission of Cambridge University Press.

Marshall Sahlins, "Cosmologies of Capitalism: The Trans-Pacific Sector of 'The World System.'" Reprinted by permission of the author.

Elizabeth G. Traube, "Secrets of Success in Postmodern Society." Reproduced by permission of the American Anthropological Association from *Cultural Anthropology* 4 (August 1989): 3. Not for further reproduction.

Raymond Williams, selections from *Marxism and Literature*, copyright Oxford University Press 1977. Reprinted from *Marxism and Literature* by Raymond Williams (1977) by permission of Oxford University Press.

Judith Williamson, "Family, Education, Photography." Reprinted from Judith Williamson, *Consuming Passions: The Dynamic of Popular Culture* (London and New York: Marion Boyars Publishers, 1986), 115–26, by permission of Marion Boyars Publishers.

Culture / Power / History

NICHOLAS B. DIRKS, GEOFF ELEY, AND SHERRY B. ORTNER

THIS READER is part of a more general effort to explore the varieties of relations among the phenomena of "culture," "power," and "history." Perhaps the best way to explain our objectives is to elaborate on the current thinking concerning these three terms and the contexts of their interpenetration.

Culture. The notion of culture has recently been undergoing some of the most radical rethinking since the early 1960s. Within anthropology, where culture was in effect the key symbol of the field, the concept has come under challenge precisely because of new understandings regarding power and history. Thus, for example, one of the core dimensions of the concept of culture has been the notion that culture is "shared" by all members of a given society. But as anthropologists have begun to study more complex societies, in which divisions of class, race, and ethnicity are fundamentally constitutive, it has become clear that if we speak of culture as shared, we must now always ask "By whom?" and "In what ways?" and "Under what conditions?"

This shift has been manifested in several very visible ways. At the level of theory, the concept of culture is being expanded by Foucauldian notions of discourse, and Gramscian notions of hegemony (on the latter point, the works of Raymond Williams have been particularly influential). Both concepts emphasize the degree to which culture is grounded in unequal relations and is differentially related to people and groups in different social positions. Connected to this point, at the level of empirical work, there has been an explosion of studies, both contemporary and historical, on the cultural worlds of different classes, ethnic groups, racial groups, and so on and the ways in which these cultural worlds interact.

Another core aspect of the concept of culture has been the notion of culture's extraordinary durability. The cultures of "traditional societies" were thought to have changed extraordinarily slowly, if at all. The virtual absence of historical investigation in anthropology, until recently, has meant that cultural systems have, indeed, appeared timeless, at least until ruptured by "culture contact." But as anthropologists have begun to adopt, at least partially, a historical perspective, the durability of culture has dissolved. In many cases, timeless traditions turn out to have been "invented," and not very long ago at that (see Hobsbawm and Ranger 1983). In other cases, long-term cultural configurations have, indeed, been very stable (e.g., Bloch 1986; Geertz 1980; Ortner 1989), but we now realize that this is a peculiar state of affairs, requiring very sharp questioning and investigation.

Finally, a central aspect of the concept of culture has been the claim of relative coherence and internal consistency—a "system of symbols," a "structure of relations." But an intriguing line of discussion in contemporary critical theory has now posed a major alternative view: culture as multiple discourses, occasionally coming together in large systemic configuration, but more often coexisting within dynamic fields of interaction and conflict.

Perhaps the main point about the current situation is that the anthropologists no longer "own" culture. At least some of the critique and transformation of the culture concept derives from its use in creative, and not simply derivative, ways in other fields—in history, philosophy, sociology, and literary criticism, to name only the most obvious cases. The field of "cultural studies," which established itself with astonishing effectiveness in the last decade, draws on literary criticism, social history, sociology, and anthropology to fashion what has become a distinct perspective on the culture of power, the culture of resistance, and the politics of cultural production and manipulation. (See Johnson 1987; Brantlinger 1990; Grossberg, Nelson, and Treichler 1992.) Which brings us to the second term for discussion:

Power. Just as the concept of culture is undergoing fragmentation, expansion, and reconstruction, so are issues of power, domination, and authority. And here, too, the questioning extends across a wide variety of fields.

One of the lasting goods of the intellectual radicalism of the 1960s—which was also the founding moment of contemporary social history—has been an expanded and more sophisticated understanding of the role and nature of "the political" in social life. This involves a radically deinstitutionalized understanding of the political process, in which questions of conformity and opposition, of the potentials for stability and cohesion in the social order, and of the strength or fragility of the dominant value system, are all displaced from the conventional institutional arena for studying them (that is, the state and public organizations in the narrower sense) onto a variety of settings previously regarded as "nonpolitical," including the workplace, the street, the deviant or criminal subculture, the recreational domain, and, above all, the family and the home. If "the personal is political" (the specifically feminist contribution to this shift of understanding), then so, too, is the wider sphere of everyday transactions.

Thus if one direction of social history, perhaps the predominant one, has been to depoliticize the social into a discrete and manageable object for study, another has been to invest it precisely with political meanings. Politics was inscribed in the texture of the everyday. The effects of these shifts on the concept of power have been multiple.

There is first of all the sense that all the relations of everyday life bear a certain stamp of power. As Foucault in particular has made us see (see esp. Foucault 1978, 1980), people acting as men and women, parents and children, teachers and students, doctors and patients, priests and penitents, can no longer be regarded simply as performing functionally defined "roles." Rather, these terms define relations in which the parties, whatever else they may do, are constantly negotiating questions of power, authority, and the control of the definitions of reality.

Second, there is the sense that everyday life and culture, in which people implicitly "conform to" or "accept" their situation, should not always be contrasted with dramatic "social movements," in which people question and challenge the status quo. Instead, while organized social movements remain enormously important in understanding large-scale transformations, much can be learned by attending to "everyday forms of resistance" as well (see Scott 1985, 1990; Lüdtke 1993).

But this, in turn, opens the question of the relationship between popular culture—in which people strive to define their identities, their boundaries, their self-respect, their "space" against the established order—and more well-defined social movements that claim to represent "the people." Such movements often themselves become removed from everyday experience, their members coming to see popular behavior as something to be educated, improved, disciplined. At the same time, the people on whose behalf such movements claim to speak often find the language and the mechanics of these movements remote and alienating. The complex and problematic relations between social movements and disorderly popular culture, involving distinctions of class and gender, ethnicity and race, roughness and respectability, are becoming central to the contemporary problematic.

Finally, the move in social history away from state politics, and toward a focus on the "small people," has often gone too far by dropping the state out of the picture. The redefinition of politics in another domain of discussion has also applied to concepts of the state; this, too, needs to be recaptured. At present much creative effort is needed to synthesize an understanding of local movements and class culture, on the one hand, and large-scale state dynamics, on the other.

Thus "power" is moving around the social space. No longer an exclusive property of "repressive apparatuses," it has invaded our sense of the smallest and most intimate of human relations as well as of the largest; it belongs to the weak as well as to the strong; and it is constituted precisely within the relations between official and unofficial agents of social control and cultural production. At the same time, there is a major recognition of the degree to which power itself is a cultural construct. The modes of expression of physical force and violence are culturally shaped, while force and violence in turn become cultural symbols, as powerful in their nonexecution as in their doing. And, of course, force in turn is only a tiny part of power, so that much of the problematic of power today is a problematic of knowledge making, universe construction, and the social production of feeling and of "reality."

History. One of the most obvious changes in the field of anthropology in recent years is the extent to which the field has been moving in a historical direction. Only slightly less obviously, history has become increasingly anthropological. On both sides, some extremely interesting and important work has come out of these shifts, yet we may now recognize that the love affair between the two fields has been relatively uncritical. On the side of anthropology, the category of "history" was for a long time captured by the so-called political economy school (see Ortner, this volume). On the history side, there was a sense that being anthropological meant studying the more "symbolic" bits of life—rituals, festivals, folklore—or alternatively simply doing "the ethnography of the past." On neither side was there a really serious assault on the question of whether history itself was inherently cultural, and culture, inherently historical.

We have already indicated the ways in which the concept of culture is being historicized. The recognition of the "invented" nature of many traditions, the recognition of cultural constancy and durability as a problem rather than a natural state of affairs, the centrality of the notion of the "constructed" nature of culture in general—all of these points are elements of a growing recognition that a historical anthropology is not just a narrativized anthropology, not just a matter of giving the present some sort of ancestral pedigree. Rather, there is a kind of dislodging of a whole series of assumptions about what culture is and how it works.

But if culture is being historicized, history is being—there is really no verb here—anthropologized? culturized? in much more profound ways than in earlier efforts. For one thing, there is a developing view that history itself has variable cultural form—that the shape of events, the pace of time, the notion of change and duration, the very question of what an event is—all of these things are not simply objective realities, but are themselves products of cultural assumptions. Moreover, there is a growing tendency to move culture out of the realm of the exotic custom, the festival, the ritual, and the like and into the center of the historical problematic, or, rather, to recognize that the rituals and festivals are sites in which larger and more dynamic fields of discourse, larger and more powerful hegemonies, are being constituted, contested, and transformed.

But here the point links up with issues of power. For the point is not simply that some generic form of historian is getting interested in culture, and some generic form of anthropologist is getting interested in history, although that is certainly true to some extent. Rather there is a very specific convergence here, and "power," in the broad range of senses discussed earlier, is the point on which that convergence is taking place. Culture as emergent from relations of power and domination, culture as a form of power and domination, culture as a medium in which power is both constituted and resisted: it is around this set of issues that certain anthropologists and certain historians (as well as fellow travelers in sociology, philosophy, literary criticism, and other fields) are beginning to work out an exciting body of thought.

MORE POWER

If two of the three key terms in our series refer as much to disciplinary cores—history and anthropology—as to a constellation of theoretical preoccupations, the third term, "power," is both more specific and more pervasive. And if our understanding of power derives from no single theoretical position, it is nevertheless linked in important ways with the writings and influence of Michel Foucault (1977a, 1977b, 1978, 1980, 1988). With all of our inevitable caveats and idiosyncratic readings, we still acknowledge the importance of Foucault's insistent and penetrating scrutiny of the field of power relations, especially in "modern" historical contexts. Two selections from Foucault appear in this volume, and it will be well to describe at the outset what we understand as Foucault's distinctive contribution.

Power is neither some universal "drive" lodged in individuals nor some elementary force transcending society and history. If historical actors sometimes embody what appears to be a Nietzschean will to power, it is equally true that any historical actor will also embody a wide range of other feelings and desires, including desires precisely antithetical to power—for love, for tenderness, for communion—although nowadays such terms can hardly be spoken with innocence, but on the contrary are also always partially implicated in power themselves. Insofar as the social world is ordered as an endlessly shifting field of inequalities, even these desires can only form themselves against a backdrop, and within the interstices, of this field, and necessarily bear its stamp. By extension, no examination of social relations or historical processes can be engaged without a relentless suspicion about power's displacements and effects.

Although Foucault is typically labeled a poststructuralist (a term that usually conceals more than it suggests), we follow Peter Dews's genealogy in placing him in the second, more "political," wave of poststructuralism, in which "attention begins to shift from language as all-embracing medium to the determinations which bear upon language; discourse starts to be seen as patterned and disrupted by non-discursive forces"(Dews 1988, 110). Dews argues that this shift was related to the events of May 1968 and entailed a recognition that "[w]hat sustains or rebels against a given social structure cannot be simply an effect of that structure itself. Social systems are both imposed by force from above—they embody relations of *power*—and are adhered to or rejected from below—they are invested or disinvested with *desire*"(Dews 1988, 110–11).

Foucault, then, takes power in all its various guises as his chief concern, but he upends the usual procedures for studying it. Whereas many would assume that power is only another term for the political, and more specifically that power is exercised chiefly by the state, Foucault seems to look everywhere else but the state. Whereas power is usually seen in opposition to freedom, particularly when opposed to its legitimated complementary term, authority, Foucault views freedom as a necessary precondition for modern forms of power. Freedom cannot abolish power; rather, it redefines power's terrain. Whereas resistance is normally seen as opposed to power, power here depends upon the possibility of resistance, and power is a field of relations from which even the purest of revolutionary struggles cannot be exempt.

However, as Foucault's own writing makes clear, the usual objections to his work—that it suggests an unbearably totalizing sense of power and affords no hope for oppositional politics—do not usually take into account the strategic character of his analysis. Indeed, Foucault's reading of power, and of discourses more generally, is always strategic, tactical, polemical, situated. Thus Foucault has examined hospitals, prisons, asylums, the truth regimes of philology and humanism, the discourses of sexuality, and what he calls "government" in a broad sense: "the government of children, of souls, of communities, of families, of the sick" (1982, 221). In subjecting to his critical scrutiny the institutions of the modern era otherwise regarded as rational and liberating, Foucault has both perfected his analytic of power and demonstrated its historicity: the success of modern forms of domination has resided in the dispersal of power from the state to a wide variety of agencies with "reasonable" claims to autonomy. This is not to say that Foucault ignores the state, only perhaps that he appreciates how misleading its obviousness can be. Indeed, Foucault reads the sinuous and subtle operations of power back into the state, which since the eighteenth century has attained an unprecedented capacity, "both an individualizing and a totalizing form of power" (1982, 213).

The triumph of modern power, however, provides us with only a partial sense of the problems of understanding its workings and is never to be construed as sufficient reason for total despair. Power exists for Foucault not as some essential thing or elementary force, but, rather, as a relation. If power is therefore everywhere, this is "not because it embraces everything, but because it comes from everywhere" (Foucault 1978, 93). Foucault continues, "[W]here there is power, there is resistance." But even as his discussion of the necessary relation of power to resistance makes clear the immanent cracks in all forms of discursive domination, we also discover that resistance itself cannot be placed outside of power, that there is "no single locus of great Refusal, no soul of revolt, source of all rebellions, or pure law of the revolutionary" (ibid, 95), no place in which the spirit of resistance may be kept wholly pure and safe. Instead, Foucault sees a plurality of resistances, which play the multiple roles of "adversary, target, support, or handle in power relations" (ibid.).

Foucault's complex understanding of power therefore invites analyses of the multiple ways in which power is deployed, engaging the myriad "points of resistance present everywhere in the power network" (ibid.). For Foucault, power is not simply juridical. Rather than exercising the negative function of limitation or repression, of just saying no, power is productive and inciting. Power cannot somehow be stripped away from social relations or discursive forms to expose the essence at the core, and the utopian prospect of eliding the relations of power in the politics of resistance can only be illusory. But far from thereby neutralizing the importance of power, Foucault instead demonstrates the complexity of its ubiquity, and compels us to assert that without it, neither history nor culture can be understood.

For the purposes of this reader, we echo Foucault's advocacy of a "new economy of power relations" (1982, 210) and see it as leading in a number of different, contestatory directions. For example, Foucault's writings on how this economy works in asylums, clinics, and prisons are taken up explicitly in Tony Bennett's paper, "The Exhibitionary Complex" (this volume), this time in terms of the institutional history of museums and exhibitions. Although Bennett begins his article with explicit acknowledgement of Foucault's method, he also seeks to qualify the terms Foucault proposes for investigating the development of power/knowledge relations during the formation of the modern period. Whereas Foucault's classic institutional mechanisms of subjection involve confinement, Bennett's examples are of exhibition, display, and spectacle. Surely the carceral system is only one aspect of the individualizing and normalizing technologies of power. Museums and exhibitions, Bennett argues, "sought to allow the people, and *en masse* rather than individually, to know rather than be known, to become the subjects rather than the objects of knowledge" to be impressed by the capacity of the state to arrange things and bodies, not least society itself, for public display.

Foucault argued in *Discipline and Punish* (1977a) that the modern prison was part of the development of a society based not on spectacle but on surveillance. The panopticon was seen from the outside simply as a sign of disciplinary power, but on the inside was a labyrinth for the disciplinary gaze, where subjects are always seen by invisible but all-invasive eyes. The great exhibitions of the nineteenth century, on the other hand, were designed so that everyone could see. One of the major objects that could be seen, of course, was society itself, an abstraction made material, an object less of discipline than of regulation. Bourgeois national culture was both celebrated and constituted by the civic instruction involved in assembling large crowds for peaceful and uplifting purposes. The rowdiness of the public fair and carnival gave way to the moral and cultural regulation of the museum.

It is interesting to compare this approach to nineteenth-century bourgeois culture with existing historical literatures, most of which have yet to register the impact of Foucauldian perspectives and are generally formed around sets of particularized national-historiographical preoccupations. In British social history, for instance, one such focus has been on religion, philanthropy, moral improvement, and the bases of associational life; in Germany attention has focused on the supposed difficulties of grounding liberal ideals of citizenship in the emergent structures of bourgeois economic power. In the massive outpouring of publications revisiting the social and cultural history of the nineteenth-century German bourgeoisie since the mid-1980s, there is no evidence of the possibilities suggested by Bennett's appropriation of Foucault or the more general literature on museums and exhibitions on which he draws (see Kocka and Mitchell 1992; Blackbourn 1991; on Britain, see Wolff and Seed [1988]). A different, but cognate, line of enquiry also stems from Jürgen Habermas's concept of the public sphere, although the persisting nervousness of Habermas before the kind of cultural analysis represented in this reader tends to position such inquiry in a somewhat different intellectual space, as, indeed, does the more vehement resistance of Habermas to a Foucauldian notion of power (see Habermas [1962] 1989; Calhoun 1992; Eley, this volume; for an extremely stimulating exploration of possible connections, see Scobey [1992]).

In the exhibitionary complex, the state not only displayed its superior power, it also linked its national past to the evolutionary chain. Anthropology and prehistory were given entertainment value, and civilizational genealogies were carefully constructed, with the self-congratulatory rhetoric of progress as the principal narrative conceit. The Eiffel Tower, built for the 1889 Paris Exhibition, was both a highly visible triumph of French technology and a means by which all of Paris was converted to spectacle. Nevertheless, Bennett (this volume) reminds us that state and society did not live by exhibition alone; the doors of the Museum stay open only because the doors of the prison are closed: "Where instruction and rhetoric failed, punishment began."

Another exemplary piece on a similar subject, Donna Haraway's paper, "Teddy Bear Patriarchy" (this volume), demonstrates what we can learn from the process of collecting and displaying the objects of "nature" in one particular exhibitionary complex, the American Museum of Natural History. Haraway shows how the hyperreal myths of the natural were appropriated by, and ordered for, a decidedly gendered bourgeois cultural form; focusing on the life/lives of the heroic taxidermist Carl Akeley, she tells "a tale of the commerce of power/knowledge in white and male supremist monopoly capitalism." Haraway follows Akeley from his first triumph, when he successfully stuffed P. T. Barnum's dead elephant, to his final apotheosis in an African jungle, where he died from tropical fever during the last of a series of brave adventures to rescue life from death and champion the causes of conservation and nature education. Along the way, Akeley gunned down myriad gorillas and elephants to present nature in the New York museum in dioramic scenes that would convey it in its truthful essence. Through taxidermy, which was art in the service of science, he conjured perfect images of natural power and beauty, noble beasts frozen forever in that moment they recognized the presence of the dangerous Other: humanity. As with Bennett's exhibitionary complex, the stress is on order, perfection, mastery, permanence. But here the violence of the museum is both celebrated and denied, the death of the displayed objects both a sign of general decadence and the transformative means for the conquest of death. Haraway tells us how the texts of the dioramas, like the texts that narrate the lives of Akeley and his wives, patrons, and African assistants, were always multivocal, always subtexts for other texts, which bring out the distortions, lies, and conceits of a dominant but frightened upper-class male world. These themes were part of the psychology of turn-of-the-century U.S. capitalism, and they became entwined in the development of eugenics, the movement "to preserve hereditary stock, to assure racial purity, to prevent race suicide."

Although Haraway's emphasis on the relations between power and knowledge, and her reading of the displacements and dispersals of the institutional complex of the museum, display a range of Foucauldian insights, she is also fascinated with the multiplication of historical narratives within institutional histories in ways that move us some distance from any Foucauldian text, though in a slightly different direction from the one urged by Bennett. Haraway employs a feminist perspective to demonstrate the gendered nature of power in ways that remind us of the general challenge of feminist theory to conventional social analysis. She rescues some of the hidden voices in her story—the secretary, Dorothy Greene, who was the actual author of Akeley's texts, the first wife, Delia, whose prowess in hunting, and in nursing her often weakened husband, is buried in archives and countertexts, the African assistant, Bill, whose provisional individuality was always constructed against the silence of his coded service and loyalty. Power never totally suppresses resistance, nor ever fully destroys the multiple subjects who resist.

Bennett extends the provenance of Foucault's text, convincing us that the process of individuation (the production of the subject) is necessarily coupled with the constitution of society (the object), that the institutional mechanisms of confinement are complemented by those of exhibition. But Bennett does not fully engage the difficulties that Haraways's account permits us to see. We might now ask about the costs of linking the constitution of the subject with the subjection of the individual. What happens when questions of agency, and of the individual's relation to power, the state, or society are asked in relation to a Foucauldian enterprise? In order to get some perspective on this question, it will be useful to step back and situate Foucault historically, among a broad range of responses to midcentury social theory.

THE SUBJECT OF PRACTICE

Although at one level Foucault has given us a crucial point of leverage out of midcentury social theory, tranforming both "culture" and "history" with a radically novel and pervasive sense of power, at another level his work requires a certain historical perspective itself. Here, Foucault's ("poststructuralist") influence must be set beside at least one other major strand of social and cultural theorizing which, rather than stressing the determination of power through history, places human agency and social practice at the very center of the problematic. Theories emphasizing practice can be traced to a number of sources (Marx, of course, but also Weber, Gramsci, and Sartre), most of which predate structuralism and continue alongside of and beyond it, insistently raising the problem of the historical actor.

As discussed in Sherry Ortner's paper, "Theory in Anthropology since the Sixties" (this volume), the 1950s and 1960s saw the near-total hegemony of social theories in which the analytic emphasis was on the ordering of the forms—institutional, ideational, psychological—within which social actors are situated (the image of enclosure and the passive voice here are both intentional). Parsonian systems theory in the United States and Lévi-Straussian structuralism in France defined the boundaries of this theoretical territory. Although Parsons claimed that the point of understanding "systems" was ultimately to understand the bases of "social action," somehow the examination of any actual instances of social action was never quite reached, being endlessly deferred as the theory of systems was refined. Lévi-Strauss on the other hand had no interest in even nodding to the actor. As the debates with Sartre made clear, the whole point of his framework was quite intentionally to get away from a philosophical tradition in which the actor (or consciousness, or will, or intention, or subject) had been endowed with far too much ontological and historical force and freedom (Lévi-Strauss 1966).

Most poststructuralists in France, including Foucault, sustained and indeed expanded the structuralist bias against theorizing the subject, particularly in the form of an agent with will and intentionality. While dropping certain aspects of Lévi-Strauss's hyperrationality, they did not drop this core tenet of the structuralist agenda, and thus should be considered late- or ultra-structuralist, rather than post- , as more or less any French thinker who became popular after Lévi-Strauss tends to be. Insofar as a subject was recognized or postulated within this framework at all, it was a radically decentered subject, often drawing from the psychoanalytic theories of Lacan. The subject had no internal coherence, and was granted neither the originary grounds of autonomous existence nor the epistemic means for self-knowledge; instead, the subject was seen as dispersed in (multiple) texts, discursive formations, fragmentary readings, and signifying practices, endless constructing and dislodging the conceit of the self.

The papers in the present collection have been selected in part to constitute a response to this position. They do so in two rather different ways. On the one hand, there is general agreement that the bourgeois agent and psyche are not the eternal subject; on the other hand, there is a clear refusal to argue that the acting subject has no ontological reality whatsoever. Thus we try to highlight efforts to understand the ways in which the subject is culturally and historically constructed in different times and places, as a being with a particular kind of affective organization, particular kinds of knowing and understanding, particular modes of gender and sexual ordering, and so forth. At the same time we seek to highlight efforts to understand the ways in which culturally and historically constituted subjects become agents in the active sense—how their actions and modes of being in the world always sustain and sometimes transform the very structures that made them.

Constituting the Subject

We must begin by confronting the ambiguity in almost all the available terms for the actor, that is, we must confront the fact that all these terms have both an active and a passive implication. Both the notion of the agent and the notion of the subject imply a person who is an active initiator of action. According to *The Concise Oxford Dictionary*, all of the primary meanings of "agent" are highly active: "One who exerts power or produces an effect; [of things] efficient cause; a natural force acting on matter . . . ; one who does the actual work." The active implications of "subject" are less prominent, but are thrown into relief when the term is contrasted with "object." In these contexts, both agents and subjects are "authors" of their actions and their projects. But "agent," of course, also means "representative"; travel agents or shipping agents act on behalf of their clients, not on their own initiative. Similarly, as Foucault in particular has emphasized, one of the meanings of "subject" is precisely a person under the dominion of an authority of some sort; a king's subjects are in a relationship of obedience to him, and laboratory subjects may do only what they are told to do by the researcher. And there are further terms, all of which carry their own nuances of activity and passivity: "person," "self," "actor," "individual," "consciousness." Given that there is no perfectly unambiguous vocabulary for the phenomenon in question, we will simply shift about between the terms undogmatically and clarify our intentions as we go.

Perhaps the most extreme position on the constitution of the subject is staked out by Foucault, who fully equates the constitution of subjects with subjection in the dominative sense. As he says at the beginning of his essay "The Subject and Power," "My objective . . . has been to create a history of the different modes by which, in our culture, human beings are made subjects . . . three modes of objectification which transform human beings into subjects"(1982, 208). He goes on to say that he is interested in exploring not so much institutions of power, but forms of power, and specifically that form of power that "categorizes the individual, marks him [sic] by his own individuality, attaches him to his own identity, imposes a law of truth on him which he must recognize and which others must recognize in him. It is a form of power which makes individuals subjects"(1982, 212).

Most of the authors in this volume do not take as uncompromising a position on the subjection of the subject as did Foucault. Nonetheless, even for authors committed to recognizing much greater scope for transformative practice, there is now a strong Foucauldian tendency to recognize that the identities culturally made available to us are often deforming and debilitating, at once constituting and limiting, providing people with a narrow sense of possibility, keeping them in their places. Through his concept of "habitus," Pierre Bourdieu develops this point extensively, arguing that the parameters of personal identity—especially of one's "place" within a system of social differences and inequalities—are structured into the objective environment (Bourdieu 1977; see esp. ch. 4, reprinted in this volume). The organization of space (in houses, in villages and cities) and time (the rhythms of work, leisure, holidays) embody the assumptions of gender, age, and social hierarchy upon which a particular way of life is built. As the actor grows up, and lives everyday life within these spatial and temporal forms, s/he comes to embody those assumptions, literally and figuratively. The effect is one of near-total naturalization of the social order, the forging of homologies between personal identity and social classification.

Bourdieu's discussion of the inculcation of doxa, of the sense that the limits of one's subjective desires are more or less isomorphic with the limits of objective possibility, is a discussion of the formation not of any particular form of subjectivity but of the limits of subjectivity itself. We will return to Bourdieu shortly, to inquire how he combines this strong sense of the constructed and limited subject with a theory of practice that professes a commitment to open-endedness and change.

Recent discussions of postmodernism, represented in this volume by Dick Hebdige's paper, "After the Masses," are important in this context for suggesting ways in which postmodern subjects are culturally and historically constructed in relation to a particular contemporary historical moment, usually described as the culture of late or postindustrial capitalism. By extension, they question certain forms of poststructuralism for celebrating and transcendentalizing this decentered and fragmented subject. As Jameson (1984) and Hebdige (this volume) argue, the death of the subject so central to poststructuralist theory is in fact merely the theoretical reflection and reification of a particular kind of subject, constructed under the regime of postmodernism. In this characterization, postmodern culture, including contemporary theory, is centrally founded on a denial of a variety of "depth models"—in persons (for example, in the notion of an inner self), in history (in the notion that the past is recoverable in some real sense), and in a variety of other contexts (for example, in buildings, which seem to consist only of external surfaces). Moreover, insofar as contemporary culture is increasingly organized in terms of surfaces, and of the interplay between surfaces (for example, in the contemporary emphasis on pastiche), it will tend to constitute subjects who are as "depthless" as postmodern society. In Jameson's terms, there is a "waning of affect" and a replacement of specific feelings with a kind of general "euphoria." The dominant form of cultural pathology shifts from "alienation" (so central in "modernist" discourse) to "fragmentation." But, again, both Jameson and Hebdige argue that the postmodern subject is not the eternal form of the ontological subject (as some poststructuralists would have it), but itself a specific historical form, constituted under the conditions of "late capitalism."

Central to such discussions is the point that a theoretical position constructed around a depthless subject with no sense of history cannot generate a coherent political actor, one who formulates a comprehensive social critique and an agenda for change. This point is also taken up by Linda Alcoff, in considering the implications of poststructuralism for feminist theory and practice in her paper, "Cultural Feminism versus Post-Structuralism" (this volume). More than perhaps anywhere else, it is in feminist theory that the problem of rescuing the subject from both poststructuralist dissolution and Foucauldian overconstructionism, has been—and is being—confronted. The attraction between feminist theory and poststructuralist theory (particularly in its early, Derridean and Lacanian forms) may have seemed strange to many observers precisely because of the dissolution of the subject, and because of the apparent impossibility of constructing an active politics within a subject-denying framework. However, the attractions of poststructuralism for British and American feminists were very similar to those for the French philosophers: they allowed an escape from the essentialized subject, in this case, from the figure of the essential woman (nurturant, relational, nonviolent, and so on), either by denying the ontological reality of the subject entirely (the early poststructuralist move) or by moving into a strong constructionist position. But once again, Alcoff points out, the problem of the acting subject immediately rears its head: "And here is precisely the dilemma for feminists: How can we ground a feminist politics that deconstructs the female subject? Nominalism [Alcoff's term for both kinds of poststructuralist move] threatens to wipe out feminism itself." Alcoff goes on to review a number of recent feminist perspectives—and to propose one of her own—that retain the benefits of poststructuralist thought and yet allow for the ways in which women have been and can continue to be the authors of their histories and politics.

Imagining Practice

In the final section of "Theory in Anthropology since the Sixties" (this volume), Sherry Ortner makes a case for the necessary centrality of social practice in understanding both the persistent structurations of culture, power, and history, and their historical transformations. Ortner traces the oscillations in anthropological theory between "objectivist" and "subjectivist," "materialist" and "idealist" perspectives. In addition, she traces the shift from a notion of practice seen as apolitical "action" and "interaction" to a notion of practice as always embedded in relations of power and inequality. Drawing on work by Sahlins (1981), Giddens (1979), and Bourdieu (1977), Ortner argues that the newer sense of practice both responds to the political naiveté of bourgeois social theory and allows for a conception of a social and historical process that holds together, rather than polarizes, structure and agency, material and cultural life: "The modern versions of practice theory . . . appear unique in accepting all three sides of the [theoretical] triangle: that society is a system, that the system is powerfully constraining, and yet that the system can be made and unmade through human action and interaction."

In reflecting on the influence of Bourdieu on this formulation, we must realize again that theory is written and produced in contexts that change dramatically when theory starts traveling, and much of the theory discussed in Ortner's essay had been on the road for a long time. When Bourdieu articulated his theory of practice, he was writing against a Lévi-Straussian structuralism that assumed certain objective mental structures in human beings, and that also assumed a methodology devoted to discovering those structures objectified in such symbolic/discursive productions as myths and rituals. Where Durkheim had argued that "mental" and symbolic representations reflected social structure, Lévi-Strauss turned Durkheim on his head. Bourdieu, in turn, was attempting to turn Durkheim back again (but with a political twist absent in both Durkheim and Lévi-Strauss), arguing that the structures to be found in cultural forms were "transformed, misrecognizable form[s] of the real divisions of the social order."

From this vantage point, Bourdieu had two principal objectives: to show how these real divisions become masked through the process of naturalization, and to chart this process as it seeped into people's heads, bodies, selves. The realization of both objectives is to be found in practice. Thus the enterprise of practice theory, in Bourdieu's hands, is largely a matter of decoding the public cultural forms within which people live their lives—the patterns and rhythms of work, eating, sleeping, leisure, sociability, patterns and rhythms that already encode the divisions, distinctions, and inequalities of the society as a whole. And the aim is to get as close as possible (both ethnographically and imaginatively) to the practical ways in which, in enacting these forms, the subject/agent comes to embody them, assume them, take them so utterly for granted that "it goes without saying because it comes without saying."

In *Marxism and Literature* (1977, excerpted in this volume) Raymond Williams works within the context of British literary studies and Marxist politics, and seems at one level to be concerned with very different kinds of issues. However, like Bourdieu, Williams is concerned with the degree to which the social and cultural process as a whole, which he interprets with his classic reading of Gramsci's theory of hegemony, shapes identities and, in his famous phrase "structures of feeling," so as to produce the naturalization of the arbitrary to which Bourdieu attends so centrally. But Williams is more directly concerned than Bourdieu with the question of resistance and social transformation, and thus attends more directly to the question of how hegemony (similar to but critically different from doxas and discourses) can be at once so powerfully defining and shaping of identities and worldviews, and at the same time limited or "open" enough that the actor is never wholly "subjected." Williams comes up with a variety of solutions, sometimes emphasizing the historical complexity of social formations, such that there are always "residual" and "emergent" arenas of practice that do not articulate fully with the current regimes of the ordinary; sometimes emphasizing the synchronic social complexity of a given social entity, such that (say) different classes will necessarily have at least partially different sets of practices and views of the world; and sometimes emphasizing the openness and inexhaustiblity of creative cultural forms, which demand interpretive flexibility and imaginativeness on the part of the actor. Recognizing the "finite but significant openness of many works of art, as signifying forms making possible but also requiring persistent and variable signifying responses" helps us see the ways in which, and the degrees to which, "the cultural process must not be assumed to be merely adaptive, extensive, and incorporative."

Calls to practice have taken diverse forms in different national contexts as well as in different disciplinary formats. Another important variant is the so-called *Alltagsgeschichte* ("everyday life") school of social history developed among German social historians. Exponents of this view, such as Hans Medick and Alf Lüdtke, examine the resources and resourcefulness of ordinary people in the conduct of their everyday lives, and find their values and experiences not easily assimilable to the conventional narratives of political history and social development (Lüdtke 1993, Eley 1989). At one level, this represents the now-familiar social historian's move, which carries analysis beneath or behind the actions of formal institutions, such as government or parties, to the structuring context of society itself. But in fact, such work is far more than this, and registers precisely the influences expounded in this introduction—above all, a turning to anthropology and a sophisticated conception of culture and power relations—so that the microcontexts of everyday analysis are less the superior realities that some populist social histories would like them to be, than the necessary ground to which the big and abstract questions of domination and subordination, power and resistance have to be chased. In other words, it is in daily experience, in the settings of ordinary desire and the trials of making it through, that the given power relations are contested or secured, in an always-incomplete process of negotiation, which is rarely unambiguously "lost" or "won."

If "power" is the term that transforms both "culture" and "history" in ways that move beyond their midcentury forms, "practice"—in the extended sense suggested here—in turn grounds both culture and power in history. In its strongest claims, practice theory is nothing less than a theory of history (thick history?), a theory "of how social beings, with their diverse motives and their diverse intentions, make and transform the world in which they live" (Ortner 1989, 193). Practice takes many forms, from the little routines of everyday life, which continually establish and naturalize the boundaries of the subject's aspirations; to the "micropractices" of relations of power and knowledge, as for example between therapist and patient, which reestablish the normalcy or deviancy and very forms of certain desires; to the practices of resistance, both daily and in large-scale social movements, which denaturalize and transform the boundaries of exploitation, oppression, and prejudice in custom and law.

Resistance

If the call to practice is an attempt at one level to repeal the normative character of social scientific assumption, it carries its own freight of problems. Practice may contest the overdeterminations of theories of power, but Bourdieu and Foucault often appear as two giants chipping away at two sides of the same theoretical coin; while Foucault uncovers the operation of power in institutional discourses and disciplinary practices, Bourdieu shows us how power inscribes its logics and scripts into the everyday lives and categories of subjects, who carry the full weight of their etymological ambivalence. It is perhaps small wonder that resistance to some of the implications of these theoretical projects, even when this resistance takes these analyses of power and practice as the point of departure, has taken the form of seeking out resistance itself.

Much of the recently intensified interest in resistance is concerned with salvaging the subject in the wake of its erosion under poststructuralism. But in the contemporary debates, both meanings of the term "subject" remain at stake. If the cultural construction of the subject is always, at least in part, a form of "subjection," then the theoretical exploration of the subject as an active agent must be concerned, at least in part, with the question of resisting or at least eluding that subjection. Again, the issues are highly complex. From a theoretical point of view we need a subject who is at once culturally and historically constructed, yet from a political perspective, we would wish this subject to be capable of acting in some sense "autonomously," not simply in conformity to dominant cultural norms and rules, or within the patterns that power inscribes. But this autonomous actor may not be defined as acting from some hidden well of innate "will" or consciousness that has somehow escaped cultural shaping and ordering. In fact, such an actor is not only possible but "normal," for the simple reason that neither "culture" itself nor the regimes of power that are imbricated in cultural logics and experiences can ever be wholly consistent or totally determining. "Identities" may be seen as (variably successful) *attempts* to create and maintain coherence out of inconsistent cultural stuff and inconsistent life experience, but every actor always carries around enough disparate and contradictory strands of knowledge and passion so as always to be in a potentially critical position. Thus the practices of everyday life may be seen as replete with petty rebellions and inchoate discontent (James Scott 1985, 1990; De Certeau 1984). Even if the subject cannot always be recuperated as a purposeful agent, neither can it any longer be seen as only the effect of subjection.

In "Authority, (White) Power and the (Black) Critic; It's All Greek to Me" (this volume), Henry Louis Gates, Jr., poses this question acutely within the domain of theory as such, a domain where battles for legitimacy, control, and "voice" have been bitterly fought in the 1980s, not just between rival theoretical schools but also between theorists and those who think theory per se is the problem. For the latter, "theory" itself is the language of power, intimidating and disabling its audience, positioning its users within privilege, and securing the status quo with its authority. Whether from the advocates of "history from below" or "people's history," some feminists, African-American and other minority militants, or anticolonial activists, "the poverty of theory" has been a recurring complaint. As a leading literary theorist and critic, centrally positioned in one of the dominant culture's leading institutions, and yet at the same time a major African-American intellectual and therefore a key voice of Black culture, Gates speaks from the heart of this contradiction.

In his discussion, Gates moves candidly back and forth between the empowering possibilities of joining the given discourse of critical theory, with its legitimating aura and access to influence—speaking the white man's language—and the presently subversive, ultimately more powerful prospect of a distinctively Black theory itself—the constructive value of the Black vernacular, "the language we use to speak to each other when no white people are around." The difficulties of embodying this claim—the difference between competing for access within an already constituted system and transforming the system itself—are familiar ones for subordinate or marginalized groups as they seek to contest the power of hegemonic formations, whether these are constituted within academic disciplines, particular institutional fields, or at the level of whole societies. But Gates formulates this constructive aspiration of resistance—its transformative and counterhegemonic opportunities as well as its negating and more purely self-protective functions—with characteristic acuity and eloquence.

The general discussion around the trope of resistance is further motivated by a reaction against totalizing formulations about power and domination. Concern about resistance seems both a way to find the cracks and fissures in the terrible proliferation of power itself (whether as repressive or terroristic domination or in the less discernible guises of late industrial technocratic capitalism) and to contest the hold that power has over us. Many recent theoretical discussions have assumed that we have a choice to make here, either for power or for resistance, a choice that is simultaneously theoretical and political. We prefer to emphasize that both Foucault, at least in his later writings, and Gramsci, certainly as interpreted by Williams, have contended that power and resistance go together, producing and reproducing each other. But once again, the demise of the standard antinomies of Western social theory leaves us groping for new formulations and different ways to think.

By now, there is a significant body of work in social history and anthropology, and to a lesser extent in sociology and political science, which explores, often movingly and with great imagination, the resilience and vitality of popular culture in the face of exploitation and repression, of crushing inequalities of access to resources and cultural goods, or simply of the snobbery and elitist disdain of their "betters" for what ordinary people are capable of achieving (Thompson 1963; Genovese 1974; Scott 1976, 1985; Willis 1977). There is now much greater sensitivity to the wide range of cultural forms and strategies through which even the most heavily dominated groups—slaves, serfs, impoverished first-generation workers, and so on—both maintain a distinct identity and express resistance, even under threat of retribution. Such cultural forms are what James Scott has called the "weapons of the weak," involving everything from exaggerated deference to petty resistance, contests that are hidden or displaced into popular cultural forms, such as folktales and festivals, in which traditions of opposition and alternative visions of the world are kept alive (Stallybrass and White 1986). There is resistance, in other words, in places we would not expect and in forms we would not recognize.

Ranajit Guha, in his paper, "The Prose of Counter-Insurgency" (this volume), has written about those instances where colonial power exercised itself in part through its capacity to silence the historical record of the subaltern classes, representing spectacular forms of popular resistance as pathologies, problems of order, and/or symptoms of religious fanaticism or cultural anomie. In this essay, Guha reads against the grain of colonial discourse to recode (semiotically and politically) the Santal insurrection of 1855; he argues that the Santals used the resources of their own cultural religiosity to engage in a decidedly political contest against British domination.

Guha, an Indian historian responsible for organizing a collective of younger Indian historians under the banner of "Subaltern Studies," takes many of his terms and cues from Gramsci. However, he begins his essay with the challenge that the texts of historical analysis are always the texts of the dominant or, in the case of modern Indian history, the colonial power, and that the voices of the subaltern are either silent or muted and transformed by the grammar of official discourse in these texts. Thus peasants are texted only in the colonial prose that contains, controls, and dismisses their subjectivity. This textualization is more than simply an abstract report: it is an expression of the colonial codes that provide the dominant structures for peasant life as well. As Guha notes, the peasant's "subalternity was materialized by the structure of property, institutionalized by law, sanctified by religion, and made tolerable—and even desirable—by tradition." So far, Guha's reasoning seems consistent with a Foucauldian understanding of the power of discourse, in this case, the truth regime that was institutionalized in the invasive colonial presence in India.

However, Guha demonstrates his departure from Foucault and his specific debt to Gramsci in taking as his primary subject the recovery and interpretation of peasant resistance. In other words, power is acknowledged and analyzed, but less because of its totalizing importance than because it has become the foil for uncovering the suppressed subject position of the subaltern. Official texts are read to show the extraordinary complexity and resilience of peasant rebellion, the expression of rebellion through the systematic (if sometimes displaced) upending of colonial codes. Guha rescues the peasant in part by reading silences, in part by explaining the necessarily "religious" character of protest in an overdetermined, "prepolitical" colonial context. The terms of analysis are structuralist and oppositional; there is a clear implication, in spite of the subsequent alignment of the Subaltern school with Foucault by some of its authors, that radical history must champion resistance rather than power, even in contexts where power seems not only triumphant, but able to trivialize the gestures and idioms of any revolt from below.

The return of the repressed, however, raises a host of theoretical and empirical problems. In particular, when Guha attempts to restore the subject position of the subaltern in history, he must resort to characterizations of peasant tradition, culture, and religion that reverberate problematically with the views of colonial anthropology itself. "Peasants" are often homogenized (not least by all being gendered as "he"), reified, and romanticized. When questioning the European constitution of the universal subject, whether for any history celebrating resistance, or for non-Western histories where European subjects are imposed, it is clear that we constantly run the risk of reinventing all-too-familiar categories, the genealogical foundations that take us right back to the heart of modern darkness: colonial history and the patriarchal anthropologies of domination. Nonetheless, Guha and the Subaltern Studies collective stake out an important pole of the resistance problematic forcefully and eloquently, insisting on the necessity for recovering not only instances of resistance but also some of the irrepressible cultural forms from which resistance can grow.

In "Ritual and Resistance: Subversion as a Social Fact" (this volume), Nicholas Dirks reviews a range of arguments about the character of resistance and its relationship to both periodic and quotidian forms of cultural practice. The essay confronts us with ethnographic examples of disorder, disruption, and dissention in a set of key village rituals in southern India, and suggests that resistance as a conceptual preoccupation may be most useful as a way of undermining the assumptions of order that undergird most of our social science. It prompts us to look not just for hidden transcripts but for systematic and pervasive disorder. In arguing that order is, at least in part, an effect of power, he proposes that the search for disorder through resistance may provide access to more critical understandings of both order and power. The recognition of disorder also opens ways to confront the ambivalent relationship of discourse and event, in terms of cultures of power where the center never holds, in which the twin processes of containment and dispersal are always in conflict (though in culturally specific contexts and ways). Thus the road to resistance might take us further than we expected, into critical forms of reflection about the foundational assumptions underlying social scientific theories about social order, in this particular instance, anthropological concepts of ritual and culture (and resistance).

Nevertheless, even anthropological approaches to the study of cultural order/orders can demonstrate, as in Marshall Sahlins's paper, "Cosmologies of Capitalism" (this volume), that the culture concept need not be on the side of power. It may even provide the basis for articulating powerful resistance, in this case to the hegemonic spread of Western capitalism. Sahlins projects his insights about the cultural character of resistance onto the largest possible screen: the interactions of Europeans with Chinese, Hawaiians, and Kwakiutl in the course of European commercial expansion from the mid-eighteenth to the mid-nineteenth century. Here, the "subjects" in question are societies, peoples with their own traditions and their own histories, who accepted (though always selectively) the material goods the Europeans had to offer, but who resisted the frames of interpretation (which of course cast the Europeans as superior) that seemed to go with them. "Resistance" here was not so much a matter of articulating opposition as of reasserting existing cultural forms and of subordinating European goods to the fulfillment of traditional ends: "[D]estiny is not history. Nor is it always tragedy. Anthropologists tell of some spectacular forms of indigenous cultural change turning into modes of political resistance—in the name of cultural persistence." Thus culture can provide instances of dramatic resistance to Western hegemony and power, at the same time that it provides the conceptual grounds for a critique of worlds that are taken as natural, in particular, the world that capitalism has given us.

THE QUESTION OF CULTURE

But if the anthropological concept of culture can be used to animate our understanding of resistance, it is also clear that culture is currently in the midst of a whirlwind of critical reflection, represented by a significant number of the articles included in this reader. As we stated at the beginning of this introduction, it is now commonplace to question whether and in what precise ways culture might be shared (or contested), durable (or constantly changing), coherent and consistent (or inchoate, contradictory, fragmented). Sahlins's own work has elsewhere demonstrated precisely how political, kinship, and gender divisions within Hawaiian society determined the kinds of responses that could be made to the disruptive presence of Captain Cook, whose life was (literally) appropriated to sustain a political cosmology that became threatened with extinction by Cook's arrival. The cultural terms of expanding Western capital transformed the death of a god into the pretext of conquest. And, through the same story, Sahlins has insisted on the destabilizing character of events for all notions of structure (see Sahlins 1981, 1985).

Clifford Geertz (1973, 1980, 1988), whose eloquent interpretations of anthropological culture have been uniquely influential, never had the same worries about structure as did Sahlins, grounding his own theory of culture in interpretive semiotics rather than structuralism. Geertz's definition of culture has always been predicated on the notion that culture has to do with meaning, with the way experience is construed rather than with some unmediated notion of experience itself, with the centrality of symbols for formulating and expressing meanings that are pervasive as well as shared. His characteristically American reading of Weber achieved its peculiar power in a succession of subtle readings of cockfights, market towns, wedding feasts, calendrical schemas, irrigation temples, and royal cremations, to mention only a few examples. For Geertz, culture became a semiotic code for reading virtually everything else (anything can be a cultural system), but he never confronted the issue of power.

Stephen Greenblatt has been among those insisting on the mutually invasive fields of the things we characterize when we say "culture" and "power." His work, now seen as the origin of the "new historicism" in literary studies, is in some ways more anthropological than historical; his sense of cultural poetics owes more to Geertz than to anyone else. In "The Circulation of Social Energy" (this volume), the opening chapter of his book, *Shakespearean Negotiations*, Greenblatt defines his enterprise as the "study of the collective making of distinct cultural practices and inquiry into the relations among these practices," but his readings constantly traverse between the cultural categories at play, so to speak, on the Elizabethan stage and the interests—institutional, personal, financial, political—that cross the aesthetic boundaries between the theater and the world (see also Greenblatt 1980).

Greenblatt's importation of anthropological methods into the Arnoldian province of Shakespearean studies may suggest precisely the kind of high culture that anthropology defined itself against, but even the distinction between high and low (one for which Greenblatt sees little place in sixteenth-century English culture, in any case) seems to be collapsing in this postmodern world of ours. At the same time that much contemporary film, music, art, and literature have challenged the conventions of the high-low categorization and its interpretive appropriation by respective culture industries (in Adorno's [1972] sense), anthropologists have had to move over and make room for an efflorescence of interest in things cultural by media specialists, film reviewers, literary critics, and an ever-widening variety of cultural theorists.

The history of cultural studies in Britain is discussed in Stuart Hall's paper, "Cultural Studies: Two Paradigms" (this volume). In its early years, British cultural studies had little impact in the United States, insulated not only by the localized character of its political concerns but also by the peculiar trajectories of the disciplines of sociology, history, anthropology, and literary studies in Britain and the United States. But in recent years it would be hard to overemphasize the importance of Cultural Studies, which has now inspired empirical studies and theoretical rethinkings with broad implications for a wide range of disciplinary configurations and projects (see Grossberg, Nelson, and Treichler 1992).

Hall's ambition, which grows out of his own committed affiliation to a specifically British tradition of cultural Marxism, is that Cultural Studies continue to hold out the "promise of a properly materialist theory of culture." However, drawing theoretical sustenance from Gramsci, Althusser, and Foucault and more directly from the work of Raymond Williams, Hall has always insisted on transcending "the endless oscillations between idealism and reductionism." As Cultural Studies has spread to America and Australia, it has predictably changed and expanded to mean a great variety of things, but it has usually maintained some kernel of this ambition. Even those who regard materialist theories as inadequate or problematic agree that wherever there is culture, there is also politics.

The work of Raymond Williams, perhaps most clearly in his succinct but powerful book, *Marxism and Literature* (1977), excerpted in this volume, has provided the theoretical inspiration for this new concern with the politics of cultural production, usually around his redefinition and deployment of Gramsci's use of the concept of hegemony. Culture is seen as political not only (or not even) in the sense that it is produced to serve certain specific interests, but rather more generally (and usefully) in that it constitutes the terrains of meaning and feeling that are central to the securing of consent and/or the incitement to rebellion in a world where brute power is only part of the story.

The politics of culture are explored in a number of essays in this volume, most directly in those by Susan McClary, Judith Williamson, Elizabeth Traube, and Susan Harding. Like Greenblatt, McClary (1990, 1992) extends the reach of critical cultural theory to "high" art. But in the paper reprinted here, "Living to Tell: Madonna's Resurrection of the Fleshly," she writes about one of the most remarkable phenomena of contemporary popular music, namely, Madonna, whose determined assault on the representational codes of both conventional morality and established left-wing and feminist critique, on the rules of sexual difference, and on public decorum and good taste, constantly inflames expectations of how public women should behave. McClary shows how Madonna "operates within a persistently repressive discourse to create liberatory musical images."

In "Family, Education, Photography" (this volume), Judith Williamson pursues what is perhaps the most populist of popular culture, photography. Williamson shows how the rise of the family photograph—both photographs of (the) family and the situating of photography within the family—is not merely an innocent pleasure, but part of the incredibly powerful (if strangely invisible) production and reproduction of the bourgeois family form. In "Secrets of Success in Postmodern Society" (this volume), Elizabeth Traube analyzes a series of popular U.S. movies produced in the 1980s. Traube traces the way the more successful ones "address the hopes and anxieties of middle-class youth regarding the corporate work world that they have joined or are about to join" in the context of the specific social and economic conjunctures of the Reagan era. The U.S. corporate ethic of entrepreneurial conformity is thus tested and reworked for a new generation in the darkened and displaced arenas of celluloid desire.

Finally, Susan Harding's paper, "The Born-Again Telescandals" (this volume), shows how television has become the principal medium not only of the sexual but of the sacred as well. In a postmodern world, ethnography has not only come home (in Williamson's case, quite literally), it makes us watch films, television, and advertisements with eyes that are constantly dazzled not only by astonishing production values, but by the ever more dizzying movement between reality and its now-receding referents.

Whether the worlds we study are postmodern or not, we are likely aware that the age of cultural innocence has escaped for good. And if the politics of culture have recently preoccupied academic concerns of the kind represented in this reader, it is also the case that we confront the politics of culture everywhere else we turn. Identity politics builds on the notion that cultural (read racial, gender, ethnic, religious) categories provide both a source of oppression and a means for empowering groups and communities to contest that oppression. Cultural politics are actively championed even by those who claim that culture should be depoliticized, for example, in the "family values" campaign of the Republican Party in 1992. While we recognize an extraordinary convergence between academic debates regarding culture and the political career of culture outside the academy, we also note the contradictions that result when recent theoretical attempts to deessentialize the categories of difference become reessentialized through the very political process that is mobilized to contest previous essences. We are learning that if all culture is political, it is accordingly impossible to establish a neutral ground for culture that would itself be exempt from the struggles, claims, contests, and chaos of the political world.

ALL THE WORLD'S A TEXT

So far we have provided only a partial description of the intellectual background to which this reader is a critical response. To understand why we have chosen these particular contents, some further history of our present concerns has to be offered. If we survey the intellectual landscape of the social sciences at the end of the twentieth century, it is hard not to be impressed by the power and popularity of literary theory, linguistic analysis, and related forms of theoretical address. Whether we look to the revival of intellectual history and the influence of Dominick LaCapra (1985), to the somewhat different convergence of intellectual historians with literary critics in a "new historicist" mold (Veeser 1989), to the enormous impact of Edward Said (1979, 1983) on intellectuals writing in and about the third world, to the interest of Joan Scott (1988) and other feminists in theories of gender and language, to the pull of reflexive anthropology toward the narrative ordering of the experienced world (Clifford and Marcus 1986; Clifford 1988), to formal analysis of the rhetoric of economics and other apparently nonliterary disciplines (McClosky 1985), or simply to the common currency of such terms as "discourse" and "deconstruction"—in all of these places, there seems to be no escape.

The transformation of literary studies by the impact of Derrida among others has played a key part in this challenge. The complexities of reading (and writing) have brought the category of the text and the work of interpretation into question. From focusing on authorial intention and the text's single attainable meaning (a chimera, which obscures the necessary openness of the text and its multiplicity of meanings), literary theory has increasingly stressed the importance of two other kinds of move—*back*, to the contexts of the text's production; and *out*, to the ways in which its meanings become constructed. In fact, rather than determining what a text "means," it may be more important to understand how the text "works," indeed, how the text itself is a "work," implicated, like all other products, in modes of production. Furthermore, this mode of analysis has been extended from written texts in the more conventional sense to all manner of documents—indeed to experience, behavior, and events as well. From assailing the transparency of the text in the discourse of literary criticism, textuality has become a metaphor for reality in general (see esp. Bennett 1982, 1990).

How have we reached this point? One key to the answer, we would argue, lies in a set of specific intellectual biographies that began somewhere in the Marxist tradition. For behind the theoretical discussions is a specific political history—the unresolved agenda of the post-1968 intellectual radicalism, which spawned the rich profusion of Marxisms and feminisms that have done so much to shape the outlook of the affected generations of scholars in the last quarter of the twentieth century. Of course, since the heady days of the 1960s, when forms of "social" explanation carried all before them, grounding the imagination in the determinant causalities of an axiomatic materialism, a veritable flood has passed beneath the bridge. And the main current of the latter, despite its materialist beginnings, has been an unrelenting antireductionism. Most important, the new diffusion of Marxism—which, for the first time, established a broad presence in the universities of the English-speaking world—took an avowedly heterodox form. The new discussions defined themselves in no uncertain terms as departures, as critical advances on the older forms of economistic theory. The "base/superstructure" model of social determination, with its assignment of logical priority to the economic, came under particular attack. The translation and reception of Althusser (1969) and Poulantzas (1973) proved the prelude for a much broader and continuing engagement with a set of mainly French theories—Lacanian psychoanalysis, Saussurian linguistics, the philosophy of science of Bachelard (McAllester Jones 1991) and Canguilhem (1978), the aesthetics of Macherey (1978), semiotics and theories of film, and so on. This freeing of politics and ideology for "relatively autonomous" analysis, anchored to the economy via "structural causality" and "determination in the last instance," opened the whole domain of the "noneconomic" to Marxist view: aesthetics, literature, the arts, theories of knowledge, science, education, religion, academic knowledge and the disciplines, intellectual life, popular culture, sexuality, and so on—in short, "culture," as it was coming to be defined by a convergent strain of British dissenting Marxism.

This is one of the histories that makes our volume a possibility. The insufficiencies of received Marxisms and other materialisms created a space from which other kinds of theory could be imagined and engaged. The interest in culture—in the politics of subjectivity—has led one substantial section of the 1960s cohort into even more radical forms of critique. Shibboleths have fallen one by one. By now, the further pursuit of the antireductionist logic in the course of the 1980s—through increasingly sophisticated readings of culture and ideology via Gramsci (1967, 1971), Foucault (1980), Voloshinov (1973) and Bakhtin (1968), French poststructuralist theory, the larger field of cultural studies in Britain (Hall 1978; Hall and Jefferson 1976; Johnson 1987), and most radically of all, the still-diversifying field of feminist theory on both sides of the Atlantic—has left the earlier intellectual moment of the 1960s far behind, to the point of bringing the original materialist inspirations radically into doubt.

As the hold of the economy has been progressively loosened, and with it, the determinative power of social structure and its causal priorities, the imaginative and epistemological needs for other kinds of analysis and understanding has grown. Moreover, this pervasive antireductionist move has had an unexpectedly powerful undertow. Following the trail of culture through the territory of power and subjectivity (to use the themes discussed in the body of this introduction), has made the home base (with its materialist securities) increasingly hard to find. In fact, for many who have taken this route, the materialist connection in its classical form has to be broken once and for all. "Society" as a unitary object can no longer be maintained. There is no structural coherence deriving from the economy, from the functional needs of the social system and its central values, or from some other overarching principle of order to which we can easily repair. Particular phenomena—events, policies, institutions, ideologies, texts—have particular social contexts in the sense of conditions, practices, and sites, which conjoin for an essential part of their meaning. But there is no underlying given structure to which they can necessarily be referred, as their essential expression or necessary effects. In other words, the major casualty of this intellectual flux has been the confidence in a notion of social totality in its various Marxist and non-Marxist forms.

The commitment to grasping society as a whole, to conceptualizing its underlying principles of unity—which is now conventionally described as the specifically "modern" or Enlightenment project—has passed into crisis. For Marxists and others on the left, this is connected to a complex of political experiences, including the numerical decline of the historical working class and its traditions; the crisis of Keynesianism, the welfare state, and statist conceptions of socialism; the economic, political, and moral collapse of communist systems; the catastrophe of the environment and of the scientific mastery of nature; and the declining purchase of straightforward class-political forms of address. In this sense, history has lost its way. The grand ideals that allowed us to read history in a particular direction, as a story of progress and emancipation, from the Industrial Revolution and the triumph of science over nature to the emancipation of the working class, the victory of socialism, and the equality of women, no longer persuade. All bets are off. "[T]here is no single right way to read history. Indeed history becomes a narrative without a teleology" (Ellis 1989, 38), a story without an end. The postmodern moment begins, it has been said, with this loss, this "incredulity with regard to the master narratives" (Lyotard 1984, xiii).

DISCOURSES OF THE SOCIAL

The last two decades have seen a dizzying intellectual history. We have moved from a time when social history and social analysis presented themselves as a kind of universal panacea and the force of social determinations seemed axiomatic, to a conjuncture in which the "social" has come to seem ever less definite and social determinations have surrendered their previous sovereignty. Moreover, this sense that the social is discursively constituted further erodes many previous certainties because of the increasingly common recognition that society has been fundamentally transformed by postmodernism. Indeed, if we follow the suggestions of Jean Baudrillard (1988), apocalyptic theorist of the postmodern, there is no longer any social referent at all. The social is produced as a simulacrum of itself, a mere chimera that the masses consult to find out what they believe and whether they exist. But Baudrillard's flight from any form of political or social determination is not shared by many who nevertheless find him correctly identifying many of the features of the postmodern age (Harvey 1989; Huyssen 1986; Lash and Urry 1987; Lash 1990; Soja 1989; Wilson 1988; Jameson 1984). It may be that the social has been transformed, but the structure of transformation seems too closely linked with the interests of late industrial capitalism and postimperial nationalism to allow the older notions of social context to be argued out of existence altogether.

One way of specifying the parameters of postmodern politics and society is provided by Susan Harding in her discussion of contemporary religious fundamentalism ("The Born-Again Telescandals," this volume). Harding uses the "born again" telescandals of 1987–1988 to delineate a rupture in what she calls the myth of modernity. Whereas fundamentalist Christians had for years been complicit in a narrative in which they accepted their position as premodern, the use of modern media, principally television, and the entry of fundamentalists into modern politics, signaled a major shift. In spite of the telescandals which brought down such religious leaders as Jim and Tammy Faye Bakker and Jimmy Swaggart, fundamentalist religion did not slide back into its earlier relationship with liberal secularists. Instead, the scandals revealed the fundamental similarities among the competing religious groups, and between them and the media establishment now clearly using the myth of the modern to service the economics of the postmodern. Here the politics of truth—the nightly docudrama of Ted Koppel—gives way to the truth of the spectacle. The most spectacular example of postmodernism as a cultural form comes in Harding's descriptions of the fundamentalist theme park Heritage U.S.A., with its depthlessness of infinite forgiveness, gratification, and incitement to consume. Thus, after modernity had appeared to install secularism as a moral value for the religious and the nonreligious alike, we have witnessed another collapse of boundaries, the merger not only of television and envangelism but of religion and politics. The dangers of postmodernism appear ironically like those we used to ascribe to the premodern, only now with a technological vengeance.

For social historians who might still claim that postmodernism is either irrelevant to their historical quest or an ideological distraction from the foundational realities of class and social determination, there are no ready-made solutions to the current conundrum. However, one extremely fruitful response has been to historicize the category of "the social" itself, by looking at the terms under which it first became abstracted into an object of theoretical knowledge, a target of policy, and a site of practice. In this context, "the social" refers not to the global analytical category of "society" in some unproblematic social science sense but to the historically located "methods, techniques, and practices" that allowed such a category to be constructed in the first place. Circling back once again to Foucault, we see that his concept of the disciplinary society is concerned directly with this process: on the one hand, as noted above, he carries the analysis of power away from the core institutions in the sense of the centralized national state toward the emergence of new individualizing strategies "that function outside, below and alongside the State apparatuses, on a much more minute and everyday level" (1980, 60); on the other hand, it is precisely through such individualizing strategies that "the social" or the "social body" became recognized, constituted, and elaborated as the main object of science, surveillance, policy, and power.

Population (fertility, age, mobility, health), economics, poverty, crime, education, and welfare became not only the main objects of governmental activity but also the measure and modalities of cohesion and solidarity in the emerging nineteenth-century social order. If we are to understand the latter, it is to the new social science and medicoadministrative discourses, their technologies, and their effects that we must look—to the new knowledges "concerning society, its health and sickness, its conditions of life, housing and habits, which served as the basic core for the 'social economy' and sociology of the nineteenth century" (Foucault 1980, 176). In the late nineteenth and early twentieth centuries, the repertoire of power-producing knowledges further expanded—psychiatry and psychology, social work and the welfare state, youth policy, industrial relations, public health, social hygiene, eugenics, and so on. As Donzelot (1979) and others have argued, the family became a particular object of such interventions and expertise. Moreover, as feminist scholars and Foucault's own final works have shown, sexuality provides a particularly rich field for showing such power relations under construction.

This "discursive" move—from the assumption of an objective "society" to the study of how the category of "the social" was formed—can be repeated for other areas too. Class may be similarly deconstructed as a category. Under the antireductionist logic described above, the process of working-class formation in the nineteenth century can no longer be presented as the logical unfolding of an economic process and its necessary effects at the levels of social organization, consciousness, and culture. At the same time, we cannot conduct the alternative analysis simply as a process of empirical disaggregation, so that a fuller grasp of the working class's compositional complexities (its sectional variety across industries, its internal differentiation according to hierarchies of seniority, status, and skill, and its cultural segmentation along lines of gender, religion, ethnicity, and race) and the time scale of its coalescence can emerge. To understand class as a political factor, in fact, we have to go further and accept the methodological and theoretical difficulties of still trying to analyze working-class politics—the rise of labor movements and socialist parties—as the expressive outcome of an economically located class interest and social-structural position.

In this sense, class as a political and cultural postulate (the assertion of a particular kind of social identity) was just as important to the process of class formation as the existence of class as a demonstrable social fact (the creation of new social positions defined by relationship to the means of production). The new insistence of the nineteenth century that class was the organizing reality of the developing capitalist societies, and the growth of specific practices and organizations around that insistence (for example, trade unions and socialist parties), is arguably a better starting point for the study of class formation than the classic one of economics and social structure, because it was at this discursive level that the operational collectivity of the class—who got to be included, who set the tone, and who received the recognized voice—was defined. In these terms, the history of class is inseparable from the history of the category. Class emerged as a set of discursive claims about the social world seeking to order the latter in terms of itself.

Much impetus for this approach was provided by Gareth Stedman Jones's *Languages of Class* (1983), which had all the more effect because of its author's standing as a leading 1960s social historian of the materialist sort. The main vehicle for Stedman Jones's new approach, a long and original essay on the political rhetoric of Chartism, argues for the constitutive importance of language in ordering perceptions of the social world, exercising political efficacy in its own right rather than being simply the expression of interests and experience formed elsewhere. Linguistically, "class" defined a constituency for the Chartist movement, and helped its parts to see themselves in a common project which the class-political form of address itself thereby constructed, rather than secondarily reflecting a unity of interest that was already given in the economy and its social relations. Moreover, Chartist ideology was less the reflection of emerging working-class interests, Stedman Jones argues, than an existing body of discourse that itself structured those interests' main direction; and Chartist politics revealed less the maturity of British working-class consciousness in the classical Marxist sense than the inherited baggage of older radical traditions.

The more important point for our immediate purposes is Stedman Jones's basic linguistic move, which simultaneously documented and strengthened the turn of many historians who considered themselves "social" to language and discourse as the key ground of a nonreductionist approach. Given social history's existing stress on the economics and sociology of working-class formation as the main key to Chartism's rise and fall (including an enormously influential essay of Stedman Jones's own [1975]), *Languages of Class* marked a major break from past work. It shifted priorities away from the recognizably materialist problematic of social history toward the very different frame of linguistic analysis; the point was to "dissociate the ambition of a theoretically informed history from any simple prejudgement about the determining role of the 'social' . . . as something outside of, and logically . . . prior to its articulation through language" (Stedman Jones 1983, 7).

Such a move allows us to free analysis from the teleology of a class consciousness thought to be inscribed in the structures of class interest and class-collective experience—and from the need to find special explanations for the many instances in which that class consciousness is imperfectly realized, if at all. Indeed, it converts the notion of "interest" itself into a problem, a discursive effect of complex histories, rather than a given and agreed-upon basis for action. Rather than asking which working-class interests were reflected in which organizations and forms of action, we should ask how particular practices and institutions encouraged or hindered particular constructions of working-class interest. Moreover, the discursive field of working-class interests is not reducible to a single essential contradiction between capital and labor. So far from such a contradiction's being structurally constitutive for the rise of a labor movement in some unmediated and straightforward way, the labor movement was actually shaped from the field of contradictions generated between the emergent conditions and their increasingly intense discursive rendition. But the unproblematic materialism of social explanation should not simply be replaced with an oversynthesized conception of public political language, as if the book on the last twenty years of innovative social history can now somehow be closed.

Discussing the impact of Stedman Jones's work and of the emerging dialogue between social history and the new forms of "postmaterialist" theory more generally, Robert Gray notes that language is "multi-layered, complex, fractured, composed of incoherences and silences, as well as the smooth flow of would-be authoritative public discourses" (1986, 367), and consequently must be read for its exclusions as well as for its unifying appeals. One of the most important of such exclusions concerns women and is ordered along lines of gender. The positive identity of the working class as it was elaborated during the nineteenth century—the ideal of the skilled male worker in industry—rested upon powerfully dichotomous assumptions about what it meant to be a man or a woman. Those assumptions were ordered into a pervasive dualism that aligned men with the world of work and the public domain of politics, and women with the home and the private realm of domesticity, the one a site of control and rationality, the other a site of emotion. Inscribed in the language of class were definite notions of masculinity and femininity which limited "women's access to knowledge, skill and independent political subjectivity" (Alexander, this volume). Consequently, the importance of gender, sexuality, and the family cannot be bracketed from an account of the politics of working-class formation. As Joan Scott says in another critical response to Stedman Jones: "These are not compartments of life but discursively related systems; 'language' makes possible the study of their interrelationships. As Chartists set forth their program they offered the terms of political collective identity. This identity rested on a set of differentiations—inclusions and exclusions, comparisons and contrasts—that relied on sexual difference for their meaning" (1988, 60).

Overcoming such exclusions means recognizing the indeterminate multiplicity of identity, and it is here that the basic poststructuralist claims about language and identity become useful. How we see ourselves as a basis for action and how we are addressed in the public arena are not fixed. Sometimes we recognize ourselves as citizens, sometimes as workers, sometimes as parents, sometimes as consumers, sometimes as enthusiasts for particular sports or hobbies, sometimes as believers in religious and other creeds, and so on; those recognitions are usually structured by power relations of different kinds; and they are usually gendered by assumptions placing us as women or men. At one level, the observation that identity or subject positions are complex and nonfixed is banal. But the important thing is that politics is usually conducted *as if* identity were fixed. The question then becomes, On what basis, at different times and in different places, does the nonfixity become temporarily fixed in such a way that individuals and groups can behave as a particular kind of agency, political or otherwise? How do people become shaped into acting subjects, understanding themselves in particular ways?

In effect, politics consists of the effort to domesticate the infinitude of identity. It is the attempt to hegemonize identity, to order it into a strong programmatic statement. If identity is decentered, politics is about the attempt to create a center. Thus the power of the socialist tradition between the late nineteenth century and the 1930s was its ability to harness and harmonize popular identities into a strong conception of the working class—that is, to construct popular political agency around the discourse of class in all the classic materialist ways. But concentrating identity in that way also has its costs. It involves a reduction to class. It involves exclusions and neglects. The positivity of the working class presumed the negativity of others—and not just other classes, but also other kinds of workers (for example, the unorganized, the rough and unrespectable, the criminal, the frivolous, the religiously devout, the ethnically different, and of course the female), and of other elements of subjectivity—in effect all those aspects of identity that could not be disciplined into a highly centered notion of class-political agency.

FEMINIST DISRUPTIONS

Throughout this essay we have pointed repeatedly to the ways in which feminist thought has challenged and undermined established categories and practices of scholarship. It is time now to pull together the various elements of contemporary feminist theory represented in this volume. "Feminist theory" is, of course, no single unitary object. It has gone through significant transformations since its emergence in the early seventies, partly in response to theoretical shifts in other fields, and partly in response to its own internal dialectics. What has unified it since the beginning, across its disparate strands, is its focus on power, on the asymmetry of the gender dichotomy and of gendered relationships.

Thus, probably the most fundamental assumption of contemporary feminist theory and practice, in all its forms, is that gender is not simply a form of difference but a form of power. This simple shift from an earlier perspective, in which gender, if it was attended to at all, was treated as a set of power-innocent "roles" (the "role of women" among tribe x, or in the xth century), not only radically reoriented the study of women and gender, but also realigned the political/intellectual matrix in which the gender problematic was situated—it became apparent that gender must be viewed as an axis of major social inequality along with race and class. The alignment of gender with race and class, in turn, has played a major role in furthering the process discussed earlier: dislodging class from its sovereign status as both the analytic key to social inequality and the primary vehicle for radical political transformation. The most prominent new forms of theorizing about social transformation argue for the necessity of recognizing diverse and multiple political initiatives (including those based not only on class, race, and gender, but on other concatenations of interests) that engage or disengage with one another in shifting and complex ways (Laclau and Mouffe 1985; Andersen and Collins 1992; Collins 1990; Sacks 1989).

Sally Alexander's piece, "Women, Class and Sexual Differences in the 1830s and 1840s" (this volume), beautifully illustrates the ways in which gender and class in particular link up with and repel each other in actual historical practice, shaping each other conceptually and practically. Alexander distinguishes between the recognition of "sexual difference" and the actual subordination of one sex by the other, a distinction that might be contested in some feminist quarters, given the point made above that gender difference is never merely difference. Drawing on Freudian and Lacanian theory, however, Alexander goes on to argue that sexual difference is always at least latently antagonistic, because of its involvement with identity formation, that is, with the shaping of the self that inevitably entails the differentiation from the nonself, the Other. It is this latent antagonism, intrinsic to the formation of gendered identities, that intersects with other forms of inequality, sometimes merging with them and sometimes disrupting them. Beatrix Campbell's *Wigan Pier Revisited* (1984), and Carolyn Steedman's *Landscape for a Good Woman* (1987) exemplify more of the surprising turns class and gender take when they are conjoined nondogmatically, that is, when neither term is allowed to dominate.

If, following our earlier arguments from Foucault, all social relations are infused with power, the same must also be said of gender: everything is gendered. This second fundamental insight of contemporary feminism has opened up another interpretive perspective, wherein seemingly gender-neutral categories, such as "class" or "the family," or the distinction between public and private spheres, are shown to encode gendered assumptions and tacitly to embody gendered images. For example, as discussed in the previous section, it is now generally accepted that the image behind the category "the working class" is basically male; insofar as the working class is primarily imaged around the industrial working class—"heavy industry"—the image is of the male as strong, physical, macho. It has similarly come to be recognized that "the family" is not simply a "haven in a heartless world," but is founded on fundamental asymmetries of power and patriarchal authority.

The argument concerning the gendered underpinnings of seemingly neutral social categories is developed most fully in Geoff Eley's paper, "Nations, Publics, and Political Cultures: Placing Habermas in the Nineteenth Century" (this volume). Eley begins from Nancy Fraser's (1989) critique of Habermas, which revealed the "gender subtext" running through all of Habermas's categories, including especially the distinction between the private sphere of the family and the public sphere of citizenship. He then goes on to link Fraser's critique to a larger body of feminist work in history and political theory that "has shown how far modern political thought is highly gendered in its basic structures . . . this was not only registered in the practical achievements of constitutions, legal codes, and political mobilization and their forms of justification, but also ordered the higher philosophical discourse around the universals of reason, law, and nature. . . ." In addition, Eley argues that the history of "associational activity," that is, of the formation of social and political groups, is also radically rewritten when one focuses on the gendered (male) nature of these groups and when one considers their particular and changing forms as both reflecting and constituting not only social and political relations in some gender-neutral sense, but specific patterns of gender as well. Finally, Eley turns these basic insights onto working-class history and picks up on (among other things) Sally Alexander's arguments about the ways in which working-class politics—again claiming universality, if only for its own class—represented not only a systematic exclusion of women and their interests from the political groupings and their agendas, but also a codification of categorical assumptions about women's and men's "natures" and "places." The effects of all this have been not only to demystify the claims made for the universality of the public sphere, but to reveal the hitherto denied universality of the private sphere, to substantiate, again and again, the feminist claim that "the personal"—the realm of "family, sexuality, self, and subjectivity"—"is political."

Embedded in these arguments is another fundamental premise of contemporary feminist thought: that gender is culturally and historically constructed. Probably the earliest proponents of this argument were anthropologists working from a position of cultural relativism. Margaret Mead, for example, argued in the 1930s that gender was culturally constructed rather than innate (1933, 1935). Building on this basically relativist insight, but enlarging it with contemporary feminist concerns, Ortner and Whitehead (1981) argued that while there are, no doubt, some natural bases of gender distinctions, and of sexual and reproductive behavior, these are relatively minimal in terms of the ways in which gender, sexuality, and reproduction are culturally defined, shaped, and woven into the social fabric in any given society at any given time. Biological sex, sexuality, and reproduction, in other words, form only a hazy and ambiguous backdrop against which cultural constructions are built, and it is the cultural and social constructions that operate as "social facts." In one of the pathbreaking essays in that volume, Jane Collier and Michelle Rosaldo convincingly argue that particular styles of manhood, womanhood, and sexuality in "simple societies" emerge from particular forms of marriage arrangements and of senior/junior power relations.

Joan Scott (1988) arrived at similar insights in the field of history. Her article had a major impact on that field, in part because of its specific feminist point, but also in part because of its participation in "the discursive turn" that the field of history was undergoing, albeit with much resistance from many quarters. Scott made a dramatic case for the importance of poststructuralism in historical analysis, linking the arbitrariness of cultural construction to the project of historicist critique. For many historians, Scott's theoretical package required a double turn, toward both feminism and "culture," and the pill was perhaps harder to swallow than it was in anthropology, where the cultural construction of gender seemed a relatively natural outgrowth of a broader cultural constructionist perspective.

Whether in its anthropological ("cultural") form, or in its historical ("discursive," frequently poststructuralist) form, however, the general point is by now fairly well established. Several of the papers in this volume carry such arguments into specific cultural fields, showing how particular representational media and associated genres both register and themselves shape the construction of gender and sexuality in very concrete historical ways. This is seen for photography (Williamson), film (Traube), television (Harding), popular music and video (McClary), and museums (Haraway). Each of these articles, in its own way, does the work of historicizing and denaturalizing gender and sexuality—the basic job of the cultural constructionist perspective. Needless to say (though, perhaps it needs to be said anyway) such analysis applies to men as well as women, male as well as female. Thus Haraway, for example, argues (this volume) that the experience constructed for the viewer by the arrangement of the American Museum of Natural History, as a "meaning machine," produces a particular, and historically emergent, form of masculinity:

> Man is not in nature partly because he is not seen, is not the spectacle. A constitutive meaning of masculine gender for us is to be the unseen, the eye (I), the author. Indeed that is part of the structure of experience in the museum, one of the reasons one has, willy nilly, the moral status of a young boy undergoing initiation through visual experience. . . . The museum is a visual technology. It works through desire for communion, not separation, and one of its products is gender.

The cultural constructionist perspective in turn allows the points made earlier to be turned around. If everything is gendered, so all aspects of gender are "classed" and "raced." Gender is never constructed in a vacuum, but always within a field of other constructions of inequality that both feed it and naturalize it. The work of Ann Stoler (e.g., 1989) has been particularly significant in this regard, showing the ways in which, in colonial regimes, race, class, gender, and generational (adult/child) categories are simultaneously, interactively—and often contradictorily—constructed.

Feminist theory, in other words, has both provoked and mirrored the interactions of culture, power, and history with which we are concerned. For it is in feminist and other forms of "minority" theory that issues of power and of cultural constructionism have a peculiar vividness and urgency. In these contexts, neither the pervasiveness of power nor the constructedness of identity is an abstract "academic" question. In these contexts, all have more than a passing stake in understanding both the invasiveness and the limits of hegemony. And in these contexts, all have more than a passing stake in understanding both the limits and the possibilities of resistance.

DISCOURSES OF CULTURE

We cannot end this discussion without confronting the fact that one of our key terms, "culture," has been subjected in recent years to very probing critique within its own field of origin, anthropology. Anthropology is a field in which the interpretive point of view has been well established, and in which the battle with some forms of reductive thinking (including various vulgar materialisms) is no longer the primary problem. For a discipline that has historically had a tentative relation to texts—focussing instead on oral cultures and primitive peoples—anthropology was much quicker to textualize culture than history has been to textualize the past. Although anthropologists for years had to confront the linguistic turn through the considerable impact of structural linguistics and symbolic analysis, the original textual turn was taken by Clifford Geertz, on the basis of a very different ensemble of theoretical influences, including Kenneth Burke, Northrup Frye, and Paul Ricoeur. Geertz wrote, in his well-known essay on the Balinese cockfight, that "[t]he culture of a people is an ensemble of texts, themselves ensembles, which the anthropologist strains to read over the shoulders of those to whom they properly belong" (1973, 452). Moreover, Geertz extended the metaphor of the text over the whole range of cultural products. As he wrote in *Negara*, "Arguments, melodies, formulas, maps, and pictures are not idealities to be stared at but texts to be read; so are rituals, palaces, technologies, and social formations" (1980, 135). All of culture is a text, not so much because it looks like one but because it can be read as one.

But then, of course, the ethnographer creates yet another text, with its own problematic character. This has generated the most recent phase of theoretical reflection in anthropology, including Geertz's own *Works and Lives* (1988), as well as the highly influential volume, *Writing Culture: The Poetics and Politics of Ethnography* (Clifford and Marcus 1986). *Writing Culture* proclaimed a crisis of representation in anthropology. The book consists almost entirely of the discussion and dissection of anthropological texts—"ethnographies" in one form or another—showing the ways in which these texts make use of various tropes, literary conventions, and narrative devices to establish ethnographic authority and/or certain kinds of unstated visions of the world. The editors and authors situate themselves firmly within the interpretive tradition established by Geertz and others over the past twenty years or so, but they argue that there is a kind of smugness to standard interpretive work. While interpretivists are happy to argue that "native" categories are culturally and historically constructed, the *Writing Culture* argument goes, they grant themselves a privileged position, in which their own categories are not subjected to this argument. But, of course, their categories are as much products of their culture, their historical moment, and their forms of power as everyone else's. Not only is this not faced and examined, it is actively obscured by the various forms of discourse construction (generally "writing") hegemonic in the academic world.

But the *Writing Culture* critique is already the focus of criticism (e.g., Sangren 1988). One cluster of questions that has been raised concerns the degree to which the *Writing Culture* argument raises self-consciousness about the writing of ethnography to the point of paralysis. If this was the case, it was only briefly so. After catching its breath, the field has collectively gone on writing, though in general with a self-awareness that has been entirely salutary.

A more serious set of questions has been raised concerning *Writing Culture*'s lack of interest in historical questions at a time when many anthropologists and others are taking "the historic turn" (McDonald, forthcoming), its virtual blindness toward feminist issues when these are so prominent in most forms of contemporary theorizing, and its narrowly disciplinary orientation at a time when interdisciplinary work is exploding all over the landscape. Of course no book can do everything. But we would suggest that the book's relative silence on issues of "power" and total silence on "history" seriously weaken the radicalness of its critique of "culture." The exclusively disciplinary focus has a similar effect, since for the most part it excludes consideration of novel—and radical—uses of the culture concept outside the field of anthropology, most notably in cultural studies.

This is not to say, however, that the question of representation raised by *Writing Culture* is trivial. The increasing attention to reflexivity of a more Saidian sort in current anthropological writing, and in particular to the way that anthropological forms of knowledge are shaped by relations of power and interest, and predetermined by tropic beginnings and procedures, has indeed led to widespread questioning of the epistemological validity of the traditional ethnographic object. Anthropologists are now rightly suspicious of the categories of "otherness" and "difference" that have historically been caught in logics of domination and denigration, whether "orientalist", "primitivist," or "colonialist." But in addressing the powerful epistemological and historical questions that compromise the objectivism of anthropological accounts, there is a danger of losing what has always been most salutary about the field. Anthropology has always promised the possibility of encountering other worlds and other modes of being that can work to defamiliarize and denaturalize the world we take for granted. How can we sustain this important project while at the same time recognizing the violence of the ("scientific") gaze and being concerned to engage in critical accounts of other cultures?

Said's *Orientalism* (1979), which in many ways parallels the *Writing Culture* arguments, broadens the issue far beyond anthropology, and powerfully establishes the point that the politics of cross-cultural representation, whether historical, literary, or anthropological, has been a colonial politics, that the construction of otherness and difference has for the last several hundred years been linked to projects of rule and domination. It is now clear that anthropology itself has been complicit (again, along with other fields), directly as well as indirectly, in colonial projects. We join with Said in challenging the procedures of cultural typification which depend upon—and perpetuate, even in a postcolonial world—the representational hubris of colonial power. But without denying that the operation of difference seems always to produce hierarchical relations between "us" and "them" (however those categories are constructed) or denying that difference cannot be thought to exist outside of representation itself, we would argue that an important part of the anthropological project must be recuperated. Further, we would argue that the anthropological project, in both its methodological and its ideological aspects, is not all that different from projects in social history (whether in colonial contexts or others) that seek to attend to those other voices—of women, workers, subalterns, even the "insane"—that have typically been suppressed and subordinated by the operations of power.

If otherness is a category that must always be suspected, nevertheless it may facilitate our attempt to listen to the voices of anthropological informants and colonized subalterns. Reflexive anthropology seems often to suggest that we must choose between reading the anthropological text as a product of either the subject or the object, either the author or the informant. This is not a choice that has to be made, any more than the recognition that meaning is contingent and conditional need necessitate a suspension of our effort to engage the world "out there." Rather, this seeming choice should lead us critically to examine the very terms of critical theory itself. By giving voice to those typically without "agency," we may find that our notion of agency is essentially and particularistically "our own"—and often alien to the cultures of subalternity we are attempting to study. In confronting categories of experience that we typically deem "religious," for example, we must beware of suggesting (as Subaltern Studies writers sometimes do), that religion is a modality of prepolitical awareness and resistance, a suggestion that emerges as unwittingly similar to colonial readings of subalterns as mystical, unworldly, and, yes, "other." Furthermore, attention to the particularities of other stories, even (perhaps especially) when these stories seem to compromise the agency of the subaltern author, necessarily subverts the way we think about power (or culture, or structure, or even theory) as a totalizing system. Informants, subalterns, subjected subjects may be necessarily complicit in the discursive formations of anthropology, colonialism, or the state (or some similar normalizing and controlling agency), as Gayatri Chakravorty Spivak has argued in her influential article, "Can the Subaltern Speak?" (1988). But they are never contained solely within them, nor are they ever totally dependent on the exemplary autonomy of the politicized intellectual.

And so there is still space for ethnography in a critically self-conscious anthropology, as there is still a past for a presentist and politicized historiography.

CULTURE / POWER / HISTORY

This volume embraces the need to explore other worlds and other modes of being, whether in history, anthropology, or other traditional disciplines in the human sciences. Critical awareness—of anthropological prejudice, colonial discourse, master narratives that tell grand stories of world history, patriarchal presuppositions, and so on—is not meant to replace the effort to write histories or ethnographies, nor is it meant simply to provide a better critique of methodological bias or partial sources, allowing us thereby to proceed with the same task we earlier left aside. Instead, the critical awareness proposed in the series, our insistence on the necessary linking of culture with power with history, is meant to challenge fundamental assumptions in academic writing.

It may be useful to think of the three terms in the set of our title as supplements, in Derrida's sense (1974). A supplement is something that is added as if an inessential extra to something else that hitherto had been perceived as standing on its own, but which at the same time paradoxically proclaims the essential inadequacy of the previous entity. The supplement coexists with that which it supplements in a deeply destabilizing way. Supplementarity suggests why every dialectical structure must remain open, why no synthesis can be anything more than provisional. Our ideas of culture and history are always to be supplemented by each other, and the resultant combinations are always to be supplemented by concerns with power. What follows in this reader is meant to point the way toward further supplements—shaping, shifting, and sharpening new disciplinary configurations and theoretical commitments, without ever losing hold of the restless and relentless concern for truth that, for all its misuses, we must continue to sustain.

REFERENCES

Adorno, Theodor, and Max Horkheimer. 1972. "The Culture Industry: Enlightenment as Mass Deception," in Adorno and Horkheimer, *The Dialectic of Enlightenment*, 120–67. New York: Herder and Herder.

Alexander, Sally. 1984. "Women, Class and Sexual Differences in the 1830s and 1840s: Some Reflections on the Writing of a Feminist History," *History Workshop Journal* 17:125–49.

Althusser, Louis. 1969. *For Marx*. London: New Left Books.

———. 1971. "Ideology and Ideological State Apparatuses (Notes towards an Investigation)," in *Lenin and Philosophy and Other Essays*, 121–73. London: New Left Books.

Althusser, Louis, and Etienne Balibar. 1970. *Reading Capital*. London: New Left Books.

Andersen, Margaret L., and Patricia Hill Collins. 1992. *Race, Class and Gender: An Anthology*. Belmont, Calif.: Wadsworth Publishing Co.

Anderson, Benedict. 1983. *Imagined Communities: Reflections on the Origin and Spread of Nationalism*. London: Verso.

Bakhtin, M. M. 1968. *Rabelais and His World*. Translated by H. Iswolsky. Cambridge, Mass.: MIT Press.

———. 1981. *The Dialogic Imagination: Four Essays*. Translated by C. Emerson and M. Holquist. Austin: University of Texas Press.

Baudrillard, Jean. 1988. *Selected Writings*. Edited by Mark Poster. Stanford: Stanford University Press.

Benjamin, Walter. 1968. *Illuminations*. New York: Harcourt, Brace, & World.

Bennett, Tony. 1982. "Text and History," in Peter Widdowson, ed., *Re-Reading English*, 223–36. London: Methuen.

———. 1990. *Outside Literature*. London: Routledge.

Benton, Ted. 1984. *The Rise and Fall of Structuralist Marxism: Althusser and His Influence*. New York: St. Martin's Press.

Blackbourn, David. 1991. "The German Bourgeoisie: An Introduction," in Blackbourn and Richard J. Evans, eds., *The German Bourgeoisie: Essays on the Social History of the German Middle Class from the Late Eighteenth to the Early Twentieth Century*, 1–45. London: Routledge.

Bloch, Maurice, ed. 1975. *Marxist Analyses and Social Anthropology*. New York: Wiley.

———. 1986. *From Blessing to Violence: History and Ideology in the Circumcision Ritual of the Merina of Madagascar*. Cambridge: Cambridge University Press.

Bourdieu, Pierre. 1977. *Outline of a Theory of Practice*. Translated by R. Nice. Cambridge: Cambridge University Press.

Brantlinger, Patrick. 1990. *Crusoe's Footprints: Cultural Studies in Britain and America*. London: Routledge.

Braverman, Harry. 1974. *Labor and Monopoly Capital*. New York: Monthly Review Press.

Calhoun, Craig, ed. 1992. *Habermas and the Public Sphere*. Cambridge, Mass.: MIT Press.

Campbell, Beatrix. 1984. *Wigan Pier Revisited: Poverty and Politics in the Eighties*. London: Virago.

Canguilhem, Georges. 1978. *On the Normal and the Pathological*. Translated by C. R. Fawcett. Boston: D. Reidel Publishing Co.

Clifford, James. 1988. *The Predicament of Culture: Twentieth-Century Ethnography, Literature, and Art*. Cambridge, Mass.: Harvard University Press.

Clifford, James, and George E. Marcus, eds. 1986. *Writing Culture: The Poetics and Politics of Ethnography*. Berkeley: University of California Press.

Cocker, Jürgen, and Mitchell, Allen. 1993. *Bourgeois Society in Nineteenth-Century Europe*. Oxford and Providence: Berg.

Collier, Jane, and Rosaldo, Michelle Z. 1981. "Gender and Sexuality in Simple Societies," in S. B. Ortner and H. Whitehead, eds., *Sexual Meanings: The Cultural Construction of Gender and Sexuality*. New York: Cambridge University Press.

Collins, Patricia Hill. 1990. *Black Feminist Thought: Knowledge, Consciousness, and the Politics of Empowerment*. Boston: Unwin Hyman.

de Certeau, Michel. 1984. *The Practice of Everyday Life*. Berkeley: University of California Press.

de Lauretis, Teresa. 1984. *Alice Doesn't: Feminism, Semiotics, Cinema*. Bloomington: Indiana University Press.

Derrida, Jacques. 1974. *Of Grammatology*. Translated by Gayatri Chakravorty Spivak. Baltimore: Johns Hopkins University Press.

———. 1991. *A Derrida Reader*. Edited by Peggy Kamuf. New York: Columbia University Press.

Dews, Peter. 1988. *Logics of Disintegration: Post-Structuralist Thought and the Claims of Critical Theory*. London: Verso.

Dirks, Nicholas B. 1987. *The Hollow Crown: Ethnohistory of an Indian Kingdom*. Cambridge: Cambridge University Press.

———. 1992a. "Castes of Mind," *Representations* 37:56–78.

———. 1992b. *Colonialism and Culture*. Ann Arbor: University of Michigan Press.

Donzelot, Jacques. 1979. *The Policing of Families*. New York: Pantheon.

Eley, Geoff. 1989. "Labor History, Social History, *Alltagsgeschichte*: Experience, Culture, and the Politics of the Everyday—A New Direction for German Social History?" *Journal of Modern History* 61:297–343.

Elliott, Gregory. 1987. *Althusser: The Detour of Theory*. London: Verso.

Ellis, Kate. 1989. "Stories without Endings: Deconstructive Theory and Political Practice," *Socialist Review* 19:37–52.

Foucault, Michel. 1977a. *Discipline and Punish: The Birth of the Prison*. Translated by Alan Sheridan. London: Allen Lane.

———. 1977b. *Language, Counter-Memory, Practice: Selected Essays and Interviews*. Translated by D. F. Bouchard and S. Simon. Ithaca, N.Y.: Cornell University Press.

———. 1978. *History of Sexuality*, vol. 1. Translated by Michael Hurley. New York: Pantheon.

———. 1980. *Power/Knowledge: Selected Interviews and Other Writings, 1972–1977*. Edited and translated by Colin Gordon. New York: Pantheon.

———. 1982. "The Subject and Power," in H. Dreyfus and P. Rabinow, eds., *Michel Foucault: Beyond Structuralism and Hermeneutics*. Translated by H. Dreyfus and P. Rabinow. Chicago: University of Chicago Press.

———. 1988. *Politics, Philosophy, Culture: Interviews and Other Writings, 1977–1984*. Edited by Lawrence D. Kritzman. New York: Routledge.

Fraser, Nancy. 1989. *Unruly Practices: Power, Discourse and Gender in Contemporary Social Theory*. Minneapolis: University of Minnesota Press.

Geertz, Clifford, 1973. "Ideology as a Cultural System" and "Deep Play: Notes on the Balinese Cockfight," in Geertz, *The Interpretation of Cultures*, 193–233 and 412–53. New York: Basic Books.

———. 1980. *Negara: The Theater State in Nineteenth-Century Bali*. Princeton, N.J.: Princeton University Press.

Geertz, Clifford. 1988. *Works and Lives: The Anthropologist as Author*. Stanford, Calif.: Stanford University Press.

Genovese, Eugene. 1974. *Roll, Jordan, Roll: The World the Slaves Made*. New York: Pantheon.

Giddens, Anthony. 1979. *Central Problems in Social Theory: Action, Structure and Contradiction in Social Analysis*. Berkeley: University of California Press.

Godelier, Mourice. 1977. *Perspectives in Marxist Anthropology*. Cambridge: Cambridge University Press.

Gramsci, Antonio, 1967. *The Modern Prince and Other Writings*. Translated by L. Marks. New York: International Publishers.

———. 1971. *Selections from the Prison Notebooks*. Translated by Q. Hoare and G. N. Smith. London: Lawrence and Wishart.

Gray, Robert. 1986. "The Deconstruction of the English Working Class," *Social History* 11:363–74.

Greenblatt, Stephen. 1980. *Renaissance Self-Fashioning*. Chicago: University of Chicago Press.

Grossberg, Lawrence, Cary Nelson, and Paula Treichler. 1992. *Cultural Studies*. New York: Routledge.

Habermas, Jürgen. [1962] 1989. *The Structural Transformation of the Public Sphere: An Inquiry into a Category of Bourgeois Society*. Reprint, Cambridge, Mass.: MIT Press.

Hall, Stuart, 1978. "Some Problems with the Ideology/Subject Couplet," *Ideology and Consciousness* 3:113–21.

Hall, Stuart, and Tony Jefferson, eds. 1976. *Resistance through Rituals: Youth Subcultures in Post-War Britain*. London: Hutchinson.

Harvey, David. 1989. *The Condition of Postmodernity: An Enquiry into the Origins of Cultural Change*. Oxford: Basil Blackwell.

Hindess, Barry, and Paul Q. Hirst. 1975. *Pre-Capitalist Modes of Production*. London: Routledge.

Hobsbawm, Eric, and Terence Ranger, eds. 1983. *The Invention of Tradition*. Cambridge: Cambridge University Press.

Hunt, Lynn, ed. 1989. *The New Cultural History*. Berkeley: University of California Press.

Huyssen, Andreas. 1986. *After the Great Divide: Modernism, Mass Culture, Postmodernism*. Bloomington: Indiana University Press.

Jameson, Frederic. 1981. *The Political Unconscious*. Ithaca, N.Y.: Cornell University Press.

———. 1984. "Postmodernism, or the Cultural Logic of Late Capitalism," *New Left Review* 146 (July–August): 53–92.

Johnson, Richard. 1987. "What Is Cultural Studies Anyway?" *Social Text* 6:38–80.

Kocka, Jürgen, and Alan Mitchell, eds. 1993. *Bourgeois Society in Nineteenth-Century Europe*. Oxford: Berg Publishers.

Lacan, Jacques. 1977. *Ecrits*. New York: Norton.

LaCapra, Dominick. 1983. *Rethinking Intellectual History: Texts, Contexts, Language*. Ithaca, N.Y.: Cornell University Press.

———. 1985. *History and Criticism*. Ithaca, N.Y.: Cornell University Press.

Laclau, Ernesto, and Chantal Mouffe. 1985. *Hegemony and Socialist Strategy: Towards a Radical Democratic Politics*. Translated by W. Moore and P. Cammack. London: Verso.

Lash, Scott. 1990. *Sociology of Postmodernism*. London: Routledge.

Lash, Scott, and John Urry. 1987. *The End of Organized Capitalism*. Cambridge: Polity Press.

Lévi-Strauss, Claude. 1966. *The Savage Mind*. No translator listed. Chicago: University of Chicago Press.

Lüdtke, Alf, ed. 1993. *The History of Everyday Life: Reconstructing Historical Experiences and Ways of Life*. Princeton, N.J.: Princeton University Press.

Lyotard, Jean-Francois. 1984. *The Postmodern Condition*. Minneapolis: University of Minnesota Press.

Macherey, Pierre. 1978. *A Theory of Literary Production*. Translated by G. Wall. London, Boston: Routledge and Kegan Paul.

Mascia-Lees, Frances E., Patricia Sharpe, and Colleen Ballerino Cohen. 1989. "The Postmodernist Turn in Anthropology: Cautions from a Feminist Perspective," *Signs* 15:7–33.

McAllester Jones, Mary. 1991. *Gaston Bachelard, Subversive Humanist: Texts and Readings*. Madison: University of Wisconsin Press.

McClary, Susan. 1990. *Feminine Endings: Music, Gender, and Sexuality*. Minneapolis: University of Minnesota Press.

———. 1992. *Georges Bizet's Carmen*. Cambridge and New York: Cambridge University Press.

McCloskey, Donald N. 1985. *The Rhetoric of Economics*. Madison: University of Wisconsin Press.

McDonald, Terrence, ed. Forthcoming. *The Historic Turn in the Human Sciences*. Ann Arbor: University of Michigan Press.

McIntosh, Mary, and Ann-Marie Wolpe, eds. 1978. *Feminism and Materialism*. London: Routledge.

Mead, Margaret. 1933. *Coming of Age in Samoa: A Psychological Study of Primitive Youth for Western Civilization*. New York: Blue Ribbon Books.

———. 1935. *Sex and Temperament in Three Primitive Societies*. London: G. Routledge and Sons.

Mohanty, S. P. 1989. "Us and Them: On the Philosophical Bases of Political Criticism," *Yale Journal of Criticism* 2(2):1–31.

Mouffe, Chantal, ed. 1979. *Gramsci and Marxist Theory*. London: Routledge.

Ortner, Sherry B. 1989. *High Religion: A Cultural and Political History of Sherpa Buddhism*. Princeton, N.J.: Princeton University Press.

———. 1991. "Reading America: Preliminary Notes on Class and Culture," in Richard G. Fox, ed., *Recapturing Anthropology: Working in the Present*, 163–89. Santa Fe, N.M.: School of American Research Press.

Ortner, Sherry B., and Harriet Whitehead, eds. 1981. *Sexual Meanings: The Cultural Construction of Gender and Sexuality*. New York: Cambridge University Press.

Poulantzas, Nicos. 1973. *Political Power and Social Classes*. Translated by T. O'Hagan. London: New Left Books.

———. 1975. *Classes in Contemporary Capitalism*. Translated by D. Fernbach. London: New Left Books.

Riley, Denise. 1983. *War in the Nursery: Theories of the Child and Mother*. London: Virago.

Sacks, Karen. 1989. "Toward a Unified Theory of Class, Race, and Gender," *American Ethnologist* 16 (3):534–50.

Sahlins, Marshall. 1981. *Historical Metaphors and Mythical Realities: Structure in the Early History of the Sandwich Islands Kingdom*. Ann Arbor: University of Michigan Press.

———. 1985. *Islands of History*. Chicago: University of Chicago Press.

Said, Edward. 1979. *Orientalism*. New York: Vintage Books.

———. 1983. *The World, the Text, and the Critic*. Cambridge, Mass.: Harvard University Press.

Sangren, P. Steven. 1988. "Rhetoric and Authority of Ethnography: 'Postmodernism' and the Social Reproduction of Texts," *Current Anthropology* 29, no. 3 (June 1988).

Saussure, Ferdinand de. 1983. *Course in General Linguistics*. Translated by R. Harris. London: Duckworth.

Scobey, David, 1992. "Anatomy of the Promenade: The Politics of Bourgeois Sociability in Nineteenth-Century New York," *Social History* 17:203–27.

Scott, James C. 1976. *The Moral Economy of the Peasant: Subsistence and Rebellion in Southeast Asia*. New Haven: Yale University Press.

———. 1985. *Weapons of the Weak: Everyday Forms of Resistance*. New Haven: Yale University Press.

———. 1990. *Domination and the Arts of Resistance: Hidden Transcripts*. New Haven: Yale University Press.

Scott, Joan Wallach. 1988. *Gender and the Politics of History*. New York: Columbia University Press.

Soja, Edward W. 1989. *Postmodern Geographies: The Reassertion of Space in Critical Social Theory*. London: Verso.

Spivak, Gayatri Chakravorty. 1988. "Can the Subaltern Speak?" in Cary Nelson and Lawrence Grossberg, eds., *Marxism and the Interpretation of Culture*, 271–313. Urbana: University of Illinois Press.

Stallybrass, Peter, and Allon White. 1986. *The Politics and Poetics of Transgression*. Ithaca, N.Y.: Cornell University Press.

Stedman Jones, Gareth. 1975. "Class Struggle and the Industrial Revolution," *New Left Review* 90:35–69. Reprinted in Jones 1983, 25–75.

———. 1983. *Languages of Class: Studies in English Working-Class History 1832–1982*. Cambridge: Cambridge University Press.

Steedman, Carolyn Kay. 1987. *Landscape for a Good Woman: A Story of Two Lives*. New Brunswick, N.J.: Rutgers University Press.

Stoler, Ann. 1989. "Rethinking Colonial Categories: European Communities and the Boundaries of Rule," *Comparative Studies in Society and History* 31 (1):134–61.

Thompson, E. P. 1963. *The Making of the English Working Class*. London: Gollancz.

Veeser, H. Aram, ed. 1989. *The New Historicism*. London: Routledge.

Voloshinov, V. N. 1973. *Marxism and the Philosophy of Language*. Translated by L. Matejka and I. R. Titunik. New York: Seminar Press.

White, Hayden. 1973. *Metahistory: The Historical Imagination in Nineteenth-Century Europe*. Baltimore: Johns Hopkins University Press.

Williams, Raymond. 1958. *Culture and Society 1780–1950*. London: Chatto and Windus.

———. 1961. *The Long Revolution*. London: Chatto and Windus.

———. 1977. *Marxism and Literature*. Oxford: Oxford University Press.

Willis, Paul. 1977. *Learning to Labor: How Working-Class Kids Get Working-Class Jobs*. New York: Columbia University Press.

Wilson, Elizabeth. 1988. *Hallucinations: Life in the Post-Modern City*. London: Hutchinson Radius.

Wolff, Janet, and John Seed, eds. 1988. *The Culture of Capital: Art, Power and the Nineteenth-Century Middle Class*. Manchester: Manchester University Press.

Wolpe, Harold, ed. 1980. *The Articulation of Modes of Production*. London: Routledge.

Wright, Erik Olin. 1978. *Class, Crisis, and the State*. London: New Left Books.

PART ONE

Culture / POWER / History

CHAPTER ONE

Teddy Bear Patriarchy: Taxidermy in the Garden of Eden, New York City, 1908–1936

DONNA HARAWAY

Nature teaches law and order and respect for property.
If these people cannot go to the country, then the
Museum must bring nature to the city.[1]

I started my thoughts on the legend of Romulus and Remus
who had been suckled by a wolf and founded Rome,
but in the jungle I had my little Lord Greystoke
suckled by an ape.[2]

THE AKELEY AFRICAN HALL AND THE THEODORE ROOSEVELT MEMORIAL IN THE AMERICAN MUSEUM OF NATURAL HISTORY: EXPERIENCE

In the heart of New York City stands Central Park—the urban garden designed by Frederick Law Olmsted to heal the overwrought or decadent city dweller with a prophylactic dose of nature. Immediately across from the park, the Theodore Roosevelt Memorial presides as the central building of the American Museum of Natural History, a monumental reproduction of the Garden of Eden. In the Garden, Western Man may begin again the first journey, the first birth from within the sanctuary of nature. An institution founded just after the Civil War and dedicated to popular education and scientific research, the American Museum of Natural History is the place to undertake this genesis, this regeneration. Passing through the Museum's Roosevelt Memorial atrium into the African Hall, opened in 1936, the ordinary citizen may enter a privileged space and time: the Age of Mammals in the heart of Africa, scene of the origin of our species.[3] A hope is implicit in every architectural detail: in immediate vision of the origin, perhaps the future can be fixed. By saving the beginnings, the end can be achieved and the present can be transcended. African Hall offers a unique communion with nature at its highest and yet most vulnerable moment, the moment of the interface of the Age of Mammals with the Age of Man. This communion is offered through the sense of vision by the craft of taxidermy.

Restoration of the origin, the task of genetic hygiene, is achieved in Carl Akeley's African Hall by an art that began for him in the 1880s with the crude stuffing of P. T. Barnum's elephant, Jumbo, who had been run down by a railroad train, the emblem of the Industrial Revolution. The end of his task came in the 1920s, with his exquisite mounting of the Giant of Karisimbi, the lone silverback male gorilla that dominates the diorama depicting the site of Akeley's own grave in the mountainous rain forest of the Congo, today's Zaire. So that it could inhabit Akeley's monument to the purity of nature, this gorilla was killed in 1921, the same year the Museum hosted the Second International Congress of Eugenics. From the dead body of the primate, Akeley crafted something finer than the living organism; he achieved its true end, a new genesis. Decadence—the threat of the city, civilization, machine—was stayed in the politics of eugenics and the art of taxidermy. And the Museum fulfilled its scientific purpose of conservation, of preservation, of the production of permanence. Life was transfigured in the principal civic arena of Western political theory—the natural body of man.[4]

Behind every mounted animal, bronze sculpture, or photograph lies a profusion of objects and social interactions among people and other animals, which in the end can be recomposed to tell a biography embracing major themes for the 20th-century United States. But the recomposition produces a story that is reticent, even mute, about Africa. H. F. Osborn, president of the American Museum from 1908–33, thought Akeley was Africa's biographer. This essay will argue that Akeley is America's biographer, or rather a biographer of a part of North America. Akeley thought that in African Hall the visitor would experience nature at its moment of highest perfection. He did not dream that he crafted the means to experience a history of race, sex, and class in New York City that reached to Nairobi. He thought he was telling the unified truth of natural history. His story will be recomposed to tell a tale of the commerce of power and knowledge in white and male supremacist monopoly capitalism, fondly named Teddy Bear Patriarchy.[5]

To enter the Theodore Roosevelt Memorial, the visitor must pass by a James Earle Fraser equestrian statue of Teddy majestically mounted as father and protector between two "primitive" men, an American Indian and an African, both standing and dressed as "savages." The facade of the memorial, funded by the State of New York and awarded to the American Museum of Natural History on the basis of its competitive application in 1923, is classical, with four Ionic columns 54 feet high, topped by statues of the great explorers Boone, Audubon, Lewis, and Clark. Reminiscent of coins, bas-relief seals of the United States and of the Liberty Bell are stamped on the front panels. Inscribed across the top are the words TRUTH, KNOWLEDGE, VISION and the dedication to Roosevelt as "a great leader of the youth of America, in energy and fortitude in the faith of our fathers, in defense of the rights of the people, in the love and conservation of nature and of the best in life and in man." Youth, paternal solicitude, virile defense of democracy, and intense emotional connection to nature are the unmistakable themes.[6]

The building presents itself in many visible faces. It is at once a Greek temple, a bank, a scientific research institution, a popular museum, a neoclassical theatre. One is entering a space that sacralizes democracy, Protestant Christianity, adventure, science, and commerce. It is impossible not to feel entering this building that a drama will be enacted inside. Experience in this public monument will be intensely personal; this structure is one of North America's spaces for joining the duality of self and community.

Just inside the portals, the visitor enters the first sacred space where transformation of consciousness and moral state will begin.[7] The walls are inscribed with Roosevelt's words under the headings "Nature," "Youth," "Manhood," the "State." The seeker begins in Nature: "There are no words that can tell the hidden spirit of the wilderness, that can reveal its mystery. . . . The nation behaves well if it treats its natural resources as assets which it must turn over to the next generation increased and not impaired in value." Nature is mystery and resource, a critical union in the history of civilization. The visitor—necessarily a boy in moral state, no matter what accidents of biology or social gender might have pertained prior to the excursion to the museum—progresses through Youth: "I want to see you game boys . . . and gentle and tender. . . . Courage, hard work, self mastery, and intelligent effort are essential to a successful life." Youth mirrors Nature, its pair across the room. The next stage is Manhood: "Only those are fit to live who do not fear to die and none are fit to die who have shrunk from the joy of life and the duty of life. Opposite is its spiritual pair, the State: "Aggressive fighting for the right is the noblest sport the world affords. . . . If I must choose between righteousness and peace, I choose righteousness." The walls of the atrium are full of murals depicting Roosevelt's life, the perfect illustration of his words. His life is inscribed in stone in a peculiarly literal way appropriate to this museum. One sees the man hunting big game in Africa, conducting diplomacy in the Philippines and China, helping boy and girl scouts, receiving academic honors, and presiding over the Panama Canal ("The land divided, the world united").

Finally, in the atrium also are the striking life-size bronze sculptures by Carl Akeley of the Nandi spearmen of East Africa on a lion hunt. These African men and the lion they kill symbolize for Akeley the essence of the hunt, of what would later be named "man the hunter." In discussing the lion spearers, Akeley always referred to them as men. In every other circumstance he referred to adult male Africans as boys. Roosevelt, the modern sportsman, and the "primitive" Nandi share in the spiritual truth of manhood. The noble sculptures express Akeley's great love for Roosevelt, his friend and hunting companion in Africa in 1910, for the killing of one of the elephants which Akeley mounted for the museum. Akeley said he would follow Roosevelt anywhere because of his "sincerity and integrity."[8]

In the museum shop in the atrium in the 1980s, one may purchase *T.R.: Champion of the Strenuous Life*, a photographic biography of the 26th president. Every aspect of the fulfillment of manhood is depicted within; even death is labeled "the Great Adventure." One learns that after his defeat in the presidential campaign of 1912, Roosevelt undertook the exploration of the Amazonian tributary, the River of Doubt, under the auspices of the American Museum of Natural History and the Brazilian Government. It was a perfect trip. The explorers nearly died, the river had never before been seen by white men, and the great stream, no longer doubtful, was renamed Rio Roosevelt by the Brazilian State. In the picture biography, which includes a print of the adventurers paddling their primitive dugout canoe (one assumes before starvation and jungle fever attenuated the ardor of the photographer in this desolate land), the former president of a great industrial power explains his return to the wilderness: "I had to go. It was my last chance to be a boy."[9]

The joining of life and death in these icons of Roosevelt's journeys and in the architecture of his stony memorial announces the central moral truth of this museum. This is the effective truth of manhood, the state conferred on the visitor who successfully passes through the trial of the museum. The body can be transcended. This is the lesson Simone de Beauvoir so painfully remembered in *The Second Sex*; man is the sex which risks life and in so doing, achieves his existence. In the upside-down world of Teddy Bear Patriarchy, it is in the craft of killing that life is constructed, not in the accident of personal, material birth. Roosevelt is clearly the perfect locus genie and patron saint for the museum and its task of regeneration of a miscellaneous, incoherent urban public threatened with genetic and social decadence, threatened with the prolific bodies of the new immigrants, threatened with the failure of manhood.[10]

The Akeley African Hall itself is simultaneously a very strange place and an ordinary experience for literally millions of North Americans over more than five decades. The types of display in this hall spread all over the country, and even the world, partly due to the craftspeople Akeley himself trained. In the 1980s sacrilege is perhaps more evident than liminal experience of nature. What is the experience of New York streetwise kids wired to Walkman radios and passing the Friday afternoon cocktail bar by the lion diorama? These are the kids who came to the museum to see the high-tech Nature-Max films. But soon, for those not physically wired into the communication system of the late 20th century, another time begins to take form. The African Hall was meant to be a time machine, and it is.[11] The individual is entering the Age of Mammals. But one is entering alone, each individual soul, as part of no stable prior community and without confidence in the substance of one's body, in order to be received into a saved community. One begins in the threatening chaos of the industrial city, part of a horde, but here one will come to belong, to find substance. No matter how many people crowd the great hall, the experience is of individual communion with nature. The sacrament will be enacted for each worshiper; here is no nature constituted from statistical reality and a probability calculus. This is not a random world, populated by late 20th-century cyborgs, for whom the threat of decadence is a nostalgic memory of a dim organic past, but the moment of origin where nature and culture, private and public, profane and sacred meet—a moment of incarnation in the encounter of man and animal.

The Hall is darkened, lit only from the display cases which line the sides of the spacious room. In the center of the Hall is a group of elephants so lifelike that a moment's fantasy suffices for awakening a premonition of their movement—perhaps an angry charge at one's personal intrusion. The elephants stand like a high altar in the nave of a great cathedral. That impression is strengthened by one's growing consciousness of the dioramas that line both sides of the Main Hall, as well as the sides of the spacious gallery above. Lit from within, the dioramas contain detailed and lifelike groups of large African mammals—game for the wealthy New York hunters who financed this experience; they are called habitat groups and are the culmination of the taxidermist's art. Called by Akeley a "peephole into the jungle,"[12] each diorama presents itself as a side altar, a stage, an unspoiled garden in nature, a hearth for home and family. As an altar, each diorama tells a part of the story of salvation history; each has its special emblems indicating particular virtues. Above all, inviting the visitor to share in its revelation, each tells the truth. Each offers a vision. Each is a window onto knowledge.

A diorama is eminently a story, a part of natural history. The story is told in the pages of nature, read by the naked eye. The animals in the habitat groups are captured in a photographer's vision and a sculptor's vision. They are actors in a morality play on the stage of nature, and the eye is the critical organ. Each diorama contains a small group of animals in the foreground, in the midst of exact reproductions of plants, insects, rocks, soil. Paintings reminiscent of Hollywood movie set art curve in back of the group and up to the ceiling, creating a great panoramic vision of a scene on the African continent. Each painting is minutely appropriate to the particular animals in the foreground. Among the 28 dioramas in the Hall, all the major geographic areas of the African continent and most of the large mammals are represented.

Gradually, the viewer begins to articulate the content of the story. Most groups are made up of only a few animals, usually including a large and vigilant male, a female or two, and one baby. Perhaps there are some other animals—a male adolescent maybe, never an aged or deformed beast. The animals in the group form a developmental series, such that the group can represent the essence of the species as a dynamic, living whole. The principles of organicism (i.e., of the laws of organic form) rule the composition.[13] There is no need for the multiplication of specimens because the series is a true biography. Each animal is an organism, and the group is an organism. Each organism is a vital moment in the narrative of natural history, condensing the flow of time into the harmony of developmental form. The groups are peaceful, composed, illuminated—in "brightest Africa." Each group forms a community structured by a natural division of function; the whole animal in the whole group is nature's truth. The physiological division of labor that has informed the history of biology is embodied in these habitat groups which tell of communities and families, peacefully and hierarchically ordered. Sexual specialization of function—the organic bodily and social sexual division of labor—is unobtrusively ubiquitous, unquestionable, right. The African buffalo, the white and black rhinos, the lion, the zebra, the mountain nyala, the okapi, the lesser koodo all find their place in the differentiated and developmental harmony of nature. The racial division of labor, the familial progress from youthful native to adult white man, was announced at the steps leading to the building itself; Akeley's original plan for African Hall included bas-relief sculptures of all the "primitive" tribes of Africa complementing the other stories of natural wildlife in the Hall. Organic hierarchies are embodied in every organ in the articulation of natural order in the museum.[14]

But there is a curious note in the story; it begins to dominate as scene after scene draws the visitor into itself through the eyes of the animals in the tableaux.[15] Each diorama has at least one animal that catches the viewer's gaze and holds it in communion. The animal is vigilant, ready to sound an alarm at the intrusion of man, but ready also to hold forever the gaze of meeting, the moment of truth, the original encounter. The moment seems fragile, the animals about to disappear, the communion about to break; the Hall threatens to dissolve into the chaos of the Age of Man. But it does not. The gaze holds, and the wary animal heals those who will look. There is no impediment to this vision. There is no mediation, nothing between the viewer and the animal. The glass front of the diorama forbids the body's entry, but the gaze invites his visual penetration. The animal is frozen in a moment of supreme life, and man is transfixed. No merely living organism could accomplish this act. The specular commerce between man and animal at the interface of two evolutionary ages is completed. The animals in the dioramas have transcended mortal life, and hold their pose forever, with muscles tensed, noses aquiver, veins in the face and delicate ankles and folds in the supple skin all prominent. No visitor to a merely physical Africa could see these animals. This is a spiritual vision made possible only by their death and literal re-presentation. Only then could the essence of their life be present. Only then could the hygiene of nature cure the sick vision of civilized man. Taxidermy fulfills the fatal desire to represent, to be whole; it is a politics of reproduction.

There is one diorama that stands out from all the others, the gorilla group. It is not simply that this group is one of the four large corner displays. There is something special in the painting with the steaming volcano in the background and lake Kivu below, in the pose of the enigmatic large silverback rising above the group in a chest-beating gesture of alarm and an unforgettable gaze in spite of the handicap of glass eyes. Here the painter's art was particularly successful in conveying the sense of limitless vision, of a panorama without end around the focal lush green garden. This is the scene that Akeley longed to return to. It is where he died, feeling he was at home as in no other place on earth. It is where he first killed a gorilla and felt the enchantment of a perfect garden. After his first visit in 1921, he was motivated to convince the Belgian government to make of this area the first African national park to ensure an absolute sanctuary for the gorilla in the future. But the viewer does not know these things when he sees the five animals in a naturalistic setting. It is plain that he is looking at a natural family of close human relatives, but that is not the essence of this diorama. The viewer sees that the elephants, the lion, the rhino, and the water hole group—with its peaceful panorama of all the grassland species, including the carnivores, caught in a moment outside the Fall—all these have been a kind of preparation, not so much for the gorilla group, as for the Giant of Karisimbi. This double for man stands in a unique personal individuality, his fixed face molded forever from the death mask cast from his corpse by a taxidermist in the Kivu Mountains. Here is natural man, immediately known. His image may be purchased on a picture postcard at the desk in the Roosevelt atrium.

It would have been inappropriate to meet the gorilla anywhere else but on the mountain. Frankenstein and his monster had Mont Blanc for their encounter; Akeley and the gorilla first saw each other on the lush volcanoes of central Africa. The glance proved deadly for them both, just as the exchange between Victor Frankenstein and his creature froze each of them into a dialectic of immolation. But Frankenstein tasted the bitter failure of his fatherhood in his own and his creature's death; Akeley resurrected his creature and his authorship in both the sanctuary of Parc Albert and the African Hall of the American Museum of Natural History. Mary Shelley's story may be read as a dissection of the deadly logic of birthing in patriarchy at the dawn of the age of biology; her tale is a nightmare about the crushing failure of the project of man. But the taxidermist labored to restore manhood at the interface of the Age of Mammals and the Age of Man. Akeley achieved the fulfillment of a sportsman in Teddy Bear Patriarchy—he died a father to the game, and their sepulcher is named after him, the Akeley African Hall.

The gorilla was the highest quarry of Akeley's life as artist, scientist, and hunter, but why? He said himself (through his ghostwriter, the invisible Dorothy Greene—is she ever absent?), "To me the gorilla made a much more interesting quarry than lions, elephants, or any other African game, for the gorilla is still comparatively unknown."[16] But so was the colobus monkey or any of a long list of animals. What qualities did it take to make an animal "game"? One answer is similarity to man, the ultimate quarry, a worthy opponent. The ideal quarry is the "other," the natural self. That is one reason Frankenstein needed to hunt down his creature. The obscurity of the gorilla was deepened and made sacred by this question, the title of Akeley's chapter urging scientific research in the new Parc Albert, "Is the gorilla almost a man?" Hunter, scientist, and artist all sought the gorilla for his revelation about the nature and future of manhood. Akeley compared and contrasted his quest for the gorilla with the French-American's, Paul du Chaillu, the first white man to kill a gorilla, in 1855, eight years after it was "discovered." Du Chaillu's account of the encounter stands as the classic portrayal of a depraved and vicious beast killed in the heroic, dangerous encounter. Akeley disbelieved du Chaillu and told his own readers how many times du Chaillu's publishers made him rewrite until the beast was fierce enough. Frankenstein plugged up his ears rather than listen to his awful son claim a gentle and peace-loving soul. Akeley was certain he would find a noble and peaceful beast; so he brought his guns, cameras, and white women into the garden to hunt, wondering what distance measured courage in the face of a charging alter-ego.

Like du Chaillu, Akeley first came upon a sign of the animal, a footprint, or in Akeley's case a handprint, before meeting face to face. "I'll never forget it. In that mud hole were the marks of four great knuckles where the gorilla had placed his hand on the ground. There is no other track like this in the world— there is no other hand in the world so large. . . . As I looked at that track I lost the faith on which I had brought my party to Africa. Instinctively I took my gun from the gun boy."[17] Later, Akeley told that the handprint, not the face, gave him his greatest thrill. In the hand the trace of kinship writ large and terrible struck the craftsman.

But then, on the first day out from camp in the gorilla country, Akeley did meet a gorilla face to face, the creature he had sought for decades, prevented from earlier success by mauling elephants, stingy millionaires, and world war. Within minutes of his first glimpse of the features of the face of an animal he longed more than anything to see, Akeley had killed him, not in the face of a charge, but through a dense forest screen within which the animal hid, rushed, and shook branches. Surely, the taxidermist did not want to risk losing his specimen, for perhaps there would be no more. He knew the Prince of Sweden was just then leaving Africa after having shot fourteen of the great apes in the same region. The animals must be wary of new hunters; collecting might be very difficult.

Whatever the exact logic that ruled the first shot, precisely placed into the aorta, the task that followed was arduous indeed—skinning the animal and transporting the various remains back to camp. The corpse had nearly miraculously lodged itself against the trunk of a tree above a deep chasm. As a result of Herculean labors, which included casting the death mask pictured in *Lions, Gorillas, and their Neighbors*,[18] Akeley was ready for his next gorilla hunt on the second day after shooting the first ape. The pace he was setting for himself was grueling, dangerous for a man ominously weakened by tropical fevers. "But science is a jealous mistress and takes little account of a man's feelings."[19] The second quest resulted in two missed males, a dead female, and her frightened baby speared by the porters and guides. Akeley and his party had killed or attempted to kill every ape they had seen since arriving in the area.

On his third day out, Akeley took his cameras and ordered his guides to lead toward easier country. With a baby, female, and male, he could do a group even if he got no more specimens. Now it was time to hunt with the camera.[20] "Almost before I knew it I was turning the crank of the camera on two gorillas in full view with a beautiful setting behind them. I do not think at the time I appreciated the fact that I was doing a thing that had never been done before."[21] But the photogenic baby and mother and the accompanying small group of other gorillas had become boring after two hundred feet of film, so Akeley provoked an action shot by standing up. That was interesting for a bit. "So finally, feeling that I had about all I could expect from that band, I picked out one that I thought to be an immature male. I shot and killed it and found, much to my regret, that it was a female. As it turned out, however, she was such a splendid large specimen that the feeling of regret was considerably lessened."[22]

Akeley commented on his satisfaction with the triumphs of his gun and camera and decided it was time to ask the rest of the party waiting in a camp below to come up and hunt gorillas. He was getting considerably sicker and feared he would not fulfill his promise to his friends to give them gorilla. His whole purpose in taking white women into gorilla country depended on meeting this commitment: "As a naturalist interested in preserving wild life, I was glad to do anything that might make killing animals less attractive."[23] The best thing to reduce the potency of game for heroic hunting is to demonstrate that inexperienced women could safely do the same thing. Science had already penetrated; women could follow.

Two days of hunting resulted in Herbert Bradley's shooting a large silverback, the one Akeley compared to Jack Dempsey and mounted as the lone male of Karisimbi in African Hall. It was now possible to admit another level of feeling: "As he lay at the base of the tree, it took all one's scientific ardour to keep from feeling like a murderer. He was a magnificent creature with the face of an amiable giant who would do no harm except perhaps in self defense or in defense of his family."[24] If he had succeeded in his aborted hunt, Victor Frankenstein could have spoken those lines.

The photograph in the American Museum film archive of Carl Akeley, Herbert Bradley, and Mary Hastings Bradley holding up the gorilla head and corpse to be recorded by the camera is an unforgettable image. The face of the dead giant looks like Bosch's conception of pain, and the lower jaw hangs slack, held up by Akeley's hand. The body looks bloated and utterly heavy. Mary Bradley gazes smilingly at the faces of the male hunters, her own eyes averted from the camera. Akeley and Herbert Bradley look directly at the camera in an unshuttered acceptance of their act. Two Africans, a young boy and a young man, perch in a tree above the scene, one looking at the camera, one at the hunting party. The contrast of this scene of death with the diorama framing the Giant of Karisimbi mounted in New York is total; the animal came to life again, this time immortal.

Akeley felt he was in the most beautiful spot on earth, and decided the scene of the death of Bradley's gorilla must be painted for the gorilla group in African Hall. There was no more need to kill after another day's observation of a multi-male, multi-female group; instead, the last capture was with the camera. "So the guns were put behind and the camera pushed forward and we had the extreme satisfaction of seeing the band of gorillas disappear over the crest of the opposite ridge none the worse for having met with white men that morning. It was a wonderful finish to a wonderful gorilla hunt."[25] Once domination is complete, conservation is urgent. But perhaps preservation comes too late.

What followed was the return to the United States and active work for an absolute gorilla sanctuary providing facilities for scientific research. Akeley feared the gorilla would be driven to extinction before it was adequately known to science.[26] His health weakened but his spirit at its height, Akeley lived to return to Kivu to prepare paintings and other material for the gorilla group diorama. Between 1921 and 1926, he mounted his precious gorilla specimens, producing that extraordinary silverback whose gaze dominates African Hall. When he did return to Kivu in 1926, he was so exhausted from his exertions to reach his goal that he died on November 17, 1926, almost immediately after he and his party arrived on the slopes of Mount Mikena, "in the land of his dreams."[27]

Akeley's was a literal science dedicated to the prevention of decadence, of biological decay. His grave was built in the heart of the rain forest on the volcano, where "all the free wild things of the forest have perpetual sanctuary."[28] Mary Jobe Akeley directed the digging of an eight-foot vault in lava gravel and rock. The hole was lined with closely set wooden beams. The coffin was crafted on the site out of solid native mahogany and lined with heavy galvanized steel salvaged from the boxes used to pack specimens to protect them from insect and other damage. Then the coffin was upholstered with camp blankets. A slab of cement ten by twelve feet and five inches thick was poured on top of the grave and inscribed with the name and date of death of the father of the game. The cement had been carried on porters' backs all the way from the nearest source in Kibale, Uganda. The men apparently ditched the first heavy load in the face of difficult trails; they were sent back for a second effort. An eight-foot stockade fence was built around the grave to deter buffalo and elephants from desecrating the site. "Dersheid, Raddatz, Bill and I worked five days and five nights to give him the best home we could build, and he was buried as I think he would have liked with a simple reading service and a prayer."[29] The grave was inviolate, and the reincarnation of the natural self would be immortal in African Hall. In 1979, "grave robbers, Zairoise poachers, violated the site and carried off [Akeley's] skeleton. . . ."[30]

CARL E. AKELEY (1864–1926), THE GUN, THE CAMERA, AND THE HUNT FOR TRUTH: BIOGRAPHY

For this untruthful picture Akeley substitutes a real gorilla.[31]

Of the two I was the savage and the aggressor.[32]

Carl Akeley's boss at the American Museum, H. F. Osborn, characterized the taxidermist as a sculptor and a biographer of African life. Akeley sought to craft a true life, a unique life. The life of Africa became his life, his telos. But it is not possible to tell his life from a single point of view. There is a polyphony of stories, and they do not harmonize. Each source for telling the story of Akeley's life speaks in an authoritative mode, but the historian felt compelled to compare the versions, and then to cast Akeley's story in an ironic mode, the register most avoided by her subject. Akeley wanted to present an immediate vision; I would like to dissect and make visible layer after layer of mediation. I want to show the reader how the experience of the diorama grew from the safari in specific times and places, how the camera and the gun together are the conduits for the spiritual commerce of man and nature, how biography is woven into and from a social and political tissue. I want to show how the stunning animals of Akeley's achieved dream in African Hall are the product of particular technologies, i.e., the techniques of effecting meanings. Technologies are concretized moments of human possibility. Marx called them dead labor, needing the animation of living labor. True enough. [Akeley's] grave was built in the heart of the rain forest on the volcano, but the relations of life and death in technologies of enforced meaning, or realist representation, are not so straightforward, even for early 20th-century organic beings, much less for ourselves, late 20th-century cyborgs, reading stories about the dead craftsman and the obsolete craft of resurrection.[33]

Life Stories

According to the available plots in U.S. history, it is necessary that Carl Akeley was born on a farm in New York State of poor, but vigorous old (white) American stock. The moment of his birth is also necessary, 1864, near the end of the Civil War. The time was an end and a beginning for so much in North America, including the history of biology and the structure of wealth and social class. His boyhood was spent in hard farm labor, in which he learned self-reliance and skill with tools and machines. From the beginning he passed long hours alone watching and hunting the wildlife of New York. By the age of 13, aroused by a borrowed book on the subject, Akeley was committed to the vocation of taxidermy. His vocation's bibliogenesis was also ordained by the plot. At that age (or age 16 in some versions), he had a business card printed up. No Yankee boy could miss the connection of life's purpose with business, although young Carl scarcely believed he could make a living at such a craft. He took lessons in painting, so that he might provide realistic backgrounds for the birds he ceaselessly mounted. From the beginning Akeley's life had a single focus: the capturing and representation of the nature he saw. On this point all the versions of Akeley's life concur.

After the crops were in, at the age of 19, Akeley set off from his father's farm "to get a wider field for my efforts."[34] First he tried to get a job with a local painter and interior decorator whose hobby was taxidermy, but this man, David Bruce, directed the young man to an institution which changed his life—Ward's Natural Science Establishment in Rochester, where Akeley would spend four years and form a friendship pregnant with consequences for the nascent science of ecology as it came to be practiced in museum exhibition. Ward's provided mounted specimens and natural history collections for practically all the museums in the nation. Several important men in the history of biology and museology in the United States passed through this curious institution, including Akeley's friend, William Morton Wheeler. Wheeler completed his eminent career in entomology at Harvard, a founder of the science of animal ecology (which he called ethology—the science of the character of nature) and a mentor in the philosophy of science and of society to the great organicists and conservative social philosophers in Harvard's biological and medical establishment.[35] Wheeler was then a young Milwaukee naturalist steeped in German "kultur" who began tutoring the rustic Akeley for entry into Yale's Sheffield Scientific School. However, 11 hours of taxidermy in the day and long hours of study proved too much; so higher education was postponed, later permanently, in order to follow the truer vocation of reading nature's book directly.

Akeley was sorely disappointed at Ward's because business imperatives allowed no room for improvement of the craft of taxidermy. He felt animals were "upholstered." He developed his own skill and technique in spite of the lack of encouragement, and the lack of money, and got a chance for public recognition when P. T. Barnum's famous elephant was run down by a locomotive in Canada in 1885. Barnum did not want to forgo the fame and profit from continuing to display the giant (who had died trying to save a baby elephant, we are told), so Akeley and a companion were dispatched to Canada from Rochester to save the situation. Six butchers from a nearby town helped with the rapidly rotting carcass; and what the young Akeley learned about very large mammal taxidermy from this experience laid the foundation for his later revolutionary innovations in producing light, strong, lifelike pachyderms. The popular press followed the monumental mounting, and the day Jumbo was launched into his own railroad car into his post-mortem career, half the population of Rochester witnessed the resurrection. The first big period of trial was over for the young taxidermist.[36]

In 1885, Wheeler had returned to Milwaukee to teach high school and soon took up a curatorship in the Milwaukee Museum of Natural History. Wheeler urged his friend to follow, hoping to continue his tutoring and to secure Akeley commissions for specimens from the museum. At this time, museums did not generally have their own taxidermy departments, although the years around 1890 were a period of flowering of taxidermic technique in Britain and the United States. Akeley opened his business shop on the Wheeler family property, and he and the naturalist spent long hours discussing natural history, finding themselves in agreement both about museum display and about the character of nature. The most important credo for them both was the need to develop scientific knowledge of the whole animal in the whole group in nature—i.e., they were committed organicists. Wheeler soon became director of the Milwaukee museum and gave Akeley significant support. Akeley had conceived the idea for habitat groups and wished to mount a series illustrating the fur-bearing animals of Wisconsin. His completed muskrat group (1889), minus the painted backgrounds, was probably the first mammalian habitat group anywhere.

As a result of a recommendation from Wheeler, in 1894 the British Museum invited Akeley to practice his trade in that world-famous institution. On the way to London, Akeley visited the Field Museum in Chicago, met Daniel Giraud Elliot, and accepted his offer of preparing the large collection of specimens the museum had bought from Ward's. In 1896, Akeley made his first collecting expedition to Africa, to British Somaliland, a trip that opened a whole new world to him. This was the first of five safaris to Africa, each escalating his sense of the purity of the continent's vanishing wildlife and the conviction that the meaning of his life was its preservation through transforming taxidermy into an art. He was again in Africa for the Field Museum in 1905, with his explorer/adventurer/author wife, Delia, to collect elephants in British East Africa. On this trip Akeley escaped with his life after killing a leopard in hand-to-fang combat.

In Chicago Akeley spent four years largely at his own expense preparing the justly famous Four Seasons deer dioramas depicting typical scenes in every detail. In 1908, at the invitation of the new [museum] president, H. F. Osborn, who was anxious to mark his office with the discovery of major new scientific laws and departures in museum exhibition and public education, Akeley moved to New York and the American Museum of Natural History in hope of preparing a major collection of large African mammals. From 1909–11 Akeley and Delia collected in British East Africa, a trip marked by a hunt with Theodore Roosevelt and his son, Kermit, who were collecting for the Washington National Museum. The safari was brought to a limping conclusion by Carl's being mauled by an elephant, thus delaying fulfillment of his dream of collecting gorillas. He spent World War I as a civilian Assistant Engineer to the Mechanical and Devices Section of the Army. He is said to have refused a commission in order to keep his freedom to speak freely to anyone in the hierarchy.

During the war, his mechanical genius had full scope, resulting in several patents in his name. The theme of Akeley the inventor recurs constantly in his life story. Included in his roster of inventions, several of which involved subsequent business development, were a motion picture camera, a cement gun, and several stages of new taxidermic processes, particularly methods of making manikins to go under the animal skins and methods of making highly naturalistic foliage.

With the close of war, Akeley focused all his energy on getting backing for the African Hall. He needed more than a million dollars. Lecture tours, articles and a book, and endless promotion brought him in touch with the major wealthy sportsmen of the state, but sufficient financial commitment eluded him. In 1921, financing half the expense himself, Akeley left for Africa again, this time accompanied by a married couple, their 5-year-old daughter, their governess, and Akeley's adult niece, whom he had promised to take hunting in Africa. Akeley felt bringing women and children to hunt gorillas was the definitive proof of this theme of brightest Africa, where the animals were noble in defense of their families, but were never wantonly ferocious. On this trip, he collected five gorillas, with the help of the Bradleys, once again nearly died from jungle fevers, and returned to New York determined to achieve permanent conservation for the gorillas in the Belgian Congo. In 1924 he married the explorer/adventurer/author Mary L. Jobe, who accompanied him on his last adventure, the Akeley-Eastman-Pomeroy African Hall Expedition, that collected for 10 dioramas of the Great Hall. George Eastman, of Eastman Kodak fortunes, and Daniel Pomeroy, the benefactors, accompanied the taxidermist-hunter to collect specimens for their bequests. Eastman, then 71 years old, went with his own physician and commanded his own railroad train for part of the excursion.

En route to Africa the Akeleys were received by the conservationist and war hero King of Belgium, Albert. He was the son of the infamous Leopold II, whose personal rapacious control of the Congo for profit was wrested away and given to the Belgian government by other European powers in 1908. Leopold II had financed Henry Stanley's explorations of the Congo. Akeley is pictured in his biographies in the line of the great explorers from Stanley and Livingstone, but also as the man who witnessed, and indeed helped birth a new bright Africa. Albert, who had been led to his views on national parks by a visit to Yosemite, confirmed plans for the Parc Albert and gave the Akeleys a commission to prepare topographical maps and descriptions of the area in cooperation with the Belgian naturalist Jean Derscheid. There was no room for a great park for the Belgians in Europe, so naturally one was established in the Congo, which was to include protection for the Pygmies who lived within park boundaries. The park was to provide sanctuary for natural primitives, as well as to foster scientific study by establishing permanent research facilities within park boundaries. After 10 months of collecting, Carl and Mary Jobe set off for the Kivu forest and the heart of remaining unspoiled Africa. Their purpose this time was not to collect gorillas, but to observe the apes, collect plants, and obtain paintings for the gorilla diorama. Carl Akeley died in November 1926, of a fever, a few days after arriving at the site of his 1921 encampment, the most beautiful spot in all of Africa for him. His wife and the other members of the expedition buried him on Mount Mikeno "in ground the hand of man can never alter or profane."[37]

Taxidermy: From Upholstery to Epiphany

Transplanted Africa stands before him—a result of Akeley's dream.[38]

The vision Carl Akeley had seen was one of jungle peace. It was this that he needed to preserve permanently for the world. His quest to embody this vision alone justified to himself his hunting, turned it into a tool of science and art, the scalpel that revealed the harmony of an organic, articulate world. Let us follow Akeley briefly through his technical contributions to taxidermy in order to grasp more fully the stories he needed to tell about the biography of Africa, the life history of nature, i.e., the natural history of life. Akeley and others have summarized many times in print how his labors transformed taxidermy from the stuffing of animals into an art capable of embodying truth, so this recapitulation will select only those themes essential to my story.[39]

It is a simple tale: Taxidermy was made into the servant of the "real." Akeley's vocation, and his achievement, was the production of an organized craft for eliciting unambiguous experience of organic perfection. Literally, Akeley "typified" nature, made nature true to type. Taxidermy was about the single story, about nature's unity, the unblemished type specimen. Taxidermy became the art most suited to the epistemological and aesthetic stance of realism. The power of this stance is in its magical effects: what is so painfully constructed appears effortlessly, spontaneously found, discovered, simply there if one will only look. Realism does not appear to be a point of view, but appears as a "peephole into the jungle" where peace may be witnessed. Epiphany comes as a gift, not as the fruit of merit and toil, soiled by the hand of man. Realistic art at its most deeply magical issues in revelation. This art repays labor with transcendence. Small wonder that artistic realism and biological science were twin brothers in the founding of the civic order of nature at the American Museum of Natural History. Both were suckled by nature, as Romulus and Remus. It is also natural that taxidermy and biology depend fundamentally upon vision in a hierarchy of the senses; they are tools for the construction, discovery of form.

Akeley's eight years in Milwaukee from 1886 to 1894 were crucial for his working out techniques that served him well the rest of his life. The culmination of that period was a head of a male Virginia deer he entered in the first Sportsman's Show, held in New York City in 1895. The judge in that national competition, in which Akeley's entry placed first, was Theodore Roosevelt, whom Akeley did not meet until they befriended each other on safari in Africa in 1906. The head, entitled "The Challenge," displayed a buck "in the full frenzy of his virility as he gave the defiant roar of the rutting season—the call to fierce combat."[40] Jungle peace was not a passive affair, nor one unmarked by gender.

The head was done in a period of experimentation leading to the production in Chicago of four habitat groups of deer displayed in the four seasons. In crafting those groups over four years, Akeley worked out his manikin method, clay-modeling, plaster-casting, vegetation-molding techniques, and early organized production system. He hired women and men workers by the hour to turn out the thousands of individual leaves needed to clothe the trees in the scenes. Background canvases were painted by Charles Abel Corwin, from studies done in the Michigan Iron Mountains, where the animals were collected. Akeley patented his vegetation process, but gave rights for its use free of charge to the Field Museum in Chicago; he did not patent his innovative methods of producing light, strong papier-mâché manikins from exact clay models and plaster casts, but allowed free worldwide use of his techniques. Cooperation in museum development was a fundamental value for this taxidermist, who did not make much money at his craft and whose inventions were a significant part of his economic survival. "Four Seasons" was installed in the Field Museum in 1902.[41]

Akeley continued to make improvements in his taxidermic technique throughout his life, and he taught several other key workers, including James Lipsitt Clark, who was the Director of Arts, Preparation and Installation at the American Museum in the years after Akeley's death when African Hall was actually constructed. While Akeley worked long hours alone, it would be a mistake to imagine taxidermy as he helped to develop its practice to be a solitary art. Taxidermy requires a complex system of coordination and division of labor, beginning in the field during the hunting of the animals and culminating in the presentation of a finished diorama allowing solitary, individual communion with nature. A minimum list of workers on one of Akeley's projects must include fellow taxidermists, other collectors, artists, anatomists, and "accessory men."[42] Pictures of work in the taxidermy studios of the American Museum show men (usually white) tanning hides, working on large clay models of sizable mammals (including elephants) or on plaster casts, assembling skeleton and wood frames, consulting scale models of the planned display, doing carpentry, making vegetation, sketching, etc. Clark reports that during the years between 1926 and 1936 when African Hall opened, still unfinished, the staff of the project usually employed about 45 men. Painting the backgrounds was itself a major artistic specialization, and the artists based their final panoramas on numerous studies done at the site of collection. In the field, the entire operation rested on the organization of the safari, a complex social institution where race, sex, and class came together intensely. The safari will be discussed more fully below, but now it is useful to note that skinning a large animal could employ 50 workers for several hours. Photographs, moving picture records, death masks of the animals, extensive anatomical measurements, initial treatment of skins, and sketches all occupied the field workers. It would not be an exaggeration to claim that the production of a modern diorama involved the work of hundreds of people in a social system embracing the major structures of skill and authority on a worldwide scale.

How can such a system produce a unified biography of nature? How is it possible to refer to *Akeley's* African Hall when it was constructed after he died? On an ideological level, the answer to these simple questions is connected to the ruling conception of organicism, an organic hierarchy, conceived as nature's principle of organization. Clark stressed the importance of "artistic composition" and described the process as a "recreation" of nature based on the principles of organic form. This process required a base of "personal experience," ideally in the form of presence in Africa, at the site of the animal's life and death. Technical crafts are always imagined to be subordinated by the ruling artistic idea, itself rooted authoritatively in nature's own life. "Such things must be felt, must be absorbed and assimilated, and then in turn, with understanding and enthusiasm, given out by the creator. . . . Therefore, our groups are very often conceived in the very lair of the animals."[43]

The credos of realism and organicism are closely connected; both are systematizations of organization by a hierarchical division of labor, perceived as natural and therefore productive of unity. Unity must be authored in the Judeo-Christian myth system, and just as nature has an Author, so does the organism or the exhibit's diorama. In this myth system, the author must be imagined with the aspects of mind, in relation to the body which executes. Akeley was intent on avoiding *lying* in his work; his craft was to tell the truth of nature. There was only one way to achieve such truth—the rule of mind rooted in the claim to experience. All the work must be done by men who did their collecting and studies on the spot because "[o]therwise, the exhibit is a lie and it would be nothing short of a crime to place it in one of the leading educational institutions of the country."[44] A single mind infused collective experience: "If an exhibition hall is to approach its ideal, its plan must be that of a master mind, while in actuality it is the product of the correlation of many minds and hands."[45] Training a school of workers was an absolutely fundamental part of Akeley's practice of taxidermy; on his success rested the possibility of telling the truth. But above all, this sense of telling a true story rested on the selection of individual animals, the formation of groups of typical specimens.

What does it mean to claim a diorama tells a unified story, a biography essential to nature? What was the meaning of "typical" for Akeley and his contemporaries in the biological departments of the American Museum of Natural History? What are the contents of these stories and what must one *do* to see these contents? To answer these questions, we must follow Carl Akeley into the field and watch him select an animal to mount. Akeley's concentration on finding the typical specimen, group, or scene cannot be overemphasized. But how could he know what was typical, or that such a state of being existed? This problem has been fundamental in the history of biology;

one effort at solution is embodied in African Hall. Three hunts illustrate Akeley's meanings of typical.

First, the concept includes the notion of perfection. The large bull giraffe in the water hole group in African Hall was the object of a hunt over many days in 1921. Several animals were passed over because they were too small or not colored beautifully enough. Remembering record trophies from late 19th-century hunters undermined satisfaction with a modern, smaller specimen taken from the depleted vanishing herds of vanishing African nature. When at last the bull was spotted and taken as the result of great skill and daring, the minute details of its preservation and recreation were lovingly described.

Similarly, in 1910–11, the hunt for a large bull elephant provided the central drama of the safari for the entire two years. An animal with asymmetrical tusks was rejected, despite his imposing size. Character, as well as mere physical appearance, was important in judging an animal to be perfect. Cowardice would disqualify the most lovely and properly proportioned beast. Ideally, the killing itself had to be accomplished as a sportsmanlike act. Perfection was heightened if the hunt were a meeting of equals. So there was a hierarchy of game according to species: lions, elephants, and giraffes far outranked wild asses or antelope. The gorilla was the supreme achievement, almost a definition of perfection in the heart of the garden at the moment of origin. Perfection inhered in the animal itself, but the fullest meanings of perfection inhered in the meeting of animal and man, the moment of perfect vision. Taxidermy was the craft of remembering this perfect experience. Realism was a supreme achievement of the art of memory, a rhetorical achievement crucial to the foundations of Western science.[46]

There is one other essential quality for the typical animal in its perfect expression: it must be an adult male. Akeley describes hunting many fine cows or lionesses, and he cared for their hides and other details of reconstruction with all his skill. But never was it necessary to take weeks and risk the success of the entire enterprise to find the perfect female. There existed an image of an animal which was somehow the gorilla or the elephant incarnate. That particular tone of perfection could only be heard in the male mode. It was a compound of physical and spiritual quality judged truthfully by the artist-scientist in the fullness of direct experience. Perfection was marked by exact quantitative measurement, but even more by virile vitality known by the hunter-scientist from visual communion. Perfection was known by natural kinship; type, kind, and kin mutually defined each other.

But Akeley hunted for a series or a group, not just for individuals. How did he know when to stop the hunt? Two groups give his criterion of wholeness, the gorilla group collected in 1921 and the original group of four elephants mounted by Akeley himself after the 1910–11 safari. At one point in his hunt for specimens, Akeley shot a gorilla, believing it to be a female, but found it to be a young male. He was disturbed because he wished to kill as few animals as possible and he believed the natural family of the gorilla did not contain more than one male. When he later saw a group made up of several males and females, he stopped his hunt with relief, confident that he could tell the truth from his existing specimens. Similarly, the photograph of Akeley's original group of four elephants unmistakably shows a perfect family. The reproductive group had the epistemological and moral status of truth tellers. It was nature's biographical unit.

Akeley wanted to be an artist and a scientist. He gave up his early plan of obtaining a degree from Yale Sheffield Scientific School and then of becoming a professional sculptor. Instead, he combined art and science in taxidermy. Since that art required that he also be a sculptor, he told some of his stories in bronzes as well as in dioramas. His criteria were similar; Akeley had many stories to tell, but they all expressed the same fundamental vision of a vanishing, threatened scene.[47] In his determination to sculpt "typical" Nandi lion spearmen, Akeley used as models extensive photographs, drawings, and "selected types of American negroes which he was using to make sure of perfect figures."[48] The variety of nature had a purpose—to lead to discovery of the highest type of each species of wild life, including human beings outside "civilization."

Besides sculpture and taxidermy, Akeley perfected another narrative tool, photography. All of his storytelling instruments relied primarily on vision. Each tool was capable of telling his truth, but each caught and held slightly different manifestations of natural history. As a visual art, taxidermy occupied for Akeley a middle ground between sculpture and photography. In a sense, both sculpture and photography were subordinate means to accomplishing the final taxidermic scene. But from another point of view, photography represented the future and sculpture the past. Let us follow Akeley into his practice of photography in the critical years suspended between the manual touch of sculpture, which produced knowledge of life in the fraternal discourses of organicist biology and realist art, and the virtual touch of the camera, which has dominated our understanding of nature since World War II. The 19th century produced the masterpieces of animal bronzes inhabiting the world's museums. Akeley's early 20th-century taxidermy, seemingly so solid and material, may be seen as a brief frozen temporal section in the incarnation of art and science, before the camera technically could pervert his single dream into the polymorphous and absurdly intimate filmic reality we now take for granted.[49] Critics accuse Akeley's taxidermy and the American Museum's expensive policy of building the great display halls in the years before World War II of being armature against the future, of having literally locked in stone one historical moment's way of seeing, while calling this vision the whole.[50] But Akeley was a leader technically and spiritually in the perfection of the camera's eye. Taxidermy was not armed against the filmic future, but froze one frame of a far more intense visual communion to be consummated in virtual images. Akeley helped produce the armature—and armament—that would advance into the future.

Photography: Hunting with the Camera

Guns have metamorphosed into cameras in this earnest comedy, the ecology
safari, because nature has ceased to be what it had always been—what
people needed protection from. Now nature—tamed, endangered, mortal—
needs to be protected from people. When we are afraid, we shoot.
But when we are nostalgic, we take pictures.[51]

This essay has repeatedly claimed Akeley and his peers feared the disappearance of their world, of their social world in the new immigrations after 1890 and the resulting dissolution of the old imagined hygienic, pre-industrial America. Civilization appeared to be a disease in the form of technological progress and the vast accumulation of wealth in the practice of monopoly capitalism by the very wealthy sportsmen who were trustees of the museum and the backers of Akeley's African Hall. The leaders of the American Museum were afraid for their health; that is, their manhood was endangered. Theodore Roosevelt knew the prophylaxis for this specific historical malaise: the true man is the true sportsman. Any human being, regardless of race, class, and gender, could spiritually participate in the moral status of healthy manhood in democracy, even if only a few (Anglo-Saxon, male, heterosexual, Protestant, physically robust, and economically comfortable) could express manhood's highest forms. From about 1890 to the 1930s, the Museum was a vast public education and research program for producing experience potent to induce the state of manhood. The Museum, in turn, was the ideological and material product of the sporting life. As Mary Jobe Akeley realized, "[The true sportsman] loves the game as if he were the father of it."[52] Akeley believed that in the end, the highest expression of sportsmanship was hunting with the camera: "Moreover, according to any true conception of sport—the use of skill, daring, and endurance in overcoming difficulties—camera hunting takes twice the man that gun hunting takes."[53] The true father of the game loves nature with the camera; it takes twice the man, and the children are in his perfect image. The eye is infinitely more potent than the gun. Both put a woman to shame—reproductively.

At the time of Akeley's first collecting safari in 1896, cameras were a nearly useless encumbrance, incapable of capturing the goal of the hunt—life. According to Akeley, the first notable camera hunters in Africa appeared around 1902.[54] The early books were based on still photographs; [motion] picture wildlife photography owes much to Akeley's own camera and did not achieve anything before the 1920s. On his 1910–11 safari to East Africa, Akeley had the best available equipment and tried to film the Nandi lion spearing. His failure due to inadequate cameras, described with great emotional intensity, led him during the next five years to design the Akeley camera, which was used extensively by the Army Signal Corps during World War I. Akeley formed the Akeley Camera Company to develop his invention, which received its civilian christening by filming Man-o-War winning the Kentucky Derby in 1920. The camera's innovative telephoto lens caught the Dempsey-Carpentier heavyweight battle. Awarded the John Price Wetherhill Medal at the Franklin Institute in 1926 for his invention, Akeley succeeded that year in filming to his satisfaction African lion spearing, on the same safari on which Rochester's George Eastman, of Eastman-Kodak fortunes, was both co-sponsor and hunter-collector.[55] Recall that Akeley's first taste of his own camera in the field was in 1921 in the Kivu forest. Within a few days, Akeley shot his first gorillas with both gun and camera, in the experiences he saw as the culmination of his life.

The ambiguity of the gun and camera runs throughout Akeley's work. He is a transitional figure from the Western image of darkest to lightest Africa, from nature worthy of manly fear to nature in need of motherly nurture. The woman/scientist/mother of orphaned apes popularized by the National Geographic Society's magazine and films in the 1970s was still half a century away.[56] With Akeley, manhood tested itself against fear, even as the lust for the image of jungle peace held the finger on the gun long enough to take the picture and even as the intellectual and mythic certainty grew that the savage beast in the jungle was human, in particular, industrial human. Even at the literal level of physical appearance, "[t]o one familiar with the old types of camera the Akeley resembled a machine gun quite as much as it resembled a camera."[57] Akeley said he set out to design a camera "that you can aim . . . with about the same ease that you can point a pistol."[58] He enjoyed retelling the apocryphal story of seven Germans in World War I mistakenly surrendering to one American in France when they found themselves faced by an Akeley. "The fundamental difference between the Akeley motion-picture camera and the others is a panoramic device which enables one to swing it all about, much as one would swing a swivel gun, following the natural line of vision."[59] Akeley semi-joked in knowing puns on the penetrating and deadly invasiveness of the camera, naming one of his image machines "The Gorilla." " 'The Gorilla' had taken 300 feet of film of the animal that had never heretofore been taken alive in its native wilds by any camera. . . . I was satisfied— more satisfied than a man ever should be— but I revelled in the feeling."[60]

The taxidermist, certain of the essential peacefulness of the gorilla, wondered how close he should let a charging male get before neglecting the camera for the gun. "I hope that I shall have the courage to allow an apparently charging gorilla to come within a reasonable distance before shooting. I hesitate to say just what I consider a reasonable distance at the present moment. I shall feel very gratified if I can get a photograph of him at twenty feet. I should be proud of my nerve if I were able to show a photograph of him at ten feet, but I do not expect to do this unless I am at the moment a victim of suicidal mania."[61] Akeley wrote these words before he had ever seen a wild gorilla. What was the boundary of courage; how much did nature or man need protecting? What if the gorilla never charged, even when provoked? What if the gorilla were a coward (or a female)? Who, precisely, was threatened in the drama of natural history in the early decades of monopoly capitalism's presence in Africa and America?

Aware of a disturbing potential of the camera, Akeley set himself against faking. He stuffed Barnum's Jumbo, but he wanted no part of the great circus magnate's cultivation of the American popular art form, the hoax.[62] But hoax luxuriated in early wildlife photography (and anthropological photography). In particular, Akeley saw unscrupulous men manipulate nature to tell the story of a fierce and savage Africa; this was the story which would sell in the motion picture emporia across America. Taxidermy had always threatened to lapse from art into deception, from life to upholstered death as a poor sportsman's trophy. Photography too was full of philistines who could debase the entire undertaking of nature work, the Museum's term for its educational work in the early decades of the 20th century. The Museum was for public entertainment (the point that kept its Presbyterian trustees resisting Sunday opening in the 1880s despite that day's fine potential for educating the new Catholic immigrants, who worked a six-day week); but entertainment only had value if it communicated the truth. Therefore, Akeley encouraged an association between the American Museum and the wildlife photographers Martin and Osa Johnson, who seemed willing and able to produce popular motion pictures telling the story of jungle peace. Johnson claimed in his 1923 prospectus to the American Museum, "The camera cannot be deceived . . . [therefore, it has] enormous scientific value."[63]

Entertainment was complexly interwoven with science, art, hunting, and education. Barnum's humbug tested the cleverness, the scientific acumen, of the observer in a republic where each citizen could find out the nakedness of the emperor and the sham of his rationality. This democracy of reason was always a bit dangerous. There is a tradition of active participation in the eye of science in America which makes the stories of nature always ready to erupt into popular politics. Natural history can be—and sometimes has been—a means for millenial expectation and disorderly action. Akeley himself is an excellent example of a self-made man who made use of the mythic resources of the independent man's honest vision, the appeal to experience, the testimony of one's own eyes. He saw the Giant of Karisimbi. The camera, an eminently democratic machine, has been crucial to the crafting of stories in biology; but its control has always eluded the professional and the moralist, the official scientist. But in Martin Johnson, Akeley hoped he had the man who would tame specular entertainment for the social uplift promised by science.

In 1906 Martin Johnson shipped out with Jack London on the *Snark* for a two-year voyage of the South Seas. The *Snark* was the photographer's *Beagle*. Its name could hardly have been better chosen for the ship that carried the two adventurers whose books and films complemented *Tarzan* for recording the dilemma of manhood in the early 20th century. Lewis Carroll's *The Hunting of the Snark* contains the lines that captured Johnson's and London's—and Akeley's—Darwinian revelation:

In one moment I've seen what has hitherto been
Enveloped in absolute mystery,
And without extra charge I will give you at large
A lesson in Natural History.[64]

From 1908 to 1913 Johnson ran five motion picture houses in Kansas. In the same period and after, he and Osa traveled in the still mysterious and potent places, filming "native life": Melanesia, Polynesia, Malekula, Borneo, Kenya Colony. In 1922 Martin and Osa sought Carl Akeley's opinion of their just-completed film, *Trailing African Wild Animals*. Akeley was delighted, and the result was the museum's setting up a special corporation to fund the Johnsons on a five-year film safari in Africa. The Johnsons' plans included making two short films, including one on "African Babies." "It will show elephant babies, lion babies, zebra babies, giraffe babies, and black babies . . . showing the play of wild animals and the maternal care that is so strange and interesting a feature of wildlife."[65] The human life of Africa was repeatedly consigned to the Age of Mammals, prior to the Age of Man. That was its only claim to protection, and of course the ultimate justification for domination. Here was a record of jungle peace.

The Johnsons planned a big animal feature film as the capstone of the safari. The museum lauded both the commercial and educational values; Osborn commented that the "double message of such photography is, first, that it brings the aesthetic and ethical influence of nature within the reach of millions of people . . . second, it spreads the idea that our generation has no right to destroy what future generations may enjoy."[66] It was perfect that the Johnson film safari overlapped with the Akeley-Eastman-Pomeroy expedition. The Akeleys spent several days helping the Johnsons film lion spearing in Tanganyika, finally capturing on film this endangered apotheosis of primitive manhood. Johnson was confident that their approach of combining truth and beauty without hoax would ultimately be commercially superior, as well as scientifically accurate. "[T]here is no limit to the money it can make. . . . My past training, my knowledge of showmanship, mixed with the scientific knowledge I have absorbed lately, and the wonderful photographic equipment . . . make me certain that this Big Feature is going to be the biggest money maker ever placed on the market, as there is no doubt it will be the last big Africa Feature made, and it will be so spectacular that there will be no danger of another film of like nature competing with it. For these reasons it will produce an income as long as we live."[67] Africa had always promised gold.

The "naked eye" science advocated by the American Museum was perfect for the camera, ultimately so superior to the gun for the possession, production, preservation, consumption, surveillance, appreciation, and control of nature. The ideology of realism essential to Akeley's aesthetic was part of his effort to touch, to see, to bridge the yawning gaps in the endangered self. To make an exact image is to insure against disappearance, to cannibalize life until it is safely and permanently a specular image, a ghost. It arrested decay. That is why nature photography is so beautiful and so religious—and such a powerful hint of an apocalyptic future. Akeley's aesthetic combined the instrumental and contemplative into a photographic technology providing a transfusion for a steadily depleted sense of reality. The image and the real mutually define each other, as all of reality in late capitalist culture lusts to become an image for its own security. Reality is assured, insured, by the image, and there is no limit to the amount of money that can be made. The camera is superior to the gun for the control of time; and Akeley's dioramas with their photographic vision, sculptor's touch, and taxidermic solidity were about the end of time.[68]

TELLING STORIES

The synthetic story told above has three major sources and several minor ones. Telling the life synthetically masks the tones and versions which emerge from listening to these sources. The single biography, the ideological achieved union of African Hall, can be brought to the edge of an imagined heteroglossic novel which has not yet been written. A polyphonic natural history waits for its sustaining social history. In order to probe more deeply into the tissue of meanings and mediations making the specific structure of experience possible for the viewer of the dioramas of African Hall—and of the Giant of Karisimbi—I would like to tease apart the sources for one major event of Akeley's life, the elephant mauling in British East Africa in 1910. This event can function as a germ for expanding my story of the structure and function of biography in the construction of a 20th-century primate order, with its specific and polymorphous hierarchies of race, sex, and class. With an ear for the tones of audience, historical moment, social interests and intentions of authors, and the material-physical appearance of sources, I would like to consider in greater detail the question of storytelling. In particular, whose stories appear and disappear in the web of social practices that constitute Teddy Bear Patriarchy? Questions of authorized writing enforced by publishing practices and of labor that never issues in acknowledged authorship (never father of the game) make up my story.[69]

Authors and Versions

She didn't write it.
She wrote it but she shouldn't have.
She wrote it, but look what she wrote about.[70]

Carl Akeley's book, *In Brightest Africa*, appears on the surface to be written by Carl Akeley. But we learn from Mary Jobe Akeley, a prolific author, that the taxidermist "hated to wield a pen."[71] She elaborates that the publishers,

Doubleday and Page (the men, not the company), were enthralled by Carl's stories told in their homes at dinner and so "determined to extract a book from him." So one evening after dinner Arthur W. Page "stationed a stenographer behind a screen, and without Carl's knowledge, she recorded everything he said while the guests lingered before the fire." The editing of this material is then ascribed to Doubleday and Page, but the author is named as Carl. The stenographer is an unnamed hand. These notes gave rise to articles in a journal called *World's Work*, but a book was still not forthcoming from the taxidermist. Then Akeley discovered a newspaper account of his Kivu journey that he greatly liked; the piece had been written by Dorothy S. Greene while she worked for the director of the American Museum. Akeley hired her as his secretary, to record his stories while he talked with other explorers or scientists or lectured to raise funds for African Hall. "She unobtrusively jotted down material which could be used in a book."[72] Who wrote *In Brightest Africa*? In the answer to that question resides a world of motivated history of the relation of mind and body in Western authorship.

The physical appearance of the books is itself an eloquent story. The stamp of approval from men like H. F. Osborn in the dignified prefaces, the presence of handsome photographs, a publishing house that catered to wealthy hunters: all compose the authority of the books. The frontispieces are like Orthodox icons; the entire story can be read from them. In *Lions, Gorillas, and Their Neighbors*, the book prepared for young people, the frontispiece shows an elderly Carl Akeley in his studio gazing intently into the eyes of the plaster death mask of the first gorilla he ever saw. Maturity in the encounter with nature is announced. *The Wilderness Lives Again*, the biography that resurrected Carl through his wife's vicarious authorship, displays in the front a young Carl, arm and hand bandaged heavily, standing outside a tent beside a dead leopard suspended by her hind legs. The caption reads: "Carl Akeley, when still in his twenties, choked this wounded infuriated leopard to death with his naked hands as it attacked him with intent to kill."

Let us turn to Carl Akeley's story of his encounter with the elephant which mauled him. The tale occurs in a chapter of Akeley's book called "Elephant Friends and Foes." Several moral lessons pervade the chapter, prominently those of human ignorance of the great animals—partly because hunters are only after ivory and trophies, so that their knowledge is only of tracking and killing, not of the animals' lives—and of Akeley's difference because of his special closeness to nature embodied in the magnificent elephants. On this safari, Akeley witnessed two elephants help a wounded comrade escape from the scene of slaughter, inspiring one of the taxidermist's bronzes. But also in this chapter, the reader sees an earthy Akeley, not above making a table to seat eight people out of elephant ears from a specimen which nearly killed him and Delia, despite each of them shooting into his head about 13 times. In this chapter, the taxidermist is hunting as an equal with his wife. He does not hide stories which might seem a bit seedy or full of personal bravado; yet his "natural nobility" pervaded all these anecdotes, particularly for an audience of potential donors to African Hall, who might quite likely find themselves shooting big game in Africa.

His near-fatal encounter with an elephant occurred when Akeley had gone off without Delia to get photographs, taking "four days' rations, gun boys, porters, camera men, and so forth—about fifteen men in all."[73] He was tracking an elephant whose trail was very fresh, when he suddenly became aware that the animal was bearing down on him directly:

> I have no knowledge of how the warning came. . . . I only know that as I picked up my gun and wheeled about I tried to shove the safety catch forward. It refused to budge. . . . My next mental record is of a tusk right at my chest. I grabbed it with my left hand, the other one with my right hand, and swinging in between them went to the ground on my back. This swinging in between the tusks was purely automatic. It was the result of many a time on the trails imagining myself caught by an elephant's rush and planning what to do, and a very profitable planning too; for I am convinced that if a man imagines such a crisis and plans what he would do, he will, when the occasion occurs, automatically do what he planned. . . . He drove his tusks into the ground on either side of me. . . . When he surged down on me, his big tusks evidently struck something in the ground that stopped them. . . . He seems to have thought me dead for he left me—by some good fortune not stepping on me—and charged off after the boys.[74]

Akeley follows this cool description full of counsel about planning for life's big moments with remarks about what elephants are reputed to do in other charges and with remarks about the behavior of his party. "I never got much information out of the boys as to what did happen, for they were not proud of their part in the adventure. . . . It is reasonable to assume that they had scattered through [the area which the elephants thoroughly trampled] like a covey of quail. . . ."[75]

Akeley tells that he lay unconscious and untouched for hours because his men felt he was dead, and they came from groups which refused ever to touch a dead man. When he came to, he shouted and got attention. He relates that word had been sent to Mrs. Akeley at base camp, who valiantly mounted a rescue party in the middle of the night against the wishes of her guides (because of the dangers of night travel through the bush), whom she pursued into their huts to force their cooperation. She sent word to the nearest government post to dispatch a doctor, and arrived at the scene of the injury by dawn. Akeley attributed his recovery to her prompt arrival, but more to the subsequent speedy arrival of a neophyte Scottish doctor, who sped through the jungle to help the injured man, partly out of his ignorance of the foolishness of hurrying to help anyone mauled by an elephant—such men simply didn't survive to pay for one's haste. The more seasoned government official, the chief medical officer, arrived considerably later.

The remainder of the chapter recounts Akeley's chat with other old hands in Africa about their experiences surviving elephant attacks. The tone is reasoned, scientific, focused on the behavior and character of those interesting aspects of elephant behavior. The constant moral of the chapter emerges again in the conclusion:

> But although the elephant is a terrible fighter in his own defense when attacked by man, that is not his chief characteristic. The things that stick in my mind are his sagacity, his versatility, and a certain comradeship which I have never noticed to the same degree in other animals. . . . I like to think back to the day I saw the group of baby elephants playing with a great ball of baked dirt. . . . I think, too, of the extraordinary fact that I have never heard or seen African elephants fighting each other. They have no enemy but man and are at peace amongst themselves. It is my friend the elephant that I hope to perpetuate in the central group in Roosevelt African Hall. . . . In this, which we hope will be an everlasting monument to the Africa that was, the Africa that is fast disappearing, I hope to place the elephant on a pedestal in the centre of the hall—the rightful place for the first among them.[76]

Akeley's interests are constantly in the perpetuation, conservation, and dignity of nature in which man is the enemy, the intruder, the dealer of death. His own exploits in the hunt stand in ironic juxtaposition only if the reader refuses to discern their true meaning—the tales of a pure man whose danger in pursuit of a noble cause brings him into communion with the beasts he kills, with nature. This nature is a worthy brother of man, a worthy foil for his manhood. Akeley's elephant is profoundly male, singular, and representative of the possibility of nobility. The mauling was an exciting tale, with parts for many actors, including Delia, but the brush with death and the details of rescue are told with the cool humor of a man ready for his end dealt by such a noble friend and brother, his best enemy, the object of his scientific curiosity. The putative behavior of the "boys" underlines the confrontation between white manhood and the noble beast. Casual and institutional racism only heightens the experience of the life story of the single adult man. The action in Akeley's stories focuses on the center of the stage, on the meeting of the singular man and animal. The entourage is inaudible, invisible, except for comic relief and anecdotes about native life. In Akeley's rendering, empowered by class and race, white woman stands without much comment in a similar moral position as white man—a hunter, an adult.

Mary L. Jobe Akeley published her biography of her husband, *The Wilderness Lives Again*, in 1940, four years after the Akeley African Hall opened to the public, his dream assured. Her purpose was no longer to raise money and tell stories to other hunters, but to promote conservation and fulfill her life's purpose—accomplishing her husband's lifework. Her biography of Carl should be taken literally. She presents herself as the inspired scribe for her husband's story. Through her vicarious authorship and through African Hall and the Parc Albert, not only the Wilderness, but Akeley himself, whose meaning was the wilderness, lives again. Mary L. Jobe had not always lived for a husband. In the years before her marriage she had completed no fewer than ten expeditions to explore British Columbian wilderness. She recounts the scene at Carl's death when she accepted his commission for her, that she would live thereafter to fulfill his work. The entire book is suffused with joy in this task. Her self-construction as the other is breathtaking in its ecstasy. The story of the elephant mauling undergoes interesting emendations to facilitate her accomplishment. One must read this book with attention because Carl's words from his field diaries and publications are quoted at great length with no typographical differentiation from the rest of the text. At no point does the wife give a source for her husband's words; they may be from conversation, lectures, anywhere. It does not matter, because the two are one flesh. The stories of Carl and Mary Jobe blend imperceptibly—until the reader starts comparing other versions of the "same" incidents, even the ones written apparently in the direct words of the true, if absent, author-husband.

The key emendation is an absence. The entire biography of Carl Akeley by Mary Jobe Akeley does not mention the name or presence of Delia. Her role in the rescue is taken by the Kikuyu man Wimbia Gikungu, called Bill, Akeley's gun bearer and native companion on several safaris. Bill is credited with rousing the recalcitrant guides and notifying the government post, thus bringing on the Scotsman posthaste.[77] The long quotation from Carl in which the whole story is told simply lacks mention of his previous wife.

Mary Jobe tells a sequel to the mauling not in Akeley's published stories, and apparently taken from his field diaries or lectures. Because it is not uncommon for a man to lose his nerve after an elephant mauling and decline to hunt elephants again, it was necessary for Akeley to face elephants again as soon as possible. Again, the first thing to notice is an absence. It is never questioned that such courage *should* be regained. But the actual story does not ennoble Akeley. He tracked an elephant before he was really healthy, needing his "boys" to carry a chair on the trail for him to sit on as he tired, and the elephant was wounded from unsportsmanlike hasty shots and not found before it died. Akeley's nobility is saved in this story by noting his humility: "The boys helped me back to camp. I felt perfectly certain that we would find him dead in the morning. The whole thing had been stupid and unsportsmanlike."[78]

Before leaving Mary Jobe Akeley's version for Delia Akeley's tale, one more aspect of the Canadian Northwest explorer deserves note. She is pictured as Carl's companion and soul mate, but not really as his co-adventurer and buddy hunter—with one exception. Mary Jobe fired two shots in Africa, and killed a magnificent male lion: "[A]n hour later we came upon a fine old lion, a splendid beast, Carl said, and good enough for me to shoot. And so I shot. . . . The lion measured nine feet six inches from top to tip, carried a dark and splendid mane; and because of its size, age, and rugged personality, Carl considered it a valuable specimen; but I was chiefly concerned that I fulfilled Carl's expectations and had killed the lion cleanly and without assistance."[79] Mary Jobe's authority as a biographer does not depend on her being a hunter, but there is no question that her status was enhanced by this most desirable transforming experience. In this act, her moral status approached that of the sportsman, a critical condition for communion with nature in the life of the American Museum of Natural History.

Delia Akeley pictures herself as a joyous and unrepentant hunter, but her husband has some warts, at least by the publication of *Jungle Portraits* in 1930. It is hard to believe her stories; she simply does not have the authorial moral status of the artist/hunter/scientist, Carl Akeley, or his socially sure second wife, who met easily with kings and commanded his safari for a major scientific institution after his death. There are some very interesting presences in Delia's tales which help highlight the kind of biography African Hall was to tell, and the kind that was to be suppressed. Experience in African Hall leads to transcendence, to the perfect type, to the heightened moment beyond mere life. First, let us look at Delia's story of the rescue. Bill appears in Delia's story, and he behaves well. But her own heroism in confronting the superstitions of the "boys" and in saving her endangered husband is, of course, the central tale in the chapter "Jungle Rescue": "Examining and cleansing Mr. Akeley's wounds were my first consideration. . . . The fact that his wounds were cared for so promptly prevented infection, and without doubt saved his life. . . . The following day Dr. Phillips, a young Scottish medical missionary, arrived."[80]

But why did Delia tell this story at all, aside from an easily imagined pain at developments in her family life and a desire to set her role on record? Whatever her personal motivation, Delia had a biographical purpose quite at odds with the official histories; she was intent on showing mediations in the form of fallible people behind the experience of natural history museums. In the opening lines of "Jungle Rescue" Delia considers at some length issues of sickness and injury for the early collectors and explorers; she remarks pointedly on insects, weariness, and failure. All this is contrasted with the experience provided the current (1930) traveler, the tourist, or indeed, even the museum visitor. She does have an interest in picturing the devoted and unremarked wife of the single-minded explorers who kept camp in the jungle and house at home. Her purpose in telling the reader that she managed Carl's safaris, that there were very material mediations in the quest for manhood and natural truth, is patent. And then there is her pique at all the attention for her scientist-husband: "The thrilling story of the accident and his miraculous escape from a frightful death has been told many times by himself from the lecture platform. But a personal account of my equally thrilling night journey to his rescue through one of the densest, elephant-infested forests on the African continent is not nearly so well known."[81] It is hard to conjure the picture of Carl Akeley talking about elephant-infested forests! This is not the wife who devotes herself to his authorship of wilderness. Indeed, she repeatedly refers to darkest Africa throughout the book.

There are other instances of Delia's insisting on her own glory at the expense of the official nobility of her husband. The reader of Delia's book discovers Carl Akeley frequently sick in his tent, an invalid dangerously close to death whose courageous wife hunts not only for food for the camp, but also for scientific specimens so that he may hasten out of this dangerous continent before it claims him. One learns again that in the elephant hunt following the mauling, Carl was searching to restore his endangered "morale." His wife was his companion in what is portrayed as a dangerous hunt terminating in a thrilling kill marked by a dangerous charge. Delia tells the story so that one cannot know who fired the fatal shot, but "fatigue and a desire to be sure of his shot made Mr. Akeley slow in getting his gun in position."[82] She includes in her chapter an extraordinary photograph of a dashing Carl Akeley smoking a pipe and lounging on top of the body of a large fallen elephant; her caption reads, "Carl Akeley and the first elephant he shot after settling the question of his morale." She concludes her narrative, "Although years have passed since that morning when I stood with my invalid husband on the edge of the vast bush-covered swamp looking for an elephant in the fog, I can see it all as clearly as if it happened yesterday. . . . [I]t is this vision which comes to my mind when I think of the monumental group of elephants which Mr. Akeley and I risked so much to obtain for the New York Natural History Museum."[83]

But hunting in the Museum's archive for that photograph of Akeley lounging astride his kill reveals something curious, and perhaps more revealing than Delia's compromising and compromised story. Delia was lying about the elephant, as the photos which accompany hers in the archive demonstrate. But the lie reveals another truth. The photos in the archive suggest a version of reality, a biography of Africa, which the Museum and its official representatives never wanted displayed in their Halls or educational publications. A reader will not find that particular photograph of Akeley in any other publication than Delia's, and even in the 1980s, archive staff are said to be leery of allowing republication of this particular photograph. The images from the photo archive upstairs haunt the mind's eye as the viewer stands before the elephant group in African Hall.

It is clear that this particular elephant with the lounging Carl could not have been killed on the occasion Delia described. The cast of accompanying characters is wrong. Another picture clearly taken on the same occasion shows the white hunter, the Scotsman Richard John Cunninghame, hired by Akeley in 1909 to teach him how to hunt elephants, lounging with Delia on the same carcass. The museum archive labels the photo "Mrs. Akeley's first elephant." It is hard not to order the separate photos in the folder into a series, hard not to tell a story. So the next snapshot shows the separated and still slightly bloody tusks of the elephant held in a gothic arch over a pleased, informal Delia. She is standing confidently under the arch, each arm reaching out to grasp a curve of the elephantine structure. But the real support for the ivory is elsewhere. Cut off at the edge of the picture are four black arms; the hands come from the framing peripheral space to encircle the tusks arching over the triumphant white woman. The museum archive labels this photo "Mrs. Akeley's ivory." The next and last photograph shows a smiling Cunninghame holding the heart of the deceased elephant and touching Mrs. Akeley's forehead with the cut edge of the animal's aorta. She stands with her head bowed under the ivory arch, now supported by a single, solemn African man. The museum's spare comment reads, "The Christening."

This, then, is also an image of an origin, a sacrament, a mark on the soul signing a spiritual transformation effected by the act of first killing. It is a sacred moment in the life of the hunter, a rebirth in the blood of the sacrifice, of conquered nature. This elephant stands a fixed witness in the Akeley African Hall to this image of an intimate touch shown by the camera's eye, which here captured an iconic moment where race, sex, and nature met for the Western hunter. In this garden, the camera captured a retelling of a Christian story of origins, a secularized Christian sacrament in a baptism of blood from the victim whose death brought spiritual adulthood, i.e., the status of hunter, the status of the fully human being who is reborn in risking life, in killing. Versions of this story recur again and again in the history of American approaches to the sciences of animal life, especially primate life. One version is the biography of white manhood told in Akeley African Hall. With Delia, the story is near parody; with Carl it is near epiphany. His was authorized to achieve a fusion of science and art. Delia, by far the more prolific author, who neither had nor was a ghostwriter, was erased—by divorce and by duplicity.

Safari: A Life of Africa

Now with few exceptions our Kivu savages, lower in the scale of intelligence than any others I had seen in Equatorial Africa, proved kindly men. . . . How deeply their sympathy affected me! As I think of them, I am reminded of the only playmate and companion of my early childhood, a collie dog. . . .[84]

The Great Halls of the American Museum of Natural History simply would not exist without the labor of Africans (or South Americans or the Irish and "Negroes" in North America). The Akeleys would be the first to acknowledge this fact; but they would always claim the principle of organization came from the white safari managers, the scientist-collector and his camp-managing wife, the elements of mind overseeing the principle of execution. From the safari of 1895, dependent upon foot travel and the strong backs of "natives," to the motor safaris of the 1920s, the everyday survival of Euro-Americans in the field depended upon the knowledge, good sense, hard work, and enforced subordination of people the white folk insisted on seeing as perpetual children or even as wildlife. If a black person accomplished some exceptional feat of intelligence or daring, the explanation was that he or she (though no examples of such a woman appear in the texts examined in this essay) was inspired, literally moved, by the spirit of the master. As Mary Jobe put it in her unself-conscious colonial voice, "It was as if the spirit of his master had descended upon him, activating him to transcendent effort."[85] This explanation was all the more powerful if the body of the master was literally, physically far removed, by death or trans-Atlantic residence.

Aristotle was as present in the safari as he was in the taxidermic studios in New York or in the physiological bodies of organisms. Labor was not authorized as action, as mind, or as form.

Both Carl and Mary Jobe Akeley's books provide important insight into the organization of the safari over the thirty-year span of Akeley's hunting life. The photographs of usually solemn African people in a semicircle around the core of white personnel, with the cars, cameras, and abundant baggage in the background, are eloquent about race, sex, and colonialism. The chapters discuss the problems of cooks, the tasks of a headman, the profusion of languages which no white person on the journey spoke, numbers of porters (about thirty for most of the 1926 trip, many more in 1895) and the problems in keeping them, the contradictory cooperation of local African leaders (often called "sultans"), the difficulty of providing white people coffee and brandy in an unspoiled wilderness, the hierarchy of pay scales and food rations for safari personnel, the behavior of gun bearers, and the punishment for perceived misdeeds. The chapters portray a social organism, properly ordered by the principles of organic form: hierarchical division of labor called cooperation and coordination. The safari was an icon of the whole enterprise in its logic of mind and body, in its scientific marking of the body for functional efficiency.[86] The Africans were inscribed with their role by the Western construction of race; they were literally written into the script of the story of life—and written out of authorship.[87]

Very few of the black personnel appear with individual biographies in the safari literature, but there are exceptions, object lessons or typ[ical] life histories. Africans were imagined as either "spoiled" or "unspoiled," like the nature they signified. Spoiled nature could not relieve decadence, the malaise of the imperialist and city dweller, but only presented evidence of decay's contagion, the germ of civilization, the infection which was obliterating the Age of Mammals. And with the end of that time came the end of the essence of manhood, hunting. But unspoiled Africans, like the Kivu forest itself, were solid evidence of the resources for restoring manhood in the healthy activity of sportsmanlike hunting. It is worth studying one of these individual biographies to glean a hint of some of the complexity of the relation of master and servant in the pursuit of science on the safari. The life story is told from the point of view of the white person; Wimbia Gikungu, the Kikuyu known as Bill who joined Carl Akeley in British East Africa in 1905 at 13 years of age, did not write my sources. He was not the author of his body, but he was the Akeleys' favorite "native."

Bill began as an assistant to Delia Akeley's tent boy, but is portrayed as rapidly learning everything there was to know about the safari through his unflagging industry and desire to please. He was said to have extraordinary intelligence and spirit, but suffered chronic difficulty with some authority and from inability to save his earnings. "He has an independence that frequently gets him into trouble. He does not like to take orders from any one of his own color."[88] He served with Akeley safaris in 1905, 1909–11, and 1926, increasing in authority and power over the years until there was no African whom Carl Akeley respected more for his trail knowledge and judgment. Akeley speaks of him sometimes as a man, but usually as a boy, like all other male Africans. Bill got into some kind of trouble serving on the Roosevelt safari, having been recommended by Akeley. Roosevelt dismissed him and had him blacklisted. Nonetheless, Akeley immediately rehired him, assuming he had had some largely innocent (i.e., not directed against a white person) eruption of his distaste for authority.[89]

Akeley describes three occasions on which he "punished" Gikungu; these episodes are condensed manifestations of Akeley's assumed paternal role. Once Bill refused to give the keys for Carl's trunk to other white people when they asked, "saying that he must have an order from his own Bwana. It was cheek, and he had to be punished; the punishment was not severe, but coming from me it went hard with him and I had to give him a fatherly talk to prevent his running away."[90] Four years later, the Kikuyu shot an elephant he believed was charging Akeley without the latter's seeing it. Akeley had seen the animal, but did not know his "gun boy" did not know. Akeley spontaneously slapped Gikungu "because he had broken one of the first rules of the game, which is that a black boy must never shoot without orders, unless his master is down and at the mercy of a beast." Akeley realized his mistake, and "my apologies were prompt and as humble as the dignity of a white man would permit."[91] The African could not be permitted to hunt independently with a gun in the presence of a white man. The entire logic of restoring threatened white manhood depended on that rule. Hunting was magic; Bill's well-meaning (and well-placed) shot was pollution, a usurpation of maturity. Finally, Akeley had Gikungu put in jail during the 1909–11 safari when "Bill" actively declined to submit when Carl "found it necessary to take him in hand for mild punishment" for another refusal of a white man's orders about baggage.[92] The African caught up with the safari weeks later after spending two weeks in jail. The white man's paternal solicitude could be quite a problem.

Repeatedly, Akeley relied on Gikungu's abilities and knowledge. Always, his performance was attributed to his loyalty for the master. Collecting the ivory of a wounded elephant, organizing the rescue after the elephant mauling, assisting Mary Jobe Akeley about Carl's death—these deeds were the manifestations of subordinate love. There is no hint that Gikungu might have had other motives—perhaps including a non-subservient pity for a white widow in the rain forest, pleasure in his superb skills, complex political dealings with other African groups, or even a superior hatred for his masters. Attributing intentions to "Bill" is without shadow of doubt; the African played his role in the safari script as the never quite tamed, permanently good boy. Bill was believed to be visible; other Africans largely remained invisible. The willed blindness of the white lover of nature remained characteristic of the scientists who went to the Garden to study primates, to study origins, until cracks began to show in this consciousness around 1970.

THE AMERICAN MUSEUM OF NATURAL HISTORY AND THE SOCIAL CONSTRUCTION OF SCIENTIFIC KNOWLEDGE: INSTITUTION

Speak to the Earth and It Shall Teach thee.[93]

Every specimen is a permanent fact.[94]

From 1890 to 1930, the "Nature Movement" was at its height in the United States. Ambivalence about "civilization" is an old theme in U.S. history, and this ambivalence was never higher than after the Civil War, and during the early decades of monopoly capital formation.[95] Civilization, obviously, refers to a complex pattern of domination of people and everybody (everything) else, often ascribed to technology—fantasized as "the Machine." Nature is such a potent symbol of innocence partly because "she" is imagined to be without technology, to be the object of vision, and so a source of both health and purity. Man is not in nature partly because he is not seen, is not the spectacle. A constitutive meaning of masculine gender for us is to be the unseen, the eye (I), the author. Indeed that is part of the structure of experience in the museum, one of the reasons one has, willy-nilly, the moral status of a young boy undergoing initiation through visual experience. Is anyone surprised that psychologists find 20th-century U.S. boys excel in dissecting visual fields? The museum is a visual technology. It works through desire for communion, not separation, and one of its products is gender. Who needs infancy in the nuclear family when we have rebirth in the ritual spaces of Teddy Bear Patriarchy?

Obviously, this essay is premised on the inversion of a causal relation of technology to the social relations of domination: the social relations of domination, I am arguing, are frozen into the hardware and logics of technology. Nature is, in "fact," constructed as a technology through social praxis. And dioramas are meaning-machines. Machines are time slices into the social organism that made them. Machines are maps of power, arrested moments of social relations that in turn threaten to govern the living. The owners of the great machines of monopoly capital—the so-called means of production—were, with excellent reason, at the forefront of nature work—because it was one of the means of production of race, gender, and class. For them, "naked eye science" could give direct vision of social peace and progress despite the appearances of class war and decadence. They required a science "instaurating" jungle peace, with its promise of restored manhood, complete with a transcendent ethic of hunting; and so they brought it.

This scientific discourse on origins was not cheap; and the servants of science, human and animal, were not tame. The relations of knowledge and power at the American Museum of Natural History are not caught by telling a tale of the great capitalists in the sky conspiring to obscure the truth. Quite the opposite, the tale must be committed Progressives struggling to dispel darkness through research, education, and reform. The great capitalists were not in the sky; they were in the field, armed with the *Gospel of Wealth*.[96] They were also often armed with an elephant gun and an Akeley camera.[97] This entire essay has been about the "social construction of knowledge." There is no boundary between the "inside" and "outside" of science, such that in one universe social relations appear, but in the other the history of ideas proceeds. Sciences are woven of social relations throughout their tissues. The concept of social relations must include the entire complex of interactions among people, as individuals and in groups of various sizes; objects, including books, buildings, and rocks; and animals, including apes and elephants.[98]

But in this section of Teddy Bear Patriarchy, I want to explore one band in the spectrum of social relations—the philanthropic activities of men in the American Museum of Natural History which fostered exhibition (including public education and scientific collecting), conservation, and eugenics. These activities are the optic tectum of naked eye science, i.e., the neural organs of integration and interpretation. This essay has moved from the immediacy of experience, through the mediations of biography and storytelling; we now must look at a synthesis of social construction.[99]

But first a word on decadence, the threat against which exhibition, conservation, and eugenics were all directed as coordinated medical interventions, as prophylaxis for an endangered body politic. The museum was a medical technology, a hygienic intervention, and the pathology was a potentially fatal organic sickness of the individual and collective body. Decadence was a venereal disease proper to the organs of social and personal reproduction: sex, race, and class. From the point of view of Teddy Bear Patriarchy, race suicide was a clinical manifestation whose mechanism was the differential reproductive rates of Anglo-Saxon vs. "non-white" immigrant women. Class war, a pathological antagonism of functionally related groups in society, seemed imminent. A burning question in the last decades of the 19th century concerned the energetic economy of middle-class women undertaking higher education: were their health, reproductive capacity, and nutritive function imperiled; were they unsexed by diverting the limited store of organic energy to their heads at crucial organic moments? Nature was threatened by the machine in the garden; the proper interface of the Age of Man and the Age of Mammals could perhaps preserve the potency of the vision of nature and so restore the energy of man. These are strange concerns for the cyborgs of the late 20th century, whose preoccupation with stress and its baroque technicist, code-implicated pathologies makes decadence seem quaint. Infection and decay have been incorporated into coding errors signified by acronyms—AIDS. But for white, middle-class Americans before World War II, decadence mattered. Lung disease (remember Teddy Roosevelt's asthma and alcoholic brother, not to mention America's version of *The Magic Mountain*), sexual disease (what was not a sexual disease, when leprosy, masturbation, and Charlotte Perkins Gilman's need to write all qualified?), and social disease (like strikes and feminism) all disclosed ontologically and epistemologically similar disorders of the relations of nature and culture. Decadence threatened in two interconnected ways, both related to functioning energy-limited productive systems. The machine (remember the iconic power of the railroad) and its fierce artificiality threatened to consume and exhaust man. And the sexual economy of man seemed vulnerable on the one hand to exhaustion and on the other to submergence in unruly and primitive excess. The trustees and officers of the museum were charged with the task of promoting public health in these circumstances.

Exhibition

The American Museum of Natural History was (and is) a "private" institution, as private could only be defined in the United States. In Europe the natural history museums were organs of the state, intimately connected to the fates of national politics.[100] Kennedy's history of the American Museum stresses how intimately connected the development of all the U.S. natural history museums was with the origins of the great class of capitalists after the Civil War. The social fate of that class was also the fate of the museum; its rearrangements and weaknesses in the 1930s were reproduced in crises in the museum, ideologically and organizationally. Philanthropy from the hands of the Rockefellers was mediated by a very complex machinery for the allocation of funds and determination of worthy recipients. The American Museum was not buffered in that way from intimate reliance on the personal beneficence of a few wealthy men. The American Museum is a particularly transparent window for spying on the wealthy in their ideal incarnation, for they made dioramas of themselves.

The great scientific collecting expeditions from the American Museum began in 1888 and stretched to the 1930s. By 1910, they had resulted in gaining for the museum a major scientific reputation in selected fields, especially paleontology, ornithology, and mammalogy. The museum in 1910 boasted nine scientific departments and twenty-five scientists. Anthropology also benefited, and the largest collecting expedition ever mounted by the museum was the 1890s Jesup North Pacific Expedition so important to Franz Boas's career.[101] The sponsors of the museum liked a science that stored facts safely; they liked the public popularity of the new exhibitions. Many people among the white, Protestant middle and upper classes in the United States were committed to nature, camping, and the outdoor life; Teddy Roosevelt embodied their politics and their ethos. Theodore Roosevelt's father was one of the incorporators of the museum in 1868. His son, Kermit, was a trustee during the building of African Hall. Others in that cohort of trustees were J. P. Morgan, William K. Vanderbilt, Henry W. Sage, H. F. Osborn, Daniel Pomeroy, E. Roland Harriman, Childs Frick, John D. Rockefeller III, and Madison Grant. These are leaders of movements for eugenics, conservation, and the rational management of capitalist society. They are patrons of science.

The first Great Hall of dioramas was Frank Chapman's Hall of North American Birds, opened in 1903. Akeley was hired to enhance the museum's ability to prepare the fascinating African game, especially elephants; and he conceived the African Hall idea on his first collecting trip for the American Museum. Osborn hoped for—and got—a North American and Asian Mammal Hall after the African one. The younger trustees in the 1920s formed an African Big Game Club that invited wealthy sportsmen to join in contributing specimens and money to African Hall. The 1920s were prosperous for these men, and they gave generously. Thirty to forty expeditions in some years were mounted in the 1920s to get the unknown facts of nature. There were over one hundred expeditions in the field for the American Museum in that decade.[102]

There was also a significant expansion of the museum's educational endeavors. Over one million children per year in New York were looking at "nature cabinets" put together by the museum. Radio talks, magazine articles, and books covered the museum's popular activities, which appeared in many ways to be a science for the people, like that of the *National Geographic*, which taught republican Americans their responsibilities in empire after 1898. Significantly, both *Natural History*, the museum's publication, and *National Geographic* relied heavily on photographs.[103] There was a big building program from 1909 to 1929; and the Annual Report of the Museum for 1921 quoted the estimate by its director that 2,452,662 (any significant decimal places?!) people were reached by the museum and its education extension program, including the nature cabinets and food exhibits circulating through the city public health department.

Osborn summarized the fond hopes of educators like himself in his claim that children who pass through the museum's halls "become more reverent, more truthful, and more interested in the simple and natural laws of their being and better citizens of the future through each visit." He maintained also that the book of nature, written only in facts, was proof against the failing of other books: "The French and Russian anarchies were based in books and in oratory in defiance of every law of nature."[104] Osborn went beyond pious hopes and constructed a Hall of the Age of Man to make the moral lessons of racial hierarchy and progress explicit, lest they be missed in gazing at elephants.[105] He countered those who criticized the Halls and educational work as too expensive, requiring too much time that would be better spent on science itself. "The exhibits in these Halls have been criticized only by those who speak without knowledge. They all tend to demonstrate the slow upward ascent and struggle of man from the lower to the higher stages, physically, morally, intellectually, and spiritually. Reverently and carefully examined, they put man upwards towards a higher and better future and away from the purely animal stage of life."[106] This is the Gospel of Wealth, reverently examined.

Prophylaxis

Two other undertakings in this period at the American Museum require comment: eugenics and conservation. They were closely linked in philosophy and in personnel at the museum, and they tied in closely with exhibition and research. For example, the notorious author of *The Passing of the Great Race*, Madison Grant, was a successful corporation lawyer, a trustee of the American Museum, an organizer of support for the North American Hall, a co-founder of the California Save-the-Redwoods League, an activist for making Mount McKinley and adjacent lands a national park, and the powerful secretary of the New York Zoological Society. His preservation of nature and germ plasm all seemed the same sort of work. Grant was not a quack or an extremist. He represented a band of Progressive opinion, one terrified of the consequences of unregulated monopoly capitalism, including failure to regulate the importation of non-white (which included Jewish and southern European) working classes who invariably had more prolific women than the "old American stock." The role of the museum in establishing Parc Albert in the Belgian Congo has already been noted. Powerful men in the American scientific establishment were involved in that significant venture in international scientific cooperation: John C. Merriam of the Carnegie Institution of Washington, George Vincent of the Rockefeller Foundation, Osborn at the American Museum. The first significant user of the sanctuary would be sent by the founder of primatology in America, Robert Yerkes, for a study of the psychobiology of wild gorillas. Yerkes was a leader in the movements for social hygiene, the category in which eugenics and conservation also fit. It was all in the service of science.

The Second International Congress of Eugenics was held at the American Museum of Natural History in 1921 while Akeley was in the field collecting gorillas and initiating plans for Parc Albert. Osborn, an ardent eugenicist, believed that it was "[p]erhaps the most important scientific meeting ever held in the Museum." All the leading U.S. universities and state institutions sent representatives, and there were many eminent foreign delegates. The proceedings were collected in a volume plainly titled, "Eugenics in Family, Race, and State." The Congress had a special fruit savored by Osborn. "The section of the exhibit bearing on immigration was then sent to Washington by the Committee on Immigration of the Congress, members of which made several visits to the Museum to study the exhibit. The press was at first inclined to treat the work of the Congress lightly . . . but as the sound and patriotic series of addresses and papers on heredity of the Congress grew and found its way into news and editorial columns of the entire press of the United States." Immigration restriction laws, to protect the Race, the only race needing a capital letter, from "submergence by the influx of other races,"[107] were passed by the U.S. Congress in 1923.

The 1930s were a hiatus for the Museum. Not only did the Depression lead to reduced contributions, but basic ideologies and politics shifted, making the formations discussed in this essay less relevant to the American ruling classes, although the Museum remained popular with New York's people way beyond the 1930s and eugenics sterilization laws have remained on the books into the late 20th century. The changes were not abrupt; but even the racial doctrines so openly championed by the Museum were publicly criticized in the 1940s, though not until then. Conservation was pursued with different political and spiritual justifications. A different biology was being born, more in the hands of the Rockefeller Foundation and in a different social womb. The issue would be molecular biology and other forms of postorganismic cyborg biology. The threat of decadence gave way to the catastrophes of the obsolescence of man (and of all organic nature) and the disease of stress, realities announced vigorously after World War II. Different forms of capitalistic patriarchy and racism would emerge, embodied as always in a retooled nature. Decadence is a disease of organisms; obsolescence and stress are conditions of technological systems. Hygiene would give way to systems engineering as the basis of medical, religious, political, and scientific storytelling practices.

To summarize the themes of Teddy Bear Patriarchy, let us compare the three public activities of the Museum, all dedicated to preserving a threatened manhood. They were exhibition, eugenics, and conservation. Exhibition has been described here at greatest length; it was a practice to produce permanence, to arrest decay. Eugenics was a movement to preserve hereditary stock, to assure racial purity, to prevent race suicide. Conservation was a policy to preserve resources, not only for industry, but also for moral formation, for the achievement of manhood. All three activities were a prescription to cure or prevent decadence, the dread disease of imperialist, capitalist, and white culture. All three activities were considered forms of education and forms of science; they were also very close to religious practice and certainly shared qualities, as well as professional interest, of medical practice. These three activities were all about preservation, purity, social order, health, and the transcendence of death, personal and collective. They attempted to insure preservation without fixation and paralysis, in the face of extraordinary change in the relations of sex, race, and class.

The leaders of the American Museum of Natural History would insist that they were trying to know and to save nature, reality. And the real was one. The explicit ontology was holism, organicism. There was also an aesthetic appropriate to exhibition, conservation, and eugenics from 1890 to 1930: realism. But in the 1920s the surrealists knew that behind the day lay the night of sexual terror, disembodiment, failure of order; in short, castration and impotence of the seminal body which had spoken all the important words for centuries, the great white father, the white hunter in the heart of Africa.[108] And the strongest evidence presented in this essay for the correctness of their judgment has been a literal reading of the realist, organicist artifacts and practices of the American Museum of Natural History. Their practice and mine have been literal, dead literal.

NOTES

First appeared in 1983.

1. Henry Fairfield Osborn, Report to the Trustees, American Museum of Natural History, May, 1908, and in John Michael Kennedy, *Philanthropy and Science in New*

York City: The American Museum of Natural History, 1868–1968, Yale University Ph.D., 1968, Univ. Microfilms, Inc., 69–13, 347 (hereafter Kennedy). The American Museum is hereafter AMNH.

2. Edgar Rice Burroughs in Irwin Porges, *Edgar Rice Burroughs: The Man Who Created Tarzan* (Provo, Utah: Brigham Young Univ., 1975), p. 129.

3. Osborn believed *Homo sapiens* arose in Asia and important Museum expeditions into the Gobi desert in the 1920s were mounted in an attempt to prove this position. However, Africa still had special meaning as the core of primitive nature, and so as origin in the sense of potential restoration, a reservoir of original conditions where "true primitives" survived. Africa was not established as the scene of the original emergence of our species until well after the 1930s. For a creative schizo-analysis of Africa as the locus for the inscription of capitalist desire in history, see William Pietz (Pitzer College), "The Phonograph in Africa: International Phonocentrism from Stanley to Sarnoff," paper from the Second International Theory and Text Conference, Southampton, England, 1983.

4. The body as generative political construction has been a major theme in feminist theory. See Nancy Hartsock, *Money, Sex, and Power* (N.Y.: Longman, 1982); Valerie Hartouni (History of Consciousness, UCSC) in ms. on Greek and Roman versions of citizenship in gendered bodies; D. J. Haraway, "Animal Sociology and a Natural Economy of the Body Politic," *Signs* 4 (1978): 21–60; and for reflections on the meanings of citizenship in this essay, *Social Research*, Winter 1974, essays from the New School for Social Research "Conference on the Meaning of Citizenship." Lacanian feminist theory has probably been the most creative and the most problematic exploration of "woman's" body as not citizen, not author, e.g., Helene Cixous, "The Laugh of the Medusa," in Elaine Marks and Isabelle de Courtivron, eds., *New French Feminisms* (Amherst: Univ. of Massachusetts Press, 1980).

5. The Deauvereaux or Hotel Colorado in Glenwood Springs, Colo., contains a plaque with one version of the origin of the Teddy Bear, emblem of Theodore Roosevelt: T. R. returned empty-handed from a hunting trip to the hotel, and so a hotel maid created a little stuffed bear and gave it to him. Word spread, and the Bear was manufactured in Germany shortly thereafter. Another version has T.R. sparing the life of a bear cub, with the stuffed version commemorating his kindness. It is a pleasure to compose an essay in feminist theory on the subject of stuffed animals.

6. Visual communion, a form of erotic fusion connected with themes of heroic action, especially death, is built into modern scientific ideologies. Its role in masculinist epistemology in science, with its politics of rebirth, is at least as crucial as ideologies of separation and objectivism. Feminist theory so far has paid more attention to gendered subject/object splitting and not enough to love in specular domination's construction of nature and her sisters. See Evelyn Fox Keller, *Reflections on Gender and Science* (New Haven: Yale [Univ. Press], 1985), Carolyn Merchant, *Death of Nature* (N.Y.: Harper and Row, 1980), and Sandra Harding and Merrill Hintikka, eds., *Discovering Reality: Feminist Perspectives on Epistemology, Metaphysics, Methodology and Philosophy of Science* (Dordrecht: Reidel, 1983), esp. E. F. Keller and C. R. Grontkowski, "The Mind's Eye."

7. I am indebted to William Pietz's 1983 UCSC slide lecture on the Chicago Field Museum for an analysis of museums as scenes of ritual transformation.

8. Carl E. Akeley, *In Brightest Africa* (N.Y.: Doubleday, Page, & Co., 1923), p. 162. Hereafter IBA.

9. William Davison Johnson, *T.R.: Champion of the Strenuous Life* (N.Y.: Theodore Roosevelt Association, 1958), pp. 138, 126–27; David McCullough, *Mornings*

on Horseback (N.Y.: Touchstone of Simon and Schuster, 1981); T. Roosevelt, *Theodore Roosevelt's America*, Farida Wiley, ed. (Devin, 1955); P. R. Cutright, *Theodore Roosevelt the Naturalist* (N.Y.: Harper and Row, 1956). For the theme of travel and the modern Western self, esp. for the penetration of Brazil, Claude Lévi-Strauss, *Tristes Tropiques*, and Daniel Defert, "The Collection of the World: Accounts of Voyages from the Sixteenth to the Eighteenth Centuries," *Dialectical Anthropology* 7 (1982): 11–20. Travel as science and as heroic quest interdigitate.

10. It is hardly irrelevant to the symbolism of fear of the new immigrants that it is the women who had all the frightening babies. It is also hardly irrelevant to the lives of the women who had to respond to the realities of immigrant life in a racist society. Linda Gordon, *Woman's Body, Woman's Right* (N.Y.: Grossman, 1976); James Reed, *From Private Vice to Public Virtue* (N.Y.: Basic Books, 1978); Carole McCann, "Politics of Birth Control and Feminist Political Options in the 1920s," ms., History of Consciousness, UCSC; John Higham, *Strangers in the Land* (Greenwood reprint of 1963 ed.). Roosevelt popularized the term "race suicide" in a 1905 speech.

11. The construction of nature, the primitive, the other through an allochronic discourse that works by temporal distancing is explored in Johannes Fabian, *Time and the Other* (N.Y.: Columbia [Univ. Press], 1983). "[G]eopolitics has its ideological foundation in chronopolitics." P. 144. "Woman" is also constructed outside shared or coeval time, as well as outside historical time.

12. Akeley to Osborn, 29 March 1911, in Kennedy, p. 186. the change from African Hall's dioramas to the radically decontextualized boutique displays of more recent AMNH practice is at least evidence for relaxed anxiety about decadence.

13. James Clark, "The Image of Africa," in *The Complete Book of African Hall* (N.Y.: AMNH, 1936), pp. 69–73 for principles of composition; special issues on African Hall, *The Mentor*, January 1926, and *Natural History*, January 1936. See also Handasyde Buchanan, *Nature into Art: A Treasury of Great Natural History Books* (Gloucester, Mass.: Smith, 1980); Donald Lowe, *The History of Bourgeois Perception* (Univ. of Chicago Press, 1982) for excellent discussion of the production of the transcendental subject from the structured relations of human eye/eye-subject/technical apparatus.

14. Malvina Hoffman's bronzes of African men and women in this hall, as well as her heads of Africans at the entrance to the hall, are extraordinary testimony to a crafted human beauty in Akeley's temple of nature. They hardly tell a story of natural primitives. On Osborn's failed effort to enlist Hoffman in his projects, see Charlotte Porter (Smithsonian), "The Rise to Parnassus: Henry Fairfield Osborn and the Hall of the Age of Man," unpublished ms.; Joshua Taylor, "Malvina Hoffman," *American Art and Antiques* 2 (July/Aug. 1979): 96–103.

15. I am indebted to James Clifford's sharp eye for this perception. He and I read the dioramas together in New York City in March 1982. For a method of reading evolutionary texts as narrative, see Misia L. Landau, *The Anthropogenic: Paleontological Writing as a Genre of Literature*, Yale Univ. Ph.D. dissertation, 1981, and "Human Evolution as Narrative," *American Scientist* 72 (May/June 1984): 262–68.

16. IBA, 190.

17. IBA, 203.

18. Carl E. Akeley and Mary L. Jobe Akeley, *Lions, Gorillas, and Their Neighbors* (N.Y.: Dodd and Mead, 1922), hereafter LGN.

19. IBA, 211. The jealous mistress trope is a ubiquitous element of the heterosexist gender anxieties pervading scientists' writing about their endeavors. See esp. Keller, *Gender and Science*.

20. William Nesbit, *How to Hunt with the Camera* (N.Y.: Dutton, 1926); G. A. Guggisberg, *Early Wildlife Photographers* (N.Y.: Talpinger, 1977); Colin Allison, *The Trophy Hunters* (Harrisburg, Pa.: Stackpole, 1981); J. L. Cloudsley-Thompson, *Animal Twilight: Man and Game in Eastern Africa* (Dufour, 1967).

21. IBA, 221.

22. IBA, 222.

23. IBA, 226. For the white woman's account of this trip, see Mary Hastings Bradley, *On the Gorilla Trail* (N.Y.: Appelton, 1922).

24. IBA, 230.

25. IBA, 235.

26. IBA, 248. Scientific knowledge canceled death; only death before knowledge was final, an abortive act in the natural history of progress.

27. Mary L. Jobe Akeley, *Carl Akeley's Africa* (N.Y.: Dodd and Mead, 1929), chpt. XV. Hereafter CAA.

28. Mary Lee Jobe Akeley, *The Wilderness Lives Again. Carl Akeley and the Great Adventure* (N.Y.: Dodd and Mead, 1940), p. 341. Hereafter WLA.

29. CAA, 189–90.

30. Dian Fossey, *Gorillas in the Mist* (Boston: Houghton Mifflin, 1983), p. 3.

31. Osborn in IBA, xii.

32. IBA, 216.

33. Cyborgs are cybernetic organisms whose birth should be sought in social reality and science fiction from the 1950s. For considerations of cyborg existence, see D. J. Haraway, "A Manifesto for Cyborgs: Science, Technology and Socialist Feminism in the 1980s," *Socialist Review* 80 (1985): 65–107. For insight on the fictions of cyborgs, see Katie King (Hist. Con. UCSC), "The Pleasures of Repetition and the Limits of Identification in Feminist Science Fiction: Reimaginations of the Body after the Cyborg"; for a theory of masculinist cyborg replication, Zoe Sofoulis (Hist. Con. UCSC), "Jupiter Space," papers delivered at the California American Studies Association meetings, 1984.

34. IBA, 1.

35. Cynthia Russett, *The Concept of Equilibrium in American Social Thought* (New Haven: Yale [Univ. Press], 1966); Mary Alice Evans and Howard Ensign Evans, *William Morton Wheeler, Biologist* (Cambridge: Harvard [Univ. Press], 1970); William Morton Wheeler, *Essays in Philosophical Biology* (Cambridge: Harvard [Univ. Press], 1939). For organicism in the history of ecology and primatology, see D. J. Haraway, "Signs of Dominance: From a Physiology to a Cybernetics of Primate Society," *Studies in History of Biology* 6 (1983): 129–219.

36. WLA, chpt. III; IBA, chpt. 1.

37. WLA, 340.

38. Clark, *Complete Book of African Hall*, p. 73.

39. IBA, II and X; WLA, VI and X; Clark.

40. WLA, 38.

41. Virtually simultaneously in New York, Frank Chapman of the Department of Mammalogy and Ornithology was working on North American bird habitat groups, which were installed for the public in a large hall in 1903, one of the first evidences of a generous policy by the trustees from about 1890 to 1930. From the mid-1880s, British Museum workers innovated methods for mounting birds, including making extremely lifelike vegetation. The American Museum founded its own department of taxidermy in 1885 and hired two London taxidermists, the brother and sister Henry

Minturn and Mrs. E. S. Mogridge, to teach how to mount the groups. Joel Asaph Abel, Head of Mammalogy and Ornithology, was able to hire Frank Chapman in 1887; Chapman is a major figure in the history of American ornithology and had an important role to play in the initiation of field primatology in the 1930s. Bird groups done at the American Museum from about 1886 on were very popular with the public and induced major changes in the fortunes of the museum. "Wealthy sportsmen, in particular, began to give to the museum." This turning point is critical in the history of the conservation movement in the United States, which will be discussed further below. Significantly because of the scientific activity of the staff of the Department of Mammalogy and Ornithology, the scientific reputation of the American Museum improved dramatically in the last years of the 19th century. Kennedy, pp. 97–104; Frank M. Chapman: *Autobiography of a Bird Lover* (N.Y.: 1933); pamphlet of Chicago Field Columbia Museum, 1902, "The Four Seasons"; "The Work of Carl E. Akeley in the Field Museum of Natural History" (Chicago: Field Museum, 1927).

42. The term is Mary Jobe Akeley's, WLA, 217.

43. Clark, 71.

44. IBA, 265.

45. IBA, 261.

46. Fabian, chpt. 4, "The Other and the Eye," in *Time and the Other*.

47. IBA, chpt. X.

48. Martin Johnson, "Camera Safaris," in *Complete Book of African Hall*, p. 47.

49. See Jane Goodall in *Among the Wild Chimpanzees* (National Geographic Society film, 1984); David Attenborough, *Life on Earth* (Boston and Toronto: Little, Brown & Co., 1979) and BBC TV series of the same name; and for astonishing pictures of human mother, baby, and wild elephant intimacy, Iain and Oria Douglas-Hamilton, *Among the Elephants* (N.Y.: Viking, 1975).

50. Kennedy, p. 204.

51. Susan Sontag, *On Photography* (N.Y.: Delta, 1977), p. 15.

52. CAA, 116.

53. IBA, 155.

54. IBA, chpt. VIII; Edward North Burton, *Two African Trips*, 1902; C. G. Schillings, *With Flashlight and Rifle*, 1905; A. Radclyffe Dugmore, *Camera Adventures in the African Wilds*, 1910.

55. CAA, 127–30; WLA, 115.

56. Jane Goodall, "My Life among the Wild Chimpanzees," *National Geographic*, August 1963, pp. 272–308; Dian Fossey, "Making Friends with Mountain Gorillas," *National Geographic*, January 1970, pp. 48–67; Birute Galdikas-Brindamour, "Orangutans, Indonesia's 'People of the Forest,'" *National Geographic*, October 1975, pp. 444–473, and "Living with the Great Orange Apes," *National Geographic*, June 1980, pp. 830–853.

57. IBA, 166.

58. IBA, 166.

59. IBA, 167.

60. IBA, 223–24. Akeley recognized the utility of his camera to anthropologists, who could (and would) use the telephoto feature "in making motion pictures of natives and of uncivilized countries without their knowledge." IBA, 1966. The photo archive of the American Museum of Natural History is a wonderful and disturbing source of early anthropological photography. These images should be systematically compared with the contemporary safari material.

61. IBA, 197.

62. Neil Harris, *Humbug, The Art of P. T. Barnum* (Boston: Little, Brown & Co., 1973); Herman Melville, *The Confidence Man*, first published 1857. The difference between Barnum in the democratic tradition of hoax and Walt Disney's proliferations of simulation matters. Jean Baudrillard, *Simulations* (N.Y.: Semiotext(e), 1983), pp. 23–26; Louis Marin, *Utopique, jeux d'espaces*; Richard Schickel, *The Disney Version* (N.Y.: Simon and Schuster, 1968).

63. October 1923, prospectus, AMNH archives; Martin Johnson, "Camera Safaris," *The Complete Book of African Hall*, 1936; CAA, 129; July 26, 1923, Akeley memorandum on Martin Johnson Film Expedition and additional material from 1923 AMNH archive, microfilm 1114a and 1114b. See Martin Johnson, *Through the South Seas with Jack London* (Dodd and Mead); *Cannibal Land* (Houghton Mifflin); *Trailing African Wild Animals* (Century); and the films *Simba*, made on the Eastman-Pomeroy expedition, and *Trailing African Wild Animals*.

64. Lewis Carroll, "The Hunting of the Snark," in *Alice in Wonderland*, Norton Critical Edition, p. 225.

65. October 1923, prospectus to the AMNH archive microfilm 1114a.

66. October 1923, Osborn endorsement, AMNH archive microfilm 1114a.

67. Martin Johnson, July 26, 1923, prospectus draft, microfilm 1114a. The expectation that a film made in the middle 1920s would be the last wildlife extravaganza is breathtaking in retrospect. But this serious hope is a wonderful statement of the belief that nature did exist in essentially one form and could be captured in one vision, if only the technology of the eye were adequate. The film made by the Johnsons was "Simba."

68. Much of this paragraph is a response to Sontag, *On Photography*. On the fears and need for mirrors of the American mythical self-made man, see G. J. Barker-Benfield, *The Horrors of the Half-Known Life* (N.Y.: Harper and Row, 1976), and Susan Griffin, *Woman and Nature* (N.Y.: Harper and Row, 1978).

69. The principal sources for this section are correspondence, annual reports, photographic archives, and artifacts in the AMNH: IBA; Mary Jobe Akeley's biography of her husband, WLA; Mary Jobe and Carl Akeley's articles in *The World's Work*; LGN; and Delia Akeley's adventure book, *Jungle Portraits* (N.Y.: Macmillan, 1930). Delia is Delia Denning, Delia Akeley, Delia A. Howe. See *N.Y. Times*, 23 May 1970, p. 23. The buoyant racism in the books and articles of this contemporary of Margaret Mead makes Mary Jobe and Carl look cautious.

70. Joanna Russ, *How to Suppress Women's Writing* (Austin: Texas [Univ. Press], 1983), p. 76. For a superb discussion of the world in which Delia and Mary Jobe worked, see Margaret W. Rossiter, *Women Scientists in America: Struggles and Strategies to 1940* (Baltimore: Johns Hopkins [Univ. Press], 1982).

71. WLA, 222.

72. WLA, 223.

73. IBA, 45.

74. IBA, 48–49.

75. IBA, 49.

76. IBA, 54–55.

77. WLA, IX.

78. WLA, 126.

79. WLA, 303.

80. JP, 249.

81. JP, 233.

82. JP, 93.

83. JP, 90, 95.

84. CAA, 300.

85. CAA, 199.

86. The literature examining functionalism in scientific discourse is large, but critical to this essay are: Alfred Sohn Rethel, *Intellectual and Manual Labor* (London: Macmillan, 1978); Bob Young, "Science *Is* Social Relations," *Radical Science Journal* 5 (1977): 65–129; Hilary Rose, "Hand, Brain, and Heart: A Feminist Epistemology for the Natural Sciences," *Signs* 9 (1983): 73–90.

87. CAA, V; WLA, XV; IBA, VII.

88. IBA, 143.

89. IBA, 144.

90. IBA, 135. "Father to the game" obviously included the highest game of all in the history of colonialism—the submission of man.

91. WLA, 132.

92. IBA, 144.

93. *Job* 12:8, engraved on a plaque at the entrance to the Earth History Hall, AMNH.

94. H. F. Osborn, 54th Annual Report to the Trustees, p. 2, AMNH archives.

95. Leo Marx, *The Machine in the Garden* (London, Oxford, and N.Y.: Oxford [Univ. Press], 1964); Roderick Nash, *Wilderness and the American Mind*, 3d rev. ed. (New Haven: Yale [Univ. Press], 1982); Roderick Nash, "The Exporting and Importing of Nature: Nature-Appreciation as a Commodity 1850–1980," *Perspectives in American History* 12 (1979): 517–60.

96. Andrew Carnegie, "The Gospel of Wealth," *North American Review*, 1889; G. William Domhoff, *Who Rules America?* ([Englewood Cliffs,] N.J.: Prentice-Hall, 1967); Waldemar A. Nielson, *The Big Foundations* (N.Y.: Columbia [Univ. Press], 1972); Gabriel Kolko, *The Triumph of Conservatism* (N.Y.: Free Press, 1977); James Weinstein, *The Corporate Ideal in the Liberal State, 1900–18* (Boston: Beacon, 1969); Robert Wiebe, *The Search for Order, 1877–1920* (N.Y.: Hill and Wang, 1966); Richard Hofstadter, *Age of Reform* (N.Y.: Knopf, 1955); E. Richard Brown, *Rockefeller Medicine Men* (Berkeley: Univ. of Calif. Press, 1978); Paul Starr, *The Social Transformation of American Medicine*, esp. chpts. 3–6 (N.Y.: Basic, 1982); Alexandra Oleson and John Voss, eds., *The Organization of Knowledge in Modern America, 1860–1920* (Baltimore: Johns Hopkins [Univ. Press], 1979).

97. One capitalist in the field with Akeley was George Eastman, an object lesson in the monopoly capitalists' greater fear of decadence than of death. I am claiming that realism is an aesthetics proper to anxiety about decadence, but what kind of realism is celebrated in a literature describing a septagenarian Eastman getting a close-up photograph at 20 feet of a charging rhino, directing his white hunter when to shoot the gun, while his personal physician looks on? "With this adventure Mr. Eastman began to enjoy Africa thoroughly. . . ." WLA, 270.

98. Bruno Latour, *Les microbes. Guerre et paix suivi de irreductions* (Paris: Metailie, 1984), pp. 171–265; Bruno Latour and Steve Woolgar, *Laboratory Life: The Social Construction of Scientific Facts* (Beverly Hills and London: Sage, 1979), esp. on inscription devices and "phenomenotechnique"; Karin Knorr-Cetina and Michael Mulkay, eds., *Science Observed* (Beverly Hills, London, and New Delhi: Sage, 1983).

99. In addition to material already cited (esp. Kennedy and AMNH archives), major sources for this section include: 1) On decadence and the crisis of white man-

hood: F. Scott Fitzgerald, *The Great Gatsby* (1925); Henry Adams, *The Education of Henry Adams* (privately printed, 1907); Ernest Hemingway, *Green Hills of Africa* (1935). 2) On the history of conservation: Roderick Nash, ed., *Environment and the Americans: Problems and Priorities* (Melbourne, Fla.: Kreiger, 1979) and *American Environment: Readings in the History of Conservation*, 2d ed. (Reading, Mass.: Addison-Wesley, 1976); Samuel Hays, *Conservation and the Gospel of Efficiency: The Progressive Conservation Movement, 1890–1920* (Cambridge: Harvard [Univ. Press], 1959). 3) On eugenics, race doctrines, and immigration: John Higham, *Send These to Me: Jews and Other Immigrants in Urban America* (N.Y.: Atheneum, 1975); John Haller, *Outcasts from Evolution* (Urbana: Illinois [Univ. Press], 1971); Allan Chase, *Legacy of Malthus* (N.Y.: Knopf, 1977); Kenneth Ludmerer, *Genetics and American Society* (Baltimore: Johns Hopkins [Univ. Press], 1972); Donald Pickens, *Eugenics and the Progressives* (Nashville[, Tenn.]: Vanderbilt [Univ. Press], 1968); S. J. Gould, *The Mismeasure of Man* (N.Y.: Norton, 1981); Stephan L. Chorover, *From Genesis to Genocide* (Cambridge: MIT Press, 1979); Hamilton Cravens, *Triumph of Evolution: American Scientists and the Heredity-Environment Controversy, 1900–41* (Philadelphia: Univ. of Pennsylvania Press, 1978). Complex concerns about sex, sexuality, hygiene, decadence, [and] birth control are crucial to the production of sex research in the early decades of the 20th century in life and social sciences. Women scientists played a key role in generating this research. Rosalind Rosenberg, *Beyond Separate Spheres: Intellectual Roots of Modern Feminism* (New Haven: Yale [Univ. Press], 1982). The incitement to discourse has been instrumental, to say the least, in the construction of "self-consciousness" and self-description of women as a social group. See Catharine A. MacKinnon, "Feminism, Marxism, Method, and the State: An Agenda for Theory," *Signs* 7, no. 3 (1982). The issue is closely connected to the "being" of woman as spectacle and the need for a feminist theory of experience. Small wonder that film theory is becoming one of the richest sites of feminist theory. Teresa de Lauretis, *Alice Doesn't: Feminism, Semiotics, and Cinema* (Bloomington: Indiana [Univ. Press], 1984); and Annette Kuhn, *Women's Pictures: Feminism and Cinema* (London, Boston, Melbourne, and Henley: Routledge & Kegan Paul, 1982).

100. Camille Limoges and his collaborators at L'Institut d'histoire et de sociopolitique des sciences, Université de Montréal, provide the most complete analysis of the Paris natural history museums from the early 19th century. Gerald Holton and William A. Blanpied, eds., *Science and Its Public: The Changing Relation* (Dordrecht: Reidel, 1976).

101. Kennedy, 141ff. Osborn presided over considerable disbursements to the Department of Anthropology, despite his own opinion that anthropology was largely "the gossip of natives." Osborn was more inclined to favor the skeletons of dinosaurs and mammals, and he is responsible for building one of the world's finest paleontology collections. H. F. Osborn, *Fifty-Two Years of Research, Observation, and Publication* (N.Y.: AMNH, 1930).

102. Kennedy, 192.

103. Philip Pauly, *American Quarterly*, 1982.

104. Osborn, "The American Museum and Citizenship," 53d Annual Report, 1922, p. 2, AMNH archives.

105. Osborn, *The Hall of the Age of Man*, AMNH Guide Leaflet Series, no. 52.

106. Osborn, "Citizenship," 54th Annual Report, p. 2.

107. Osborn, 53d Annual Report, 1921, pp. 31–32. Ethel Tobach of the AMNH helped me interpret and find material on social networks, eugenics, racism, and sexism

at the Museum. The organizing meetings for the Galton Society were held in Osborn's home.

108. Joseph Conrad, esp., *Heart of Darkness*, is crucial to this aspect of my story, especially for exploring complexities of language and desire. See also Fredric Jameson, "Romance and Reification: Plot Construction and Ideological Closure in Joseph Conrad," *The Political Unconscious* (Ithaca: Cornell [Univ. Press], 1981).

Cultural Feminism versus Post-Structuralism: The Identity Crisis in Feminist Theory

LINDA ALCOFF

FOR MANY contemporary feminist theorists, the concept of woman is a problem. It is a problem of primary significance because the concept of woman is the central concept for feminist theory and yet it is a concept that is impossible to formulate precisely for feminists. It is the central concept for feminists because the concept and category of woman is the necessary point of departure for any feminist theory and feminist politics, predicated as these are on the transformation of women's lived experience in contemporary culture and the reevaluation of social theory and practice from a woman's point of view. But as a concept it is radically problematic precisely for feminists because it is crowded with the overdeterminations of male supremacy, invoking in every formulation the limit, contrasting Other, or mediated self-reflection of a culture built on the control of females. In attempting to speak for women, feminism often seems to presuppose that it knows what women truly are, but such an assumption is foolhardy given that every source of knowledge about women has been contaminated with misogyny and sexism. No matter where we turn—to historical documents, philosophical constructions, social scientific statistics, introspection, or daily practices—the mediation of female bodies into constructions of woman is dominated by misogynist discourse. For feminists, who must transcend this discourse, it appears we have nowhere to turn.[1]

Thus the dilemma facing feminist theorists today is that our very self-definition is grounded in a concept that we must deconstruct and de-essentialize in all of its aspects. Man has said that woman can be defined, delineated, captured—understood, explained, and diagnosed—to a level of determination never accorded to man himself, who is conceived as a rational animal with free will. Where man's behavior is underdetermined, free to construct its own future along the course of its rational choice, woman's nature has overdetermined her behavior, the limits of her intellectual endeavors, and the inevitabilities of her emotional journey through life. Whether she is construed as essentially immoral and irrational (à la Schopenhauer) or essentially kind and benevolent (à la Kant), she is always construed as an essential *something* inevitably accessible to direct intuited apprehension by males.[2] Despite the variety of ways in which man has construed her essential characteristics, she is always the Object, a conglomeration of attributes to be predicted and controlled along with other natural phenomena. The place of the free-willed subject who can transcend nature's mandates is reserved exclusively for men.[3]

Feminist thinkers have articulated two major responses to this situation over the last ten years. The first response is to claim that feminists have the exclusive right to describe and evaluate woman. Thus cultural feminists argue that the problem of male supremacist culture is the problem of a process in which women are defined by men, that is, by a group which has a contrasting point of view and set of interests from women, not to mention a possible fear and hatred of women. The result of this has been a distortion and devaluation of feminine characteristics, which now can be corrected by a more accurate feminist description and appraisal. Thus the cultural feminist reappraisal construed women's passivity as her peacefulness, her sentimentality as her proclivity to nurture, her subjectiveness as her advanced self-awareness, and so forth. Cultural feminists have not challenged the defining of woman but only that definition given by men.

The second major response has been to reject the possibility of defining women as such at all. Feminists who take this tactic go about the business of deconstructing all concepts of woman and argue that both feminist and misogynist attempts to define woman are politically reactionary and ontologically mistaken. Replacing woman-as-housewife with woman-as-supermom (or earth mother or superprofessional) is no advance. Using French post-structuralist theory, these feminists argue that such errors occur because we are in fundamental ways duplicating misogynist strategies when we try to define women, characterize women, or speak for women, even though allowing for a range of differences within the gender. The politics of gender or sexual difference must be replaced with a plurality of difference where gender loses its position of significance.

Briefly put, then, the cultural feminist response to Simone de Beauvoir's question, "Are there women?" is to answer yes and to define women by their activities and attributes in the present culture. The post-structuralist response is to answer no and attack the category and the concept of woman through problematizing subjectivity. Each response has serious limitations, and it is becoming increasingly obvious that transcending these limitations while retaining the theoretical framework from which they emerge is impossible. As a result, a few brave souls are now rejecting these choices and attempting to map out a new course, a course that will avoid the major problems of the earlier responses. In this paper I will now discuss some of the pioneer work being done to develop a new concept of woman and offer my own contribution toward it.[4] But first, I must spell out more clearly the inadequacies of the first two responses to the problem of woman and explain why I believe these inadequacies are inherent.

CULTURAL FEMINISM

Cultural feminism is the ideology of a female nature or female essence re-appropriated by feminists themselves in an effort to revalidate undervalued female attributes. For cultural feminists, the enemy of women is not merely a social system or economic institution or set of backward beliefs but masculinity itself and in some cases male biology. Cultural feminist politics revolve around creating and maintaining a healthy environment—free of masculinist values and all their offshoots, such as pornography—for the female principle. Feminist theory, the explanation of sexism, and the justification of feminist demands can all be grounded securely and unambiguously on the concept of the essential female.

Mary Daly and Adrienne Rich have been influential proponents of this position.[5] Breaking the trend toward androgyny and the minimizing of gender differences that was popular among feminists in the early seventies, both Daly and Rich argue for a returned focus on femaleness.

For Daly, male barrenness leads to parasitism on female energy, which flows from our life-affirming, life-creating, biological condition: "Since female energy is essentially biophilic, the female spirirt/body is the primary target in this perpetual war of aggression against life. Gyn/Ecology is the re-claiming of life-loving female energy." [6] Despite Daly's warnings against biological reductionism,[7] her own analysis of sexism uses gender-specific biological traits to explain male hatred for women. The childless state of "all males" leads to a dependency on women, which in turn leads men to "deeply identify with 'unwanted female tissue.'"[8] Given their state of fear and insecurity it becomes almost understandable, then, that men would desire to dominate and control that which is so vitally necessary to them: the life-energy of women. Female energy, conceived by Daly as a natural essence, needs to be freed from its male parasites, released for creative expression and recharged through bonding with other women. In this free space women's "natural" attributes of love, creativity, and the ability to nurture can thrive.

Women's identification as female is their defining essence for Daly, their haecceity, overriding any other way in which they may be defined or may define themselves. Thus Daly states: "Women who accept false inclusion among the fathers and sons are easily polarized against other women on the basis of ethnic, national, class, religious and other *male-defined differences*, applauding the defeat of 'enemy' women."[9] These differences are apparent rather than real, inessential rather than essential. The only real difference, the only difference that can change a person's ontological placement on Daly's dichotomous map, is sex difference. Our essence is defined here, in our sex, from which flow all the facts about us: who are our potential allies, who is our enemy, what are our objective interests, what is our true nature. Thus, Daly defines women again and her definition is strongly linked to female biology.

Many of Rich's writings have exhibited surprising similarities to Daly's position described above, surprising given their difference in style and temperament. Rich defines a "female consciousness"[10] that has a great deal to do with the female body.

> I have come to believe . . . that the female biology—the diffuse, intense sensuality radiating out from clitoris, breasts, uterus, vagina; the lunar cycles of menstruation; the gestation and fruition of life which can take place in the female body—has far more radical implications than we have yet come to appreciate. Patriarchical thought has limited female biology to its own narrow specifications. The feminist vision has recoiled from female biology for these reasons; it will, I believe, come to view our physicality as a resource, rather than a destiny. . . . We must touch the unity and resonance of our physicality, our bond with the natural order, the corporeal ground of our intelligence.[11]

Thus Rich argues that we should not reject the importance of female biology simply because patriarchy had used it to subjugate us. Rich believes that "our biological grounding, the miracle and paradox of the female body and its spiritual and political meanings" holds the key to our rejuvenation and our reconnection with our specific female attributes, which she lists as "our great mental capacities . . .; our highly developed tactile sense; our genius for close observation; our complicated, pain-enduring, multi-pleasured physicality."[12]

Rich further echoes Daly in her explanation of misogyny: "The ancient, continuing envy, awe, and dread of the male for the female capacity to create life has repeatedly taken the form of hatred for every other female aspect of creativity."[13] Thus Rich, like Daly, identifies a female essence, defines patriarchy as the subjugation and colonization of this essence out of male envy and need, and then promotes a solution that revolves around rediscovering our essence and bonding with other women. Neither Rich nor Daly espouses biological reductionism, but this is because they reject the oppositional dichotomy of mind and body that such a reductionism presupposes. The female essence for Daly and Rich is not simply spiritual or simply biological—it is both. Yet the key point remains that it is our specifically female anatomy that is the primary constituent of our identity and the source of our female essence. Rich prophesies that "the repossession by women of our bodies will bring far more essential change to human society than the seizing of the means of production by workers. . . . In such a world women will truly create new life, bringing forth not only children (if and as we choose) but the visions, and the thinking, necessary to sustain, console and alter human existence—a new relationship to the universe. Sexuality, politics, intelligence, power, motherhood, work, community, intimacy will develop new meanings; thinking itself will be transformed."[14]

The characterization of Rich's and Daly's views as part of a growing trend within feminism toward essentialism has been developed most extensively by Alice Echols.[15] Echols prefers the name "cultural feminism" for this trend because it equates "women's liberation with the development and preservation of a female counter culture."[16] Echols identifies cultural feminist writings by their denigration of masculinity rather than male roles or practices, by their valorization of female traits, and by their commitment to preserve rather than diminish gender differences. Besides Daly and Rich, Echols names Susan Griffin, Kathleen Barry, Janice Raymond, Florence Rush, Susan Brownmiller, and Robin Morgan as important cultural feminist writers, and she documents her claim persuasively by highlighting key passages of their work. Although Echols finds a prototype of this trend in early radical feminist writings by Valerie Solanis and Joreen, she is careful to distinguish cultural feminism from radical feminism as a whole. The distinguishing marks between the two include their position on the mutability of sexism among men, the connection between biology and misogyny, and the degree of focus on valorized female attributes. As Hester Eisenstein has argued, there is a tendency within many radical feminist works toward setting up an ahistorical and essentialist conception of female nature, but this tendency is developed and consolidated by cultural feminists, thus rendering their work significantly different from radical feminism.

However, although cultural feminist views sharply separate female from male traits, they certainly do not all give explicitly essentialist formulations of what it means to be a woman. So it may seem that Echols's characterization of cultural feminism makes it appear too homogeneous and that the charge of essentialism is on shaky ground. On the issue of essentialism Echols states:

> This preoccupation with defining the female sensibility not only leads these feminists to indulge in dangerously erroneous generalizations about women, but to imply that this identity is innate rather than socially constructed. At best, there has been a curiously cavalier disregard for whether these differences are biological or cultural in origin. Thus Janice Raymond argues: "Yet there are differences, and some feminists have come to realize that those differences are important whether they spring from socialization, from biology, or from the total history of existing as a woman in a patriarchal society."[17]

Echols points out that the importance of the differences varies tremendously according to their source. If that source is innate, the cultural feminist focus on building an alternative feminist culture is politically correct. If the differences are not innate, the focus of our activism should shift considerably. In the absence of a clearly stated position on the ultimate source of gender difference, Echols infers from their emphasis on building a feminist free-space and women-centered culture that cultural feminists hold some version of essentialism. I share Echols's suspicion. Certainly, it is difficult to render the views of Rich and Daly into a coherent whole without supplying a missing premise that there is an innate female essence.

Interestingly, I have not included any feminist writings from women of oppressed nationalities and races in the category of cultural feminism, nor does Echols. I have heard it argued that the emphasis placed on cultural identity by such writers as Cherríe Moraga and Audre Lorde reveals a tendency toward essentialism also. However, in my view their work has consistently rejected essentialist conceptions of gender. Consider the following passage from Moraga: "When you start to talk about sexism, the world becomes increasingly complex. The power no longer breaks down into neat little hierarchical categories, but becomes a series of starts and detours. Since the categories are not easy to arrive at, the enemy is not easy to name. It is all so difficult to unravel."[18] Moraga goes on to assert that "some men oppress the very women they love," implying that we need new categories and new concepts to describe such complex and contradictory relations of oppression. In this problematic understanding of sexism, Moraga seems to me light-years ahead of Daly's Manichaean ontology or Rich's romanticized conception of the female. The simultaneity of oppressions experienced by women such as Moraga resists essentialist conclusions. Universalist conceptions of female or male experiences and attributes are not plausible in the context of such a complex network of relations, and without an ability to universalize, the essentialist argument is difficult if not impossible to make. White women cannot be all good or all bad; neither can men from oppressed groups. I have simply not found writings by feminists who are oppressed also by race and/or class that place or position maleness wholly as Other. Reflected in their problematized understanding of masculinity is a richer and likewise problematized concept of woman.[19]

Even if cultural feminism is the product of white feminists, it is not homogeneous, as Echols herself points out. The biological accounts of sexism given by Daly and Brownmiller, for example, are not embraced by Rush or Dworkin. But the key link between these feminists is their tendency toward invoking universalizing conceptions of woman and mother in an essentialist way. Therefore, despite lack of complete homogeneity within the category, it seems still justifiable and important to identify (and criticize) within these sometimes disparate works their tendency to offer an essentialist response to misogyny and sexism through adopting a homogeneous, unproblematized, and ahistorical conception of woman.

One does not have to be influenced by French post-structuralism to disagree with essentialism. It is well documented that the [assertion of] innateness of gender differences in personality and character is at this point factually and philosophically indefensible.[20] There are a host of divergent ways gender divisions occur in different societies, and the differences that appear to be universal can be explained in nonessentialist ways. However, belief in women's innate peacefulness and ability to nurture has been common among feminists since the nineteenth century and has enjoyed a resurgence in the last decade, most notably among feminist peace activists. I have met scores of young feminists drawn to actions like the Women's Peace Encampment and to groups like Women for a Non-Nuclear Future by their belief that the maternal love women have for their children can unlock the gates of imperialist oppression. I have great respect for Echols's fear that their effect is to "reflect and reproduce dominant cultural assumptions about women," which not only fail to represent the variety in women's lives but promote unrealistic expectations about "normal" female behavior that most of us cannot satisfy.[21] Our gender categories are positively constitutive and not mere hindsight descriptions of previous activities. There is a self-perpetuating circularity between defining woman as essentially peaceful and nurturing and the observations and judgments we shall make of future women and the practices we shall engage in as women in the future. Do feminists want to buy another ticket for women of the world on the merry-go-round of feminine constructions? Don't we want rather to get off the merry-go-round and run away?

This should not imply that the political effects of cultural feminism have all been negative.[22] The insistence on viewing traditional feminine characteristics from a different point of view, to use a "looking glass" perspective, as a means of engendering a gestalt switch on the body of data we all currently share about women, has had positive effect. After a decade of hearing liberal feminists advising us to wear business suits and enter the male world, it is a helpful corrective to have cultural feminists argue instead that women's world is full of superior virtues and values, to be credited and learned from rather than despised. Herein lies the positive impact of cultural feminism. And surely much of their point is well taken, that it was our mothers who made our families survive, that women's handiwork is truly artistic, that women's caregiving is really superior in value to male competitiveness.

Unfortunately, however, the cultural feminist championing of a redefined "womanhood" cannot provide a useful long-range program for a feminist movement and, in fact, places obstacles in the way of developing one. Under conditions of oppression and restrictions on freedom of movement, women, like other oppressed groups, have developed strengths and attributes that should be correctly credited, valued, and promoted. What we should not promote, however, are the restrictive conditions that gave rise to those attributes: forced parenting, lack of physical autonomy, dependency for survival on mediation skills, for instance. What conditions for women do we want to promote? A freedom of movement such that we can compete in the capitalist world alongside men? A continued restriction to child-centered activities? To the extent cultural feminism merely valorizes genuinely positive attributes developed under oppression, it cannot map our future long-range course. To the extent that it reinforces essentialist explanations of these attributes, it is in danger of solidifying an important bulwark for sexist oppression: the belief in an innate "womanhood" to which we must all adhere lest we be deemed either inferior or not "true" women.

POST-STRUCTURALISM

For many feminists, the problem with the cultural feminist response to sexism is that it does not criticize the fundamental mechanism of oppressive power used to perpetuate sexism and in fact reinvokes that mechanism in its supposed solution. The mechanism of power referred to here is the construction of the subject by a discourse that weaves knowledge and power into a coercive structure that "forces the individual back on himself and ties him to his own identity in a constraining way."[23] On this view, essentialist formulations of womanhood, even when made by feminists, "tie" the individual to her identity as a woman and thus cannot represent a solution to sexism.

This articulation of the problem has been borrowed by feminists from a number of recently influential French thinkers who are sometimes called post-structuralist but who also might be called post-humanist and post-essentialist. Lacan, Derrida, and Foucault are the front-runners of this group. Disparate as these writers are, their (one) common theme is that the self-contained, authentic subject conceived by humanism to be discoverable below a veneer of cultural and ideological overlay is in reality a construct of that very humanist discourse. The subject is not a locus of authorial intentions or natural attributes or even a privileged, separate consciousness. Lacan uses psychoanalysis, Derrida uses grammar, and Foucault uses the history of the discourses all to attack and "deconstruct"[24] our concept of the subject as having an essential identity and an authentic core that has been repressed by society. There is no essential core "natural" to us, and so there is no repression in the humanist sense.

There is an interesting sort of neodeterminism in this view. The subject of self is never determined by biology in such a way that human history is predictable or even explainable, and there is no unilinear direction of a determinist arrow pointing from some fairly static, "natural" phenomena to human experience. On the other hand, this rejection of biological determinism is not grounded in the belief that human subjects are underdetermined but, rather, in the belief that we are overdetermined (i.e., constructed) by a social discourse and/or cultural practice. The idea here is that we individuals really have little choice in the matter of who we are, for as Derrida and Foucault like to remind us, individual motivations and intentions count for nil or almost nil in the scheme of social reality. We are constructs mediated by and/or grounded on a social discourse beyond (way beyond) individual control. As Foucault puts it, we are bodies "totally imprinted by history."[25] Thus, subjective experiences are determined in some sense by macro forces. However, these macro forces, including some social discourses and social practices, are apparently not overdetermined, resulting as they do from such a complex and unpredictable network of overlapping and crisscrossing elements that no unilinear directionality is perceivable and in fact no final or efficient cause exists. There may be, and Foucault hoped at one point to find them,[26] perceivable processes of change within the social network, but beyond schematic rules of thumb neither the form nor the content of discourse has a fixed or unified structure that can be predicted or mapped out via an objectified, ultimate realm. To some extent, this view is similar to contemporary methodological individualism, whose advocates will usually concede that the complex of human intentions results in a social reality bearing no resemblance to the summarized categories of intentions but looking altogether different than any one party or sum of parties ever envisaged or desired. The difference, however, is that while methodological individualists admit that human intentions are ineffective, post-structuralists deny not only the efficacy but also the ontological autonomy and even the existence of intentionality.

Post-structuralists unite with Marx in asserting the social dimension of individual traits and intentions. Thus, they say we cannot understand society as the conglomerate of individual intentions but, rather, must understand individual intentions as constructed within a social reality. To the extent post-structuralists emphasize social explanations of individual practices and experiences I find their work illuminating and persuasive. My disagreement occurs, however, when they seem totally to erase any room for maneuver by the individual within a social discourse or set of institutions. It is that totalization of history's imprint that I reject. In their defense of a total construction of the subject, post-structuralists deny the subject's ability to reflect on the social discourse and challenge its determinations.

Applied to the concept of woman, the post-structuralist's view results in what I shall call nominalism: the idea that the category "woman" is a fiction and that feminist efforts must be directed toward dismantling this fiction. "Perhaps . . . 'woman' is not a determinable identity. Perhaps woman is not some thing which announces itself from a distance, at a distance from some other thing. . . . Perhaps woman—a non-identity, non-figure, a simulacrum—is distance's very chasm, the out-distancing of distance, the interval's cadence, distance itself."[27] Derrida's interest in feminism stems from his belief, expressed above, that woman may represent the rupture in the functional discourse that entails hierarchies of difference and a Kantian ontology. Because woman has in a sense been excluded from this discourse, it is possible to hope that she might provide a real source of resistance. But her resistance will not be at all effective if she continues to use the mechanism of logocentrism to redefine woman: she can be an effective resister only if she drifts and dodges all attempts to capture her. Then, Derrida hopes, the following futuristic picture will come true: "Out of the depths, endless and unfathomable, she engulfs and distorts all vestige of essentiality, of identity, of property. And the philosophical discourse, blinded, founders on these shoals and is hurled down these depths to its ruin."[28] For Derrida, women have always been defined as a subjugated difference within a binary opposition: man/woman, culture/nature, positive/negative, analytical/intuitive. To assert an essential gender difference as cultural feminists do is to reinvoke this oppositional structure. The only way to break out of this structure, and in fact to subvert the structure itself, is to assert total difference, to be that which cannot be pinned down or subjugated within a dichotomous hierarchy. Paradoxically, it is to be what is not. Thus feminists cannot demarcate a definitive category of "woman" without eliminating all possibility for the defeat of logocentrism and its oppressive power.

Foucault similarly rejects all constructions of oppositional subjects—whether the "proletariat," "woman," or "the oppressed"—as mirror images that merely recreate and sustain the discourse of power. As Biddy Martin points out, "The point from which Foucault deconstructs is off-center, out of line, apparently unaligned. It is not the point of an imagined absolute otherness, but an 'alterity' which understands itself as an internal exclusion."[29]

Following Foucault and Derrida, an effective feminism could only be a wholly negative feminism, deconstructing everything and refusing to construct anything. This is the position Julia Kristeva adopts, herself an influential French post-structuralist. She says: "A woman cannot be; it is something which does not even belong in the order of being. *It follows that a feminist practice can only be negative*, at odds with what already exists so that we may say 'that's not it' and 'that's still not it.'"[30] The problemative character of subjectivity does not mean, then, that there can be no political struggle, as one might surmise from the fact that post-structuralism deconstructs the position of the revolutionary in the same breath as it deconstructs the position of the reactionary. But the political struggle can have only a "negative function," rejecting "everything finite, definite, structured, loaded with meaning, in the existing state of society."[31]

The attraction of the post-structuralist critique of subjectivity for feminists is twofold. First, it seems to hold out the promise of an increased freedom for women, the "free play" of a plurality of differences unhampered by any predetermined gender identity as formulated by either patriarchy or cultural feminism. Second, it moves decisively beyond cultural feminism and liberal feminism in further theorizing what they leave untouched: the construction of subjectivity. We can learn a great deal here about the mechanisms of sexist oppression and the construction of specific gender categories by relating these to social discourse and by conceiving of the subject as a cultural product. Certainly, too, this analysis can help us understand right-wing women, the reproduction of ideology, and the mechanisms that block social progress. However, adopting nominalism creates significant problems for feminism. How can we seriously adopt Kristeva's plan for only negative struggle? As the Left should by now have learned, you cannot mobilize a movement that is only and always against: you must have a positive alternative, a vision of a better future that can motivate people to sacrifice their time and energy toward its realization. Moreover, a feminist adoption of nominalism will be confronted with the same problem theories of ideology have, that is, Why is a right-wing woman's consciousness constructed via social discourse but a feminist's consciousness not? Post-structuralist critiques of subjectivity pertain to the construction of all subjects or they pertain to none. And here is precisely the dilemma for feminists: How can we ground a feminist politics that deconstructs the female subject? Nominalism threatens to wipe out feminism itself.

Some feminists who wish to use post-structuralism are well aware of this danger. Biddy Martin, for example, points out that "we cannot afford to refuse to take a political stance 'which pins us to our sex' for the sake of an abstract theoretical correctness. . . . There is the danger that Foucault's challenges to traditional categories, if taken to a logical conclusion . . . could make the question of women's oppression obsolete."[32] Based on her articulation of the problem with Foucault, we are left hopeful that Martin will provide a solution that transcends nominalism. Unfortunately, in her reading of Lou Andreas-Salome, Martin valorizes undecidability, ambiguity, and elusiveness and intimates that by maintaining the undecidability of identity the life of Andreas-Salome provides a text from which feminists can usefully learn.[33]

However, the notion that all texts are undecidable cannot be useful for feminists. In support of his contention that the meaning of texts is ultimately undecidable, Derrida offers us in *Spurs* three conflicting but equally warranted interpretations of how Nietzsche's texts construct and position the female. In one of these interpretations, Derrida argues, we can find purportedly feminist propositions.[34] Thus, Derrida seeks to demonstrate that even the seemingly incontrovertible interpretation of Nietzsche's works as misogynist can be challenged by an equally convincing argument that they are not. But how can this be helpful to feminists, who need to have their accusations of misogyny validated rather than rendered "undecidable"? The point is not that Derrida himself is antifeminist, nor that there is nothing at all in Derrida's work that can be useful for feminists. But the thesis of undecidability as it is applied in the case of Nietzsche sounds too much like yet another version of the antifeminist argument that our perception of sexism is based on a skewed, limited perspective and that what we take to be misogyny is in reality helpful rather than hurtful to the cause of women. The declaration of undecidability must inevitably return us to Kristeva's position, that we can give only negative answers to the question, What is a woman? If the category "woman" is fundamentally undecidable, then we can offer no positive conception of it that is immune to deconstruction, and we are left with a feminism that can be only deconstructive and, thus, nominalist once again.[35]

A nominalist position on subjectivity has the deleterious effect of de-gendering our analysis, of in effect making gender invisible once again. Foucault's ontology includes only bodies and pleasures, and he is notorious for not including gender as a category of analysis. If gender is simply a social construct, the need and even the possibility of a feminist politics becomes immediately problematic. What can we demand in the name of women if "women" do not exist and demands in their name simply reinforce the myth that they do? How can we speak out against sexism as detrimental to the interests of women if the category is a fiction? How can we demand legal abortions, adequate child care, or wages based on comparable worth without invoking the concept of "woman"?

Post-structuralism undercuts our ability to oppose the dominant trend (and, one might argue, the dominant danger) in mainstream Western intellectual thought, that is, the insistence on a universal, neutral, perspectiveless epistemology, metaphysics, and ethics. Despite rumblings from the Continent, Anglo-American thought is still wedded to the idea (1) of a universalizable, apolitical methodology and set of transhistorical basic truths unfettered by associations with particular genders, races, classes, or cultures. The rejection of subjectivity, unintentionally but nevertheless, colludes with this "generic human" thesis of classical liberal thought, that particularities of individuals are irrelevant and improper influences on knowledge. By designating individual particularities such as subjective experience as a social construct, post-structuralism's negation of the authority of the subject coincides nicely with the classical liberal's view that human particularities are irrelevant. (For the liberal, race, class, and gender are ultimately irrelevant to the questions of justice and truth because "underneath we are all the same." For the post-structuralist, race, class, and gender are constructs and, therefore, incapable of decisively validating conceptions of justice and truth because underneath there lies no natural core to build on or liberate or maximize. Hence, once again, underneath we all are the same.) It is, in fact, a desire to topple this commitment to the possibility of a worldview—purported in fact as the best of all possible worldviews—grounded in a generic human that motivates much of the cultural feminist glorification of femininity as a valid specificity legitimately grounding feminist theory.[36]

The preceding characterizations of cultural feminism and post-structuralist feminism will anger many feminists by assuming too much homogeneity and by blithely pigeonholing large and complex theories. However, I believe the tendencies I have outlined toward essentialism and toward nominalism represent the main current responses by feminist theory to the task of reconceptualizing "woman." Both responses have significant advantages and serious shortcomings. Cultural feminism has provided a useful corrective to the "generic human" thesis of classical liberalism and has promoted community and self-affirmation, but it cannot provide a long-range future course of action for feminist theory or practice, and it is founded on a claim of essentialism that we are far from having the evidence to justify. The feminist appropriation of post-structuralism has provided suggestive insights on the construction of female and male subjectivity and has issued a crucial warning against creating a feminism that reinvokes the mechanisms of oppressive power. Nonetheless, it limits feminism to the negative tactics of reaction and deconstruction and endangers the attack against classical liberalism by discrediting the notion of an epistemologically significant, specific subjectivity. What's a feminist to do?

We cannot simply embrace the paradox. In order to avoid the serious disadvantages of cultural feminism and post-structuralism, feminism needs to transcend the dilemma by developing a third course, an alternative theory of the subject that avoids both essentialism and nominalism. This new alternative might share the post-structuralist insight that the category "woman" needs to be theorized through an exploration of the experience of subjectivity, as opposed to a description of current attributes, but it need not concede that such an exploration will necessarily result in a nominalist position on gender, or an erasure of it. Feminists need to explore the possibility of a theory of the gendered subject that does not slide into essentialism. In the following two sections I will discuss recent work that makes a contribution to the development of such a theory, or so I shall argue, and in the final section I will develop my own contribution in the form of a concept of gendered identity as positionality.

TERESA DE LAURETIS

Lauretis's influential book *Alice Doesn't*, is a series of essays organized around an exploration of the problem of conceptualizing woman as subject. This problem is formulated in her work as arising out of the conflict between "woman" as a "fictional construct" and "women" as "real historical beings."[37] She says: "The relation between women as historical subjects and the notion of woman as it is produced by hegemonic discourses is neither a direct relation of identity, a one-to-one correspondence, nor a relation of simple implication. Like all other relations expressed in language, it is an arbitrary and symbolic one, that is to say, culturally set up. The manner and effects of that set-up are what the book intends to explore."[38] The strength of Lauretis's approach is that she never loses sight of the political imperative of feminist theory and, thus, never forgets that we must seek not only to describe this relation in which women's subjectivity is grounded, but also to change it. And yet, given her view that we are constructed via a semiotic discourse, this political mandate becomes a crucial problem. As she puts it, "Paradoxically, the only way to position oneself outside of that discourse is to displace oneself within it—to refuse the question as formulated, or to answer deviously (though in its words), even to quote (but against the grain). The limit posed but not worked through in this book is thus the contradiction of feminist theory itself, at once excluded from discourse and imprisoned within it."[39] As with feminist theory, so, too, is the female subject "at once excluded from discourse and imprisoned within it." Constructing a theory of the subject that both concedes these truths and yet allows for the possibility of feminism is the problem Lauretis tackles throughout *Alice Doesn't*. To concede the construction of the subject via discourse entails that the feminist project cannot be simply "how to make visible the invisible" as if the essence of gender were out there waiting to be recognized by the dominant discourse. Yet Lauretis does not give up on the possibility of producing "the condition of visibility for a different social subject."[40] In her view, a nominalist position on subjectivity can be avoided by linking subjectivity to a Peircean notion of practices and a further theorized notion of experience.[41] I shall look briefly at her discussion of this latter claim.

Lauretis's main thesis is that subjectivity, that is, what one "perceives and comprehends as subjective," is constructed through a continuous process, and ongoing constant renewal based on an interaction with the world, which she defines as experience: "And thus [subjectivity] is produced not by external ideas, values, or material causes, but by one's personal, subjective engagement in the practices, discourses, and institutions that lend significance (value, meaning, and affect) to the events of the world."[42] This is the process through which one's subjectivity becomes en-gendered. But describing the subjectivity that emerges is still beset with difficulties, principally the following: "The feminist efforts have been more often than not caught in the logical trap set up by [a] paradox. Either they have assumed that 'the subject,' like 'man,' is a generic term, and as such can designate equally and at once the female and male subjects, with the result of erasing sexuality and sexual difference from subjectivity. Or else they have been obliged to resort to an oppositional notion of 'feminine' subject defined by silence, negativity, a natural sexuality, or a closeness to nature not compromised by patriarchal culture."[43] Here again is spelled out the dilemma between a post-structuralist genderless subject and a cultural feminist essentialized subject. As Lauretis points out, the latter alternative is constrained in its conceptualization of the female subject by the very act of distinguishing female from male subjectivity. This appears to produce a dilemma, for if we de-gender subjectivity, we are committed to a generic subject and thus undercut feminism, while on the other hand if we define the subject in terms of gender, articulating female subjectivity in a space clearly distinct from male subjectivity, then we become caught up in an oppositional dichotomy controlled by a misogynist discourse. A gender-bound subjectivity seems to force us to revert "women to the body and to sexuality as an immediacy of the biological, as nature."[44] For all her insistence on a subjectivity constructed through practices, Lauretis is clear that *that* conception of subjectivity is not what she wishes to propose. A subjectivity that is fundamentally shaped by gender appears to lead irrevocably to essentialism, the posing of male/female opposition as universal and ahistorical. A subjectivity that is not fundamentally shaped by gender appears to lead to the conception of a generic human subject, as if we could peel away our "cultural" layers and get to the real root of human nature, which turns out to be genderless. Are these really our only choices?

In *Alice Doesn't* Lauretis develops the beginnings of a new conception of subjectivity. She argues that subjectivity is neither (over)determined by biology nor by "free, rational, intentionality" but, rather, by experience, which she defines (via Lacan, Eco, and Pierce) as "a complex of habits resulting from the semiotic interaction of our 'outer world' and 'inner world,' the continuous engagement of a self or subject in social reality."[45] Given this definition, the question obviously becomes, Can we ascertain a "female experience"? This is the question Lauretis prompts us to consider, more specifically, to analyze "that complex of habits, dispositions, associations and perceptions, which en-genders one as female."[46] Lauretis ends her book with an insightful observation that can serve as a critical starting point:

> This is where the specificity of a feminist theory may be sought: not in femininity as a privileged nearness to nature, the body, or the unconscious, an essence which inheres in women but to which males now too lay a claim; not in female

tradition simply understood as private, marginal, and yet intact, outside of history but fully there to be discovered or recovered; not, finally, in the chinks and cracks of masculinity, the fissures of male identity or the repressed of phallic discouse; *but rather in that political, theoretical, self-analyzing practice* by which the relations of the subject in social reality can be rearticulated from the historical experience of women. Much, very much, is still to be done.[47]

Thus Lauretis asserts that the way out of the totalizing imprint of history and discourse is through our "political, theoretical self-analyzing practice." This should not be taken to imply that only intellectual articles in academic journals represent a free space or ground for maneuver but, rather, that all women can (and do) think about, criticize, and alter discourse and, thus, that subjectivity can be reconstructed through the process of reflexive practice. The key component of Lauretis's formulation is the dynamic she poses at the heart of subjectivity: a fluid interacting in constant motion and open to alteration by self-analyzing practice.

Recently, Lauretis has taken off from this point and developed further her conception of subjectivity. In the introductory essay for her latest book, *Feminist Studies/Critical Studies*, Lauretis claims that an individual's identity is constituted with a historical process of consciousness, a process in which one's history "is interpreted or reconstructed by each of us within the horizon of meanings and knowledges available in the culture at given historical moments, a horizon that also includes modes of political commitment and struggle. . . .Consciousness, therefore, is never fixed, never attained once and for all, because discursive boundaries change with historical conditions."[48]Here Lauretis guides our way out of the dilemma she articulated for us in *Alice Doesn't*. The agency of the subject is made possible through this process of political interpretation. And what emerges is multiple and shifting, neither "prefigured . . . in an unchangeable symbolic order" nor merely "fragmented, or intermittent."[49] Lauretis formulates a subjectivity that gives agency to the individual while at the same time placing her within "particular discursive configurations" and, moreover, conceives of the process of consciousness as a strategy. Subjectivity may thus become imbued with race, class, and gender without being subjected to an overdetermination that erases agency.

DENISE RILEY

Denise Riley's *War in the Nursery: Theories of the Child and Mother* is an attempt to conceptualize women in a way that avoids what she calls the biologism/culturalist dilemma: that women must be either biologically determined or entirely cultural constructs. Both of these approaches to explaining sexual difference have been theoretically and empirically deficient, Riley claims. Biological deterministic accounts fail to problematize the concepts they use, for example, "biology," "nature," and "sex" and attempt to reduce "everything to the workings of a changeless biology."[50] On the other hand, the "usual corrective to biologism"[51]—the feminist-invoked cultural construction thesis—"ignores the fact that there really is a biology, which must be conceived more clearly" and moreover "only substitutes an unbounded sphere of social determination for that of biological determination."[52]

In her attempt to avoid the inadequacies of these approaches, Riley states: "The tactical problem is in naming and specifying sexual difference where it has been ignored or misread; but without doing so in a way which guarantees it an eternal life of its own, a lonely trajectory across infinity which spreads out over the whole of being and the whole of society—as if the chance of one's gendered conception mecilessly guaranteed every subsequent facet of one's existence at all moments."[53] Here I take Riley's project to be an attempt to conceptualize the subjectivity of woman as gendered subject, without essentializing gender such that it takes on "an eternal life of its own"; to avoid both the denial of sexual difference (nominalism) and an essentializing of sexual difference.

Despite this fundamental project, Riley's analysis in this book is mainly centered on the perceivable relations between social policies, popularized psychologies, the state, and individual practices, and she does not often ascend to the theoretical problem of conceptions of woman. What she does do is proceed with her historical and sociological analysis *without ever losing sight of the need to problematize her key concepts*, for example, woman and mother. In this she provides an example, the importance of which cannot be overestimated. Moreover, Riley discusses in her last chapter a useful approach to the political tension that can develop between the necessity of problematizing concepts on the one hand and justifying political action on the other.

In analyzing the pros and cons of various social policies, Riley tries to take a feminist point of view. Yet any such discussion must necessarily presuppose, even if it is not openly acknowledged, that needs are identifiable and can therefore be used as a yardstick in evaluating social policies. The reality is, however, that needs are terribly difficult to identify, since most if not all theories of need rely on some naturalist conception of the human agent, an agent who either can consciously identify and state all of her or his needs, or whose "real" needs can be ascertained by some external process of analysis. Either method produces problems: it seems unrealistic to say that only if the agent can identify and articulate specific needs do the needs exist, and yet there are obvious dangers to relying on "experts" or others to identify the needs of an individual. Further, it is problematic to conceptualize the human agent as having needs in the same way a table has properties, since the human agent is an entity in flux in a way that the table is not and is subject to forces of social construction that affect her subjectivity and thus her needs. Utilitarian theorists, especially desire and welfare utilitarian theorists, are particularly vulnerable to this problem, since the standard of moral evaluation they advocate using is precisely needs (or desires, which are equally problemàtic).[54] Feminist evaluations of social policy that use a concept of "women's needs" must run into the same difficulty. Riley's approach to this predicament is as follows: "I've said that people's needs obviously can't be revealed by a simple process of historical unveiling, while elsewhere I've talked about the 'real needs' of mothers myself. I take it that it's necessary both to stress the non-self-evident nature of need and the intricacies of its determinants, and also to act politically as if needs could be met, or at least met halfway."[55] Thus Riley asserts the possibility and even the necessity of combining decisively fomulated political demands with an acknowledgment of their essentialist danger. How can this be done without weakening our political struggle?

On the one hand, as Riley argues, the logic of concrete demands does not entail a commitment to essentialism. She says: "Even though it is true that arguing for adequate childcare as one obvious way of meeting the needs of mothers does suppose an orthodox division of labor, in which responsibility for children is the province of women and not of men, nevertheless this division is what, by and large, actually obtains. Recognition of that in no way commits you to supposing that the care of children is fixed eternally as female."[56] We need not invoke a rhetoric of idealized motherhood to demand that women here and now need childcare. On the other hand, the entire corpus of Riley's work on social policies is dedicated to demonstrating the dangers that such demands can entail. She explains these as follows: "Because the task of illuminating 'the needs of mothers' starts out with gender at its most decisive and inescapable point—the biological capacity to bear children—there's the danger that it may fall back into a conservative restating and confirming of social-sexual difference as timeless too. This would entail making the needs of mothers into fixed properties of 'motherhood' as a social function: I believe this is what happened in postwar Britain."[57] Thus, invoking the demands of women with children also invokes the companion belief in our cultural conception of essentialized motherhood.

As a way of avoiding this particular pitfall, Riley recommends against deploying any version of "motherhood" *as such*. I take it that what Riley means here is that we can talk about the needs of women with children and of course refer to these women as mothers but that we should eschew all reference to the idealized institution of motherhood as women's privileged vocation or the embodiment of an authentic or natural female practice.

The light that Riley sheds on our problem of woman's subjectivity is threefold. First, and most obviously, she articulates the problem clearly and deals with it head on. Second, she shows us a way of approaching child-care demands without essentializing femininity, that is, by keeping it clear that these demands represent only current and not universal or eternal needs of women and by avoiding invocations of motherhood altogether. Third, she demands that our problematizing of concepts like "woman's needs" coexist alongside a political program of demands in the name of women, without either countermanding the other. This is not to embrace the paradox but, rather, to call for a new understanding of subjectivity that can bring into harmony both our theoretical and our political agendas.

Denise Riley presents a useful approach to the political dimension of the problem of conceptualizing woman by discussing ways to avoid essentialist political demands. She reminds us that we should not avoid political action because our theory has uncovered chinks in the formulation of our key concepts.

A Concept of Positionality

Let me state initally that my approach to the problem of subjectivity is to treat it as a metaphysical problem rather than an empirical one. For readers coming from a post-structuralist tradition this statement will require immediate clarification. Continental philosophers from Nietzsche to Derrida have rejected the discipline of metaphysics in toto because they say it assumes a naive ontological connection between knowledge and a reality conceived as a thing-in-itself, totally independent of human practices and methodology. Echoing the logical positivists here, these philosophers have claimed that metaphysics is nothing but an exercise in mystification, presuming to make knowledge claims about such things as souls and "necessary" truths that we have no way of justifying. Perhaps the bottom line criticism has been that metaphysics defines truth in such a way that it is impossible to attain, and then claims to have attained it. I agree that we should reject the metaphysics of transcendent things-in-themselves and the presumption to make claims about the noumena, but this involves a rejection of a specific ontology of truth and a particular tradition in the history of metaphysics and not a rejection of metaphysics itself. If metaphysics is conceived not as any particular ontological commitment but as the attempt to reason through ontological issues that cannot be decided empirically, then metaphysics continues today in Derrida's analysis of language, Foucault's conception of power, and all of the post-structuralist critiques of humanist theories on the subject. Thus, on this view, the assertion that someone is "doing metaphysics" does not serve as a pejorative. There are questions of importance to human beings that science alone cannot answer (including what science is and how it functions), and yet these are questions that we can usefully address by combining scientific data with other logical, political, moral, pragmatic, and coherence considerations. The distinction between what is normative and what is descriptive breaks down here. Metaphysical problems are problems that concern factual claims about the world (rather than simply expressive, moral, or aesthetic assertions, e.g.) but are problems that cannot be determined through empirical means alone.[58]

In my view the problem of the subject and, within this, the problem of conceptualizing "woman," is such a metaphysical problem. Thus, I disagree with both phenomenologists and psychoanalysts who assert that the nature of subjectivity can be discovered via a certain methodology and conceptual apparatus, either the epoch or the theory of the unconcious.[59] Neurophysiologi-cal reductionists likewise claim to be able to produce empirical explanations of subjectivity, but they will by and large admit that their physicalist explana-tions can tell us little about the experiential reality of subjectivity.[60] More-over, I would assert that physicalist explanations can tell us little about how the concept of subjectivity should be construed, since this concept necessarily entails considerations not only of the empirical data but also of the political and ethical implications as well. Like the determination of when "human" life begins—whether at conception, full brain development, or birth—we cannot through science alone settle the issue since it turns on how we (to some ex-tent) choose to define concepts like "human" and "woman." We cannot dis-cover the "true meaning" of these concepts but must decide how to define them using all the empirical data, ethical arguments, political implications, and coherence constraints at hand.

Psychoanalysis should be mentioned separately here since it was Freud's initial problematizing of the subject from which developed post-structuralist rejection of the subject. It is the psychoanalytic conception of the uncon-scious that "undermines the subject from any position of certainty" and in fact claims to reveal that the subject is a fiction.[61] Feminists, then, use psy-choanalysis to problematize the gendered subject to reveal "the fictional na-ture of the sexual category to which every human subject is none the less assigned."[62] Yet while a theorizing of the unconscious is used as a primary means of theorizing the subject, certainly psychoanalysis alone cannot pro-vide all of the answers we need for a theory of the gendered subject.[63]

As I have already stated, it seems important to use Teresa de Lauretis's conception of experience as a way to begin to describe the features of human subjectivity. Lauretis starts with no given biological or psychological fea-tures and thus avoids assuming an essential characterization of subjectivity, but she also avoids the idealism that can follow from a rejection of materialist analyses by basing her conception on real practices and events. The impor-tance of this focus on practices is, in part, Lauretis's shift away from the be-lief in the totalization of language or textuality to which most antiessentialist analyses become wedded. Lauretis wants to argue that language is not the sole source and locus of meaning, that habits and practices are crucial in the construction of meaning, and that through self-analyzing practices we can rearticulate female subjectivity. Gender is not a point to start from in the sense of being a given thing but is, instead, a posit or construct, formalizable in a nonarbitrary way through a matrix of habits, practices, and discourses. Further, it is an interpretation of our history within a particular discursive constellation, a history in which we are both subjects of and subjected to social construction.

The advantage of such an analysis is its ability to articulate a concept of gendered subjectivity without pinning it down one way or another for all time. Given this and given the danger that essentialist conceptions of the sub-ject pose specifically for women, it seems both possible and desirable to construe a gendered subjectivity in relation to concrete habits, practices, and discourses while at the same time recognizing the fluidity of these.

As both Lacan and Riley remind us, we must continually emphasize within any account of subjectivity the historical dimension.[64] This will waylay the tendency to produce general, universal, or essential accounts by making all our conclusions contingent and revisable. Thus, through a conception of human subjectivity as an emergent property of a historicized experience, we can say "feminine subjectivity is construed here and now in such and such a way" without this ever entailing a universalizable maxim about the "feminine."

It seems to me equally important to add to this approach an "identity politics," a concept that developed from the Combahee River Collective's "A Black Feminist Statement."[65] The idea here is that one's identity is taken (and defined) as a political point of departure, as a motivation for action, and as a delineation of one's politics. Lauretis and the authors of *Yours in Struggle* are clear about the problematic nature of one's identity, one's subject-ness, and yet argue that the concept of identity politics is useful because identity is a posit that is politically paramount. Their suggestion is to recognize one's identity as always a construction, yet also a necessary point of departure.

I think this point can be readily instituted by people of mixed races and cultures who have had to choose in some sense their identity.[66] For example, assimilated Jews who have chosen to become Jewish-identified as a political tactic against anti-Semitism are practicing identity politics. It may seem that members of more easily identifiable oppressed groups do not have this luxury, but I think that just as Jewish people can choose to assert their Jewishness, so black men, women of all races, and other members of more immediately recognized oppressed groups can practice identity politics by choosing their identity as a member of one or more groups as their political point of departure. This, in fact, is what is happening when women who are not feminists downplay their identity as women and who, on becoming feminists, then begin making an issue of their femaleness. It is the claiming of their identity as women as a political point of departure that makes it possible to see, for instance, gender-biased language that in the absence of that departure point women often do not even notice.

It is true that antifeminist women can and often do identify themselves strongly as women and with women as a group, but this is usually explained by them within the context of an essentialist theory of femininity. Claiming that one's politics are grounded in one's essential identity avoids problematizing both identity and the connection between identity and politics and thus avoids the agency involved in underdetermined actions. The difference between feminists and antifeminists strikes me as precisely this: the affirmation or denial of our right and our ability to construct, and take responsibility for, our gendered identity, our politics, and our choices.[67]

Identity politics provides a decisive rejoinder to the generic human thesis and the mainstream methodology of Western political theory. According to

the latter, the approach to political theory must be through a "veil of ignorance" where the theorist's personal interests and needs are hypothetically set
aside. The goal is a theory of universal scope to which all ideally rational,
disinterested agents would acquiesce if given sufficient information. Stripped
of their particularities, these rational agents are considered to be potentially
equally persuadable. Identity politics provides a materialist response to this
and, in so doing, sides with Marxist class analysis. The best political theory
will not be one ascertained through a veil of ignorance, a veil that is impossible to construct. Rather, political theory must base itself on the initial premise
that all persons, including the theorist, have a fleshy, material identity that
will influence and pass judgment on all political claims. Indeed, the best political theory for the theorist herself will be one that acknowledges this fact.
As I see it, the concept of identity politics does not presuppose a prepackaged
set of objective needs or political implications but problematizes the connection of identity and politics and introduces identity as a factor in any political
analysis.

If we combine the concept of identity politics with a conception of the
subject as positionality, we can conceive of the subject as nonessentialized
and emergent from a historical experience and yet retain our political ability
to take gender as an important point of departure. Thus we can say at one and
the same time that gender is not natural, biological, universal, ahistorical, or
essential and yet still claim that gender is relevant because we are taking gender as a position from which to act politically. What does position mean here?

When the concept "woman" is defined not by a particular set of attributes
but by a particular position, the internal characteristics of the person thus
identified are not denoted so much as the external context within which that
person is situated. The external situation determines the person's relative
position, just as the position of a pawn on a chessboard is considered safe
or dangerous, powerful or weak, according to its relation to the other chess
pieces. The essentialist definition of woman makes her identity independent
of her external situation: since her nurturing and peaceful traits are innate
they are ontologically autonomous of her position with respect to others or to
the external historical and social conditions generally. The positional definition, on the other hand, makes her identity relative to a constantly shifting
context, to a situation that includes a network of elements involving others,
the objective economic conditions, cultural and political institutions and ideologies, and so on. If it is possible to identify women by their position within
this network of relations, then it becomes possible to ground a feminist argument for women, not on a claim that their innate capacities are being stunted,
but that their position within the network lacks power and mobility and requires radical change. The position of women is relative and not innate, and
yet neither is it "undecidable." Through social critique and analysis we can
identify women via their position relative to an existing cultural and social
network.

It may sound all too familiar to say that the oppression of women involves their relative position within a society; but my claim goes further than this. I assert that the very subjectivity (or subjective experience of being a woman) and the very identity of women is constituted by women's position. However, this view should not imply that the concept of "woman" is determined solely by external elements and that the woman herself is merely a passive recipient of an identity created by these forces. Rather, she herself is part of the historicized, fluid movement, and she therefore actively contributes to the context within which her position can be delineated. I would include Lauretis's point here, that the identity of a woman is the product of her own interpretation and reconstruction of her history, as mediated through the cultural discursive context to which she has access.[68] Therefore, the concept of positionality includes two points: first, as already stated, that the concept of woman is a relational term identifiable only within a (constantly moving) context; but, second, that the position that women find themselves in can be actively utilized (rather than transcended) as a location for the construction of meaning, a place from where meaning can be *discovered* (the meaning of femaleness). The concept of woman as positionality shows how women use their positional perspective as a place from which values are interpreted and constructed rather than as a locus of an already determined set of values. When women become feminists the crucial thing that has occurred is not that they have learned any new facts about the world but that they have come to view those facts from a different position, from their own position as subjects. When colonial subjects begin to be critical of the formerly imitative attitude they had toward the colonists, what is happening is that they begin to identify with the colonized rather than the colonizers.[69] This difference in positional perspective does not necessitate a change in what are taken to be facts, although new facts may come into view from the new position, but it does necessitate a political change in perspective since the point of departure, the point from which all things are measured, has changed.

In this analysis, then, the concept of positionality allows for a determinate though fluid identity of woman that does not fall into essentialism: woman is a position from which a feminist politics can emerge rather than a set of attributes that are "objectively identifiable." Seen in this way, being a "woman" is to take up a position within a moving historical context and to be able to choose what we make of this position and how we alter this context. From the perspective of that fairly determinate though fluid and mutable position, women can themselves articulate a set of interests and ground a feminist politics.

The concept and the position of women is not ultimately undecidable or arbitrary. It is simply not possible to interpret our society in such a way that women have more power or equal power relative to men. The conception of woman that I have outlined limits the construction of woman we can offer by defining subjectivity as positionality within a context. It thus avoids nominalism but also provides us with the means to argue against views like "oppression is all in your head" or the view that antifeminist women are not oppressed.

At the same time, by highlighting historical movement and the subject's ability to alter her context, the concept of positionality avoids essentialism. It even avoids tying ourselves to a structure of gendered politics conceived as historically infinite, though it allows for the assertion of gender politics on the basis of positionality at any time. Can we conceive of a future in which oppositional gender categories are not fundamental to one's self-concept? Even if we cannot, our theory of subjectivity should not preclude, and moreover, prevent, that eventual possibility. Our concept of woman as a category, then, needs to remain open to future radical alteration; else we will preempt the possible forms eventual stages of the feminist transformation can take.

Obviously, there are many theoretical questions on positionality that this discussion leaves open. However, I would like to emphasize that the problem of woman as subject is a real one for feminism and not just on the plane of high theory. The demands of millions of women for childcare, reproductive control, and safety from sexual assult can reinvoke the cultural assumption that these are exclusively feminine issues and can reinforce the right wing's reification of gender differences unless and until we can formulate a political program that can articulate these demands in a way that challenges rather than utilizes sexist discourse.

Recently, I heard an attack on the phrase "woman of color" by a woman, dark-skinned herself, who was arguing that the use of this phrase simply reinforces the significance of that which should have no significance—skin color. To a large extent I agreed with this woman's argument: we must develop the means to address the wrongs done to us without reinvoking the basis of these wrongs. Likewise, women who have been eternally construed must seek a means of articulating a feminism that does not continue construing us in any set way. At the same time, I believe we must avoid buying into the neuter, universal "generic human" thesis that covers the West's racism and androcentrism with a blindfold. We cannot resolve this predicament by ignoring one half of it or by attempting to embrace it. The solution lies, rather, in formulating a new theory within the process of reinterpreting our position, and reconstructing our political identity, as women and feminists in relation to the world and to one another.

NOTES

First appeared in 1988.

1. It may seem that we can solve this dilemma easily enough by simply defining women as those with female anatomies, but the question remains, What is the significance, if any, of those anatomies? What is the connection between female anatomy and the concept of woman? It should be remembered that the dominant discourse does

not include in the category woman everyone with a female anatomy: it is often said that aggressive, self-serving, or powerful women are not "true" or "real" women. Moreover, the problem cannot be avoided by simply rejecting the concept of "woman" while retaining the category of "women." If there are women, then there must exist a basis for the category and a criterion for inclusion within it. This criterion need not posit a universal, homogeneous essence, but there must be a criterion nonetheless.

2. For Schopenhauer's, Kant's, and nearly every other major Western philosopher's conception of woman, and for an insight into just how contradictory and incoherent these are, see Linda Bell's excellent anthology, *Visions of Women* (Clifton, N.J.: Humana Press, 1983).

3. For an interesting discussion of whether feminists should even seek such transcendence, see Genevieve Lloyd, *The Man of Reason* (Minneapolis: University of Minnesota Press, 1984), 86–102.

4. Feminist works I would include in the group but which I won't be able to discuss in this essay are Elizabeth L. Berg, "The Third Woman," *Diacritics* 12 (1982): 11–20; and Lynne Joyrich, "Theory and Practice: The Project of Feminist Criticism," unpublished manuscript (Brown University, 1984). Luce Irigaray's work may come to mind for some readers as another proponent of a third way, but for me Irigaray's emphasis on female anatomy makes her work border too closely on essentialism.

5. Rich has recently departed from this position and in fact begun to move in the direction of the concept of woman I defend in this essay (Adrienne Rich, "Notes toward a Politics of Location," in her *Blood, Bread, and Poetry* [New York: Norton, 1986]).

6. Mary Daly, *Gyn/Ecology* (Boston: Beacon, 1978), 355.

7. Ibid., 60.

8. Ibid., 59.

9. Ibid., 365 (my emphasis).

10. Adrienne Rich, *On Lies, Secrets, and Silence* (New York: Norton, 1979), 18.

11. Adrienne Rich, *Of Woman Born* (New York: Bantam, 1977), 21.

12. Ibid., 290.

13. Ibid., 21.

14. Ibid., 292. Three pages earlier Rich castigates the view that we need only release on the world women's ability to nurture in order to solve the world's problems, which may seem incongruous given the above passage. The two positions are consistent, however: Rich is trying to correct the patriarchal conception of women as essentially nurturers with a view of women that is more comprehensive and complicated than the patriarchal one.

15. See Alice Echols, "The New Feminism of Yin and Yang," in *Powers of Desire: The Politics of Sexuality*, eds. Ann Snitow, Christine Stansell, and Sharon Thompson (New York: Monthly Review Press, 1983), 439–59, and "The Taming of the Id: Feminist Sexual Politics, 1968–1983," in *Pleasure and Danger: Exploring Female Sexuality*, ed. Carole S. Vance (Boston: Routledge & Kegan Paul, 1984), 50–72. Hester Eisenstein paints a similar picture of cultural feminism in her *Contemporary Feminist Thought* (Boston: G. K. Hall, 1983), esp. xvii–xix and 105–45. Josephine Donovan has traced the more recent cultural feminism analyzed by Echols and Eisenstein to the earlier matriarchal vision of feminists like Charlotte Perkins Gilman (Josephine Donovan, *Feminist Theory: The Intellectual Traditions of American Feminism* [New York: Ungar, 1985], esp. chap. 2).

16. Echols, "The New Feminism of Yin and Yang," 441.

17. Ibid., 440.

18. Cherríe Moraga, "From a Long Line of Vendidas: Chicanas and Feminism," in *Feminist Studies/Critical Studies*, ed. Teresa de Lauretis (Bloomington: Indiana University Press, 1986), 180.

19. See also Moraga, "From a Long Line of Vendidas," 187; and Cherríe Moraga, "La Guerra," in *This Bridge Is Called My Back: Writings by Radical Women of Color*, eds. Cherríe Moraga and Gloria Anzaldúa (New York: Kitchen Table, 1983), 32–33; Barbara Smith, "Introduction," in *Home Girls: A Black Feminist Anthology*, ed. Barbara Smith (New York: Kitchen Table, 1983), xix–lvi; "The Combahee River Collective Statement," in Smith, ed., 272–82; Audre Lorde, "Age, Race, Class, and Sex: Women Redefining Difference," in her *Sister Outsider* (Trumansburg, N.Y.: Crossing, 1984), 114–23; and bell hooks, *Feminist Theory: From Margin to Center* (Boston: South End, 1984). All of these works resist the universalizing tendency of cultural feminism and highlight the differences between women, and between men, in a way that undercuts arguments for the existence of an overarching gendered essence.

20. There is a wealth of literature on this, but two good places to begin are Anne Fausto-Sterling, *Myths of Gender: Biological Theories about Women and Men* (New York: Basic, 1986); and Sherry Ortner and Harriet Whitehead, eds., *Sexual Meanings: The Cultural Construction of Gender and Sexuality* (New York: Cambridge University Press, 1981).

21. Echols, "The New Feminism of Yin and Yang," 440.

22. Hester Eisenstein's treatment of cultural feminism, though critical, is certainly more two-sided than Echols's. While Echols apparently sees only the reactionary results of cultural feminism, Eisenstein sees in it a therapeutic self-affirmation necessary to offset the impact of a misogynist culture (see Eisenstein [n. 15 above]).

23. Michel Foucault, "Why Study Power: The Question of the Subject," in *Beyond Structuralism and Hermeneutics: Michel Foucault*, ed. Hubert L. Dreyfus and Paul Rabinow, 2d ed. (Chicago: University of Chicago Press, 1983), 212.

24. This term is principally associated with Derrida, for whom it refers specifically to the process of unraveling metaphors in order to reveal their underlying logic, which usually consists of a simple binary opposition, such as man/woman, subject/object, culture/nature, etc. Derrida has demonstrated that within such oppositions one side is always superior to the other side, such that there is never any pure difference without domination. The term "deconstruction" has also come to mean more generally any exposure of a concept as ideologically or culturally constructed rather than natural or a simple reflection of reality (see Derrida, *Of Grammatology*, trans. G. Spivak [Baltimore: Johns Hopkins University Press, 1976]; also helpful is Jonathan Culler's *On Deconstruction* [Ithaca, N.Y.: Cornell University Press, 1982]).

25. Michel Foucault, "Nietzsche, Genealogy, History," in *The Foucault Reader*, ed. Paul Rabinow (New York: Pantheon, 1984), 83.

26. This hope is evident in Michel Foucault's *The Order of Things: An Archaeology of the Human Sciences* (New York: Random House, 1973).

27. Jacques Derrida, *Spurs*, trans. Barbara Harlow (Chicago: University of Chicago Press, 1978), 49.

28. Ibid., 51.

29. Biddy Martin, "Feminism, Criticism, and Foucault," *New German Critique* 27 (1982): 11.

30. Julia Kristeva, "Woman Can Never Be Defined," in *New French Feminisms*, ed. Elaine Marks and Isabelle de Courtivron (New York: Schocken, 1981), 137 (my italics).

31. Julia Kristeva, "Oscillation between Power and Denial," in Marks and Courtivron, eds., 166.

32. Martin, 16–17.

33. Ibid., esp. 21, 24, and 29.

34. See Derrida, *Spurs*, esp. 57 and 97.

35. Martin's most recent work departs from this in a positive direction. In an essay coauthored with Chandra Talpade Mohanty, Martin points out "the political limitations of an insistence on 'interdeterminacy' which implicitly, when not explicitly, denies the critic's own situatedness in the social, and in effect refuses to acknowledge the critic's own institutional home." Martin and Mohanty seek to develop a more positive, though still problematized, conception of the subject as having a "multiple and shifting" perspective. In this, their work becomes a significant contribution toward the development of an alternative conception of subjectivity, a conception unlike the one that I will discuss in the rest of this essay ("Feminist Politics: What's Home Got to Do with It?" in Lauretis, ed. [n. 18 above], 191–212, esp. 194).

36. A wonderful exchange on this between persuasive and articulate representatives of both sides was printed in *Diacritics* (Peggy Kamuf, "Replacing Feminist Criticism," *Diacritics* 12 [1982]: 42–47; and Nancy Miller, "The Text's Heroine: A Feminist Critic and Her Fictions," *Diacritics* 12 [1982]: 48–53).

37. Teresa de Lauretis, *Alice Doesn't* (Bloomington: Indiana University Press, 1984), 5.

38. Ibid., 5–6.

39. Ibid., 7.

40. Ibid., 8–9.

41. Ibid., 11.

42. Ibid., 159.

43. Ibid., 161.

44. Ibid.

45. Ibid., 182. The principal texts Lauretis relies on in her exposition of Lacan, Eco, and Peirce are Jacques Lacan, *Escrits* (Paris: Seuil, 1966); Umberto Eco, *A Theory of Semiotics* (Bloomington: Indiana University Press, 1976), and *The Role of the Reader: Explorations in the Semiotic of Texts* (Bloomington: Indiana University Press, 1979); and Charles Sanders Peirce, *Collected Papers*, vols. 1–8 (Cambridge, Mass.: Harvard University Press, 1931–1958).

46. Lauretis, *Alice Doesn't* (n. 37 above), 182.

47. Ibid., 186 (my italics).

48. Lauretis, ed. (n. 18 above), 8.

49. Ibid., 9.

50. Denise Riley, *War in the Nursery: Theories of the Child and Mother* (London: Virago, 1983), 2.

51. Ibid., 6.

52. Ibid., 2, 3.

53. Ibid., 4.

54. For a lucid description of just how difficult this problem is for utilitarians, see John Elster, "Sour Grapes—Utilitarianism and the Genesis of Wants," in *Utilitarianism and Beyond*, ed. Amartya Sen and Bernard Williams (Cambridge: Cambridge University Press, 1982), 219–38.

55. Riley, 193–194.

56. Ibid., 194.

57. Ibid., 194–95.

58. In this conception of the proper dimension of and approach to metaphysics (as a conceptual enterprise to be decided partially by pragmatic methods), I am following in the tradition of the later Rudolf Carnap and Ludwig Wittgenstein, among others (Rudolf Carnap, "Empiricism, Semantics, and Ontology," and "On the Character of Philosophical Problems," both in *The Linguistic Turn*, ed. R. Rorty [Chicago: University of Chicago Press, 1967]; and Ludwig Wittgenstein, *Philosophical Investigations*, trans. G. E. M. Anscombe [New York: Macmillan, 1958]).

59. I am thinking particularly of Husserl and Freud here. The reason for my disagreement is that both approaches are in reality more metaphysical than their proponents would admit and, further, that I have only limited sympathy for the metaphysical claims they make. I realize that to explain this fully would require a long argument, which I cannot give in this essay.

60. See, e.g., Donald Davidson, "Psychology as Philosophy," in his *Essays on Actions and Interpretations* (Oxford: Clarendon Press, 1980), 230.

61. Jacqueline Rose, "Introduction II," in *Feminine Sexuality: Jacques Lacan and the École Freudienne*, ed. Juliet Mitchell and Jacqueline Rose (New York: Norton, 1982), 29, 30.

62. Ibid., 29.

63. Psychoanalysis must take credit for making subjectivity a problematic issue, and yet I think a view that gives psychoanalysis hegemony in this area is misguided, if only because psychoanalysis is still extremely hypothetical. Let a hundred flowers bloom.

64. See Juliet Mitchell, "Introduction I," in Mitchell and Rose, eds., 4–5.

65. This was suggested to me by Teresa de Lauretis in an informal talk she gave at the Pembroke Center, 1984–1985. A useful discussion and application of this concept can be found in Elly Bulkin, Minnie Bruce Pratt, and Barbara Smith, *Yours in Struggle: Three Feminist Perspectives on Anti-Semitism and Racism* (Brooklyn, N.Y.: Long Haul Press, 1984), 98–99. Martin and Mohanty's paper (n. 35 above) offers a fruitful reading of the essay in *Yours in Struggle* by Minnie Bruce Pratt entitled "Identity: Skin Blood Heart" and brings into full relief the way in which she uses identity politics. See also "The Combahee River Collective" (n. 19 above).

66. This point has been the subject of long, personal reflection for me, as I myself am half Latina and half white. I have been motivated to consider it also since the situation is even more complicated for my children, who are half mine, and half a Jewish father's.

67. I certainly do not believe that most women have the freedom to choose their situation in life, but I do believe that of the multiple ways we are held in check, internalized oppressive mechanisms play a significant role, and we can achieve control over these. On this point I must say I have learned from and admired the work of Mary Daly, particularly *Gyn/Ecology* (n. 6 above), which reveals and describes these internal mechanisms and challenges us to repudiate them.

68. See Teresa de Lauretis, "Feminist Studies/Critical Studies: Issues, Terms, Contexts," in Lauretis, ed. (n. 18 above), 8–9.

69. This point is brought out by Homi Bhabha in his "Of Mimicry and Man: The Ambivalence of Colonial Discourse," *October* 28 (1984): 125–33, and by Abdur Rahman in his *Intellectual Colonization* (New Delhi: Vikas, 1983).

The Exhibitionary Complex

TONY BENNETT

IN REVIEWING Foucault on the asylum, the clinic, and the prison as institutional articulations of power and knowledge relations, Douglas Crimp suggests that there "is another such institution of confinement ripe for analysis in Foucault's terms—the museum—and another discipline—art history"[1] Crimp is no doubt right, although the terms of his proposal are misleadingly restrictive. For the emergence of the art museum was closely related to that of a wider range of institutions—history and natural science museums, dioramas and panoramas, national and, later, international exhibitions, arcades and department stores—which served as linked sites for the development and circulation of new disciplines (history, biology, art history, anthropology) and their discursive formations (the past, evolution, aesthetics, man) as well as for the development of new technologies of vision. Furthermore, while these comprised an intersecting set of institutional and disciplinary relations which might be productively analyzed as particular articulations of power and knowledge, the suggestion that they should be construed as institutions of confinement is curious. It seems to imply that works of art had previously wandered through the streets of Europe like the Ships of Fools in Foucault's *Madness and Civilization*; or that geological and natural history specimens had been displayed before the world, like the condemned on the scaffold, rather than being withheld from public gaze, secreted in the *studiolo* of princes, or made accessible only to the limited gaze of high society in the *cabinets des curieux* of the aristocracy. Museums may have enclosed objects within walls, but the nineteenth century saw their doors opened to the general public—witnesses whose presence was just as essential to a display of power as had been that of the people before the spectacle of punishment in the eighteenth century.

Institutions, then, not of confinement but of exhibition, forming a complex of disciplinary and power relations whose development might more fruitfully be juxtaposed to, rather than aligned with, the formation of Foucault's "carceral archipelago." For the movement Foucault traces in *Discipline and Punish* is one in which objects and bodies—the scaffold and the body of the condemned—which had previously formed a part of the public display of power were withdrawn from the public gaze as punishment increasingly took the form of incarceration. No longer inscribed within a public dramaturgy of power, the body of the condemned comes to be caught up within an inward-looking web of power relations. Subjected to omnipresent forms of surveillance through which the message of power was carried directly to it so as to render it docile, the body no longer served as the surface on which, through the system of retaliatory marks inflicted on it in the name of the sovereign, the lessons of power were written for others to read:

> The scaffold, where the body of the tortured criminal had been exposed to the ritually manifest force of the sovereign, the punitive theatre in which the representation of punishment was permanently available to the social body, was replaced by a great enclosed, complex and hierarchised structure that was integrated into the very body of the state apparatus.[2]

The institutions comprising "the exhibitionary complex," by contrast, were involved in the transfer of objects and bodies from the enclosed and private domains in which they had previously been displayed (but to a restricted public) into progressively more open and public arenas where, through the representations to which they were subjected, they formed vehicles for inscribing and broadcasting the messages of power (but of a different type) throughout society.

Two different sets of institutions and their accompanying knowledge/power relations, then, whose histories, in these respects, run in opposing directions. Yet they are also parallel histories. The exhibitionary complex and the carceral archipelago develop over roughly the same period—the late eighteenth to the mid-nineteenth century—and achieve developed articulations of the new principles they embodied within a decade or so of one another. Foucault regards the opening of the new prison at Mettray in 1840 as a key moment in the development of the carceral system. Why Mettray? Because, Foucault argues, "it is the disciplinary form at its most extreme, the model in which are concentrated all the coercive technologies of behavior previously found in the cloister, prison, school or regiment and which, in being brought together in one place, served as a guide for the future development of carceral institutions" (p. 293). In Britain, the opening of Pentonville Model Prison in 1842 is often viewed in a similar light. Less than a decade later, the Great Exhibition of 1851 brought together an ensemble of disciplines and techniques of display that had been developed within the previous histories of museums, panoramas, Mechanic's Institute exhibitions, art galleries, and arcades. In doing so, it translated these into exhibitionary forms which, in simultaneously ordering objects for public inspection and ordering the public that inspected, were to have a profound and lasting influence on the subsequent development of museums, art galleries, expositions, and department stores.

Nor are these entirely separate histories. At certain points they overlap, often with a transfer of meanings and effects between them. To understand their interrelations, however, it will be necessary, in borrowing from Foucault, to qualify the terms he proposes for investigating the development of power/knowledge relations during the formation of the modern period. For the set of such relations associated with the development of the exhibitionary

The cabinet of curiosities: the *Metallotheca* of Michele Mercati in the Vatican, 1719

The Great Exhibition, 1851: the Western, or British, Nave, looking east
(plate by H. Owen and M. Ferrier)

complex serves as a check to the generalizing conclusions Foucault derives from his examination of the carceral system. In particular, it calls into question his suggestion that the penitentiary merely perfected the individualizing and normalizing technologies associated with a veritable swarming of forms of surveillance and disciplinary mechanisms which came to suffuse society with a new—and all-pervasive—political economy of power. This is not to suggest that technologies of surveillance had no place in the exhibitionary complex but rather that their intrication with new forms of spectacle produced a more complex and nuanced set of relations through which power was exercised and relayed to—and, in part, through and by—the populace than the Foucauldian account allows.

Foucault's primary concern, of course, is with the problem of order. He conceived the development of new forms of discipline and surveillance, as Jeffrey Minson puts it, as an "attempt to reduce an ungovernable *populace* to a multiply differentiated *population*," parts of "an historical movement aimed at transforming highly disruptive economic conflicts and political forms of disorder into quasi-technical or moral problems for social administration." These mechanisms assumed, Minson continues, "that the key to the populace's social and political unruliness and also the means of combating it lies in the 'opacity' of the populace to the forces of order."[3] The exhibitionary complex was also a response to the problem of order, but one which worked differently in seeking to transform that problem into one of culture—a question of winning hearts and minds as well as the disciplining and training of bodies. As such, its constituent institutions reversed the orientations of the disciplinary apparatuses in seeking to render the forces and principles of order visible to the populace—transformed, here, into a people, a citizenry—rather than vice versa. They sought not to map the social body in order to know the populace by rendering it visible to power. Instead, through the provision of object lessons in power—the power to command and arrange things and bodies for public display—they sought to allow the people, *en masse* rather than individually, to know rather than be known, to become the subjects rather than the objects of knowledge. Yet, ideally, they sought also to allow the people to know and thence to regulate themselves; to become, in seeing themselves from the side of power, both the subjects and the objects of knowledge, knowing power and what power knows, and knowing themselves as (ideally) known by power, interiorizing its gaze as a principle of self-surveillance and, hence, self-regulation.

It is, then, as a set of cultural technologies concerned to organize a voluntarily self-regulating citizenry that I propose to examine the formation of the exhibitionary complex. In doing so, I shall draw on the Gramscian perspective of the ethical and educative function of the modern state to account for the relations of this complex to the development of the bourgeois democratic polity. Yet, while wishing to resist a tendency in Foucault toward misplaced generalizations, it is to Foucault's work that I shall look to unravel the relations between knowledge and power effected by the technologies of vision embodied in the architectural forms of the exhibitionary complex.

DISCIPLINE, SURVEILLANCE, SPECTACLE

In discussing the proposals of late-eighteenth-century penal reformers, Foucault remarks that punishment, while remaining a "legible lesson" organized in relation to the body of the offended, was envisioned as "a school rather than a festival; an ever-open book rather than a ceremony" (p. 111). Hence, in schemes to use convict labor in public contexts, it was envisaged that the convict would repay society twice: once by the labor he provided, and a second time by the signs he produced, a focus of both profit and signification in serving as an ever-present reminder of the connection between crime and punishment:

> Children should be allowed to come to the places where the penalty is being carried out; there they will attend their classes in civics. And grown men will periodically relearn the laws. Let us conceive of places of punishment as a Garden of the Laws that families would visit on Sundays. (p. 111)

In the event, punishment took a different path with the development of the carceral system. Under both the *ancien régime* and the projects of the late-eighteenth-century reformers, punishment had formed part of a public system of representation. Both regimes obeyed a logic according to which "secret punishment is a punishment half-wasted" (p. 111). With the development of the carceral system, by contrast, punishment was removed from the public gaze in being enacted behind the closed walls of the penitentiary, and had in view not the production of signs for society but the correction of the offender. No longer an art of public effects, punishment aimed at a calculated transformation in the behavior of the convicted. The body of the offended, no longer a medium for the relay of signs of power, was zoned as the target for disciplinary technologies which sought to modify behavior through repetition.

> The body and the soul, as principles of behaviour, form the element that is now proposed for punitive intervention. Rather than on an art of representation, this punitive intervention must rest on a studied manipulation of the individual. . . . As for the instruments used, these are no longer complexes of representation, reinforced and circulated, but forms of coercion, schemata of restraint, applied and repeated. Exercises, not signs. . . . (p. 128)

It is not this account itself that is in question here but some of the more general claims Foucault elaborates on its basis. In his discussion of "the swarming of disciplinary mechanisms," Foucault argues that the disciplinary technologies and forms of observation developed in the carceral system—and especially the principle of panopticism, rendering everything visible to the eye of power—display a tendency "to become 'de-institutionalized,' to emerge from the closed fortresses in which they once functioned and to circulate in a 'free' state" (p. 211). These new systems of surveillance, mapping the social body so as to render it knowable and amenable to social regulation, mean, Foucault argues, that "one can speak of the formation of a disciplinary society . . . that stretches from the enclosed disciplines, a sort of social 'quar-antine,' to an indefinitely generalizable mechanism of 'panopticism'" (p. 216). A society, according to Foucault in his approving quotation of Julius, that "is one not of spectacle, but of surveillance":

> Antiquity had been a civilisation of spectacle. "To render accessible to a multi-tude of men the inspection of a small number of objects": this was the problem to which the architecture of temples, theatres and circuses responded. . . . In a soci-ety in which the principal elements are no longer the community and public life, but on the one hand, private individuals and, on the other, the state, relations can be regulated only in a form that is the exact reverse of the spectacle. It was to the modern age, to the ever-growing influence of the state, to its ever more profound intervention in all the details and all the relations of social life, that was reserved the task of increasing and perfecting its guarantees, by using and directing to-wards that great aim the building and distribution of buildings intended to ob-serve a great multitude of men at the same time. (pp. 216–17)

A disciplinary society: this general characterization of the modality of power in modern societies has proved one of the more influential aspects of Foucault's work. Yet it is an incautious generalization and one produced by a peculiar kind of misattention. For it by no means follows from the fact that punishment had ceased to be a spectacle that the function of displaying power—of making it visible for all to see—had itself fallen into abeyance.[4] Indeed, as Graeme Davison suggests, the Crystal Palace might serve as the emblem of an architectural series which could be ranged against that of the asylum, school, and prison in its continuing concern with the display of ob-jects to a great multitude:

> The Crystal Palace reversed the panoptical principle by fixing the eyes of the multitude upon an assemblage of glamorous commodities. The Panopticon was designed so that everyone could be seen; the Crystal Palace was designed so that everyone could see.[5]

This opposition is a little overstated in that one of the architectural innova-tions of the Crystal Palace consisted in the arrangement of relations between the public and exhibits so that, while everyone could see, there were also vantage points from which everyone could be seen, thus combining the func-tions of spectacle and surveillance. Nonetheless, the shift of emphasis is worth preserving for the moment, particularly as its force is by no means limited to the Great Exhibition. Even a cursory glance through Richard Al-tick's *The Shows of London* convinces that the nineteenth century was quite unprecedented in the social effort it devoted to the organization of spectacles arranged for increasingly large and undifferentiated publics.[6] Several aspects of these developments merit a preliminary consideration.

First: The tendency for society itself—in its constituent parts and as a whole—to be rendered as a spectacle. This was especially clear in attempts to render the city visible, and hence knowable, as a totality. While the depths of city life were penetrated by developing networks of surveillance, cities increasingly opened up their processes to public inspection, laying their secrets open not merely to the gaze of power but, in principle, to that of everyone; indeed, making the specular dominance of the eye of power available to all. By the turn of the century, Dean MacCannell notes, sightseers in Paris "were given tours of the sewers, the morgue, a slaughterhouse, a tobacco factory, the government printing office, a tapestry works, the mint, the stock exchange and the supreme court in session."[7] No doubt such tours conferred only an imaginary dominance over the city, an illusory rather than substantive controlling vision, as Dana Brand suggests was the case with earlier panorama.[8] Yet the principle they embodied was real enough and, in seeking to render cities knowable in exhibiting the workings of their organizing institutions, they are without parallel in the spectacles of earlier regimes where the view of power was always "from below." This ambition toward a specular dominance over a totality was even more evident in the conception of international exhibitions which, in their heyday, sought to make the whole world, past and present, metonymically available in the assemblage of objects and peoples they brought together and, from their towers, to lay it before a controlling vision.

Second: The increasing involvement of the state in the provision of such spectacles. In the British case, and even more so the American, such involvement was typically indirect.[9] Nicholas Pearson notes that while the sphere of culture fell increasingly under governmental regulation in the second half of the nineteenth century, the preferred form of administration for museums, art galleries, and exhibitions was (and remains) via boards of trustees. Through these, the state could retain effective direction over policy by virtue of its control over appointments but without involving itself in the day-to-day conduct of affairs and so, seemingly, violating the Kantian imperative in subordinating culture to practical requirements.[10] Although the state was initially prodded only reluctantly into this sphere of activity, there should be no doubt of the importance it eventually assumed. Museums, galleries, and, more intermittently, exhibitions played a pivotal role in the formation of the modern state and are fundamental to its conception as, among other things, a set of educative and civilizing agencies. Since the late nineteenth century, they have been ranked highly in the funding priorities of all developed nation-states and have proved remarkably influential cultural technologies in the degree to which they have recruited the interest and participation of their citizenries.

Finally: The exhibitionary complex provided a context for the *permanent* display of power/knowledge. In his discussion of the display of power in the *ancien régime*, Foucault stresses its episodic quality. The spectacle of the scaffold formed part of a system of power which "in the absence of continual supervision, sought a renewal of its effect in the spectacle of its individual manifestations; of a power that was recharged in the ritual display of its reality as 'super-power'" (p. 57). It is not that the nineteenth century dispensed entirely with the need for the periodic magnification of power through its excessive display, for the expositions played this role. They did so, however, in relation to a network of institutions which provided mechanisms for the permanent display of power. And for a power which was not reduced to periodic effects but which, to the contrary, manifested itself precisely in continually displaying its ability to command, order, and control objects and bodies, living or dead.

There is, then, another series from the one Foucault examines in tracing the shift from the ceremony of the scaffold to the disciplinary rigors of the penitentiary. Yet it is a series which has its echo and, in some respects, model in another section of the socio-juridical apparatus: the trial. The scene of the trial and that of punishment traversed one another as they moved in opposite directions during the early modern period. As punishment was withdrawn from the public gaze and transferred to the enclosed space of the penitentiary, so the procedures of trial and sentencing—which, except for England, had hitherto been mostly conducted in secret, "opaque not only to the public but also to the accused himself" (p. 35)—were made public as part of a new system of judicial truth which, in order to function as truth, needed to be made known to all. If the asymmetry of these movements is compelling, it is no more so than the symmetry of the movement traced by the trial and the museum in the transition they make from closed and restricted to open and public contexts. And, as a part of a profound transformation in their social functioning, it was ultimately to these institutions—and not by witnessing punishment enacted in the streets or, as Bentham had envisaged, by making the penitentiaries open to public inspection—that children, and their parents, were invited to attend their lessons in civics.

Moreover, such lessons consisted not in a display of power which, in seeking to terrorize, positioned the people on the other side of power as its potential recipients but sought rather to place the people—conceived as a nationalized citizenry—on this side of power, both its subject and its beneficiary. To identify with power, to see it as, if not directly theirs, then indirectly so, a force regulated and channeled by society's ruling groups but for the good of all: this was the rhetoric of power embodied in the exhibitionary complex— a power made manifest not in its ability to inflict pain but by its ability to organize and coordinate an order of things and to produce a place for the people in relation to the order. Detailed studies on nineteenth-century expositions thus consistently highlight the ideological economy of their organizing principles, transforming displays of machinery and industrial processes, of finished products and *objets d'art*, into material signifiers of progress—but of progress as a collective national achievement with capital as the great coordinator.[11] This power thus subjugated by flattery, placing itself on the side of the people by affording them a place within its workings—a power which placed the people behind it, inveigled into complicity with it rather than cowed into submission before it. And this power marked out the distinction between the subjects and the objects of power not within the national body but, as organized by the many rhetorics of imperialism, between that body and other, "non-civilized" peoples upon whose bodies the effects of power were unleashed with as much force and theatricality as had been manifest on the scaffold. This was, in other words, a power which aimed at a rhetorical effect through its representation of otherness rather than at any disciplinary effects.

Yet it is not merely in terms of its ideological economy that the exhibitionary complex must be assessed. While museums and expositions may have set out to win the hearts and minds of their visitors, these also brought their bodies with them, creating architectural problems as vexing as any posed by the development of the carceral archipelago. The birth of the latter, Foucault argues, required a new architectural problematic:

> that of an architecture that is no longer built simply to be seen (as with the ostentation of palaces), or to observe the external space (cf. the geometry of fortress), but to permit an internal, articulated and detailed control—to render visible those who are inside it; in more general terms, an architecture that would operate to transform individuals: to act on those it shelters, to provide a hold on their conduct, to carry the effects of power right to them, to make it possible to know them, to alter them. (p. 172)

As Davison notes, the development of the exhibitionary complex also posed a new demand: that everyone should see, and not just the ostentation of imposing facades but their contents too. This, too, created a series of architectural problems which were ultimately resolved only through a "political economy of detail" similar to that applied to the regulation of the relations between bodies, space, and time within the penitentiary. In Britain, France, and Germany, the late eighteenth and early nineteenth centuries witnessed a spate of state-sponsored architectural competitions for the design of museums in which the emphasis shifted progressively away from organizing spaces of display for the private pleasure of the prince or aristocrat and toward an organization of space and vision that would enable museums to function as organs of public instruction.[12] Yet, as I have already suggested, it is misleading to view the architectural problematics of the exhibitionary complex as simply reversing the principles of panopticism. The effect of these principles, Foucault argues, was to abolish the crowd conceived as "a compact mass, a locus of multiple exchanges, individualities merging together, a collective effect" and to replace it with "a collection of separated individualities" (p. 201). However, as John MacArthur notes, the Panopticon is simply a technique, not itself a disciplinary regime or essentially a part of one, and, like all techniques, its potential effects are not exhausted by its deployment within any of the regimes in which it happens to be used.[13] The peculiarity of the exhibitionary complex is not to be found in its reversal of the principles of the Panopticon. Rather, it consists in its incorporation of aspects of those principles together with those of the panorama, forming a technology of vision which served not to atomize and disperse the crowd but to regulate it, and to

The Paris Exhibition, 1855

do so by rendering it visible to itself, by making the crowd itself the ultimate spectacle.

An instruction from a "Short Sermon to Sightseers" at the 1901 Pan-American Exposition enjoined: "Please remember when you get inside the gates you are part of the show."[14] This was also true of museums and department stores, which, like many of the main exhibition halls of expositions, frequently contained galleries affording a superior vantage point from which the layout of the whole and the activities of other visitors could also be observed.[15] It was, however, the expositions which developed this characteristic furthest in constructing viewing positions from which they could be surveyed as totalities: the function of the Eiffel Tower at the 1889 Paris exposition, for example. To see and be seen, to survey yet always be under surveillance, the object of an unknown but controlling look: in these ways, as micro-worlds rendered constantly visible to themselves, expositions realized some of the ideals of panopticism in transforming the crowd into a constantly surveyed, self-watching, self-regulating, and, as the historical record suggests, consistently orderly public—a society watching over itself.

Within the hierarchically organized systems of looks of the penitentiary in which each level of looking is monitored by a higher one, the inmate constitutes the point at which all these looks culminate but he is unable to return a look of his own or move to a higher level of vision. The exhibitionary complex, by contrast, perfected a self-monitoring system of looks in which the subject and object positions can be exchanged, in which the crowd comes to commune with and regulate itself through interiorizing the ideal and ordered view of itself as seen from the controlling vision of power—a site of sight accessible to all. It was in thus democratizing the eye of power that the expositions realized Bentham's aspiration for a system of looks within which the central position would be available to the public at all times, a model lesson in civics in which a society regulated itself through self-observation. But, of course, self-observation from a certain perspective. As Manfredo Tafuri puts it:

> The arcades and the department stores of Paris, like the great expositions, were certainly the places in which the crowd, itself become a spectacle, found the spatial and visual means for a self-education from the point of view of capital.[16]

However, this was not an achievement of architecture alone. Account must also be taken of the forces which, in shaping the exhibitionary complex, formed both its publics and its rhetorics.

SEEING THINGS

It seems unlikely, come the revolution, that it will occur to anyone to storm the British Museum. Perhaps it always was. Yet, in the early days of its history, the fear that it might incite the vengeance of the mob was real enough. In 1780, in the midst of the Gordon Riots, troops were housed in the gardens and building and, in 1848, when the Chartists marched to present the People's Charter to Parliament, the authorities prepared to defend the museum as vigilantly as if it had been a penitentiary. The museum staff were sworn in as special constables; fortifications were constructed around the perimeter; a garrison of museum staff, regular troops, and Chelsea pensioners, armed with muskets, pikes, and cutlasses, and with provisions for a three-day siege, occupied the buildings; stones were carried to the roof to be hurled down on the Chartists should they succeed in breaching the outer defenses.[17]

This fear of the crowd haunted debates on the museum's policy for over a century. Acknowledged as one of the first public museums, its conception of the public was a limited one. Visitors were admitted only in groups of fifteen and were obliged to submit their credentials for inspection prior to admission, which was granted only if they were found to be "not exceptionable."[18] When changes to this policy were proposed, they were resisted by both the museum's trustees and its curators, apprehensive that the unruliness of the mob would mar the ordered display of culture and knowledge. When, shortly after the museum's establishment, it was proposed that there be public days on which unrestricted access would be allowed, the proposal was scuttled on the grounds, as one trustee put it, that some of the visitors from the streets would inevitably be "in liquor" and "will never be kept in order." And if public days should be allowed, Dr. Ward continued,

> then it will be necessary for the Trustees to have a presence of a Committee of themselves attending, with at least two Justices of the Peace and the constables of the division of Bloomsbury . . . supported by a guard such as one as usually attends at the Play-House, and even after all this, Accidents must and will happen.[19]

Similar objections were raised when, in 1835, a select committee was appointed to inquire into the management of the museum and suggested that it might be opened over Easter to facilitate attendance by the laboring classes. A few decades later, however, the issue had been finally resolved in favor of the reformers. The most significant shift in the state's attitude toward museums was marked by the opening of the South Kensington Museum in 1857. Administered, eventually, under the auspices of the Board of Education, the museum was officially dedicated to the service of an extended and undifferentiated public, with opening hours and an admissions policy designed to maximize its accessibility to the working classes. It proved remarkably successful, too, attracting over 15 million visits between 1857 and 1883, over 6.5 million of which were recorded in the evenings, the most popular time for working-class visitors, who, it seems, remained largely sober. Henry Cole, the first director of the museum and an ardent advocate of the role museums should play in the formation of a rational public culture, pointedly rebutted the conceptions of the unruly mob which had informed earlier objections to open admissions policies. Informing a House of Commons committee in 1860 that only one person had had to be excluded for not being able to walk steadily, he went on to note that the sales of alcohol in the refreshment rooms had averaged out, as Altick summarizes it, at "two and a half drops of wine, fourteen-fifteenths of a drop of brandy, and ten and half drops of bottled ale per capita."[20] As the evidence of the orderliness of the newly extended mu-

The South Kensington Museum (later the Victoria and Albert): interior of the South Court, eastern portion, from the south, circa 1876 (drawing by John Watkins)

seum public mounted, even the British Museum relented and, in 1883, embarked on a program of electrification to permit evening opening.

The South Kensington Museum thus marked a significant turning point in the development of British museum policy in clearly enunciating the principles of the modern museum conceived as an instrument of public education. It provided the axis around which London's museum complex was to develop throughout the rest of the century and exerted a strong influence on the development of museums in the provincial cities and towns. These now rapidly took advantage of the Museum Bill of 1845 (hitherto used relatively sparingly), which empowered local authorities to establish museums and art galleries: the number of public museums in Britain increased from 50 in 1860 to 200 in 1900.[21] In its turn, however, the South Kensington Museum had derived its primary impetus from the Great Exhibition, which, in developing a new pedagogic relation between state and people, had also subdued the specter of the crowd. This specter had been raised again in the debates set in motion by the proposal that admission to the exhibition should be free. It could only be expected, one correspondent to *The Times* argued, that both the rules of decorum and the rights of property would be violated if entry were made free to "his majesty the mob." These fears were exacerbated by the revolutionary upheavals of 1848, occasioning several European monarchs to petition that the public be banned from the opening ceremony (planned for May Day) for fear that this might spark off an insurrection which, in turn, might give rise to a general European conflagration.[22] And then there was the fear of social contagion should the laboring classes be allowed to rub shoulders with the upper classes.

In the event, the Great Exhibition proved a transitional form. While open to all, it also stratified its public in providing different days for different classes of visitors regulated by varying prices of admission. In spite of this limitation, the exhibition proved a major spur to the development of open-door policies. Attracting over 6 million visitors itself, it also vastly stimulated the attendance at London's main historic sites and museums: visits to the British Museum, for example, increased from 720,643 in 1850 to 2,230,242 in 1851.[23] Perhaps more important, though, was the orderliness of the public, which in spite of the thousand extra constables and ten thousand troops kept on standby, proved duly appreciative, decorous in its bearing, and entirely apolitical. More than that, the exhibition transformed the many-headed mob into an ordered crowd, a part of the spectacle and a sight of pleasure in itself. Victoria, in recording her impressions of the opening ceremony, dwelt particularly on her pleasure in seeing so large, so orderly, and so peaceable a crowd assembled in one place:

> The Green Park and Hyde Park were one mass of densely crowded human beings, in the highest good humour and most enthusiastic. I never saw Hyde Park look as it did, being filled with crowds as far as the eye could see.[24]

Nor was this entirely unprepared for. The working-class public the exhibition attracted was one whose conduct had been regulated into appropriate forms in the earlier history of the Mechanics Institute exhibitions. Devoted largely to the display of industrial objects and processes, these exhibitions pioneered policies of low admission prices and late opening hours to encourage working-class attendance long before these were adopted within the official museum complex. In doing so, moreover, they sought to tutor their visitors on the modes of deportment required if they were to be admitted. Instruction booklets advised working-class visitors how to present themselves, placing particular stress on the need to change out of their working clothes—partly so as not to soil the exhibits, but also so as not to detract from the pleasures of the overall spectacle; indeed, to become parts of it:

> Here is a visitor of another sort; the mechanic has resolved to treat himself with a few hours holiday and recreation; he leaves the "grimy shop," the dirty bench, and donning his Saturday night suit he appears before us—an honourable and worthy object.[25]

In brief, the Great Exhibition and, subsequently, the public museums developed in its wake found themselves heirs to a public which had already been formed by a set of pedagogic relations which, developed initially by voluntary organizations—in what Gramsci would call the realm of civil society—

were henceforward to be more thoroughgoingly promoted within the social body in being subjected to the direction of the state.

Not, then, a history of confinement but one of the opening up of objects to more public contexts of inspection and visibility: this is the direction of movement embodied in the formation of the exhibitionary complex. A movement which simultaneously helped to form a new public and inscribe it in new relations of sight and vision. Of course, the precise trajectory of these developments in Britain was not followed elsewhere in Europe. Nonetheless, the general direction of development was the same. While earlier collections (whether of scientific objects, curiosities, or works of art) had gone under a variety of names (museums, *studiolo*, *cabinets des curieux*, *Wunderkammer*, *Kunstkammer*) and fulfilled a variety of functions (the storing and dissemination of knowledge, the display of princely and aristocratic power, the advancement of reputations and careers), they had mostly shared two principles: that of private ownership and that of restricted access.[26] The formation of the exhibitionary complex involved a break with both in effecting the transfer of significant quantities of cultural and scientific property from private into public ownership, where they were housed within institutions administered by the state for the benefit of an extended general public.

The significance of the formation of the exhibitionary complex, viewed in this perspective, was that of providing new instruments for the moral and cultural regulation of the working classes. Museums and expositions, in drawing on the techniques and rhetorics of display and pedagogic relations developed in earlier nineteenth-century exhibitionary forms, provided a context in which the working- and middle-class publics could be brought together and the former—having been tutored into forms of behavior to suit them for the occasion—could be exposed to the improving influence of the latter. A history, then, of the formation of a new public and its inscription in new relations of power and knowledge. But a history accompanied by a parallel one aimed at the destruction of earlier traditions of popular exhibitions and the publics they implied and produced. In Britain, this took the form, *inter alia*, of a concerted attack on popular fairs owing to their association with riot, carnival, and in their sideshows, the display of monstrosities and curiosities, which, no longer enjoying elite patronage, were now perceived as impediments to the rationalizing influence of the restructured exhibitionary complex.

Yet, by the end of the century, fairs were to be actively promoted as an aid rather than a threat to public order. This was partly because the mechanization of fairs meant that their entertainments were increasingly brought into line with the values of industrial civilization, a testimony to the virtues of progress.[27] But it was also a consequence of changes in the conduct of fairgoers. By the end of the century, Hugh Cunningham argues, "fairgoing had become a relatively routine ingredient in the accepted world of leisure" as "fairs became tolerated, safe, and in due course a subject for nostalgia and revival."[28] The primary site for this transformation of fairs and the conduct of

their publics—although never quite so complete as Cunningham suggests—
was supplied by the fair zones of the late-nineteenth-century exhibitions. It
was here that two cultures abutted . . . [each] other, the fair zones forming a
kind of buffer region between the official and the popular culture, with the
former seeking to reach into the latter and moderate it. Initially, these fair
zones established themselves independently of the official expositions and
their organizing committees. The product of the initiative of popular show-
men and private traders eager to exploit the market the expositions supplied,
they consisted largely of an *ad hoc* mélange of both new (mechanical rides)
and traditional popular entertainments (freak shows, etc.), which frequently
mocked the pretensions of the expositions they adjoined. Burton Benedict
summarizes the relations between expositions and their amusement zones in
late-nineteenth-century America as follows:

> Many of the display techniques used in the amusement zone seemed to parody
> those of the main fair. Gigantism became enormous toys or grotesque monsters.
> Impressive high structures became collapsing or whirling amusement "rides."
> The solemn female allegorical figures that symbolised nations (Miss Liberty,
> Britannia) were replaced by comic male figures (Uncle Sam, John Bull). At the
> Chicago fair of 1893 the gilded female statue of the Republic on the Court of
> Honour contrasted with a large mechanical Uncle Sam on the Midway that deliv-
> ered forty thousand speeches on the virtues of Hub Gore shoe elastics. Serious
> propagandists for manufacturers and governments in the main fair gave way to
> barkers and pitchmen. The public no longer had to play the role of impressed
> spectators. They were invited to become frivolous participants. Order was re-
> placed by jumble, and instruction by entertainment.[29]

As Benedict goes on to note, the resulting tension between unofficial fair
and official exposition led to "exposition organisers frequently attempting to
turn the amusement zone into an educational enterprise or at least to regulate
the type of exhibit shown." In this, they were never entirely successful. Into
the twentieth century, the amusement zones remained sites of illicit pleasures—of burlesque shows and prostitution—and of ones which the expositions themselves aimed to render archaic. Altick's "monster-mongers and re-
tailers of other strange sights" seem to have been as much in evidence at the
Panama Pacific Exhibition of 1915 as they had been, a century earlier, at St.
Bartholomew's Fair, Wordsworth's Parliament of Monsters.[30] Nonetheless,
what was evident was a significant restructuring in the ideological economy
of such amusement zones as a consequence of the degree to which, in subjecting them to more stringent forms of control and direction, exposition authorities were able to align their thematics to those of the official expositions
themselves and, thence, to those of the rest of the exhibitionary complex.
Museums, the evidence suggests, appealed largely to the middle classes and
the skilled and respectable working classes and it seems likely that the same
was true of expositions. The link between expositions and their adjoining fair

zones, however, provided a route through which the exhibitionary complex and the disciplines and knowledges which shaped its rhetorics acquired a far wider and more extensive social influence.

THE EXHIBITIONARY DISCIPLINES

The space of representation constituted by the exhibitionary complex was shaped by the relations between an array of new disciplines: history, art history, archaeology, geology, biology, and anthropology. Whereas the disciplines associated with the carceral archipelago were concerned to reduce aggregates to individualities, rendering the latter visible to power and so amenable to control, the orientation of these disciplines—as deployed in the exhibitionary complex—might best be summarized as that of "show and tell." They tended also to be generalizing in their focus. Each discipline, in its museological deployment, aimed at the representation of a type and its insertion in a developmental sequence for display to a public.

Such principles of classification and display were alien to the eighteenth century. Thus, in Sir Hans Soane's Museum, architectural styles are displayed in order to demonstrate their essential permanence rather than their change and development.[31] The emergence of a historicized framework for the display of human artifacts in early-nineteenth-century museums was thus a significant innovation. But not an isolated one. As Stephen Bann shows, the emergence of a "historical frame" for the display of museum exhibits was concurrent with the development of an array of disciplinary and other practices which aimed at the lifelike reproduction of an authenticated past and its representation as a series of stages leading to the present—the new practices of history writing associated with the historical novel and the development of history as an empirical discipline, for example.[32] Between them, these constituted a new space of representation concerned to depict the development of peoples, states, and civilizations through time conceived as a progressive series of developmental stages.

The French Revolution, Germaine Bazin suggests, played a key role in opening up this space of representation by breaking the chain of dynastic succession that had previously vouchsafed a unity to the flow and organization of time.[33] Certainly, it was in France that historicized principles of museum display were first developed. Bazin stresses the formative influence of the Museum des monuments français (1795) in exhibiting works of art in galleries devoted to different periods, the visitor's route leading from earlier to later periods, with a view to demonstrating both the painterly conventions peculiar to each epoch and their historical development. He accords a similar significance to Alexandre du Sommerard's collection at the Hôtel de Cluny, which, as Bann shows, aimed at "an integrative construction of historical totalities," creating the impression of a historically authentic milieu by suggest-

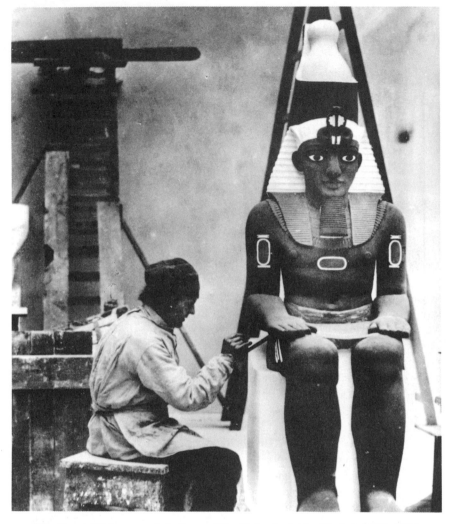

The Crystal Palace: model of one of the Colossi of Abu Simbel, 1852–1853
(plate by Philip Henry Delamotte)

ing an essential and organic connection between artifacts displayed in rooms classified by period.[34]

Bann argues that these two principles—the *galleria progressiva* and the period room, sometimes employed singly, at others in combination—constitute the distinctive poetics of the modern historical museum. It is important to add, though, that this poetics displayed a marked tendency to be nationalized. If, as Bazin suggests, the museum became "one of the fundamental institutions of the modern state,"[35] that state was also increasingly a nation-state. The significance of this was manifested in the relations between two new historical times—national and universal—which resulted from an increase in the vertical depth of historical time as it was both pushed further and further back into the past and brought increasingly up to date. Under the impetus of the rivalry between France and Britain for dominion in the Middle East, museums, in close association with archaeological excavations of progressively deeper pasts, extended their time horizons beyond the medieval period and the classical antiquities of Greece and Rome to encompass the remnants of the Egyptian and Mesopotamian civilizations. At the same time, the recent past was historicized as the newly emerging nation-states sought to preserve and immemorialize their own formation as a part of that process of "nationing" their populations that was essential to their further development. It was as a consequence of the first of these developments that the prospect of a universal history of civilization was opened up to thought and materialized in the archaeological collections of the great nineteenth-century museums. The second development, however, led to these universal histories' being annexed to national histories as, within the rhetorics of each national museum complex, collections of national materials were represented as the outcome and culmination of the universal story of civilization's development.

Nor had displays of natural or geological specimens been organized historically in the various precursors of nineteenth-century public museums. Throughout the greater part of the eighteenth century, principles of scientific classification testified to a mixture of theocratic, rationalist, and proto-evolutionist systems of thought. Translated into principles of museological displays, the result was the table, not the series, with species being arranged in terms of culturally codified similarities/dissimilarities in their external appearances rather than being ordered into temporally organized relations of precession/succession. The crucial challenges to such conceptions came from developments within geology and biology, particularly where their researches overlapped in the stratigraphical study of fossil remains.[36] However, the details of these developments need not concern us here. So far as their implications for museums were concerned, their main significance was that of allowing for organic life to be conceived and represented as a temporally ordered succession of different forms of life, where the transitions between them were accounted for not as a result of external shocks (as had been the case in the eighteenth century) but as the consequence of an inner momentum inscribed within the concept of life itself.[37]

If developments within history and archaeology thus allowed for the emergence of new forms of classifications and display through which the stories of nations could be told and related to the longer story of Western civilization's development, the discursive formations of nineteenth-century geology and biology allowed these cultural series to be inserted within the longer developmental series of geological and natural time. Museums of science and technology, heirs to the rhetorics of progress developed in national and international exhibitions, completed the evolutionary picture in representing the history of industry and manufacture as a series of progressive innovations leading up to the contemporary triumphs of industrial capitalism.

The cabinet of curiosities: Ferrante Imperato's museum in Naples, 1599

The Crystal Palace: stuffed animals and ethnographic figures (plate by Delamotte)

Yet, in the context of late-nineteenth-century imperialism, it was arguably the employment of anthropology within the exhibitionary complex which proved most central to its ideological functioning. For it played the crucial role of connecting the histories of Western nations and civilizations to those of other peoples, but only by separating the two in providing for an interrupted continuity in the order of peoples and races—one in which "primitive peoples" dropped out of history altogether in order to occupy a twilight zone between nature and culture. This function had been fulfilled earlier in the century by the museological display of anatomical peculiarities which seemed to confirm polygenetic conceptions of mankind's origins. The most celebrated instance was that of Saartjie Baartman, the "Hottentot Venus," whose protruding buttocks—interpreted as a sign of separate development— occasioned a flurry of scientific speculation when she was displayed in Paris and London. On her death in 1815, an autopsy revealed alleged peculiarities in her genitalia, which, likened to those of the orangutan, were cited as proof positive of the claim that black peoples were the product of a separate—and, of course, inferior, more primitive, and bestial—line of descent. No less an authority than Cuvier lent his support to this conception in circulating a report of Baartman's autopsy and presenting her genital organs—"prepared in a way so as to allow one to see the nature of the labia"[38]—to the French Academy, which arranged for their display in the Musée d'Ethnographie de Paris (now the Musée de l'Homme).

Darwin's rebuttal of theories of polygenesis entailed that different means be found for establishing and representing the fractured unity of the human species. By and large, this was achieved by the representation of "primitive peoples" as instances of arrested development, as examples of an earlier stage of species development which Western civilizations had long ago surpassed. Indeed, such peoples were typically represented as the still-living examples of *the* earliest stage in human development, the point of transition between nature and culture, between ape and man, the missing link necessary to account for the transition between animal and human history. Denied any history of their own, it was the fate of "primitive peoples" to be dropped out of the bottom of human history in order that they might serve, representationally, as its support—underlining the rhetoric of progress by serving as its counterpoints, representing the point at which human history emerges from nature but has not yet properly begun its course.

So far as the museological display of artifacts from such cultures was concerned, this resulted in their arrangement and display—as at the Pitt-Rivers Museum—in accordance with the genetic or typological system which grouped together all objects of a similar nature, irrespective of their ethnographic groupings, in an evolutionary series leading from the simple to the complex.[39] However, it was with regard to the display of human remains that the consequences of these principles of classification were most dramatically manifested. In eighteenth-century museums, such displays had placed the accent on anatomical peculiarities, viewed primarily as a testimony to the rich diversity of the chain of universal being. By the late nineteenth century, however, human remains were most typically displayed as parts of evolutionary series, with the remains of still-extant peoples being allocated the earliest position within them. This was particularly true for the remains of Australian Aborigines. In the early years of Australian settlement, the colony's museums had displayed little or no interest in Aboriginal remains.[40] The triumph of evolutionary theory transformed this situation, leading to a systematic rape of Aboriginal sacred sites—by the representatives of British, European, and American as well as Australian museums—for materials to provide a representational foundation for the story of evolution within, tellingly enough, natural history displays.[41]

The space of representation constituted in the relations between the disciplinary knowledges deployed within the exhibitionary complex thus permitted the construction of a temporally organized order of things and peoples. Moreover, that order was a totalizing one, metonymically encompassing all things and all peoples in their interactions through time. And an order which organized the implied public—the white citizenries of the imperialist powers—into a unity, representationally effacing divisions within the body politic in constructing a "we" conceived as the realization, and therefore just beneficiaries, of the processes of evolution and identified as a unity in opposition to the primitive otherness of conquered peoples. This was not entirely new. As Peter Stallybrass and Allon White note, the popular fairs of the late eighteenth and early nineteenth centuries had exoticized the grotesque imagery of the carnival tradition by projecting it onto the representatives of alien cultures. In thus providing a normalizing function via the construction of a radically different Other, the exhibition of other peoples served as a vehicle for "the edification of a national public and the confirmation of its imperial superiority."[42] If, in its subsequent development, the exhibitionary complex latched on to this preexisting representational space, what it added to it was a historical dimension.

THE EXHIBITIONARY APPARATUSES

The space of representation constituted by the exhibitionary disciplines, while conferring a degree of unity on the exhibitionary complex, was also somewhat differently occupied—and to different effect—by the institutions comprising that complex. If museums gave this space a solidity and permanence, this was achieved at the price of a lack of ideological flexibility. Public museums instituted an order of things that was meant to last. In doing so, they provided the modern state with a deep and continuous ideological backdrop but one which, if it was to play this role, could not be adjusted to respond to shorter-term ideological requirements. Exhibitions met this need, injecting new life into the exhibitionary complex and rendering its ideological configurations more pliable in bending them to serve the conjuncturally specific hegemonic strategies of different national bourgeoisies. They made the order of things dynamic, mobilizing it strategically in relation to the more immediate ideological and political exigencies of the particular moment.

This was partly an effect of the secondary discourses which accompanied exhibitions. Ranging from the state pageantry of their opening and closing ceremonies through newspaper reports to the veritable swarming of pedagogic initiatives organized by religious, philanthropic, and scientific associations to take advantage of the publics which exhibitions produced, these often forged very direct and specific connections between the exhibitionary rhetoric of progress and the claims to leadership of particular social and political forces. The distinctive influence of the exhibitions themselves, however, consisted in their articulation of the rhetoric of progress to the rhetorics of nationalism and imperialism and in producing, via their control over their adjoining popular fairs, an expanded cultural sphere for the deployment of the exhibitionary disciplines.

The basic signifying currency of the exhibitions, of course, consisted in their arrangement of displays of manufacturing processes and products. Prior to the Great Exhibition, the message of progress had been carried by the arrangement of exhibits in, as Davison puts it, "a series of classes and subclasses ascending from raw products of nature, through various manufactured goods and mechanical devices, to the 'highest' forms of applied and fine art."[43] As such, the class articulations of this rhetoric were subject to some variation. Mechanics Institutes' exhibitions placed considerable stress on the centrality of labor's appropriation of their message. "The machinery of wealth, here displayed," the *Leeds Times* noted in reporting an 1839 exhibition, "has been created by the men of hammers and papercaps; more honourable than all the sceptres and coronets in the world."[44] The Great Exhibition introduced two changes which decisively influenced the future development of the form.

First, the stress was shifted from the *processes* to the *products* of production, divested of the marks of their making and ushered forth as signs of the productive and coordinating power of capital and the state. After 1851, world fairs were to function less as vehicles for the technical education of the working classes than as instruments for their stupefaction before the reified products of their own labor, "places of pilgrimage," as Benjamin put it, "to the fetish Commodity."[45]

Second, while not entirely abandoned, the earlier progressivist taxonomy based on stages of production was subordinated to the dominating influence of principles of classification based on nations and the supra-national constructs of empires and races. Embodied, at the Crystal Palace, in the form of national courts or display areas, this principle was subsequently developed into that of separate pavilions for each participating country. Moreover, following an innovation of the Centennial Exhibition held at Philadelphia in 1876, these pavilions were typically zoned into racial groups: the Latin, Teutonic, Anglo-Saxon, American, and Oriental being the most favored classifications, with black peoples and the aboriginal populations of conquered terri-

The Great Exhibition, 1851: stands of Egypt, Turkey, and Greece
(plate by Owen and Ferrier)

tories, denied any space of their own, being represented as subordinate adjuncts to the imperial displays of the major powers. The effect of these developments was to transfer the rhetoric of progress from the relations between stages of production to the relations between races and nations by superimposing the associations of the former onto the latter. In the context of imperial displays, subject peoples were thus represented as occupying the lowest levels of manufacturing civilization. Reduced to displays of "primitive" handicrafts and the like, they were represented as cultures without momentum except for that benignly bestowed on them from without through the improving mission of the imperialist powers. Oriental civilizations were allotted an intermediate position in being represented either as having at one time been subject to development but subsequently degenerating into stasis or as embodying achievements of the standards set by Europe.[46] In brief, a progressivist taxonomy for the classification of goods and manufacturing processes was laminated onto a crudely racist teleological conception of the relations between peoples and races, which culminated in the achievements of the metropolitan powers, invariably most impressively displayed in the pavilions of the host country.

Exhibitions thus located their preferred audiences at the very pinnacle of the exhibitionary order of things they constructed. They also installed them at the threshold of greater things to come. Here, too, the Great Exhibition led the way in sponsoring a display of architectural projects for the improvement of social conditions in the areas of health, sanitation, education, and welfare—promissory notes that the engines of progress would be harnessed for the general good. Indeed, exhibitions came to function as promissory notes in their totalities, embodying, if just for a season, utopian principles of social organization which, when the time came for the notes to be redeemed, would eventually be realized in perpetuity. As world fairs fell increasingly under the influence of modernism, the rhetoric of progress tended, as Rydell puts it, to be "translated into a utopian statement about the future," promising the imminent dissipation of social tensions once progress had reached the point where its benefits might be generalized.[47]

Iain Chambers has argued that working- and middle-class cultures became sharply distinct in late-nineteenth-century Britain as an urban commercial popular culture developed beyond the reach of the moral economy of religion and respectability. As a consequence, he argues, "official culture was publicly limited to the rhetoric of monuments in the centre of town: the university, the museum, the theatre, the concert hall; otherwise it was reserved for the 'private' space of the Victorian residence."[48] While [one would] not disput[e] the general terms of this argument, it does omit any consideration of the role of exhibitions in providing official culture with powerful bridgeheads into the newly developing popular culture. Most obviously, the official zones of exhibitions offered a context for the deployment of the exhibitionary disciplines which reached a more extended public than that ordinarily reached by the public museum system. The exchange of both staff and exhibits between museums and exhibitions was a regular and recurrent aspect of their relations, furnishing an institutional axis for the extended social deployment of a distinctively new ensemble of disciplines. Even within the official zones of exhibitions, the exhibitionary disciplines thus achieved an exposure to publics as large as any to which even the most commercialized forms of popular culture could lay claim: 32 million people attended the Paris Exposition of 1889; 27.5 million went to Chicago's Columbian Exposition in 1893 and nearly 49 million to Chicago's 1933/4 Century of Progress Exposition; the Glasgow Empire Exhibition of 1938 attracted 12 million visitors, and over 27 million attended the Empire Exhibition at Wembley in 1924/5.[49] However, the ideological reach of exhibitions often extended significantly further as they established their influence over the popular entertainment zones which, while initially deplored by exhibition authorities, were subsequently to be managed as planned adjuncts to the official exhibition zones and, sometimes, incorporated into the latter. It was through this network of relations that the official public culture of museums reached into the developing urban popular culture, shaping and directing its development in subjecting the ideological thematics of popular entertainments to the rhetoric of progress.

The most critical development in this respect consisted in the extension of anthropology's disciplinary ambit into the entertainment zones, for it was here that the crucial work of transforming non-white peoples themselves—and not just their remains or artifacts—into object lessons of evolutionary theory was accomplished. Paris led the way here in the colonial city it constructed as part of its 1889 Exposition. Populated by Asian and African peoples in simulated "native" villages, the colonial city functioned as the showpiece of French anthropology and, through its influence on delegates to the tenth Congrès Internationale d'Anthropologie et d'Archéologie Préhistorique held in association with the exposition, had a decisive bearing on the future modes of the discipline's social deployment. While this was true internationally, Rydell's study of American world fairs provides the most detailed demonstration of the active role played by museum anthropologists in transforming the midways into living demonstrations of evolutionary theory by arranging non-white peoples into a "sliding-scale of humanity," from the barbaric to the nearly civilized, thus underlining the exhibitionary rhetoric of progress by serving as visible counterpoints to its triumphal achievements. It was here that relations of knowledge and power continued to be invested in the public display of bodies, colonizing the space of earlier freak and monstrosity shows in order to personify the truths of a new regime of representation.

In their interrelations, then, the expositions and their fair zones constituted an order of things and of peoples which, reaching back into the depths of prehistoric time as well as encompassing all corners of the globe, rendered the whole world metonymically present, subordinated to the dominating gaze of the white, bourgeois, and (although this is another story) male eye of the metropolitan powers. But an eye of power which, through the development of the technology of vision associated with exposition towers and the positions for seeing these produced in relation to the miniature ideal cities of the expositions themselves, was democratized in being made available to all. Earlier attempts to establish a specular dominance over the city had, of course, been legion—the camera obscura, the panorama—and often fantastic in their technological imaginings. Moreover, the ambition to render the whole world, as represented in assemblages of commodities, subordinate to the controlling vision of the spectator was present in world exhibitions from the outset. This was represented synechdochically at the Great Exhibition by Wylde's Great Globe, a brick rotunda which the visitor entered to see plaster casts of the world's continents and oceans. The principles embodied in the Eiffel Tower, built for the 1889 Paris Exposition and repeated in countless subsequent expositions, brought these two series together, rendering the project of specular dominance feasible in affording an elevated vantage point over a micro-world which claimed to be representative of a larger totality.

Barthes has aptly summarized the effects of the technology of vision embodied in the Eiffel Tower. Remarking that the tower overcomes "the habit-

The Chicago Columbian Exposition, 1893: view from the roof of the Manufactures
and Liberal Arts Building

ual divorce between *seeing* and *being seen*," Barthes argues that it acquires a
distinctive power from its ability to circulate between these two functions
of sight:

> An object when we look at it, it becomes a lookout in its turn when we visit it,
> and now constitutes as an object, simultaneously extended and collected beneath
> it, that Paris which just now was looking at it.[50]

A sight itself, it becomes the site for a sight; a place both to see and be seen
from, which allows the individual to circulate between the object and subject
positions of the dominating vision it affords over the city and its inhabitants.
In this, its distancing effect, Barthes argues, "the Tower makes the city into a
kind of nature; it constitutes the swarming of men into a landscape, it adds to
the frequently grim urban myth a romantic dimension, a harmony, a mitiga-
tion," offering "an immediate consumption of a humanity made natural by
that glance which transforms it into space,"[51] It is because of the dominating
vision it affords, Barthes continues, that, for the visitor, "the Tower is the first
obligatory monument; it is a Gateway, it marks the transition to a knowledge."[52] And to the power associated with that knowledge: the power to order
objects and persons into a world to be known and to lay it out before a vision
capable of encompassing it as a totality.

In "The Prelude," Wordsworth, seeking a vantage point from which to quell the tumultuousness of the city, invites his reader to ascend with him "Above the press and danger of the crowd/Upon some showman's platform" at St. Bartholomew's Fair, likened to mobs, riotings, and executions as occasions when the passions of the city's populace break forth into unbridled expression. The vantage point, however, affords no control:

> All moveables of wonder, from all parts,
> Are here—Albinos, painted Indians, Dwarfs,
> The Horse of knowledge, and the learned Pig,
> The Stone-eater, the man that swallows fire,
> Giants, Ventriloquists, the Invisible Girl,
> The Bust that speaks and moves its goggling eyes,
> The Wax-work, Clock-work, all the marvellous craft
> Of modern Merlins, Wild Beasts, Puppet-shows,
> All out-o'-the-way, far-fetched, perverted things,
> All freaks of nature, all Promethean thoughts
> Of man, his dullness, madness, and their feats
> All jumbled up together, to compose
> A Parliament of Monsters.[53]

Stallybrass and White argue that this Wordsworthian perspective was typical of the early-nineteenth-century tendency for the educated public, in withdrawing from participation in popular fairs, also to distance itself from, and seek some ideological control over, the fair by the literary production of elevated vantage points—from which it might be observed. By the end of the century, the imaginary dominance over the city afforded by the showman's platform had been transformed into a cast-iron reality while the fair, no longer a symbol of chaos, had become the ultimate spectacle of an ordered totality. And the substitution of observation for participation was a possibility open to all. The principle of spectacle—that, as Foucault summarizes it, of rendering a small number of objects accessible to the inspection of a multitude of men—did not fall into abeyance in the nineteenth century; it was surpassed through the development of technologies of vision which rendered the multitude accessible to its own inspection.

CONCLUSION

I have sought, in this article, to tread a delicate line between Foucault's and Gramsci's perspective on the state, but without attempting to efface their differences so as to forge a synthesis between them. Nor is there a compelling need for such a synthesis. The concept of the state is merely a convenient shorthand for an array of governmental agencies which—as Gramsci was among the first to argue in distinguishing between the coercive apparatuses of the state and those engaged in the organization of consent—need not be conceived as unitary with regard to either their functioning or the modalities of power they embody.

That said, however, my argument has been mainly with (but not against) Foucault. In the study already referred to, Pearson distinguishes between the "hard" and the "soft" approaches to the nineteenth-century state's role in the promotion of art and culture. The former consisted of "a systematic body of knowledge and skills promulgated in a systematic way to specified audiences." Its field was comprised by those institutions of schooling which exercised a forcible hold or some measure of constraint over their members and to which the technologies of self-monitoring developed in the carceral system undoubtedly migrated. The "soft" approach, by contrast, worked "by example rather than by pedagogy; by entertainment rather than by disciplined schooling; and by subtlety and encouragement."[54] Its field of application consisted of those institutions whose hold over their publics depended on their voluntary participation.

There seems no reason to deny the different sets of knowledge/power relations embodied in these contrasting approaches, or to seek their reconciliation in some common principle. For the needs to which they responded were different. The problem to which the "swarming of disciplinary mechanism" responded was that of making extended populations governable. However, the development of bourgeois democratic polities required not merely that the populace be governable but that it assent to its governance, thereby creating a need to enlist active popular support for the values and objectives enshrined in the state. Foucault knows well enough the symbolic power of the penitentiary:

> The high wall, no longer the wall that surrounds and protects, no longer the wall that stands for power and wealth, but the meticulously sealed wall, uncrossable in either direction, closed in upon the now mysterious work of punishment, will become, near at hand, sometimes even at the very centre of the cities of the nineteenth century, the monotonous figure, at once material and symbolic, of the power to punish. (p. 116)

Museums were also typically located at the center of cities where they stood as embodiments, both material and symbolic, of a power to "show and tell" which, in being deployed in a newly constituted open and public space, sought rhetorically to incorporate the people within the processes of the state. If the museum and the penitentiary thus represented the Janus face of power, there was nonetheless—at least symbolically—an economy of effort between them. For those who failed to adopt the tutelary relation to the self promoted by popular schooling or whose hearts and minds failed to be won in the new pedagogic relations between state and people symbolized by the open doors of the museum, the closed walls of the penitentiary threatened a sterner instruction in the lessons of power. Where instruction and rhetoric failed, punishment began.

NOTES

First appeared in 1988.

1. Douglas Crimp, "On the museum's ruins," in Hal Foster (ed.), *The Anti-Aesthetic: Essays on Postmodern Culture* (Washington, D.C.: Bay Press, 1985), 45.

2. Michael Foucault, *Discipline and Punish: The Birth of the Prison*, trans. by A. Sheridan (London: Allen Lane, 1977), 115–16; further page references will be given in the text.

3. Jeffrey Minson, *Genealogies of Morals: Nietzche, Foucault, Donzelot and the Eccentricity of Ethics* (London: Macmillan, 1985), 24.

4. This point is well made by MacArthur, who sees this aspect of Foucault's argument as inimical to the overall spirit of his work in suggesting a "historical division which places theatre and spectacle as past." John MacArthur, "Foucault, Tafuri, Utopia: Essays in the history and theory of architecture" (unpublished M. Phil. thesis, University of Queensland, 1983), 192.

5. Graeme Davison, "Exhibitions," *Australian Cultural History* (Canberra: Australian Academy of the Humanities and the History of Ideas Unit, A.N.U.), no. 2 (1982/3) 7.

6. See Richard D. Altick, *The Shows of London* (Cambridge, Mass., and London: the Belknap Press of Harvard University Press, 1978).

7. Dean MacCannell, *The Tourist: A New Theory of the Leisure Class* (New York: Schocken Books, 1976, 57).

8. See Dana Aron Brand, *The Spectator and the City: Fantasies of Urban Legibility in Nineteenth-Century England and America* (Ann Arbor, Mich.: University Microfilms International, 1986).

9. For discussions of the role of the American state in relation to museums and expositions, see, respectively, K. E. Meyer, *The Art Museum: Power, Money, Ethics* (New York: William Morrow & Co., 1979), and Reid Badger, *The Great American Fair: The World's Columbian Exposition and American Culture* (Chicago: Nelson Hall, 1979).

10. Nicholas Pearson, *The State and the Visual Arts: A Discussion of State Intervention in the Visual Arts in Britain, 1780–1981* (Milton Keynes: Open University Press, 1982), 8–13, 46–7.

11. See Debora Silverman, "The 1889 exhibition: The crisis of bourgeois individualism," *Oppositions: A Journal of Ideas and Criticism in Architecture*, Spring 1977; and Robert W. Rydell, *All the World's a Fair: Visions of Empire at American International Expositions, 1876–1916* (Chicago: University of Chicago Press, 1984).

12. See H. Seling, "The genesis of the museum," *Architectural Review*, no. 131 (1967).

13. MacArthur, ["Foucault, Tafuri, Utopia,"] 192–3.

14. Cited in Neil Harris, "Museums, merchandising and popular taste: The struggle for influence," in I. M. G. Quimby (ed.), *Material Culture and the Study of American Life* (New York: W. W. Norton, 1978), 144.

15. For details of the use of rotundas and galleries to this effect in department stores, see John William Ferry, *A History of the Department Store* (New York: Macmillan, 1960).

16. Manfredo Tafuri, *Architecture and Utopia: Design and Capitalist Development* (Cambridge, Mass.: MIT Press, 1976), 83.

17. For further details, see Edward Millar, *That Noble Cabinet: A History of the British Museum* (Athens, Ohio: Ohio University Press, 1974).

18. A. S. Wittlin, *The Museum: Its History and Its Tasks in Education* (London: Routledge & Kegan Paul, 1949), 113.

19. Cited in Millar, [*That Noble Cabinet,*] 62.

20. Altick, [*Shows of London,*] 500.

21. See David White, "Is Britain becoming one big museum?" *New Society*, 20 October 1983.

22. See Audrey Shorter, "Workers under glass in 1851," *Victorian Studies*, 10, 2 (1966).

23. See Altick, [*Shows of London,*] 467.

24. Cited in C. H. Gibbs-Smith, *The Great Exhibition of 1851* (London: HMSO, 1981), 18.

25. Cited in Toshio Kusamitsu, "Great exhibitions before 1851," *History Workshop*, no. 9 (1980), 77.

26. A comprehensive introduction to these earlier forms is offered by Olive Impey and Arthur MacGregor (eds.), *The Origins of Museums: The Cabinet of Curiosities in Sixteenth- and Seventeenth-Century Europe* (Oxford: Clarendon Press, 1985). See also Bazin, [note 33] below.

27. I have touched on these matters elsewhere. See Tony Bennett, "A thousand and one troubles: Blackpool Pleasure Beach," in *Formations of Pleasure* (London: Routledge & Kegan Paul, 1983), and "Hegemony, ideology, pleasure: Blackpool," in Tony Bennett, Colin Mercer, and Janet Woollacott (eds.), *Popular Culture and Social Relations* (Milton Keynes: Open University Press, 1986).

28. Hugh Cunningham, *Leisure in the Industrial Revolution* (London: Croom Helm, 1980). As excerpted in Bernard Waites, Tony Bennett, and Graham Martin (eds.), *Popular Culture: Past and Present* (London: Croom Helm, 1982), 163.

29. Burton Benedict, "The anthropology of world's fairs," in Burton Benedict (ed.), *The Anthropology of World's Fairs: San Francisco's Panama Pacific Exposition of 1915* (New York: Scolar Press, 1983), 53–4.

30. For details, see E. McCullough, *World's Fair Midways: An Affectionate Account of American Amusement Areas* (New York: Exposition Press, 1966), 76.

31. See Colin Davies, "Architecture and remembrance," *Architectural Review* (February, 1984), 54.

32. See Stephen Bann, *The Clothing of Clio: A Study of the Representation of History in Nineteenth-Century Britain and France* (Cambridge: Cambridge University Press, 1984).

33. G. Bazin, *The Museum Age* (New York: Universal Press, 1967), 218.

34. Bann, [*Clothing of Clio,*] 85.

35. Bazin, [*Museum Age,*] 169.

36. For details of these interactions, see Martin J. S. Rudwick, *The Meaning of Fossils: Episodes in the History of Palaeontology* (Chicago: University of Chicago Press, 1985).

37. I draw here on Michael Foucault, *The Order of Things: An Archaeology of the Human Sciences* (London: Tavistock, 1970).

38. Cuvier, cited in Sander L. Gilman, "Black bodies, white bodies: Toward an iconography of female sexuality in late nineteenth-century art, medicine and literature," *Critical Inquiry*, 21, I (autumn, 1985), 214–15.

39. See David K. van Keuren, "Museums and ideology: Augustus Pitt-Rivers, an-

thropological museums, and social change in later Victorian Britain," *Victorian Studies*, 28, 1 (Autumn, 1984).

40. See S. G. Kohlstedt, "Australian museums of natural history: Public practices and scientific initiatives in the 19th century," *Historical Records of Australian Science* vol. 5 (1983).

41. For the most thorough account, see D. J. Mulvaney, "The Australian Aborigines 1606–1929: Opinion and fieldwork," *Historical Studies*, 8, 30–1 (1958).

42. Peter Stallybrass and Allon White, *The Politics and Poetics of Transgression* (London: Methuen, 1986), 42.

43. Davison, ["Exhibitions,"] 8.

44. Cited in Kusamitsu, ["Great exhibitions,"] 79.

45. Walter Benjamin, *Charles Baudelaire: A Lyric Poet in the Era of High Capitalism* (London: New Left Books, 1973), 165.

46. See Neil Harris, "All the world a melting pot? Japan at American fairs, 1876–1904," in Ireye Akira (ed.), *Mutual Images: Essays in American-Japanese Relations* (Cambridge, Mass: Harvard University Press, 1975).

47. Rydell, [*All the World's,*] 4.

48. Iain Chambers, "The obscured metropolis," *Australian Journal of Cultural Studies*, 3, 2 (December, 1985), 9.

49. John M. MacKenzie, *Propaganda and Empire: The Manipulation of British Public Opinion, 1880–1960* (Manchester: Manchester University Press, 1984), 101.

50. Roland Barthes, *The Eiffel Tower, and Other Mythologies* (New York: Hill & Wang, 1979), 4.

51. Ibid., 8.

52. Ibid., 14.

53. VII, 684–5; 706–18.

54. Pearson, [*The State,*] 35.

Structures, Habitus, Power: Basis for a Theory of Symbolic Power

PIERRE BOURDIEU

DOXA, ORTHODOXY, HETERODOXY

There is, perhaps, no better way of *making felt* the real function of classificatory systems than to evoke as concretely as possible the abrupt and total transformation of daily life which occurs [for the Kabyle of Algeria] on the "return of *azal* [midday, dry season]." Everything, without exception, in the activities of the men, the women, and the children, is abruptly altered by the adoption of a new rhythm: the movements of the flock, of course, but also the men's work and the domestic activities of the women, the place where the cooking is done, the rest periods, the food eaten, the times and the itinerary of the women's movements and outdoor work, the rhythm of the men's assembly meetings, of the ceremonies, prayers, markets, and meetings outside the village.

In the wet season, in the morning, before *eddoḥa*, all the men are in the village; with the exception of the meeting sometimes held on a Friday after collective prayer, this is the time of day for meetings of the clan assembly and all the conciliation committees (before a divorce, or to prevent a divorce, before division of an estate or to avoid division); this is also the time when announcements concerning all the men are made from the top of the minaret (summoning them to participate in collective work, repairing roads, digging drains, transporting flagstones, etc.). About the time of *eddoḥa* the shepherd sets out with his flock and the men go off to the fields and gardens, either to work on the major seasonal tasks such as plowing or digging or to spend their time on the minor activities which occupy the slack periods of the agrarian year or day (collecting grass or diss, digging or clearing ditches, gathering wood, digging up tree-stumps, etc.). When rain, snow, or cold rule out work in the fields and the earth is too wet to be trodden on without jeopardizing the future crop or the plowing to come, and when the state of the roads and the fear of being weather-bound far from the house suspend traditional relation with the outside world, the men's imperative duty to be outside brings them all to the communal house (even across clan and/or league divisions). Indeed at that time of the year, not a man is missing from the village (to which the inhabitants of the *azib*—hamlet—return at *thaqachachth*—end of October).

The evening meal (*imensi*) is served very early, as soon as the men have taken off their moccasins and work-clothes and have had a short rest. By nightfall, everyone is at home, except those who want to offer evening prayer in the mosque, where the last prayer (*el'icha*) is generally brought forward so as to be said at the same time as *maghreb*. Because the men eat all their meals indoors (except the afternoon snack), the women, ousted from their own space, strive to reconstitute a separate universe, making the preparations for the meal over by the wall of darkness, during the afternoon, while the men are away, taking care not to attract attention, even when busy, or be found doing nothing: the loom, which is up throughout the wet season, affords them a sort of veil, behind which they can withdraw, and also the alibi of a permanently available activity. The same strategies appear in the use made of the village space: if the men are present, the wife cannot go to the fountain all morning, especially since the risk of a fall requires special precautions; so the "old woman" is the one who goes and gets the water in the morning and, if there is no little girl available, keeps chickens and animals away from the matting on which the olives or grain are spread out before being taken to the press or the mill.

The group's withdrawal into itself, and also into its own past, its traditions—with the tales and legends in the long evenings in the room reserved for the men—is followed by the opening onto the outside world in the dry season.[1] Whereas during the wet season the village awoke every morning without much ado, once *azal* returns it awakes with a great deal of noise and bustle: the tread of mules as men make their way to market is followed by the uninterrupted tread of the outgoing flocks, and then by the clattering hooves of the asses ridden or led by the men going off to the fields or the forest. About the time of *eddoḥa*, the shepherd brings back his flock and some of the men return to the village for their midday rest. The muezzin's call to *eddoḥa* is the signal for the second going out of the day. In less than half an hour, the village is this time almost completely emptied: in the morning, the women were kept in the house by their domestic tasks and above all by the impropriety there would be in taking their midday rest outside, under a tree, like the men, or in hurrying to get home, which is a woman's proper place at a moment reserved for intimacy; by contrast, in the afternoon, all but a few of the women accompany the men, at least on certain occasions: there are first, of course, the "old women," who, after "giving their orders" to the daughters-in-law whose turn it is to prepare dinner, taking the measure of flour from the *akufi*, getting the bunch of onions and the other vegetables required for *imensi* out of *tha'richth*, and putting the keys to all the stores back on their girdles, go and make their contribution to the work and assert their authority in their own way, by inspecting the gardens, making good the men's negligence—the stray piece of wood, the handful of fodder dropped on the way, the branch left under a tree—and in the evening bringing back, on top of the jar of water from the spring in the garden, a bunch of herbs, vine-leaves, or maize for the domestic animals. There are also the young wives who, especially at the time of the fig-harvest, follow their husbands around the orchard, picking up the fruit the men have beaten down, sorting it and setting it out on trays, and go home in the evening, each a few paces behind her husband, alone, or accompanied by the "old woman."

Thus the double going out delimits *azal*, a sort of "dead" time which everyone feels he must respect: all is silent, still, and austere; the streets are "desertlike." Most of the men are scattered far from the village, some living in the *azib*, others away from home for long periods looking after the garden and the pair of oxen that are being fatted, others watching over the fig-drying shed (in this season every family's fear is that in an emergency it would not be able to assemble its men). No one can say whether the public space of the village belongs to man or to woman. So each of them takes care not to occupy it: there is something suspicious about anyone who ventures into the streets at that hour. The few men who have not stayed in the fields to sleep under a tree take their siesta in any spot that is to hand, in the shade of a porch or a hedge, in front of the mosque, on the flagstones or indoors, in the courtyards of their houses, or in side rooms if they have one. Furtive shadows slip across the street from one house to another: the women, equally unoccupied, are taking advantage of the limited presence of the men to meet together or visit one another. Only the shepherds[2] who have returned to the village with their flocks bring life to the outer crossroads and the minor meeting-places with their games—*thigar*, a kicking contest, *thighuladth*, stone-throwing at targets, *thimrith*, a sort of draughts, etc.

Doing one's duty as a man means conforming to the social order, and this is fundamentally a question of respecting rhythms, keeping pace, not falling out of line. "Don't we all eat the same wheatcake (or the same barley)?" "Don't we all get up at the same time?" These various ways of reasserting solidarity contain an implicit definition of the fundamental virtue of conformity, the opposite of which is the desire to stand apart from others. Working while others are resting, staying in the house while the others are working in the fields, traveling on deserted roads, wandering round the streets of the village while the others are asleep or at the market—these are all suspicious forms of behavior. The eccentric who does everything differently from other people is called *amkhalef* (from *khalef*, to stand out, to transgress) and there is often a play on words to the effect that *amkhalef* is also the man who arrives late (from *khellef*, to leave behind). Thus, as we have seen, a worthy man, conscious of his responsibilities, must get up early.[3] "The man who does not settle his business early in the morning will never settle it"; "It's the morning that gives the hunters their game; bad luck for late sleepers!" and again "The *suq* is the morning"; "The man who sleeps until the middle of *azal* will find the market empty" (*sebah*, to be present in the morning, also means to be fitting, becoming).[4] But getting up early is not a virtue in itself: if they are ill-used, wasted, the first hours are no more than "time taken from the night," an offense against the principle that "there is a time for everything," and that "everything should be done in its time" (*kul waqth salwaqth-is*, "everthing in its time"). What is the use of a man's getting up at the muezzin's call if he is not going to say the morning prayer? There is only mockery for the man who, despite getting up "under the stars" or when "dawn has not taken shape" (*'alam*) has achieved little. Respect for collective rhythms implies respect for *the* rhythm that is appropriate to each action—neither excessive haste nor sluggishness. It is simply a question of being in the proper place at the proper time. A man must walk with a "measured pace" (*ikthal uqudmis*), neither lagging behind nor running like a "dancer," a shallow, frivolous way to behave, unworthy of a man of honor. So there is mockery, too, for the man who hurries without thinking, who runs to catch up with someone else, who works so hastily that he is likely to "maltreat the earth," forgetting the teachings of wisdom:

> It is useless to pursue the world,
> No one will ever overtake it.
>
> You who rush along,
> Stay and be rebuked;
> Daily bread comes from God,
> It is not for you to concern yourself.

The overeager peasant moves ahead of the collective rhythms which assign each act its particular moment in the space of the day, the year, or human life; his race with time threatens to drag the whole group into the escalation of diabolic ambition, *thahraymith*, and thus to turn circular time into linear time, simple reproduction into indefinite accumulation.[5]

The tasks of farming, *horia erga*, seasonal works, as the Greeks called them, are defined as much in their rhythm, which determines their duration, as in their moment. The sacred tasks, such as plowing and sowing, fall to those who are capable of treating the land with the respect it deserves, of approaching it (*qabel*) with the measured pace of man meeting a partner whom he wants to welcome and honor. This is underlined by the myth of the origin of wheat and barley. Adam was sowing wheat; Eve brought him some wheatcake. She saw him sowing grain by grain, "covering each seed with earth," and invoking God each time. She accused him of *wasting his time*. While her husband was busy eating, she started to broadcast the grain, without invoking the name of God. When the crop came up, Adam found his field full of strange ears, delicate and brittle, like woman. He called this plant (barley) *ech'ir*—"weak." One of the effects of the ritualization of practices is precisely that of assigning them a time—i.e., a moment, a tempo, and a duration—which is relatively independent of external necessities, those of climate, technique, or economy, thereby conferring on them the sort of arbitrary necessity which specifically defines cultural arbitrariness.

The reason why submission to the collective rhythms is so rigorously demanded is that the temporal forms or the spatial structures structure not only the group's representation of the world but the group itself, which orders itself in accordance with this representation: this may be clearly seen, for example, in the fact that the organization of the existence of the men and the women in accordance with different times and different places constitutes two interchangeable ways of securing separation and hierarchization of the male and female worlds, the women going to the fountain at an hour when the men are not in the streets, or by a special path, or both at once.[6] The social calendar tends to secure integration by compounding the *synchronization* of identical practices with the *orchestration* of different but structurally homologous practices (such as plowing and weaving).[7] All the divisions of the group are projected at every moment into the spatio-temporal organization which assigns each category its place and time: it is here that the fuzzy logic of practice works wonders in enabling the group to achieve as much *social and logical* integration as is compatible with the diversity imposed by the division of labor between the sexes, the ages, and the "occupations" (smith, butcher).[8] Synchronization, in the case of rites or tasks, is that much more associated with spatial grouping the more there is collectively at stake: rites thus range in importance from the great solemn rites (e.g., *awdjeb*) enacted by everyone at the same time, through the rites performed at the same time but by each family separately (the sacrifice of a sheep at the Aid), through those which may be practiced at any time (e.g., the rite to cure sties), and finally to those which must only take place in secret and at unusual hours (the rites of love magic).

Practical taxonomies, which are a transformed, misrecognizable form of the real divisions of the social order, contribute to the reproduction of that order by producing objectively orchestrated practices adjusted to those divisions. Social time as *form*, in the musical sense, as succession organized by the application to passing time of the principle which organizes all dimensions of practice, tends to fulfill, even more effectively than the division of space, a function of integration in and through division, i.e., through hierarchization. But more profoundly, the organization of time and the group in accordance with mythical structures leads collective practice to appear as "realized myth," in the sense in which for Hegel tradition is "realized morality" (*Sittlichkeit*), the reconciliation of subjective demand and objective (i.e., collective) necessity which grounds the *belief* of a whole group in what the group believes, i.e., in the group: a reflexive return to the principles of the operations of objectification, practices or discourses, is prevented by the very reinforcement which these productions continuously draw from a world of objectifications produced in accordance with the same subjective principles.

Every established order tends to produce (to very different degrees and with very different means) the naturalization of its own arbitrariness. Of all the mechanisms tending to produce this effect, the most important and the best concealed is undoubtedly the dialectic of the objective chances and the agents' aspirations, out of which arises the *sense of limits*, commonly called the *sense of reality*, i.e., the correspondence between the objective classes and the internalized classes, social structures, and mental structures, which is the basis of the most ineradicable adherence to the established order. Systems of classification which reproduce, in their own specific logic, the objective classes, i.e., the divisions by sex, age, or position in the relations of production, make their specific contribution to the reproduction of the power relations of which they are the product, by securing the misrecognition, and hence the recognition, of the arbitrariness on which they are based: in the extreme case, that is to say, when there is a quasi-perfect correspondence between the objective order and the subjective principles of organization (as in ancient societies) the natural and social world appears as self-evident. This experience we shall call *doxa*, so as to distinguish it from an orthodox or heterodox belief implying awareness and recognition of the possibility of different or antagonistic beliefs. Schemes of thought and perception can produce the objectivity that they do produce only by producing misrecognition of the limits of the cognition that they make possible, thereby founding immediate adherence, in the doxic mode, to the world of tradition experienced as a "natural world" and taken for granted. The instruments of knowledge of the social world are in this case (objectively) political instruments which contribute to the reproduction of the social world by producing immediate adherence to the world, seen as self-evident and undisputed, of which they are the product and of which they reproduce the structures in a transformed form. The political function of classifications is never more likely to pass unnoticed than in the case of relatively undifferentiated social formations, in which the prevailing classificatory system encounters no rival or antagonistic principle. . . . [I]n the case of the domestic conflicts to which marriages often give rise, social categories disadvantaged by the symbolic order, such as women and the young, cannot but recognize the legitimacy of the dominant classification in the very fact that their only chance of neutralizing those of its effects most contrary to their own interests lies in submitting to them in order to make use of them (in accordance with the logic of the *éminence grise*).

The taxonomies of the mythico-ritual system at once divide and unify, legitimating unity in division, that is to say, hierarchy.[9] There is no need to insist on the function of legitimation of the division of labor and power between the sexes that is fulfilled by a mythico-ritual system entirely dominated by male values. It is perhaps less obvious that the social structuring of temporality which organizes representations and practices, most solemnly reaffirmed in the rites of passage, fulfills a political function by symbolically manipulating *age limits*, i.e., the boundaries which define age-groups, but also the limitations imposed at different ages. The mythico-ritual categories cut up the age continuum into discontinuous segments, constituted not biologically (like the physical signs of aging) but socially, and marked by the symbolism of cosmetics and clothing, decorations, ornaments, and emblems, the tokens which express and underline the representations of the uses of the body that are legitimately associated with each socially defined age, and also those which are ruled out because they would have the effect of disrupting the system of oppositions between the generations (such as rejuvenation rites, which are the exact inversion of the rites of passage). Social representations of the different ages of life, and of the properties attached by definition to them, express, in their own logic, the power relations between the age-classes, helping to reproduce at once the union and the division of those classes by means of temporal divisions tending to produce both continuity and rupture. They thereby rank among the institutionalized instruments for maintenance of the symbolic order, and hence among the mechanisms of the reproduction of the social order whose very functioning serves the interests of those occupying a dominant position in the social structure, the men of mature age.[10]

We see yet again how erroneous it would be to consider only the cognitive or, as Durkheim put it, "speculative," functions of mythico-ritual representations: these mental structures, a transfigured reproduction of the structures constituting a mode of production and a mode of biological and social reproduction, contribute at least as efficaciously as the provisions of custom toward defining and maintaining the delimitation of powers between the sexes and generations, through the ethical dispositions they produce, such as the sense of honor or respect for elders and ancestors. The theory of knowledge is a dimension of political theory because the specifically symbolic power to impose the principles of the construction of reality—in particular, social reality—is a major dimension of political power.

In a determinate social formation, the stabler the objective structures and the more fully they reproduce themselves in the agents' dispositions, the greater the extent of the field of doxa, of that which is taken for granted. When, owing to the quasi-perfect fit between the objective structures and the internalized structures which results from the logic of simple reproduction, the established cosmological and political order is perceived not as arbitrary, i.e., as one possible order among others, but as a self-evident and natural order which goes without saying and therefore goes unquestioned, the agents' aspirations have the same limits as the objective conditions of which they are the product.

It is not easy to evoke the subjective experience associated with this world of the realized ought-to-be, in which things that could scarcely be otherwise nonetheless are what they are only because they are what they ought to be, in which an agent can have at one and the same time the feeling that there is nothing to do except what he is doing and also that he is only doing what he ought.[11] And so it is in all seriousness that I juxtapose two particularly striking evocations of this experience, one by an old Kabyle woman, underlining the fact that to be ill and dying was a social status, with its attendant rights and duties, and the other by Marcel Proust, describing the subjective effects of the ritualization of practices:

> In the old days, folk didn't know what illness was. They went to bed and they died. It's only nowadays that we're learning words like liver, lung [*albumun*; Fr. *le poumon*], intestines, stomach [*listuma*, Fr. *l'estomac*], and I don't know what! People only used to know [pain in] the belly [*th'abut*]; that's what every-

one who died died of, unless it was fever [*thawla*]. . . . In the old days sick people used to call for death, but it wouldn't come. When someone was ill, the news soon spread everywhere, not just in the village, but all over the *'arch.* Besides, a sick man's house is never empty: in the daytime all his relatives, men and women, come for news. . . . At nightfall, all the women relatives, even the youngest, would be taken to his bedside. And once a week there was "the sick man's market" [*suq umutin*]: they would send someone to buy him meat or fruit. All that's forgotten nowadays; it's true, there aren't any sick people now, not as there used to be. Now everyone's sick, everyone's complaining of something. Those who were dying used to suffer a lot; death came slowly, it could take a night and a day or two nights and a day. Death "always struck them through their speech": first they became dumb. Everyone had time to see them one last time; the relatives were given time to assemble and to prepare the burial. They would give alms to make the dying easier: they would give the community a tree, generally a fig-tree planted beside the road. Its fruit would not be picked, but left for passing travellers and the poor [*chajra usufagh*, the tree of the outgoing; *chajra n'esadhaqa*, the alms tree]. . . . Who's ill nowadays? Who's well? Everyone complains but no one stays in bed; they all run to the doctor. Everyone knows what's wrong with him now.[12]

From the position of the bed, my side recalled the place where the crucifix used to be, the breadth of the recess in the bedroom in my grandparents' house, in the days when there were still bedrooms and parents, a time for each thing, when you loved your parents not because you found them intelligent but because they were your parents, when you went to bed not because you wanted to but because it was time, and when you marked the desire, the acceptance and the whole ceremony of sleeping by going up two steps to the big bed, where you closed the blue rep curtains with their raised-velvet bands, and where, when you were ill, the old remedies kept you for several days on end, with a nightlight on the Siena marble mantlepiece, without any of the immoral medicines that allow you to get up and imagine you can lead the life of a healthy man when you are ill, sweating under the blankets thanks to perfectly harmless infusions, which for two thousand years have contained the flowers of the meadows and the wisdom of old women.[13]

Moreover, when the conditions of existence of which the members of a group are the product are very little differentiated, the dispositions which each of them exercised in his practice are confirmed and hence reinforced both by the practice of the other members of the group (one function of symbolic exchanges such as feasts and ceremonies being to favor the circular reinforcement which is the foundation of *collective belief*) and also by institutions which constitute collective thought as much as they express it, such as language, myth, and art. The self-evidence of the world is reduplicated by the instituted discourses about the world in which the whole group's adherence to that self-evidence is affirmed. The specific potency of the explicit statement that brings subjective experiences into the reassuring unanimity of a socially approved collectively attested sense imposes itself with the *authority* and *necessity* of a collective position adopted on data intrinsically amenable to many other structurations.

"Nature" as science understands it—a cultural fact which is the historical product of a long labor of "disenchantment" (*Entzauberung*)—is never encountered in such a universe. Between the child and the world the whole group intervenes, not just with the warnings that inculcate a fear of supernatural dangers,[14] but with a whole universe of ritual practices and also of discourses, sayings, proverbs, all structured in concordance with the principles of the corresponding habitus. Furthermore, through the acts and symbols that are intended to contribute to the reproduction of nature and of the group by the analogical reproduction of natural processes, mimetic representation helps to produce in the agents temporary reactions (such as, for example, the collective excitement associated with *lakhrif*) or even *lasting dispositions* (such as the generative schemes incorporated in the body schema) attuned to the objective processes expected from the ritual action—helps, in other words, to make the world conform to the myth.

Because the subjective necessity and self-evidence of the commonsense world are validated by the objective consensus on the sense of the world, what is essential *goes without saying because it comes without saying*: the tradition is silent, not least about itself as a tradition; customary law is content to enumerate specific applications of principles which remain implicit and unformulated, because unquestioned; the play of the mythico-ritual homologies constitutes a perfectly closed world, each aspect of which is, as it were, a reflection of all others, a world which has no place for *opinion* as liberal ideology understands it, i.e., as one of the different and equally legitimate answers which can be given to an explicit question about the established political order; and nothing is further from the correlative notion of the *majority* than the *unanimity* of doxa, the aggregate of the "choices" whose subject is everyone and no one because the questions they answer cannot be explicitly asked. The adherence expressed in the doxic relation to the social world is the absolute form of recognition of legitimacy through misrecognition of arbitrariness, since it is unaware of the very question of legitimacy, which arises from competition for legitimacy, and hence from conflict between groups claiming to possess it.

The truth of a doxa is only ever fully revealed when negatively constituted by the constitution of a *field of opinion*, the locus of the confrontation of competing discourses—whose political truth may be overtly declared or may remain hidden, even from the eyes of those engaged in it, under the guise of religious or philosophical oppositions. It is by reference to the universe of opinion that the complementary class is defined, the class of that which is taken for granted, doxa, the sum total of the theses tacitly posited on the hither side of all inquiry, which appear as such only retrospectively, when they come to be suspended practically. The practical questioning of the theses implied in a particular way of living that is brought about by "culture contact" or by the political and economic crises correlative with class division is

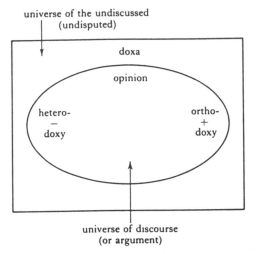

not the purely intellectual operation which phenomenology designates by the term *epoche*, the deliberate, methodical suspension of naive adherence to the world.[15] The critique which brings the undiscussed into discussion, the unformulated into formulation, has as the condition of its possibility objective crisis, which, in breaking the immediate fit between the subjective structures and the objective structures, destroys self-evidence practically. It is when the social world loses its character as a natural phenomenon that the question of the natural or conventional character (*phusei* or *nomo*) of social facts can be raised.[16] It follows that the would-be most radical critique always has the limits that are assigned to it by the objective conditions. Crisis is a necessary condition for a questioning of doxa but is not in itself a sufficient condition for the production of a critical discourse. In class societies, in which the definition of the social world is at stake in overt or latent class struggle, the drawing of the line between the field of opinion, of that which is explicitly questioned, and the field of *doxa*, of that which is beyond question and which each agent tacitly accords by the mere fact of acting in accord with social convention, is itself a fundamental objective at stake in that form of class struggle which is the struggle for the imposition of the dominant systems of classification. The dominated classes have an interest in pushing back the limits of *doxa* and exposing the arbitrariness of the taken for granted; the dominant classes have an interest in defending the integrity of doxa or, short of this, of establishing in its place the necessarily imperfect substitute, *orthodoxy*.

It is only when the dominated have the material and symbolic means of rejecting the definition of the real that is imposed on them through logical structures reproducing the social structures (i.e., the state of the power relations) and to lift the (institutionalized or internalized) censorships which it implies, i.e., when social classifications become the object and instrument of class struggle, that the arbitrary principles of the prevailing classification can appear as such and it therefore becomes necessary to undertake the work of conscious systematization and express rationalization which marks the passage from doxa to orthodoxy.

Orthodoxy, straight, or rather *straightened*, opinion, which aims, without ever entirely succeeding, at restoring the primal state of innocence of doxa, exists only in the objective relationship which opposes it to heterodoxy, that is, by reference to the choice—*hairesis*, heresy—made possible by the existence of *competing possibles* and to the explicit critique of the sum total of the alternatives not chosen that the established order implies. It is defined as a system of euphemisms, of acceptable ways of thinking and speaking the natural and social world, which rejects heretical remarks as blasphemies.[17] But the manifest censorship imposed by orthodox discourse, the official way of speaking and thinking the world, conceals another, more radical censorship: the overt opposition between "right" opinion and "left" or "wrong" opinion, which delimits *the universe of possible discourse*, be it legitimate or illegitimate, euphemistic or blasphemous, masks in its turn the fundamental opposition between the universe of things that can be stated, and hence thought, and the universe of that which is taken for granted. The universe of discourse, in the classic definition given by A. de Morgan in his *Formal Logic*, "a range of ideas which is either expressed or understood as containing the whole matter under discussion,"[18] is practically defined in relation to the necessarily unnoticed complementary class that is constituted by the universe of that which is undiscussed, unnamed, admitted without argument or scrutiny. Thus in class societies, everything takes place as if the struggle for the power to impose the legitimate mode of thought and expression that is unceasingly waged in the field of the production of symbolic goods tended to conceal, not least from the eyes of those involved in it, the contribution it makes to the delimitation of the universe of discourse, that is to say, the universe of the thinkable, and hence to the delimitation of the universe of the unthinkable; as if euphemism and blasphemy, through which the expressly censored unnameable nonetheless finds its way into the universe of discourse, conspired in their very antagonism to occult the "aphasia" of those who are denied access to the instruments of the struggle for the definition of reality. If one accepts the equation made by Marx in *The German Ideology*, that "language is real, practical consciousness," it can be seen that the boundary between the universe of (orthodox or heterodox) discourse and the universe of doxa, in the twofold sense of what goes without saying and what cannot be said for lack of an available discourse, represents the dividing-line between the most radical form of misrecognition and the awakening of political consciousness.

The relationship between language and experience never appears more clearly than in crisis situations in which the everyday order (*Alltäglichkeit*) is challenged, and with it the language of order, situations which call for an extraordinary discourse (the *Ausseralltäglichkeit* which Weber presents as the decisive characteristic of charisma) capable of giving systematic expression to the gamut of extraordinary experiences that this, so to speak, objective *epoche* has provoked or made possible. "Private" experiences undergo nothing less than a change of state when they recognize themselves in the *public objectivity* of an already constituted discourse, the objective sign of recognition of their right to be spoken and to be spoken publicly: "Words wreak havoc," says Sartre, "when they find a name for what had up to then been lived namelessly."[19] Because any language that can command attention is an "authorized language," invested with the authority of a group, the things it designates are not simply expressed but also authorized and legitimated. This is true not only of establishment language but also of the heretical discourses which draw their legitimacy and authority from the very groups over which they exert their power and which they literally produce by expressing them: they derive their power from their capacity to *objectify* unformulated experiences, to make them public—a step on the road to officialization and legitimation—and, when the occasion arises, to manifest and reinforce their concordance. Heretical power, the strength of the sorcerer who wields a liberating potency—that of all logotherapies—in offering the means of expressing experiences usually repressed, the strength of the prophet or political leader who mobilizes the group by announcing to them what they want to hear, rests on the dialectical relationship between authorized, authorizing language and the group which authorizes it and acts on its authority.

SYMBOLIC CAPITAL

The theoretical construction which retrospectively projects the counter-gift into the project of the gift has the effect of transforming into mechanical sequences of obligatory acts the at once risky and necessary improvisation of the everyday strategies which owe their infinite complexity to the fact that the giver's undeclared calculation must reckon with the receiver's undeclared calculation, and hence satisfy his expectations without appearing to know what they are. In the same operation, it removes the conditions making possible the *institutionally organized and guaranteed misrecognition*[20] which is the basis of gift exchange and, perhaps, of all the symbolic labor intended to transmute, by the sincere fiction of a disinterested exchange, the inevitable, and inevitably interested, relations imposed by kinship, neighborhood, or work into elective relations of reciprocity: in the work of reproducing established relations—through feasts, ceremonies, exchanges of gifts, visits or courtesies, and above all, marriages—which is no less vital to the existence of the group than the reproduction of the economic bases of its existence, the labor required to conceal the function of the exchanges is as important an element as the labor needed to carry out the function.[21] If it is true that the lapse of time interposed is what enables the gift or the counter-gift to be seen and experienced as an inaugural act of generosity, without any past or future, i.e., without *calculation*, then it is clear that in reducing the polythetic to the monothetic, objectivism destroys the specificity of all practices which, like gift exchange, tend or pretend to put the law of self-interest into abeyance. A rational contract would telescope into an instant a transaction which gift exchange disguises by stretching it out in time; and because of this, gift exchange is, if not the only mode of commodity circulation practiced, at least the only mode to be fully recognized, in societies which, because they deny "the true soil of their life," as Lukács puts it, have an economy in itself and not for itself. Everything takes place as if the essence of the "archaic" economy lay in the fact that economic activity cannot explicitly acknowledge the economic ends in relation to which it is objectively oriented: the "idolatry of nature" which makes it impossible to think of nature as a raw material, or consequently, to see human activity as *labor*, i.e., as man's struggle against nature, tends, together with the systematic emphasis on the symbolic aspect of the activities and relations of production, to prevent the economy from being grasped *as* an economy, i.e., as a system governed by the laws of interested calculation, competition, or exploitation.

In reducing the economy to its objective reality, economism annihilates the specificity located precisely in the socially maintained discrepancy between the misrecognized or, as one might say, socially repressed objective truth of economic activity, and the social representation of production and exchange. It is no accident that the vocabulary of the archaic economy should be entirely composed of double-sided notions that are condemned to disintegrate in the course of the history of the economy, since, owing to their duality, the social relations they designate represent unstable structures which are condemned to split in two as soon as there is any weakening of the social mechanisms aimed at maintaining them. Thus, to take an extreme example, *rahnia*, a contract by which the borrower grants the lender the usufruct of some of his land for the duration of the loan, and which is regarded as the worst form of usury when it leads to dispossession, differs only in the nature of the social relation between the two parties, and thus in the detailed terms of the agreement, from the aid granted to a relative in difficulties so as to save him from having to sell a piece of land, which, even when it continues to be used by its owner, constitutes a sort of security on the loan.[22] "It was precisely the Romans and Greeks," writes Mauss, "who, possibly following the Northern and Western Semites, drew the distinction between personal rights and real rights, separated purchases from gifts and exchanges, dissociated moral obligations from contracts, and, above, all, conceived of the difference between ritual, rights and interests. By a genuine, great, and venerable revolution they passed beyond the excessively hazardous, costly and elaborate gift economy, which was encumbered with personal considerations, incompatible with the development of the market, trade and production, and, in a word, uneconomic."[23] The historical situations in which the unstable, artificially maintained structures of the good-faith economy break up and make way for the *clear, economic* (i.e., *economical*) concepts of the undisguised self-interest economy reveal the cost of operating an economy which, by its refusal to acknowledge and confess itself as such, is forced to devote as much time to concealing the reality of economic acts as it expends in carrying them out: the generalization of monetary exchange, which exposes the objective workings of the economy, also brings to light the institutional mechanisms, proper to the archaic economy, which have the function of limiting and disguising the play of economic interest and calculation (economic in the narrow sense of the word). For example, a well-known mason, who had learned his trade in France, caused a scandal, around 1955, by going home when his work was finished without eating the meal traditionally given in the mason's honor when a house is built, and then demanding, in addition to the price of his day's work (one thousand old francs), an allowance of two hundred francs in lieu of the meal: his demand for the cash equivalent of the meal was a sacrilegious reversal of the formula used by symbolic alchemy to transmute the price of labor into an unsolicited gift, and it thus exposed the device most commonly employed to keep up appearances by means of a collectively concerted make-believe. As an act of exchange setting the seal on the alliances ("I set the wheatcake and the salt between us"), the final meal at the time of the *thiwizi* of harvest or house-building naturally became a *closing rite* intended to transmute an interested transaction retrospectively into a generous exchange (like the gifts which mark the successful conclusion of a deal).[24] Whereas the greatest indulgence was accorded to the subterfuges used by some to minimize the cost of the meals at the end of the *thiwizi* (e.g., inviting only the "notables" of each group, or one man from each family)—a departure from principles which at least paid lip service to their legitimacy—the reaction could only be scandal and shock when a man took it upon himself to declare that the meal had a cash equivalent, thus betraying the best-kept and worst-kept secret (one that everyone must keep), and breaking the law of silence which guarantees the complicity of collective bad faith in the good-faith economy.

The *good-faith economy* calls forth the strange incarnation of *homo economicus* known as the *bu niya* (or *bab niya*), the man of good faith (*niya* or *thi'ugganth*, from *a'ggun*, the child still unable to speak, contrasted with *thahraymith*, calculating, technical intelligence). The man of good faith would not think of selling certain fresh food products—milk, butter, cheese, vegetables, fruit—to another peasant, but always distributes them among friends or neighbors. He practices no exchanges involving money and all his relations are based on total confidence; unlike the shady dealer, he has recourse to none of the guarantees (witnesses, written documents, etc.) with which commercial transactions are surrounded. The general law of exchanges means that the closer the individuals or groups are in the genealogy, the easier it is to make agreements, the more frequent they are, and the more completely they are entrusted to good faith. Conversely, as the relationship becomes more impersonal, i.e., as one moves out from the relationship between brothers to that between virtual strangers (people from two different villages) or even complete strangers, . . . a transaction is less likely to occur at all, but it can become and increasingly does become purely "economic" in character, i.e., closer to its economic reality, and the interested calculation which is never absent even from the most generous exchange (in which both parties account—i.e., count—themselves satisfied) can be more and more openly revealed. This explains why recourse to formal guarantees becomes more and more exceptional as the social distance between the parties decreases, and also as the solemnity of the guarantees increases, because the authorities responsible for authenticating and enforcing them are more remote and/or more venerated. (First there is the word of witnesses, which is enhanced if they are distant and influential; then there is a simple paper drawn up by someone not specialized in the production of legal documents; then the contract signed before a taleb, providing a religious but not a legal guarantee, which is less solemn when drawn up by the village taleb than by a well-known taleb; then the Cadi's written document; and finally the contract signed in front of a lawyer.) It would be insulting to presume to authenticate a transaction based on trust between trustworthy people, and still more so between relatives, before a lawyer, a cadi, or even witnesses. Similarly, the share of the loss which partners agree to accept when there is an accident to an animal may be entirely different depending on the assessment of their responsiblities which they come to in accordance with the relationship between them: a man who has lent an animal to a close relative feels he must minimize his partner's responsibility. By contrast, a regular contract, signed before the Cadi or before witnesses, governed the arrangement by which the Kabyles handed over their oxen to the southern Nomads to be looked after for one, two, or three working years (from autumn to autumn) in exchange for twenty-two double decaliters of barley per ox per year, with costs to be shared in the case of loss and profits shared in the case of sale. Private arrangements between kin and affines are to market transactions what ritual war is to total war. The "goods or beasts of the fellah" are traditionally contrasted with the "goods or beasts of the market": old informants will talk endlessly of the tricks and frauds which are common practice in the "big markets," that is to say, in the exchanges between strangers. There are countless tales of mules which run off as soon as the purchaser has got them home, oxen made to look fatter by rubbing them with a plant which makes them swell (*adhris*), and purchasers who band together to force prices down. The incarnation of economic war is the shady dealer, the man who fears neither God nor man. Men avoid buying animals from him, just as they avoid buying from any complete stranger: as one informant said, for straightforward goods such as land, it is the choice of the thing to be purchased which determines the buyer's decision; for problematic goods, such as beasts of burden, especially mules, it is the choice of seller which decides, and at least an effort is made to substitute a personalized relationship ("on behalf of . . .") for a completely impersonal, anonymous one. Every intermediate stage can be found, from transactions based on complete distrust, such as that between the peasant and the shady dealer, who cannot demand or obtain guarantees because he cannot guarantee the quality of his product or find guarantors, to the exchange of honor which can dispense with conditions and depend entirely on the good faith of the "contracting parties." But in most transactions the notions of buyer and seller tend to be dissolved in the network of middlemen and guarantors designed to transform the purely economic relationship between supply and demand into a genealogically based and genealogically guaranteed relationship. Marriage itself is no exception: quite apart from parallel-cousin marriage, it almost always occurs between families already linked by a whole network of previous exchanges, underwriting the specific new agreement. It is significant that in the first phase of the highly complex negotiations leading up to the marriage agreement, the families bring in prestigious kinsmen or affines as "guarantors," the symbolic capital thus displayed serving both to strengthen their hand in the negotiations and to guarantee the deal once it has been concluded.

Similarly, the indignant comments provoked by the heretical behavior of peasants who have departed from traditional ways draw attention to the mechanisms which formerly inclined the peasant to maintain a magical relationship with the land and made it impossible for him to see his toil as labor: "It's sacrilege, they have profaned the land; they have done away with fear [*elhiba*]. Nothing intimidates them or stops them; they turn everything upside down, I'm sure they'll end up plowing in *lakhrif* if they are in a hurry and if they mean to spend *lahal* [the licit period for plowing] doing something else, or in *rbi'* [spring] if they've been too lazy in *lahal*. It's all the same to them." Everything in the peasant's practice actualizes, in a different mode, the objective intention revealed by ritual. The land is never treated as a raw material to be exploited, but always as the object of respect mixed with fear (*elhiba*): it will "settle its scores," they say, and take revenge for the bad treatment it receives from a clumsy or over-hasty farmer. The accomplished peasant "presents himself" to his land with the stance appropriate when one man meets another (i.e., face to face), and with the attitude of trusting familiarity he would show a respected kinsman. During the plowing, he would not think of delegating the task of leading the team and the only task he leaves for his "clients" (*ichikran*) is that of breaking up the soil behind the plow. "The old men used to say that to plow properly, you had to be the master of the land. The young men were left out of it: it would have been an insult to the land to 'present' it [*qabel*] with men one would not dare to present to other men." "It is the man who confronts [receives] other men," says a proverb, "who must confront the land." To take up Hesiod's opposition between *ponos* and *ergon*, the peasant does not work; he takes *pains*. "Give to the earth and the earth will give to you," says a proverb. This can be taken to mean that in obedience to the logic of gift exchange, nature bestows its bounty only on those who bring it their care as a tribute. And the heretical behavior of those who leave to the young the task of "opening the earth and plowing into it the wealth of the new year" provokes the older peasants to express the principle of the relationship between men and the land, which could remain unformulated as long as it was taken for granted: "The earth no longer gives because we give it nothing. We openly mock the earth and it is only right that it should pay us back with lies." The self-respecting man should always be busy doing something; if he cannot find anything to do, "at least he can carve his spoon." Activity is as much a duty of communal life as an economic necessity. What is valued is activity for its own sake, regardless of its strictly economic function, inasmuch as it is regarded as appropriate to the function of the person doing it.[25] Only the application of categories alien to the peasant experience (those imposed by economic domination and the generalization of monetary exchanges) brings up the distinction between the technical aspect and the ritual or symbolic aspect of agricultural activity. The distinction between productive and unproductive work or between profitable and unprofitable work is unknown: the ancient economy knows only the opposition between the idler who fails in his social duty and the worker who performs his socially defined proper function, whatever the product of his effort.

Everything conspires to conceal the relationship between work and its product. Thus the distinction which Marx makes between the *working period* proper—the time devoted to plowing and harvest—and the *production period*—the nine months or so between sowing and harvesting, during which time there is hardly any productive work to be done—is disguised in practice by the apparent continuity conferred on agricultural activity by the countless minor tasks intended to assist nature in its labor. No one would have thought of assessing the technical efficiency or economic usefulness of these indissolubly technical *and* ritual acts, the peasant's version, as it were, of art for art's sake, such as fencing the fields, pruning the trees, protecting the new shoots from the animals, or "visiting" (*asafqadh*) and looking after the fields, not to mention practices generally regarded as rites, such as actions intended to expel or transfer evil (*asifedh*) or celebrate the coming of spring. Similarly, no one would dream of trying to evaluate the profitability of all the activities which the application of alien categories would lead one to regard as unproductive, such as the functions carried out by the head of the family as leader and representative of the group—coordinating the work, speaking in the men's assembly, bargaining in the market, and reading in the mosque. "If the peasant counted," runs a proverb, "he would not sow." Perhaps we should say that the relationship between work and its product is in reality not unknown, but *socially repressed*; that the productivity of labor is so low that the peasant must refrain from counting his time, in order to preserve the meaningfulness of his work; or—and this is only an apparent contradiction—that in a world in which time is so plentiful and goods are so scarce, his best and indeed only course is to spend his time without counting it, to squander the one thing which exists in abundance.[26]

In short, the reality of production is no less repressed than the reality of circulation, and the peasant's "pains" are to *labor* what the gift is to commerce (an activity for which, as Emile Benveniste points out, the Indo-European languages had no name). The discovery of labor presupposes the constitution of the common ground of production, i.e., the disenchantment of a natural world henceforward reduced to its economic dimension alone; ceasing to be the tribute paid to a necessary order, activity can be directed toward an exclusively economic end, the end which money, henceforward the measure of all things, starkly designates. This means the end of the primal undifferentiatedness which made possible the play of individual and collective misrecognition: measured by the yardstick of monetary profit, the most sacred activities find themselves constituted negatively, as *symbolic*, i.e., in a sense the word sometimes receives, as lacking contrete or material effect, in short, *gratuitous*, i.e., disinterested but also useless.

Those who apply the categories and methods of economics to archaic economies without taking into account the ontological transmutation they impose on their object are certainly not alone nowadays in treating this type of economy "as the Fathers of the church treated the religions which preceded Christianity": Marx's phrase could also be applied to those Marxists who tended to limit research on the formations they call "pre-capitalist" to scholastic discussion about the typology of modes of production. The common root of this ethnocentrism is the unconscious acceptance of a *restricted definition* of economic interest, which, in its explicit form, is the historical product of capitalism: the constitution of relatively autonomous areas of practice is accompanied by a process through which symbolic interests (often described as "spiritual" or "cultural") come to be set up in opposition to strictly economic interests as defined in the field of economic transactions by the fundamental tautology "business is business"; strictly "cultural" or "aesthetic" interest, disinterested interest, is the paradoxical product of the ideological labor in which writers and artists, those most directly interested, become autonomous by being opposed to material interests, i.e., by being symbolically nullified as interests. Economism knows no other interest than that which capitalism has produced, through a sort of concrete application of abstraction, by establishing a universe of relations between man and man based, as Marx says, on "callous cash payment." Thus it can find no place in its analyses, still less in its calculations, for the strictly symbolic interest which is occasionally recognized (when too obviously entering into conflict with "interest" in the narrow sense, as in certain forms of nationalism or regionalism) only to be reduced to the irrationality of feeling or passion. In fact, in a universe characterized by the more or less perfect interconvertibility of economic capital (in the narrow sense) and symbolic capital, the *economic calculation* directing the agents' strategies takes indissociably into account profits and losses which the narrow definition of economy unconsiously rejects as *unthinkable* and *unnameable*, i.e., as economically irrational. In short, contrary to naively idyllic representations of "pre-capitalist" societies (or of the "cultural" sphere of capitalist societies), practice never ceases to conform to economic calculation even when it gives every appearance of disinterestedness by departing from the logic of interested calculation (in the narrow sense) and playing for stakes that are non-material and not easily quantified.

Thus the theory of strictly economic practice is simply a particular case of a general theory of the economics of practice. The only way to escape from the ethnocentric naiveties of economism, without falling into populist exaltation of the generous naivety of earlier forms of society, is to carry out in full what economism does only partially, and to extend economic calculation to *all* the goods, material and symbolic, without distinction, that present themselves as *rare* and worthy of being sought after in a particular social formulation—which may be "fair words" or smiles, handshakes or shrugs, compliments or attention, challenges or insults, honor or honors, powers or pleasures, gossip or scientific information, distinction or distinctions, etc. Economic calculation has hitherto managed to appropriate the territory objectively surrendered to the remorseless logic of what Marx calls "naked self-interest" only by setting aside a "sacred" island miraculously spared by the "icy water of egotistical calculation" and left as a sanctuary for the priceless or worthless things it cannot assess. But an accountancy of symbolic exchanges would itself lead to a distorted representation of the archaic economy if it were forgotten that, as the product of a principle of differentiation alien to the universe to which it is applied—the distinction between economic and symbolic capital—the only way in which such accountancy can apprehend the undifferentiatedness of economic and symbolic capital is in the form of their perfect interconvertibility. If the constitution of art *qua* art, accompanying the development of a relatively autonomous artistic field, leads one to conceive of certain primitive or popular practices as aesthetic, one inevitably falls into the ethnocentric errors unavoidable when one forgets that those practices cannot be conceived as such from within; similarly, any partial or total objectification of the ancient economy that does not include a theory of the *theorization effect* and of the social conditions of objective apprehension, together with a theory of that economy's relation to its objective reality (a relation of misrecognition), succumbs to the subtlest and most irreproachable form of ethnocentrism.

In its full definition, the patrimony of a family or lineage includes not only their land and instruments of production but also their kin and their clientele, *nesba*, the network of alliances, or, more broadly, of relationships, to be kept up and regularly maintained, representing a heritage of commitments and debts of honor, a capital of rights and duties built up in the course of successive generations and providing an additional source of strength which can be called upon when extraordinary situations break in upon the daily routine. For all its power to regulate the routine of the ordinary course of events through ritual stereotyping, and to overcome crises by producing them symbolically or ritualizing them as soon as they appear, the archaic economy is nonetheless familiar with the opposition between ordinary and extraordinary occasions, between the regular needs which the household can satisfy and the exceptional needs for material and symbolic goods and services (in unusual circumstances of economic crisis, political conflict, or simply urgent farm work) requiring the unpaid assistance of a more extended group. If this is so, it is because, contrary to what Max Weber suggests when he draws a crude contrast between the traditionalist type and the charismatic type, the ancient economy has its discontinuities, not only in the political sphere, with conflicts which may start with a chance incident and escalate into tribal war through the interplay of the "leagues," but also in the economic sphere, with the opposition between the *labor period*, which in traditional cereal cultivation is particularly short, and the *production period*—an opposition giving rise to one of the basic contradictions of that social formation and also, in consequence, to the strategies designed to overcome it.[27] The strategy of accumulating a capital of honor and prestige, which produces the clients as much as they produce it, provides the optimal solution to the problem the group would face if it had to *maintain continuously* (throughout the production period as well) the whole (human and animal) workforce it needs during the labor period: it allows the great families to make use of the maximum workforce during the labor period, and to [reduce] consumption to a minimum during the unavoidably long production period. Both human and animal consumption are cut, the former by the reduction of the group to the minimal unit, the family; and the latter through hire contracts, such as the *charka* of an ox, by which the owner lends his animal in exchange for nothing more than compensation in cash or in kind for "depreciation of the capital." These services, provided at precise moments and limited [to] periods of intense activity, such as harvest time, are repaid either in the form of labor, at other times of the year, or with other services such as protection, the loan of animals, etc.

Thus we see that symbolic capital, which in the form of the prestige and renown attached to a family and a name is readily convertible back into economic capital, is perhaps *the most valuable form of accumulation* in a society in which the severity of the climate (the major work—plowing and harvesting—having to be done in a very short space of time) and the limited technical resources (harvesting is done with the sickle) demand collective labor. Should one see in it a disguised form of purchase of labor power, or a covert exaction of corvées? By all means, as long as the analysis holds together what holds together in practice, the *double reality* of intrinsically *equivocal*, *ambiguous* conduct. This is the pitfall awaiting all those whom a naively dualistic representation of the relationship between practice and ideology, between the "native" economy and the "native" representation of that economy, leads into self-mystifying demystifications:[28] the complete reality of this appropriation of services lies in the fact that it *can only* take place in the disguise of the *thiwizi*, the voluntary assistance which is also a corvée and is thus a voluntary corvée and forced assistance, and that, to use a geometrical metaphor, it implies a double half-rotation returning to the starting-point, i.e., a conversion of material capital into symbolic capital itself reconvertible into material capital.

The acquisition of a clientele, even an inherited one, implies considerable *labor* devoted to making and maintaining relations, and also substantial material and symbolic *investments*, in the form of political aid against attack, theft, offense, and insult, or economic aid, which can be very costly, especially in times of scarcity. As well as material wealth, *time* must be invested, for the value of symbolic labor cannot be defined without reference to the time devoted to it, *giving* or *squandering time* being one of the most precious of gifts.[29] It is clear that in such conditions symbolic capital can only be accumulated at the expense of the accumulation of economic capital. Combining with the objective obstacles stemming from the inefficiency of the means of production, the action of the social mechanisms inclining agents to repress or disguise economic interest and tending to make the accumulation of symbolic capital the only recognized, legitimate form of accumulation was sufficient to restrain and even prohibit the accumulation of material capital; and it was no doubt rare for the assembly to have to step in and order someone "not to get any richer."[30] It is a fact that collective pressure—with which the wealthy members of the group have to reckon, because they draw from it not only their authority but also, at times, political power, the strength of which ultimately reflects their capacity to mobilize the group for or against individuals or groups—requires the rich not only to pay the largest share of the cost of ceremonial exchanges (*tawsa*) but also to make the biggest contributions to the maintenance of the poor, the lodging of strangers, and the organization of festivals. Above all, wealth implies duties. "The generous man," it is said, "is the friend of God." Belief in immanent justice, which inspires a number of practices (such as collective oath-swearing), no doubt helps to make of generosity a sacrifice designed to win in return the blessing of prosperity: "Eat, you who are used to feeding others"; "Lord, give unto me that I may give." But the two forms of capital are so inextricably linked that the mere exhibition of the material and symbolic strength represented by prestigious affines is likely to be in itself a source of material profit in a good-faith economy in which good repute is the best, if not the only, economic guarantee: it is easy to see why the great families never miss a chance (and this is one reason for their predilection for distant marriages and vast processions) to organize exhibitions of symbolic capital (in which conspicuous consumption is only the most visible aspect), with processions of relatives and friends to solemnize the pilgrim's departure or return; the bride's escort, assessed in terms of the number of "rifles" and the intensity of the salutes fired in the couple's honor; prestigious gifts, including sheep, given on the occasion of the marriage; witnesses and guarantors who can be mobilized at any time and place, to attest the good faith of a market transaction or to strengthen the position of the lineage in matrimonial negotiation and to solemnize the contract. Once one realizes that symbolic capital is always *credit*, in the widest sense of the word, i.e., a sort of advance which the group alone can grant those who give it the best material and symbolic *guarantees*, it can be seen that the exhibition of symbolic capital (which is always very expensive in economic terms) is one of the mechanisms which (no doubt universally) make capital go to capital.

It is thus by drawing up a *comprehensive balance-sheet* of symbolic profits, without forgetting the undifferentiatedness of the symbolic and material

aspects of the patrimony, that it becomes possible to grasp the economic rationality of conduct which economism dismisses as absurd: the decision to
buy a second pair of oxen after the harvest, on the grounds that they are
needed for treading out the grain—which is a way of making it known the
crop has been plentiful—only to have to sell them again for lack of fodder,
before the autumn plowing, when they would be technically necessary, seems
economically aberrant only if one forgets all the material and symbolic profit
accruing from this (albeit fictitious) addition to the family's symbolic capital
in the late-summer period in which marriages are negotiated. The perfect rationality of this strategy of bluff lies in the fact that marriage is the occasion
for an (in the widest sense) economic circulation which cannot be seen purely
in terms of material goods; the profit a group can expect to draw from the
transaction rises with its material and especially its symbolic patrimony, in
other words, its standing in the eyes of other groups. This standing, which
depends on the capacity of the group's point of honor to guarantee the invul-
nerability of its honor, and constitutes an undivided whole indissolubly uniting the quantity and quality of its goods and the quantity and quality of the
men capable of turning them to good account, is what enables the group,
mainly through marriage, to acquire powerful affines (i.e., wealth in the form
of "rifles," measured not only by the number of men but also by their quality,
i.e., their point of honor), and defines the group's capacity to preserve its land
and honor, and in particular the honor of its women (i.e., the capital of material and symbolic strength which can actually be mobilized for market transactions, contests of honor, or work on the land). Thus the interest at stake in
the conduct of honor is one for which economism has no name, and which
has to be called symbolic, although it is such as to inspire actions which are
very directly material; just as there are professions, like law and medicine, in
which those who practice them must be "above suspicion," so a family has a
vital interest in keeping its capital of honor, i.e., its capital of honorability,
safe from suspicion. And the hypersensitivity to the slightest slur or innuendo
(*thasalqubth*), and the multiplicity of strategies designed to belie or avert
them, can be explained by the fact that symbolic capital is less easily measured and counted than livestock and that the group, ultimately the only
source of credit for it, will readily withdraw that credit and direct its suspi-
cions at the strongest members, as if in matters of honor, as in land, one
man's greater wealth made the others that much poorer.

We must analyze in terms of the same logic the mechanisms which sometimes endow a piece of land with a value not always corresponding to its
strictly technical and (in the narrow sense) economic qualities. Doubtless the
nearest fields, those best maintained and best farmed, and hence the most
"productive," those most accessible to the women (by private paths, *thikhu-
radjiyin*), are predisposed to be more highly valued by *any* purchaser; however, a piece of land will sometimes take on a symbolic value disproportion-
ate to its economic value, as a function of the socially accepted definition of
the symbolic patrimony. Thus the first plots to be relinquished will be the

land least integrated into the estate, least associated with the name of its present owners, the land which was bought (especially by a recent purchase) rather than inherited, the land bought from strangers rather than bought from kinsmen. When a field endowed with all the properties which define a strong integration into the patrimonial estate is owned by strangers, buying it back becomes a question of honor, analogous to avenging an insult, and it may rise to exorbitant prices. They are purely theoretical prices most of the time, since, within this logic, the symbolic profits of making the challenge are greater than the material profits that would accrue from cynical (hence reprehensible) exploiting of the situation. So, the point of honor the possessors set on keeping the land, especially if their appropriation is sufficiently recent to retain its value as a challenge to the alien group, is equal to the other side's determination to buy it back and to avenge the injury done to the *hurma* of their land. It may happen that a third group will step in with a higher bid, thereby challenging not the seller, who only profits from the competition, but the "legitimate" owners.[31]

Only an inconsistent—because reduced and reductive—materialism can fail to see that strategies whose object is to conserve or increase the honor of the group, in the forefront of which stand blood vengeance and marriage, are dictated by interests no less vital than are inheritance or fertility strategies.[32] The interest leading an agent to defend his symbolic capital is inseparable from the tacit adherence, inculcated in the earliest years of life and reinforced by all subsequent experience, to the axiomatics objectively inscribed in the regularities of the (in the broad sense) economic order which constitutes a determinate type of symbolic capital as worthy of being pursued and preserved. The objective harmony between the agents' dispositions (here, their propensity and capacity to play the game of honor) and the objective regularities of which their dispositions are the product means that membership in this economic cosmos implies unconditional recognition of the stakes which, by its very existence, it presents as *taken for granted*, that is, misrecognition of the arbitrariness of the value it confers on them. This value is such as to induce investments and over-investments (in both the economic and the psychoanalytic senses) which tend, through the ensuing competition and rarity, to reinforce the well-grounded illusion that the value of symbolic goods is inscribed in the nature of things, just as interest in these goods is inscribed in the nature of men.

Thus, the homologies established between the circulation of land sold and bought, the circulation of "throats" "lent" and "returned" (murder and vengeance), and the circulation of women given and received, that is, between the different forms of capital and the corresponding modes of circulation, oblige us to abandon the dichotomy of the economic and the non-economc which stands in the way of seeing the science of economic practices as a particular case of a *general science of the economy of practices*, capable of treating all practices, including those purporting to be disinterested or gratuitous, and hence non-economic, as economic practices directed toward the maximizing of material or symbolic profit. The capital accumulated by groups, the energy of social dynamics—in this case their capital of physical strength (related to their mobilizing capacity, and hence to the number of men and their readiness to fight), their economic capital (land and livestock), and their symbolic capital, always additionally associated with possession of the other kinds of capital, but susceptible of increase or decrease depending on how they are used—can exist in *different forms* which, although subject to strict laws of equivalence and hence mutually convertible, produce specific effects.[33] Symbolic capital, a transformed and thereby *disguised* form of physical "economic" capital, produces its proper effect inasmuch, and only inasmuch, as it conceals the fact that it originates in "material" forms of capital which are also, in the last analysis, the source of its effects.

MODES OF DOMINATION

In societies which have no "self-regulating market" (in Karl Polyani's sense), no educational system, no juridical apparatus, and no State, relations of domination can be set up and maintained only at the cost of strategies which must be endlessly renewed, because the conditions required for a *mediated, lasting appropriation* of other agents' labor, services, or homage have not been brought together. By contrast, domination no longer needs to be exerted in a direct, personal way when it is entailed in possession of the means (economic or cultural capital) of appropriating the mechanisms of the field of production and the field of cultural production, which tend to assure their own reproduction by their very functioning, independently of any deliberate intervention by the agents. So it is in the degree of objectification of the accumulated social capital that one finds the basis of all the pertinent differences between the modes of domination: that is, very schematically, between, on the one hand, social universes in which relations of domination are made, unmade, and remade in and by the interactions between persons, and on the other hand, social formations in which, mediated by objective, institutionalized mechanisms, such as those producing and guaranteeing the distribution of "titles" (titles of nobility, deeds of possession, academic degrees, etc.), relations of domination have the opacity and permanence of things and escape the grasp of individual consciousness and power. Objectification guarantees the permanence and cumulativity of material and symbolic acquisitions, which can then subsist without the agents' having to recreate them continuously and in their entirety by deliberate action; but, because the profits of these institutions are the object of differential appropriation, objectification also and inseparably ensures the reproduction of the structure of the distribution of the capital which, in its various forms, is the precondition for such appropriation, and in so doing, reproduces the structure of the relations of domination and dependence.

Paradoxically, it is precisely because there exist relatively autonomous fields, functioning in accordance with rigorous mechanisms capable of imposing their necessity on the agents, that those who are in a position to command these mechanisms and to appropriate the material and/or symbolic profits accruing from their functioning are able to *dispense with* strategies aimed expressly (which does not mean manifestly) and directly (i.e., without being mediated by the mechanisms) at the domination of individuals, a domination which in this case is the condition of the appropriation of the material and symbolic profits of their labor. The saving is a real one, because strategies designed to establish or maintain lasting relations of a dependence are generally very expensive in terms of material goods (as in the potlatch or in charitable acts), services, or simply *time*, which is why, by a paradox constitutive of this mode of domination, the means eat up the end, and the actions necessary to ensure the continuation of power themselves help to weaken it.[34]

Economic power lies not in wealth but in the relationship between wealth and a field of economic relations, the constitution of which is inseparable from the development of a *body of specialized agents*, with specific interests; it is in this relationship that wealth is constituted, in the form of capital, that is, as the instrument for appropriating the institutional equipment and the mechanisms indispensable to the functioning of the field thereby also appropriating the profits from it. Thus Moses Finley convincingly shows that the ancient economy lacked not resources but the means "to overcome the limits of individual resources." "There were no proper credit instruments—no negotiable paper, no book clearance, no credit payments. . . . There was money-lending in plenty but it was concentrated on small usurious loans to peasants or consumers, and in large borrowings to enable men to meet the political or other conventional expenditures of the upper classes. . . . Similarly in the field of business organization: there were no long-term partnerships or corporations, no brokers or agents, no guilds—again with the occasional and unimportant exception. In short, both the organizational and the operational devices were lacking for the mobilization of private capital resources."[35] This analysis is even more relevant to ancient Kabylia, which lacked even the most elementary instruments of an economic institution. Land was in fact more or less totally excluded from circulation (though, occasionally serving as security, it was liable to pass from one group to another). Village and tribal markets remained isolated and there was no way in which they could be linked up in a single mechanism. The opposition made by traditional morality, incarnated by the *bu niya*, between the "sacrilegious cunning" customary in market transactions and the good faith appropriate to exchanges among kinsmen and friends[36]—which was marked by the spatial distinction between the place of residence, the village, and the place of transactions, the market—must not be allowed to mask the opposition between the small local market, still "embedded in social relationships," as Polyani puts it, and the market when it has become the "dominant transaction mode."[37]

The strategies of honor are not banished from the market: though a man may enhance his prestige by tricking a stranger, he may also take pride in having bought something at an exorbitant price, to satisfy his point of honor, just "to show he could do it"; or he may boast of having managed to strike a bargain without laying out a penny in cash, either by mobilizing a number of guarantors, or, better still, by drawing on the *credit* and the *capital of trust* which come as much from a reputation for honor as from a reputation for wealth. It is said of such a man that "he could come back with the whole market even if he left home with nothing in his pockets." Men whose reputation is known to all are predisposed to play the part of guarantors—either for the seller, who vouches for the quality of his animal in their presence, or for the buyer, who, if he is not paying in cash, promises that he will repay his debt promptly.[38] The trust in which they are held, and the connections which they can mobilize, enable them to "go to the market with only their faces, their names, and their honor for money"—in other words, the only things which can take the place of money in this economy—and even "to wager [to make an offer], *whether they have money on them or not.*" *Strictly personal qualities*, "which cannot be borrowed or lent," count at least as much as wealth or solvency. In reality, even in the market the degree of mutual information is such as to leave little scope for overpricing, cheating, and bluff. If, exceptionally, a man "who has not been brought up for the market" tries to "make a bid," he is soon put in his place. "The market will judge," they say, meaning by "market" not the laws of the market, which in a very different universe sanction reckless undertakings, but rather the collective judgment shaped and manifested in the market. Either a man *is* a "market man" (*argaz nasuq*) or he isn't; a total judgment is passed on *the whole man*, and like all such judgments in every society, it involves the ultimate values laid down in the mythical taxonomies. A "house man" (*argaz ukhamis*) who takes it upon himself to overstep his "natural" limits is put in his place with the words, "Since you're only a fireside man, remain a fireside man" (*thakwath*, the alcove in the wall of the house which is used to hide the small, typically female objects which must not be seen in broad daylight—spoons, rags, weaving tools, etc.).

The village/market dichotomy is no doubt a means of preventing the impersonal exchanges of the market from obtruding the dispositions of calculation into the world of reciprocity relationships. In fact, whether a small tribal market or a big regional market, the *suq* represents a transactional mode intermediate between two extremes, neither of which is ever fully actualized: on the one hand there are the exchanges of the familiar world of acquaintance, based on the *trust* and *good faith* that are possible when the purchaser is well informed about the products exchanged and the seller's strategies, and when the relationship between the parties concerned exists before and after the exchange; and on the other hand there are the rational strategies of the self-regulating market, which are made possible by the standardization of its products and the quasi-mechanical necessity of its processes. The *suq* does not provide all the traditional information, but neither does it create the conditions for rational information. This is why all the strategies applied by the peasants aim to minimize the risk implied in the unpredictability of the outcome, by transforming the impersonal relationships of commercial transactions, which have neither past nor future, into lasting relationships of reciprocity: by calling upon guarantors, witnesses, and mediators they are able to establish, or re-establish, the functional equivalent of a traditional network of relationships between the contracting parties.

Just as economic wealth cannot function as capital until it is linked to an economic apparatus, so cultural competence in its various forms cannot be constituted as cultural capital until it is inserted into the objective relations between the system of economic production and the system producing the producers (which is itself constituted by the relation between the school system and the family). When a society lacks both the literacy which would enable it to preserve and accumulate in objectified form the cultural resources it has inherited from the past, and also the educational system which would give its agents the aptitudes and dispositions required for the symbolic reappropriation of those resources, it can only preserve them *in their incorporated state*.[39] Consequently, to ensure the perpetuation of cultural resources which would otherwise disappear along with the agents who bear them, it has to resort to systematic inculcation, a process which, as is shown by the case of the bards, may last as long as the period during which the resources are actually used. The transformations made possible by an instrument of cultural communication such as writing have been abundantly described:[40] by detaching cultural resources from persons, literacy enables a society to move beyond immediate human limits—in particular, those of individual memory—and frees it from the constraints implied by mnemonic devices such as poetry, the preservation technique par excellence in non-literate societies;[41] it enables a society to accumulate culture hitherto preserved in embodied form, and correlatively enables particular groups to practice *primitive accumulation of cultural capital*, the partial or total monopolizing of the society's symbolic resources in religion, philosophy, art, and science, by monopolizing the instruments for appropriation of those resources (writing, reading, and other decoding techniques), henceforward preserved not in memories but in texts.

But the objectification effects of literacy are nothing in comparison with those produced by the educational system. Without entering into detailed analysis, it must suffice to point out that academic qualifications are to cultural capital what money is to economic capital.[42] By giving the same value to all holders of the same certificate, so that any one of them can take the place of any other, the educational system minimizes the obstacles to the free circulation of cultural capital which result from its being incorporated in individual persons (without, however, sacrificing the advantages of the charismatic ideology of the irreplaceable individual); it makes it possible to relate all qualification holders (and also, negatively, all unqualified individuals) to a single standard, thereby setting up a *single market* for all cultural capacities and guaranteeing the convertibility of cultural capital into money, at a determinate cost in labor and time. Academic qualifications, like money, have a conventional, fixed value which, being guaranteed by law, is freed from local limitations (in contrast to scholastically uncertified cultural capital) and temporal fluctuations: the cultural capital which they in a sense guarantee once and for all does not constantly need to be proved. The objectification accomplished by academic degrees and diplomas and, in a more general way, by all forms of credentials, is inseparable from the objectification which the law guarantees by defining *permanent positions* which are distinct from the biological individuals holding them, and may be occupied by agents who are biologically different but interchangeable in terms of the qualifications required. Once this state of affairs is established, relations of power and domination no longer exist directly between individuals; they are set up in pure objectivity between institutions, i.e., between socially guaranteed qualifications and socially defined positions, and through them, between the social mechanisms which produce and guarantee both the social value of the qualifications and the positions and also the distribution of these social attributes, among biological individuals.[43]

Law does no more than symbolically consecrate—by *recording* it in a form which renders it both eternal and universal—the structure of the power relation between groups and classes which is produced and guaranteed practically by the functioning of these mechanisms. For example, it records and legitimates the distinction between the position and the person, the power and its holder, together with the relationship obtaining at a particular moment between qualifications and jobs (reflecting the relative bargaining power of the buyers and sellers of qualified, i.e., scholastically guaranteed, labor power) which appears concretely in a particular distribution of the material and symbolic profits assigned to the holders (or non-holders) of qualifications. The law thus contributes its own (specifically symbolic) force to the action of the various mechanisms which render it superfluous constantly to reassert power relations by overtly resorting to force.

Thus the task of legitimating the established order does not fall exclusively to the mechanisms traditionally regarded as belonging to the order of ideology, such as law. The system of symbolic goods production and the system producing the producers fulfill in addition, i.e., by the very logic of their normal functioning, ideological functions, by virtue of the fact that the mechanisms through which they contribute to the reproduction of the established order and to the perpetuation of domination remain hidden. The educational system helps to provide the dominant class with what Max Weber terms "a theodicy of its own privilege," not so much through the ideologies it produces or inculcates (as those who speak of "ideological apparatuses" would have it); but rather through the practical justification of the established order which it achieves by using the overt connection between qualifications and jobs as a smokescreen for the connection—which it *records surreptitiously*, under cover of formal equality—between the qualifications people obtain and the cultural capital they have inherited—in other words, through the legitimacy it confers on the transmission of this form of heritage. The most successful ideological effects are those which have no need of words, and ask no more than complicitous silence. It follows, incidentally that any analysis of ideologies, in the narrow sense of "legitimating discourses," which fails to include an analysis of the corresponding institutional mechanisms is liable to be no more than a contribution to the efficacy of those ideologies: this is true of all internal (semiological) analyses of political, educational, religious, or aesthetic ideologies which forget that the political function of these ideologies may in some cases be reduced to the effect of displacement and diversion, camouflage and legitimation, which they produce by reproducing—through their oversights and omissions, and in their deliberately or involuntarily complicitous silences—the effects of the objective mechanisms.[44]

It has been necessary at least to sketch an analysis of the objective mechanisms which play a part both in setting up and in concealing lasting relations of domination, in order to understand fully the radical difference between the different modes of domination and the different political strategies for conservation characteristic of social formations whose accumulated social energy is unequally objectified in mechanisms. On the one side there are social relations which, not containing within themselves the principle of their own reproduction, must be kept up through nothing less than a process of continuous creation; on the other side, a social world which, containing within itself the principle of its own continuation, frees agents from the endless work of creating or restoring social relations. This opposition finds expression in the history or prehistory of sociological thought. In order to "ground social being in nature," as Durkheim puts it,[45] it has been necessary to break with the propensity to see it as founded on the arbitrariness of individual wills, or, with Hobbes, on the arbitrariness of a sovereign will: "For Hobbes," writes Durkheim, "it is an act of will which gives birth to the social order and it is a perpetually renewed act of will which upholds it.[46] And there is every reason to believe that the break with this artificialist vision, which is the precondition for scientific apprehension, could not be made before the constitution, in reality, of objective mechanisms like the self-regulating market, which, as Polyani points out, was intrinsically conducive to belief in determinism. But social reality had another trap in store for science: the existence of mechanisms capable of reproducing the political order, independently of any deliberate intervention, makes it possible to recognize as political, amongst the different types of conduct directed toward gaining or keeping power, only such practices as tacitly exclude control over the reproduction mechanisms from the area of legitimate competition. In this way, social science, taking for its object the sphere of legitimate politics (as so-called "political science" does nowadays) adopted the preconstructed object which reality foisted upon it.

The greater the extent to which the task of reproducing the relations of domination is taken over by objective mechanisms, which serve the interests of the dominant group without any conscious effort on the latter's part, the more indirect and, in a sense, impersonal, become the strategies objectively oriented toward reproduction: it is not by lavishing generosity, kindness, or politeness on his charwoman (or on any other "socially inferior" agent), but by choosing the best investment for his money, or the best school for his son, that the possessor of economic or cultural capital perpetuates the relationship of domination which objectively links him with his charwoman and even her descendants. Once a system of mechanisms has been constituted capable of objectively ensuring the reproduction of the established order by its own motion (*apo tou automatou*, as the Greeks put it), the dominant class has only to *let the system they dominate take its own course* in order to exercise their domination; but until such a system exists, they have to work directly, daily, personally, to produce and reproduce conditions of domination which are even then never entirely trustworthy. Because they cannot be satisfied with appropriating the profits of a social machine which has not yet developed the power of self-perpetuation, they are obliged to resort to *the elementary forms of domination*, in other words, the direct domination of one person by another, the limiting case of which is appropriation of persons, i.e., slavery. They cannot appropriate the labor, services, goods, homage, and respect of others without "winning" them personally, "tying" them—in short, creating a bond between persons.

This is why a social relationship such as that between the master and his *khammes* (a sort of *metayer*, who gets only a very small share of the crop, usually a fifth, with local variations), which might at first seem very close to a simple capital-labor relation, cannot in fact be kept up without the direct application of material or symbolic violence to the person who is being tied. The master may bind his *khammes* by a debt which forces him to keep renewing his contract until he finds a new master willing to pay off the debt to the former employer—in other words, indefinitely. He may also resort to brutal measures such as seizing the entire crop in order to recover his loan. But each particular relationship is the product of complex strategies whose efficacy depends not only on the material and symbolic strength of either party but also on their skill in arousing sympathy or indignation so as to mobilize the group. The value of the relationship for the dominator does not lie exclusively in the resultant material profits, and many masters who are not much richer than their *khammes* and would gain by cultivating their lands themselves refrain from doing so because they prefer the prestige of possessing a "clientele." But a man who wants to be treated as a "master" must show he has the virtues corresponding to his status, and the first of these is generosity and dignity in his relations with his "clients." The compact uniting the master and his *khammes* is an arrangement between one man and another guaranteed by nothing beyond the "loyalty" which honor demands. But the "great" are expected to show that they are worthy of their rank by affording material and symbolic "protection" to those dependent upon them.

Here again, it is all a question of strategy, and the reason why the "enchanted" relations of the pact of honor are so frequent is that, in this economy, the strategies of symbolic violence are often ultimately more economical than pure "economic" violence. Given that there is no real labor market, and that money is rare (and therefore dear), the best way in which the master can serve his own interests is to work away, day in, day out, with constant care and attention, weaving the ethical and affective, as well as economic, bonds which durably tie his *khammes* to him. To reinforce the bonds of obligation, the master may arrange the marriage of his *khammes* (or his son) and install him, with his family, in the master's own house; the children, brought up together, with the goods (the flock, fields, etc.) being owned in common, often take a long time to discover what their position is. It is not uncommon for one of the sons of a *khammes* to go and work for wages in the town, together with one of the master's sons, and like him, bring back his savings to the master. In short, if the master wants to persuade the *khammes* to devote himself over a long period to the pursuit of the master's interests, he has to *associate* him completely with those interests, masking the dyssymmetry of the relationship by symbolically denying it in his behavior. The *khammes* is the man to whom one entrusts one's goods, one's house, and one's honor (as is shown by the formula used by a master leaving to go and work in a town or in France: "Associate, I'm counting on you; I'm going off to be an associate myself"). The *khammes* "treats the land as if he owned it," because there is nothing in his master's conduct to belie his claim to have rights over the land on which he works; and it is not unusual to hear a *khammes* saying, long after leaving his "master," that the sweat of his brow entitles him to pick fruit or enter the estate. And just as he never feels entirely freed from his obligations toward his former master, so, after what he calls a "change of heart" he may accuse his master of "treachery" in abandoning someone he had "adopted."

Thus the system contains only two ways (and they prove in the end to be just one way) of getting and keeping a lasting hold over someone: gifts or debts, the overtly economic obligations of debt, or the "moral," "affective" obligations created and maintained by exchange, in short, overt (physical or economic) violence, or symbolic violence—*censored, euphemized,* i.e., unrecognizable, socially recognized violence. There is an intelligible relation—not a contradiction—between these two forms of violence, which coexist in the same social formation and sometimes in the same relationship:[47] when domination can only be exercised in its *elementary form,* i.e., directly, between one person and another, it cannot take place overtly and must be disguised under the veil of enchanted relationships, the official model of which is presented by relations between kinsmen; in order to be socially recognized it must get itself misrecognized.[48] The reason for the pre-capitalist economy's great need for symbolic violence is that the only way in which relations of domination can be set up, maintained, or restored, is through strategies which, being expressly oriented toward the establishment of relations of personal dependence, must be disguised and transfigured lest they destroy themselves by revealing their true nature; in a word, they must be *euphemized.*

Hence the *censorship* to which the overt manifestation of violence, especially in its naked economic form, is subjected by the logic characteristic of an economy in which interests can only be satisfied on condition that they be disguised in and by the strategies aiming to satisfy them.[49] It would be a mistake to see a contradiction in the fact that violence is here both more present and more hidden.[50] Because the pre-capitalist economy cannot count on the implacable, hidden violence of objective mechanisms, it resorts *simultaneously* to forms of domination which may strike the modern observer as more brutal, more primitive, more barbarous, or at the same time, as gentler, more humane, more respectful of persons.[51] This coexistence of overt physical and economic violence and of the most refined symbolic violence is found in all the institutions characteristic of this economy, and at the heart of every social relationship: it is present both in the debt and in the gift, which, in spite of their apparent opposition, have in common the power of founding either dependence (and even slavery) or solidarity, depending on the strategies within which they are deployed. The fundamental ambiguity of all the institutions which modern taxonomies tend to present as economic is evidence that contrary strategies, which, as we have also seen in the case of the master-*khammes* relationship, may coexist under the same name, are *interchangeable* ways of performing the same function, with the "choice" between overt violence and gentle, hidden violence depending on the relative strengths of the two parties at a particular time, and on the degree of integration and ethical integrity of the arbitrating group. In a society in which overt violence, the violence of the usurer or the merciless master, meets with collective reprobation[52] and is liable either to provoke a violent riposte from the victim or to force him to flee (that is to say, in either case, in *the absence of any other recourse*, to provoke the annihilation of the very relationship which was intended to be exploited), symbolic violence, the gentle, invisible form of violence, which is never recognized as such, and is not so much undergone as chosen, the violence of credit, confidence, obligation, personal loyalty, hospitality, gifts, gratitude, piety—in short, all the virtues honored by the code of honor—cannot fail to be seen as the most economical mode of domination, i.e., the mode which best corresponds to the economy of the system.

Gentle, hidden exploitation is the form taken by man's exploitation of man whenever overt, brutal exploitation is impossible. It is as false to identify this essentially *dual* economy with its official reality (generosity, mutual aid, etc.), i.e., the form which exploitation has to adopt in order to take place, as it is to reduce it to its objective reality, seeing mutual aid as a corvée, the *khammes* as a sort of slave, and so on. The gift, generosity, conspicuous distribution—the most extreme case of which is the potlatch—are operations of social alchemy which may be observed whenever the direct application of overt physical or economic violence is negatively sanctioned, and which tend to bring about the transmutation of economic capital into symbolic capital. Wastage of money, energy, time, and ingenuity is the very essence of the social alchemy through which an interested relationship is transmuted into a disinterested, gratuitous relationship, overt domination into misrecognized, "socially recognized" domination, in other words, *legitimate authority*. The active principle is the labor, time, care, attention, and savoir-faire which must be squandered to produce a personal gift irreducible to its equivalent in money, a present in which what counts is not so much what you give as the way you give it, the seemingly "gratuitous" surrender not only of goods or women but of things that are even more personal and therefore more precious, because, as the Kabyles say, they can "neither be borrowed nor lent," such as *time*—the time that has been taken to do the things that "won't be forgotten," because they are done the right way at the right time—marks of appreciation, "gestures," "kindnesses," and "considerations."[53] The exercise of gentle violence demands a *"personal"* price from its users. Authority, charisma, grace, or, for the Kabyles, *sar*, are always seen as a property of the person. *Fides*, as Benveniste points out, is not "trust" but the fact that "the inherent quality of a person inspires confidence in him and is exercised in the form of a protective authority over those who entrust themselves to him."[54] The illusion implied by personal fidelity—that the object is the source of the feelings responsible for the particular representation of the object—is not entirely an illusion; the "grace" which gratitude recognizes is indeed, as Hobbes observes, the recognition of an *"antecedent grace."*

Gentle exploitation is much more costly—and not only in economic terms—for those who pratice it. "Responsibilities" such as those of the *tamen*, the "spokesman" or "guarantor" who represented his group (*thakharrubth* or *adhrum*) at the meetings of the men's assembly and on all solemn occasions, gave rise to little competition or envy, and it was not uncommon for the most influential and most important members of a group to refuse the job or soon ask to be replaced: the tasks of representation and mediation which fell to the *tamen* did indeed demand a great deal of time and effort. Those on whom the group bestows the title "wise men" or "great men," and who, in the absence of any official mandate, find themselves invested with a sort of tacit delegation of the group's authority, feel *obliged* (by a sense of duty toward themselves resulting from considerable self-esteem) constantly to recall the group to the values it officially recognizes, both by their exemplary conduct and by their express utterances; if they see two women of their group quarreling they feel it incumbent upon them to separate them and even to beat them (if they are widows or if the men responsible for them are without authority) or fine them; in cases of serious conflict between members of their own clan, they feel required to recall both parties to wisdom, never an easy task and sometimes a dangerous one; in any situation liable to lead to inter-clan conflict (in cases of crime, for example) they meet together in an assembly with the marabout so as to reconcile the antagonists; they feel it their duty to protect the interests of the clients and the poor, to give them presents when the traditional collections are made (for the *thimechret*, for example), to send them food at feast times, to assist the widows, to arrange marriages for the orphans, etc.

In short, because the delegation which is the basis of personal authority remains diffuse and is neither officially declared nor institutionally guaranteed, it can only be lastingly maintained through actions whose conformity to the values recognized by the group is a practical reaffirmation of that authority.[55] It follows that in such a system, the "great" are those who can least afford to take liberties with the official norms, and that the price to be paid for their outstanding value is outstanding conformity to the values of the group, the source of all symbolic value. The constitution of institutionalized mechanisms makes it possible for a single agent (a party leader or union delegate, a member of a board of directors, a member of an academy, etc.) to be entrusted with the totality of the capital which is the basis of the group, and to exert over this capital, collectively owned by all the "shareholders," a delegated authority not strictly related to his personal contribution; but in pre-capitalist societies, each agent shares directly in the collective capital, symbolized by the name of the family or lineage, to an extent directly proportionate to his own contribution, i.e., exactly to the extent that his words, deeds, and person are a credit to the group.[56] The system is such that the dominant agents have a vested interest in virtue; they can accumulate political power only by paying a *personal* price, and not simply by redistributing their goods and money; they must have the "virtues" of their power because the only basis of their power is "virtue."

Generous conduct, of which the potlatch (a curio for anthropologists) is simply the extreme case, might seem to suspend the universal law of interest and "fair exchange," whereby nothing is ever given for nothing, and to set up instead relationships which are their own end—conversation for conversation's sake (and not in order to say something), giving for giving's sake, and so on. But in reality such denials of interest are never more than *practical disclaimers*: like Freud's *Verneinung*, the discourse which says what it says only in a form that tends to show that it is not saying it, they satisfy interest in a (disinterested) manner designed to show that they are not satisfying interest. (A parenthesis of the benefit of the moralists: an absolute, i.e., ethical, justification of the enchantment felt by the observer of enchanted social relations may be found in the fact that, as with desire, so with material interest: society cannot ask or expect of its members anything more or better than denial, a "lifting of repression," which, as Freud says, does not amount to "an acceptance of what is repressed.")[57] Everyone knows that "it's not what you give but the way you give it" that counts, that what distinguishes the gift from mere "fair exchange" is the labor devoted to *form*: the *presentation*, the manner of giving, must be such that the outward forms of the act present a practical denial of the content of the act, symbolically transmuting an interested exchange or a simple power relation into a relationship set up in due form for form's sake, i.e., inspired by pure respect for the customs and conventions recognized by the group. (A parenthesis for the benefit of the aesthetes: archaic societies devote more time and effort to the forms, because in them the censorship of direct expression of personal interest is stronger; they thus offer connoisseurs of beautiful forms the enchanting spectacle of an art of living raised to the level of art for art's sake founded on the refusal to acknowledge self-evident realities such as "business is business" or "time is money" on which the unaesthetic lifestyle of the *harried leisure classes*[58] in so-called advanced societies is based.)

Goods are for giving. The rich man is "rich so as to be able to give to the poor," say the Kabyles.[59] This is an exemplary disclaimer: because giving is also a way of possessing (a gift which is not matched by a counter-gift creates a lasting bond, restricting the debtor's freedom and forcing him to adopt a peaceful, cooperative, prudent attitude); because in the absence of any juridical guarantee, or any coercive force, one of the few ways of "holding" someone is to *keep up* a lasting asymmetrical relationship such as indebtedness; and because the only recognized, legitimate form of possession is that achieved by dispossessing oneself—i.e., obligation, gratitude, prestige, or personal loyalty. Wealth, the ultimate basis of power, can exert power, and exert it durably, only in the form of symbolic capital; in other words, economic capital can be accumulated only in the form of symbolic capital, the unrecognizable, and hence socially recognizable, form of the other kinds of capital. The chief is indeed, in Malinowski's phrase, a "tribal banker," amassing food only to lavish it on others, in order to build up a capital of obligations and debts which will be repaid in the form of homage, respect, loyalty, and, when the opportunity arises, work and services, which may be the bases of a new accumulation of material goods.[60] Processes of circular circulation, such as the levying of a tribute followed by hierarchical redistribution, would appear absurd but for the effect they have of transmuting the nature of the social relation between the agents or groups involved. Wherever they are observed, these *consecration cycles* perform the fundamental operation of social alchemy, the transformation of arbitrary relations, *de facto* differences into officially recognized distinctions. Distinctions and lasting associations are founded in the circular circulation from which the legitimation of power arises as a symbolic surplus value. If, like Lévi-Strauss, one considers only the *particular case* of exchanges of material and/or symbolic goods intended to legitimate relations of reciprocity, one is in danger of forgetting that all structures of inseparably material and symbolic exchange (i.e., involving both circulation and communication) function as ideological machines whenever the *de facto* state of affairs which they tend to legitimate by transforming a contingent social relationship into a recognized relationship is an unequal balance of power.

The endless reconversion of economic capital into symbolic capital, at the cost of a wastage of social energy, which is the condition for the permanence of domination, cannot succeed without the complicity of the whole group: the work of denial which is the source of social alchemy is, like magic, a collective undertaking. As Mauss puts it, the whole society pays itself in the false coin of its dream. The collective misrecognition which is the basis of the ethic of honor, a collective denial of the economic reality of exchange, is only possible because, when the group lies to itself in this way, there is neither deceiver nor deceived: the peasant who treats his *khammes* as an associate, because that is the custom and because honor requires him to do so, deceives himself as much as he deceives his *khammes*, since the only form in which he can serve his interest is the euphemistic form presented by the ethic of honor; and nothing suits the *khammes* better than to play his part in an interested fiction which offers him an honorable representation of his condition. Thus the mechanisms responsible for reproducing the appropriate habitus are here an integral part of an apparatus of production which could not function without them. Agents lastingly "bind" each other, not only as parents and children, but also as creditor and debtor, master and *khammes*, only through the dispositions which the group inculcates in them and continuously reinforces, and which render *unthinkable* practices which would appear as legitimate and even be taken for granted in the disenchanted economy of "naked self-interest."[61]

The official truth produced by the collective work of euphemization, an elementary form of the labor of objectification which eventually leads to the juridical definition of acceptable behavior, is not simply the group's means of saving its "spiritual point of honor"; it also has a practical efficacy, for, even if it were contradicted by everyone's behavior, like a rule to which every case proved an exception, it would still remain a true description of such behavior as is intended to be acceptable. The code of honor weighs on each agent with the weight of all the other agents, and the disenchantment which leads to the progressive unveiling of repressed meanings and functions can only result from a collapse of the social conditions of the *cross-censorship* to which each agent submits with impatience but which he imposes on all the others.[62]

If it be true that symbolic violence is the gentle, hidden form which violence takes when overt violence is impossible, it is understandable why symbolic forms of domination should have progressively withered away as objective mechanisms came to be constituted which, in rendering superfluous the work of euphemization, tended to produce the "disenchanted" dispositions their development demanded. It is equally clear why the progressive uncovering and neutralization of the ideological and practical effects of the mechanisms assuring the reproduction of the relations of domination should determine a return to forms of symbolic violence again based on dissimulation of the mechanisms of reproduction through the conversion of economic into symbolic captial: it is through legitimacy-giving redistribution, public ("social" policies) and private (financing of "disinterested" foundations, grants to hospitals and to academic and cultural institutions), which they make possible, that the efficacy of the mechanisms of reproduction is exerted.

To these forms of legitimate accumulation, through which the dominant groups or classes secure a capital of "credit" which seems to owe nothing to the logic of exploitation,[63] must be added another form of accumulation of symbolic capital, the collection of luxury goods attesting the taste and distinction of their owner. The denial of economy and of economic interest, which in pre-capitalist societies at first took place on a ground from which it had to be expelled in order for economy to be constituted as such, thus finds its favorite refuge in the domain of art and culture, the site of pure consumption—of money, of course, but also of time convertible into money. The world of art, a sacred island systematically and ostentatiously opposed to the profane, everyday world of production, a sanctuary for gratuitous, disinterested activity in a universe given over to money and self-interest, offers, like theology in a past epoch, an imaginary anthropology obtained by denial of all the negations really brought about by the economy.

NOTES

First appeared in 1977.

1. The wet season is the time for *oral* instruction through which the group memory is forged. In the dry season, that memory is acted out and enriched through participation in the acts and ceremonies which set the seal on group unity: it is in summer that the children undergo practical training in their future tasks as peasants and their obligations as men of honor.

2. The "shepherds" are the small boys of the village. (Translator.)

3. A principle which, as we have seen, belongs as much to magic as to morality. For example, there is a saying, *leftar n-esbah d-esbuh erbah*, breakfast in the morning is the first well-omened encounter (*erbah*, to succeed, prosper).

4. Early rising to let out the animals, to go to Koran school, or simply to be outside with the men, at the same time as the men, is an element of the conduct of honor which boys are taught to respect from an early age. On the first day of spring, the mistress of the house, who alone has a right to wake up the daughters and daughters-in-law, calls the children: "Wake up, children! The longer you walk before sunrise, the longer you will live!" The women, for their part, set their point of honor on getting up at the same time as the men, if not earlier (the only way they can get all the time they want to attend to their appearance without being watched by the men, who pretend to be ignorant of the women's behavior on this point).

5. The young incur even greater disapproval when they try to set up a power struggle between the generations, jeopardizing an order based on the maintenance of temporal distance; the generations are separated only by time, which is as much as to say nothing, for one only has to wait and the difference will disappear; but the gap maintaining and maintained by the gerontocratic order is in fact unbridgeable, since the only way to cross it, short of refusing the game, is to wait.

6. It follows that disorganization of its temporal rhythms and spatial framework is one of the basic factors in the disorganization of the group; thus the concentrations of population imposed by the French Army during the war of liberation led to a profound

(and often lasting) change in the status of the women, who, when deprived of the autonomy they derived from access to a separate place and time, were condemned either to be cloistered or to wear the veil, which, after the concentration, made its appearance among Berber populations where it was previously unknown.

7. It is understandable that collective dancing or singing, particularly spectacular cases of the synchronization of the homogeneous and the orchestration of the heterogeneous, are everywhere predisposed to symbolize group integration and, by symbolizing it, to strengthen it.

8. It goes without saying that logical integration is never total, though always sufficient to ensure the more-or-less-perfect predictability of all members of the group (setting aside the *amahbul* who takes it upon himself to break with the collective rhythms).

9. Brutal reduction of this twofold, two-faced discourse to its objective (or at least, objectivist) truth neglects the fact that it only produces its specifically symbolic effects inasmuch as it never directly imparts that truth; the enchanted relationship which scientific objectification has to destroy in order to constitute itself is an integral part of the full truth of practice. Science must integrate the objectivist truth of practice and the equally objective misrecognition of that truth into a higher definition of objectivity.

10. Whether through the intermediary of their control over inheritance, which lends itself to all sorts of strategic manipulation, from sheer delay in the effective transmission of powers to the threat of disinheritance, or through the intermediary of the various strategic uses to which they can put their officially recognized monopoly of matrimonial negotiations, the elders have the means of taking advantage of the socially recognized limits of youth. An analysis of the strategies used by the heads of noble houses to keep their heirs in a subordinate position, forcing them to go out on dangerous adventures far from home, is to be found in G. Duby, *Hommes et structures du Moyen-Age* (Paris and The Hague: Mouton, 1973), pp. 213–25, esp. p. 219.

11. Love, not immune to such ritualization, also conforms to this logic, as is well illustrated by the words of a young Kabyle woman: "A girl doesn't know her husband beforehand and she looks to him for everything. She loves him even before they marry, because she must; she has to love him, there is no other 'door.'"

12. The full text of this conversation can be found in P. Bourdieu and A. Sayad, *Le Déracinement* (Paris: Minuit, 1964), pp. 215–20.

13. M. Proust, *Contre Sainte-Beuve* (Paris: Gallimard, 1965), pp. 74–5.

14. Cf. J. M. W. Whiting, *Becoming a Kwoma* (New Haven, Conn.: Yale University Press, 1941), p. 215.

15. The phenomenologists systematically forget to carry out an ultimate "reduction," the one which would reveal to them the social conditions of the possibility of the "reduction" and the *epoche*. What is radically excluded from phenomenological analysis of the "general thesis of the natural standpoint" which is constitutive of "primary experience" of the social world is the question of the economic and social conditions of the *belief* which consists in "taking the 'factworld' (*Wirklichkeit*) just as it gives itself" (E. Husserl, *Ideas* (New York: Collier-Macmillan, 1962), p. 96), a belief which the reduction subsequently causes to appear as a "thesis," or, more precisely, as an *epoche* of the *epoche*, a suspension of doubt as to the possibility that the world of the natural standpoint could be otherwise.

16. If the emergence of a field of discussion is historically linked to the development of cities, this is because the concentration of different ethnic and/or professional

groups in the same space, with in particular the overthrow of spatial and temporal frameworks, favors the confrontation of different cultural traditions, which tends to expose their arbitrariness *practically*, through first-hand experience, in the very heart of the routine of the everyday order, of the possibility of doing the same things differently, or, no less important, of doing something different at the same time; and also because it permits and requires the development of a body of specialists charged with raising to the level of discourse, so as to rationalize and systematize them, the presuppositions of the traditional world-view, hitherto mastered in their practical state.

17. A whole aspect of what is nowadays referred to as sociology (or anthropology) partakes of this logic.

18. *Formal Logic: Or, the Calculus of Inference, Necessary and Probable* (London: Taylor and Walton, 1847), p. 41.

19. J.-P. Sartre, *L'Idiot de la famille* (Paris: Gallimard, 1971), vol. 1, p. 783.

20. On belief as individual bad faith maintained and supported by collective bad faith, see P. Bourdieu, "Genèse et structure du champ religeux," *Revue française de sociologie*, 12, 3 (1971), p. 318.

21. To convince oneself that this is so, one only has to remember the tradition of "confraternity" within the medical profession. No doctor ever pays a fellow doctor a fee; instead he has to find him a present—without knowing what he wants or needs—not costing too much more or too much less than the consultation, but also not coming too close, because that would amount to stating the price of the consultation, thereby giving away the interested fiction that it was free.

22. "You've saved me from having to sell" is what is said in such cases to the lender who prevents land from falling into the hands of a stranger, by means of a sort of fictitious sale (he gives the money while allowing the owner the continued use of his property).

23. M. Mauss, "Essai sur le don," in *Sociologie et anthropologie* (Paris: PUF, 1950), p. 239; trans. I Cunnison as *The Gift* (London, 1966), p. 52.

24. The sacred character of the meal appears in the formulae used in swearing an oath: "By the food and the salt before us" or "By the food and the salt we have shared." A pact sealed by eating together would become a curse for the man who betrayed it: "I do not curse him, the broth and the salt curse him." To invite one's guest to take a second helping, one says: "There's no need to swear, the food does it [for you]"; "The food will settle its score with you [if you leave it]." A shared meal is also a ceremony of reconciliation, leading to the abandonment of vengeance. Similarly, an offering of food to a patron saint or the group's ancestor implies a contract of alliance. The *thiwizi* is inconceivable without the final meal: and thus it usually only brings together people of the same *adhrum* or the same *thakharubth*.

25. There is strong disapproval of individuals who are no use to their family or the group, "dead men whom God has drawn from living men," in the words of the verse of the Koran often applied to them: they are incapable of "pulling any weight." To remain idle, especially when one belongs to a great family, is to shirk the duties and tasks which are an inseparable part of belonging to the group. And so a man who has been out of farming for some time, because he has been away or been ill, is quickly found a place in the cycle of work and the circuit of the exchange of services. The group has the right to demand of each of its members that he should have an occupation, however unproductive, and it must therefore make sure that everyone is found an occupation, even a purely symbolic one: the peasant who provides idlers with an opportunity to work on his land is universally approved, because he is giving mar-

ginal individuals a chance to integrate themselves into the group by doing their duty as men.

26. The cost of time rises with rising productivity (i.e., the quantity of goods offered for consumption, and hence consumption itself, which also takes time); time thus tends to become scarcer, while the scarcity of goods diminishes. Squandering of goods may even become the only way of saving time, which is now more valuable than the products which could be saved if time were devoted to maintenance and repair, etc. (cf. G. S. Becker, "A Theory of the Allocation of Time," *Economic Journal*, 75, no. 289 (September 1965), pp. 493–517). This is no doubt the objective basis of the contrast in attitudes to time which has often been described.

27. A variant of this contradiction is expressed in the saying, "When the year is bad, there are always too many bellies to be filled; when it is good, there are never enough hands to do the work."

28. It would not be difficult to show that debates about Berber (and more generally, ancient) "democracy" similarly oppose first-degree naivety to second-degree naivety; the latter is perhaps the more pernicious, because the satisfaction derived from false lucidity makes it impossible to attain the adequate knowledge which simultaneously transcends and conserves the two forms of naivety: "*ancient democracy*" owes its specificity to the fact that it leaves implicit and unquestioned (doxa) the principles which liberal "democracy" can and must profess (orthodoxy) because they have ceased to govern conduct in the practical state.

29. The man who "gives others no more than the time he owes them" is reproached in terms like these: "You've only just arrived, and now you're off again." "Are you leaving us? We've only just sat down. . . . We've hardly spoken." The analogy between a man's relationships with others and his relationship to the land leads to condemnation of the man who thoughtlessly hurries in his work and, like the guest who leaves almost as soon as he arrives, does not give it the care and time, i.e., the respect, which are its due.

30. R. Maunier, *Mélanges de sociologie nord-africaine* (Paris: Alcan, 1930), p. 68.

31. Such tactics are, as far as possible, kept out of transactions between kinsmen, and there is disapproval of the man who takes advantage of the destitution of the person forced to sell.

32. The trap is all the more infallible when, as in marriage, the circulation of immediately perceptible material goods, such as the bridewealth, the apparent issue at stake in matrimonial negotiations, conceals the total circulation, actual or potential, of goods that are indissociably material and symbolic, of which they are only the aspect most visible to the eye of the capitalist *homo economicus*. The amount of the payment, always of small value in relative and absolute terms, would not justify the hard bargaining to which it gives rise, did it not take on a symbolic value of the highest importance as the unequivocal demonstration of the worth of a family's products on the matrimonial exchange market, and of the capacity of the heads of the family to obtain the best price for their products through their negotiating skills. The best proof of the irreducibility of the stakes of matrimonial strategy to the amount of bridewealth is provided by history, which here too has dissociated the symbolic and material aspects of transactions: once reduced to its purely monetary value, the bridewealth lost its significance as a symbolic rating, and the bargains of honor, thus reduced to the level of mere haggling, were from then on considered shameful.

33. Although he fails to draw any real conclusions from it, in a work which proves disappointing, Bertrand Russell admirably expresses an insight into the analogy be-

tween energy and power which could serve as the basis for a unification of social science: "Like energy, power has many forms, such as wealth, armaments, civil authority, influence, or opinion. No one of these can be regarded as subordinate to any other, and there is no one form which the others are derivative. The attempt to treat one form of power, say wealth, in isolation, can only be partially successful, just as the study of one form of energy will be defective at certain points, unless other forms are taken into account. Wealth may result from military power or from influence over opinion, just as either of these may result from wealth" (*Power: A New Social Analysis* [London: Allen and Unwin, 1938]), pp. 12–13). And he goes on to define the program for this unified science of social energy: "Power, like energy, must be regarded as continually passing from any one of its forms into any other, and it should be the business of social science to seek the laws of such transformations" (pp. 13–14).

34. It has often been pointed out that the logic which makes the redistribution of goods the *sine qua non* of the continuation of power tends to reduce or prevent the primitive accumulation of economic capital and the development of class division (cf., for example, E. Wolf, *Sons of the Shaking Earth* [Chicago: University of Chicago Press, 1959], p. 216).

35. M. I. Finley, "Technical Innovation and Economic Progress in the Ancient World," *Economic History Review*, 18, 1 (August 1965), pp. 29–45, esp. p. 37; and see "Land Debt and the Man of Property in Classical Athens," *Political Science Quarterly*, 68 (1953), pp. 249–68.

36. See P. Bohannan, "Some Principles of Exchange and Investment among the Tiv," *American Anthropologist*, 57, 1 (1955), pp. 60–70.

37. K. Polyani, *Primitive Archaic and Modern Economics*, ed. George Dalton (New York: Doubleday, 1968), and *The Great Transformation* (New York: Rinehart, 1944). It is rather paradoxical that in his contribution to a collection of essays edited by Karl Polyani, Francisco Benet pays so much attention to the contrast between the market and the village and scarcely mentions the factors which keep the local *suq* under the control of the good-faith economy (see F. Benet, "Explosive Markets: The Berber Highlands," in K. Polyani, C. M. Arensberg, and H. W. Pearson [eds.], *Trade and Market in the Early Empires* [New York: Free Press, 1957]).

38. The shady dealer cannot find anyone to answer for him (or his wares) and so he cannot demand guarantees from the buyer.

39. The belief, often held in gnostic religions, that knowledge may be transmitted through various forms of magical contact—most typically, through a kiss—may be seen as an attempt to transcend the limits of this mode of preservation: "Whatever it is that the practitioner learns, he learns from another *dukun*, who is his *guru* (teacher); and whatever he learns, he and others call his *ilmu* (science). *Ilmu* is generally considered to be a kind of abstract knowledge or supernormal skill, but by the more concrete-minded and "old fashioned," it is sometimes viewed as a kind of substantive magical power, in which case, its transmission may be more direct than through teaching" (C. Geertz, *The Religion of Java* (London: Collier-Macmillan, 1960), p. 88).

40. See in particular J. Goody and I. Watt, "The Consequences of Literacy," *Comparative Studies in Society and History*, 5 (1962–3), pp. 304ff., and J. Goody (ed.), *Literacy in Traditional Societies* (Cambridge: [Cambridge] University Press, 1968).

41. "The poet is the incarnate book of the oral people" (J. A. Notopoulos, "Mnemosyne in Oral Literature," *Transactions and Proceedings of the American Philological Association*, 69 (1938), pp. 465–93, esp. p. 469). In a very impressive article, William C. Greene shows how a change in the mode of accumulation, circulation, and

reproduction of culture results in a change in the function it is made to perform, together with a change in the structure of cultural products ("The Spoken and the Written Word," *Harvard Studies in Classical Philology*, 9 [1951], pp. 24–58). And Eric A. Havelock similarly shows that even the content of cultural resources is transformed by the transformation of "the technology of preserved communication," and in particular, by the abandonment of *mimesis*, a practical reactivation mobilizing all the resources of a "pattern of organized actions"—music, rhythm, words—for mnemonic purposes in an act of affective identification, in favor of written discourse, which, because it exists as a text, is repeatable, reversable, detached from the situation, and predisposed by its permanence to become the object of analysis, comparison, contrast, and reflection (*Preface to Plato* [Cambridge, Mass.: Harvard University Press, 1963]). Until language is objectified in the written text, speech is inseparable from the speaker's whole person, and in his absence it can be manipulated only in the mode of *mimesis*, which is not open to analysis or criticism.

42. A social history of all forms of *distinction* (of which the *title* is a particular case) would have to show the social conditions and the consequences of the transition from a personal authority which can neither be delegated nor inherited (e.g., the *gratia*, esteem, influence, of the Romans) to the *title*—from honor to the *jus honorum*. In Rome, for example, the use of titles (e.g., *eques Romanus*) defining a *dignitas*, an officially recognized position in the State (as distinct from a purely personal quality), was, like the use of *insignia*, progressively subjected to detailed control by custom or law (cf. C. Nicolet, *L'Ordre équestre à l'époque republicaine*, vol. 1: *Definitions juridiques et structures sociales* [Paris, 1966], pp. 236–41).

43. On this point, see P. Bourdieu and L. Boltanksi, "Le Titre et le poste: rapports entre le système de production et le système de réproduction," *Actes de la récherche en sciences sociales*, no. 2, March 1975; trans. "Qualifications and Jobs," *CCCS Stencilled Paper 46* (University of Birmingham, 1977).

44. This is true, for example, of the charismatic (or meritocratic) ideology which explains the differential probability of access to academic qualifications by reference to the inequality of innate talent, thus reproducing the effect of the mechanisms which dissimulate the relationship between academic attainment and inherited cultural capital.

45. E. Durkheim, *Montesquieu et Rousseau* (Paris: Rivière, 1953), p. 197.

46. *Ibid.* p. 195. The analogy with the Cartesian theory of continuous creation is perfect. And when Leibniz criticized a conception of God condemned to move the world "as a carpenter moves his axe or as a miller drives his millstone by directing water towards the wheel" (G. W. Leibniz, "De ipsa natura," *Opuscula philosophica selecta*, ed. P. Shrecker [Paris: Boivin, 1939], p. 92), and put forward in place of the Cartesian universe, which cannot exist without unremitting divine attention, a physical universe endowed with a *vis propria*, he was initiating the critique, which did not find expression until much later (i.e., in Hegel's introduction to the *Philosophy of Right*), of all forms of the refusal to acknowledge that the social world has a nature, i.e., an immanent necessity.

47. If acts of communication—exchanges of gifts, challenges, or words—always bear within them a potential conflict, it is because they always contain the possibility of domination. *Symbolic violence* is that form of domination which, transcending the opposition usually drawn between sense relations and power relations, communication and domination, is only exerted *through* the communication in which it is disguised.

48. It can be seen that if one is trying to account for the *specific* form in which domination is realized in the pre-capitalist economy, it is not sufficient to observe, as Marshall D. Sahlins does, that the pre-capitalist economy does not provide the conditions necessary for an indirect, impersonal mode of domination, in which the worker's dependence on the employer is the quasi-automatic product of the mechanisms of the labor market (cf. "Political Power and the Economy in Primitive Society," in G. E. Dole and R. L. Carneiro [eds.], *Essays in the Science of Culture* [New York: Crowell, 1960], pp. 390–415; "Poor Man, Rich Man, Big Man, Chief: Political Types in Melanesia and Polynesia," *Comparative Studies in Society and History*, 5 [1962–3], pp. 285–303; "On the Sociology of Primitive Exchange," in M. Banton [ed.], *The Relevance of Models for Social Anthropology* [London: Tavistock, 1965], pp. 139–236). These *negative conditions* (which one is amply justified in pointing to when it is a question of countering any form of idealism or idealization) do not account for the internal logic of symbolic violence, any more than the absence of the lightning rod and the electric telegraph, which Marx refers to in a famous passage in the introduction to the *Grundrisse*, can be used to explain Jupiter and Hermes, i.e., the internal logic of Greek mythology and art.

49. The interactionist "gaze," which ignores the objective mechanisms and their operation, in order to look into the direct interactions between agents, would find an ideal terrain in this sort of society, i.e., precisely in the case in which, because of the relationship normally existing between the anthropologist and his object, it is the least likely to be possible. Another paradox appears in the fact that structuralism, in the strict sense of the word, i.e., the sciences of the objective structures of the social world (and not simply of agents' images of them), is least adequate and least fruitful when applied to societies in which relations of domination and dependence are the product of continuous creation (unless one chooses to posit, as the structuralism of Lévi-Strauss implicitly does, that in such cases the structure lies in the ideology, and that power lies in the possession of the instrument of appropriation of these structures, i.e., in a form of cultural capital).

50. Emile Benveniste's history of the vocabulary of Indo-European institutions charts the linguistic milestones in the process of *unveiling* and *disenchantment* which runs from physical or symbolic violence to law and order, from ransom to purchase, from the prize for a notable action to the rate for the job, from recognition of services to recognition of debts, from moral worth to creditworthiness, and from moral obligation to the court order (*Indo-European Language and Society* [London: Faber, 1973], esp. pp. 101–62). And similarly, Moses Finley shows how debts which were sometimes contrived so as to produce situations of enslavement could also serve to create relations of solidarity between equals ("La servitude pour dettes," *Revue d'histoire du Droit français et étranger*, 4th series, 43, 2 [April–June 1965], pp. 159–84).

51. The question of the relative worth of the different modes of domination—a question raised, implicitly at least, by Rousseauistic accounts of primitive paradises and disquisitions on "modernization"—is totally meaningless and can only give rise to necessarily interminable debates on *the advantages and disadvantages of the situations before and after*, the only interest of which lies in the revelation of the researcher's social phantasms, i.e., his unanalyzed relationship with his own society. As in all comparisons of one system with another, it is possible *ad infinitum* to contrast representations of the two systems (e.g., enchantment versus disenchantment) differing in their affective coloring and ethical connotations depending on which of the two

is taken as a standpoint. The only legitimate object of comparison is each system considered *as* a system, and this precludes any evaluation other than that implied in the immanent logic of its evolution.

52. Certain usurers, fearing dishonor and ostracism by the group, prefer to grant their debtors new time-limits for repayment (e.g., until the olive harvest) to save them from having to sell land in order to pay. Many of those who had been prepared to flout public opinion paid the price of their defiance, sometimes with their lives, during the war of liberation.

54. E. Benveniste, *Indo-European Language and Society*, pp. 84ff.

55. The marabouts are in a different position, because they wield an institutionally delegated authority as members of a respected body of "religious officials" and because they keep up a separate status—in particular, through fairly strict endogamy and a whole set of traditions, such as the practice of confining their women to the house. The fact remains that the only occasions on which men who "like the mountain torrents, grow greater in stormy times" can, as the proverb suggests, take advantage of their quasi-institutionalized role as mediators, are when their knowledge of the traditions and acquaintance with the persons involved enable them to exercise a symbolic authority which can only exist through direct delegation by the group: the marabouts are most often simply the loophole, the "door," as the Kabyles say, which enables groups in conflict to reach an agreement without losing face.

56. Conversely, whereas institutionalized delegation of authority, which is accompanied by an explicit definition of responsibilities, tends to limit the consequences of individual shortcomings, diffuse delegation, which comes as the corollary of membership [in] the group, underwrites all members of the group, without distinction, with the guarantee of the collectively owned capital, but does not cover the group against the discredit which it may incur from the conduct of any member; this accounts for the importance which the "great" attach to defending the collective honor in the honor of the weakest member of their group.

57. See S. Freud, "Negation," *Complete Psychological Works* (standard ed.), ed. J. Strachey, vol. 29 (London: Hogarth Press, 1961), pp. 235–6.

58. See S. B. Linder, *The Harried Leisure Class* (New York and London: Columbia University Press, 1970).

59. "Lord, give to me that I may give" (only the saint can give without possessing). Wealth is God's gift to man to enable him to relieve the poverty of others. "A generous man is the friend of Allah." Both worlds belong to him. He who wishes to keep his wealth must show he is worthy of it, by showing that he is generous; otherwise his wealth will be taken from him.

60. It would be a mistake to overemphasize the contrast between the symmetry of gift-exchange and the asymmetry of the ostentatious distribution which is the basis of the constitution of political authority. It is possible to move by successive degrees from one pattern to the other: as one moves away from perfect reciprocity, so an increasing proportion of the counter-prestations come to be made up of homage, respect, obligations, and moral debts. Those who, like Polyani and Sahlins, have seen clearly the determining function of redistribution in the constitution of political authority and in the operation of tribal economy (with the circuit of accumulation and redistribution functioning in a similar way to a State's budget) have not analyzed the way in which this process, the device par excellence for conversion of economic capital into symbolic capital, creates lasting relations of dependence which, though economically based, are disguised under the veil of moral relations.

61. It follows that the objectivist error—in particular the mistake of ignoring the effects of objectifying the non-objectified—is more far-reaching in its consequences in a world in which, as here, reproduction of the social order depends more on the unceasing reproduction of concordant habitus than on the automatic reproduction of structures capable of producing or selecting concordant habitus.

62. Urbanization, which brings together groups with different traditions and weakens reciprocal controls (and, even before urbanization, the generalization of monetary exchanges and the introduction of wage labor), results in the collapse of the collectively maintained collective fiction of the religion of honor. *Trust* is replaced by *credit* (*talq*), which was formerly cursed or despised (as is shown by the insult "Face of credit!"—the face of the man who has ceased to feel dishonor—and by the fact that repudiation without restitution, the greatest offense imaginable, is called *berru natalq*). "In the age of credit," said an informant, "wretched indeed are those who can only appeal to the trust in which their parents were held. All that counts now is the goods you have immediately to hand. Everyone wants to be a market man. Everyone thinks he has a right to trust, so that there's no trust anywhere now."

63. It was not a sociologist but a group of American industrialists who conceived the "bank-account" theory of public relations: "It necessitates making *regular and frequent* deposits on the Bank of Public Good-Will, so that valid checks can be drawn on this account when it is desirable" (quoted in Dayton MacKean, *Party and Pressure Politics* [New York: Houghton Mifflin, 1944]). See also R. W. Gable, "N.A.M.: Influential Lobby or Kiss of Death?" *Journal of Politics*, 15, 2 (May 1953), p. 262 (on the different ways in which the National Association of Manufacturers tries to influence the general public, educators, churchmen, women's club leaders, farmers' leaders, etc.); and H. A. Turner "How Pressure Groups Operate," *Annals of the American Academy of Political and Social Science*, 319 (September 1958), pp. 63–72 (on the way in which "an organization elevates itself in the esteem of the general public and conditions their attitudes so that a state of public opinion will be created in which the public will almost automatically respond with favor to the programs desired by the group").

Two Lectures

MICHEL FOUCAULT

LECTURE ONE: 7 JANUARY 1976

I have wanted to speak to you of my desire to be finished with, and to somehow terminate a series of researches that have been our concern for some four or five years now, in effect, from the date of my arrival here, and which, I am well aware, have met with increasing difficulties, both for you and for myself. Though these researches were very closely related to each other, they have failed to develop into any continuous or coherent whole. They are fragmentary researches, none of which in the last analysis can be said to have proved definitive, nor even to have led anywhere. Diffused and at the same time repetitive, they have continually re-trod the same ground, invoked the same themes, the same concepts, etc.

You will recall my work here, such as it has been: some brief notes on the history of penal procedure, a chapter or so on the evolution and institutionalization of psychiatry in the nineteenth century, some observations on sophistry, on Greek money, on the medieval Inquisition. I have sketched a history of sexuality or at least a history of knowledge of sexuality on the basis of the confessional practice of the seventeenth century or the forms of control of infantile sexuality in the eighteenth to nineteenth century. I have sketched a genealogical history of the origins of a theory and a knowledge of anomaly and of the various techniques that relate to it. None of it does more than mark time. Repetitive and disconnected, it advances nowhere. Since indeed it never ceases to say the same thing, it perhaps says nothing. It is tangled up into an indecipherable, disorganized muddle. In a nutshell, it is inconclusive.

Still, I could claim that after all these were only trails to be followed, it mattered little where they led; indeed, it was important that they did not have a predetermined starting point and destination. They were merely lines laid down for you to pursue or to divert elsewhere, for me to extend upon or re-design as the case might be. They are, in the final analysis, just fragments, and it is up to you or me to see what we can make of them. For my part, it has struck me that I might have seemed a bit like a whale that leaps to the surface of the water disturbing it momentarily with a tiny jet of spray and lets it be believed, or pretends to believe, or wants to believe, or himself does in fact indeed believe, that down in the depths where no one sees him any more, where he is no longer witnessed nor controlled by anyone, he follows a more profound, coherent and reasoned trajectory. Well, anyway, that was more or less how I at least conceived the situation; it could be that you perceived it differently.

After all, the fact that the character of the work I have presented to you has been at the same time fragmentary, repetitive, and discontinuous could well be a reflection of something one might describe as a febrile indolence—a typical affliction of those enamored of libraries, documents, reference works, dusty tomes, texts that are never read, books that are no sooner printed than they are consigned to the shelves of libraries where they thereafter lie dormant to be taken up only some centuries later. It would accord all too well with the busy inertia of those who profess an idle knowledge, a species of luxuriant sagacity, the rich hoard of the *parvenus* whose only outward signs are displayed in footnotes at the bottom of the page. It would accord with all those who feel themselves to be associates of one of the more ancient or more typical secret societies of the West, those oddly indestructible societies unknown it would seem to Antiquity, which came into being with Christianity, more likely at the time of the first monasteries, at the periphery of the invasions, the fires and the forests: I mean to speak of the great warm and tender Freemasonry of useless erudition.

However, it is not simply a taste for such Freemasonry that has inspired my course of action. It seems to me that the work we have done could be justified by the claim that it is adequate to a restricted period, that of the last ten, fifteen, at most twenty years, a period notable for two events which for all they may not be really important are nonetheless to my mind quite interesting.

On the one hand, it has been a period characterized by what one might term the efficacy of dispersed and discontinuous offensives. There are a number of things I have in mind here. I am thinking, for example, where it was a case of undermining the function of psychiatric institutions, of that curious efficacy of localized anti-psychiatric discourses. These are discourses which you are well aware lacked and still lack any systematic principles of coordination of the kind that would have provided or might today provide a system of reference for them. I am thinking of the original reference towards existential analysis or of certain directions inspired in a general way by Marxism, such as Reichian theory. Again, I have in mind that strange efficacy of the attacks that have been directed against traditional morality and hierarchy, attacks which again have no reference except perhaps in a vague and fairly distant way to Reich and Marcuse. On the other hand there is also the efficacy of the attacks upon the legal and penal system, some of which had a very tenuous connection with the general and in any case pretty dubious notion of class justice, while others had a rather more precisely defined affinity with anarchist themes. Equally, I am thinking of the efficacy of a book such as *L'Anti-Oedipe*, which really has no other source of reference than its own prodigious theoretical inventiveness: a book, or rather a thing, an event, which has managed, even at the most mundane level of psychoanalytic practice, to introduce a note of shrillness into that murmured exchange that has for so long continued uninterrupted between couch and armchair.

I would say, then, that what has emerged in the course of the last ten or fifteen years is a sense of the increasing vulnerability to criticism of things, institutions, practices, discourses. A certain fragility has been discovered in the very bedrock of existence—even, and perhaps above all, in those aspects of it that are most familiar, most solid, and most intimately related to our bodies and to our everyday behavior. But together with this sense of instability and this amazing efficacy of discontinuous, particular, and local criticism, one in fact also discovers something that perhaps was not initially foreseen, something one might describe as precisely the inhibiting effect of global, *totalitarian theories*. It is not that these global theories have not provided nor continue to provide in a fairly consistent fashion useful tools for local research: Marxism and psychoanalysis are proofs of this. But I believe these tools have only been provided on the condition that the theoretical unity of these discourses was in some sense put in abeyance, or at least curtailed, divided, overthrown, caricatured, theatricalized, or what you will. In each case, the attempt to think in terms of a totality has in fact proved a hindrance to research.

So, the main point to be gleaned from these events of the last fifteen years, their predominant feature, is the *local* character of criticism. That should not, I believe, be taken to mean that its qualities are those of an obtuse, naive, or primitive empiricism; nor is it a soggy eclecticism, an opportunism that laps up any and every kind of theoretical approach; nor does it mean a self-imposed asceticism which taken by itself would reduce to the worst kind of theoretical impoverishment. I believe that what this essentially local character of criticism indicates in reality is an autonomous, non-centralized kind of theoretical production, one, that is to say, whose validity is not dependent on the approval of the established regimes of thought.

It is here that we touch upon another feature of these events that has been manifest for some time now: it seems to me that this local criticism has proceeded by means of what one might term "a return of knowledge." What I mean by that phrase is this: it is a fact that we have repeatedly encountered, at least at a superficial level, in the course of most recent times, an entire thematic to the effect that it is not theory but life that matters, not knowledge but reality, not books but money, etc.; but it also seems to me that over and above, and arising out of this thematic, there is something else to which we are witness, and which we might describe as an *insurrection of subjugated knowledges*.

By subjugated knowledges I mean two things: on the one hand, I am referring to the historical contents that have been buried and disguised in a functionalist coherence or formal systemization. Concretely, it is not a semiology of the life of the asylum, it is not even a sociology of delinquency, that has made it possible to produce an effective criticism of the asylum and likewise of the prison, but rather the immediate emergence of historical contents. And this is simply because only the historical contents allow us to rediscover the ruptural effects of conflict and struggle that the order imposed by functionalist or systematizing thought is designed to mask. Subjugated knowledges are thus those blocs of historical knowledge which were present but disguised within the body of functionalist and systematizing theory and which criticism—which obviously draws upon scholarship—has been able to reveal.

On the other hand, I believe that by subjugated knowledges one should understand something else, something which in a sense is altogether different, namely, a whole set of knowledges that have been disqualified as inadequate to their task or insufficiently elaborated: naive knowledges, located low down on the hierarchy, beneath the required level of cognition or scientificity. I also believe that it is through the re-emergence of these low-ranking knowledges, these unqualified, even directly disqualified knowledges (such as that of the psychiatric patient, of the ill person, of the nurse, of the doctor—parallel and marginal as they are to the knowledge of medicine—that of the delinquent, etc.), and which involve what I would call a popular knowledge (*le savoir des gens*) though it is far from being a general commonsense knowledge, but is on the contrary a particular, local, regional knowledge, a differential knowledge incapable of unanimity and which owes its force only to the harshness with which it is opposed by everything surrounding it—that it is through the re-appearance of this knowledge, of these local popular knowledges, these disqualified knowledges, that criticism performs its work.

However, there is a strange kind of paradox in the desire to assign to this same category of subjugated knowledges what are on the one hand the products of meticulous, erudite, exact historical knowledge, and on the other hand local and specific knowledges which have no common meaning and which are in some fashion allowed to fall into disuse whenever they are not effectively and explicitly maintained in themselves. Well, it seems to me that our critical discourses of the last fifteen years have in effect discovered their essential force in this association between the buried knowledges of erudition and those disqualified from the hierarchy of knowledges and sciences.

In the two cases—in the case of the erudite as in that of the disqualified knowledges—with what in fact were these buried, subjugated knowledges really concerned? They were concerned with a *historical knowledge of struggles*. In the specialized areas of erudition as in the disqualified, popular knowledge there lay the memory of hostile encounters which even up to this day have been confined to the margins of knowledge.

What emerges out of this is something one might call a genealogy, or rather a multiplicity of genealogical researches, a painstaking rediscovery of struggles together with the rude memory of their conflicts. And these genealogies, that are the combined product of an erudite knowledge and a popular knowledge, were not possible and could not even have been attempted except on one condition, namely that the tyranny of globalizing discourses with their hierarchy and all their privileges of a theoretical *avant-garde* was eliminated.

Let us give the term *genealogy* to the union of erudite knowledge and local memories which allows us to establish a historical knowledge of struggles and to make use of this knowledge tactically today. This then will be a provisional definition of the genealogies which I have attempted to compile with you over the last few years.

You are well aware that this research activity, which one can thus call genealogical, has nothing at all to do with an opposition between the abstract unity of theory and the concrete multiplicity of facts. It has nothing at all to do with a disqualification of the speculative dimension which opposes to it, in the name of some kind of scientism, the rigor of well established knowledges. It is not therefore via an empiricism that the genealogical project unfolds, nor even via a positivism in the ordinary sense of that term. What it really does is to entertain the claims to attention of local, discontinuous, disqualified, illegitimate knowledges against the claims of a unitary body of theory which would filter, hierarchize, and order them in the name of some true knowledge and some arbitrary idea of what constitutes a science and its objects. Genealogies are therefore not positivistic returns to a more careful or exact form of science. They are precisely anti-sciences. Not that they vindicate a lyrical right to ignorance or non-knowledge: it is not that they are concerned to deny knowledge or that they esteem the virtues of direct cognition and base their practice upon an immediate experience that escapes encapsulation in knowledge. It is not that with which we are concerned. We are concerned, rather, with the insurrection of knowledges that are opposed primarily not to the contents, methods, or concepts of a science, but to the effects of the centralizing powers which are linked to the institution and functioning of an organized scientific discourse within a society such as ours. Nor does it basically matter all that much that this institutionalization of scientific discourse is embodied in a university, or, more generally, in an educational apparatus, in a theoretical-commercial institution such as psychoanalysis or within the framework of reference that is provided by a political system such as Marxism; for it is really against the effects of the power of a discourse that is considered to be scientific that the genealogy must wage its struggle.

To be more precise, I would remind you how numerous have been those who for many years now, probably for more than half a century, have questioned whether Marxism was, or was not, a science. One might say that the same issue has been posed, and continues to be posed, in the case of psychoanalysis, or even worse, in that of the semiology of literary texts. But to all these demands of: "Is it or is it not a science?" the genealogies or genealogists would reply: "If you really want to know, the fault lies in your very determination to make a science out of Marxism or psychoanalysis or this or that study." If we have any objection against Marxism, it lies in the fact that it could effectively be a science. In more detailed terms, I would say that even before we can know the extent to which something such as Marxism or psychoanalysis can be compared to a scientific practice in its everyday functioning, its rules of construction, its working concepts, that even before we can pose the question of a formal and structural analogy between [science and] Marxist or psychoanalytic discourse, it is surely necessary to question ourselves about our aspirations to the kind of power that is presumed to accompany such a science. It is surely the following kinds of questions that would need to be posed: What types of knowledge do you want to disqualify in the very instant of your demand: "Is it a science"? Which speaking, discoursing subjects—which subjects of experience and knowledge—do you then want to "diminish" when you say: "I who conduct this discourse am conducting a scientific discourse, and I am a scientist"? Which theoretical-political *avant-garde* do you want to enthrone in order to isolate it from all the discontinuous forms of knowledge that circulate about it? When I see you straining to establish the scientificity of Marxism I do not really think that you are demonstrating once and for all that Marxism has a rational structure and that therefore its propositions are the outcome of verifiable procedures; for me you are doing something altogether different, you are investing Marxist discourses and those who uphold them with the effects of a power which the West since Medieval times has attributed to science and has reserved for those engaged in scientific discourse.

By comparison, then, and in contrast to the various projects which aim to inscribe knowledges in the hierarchical order of power associated with science, a genealogy should be seen as a kind of attempt to emancipate historical knowledges from that subjection, to render them, that is, capable of opposition and of struggle against the coercion of a theoretical, unitary, formal, and scientific discourse. It is based on a reactivation of local knowledges—of minor knowledges, as Deleuze might call them—in opposition to the scientific hierarchization of knowledges and the effects intrinsic to their power: this, then, is the project of these disordered and fragmentary genealogies. If we were to characterize it in two terms, then "archaeology" would be the appropriate methodology of this analysis of local discursivities, and "genealogy" would be the tactics whereby, on the basis of the descriptions of these local discursivities, the subjected knowledges which were thus released would be brought into play.

So much can be said by way of establishing the nature of the project as a whole. I would have you consider all these fragments of research, all these discourses, which are simultaneously both superimposed and discontinuous, which I have continued obstinately to pursue for some four or five years now, as elements of these genealogies which have been composed—and by no means by myself alone—in the course of the last fifteen years. At this point, however, a problem arises, and a question: why not continue to pursue a theory which in its discontinuity is so attractive and plausible, albeit so little verifiable? Why not continue to settle upon some aspect of psychiatry or of the theory of sexuality, etc.? It is true, one could continue (and in a certain sense I shall try to do so) if it were not for a certain number of changes in the current situation. By this I mean that it could be that in the course of the last five, ten, or even fifteen years, things have assumed a different complexion—the contest could be said to present a different physiognomy. Is the relation of forces today still such as to allow these disinterred knowledges some kind of autonomous life? Can they be isolated by these means from every subjugating relationship? What force do they have taken in themselves? And, after all, is it not perhaps the case that these fragments of genealogies are no sooner brought to light, that the particular elements of the knowledge that one seeks to disinter are no sooner accredited and put into circulation, than they run the risk of re-codification, re-colonization? In fact, those unitary discourses, which first disqualified and then ignored them when they made their appearance, are, it seems, quite ready now to annex them, to take them back within the fold of their own discourse and to invest them with everything this implies in terms of their effects of knowledge and power. And if we want to protect these only lately liberated fragments are we not in danger of ourselves constructing, with our own hands, that unitary discourse to which we are invited, perhaps to lure us into a trap, by those who say to us: "All this is fine, but where are you heading? What kind of unity are you after?" The temptation, up to a certain point, is to reply: "Well, we just go on, in a cumulative fashion; after all, the moment at which we risk colonization has not yet arrived." One could even attempt to throw out a challenge: "Just try to colonize us then!" Or one might say, for example, "Has there been, from the time when anti-psychiatry or the genealogy of psychiatric institutions w[as] launched—and it is now a good fifteen years ago—a single Marxist, or a single psychiatrist, who has gone over the same ground in his own terms and shown that these genealogies that we produced were false, inadequately elaborated, poorly articulated, and ill-founded?" In fact, as things stand in reality, these collected fragments of a genealogy remain as they have always been, surrounded by a prudent silence. At most, the only arguments that we have heard against them have been of the kind I believe were voiced by Monsieur Juquin:[1] "All this is all very well, but Soviet psychiatry nonetheless remains the foremost in the world." To which I would reply: "How right you are; Soviet psychiatry is indeed the foremost in the world and it is precisely that which one would hold against it."

The silence, or rather the prudence, with which the unitary theories avoid the genealogy of knowledges might therefore be a good reason to continue to pursue it. Then at least one could proceed to multiply the genealogical fragments in the form of so many traps, demands, challenges, what you will. But in the long run, it is probably over-optimistic, if we are thinking in terms of a contest—that of knowledge against the effects of the power of scientific discourse—to regard the silence of one's adversaries as indicative of a fear we have inspired in them. For perhaps the silence of the enemy—and here at the very least we have a methodological or tactical principle that it is always useful to bear in mind—can also be the index of our failure to produce any such fear at all. At all events, we must proceed just as if we had not alarmed them at all, in which case it will be no part of our concern to provide a solid and homogeneous theoretical terrain for all these dispersed genealogies, nor to descend upon them from on high with some kind of halo of theory that would unite them. Our task, on the contrary, will be to expose and specify the issue at stake in this opposition, this struggle, this insurrection of knowledges against the institutions and against effects of the knowledge and power that invests scientific discourse.

What is at stake in all these genealogies is the nature of this power which has surged into view in all its violence, aggression, and absurdity in the course of the last forty years, contemporaneously, that is, with the collapse of Fascism and the decline of Stalinism. What, we must ask, is this power—or rather, since that is to give a formulation to the question that invites the kind of theoretical coronation of the whole which I am so keen to avoid—what are these various contrivances of power, whose operations extend to such differing levels and sectors of society and are possessed of such manifold ramifications? What are their mechanisms, their effects, and their relations? The issue here can, I believe, be crystallized essentially in the following question: is the analysis of power or of powers to be deduced in one way or another from the economy? Let me make this question and my reasons for posing it somewhat clearer. It is not at all my intention to abstract from what are innumerable and enormous differences; yet despite, and even because of these differences, I consider there to be a certain point in common between the juridical, and let us call it, liberal, conception of political power (found in the *philosophies* of the eighteenth century) and the Marxist conception, or at any rate a certain conception currently held to be Marxist. I would call this common point an economism in the theory of power. By that I mean that in the case of the classic, juridical theory, power is taken to be a right, which one is able to possess like a commodity, and which one can in consequence transfer or alienate, either wholly or partially, through a legal act or through some act that establishes a right, such as takes place through cession or contract. Power is that concrete power which every individual holds, and whose partial or total cession enables political power or sovereignty to be established. This theoretical construction is essentially based on the idea that the constitution of political power obeys the model of a legal transaction involving a contractual type of exchange (hence the clear analogy that runs through all these theories between power and commodities, power and wealth). In the other case—I am thinking here of the general Marxist conception of power—one finds none of all that. Nonetheless, there is something else inherent in this latter conception, something which one might term an economic functionality of power. This economic functionality is present to the extent that power is conceived primarily in terms of the role that it plays in the maintenance simultaneously of the relations of production and of a class domination which the development and specific forms of the forces of production have rendered possible. On this view, then, the historical *raison d'être* of political power is to be found in the economy. Broadly speaking, in the first case we have a political power whose formal model is discoverable in the process of exchange, the economic circulation of commodities; in the second case, the historical *raison d'être* of political power and the principle of its concrete forms and actual functioning, is located in the economy. Well then, the problem involved in the researches to which I refer can, I believe, be broken down in the following manner: in the first place, is power always in a subordinate position relative to the economy? Is it always in the service of, and ultimately answerable to, the economy? Is its essential end and purpose to serve the economy? Is it destined to realize, consolidate, maintain, and reproduce the relations appropriate to the economy and essential to its functioning? In the second place, is power modeled upon the commodity? Is it something that one possesses, acquires, cedes through force or contract, that one alienates or recovers, that circulates, that voids this or that region? Or, on the contrary, do we need to employ varying tools in its analysis—even, that is, when we allow that it effectively remains the case that the relations of power do indeed remain profoundly enmeshed in and with economic relations and participate with them in a common circuit? If that is the case, it is not the models of functional subordination or formal isomorphism that will characterize the interconnection between politics and the economy. Their indissolubility will be of a different order, one that it will be our task to determine.

What means are available to us today if we seek to conduct a non-economic analysis of power? Very few, I believe. We have in the first place the assertion that power is neither given, nor exchanged, nor recovered, but rather exercised, and that it only exists in action. Again, we have at our disposal another assertion to the effect that power is not primarily the maintenance and reproduction of economic relations, but is above all a relation of force. The questions to be posed would then be these: if power is exercised, what sort of exercise does it involve? In what does it consist? What is its mechanism? There is an immediate answer that many contemporary analyses would appear to offer: power is essentially that which represses. Power represses nature, the instincts, a class, individuals. Though one finds this definition of power as repression endlessly repeated in present-day discourse, it is not that discourse which invented it—Hegel first spoke of it, then Freud and later Reich. In any case, it has become almost automatic in the parlance of the times to define power as an organ of repression. So should not the analysis of power be first and foremost an analysis of the mechanisms of repression?

Then again, there is a second reply we might make: if power is properly speaking the way in which relations of force are deployed and given concrete expression, rather than analyzing it in terms of cession, contract, or alienation, or functionally in terms of its maintenance of the relations of production, should we not analyze it primarily in terms of *struggle, conflict,* and *war*? One would then confront the original hypothesis, according to which power is essentially repression, with a second hypothesis to the effect that power is war, a war continued by other means. This reversal of Clausewitz's assertion that war is politics continued by other means has a triple significance: in the first place, it implies that the relations of power that function in a society such as ours essentially rest upon a definite relation of forces that is established at a determinate, historically specifiable moment, in war and by war. Furthermore, if it is true that political power puts an end to war, that it installs, or tries to install, the reign of peace in civil society, this by no means implies that it suspends the effects of war or neutralizes the disequilibrium revealed in the final battle. The role of political power, on this hypothesis, is perpetually to reinscribe it in social institutions, in economic inequalities, in language, in the bodies themselves of each and every one of us.

So this would be the first meaning to assign to the inversion of Clausewitz's aphorism that war is politics continued by other means. It consists in seeing politics as sanctioning and upholding the disequilibrium of forces that was displayed in war. But there is also something else that the inversion signifies, namely, that none of the political struggles, the conflicts waged over power, with power, for power, the alterations in the relations of force, the favoring of certain tendencies, the reinforcements, etc., etc., that come about within this "civil peace"—that none of these phenomena in a political system should be interpreted except as the continuation of war. They should, that is to say, be understood as episodes, factions, and displacements in that same war. Even when one writes the history of peace and its institutions, it is always the history of this war that one is writing. The third, and final, meaning to be assigned to the inversion of Clausewitz's aphorism, is that the end result can only be the outcome of war, that is, of a contest of strength, to be decided in the last analys[i]s by recourse to arms. The political battle would cease with this final battle. Only a final battle of that kind would put an end, once and for all, to the exercise of power as continual war.

So, no sooner do we attempt to liberate ourselves from economistic analyses of power, than two solid hypotheses offer themselves: the one argues that the mechanisms of power are those of repression. For convenience' sake, I shall term this Reich's hypothesis. The other argues that the basis of the relationship of power lies in the hostile engagement of forces. Again for convenience, I shall call this Nietzsche's hypothesis.

These two hypotheses are not irreconcilable; they even seem to be linked in a fairly convincing manner. After all, repression could be seen as the political consequence of war, somewhat as oppression, in the classic theory of political right, was seen as the abuse of sovereignty in the juridical order.

One might thus contrast two major systems of approach to the analysis of power: in the first place, there is the old system as found in the *philosophes* of the eighteenth century. The conception of power as an original right that is given up in the establishment of sovereignty, and the contract, as matrix of political power, provide its points of articulation. A power so constituted risks becoming oppression whenever it over-extends itself, whenever, that is, it goes beyond the terms of the contract. Thus we have contract-power, with oppression as its limit, or rather as the transgression of this limit. In contrast, the other system of approach no longer tries to analyze political power according to the schema of contract-oppression, but in accordance with that of war-repression, and, at this point, repression no longer occupies the place that oppression occupies in relation to the contract, that is, it is not abuse, but is, on the contrary, the mere effect and continuation of a relation of domination. On this view, repression is none other than the realization, within the continual warfare of this pseudo-peace, of a perpetual relationship of force.

Thus we have two schemes for the analysis of power. The contract-oppression schema, which is the juridical one, and the domination-repression or war-repression schema for which the pertinent opposition is not between the legitimate and the illegitimate, as in the first schema, but between struggle and submission.

It is obvious that all my work in recent years has been couched in the schema of struggle-repression, and it is this—which I have hitherto been attempting to apply—which I have now been forced to reconsider, both because it is still insufficiently elaborated at a whole number of points, and because I believe that these two notions of repression and war must themselves be considerably modified if not ultimately abandoned. In any case, I believe that they must be submitted to closer scrutiny.

I have always been especially diffident of this notion of repression: it is precisely with reference to those genealogies of which I was speaking just now—of the history of penal right, of psychiatric power, of the control of infantile sexuality, etc.—that I have tried to demonstrate to you the extent to which the mechanisms that were brought into operation in these power formations were something quite other, or in any case something much more, than repression. The need to investigate this notion of repression more thoroughly springs therefore from the impression I have that it is wholly inadequate to the analysis of the mechanisms and effects of power that it is so pervasively used to characterize today.

LECTURE TWO: 14 JANUARY 1976

The course of study that I have been following until now—roughly since 1970–71—has been concerned with the *how* of power. I have tried, that is, to relate its mechanisms to two points of reference, two limits: on the one hand, to the rules of right that provide a formal delimitation of power; on the other, to the effects of truth that this power produces and transmits, and which in their turn reproduce this power. Hence we have a triangle: power, right, truth.

Schematically, we can formulate the traditional questions of political philosophy in the following terms: how is the discourse of truth, or quite simply, philosophy as that discourse which *par excellence* is concerned with truth, able to fix limits to the rights of power? That is the traditional question. The one I would prefer to pose is rather different. Compared to the traditional, noble, and philosophic question it is much more down to earth and concrete. My problem is rather this: what rules of right are implemented by the relations of power in the production of discourses of truth? Or alternatively, what type of power is susceptible of producing discourses of truth that in a society such as ours are endowed with such potent effects? What I mean is this: in a society such as ours, but basically in any society, there are manifold relations of power which permeate, characterize, and constitute the social body, and these relations of power cannot themselves be established, consolidated, nor implemented without the production, accumulation, circulation, and functioning of a discourse. There can be no possible exercise of power without a certain economy of discourses of truth which operates through and on the basis of this association. We are subjected to the production of truth through power and we cannot exercise power except through the production of truth. This is the case for every society, but I believe that in ours the relationship between power, right, and truth is organized in a highly specific fashion. If I were to characterize, not its mechanism itself, but its intensity and constancy, I would say that we are forced to produce the truth of power that our society demands, of which it has need, in order to function: we *must* speak the truth; we are constrained or condemned to confess or to discover the truth. Power never ceases its interrogation, its inquisition, its registration of truth: it institutionalizes, professionalizes, and rewards its pursuit. In the last analysis, we must produce truth as we must produce wealth, indeed we must produce truth in order to produce wealth in the first place. In another way, we are also subjected to truth in the sense in which it is truth that makes the laws, that produces the true discourse which, at least partially, decides, transmits, and itself extends upon the effects of power. In the end, we are judged, condemned, classified, determined in our undertakings, destined to a certain mode of living or dying, as a function of the true discourses which are the bearers of the specific effects of power.

So, it is the rules of right, the mechanisms of power, the effects of truth or if you like, the rules of power and the powers of true discourses, that can be said more or less to have formed the general terrain of my concern, even if, as I know full well, I have traversed it only partially and in a very zigzag fashion. I should like to speak briefly about this course of research, about what I have considered as being its guiding principle and about the methodological imperatives and precautions which I have sought to adopt. As regards the general principle involved in a study of the relations between right and power, it seems to me that in Western societies since Medieval times it has been royal power that has provided the essential focus around which legal thought has been elaborated. It is in response to the demands of royal power, for its profit and to serve as its instrument or justification, that the juridical edifice of our own society has been developed. Right in the West is the King's right. Naturally everyone is familiar with the famous, celebrated, repeatedly emphasized role of the jurists in the organization of royal power. We must not forget that the revitalization of Roman Law in the twelfth century was the major event around which, and on whose basis, the juridical edifice which had collapsed after the fall of the Roman Empire was reconstructed. This resurrection of Roman Law had in effect a technical and constitutive role to play in the establishment of the authoritarian, administrative, and in the final analysis, absolute power of the monarchy. And when this legal edifice escapes in later centuries from the control of the monarch, when, more accurately, it is turned against that control, it is always the limits of this sovereign power that are put in question, its prerogatives that are challenged. In other words, I believe that the King remains the central personage in the whole legal edifice of the West. When it comes to the general organization of the legal system in the West, it is essentially with the King, his rights, his power and its eventual limitations, that one is dealing. Whether the jurists were the King's henchmen or his adversaries, it is of royal power that we are speaking in every case when we speak of these grandiose edifices of legal thought and knowledge.

There are two ways in which we do so speak. Either we do so in order to show the nature of the juridical armory that invested royal power, to reveal the monarch as the effective embodiment of sovereignty, to demonstrate that his power, for all that it was absolute, was exactly that which befitted his fundamental right. Or, by contrast, we do so in order to show the necessity of imposing limits upon this sovereign power, of submitting it to certain rules of right, within whose confines it had to be exercised in order for it to remain legitimate. The essential role of the theory of right, from medieval times onwards, was to fix the legitimacy of power; that is the major problem around which the whole theory of right and sovereignty is organized.

When we say that sovereignty is the central problem of right in Western societies, what we mean basically is that the essential function of the discourse and techniques of right has been to efface the domination intrinsic to power in order to present the latter at the level of appearance under two different aspects: on the one hand, as the legitimate rights of sovereignty, and on the other, as the legal obligation to obey it. The system of right is centered entirely upon the King, and it is therefore designed to eliminate the fact of domination and its consequences.

My general project over the past few years has been, in essence, to reverse the mode of analysis followed by the entire discourse of right from the time of the Middle Ages. My aim, therefore, was to invert it, to give due weight, that is, to the fact of domination, to expose both its latent nature and its brutality. I then wanted to show not only how right is, in a general way, the instrument of this domination—which scarcely needs saying—but also to show the extent to which, and the forms in which, right (not simply the laws but the whole complex of apparatuses, institutions, and regulations responsible for their application) transmits and puts in motion relations that are not relations of sovereignty, but of domination. Moreover, in speaking of domination I do not have in mind that solid and global kind of domination that one person exercises over others, or one group over another, but the manifold forms of domination that can be exercised within society. Not the domination of the King in his central position, therefore, but that of his subjects in their mutual relations: not the uniform edifice of sovereignty, but the multiple forms of subjugation that have a place and function within the social organism.

The system of rights, the domain of the law, are permanent agents of these relations of domination, these polymorphous techniques of subjugation. Right should be viewed, I believe, not in terms of a legitimacy to be established, but in terms of the methods of subjugation that it instigates.

The problem for me is how to avoid this question, central to the theme of right, regarding sovereignty and the obedience of the individual subjects in order that I may substitute the problem of domination and subjugation for that of sovereignty and obedience. Given that this was to be the general line of my analysis, there were a certain number of methodological precautions that seemed requisite to its pursuit. In the very first place, it seemed important to accept that the analysis in question should not concern itself with the regulated and legitimate forms of power in their central locations, with the general mechanisms through which they operate, and the continual effects of these. On the contrary, it should be concerned with power at its extremities, in its ultimate destinations, with those points where it becomes capillary, that is, in its more regional and local forms and institutions. Its paramount concern, in fact, should be with the point where power surmounts the rules of right which organize and delimit it and extends itself beyond them, invests itself in institutions, becomes embodied in techniques, and equips itself with instruments and eventually even violent means of material intervention. To give an example: rather than try to discover where and how the right of punishment is founded on sovereignty, how it is presented in the theory of monarchical right or in that of democratic right, I have tried to see in what ways punishment and the power of punishment are effectively embodied in a certain number of local, regional, material institutions, which are concerned with torture or imprisonment, and to place these in the climate—at once institutional and physical, regulated and violent—of the effective apparatuses of punishment. In other words, one should try to locate power at the extreme points of its exercise, where it is always less legal in character.

A second methodological precaution urged that the analysis should not concern itself with power at the level of conscious intention or decision; that it should not attempt to consider power from its internal point of view and that it should refrain from posing the labyrinthine and unanswerable question: "Who then has power and what has he in mind? What is the aim of someone who possesses power?" Instead, it is a case of studying power at the point where its intention, if it has one, is completely invested in its real and effective practices. What is needed is a study of power in its external visage, at the point where it is in direct and immediate relationship with that which we can provisionally call its object, its target, its field of application, there— that is to say, where it installs itself and produces its real effects.

Let us not, therefore, ask why certain people want to dominate, what they seek, what is their overall strategy. Let us ask, instead, how things work at the level of ongoing subjugation, at the level of those continuous and uninterrupted processes which subject our bodies, govern our gestures, dictate our behaviors, etc. In other words, rather than ask ourselves how the sovereign appears to us in his lofty isolation, we should try to discover how it is that subjects are gradually, progressively, really, and materially constituted through a multiplicity of organisms, forces, energies, materials, desires, thoughts, etc. We should try to grasp subjection in its material instance as a constitution of subjects. This would be the exact opposite of Hobbes' project in *Leviathan*, and of that, I believe, of all jurists for whom the problem is the distillation of a single will—or rather, the constitution of a unitary, singular body animated by the spirit of sovereignty—from the particular wills of a multiplicity of individuals. Think of the scheme of Leviathan: insofar as he is a fabricated man, Leviathan is no other than the amalgamation of a certain number of separate individualities, who find themselves reunited by the complex of elements that go to compose the State; but at the heart of the State, or rather, at its head, there exists something which constitutes it as such, and this is sovereignty, which Hobbes says is precisely the spirit of Leviathan. Well, rather than worry about the problem of the central spirit, I believe that we must attempt to study the myriad of bodies which are constituted as peripheral *subjects* as a result of the effects of power.

A third methodological precaution relates to the fact that power is not to be taken as a phenomenon of one individual's consolidated and homogeneous domination over others, or that of one group or class over others. What, by contrast, should always be kept in mind is that power, if we do not take too distant a view of it, is not that which makes the difference between those who exclusively possess and retain it and those who do not have it and submit to it. Power must be analyzed as something which circulates, or rather as something which only functions in the form of a chain. It is never localized here or there, never in anybody's hands, never appropriated as a commodity or piece of wealth. Power is employed and exercised through a net-like organization. And not only do individuals circulate between its threads; they are always in the position of simultaneously undergoing and exercising this power. They are not only its inert or consenting target; they are always also the elements of its articulation. In other words, individuals are the vehicles of power, not its points of application.

The individual is not to be conceived as a sort of elementary nucleus, a primitive atom, a multiple and inert material on which power comes to fasten or against which it happens to strike, and in so doing subdues or crushes individuals. In fact, it is already one of the prime effects of power that certain bodies, certain gestures, certain discourses, certain desires, come to be identified and constituted as individuals. The individual, that is, is not the *vis-à-vis* of power; it is, I believe, one of its prime effects. The individual is an effect of power, and at the same time, or precisely to the extent to which it is that effect, it is the element of its articulation. The individual which power has constituted is at the same time its vehicle.

There is a fourth methodological precaution that follows from this: when I say that power establishes a network through which it freely circulates, this is

true only up to a certain point. In much the same fashion we could say therefore that we all have a fascism in our heads, or, more profoundly, that we all
have a power in our bodies. But I do not believe that one should conclude
from that that power is the best distributed thing in the world, although in
some sense that is indeed so. We are not dealing with a sort of democratic or
anarchic distribution of power through bodies. That is to say, it seems to
me—and this then would be the fourth methodological precaution—that the
important thing is not to attempt some kind of deduction of power starting
from its center and aimed at the discovery of the extent to which it permeates
into the base, of the degree to which it reproduces itself down to and including the most molecular elements of society. One must rather conduct an *ascending* analysis of power, starting, that is, from its infinitesimal mechanisms, which each have their own history, their own trajectory, their own
techniques and tactics, and then see how these mechanisms of power have
been—and continue to be—invested, colonized, utilized, involuted, transformed, displaced, extended, etc., by ever more general mechanisms and by
forms of global domination. It is not that this global domination extends itself
right to the base in a plurality of repercussions: I believe that the manner in
which the phenomena, the techniques, and the procedures of power enter into
play at the most basic levels must be analyzed, that the way in which these
procedures are displaced, extended, and altered must certainly be demonstrated; but above all what must be shown is the manner in which they are
invested and annexed by more global phenomena and the subtle fashion in
which more general powers or economic interests are able to engage with
these technologies that are at once both relatively autonomous of power and
act as its infinitesimal elements. In order to make this clearer, one might cite
the example of madness. The descending type of analysis, the one of which I
believe one ought to be wary, will say that the bourgeoisie has, since the
sixteenth or seventeenth century, been the dominant class; from this premise,
it will then set out to deduce the internment of the insane. One can always
make this deduction, it is always easily done and that is precisely what I
would hold against it. It is in fact a simple matter to show that since lunatics
are precisely those persons who are useless to industrial production, one is
obliged to dispense with them. One could argue similarly in regard to infantile sexuality—and several thinkers, including Wilhelm Reich, have indeed
sought to do so up to a certain point. Given the domination of the bourgeois
class, how can one understand the repression of infantile sexuality? Well,
very simply—given that the human body had become essentially a force of
production from the time of the seventeenth and eighteenth century, all the
forms of its expenditure which did not lend themselves to the constitution of
the productive forces—and were therefore exposed as redundant—were
banned, excluded, and repressed. These kinds of deduction are always possible. They are simultaneously correct and false. Above all they are too glib,
because one can always do exactly the opposite and show, precisely by appeal to the principle of the dominance of the bourgeois class, that the forms of

control of infantile sexuality could in no way have been predicted. On the contrary, it is equally plausible to suggest that what was needed was sexual training, the encouragement of a sexual precociousness, given that what was fundamentally at stake was the constitution of a labor force whose optimal state, as we well know, at least at the beginning of the nineteenth century, was to be infinite: the greater the labor force, the better able would the system of capitalist production have been to fulfill and improve its functions.

I believe that anything can be deduced from the general phenomenon of the domination of the bourgeois class. What needs to be done is something quite different. One needs to investigate historically, and beginning from the lowest level, how mechanisms of power have been able to function. In regard to the confinement of the insane, for example, or the repression and interdiction of sexuality, we need to see the manner in which, at the effective level of the family, of the immediate environment, of the cells and most basic units of society, these phenomena of repression or exclusion possessed their instruments and their logic, in response to a certain number of needs. We need to identify the agents responsible for them, their real agents (those which constituted the immediate social *entourage*, the family, parents, doctors, etc.), and not be content to lump them under the formula of a generalized bourgeoisie. We need to see how these mechanisms of power, at a given moment, in a precise conjuncture and by means of a certain number of transformations, have begun to become economically advantageous and politically useful. I think that in this way one could easily manage to demonstrate that what the bourgeoisie needed, or that in which its system discovered its real interests, was not the exclusion of the mad or the surveillance and prohibition of infantile masturbation (for, to repeat, such a system can perfectly well tolerate quite opposite practices), but rather, the techniques and procedures themselves of such an exclusion. It is the mechanisms of that exclusion that are necessary, the apparatuses of surveillance, the medicalization of sexuality, of madness, of delinquency, all the micro-mechanisms of power, that came, from a certain moment in time, to represent the interests of the bourgeoisie. Or even better, we could say that to the extent to which this view of the bourgeoisie and of its interests appears to lack content, at least in regard to the problems with which we are here concerned, it reflects the fact that it was not the bourgeoisie itself which thought that madness had to be excluded or infantile sexuality repressed. What in fact happened instead was that the mechanisms of the exclusion of madness, and of the surveillance of infantile sexuality, began from a particular point in time, and for reasons which need to be studied, to reveal their political usefulness and to lend themselves to economic profit, and that as a natural consequence, all of a sudden, they came to be colonized and maintained by global mechanisms and the entire State system. It is only if we grasp these techniques of power and demonstrate the economic advantages or political utility that derives from them in a given context for specific reasons, that we can understand how these mechanisms come to be effectively incorporated into the social whole.

To put this somewhat differently: the bourgeoisie has never had any use for the insane; but the procedures it has employed to exclude them have revealed and realized—from the nineteenth century onwards, and again on the basis of certain transformations—a political advantage, on occasion even a certain economic utility, which have consolidated the system and contributed to its overall functioning. The bourgeoisie is interested in power, not in madness, in the system of control of infantile sexuality, not in that phenomenon itself. The bourgeoisie could not care less about delinquents, about their punishment and rehabilitation, which economically have little importance, but it is concerned about the complex of mechanisms with which delinquency is controlled, pursued, punished, and reformed, etc.

As for our fifth methodological precaution: it is quite possible that the major mechanisms of power have been accompanied by ideological productions. There has, for example, probably been an ideology of education, and ideology of the monarchy, an ideology of parliamentary democracy, etc., but basically I do not believe that what has taken place can be said to be ideological. It is both much more and much less than ideology. It is the production of effective instruments for the formation and accumulation of knowledge—methods of observation, techniques of registration, procedures for investigation and research, apparatuses of control. All this means that power, when it is exercised through these subtle mechanisms, cannot but evolve, organize, and put into circulation a knowledge, or rather apparatuses of knowledge, which are not ideological constructs.

By way of summarizing these five methodological precautions, I would say that we should direct our researches on the nature of power not toward the juridical edifice of sovereignty, the State apparatuses and the ideologies which accompany them, but toward domination and the material operators of power, toward forms of subjection and the inflections and utilizations of their localized systems, and toward strategic apparatuses. We must eschew the model of Leviathan in the study of power. We must escape from the limited field of juridical sovereignty and State institutions, and instead base our analysis of power on the study of the techniques and tactics of domination.

This, in its general outline, is the methodological course that I believe must be followed, and which I have tried to pursue in the various researches that we have conducted over recent years on psychiatric power, on infantile sexuality, on political systems, etc. Now as one explores these fields of investigation, observing the methodological precautions I have mentioned, I believe that what then comes into view is a solid body of historical fact, which will ultimately bring us into confrontation with the problems of which I want to speak this year.

This solid, historical body of fact is the juridical-political theory of sovereignty of which I spoke a moment ago, a theory which has had four roles to play. In the first place, it has been used to refer to a mechanism of power that was effective under the feudal monarchy. In the second place, it has served as instrument and even as justification for the construction of the large-scale administrative monarchies. Again, from the time of the sixteenth century and more than ever from the seventeenth century onward, but already at the time of the wars of religion, the theory of sovereignty has been a weapon which has circulated from one camp to another, which has been utilized in one sense or another, either to limit or else to reinforce royal power: we find it among Catholic monarchists and Protestant anti-monarchists, among Protestant and more-or-less liberal monarchists, but also among Catholic partisans of regicide or dynastic transformation. It functions both in the hands of aristocrats and in the hands of parliamentarians. It is found among the representatives of royal power and among the last feudatories. In short, it was the major instrument of political and theoretical struggle around the systems of power of the sixteenth and seventeenth centuries. Finally, in the eighteenth century, it is again this same theory of sovereignty, reactivated through the doctrine of Roman law, that we find in its essentials in Rousseau and his contemporaries, but now with a fourth role to play: now it is concerned with the construction, in opposition to the administrative, authoritarian, and absolutist monarchies, of an alternative model, that of parliamentary democracy. And it is still this role that it plays at the moment of the Revolution.

Well, it seems to me that if we investigate these four roles there is a definite conclusion to be drawn: as long as a feudal type of society survived, the problems to which the theory of sovereignty was addressed were in effect confined to the general mechanisms of power, to the way in which its forms of existence at the higher level of society influenced its exercise at the lowest levels. In other words, the relationship of sovereignty, whether interpreted in a wider or narrower sense, encompasses the totality of the social body. In effect, the mode in which power was exercised could be defined in its essentials in terms of the relationship sovereign-subject. But in the seventeenth and eighteenth centuries, we have the production of an important phenomenon, the emergence, or rather the invention, of a new mechanism of power possessed of highly specific procedural techniques, completely novel instruments, quite different apparatuses, and which is also, I believe, absolutely incompatible with the relations of sovereignty.

This new mechanism of power is more dependent upon bodies and what they do than upon the Earth and its products. It is a mechanism of power which permits time and labor, rather than wealth and commodities, to be extracted from bodies. It is a type of power which is constantly exercised by means of a system of levies or obligations distributed over time. It presupposes a tightly knit grid of material coercions rather than the physical existence of a sovereign. It is ultimately dependent upon the principle, which introduces a genuinely new economy of power, that one must be able simultaneously both to increase the subjected forces and to improve the force and efficacy of that which subjects them.

This type of power is in every aspect the antithesis of that mechanism of power which the theory of sovereignty described or sought to transcribe. The latter is linked to a form of power that is exercised over the Earth and its products, much more than over human bodies and their operations. The theory of sovereignty is something which refers to the displacement and appropriation on the part of power, not of time and labor, but of goods and wealth. It allows discontinuous obligations distributed over time to be given legal expression but it does not allow for the codification of a continuous surveillance. It enables power to be founded in the physical existence of the sovereign, but not in continuous and permanent systems of surveillance. The theory of sovereignty permits the foundation of an absolute power in the absolute expenditure of power. It does not allow for a calculation of power in terms of the minimum expenditure for the maximum return.

This new type of power, which can no longer be formulated in terms of sovereignty, is, I believe, one of the great inventions of bourgeois society. It has been a fundamental instrument in the constitution of industrial capitalism and of the type of society that is its accompaniment. This non-sovereign power, which lies outside the form of sovereignty, is disciplinary power. Impossible to describe in the terminology of the theory of sovereignty from which it differs so radically, this disciplinary power ought by rights to have led to the disappearance of the grand juridical edifice created by that theory. But in reality, the theory of sovereignty has continued not only to exist as an ideology of right, but also to provide the organizing principle of the legal codes which Europe acquired in the nineteenth century, beginning with the Napoleonic Code.

Why has the theory of sovereignty persisted in this fashion as an ideology and an organizing principle of these major legal codes? For two reasons, I believe. On the one hand, it has been, in the eighteenth and again in the nineteenth century, a permanent instrument of criticism of the monarchy and of all the obstacles that can thwart the development of disciplinary society. But at the same time, the theory of sovereignty, and the organization of a legal code centered upon it, have allowed a system of right to be superimposed upon the mechanisms of discipline in such a way as to conceal its actual procedures, the element of domination inherent in its techniques, and to guarantee to everyone, by virtue of the sovereignty of the State, the exercise of his proper sovereign rights. The juridical systems—and this applies both to their codification and to their theorization—have enabled sovereignty to be democratized through the constitution of a public right articulated upon collective sovereignty, while at the same time this democratization of sovereignty was fundamentally determined by and grounded in mechanisms of disciplinary coercion.

To put this in more rigorous terms, one might say that once it became necessary for disciplinary constraints to be exercised through mechanisms of domination and yet at the same time for their effective exercise of power to be disguised, a theory of sovereignty was required to make an appearance at the level of the legal apparatus, and to re-emerge in its codes. Modern society, then, from the nineteenth century up to our own day, has been characterized on the one hand, by a legislation, a discourse, an organization based on public right, whose principle of articulation is the social body and the delegative status of each citizen; and, on the other hand, by a closely linked grid of disciplinary coercions whose purpose is in fact to assure the cohesion of this same social body. Though a theory of right is a necessary companion to this grid, it cannot in any event provide the terms of its endorsement. Hence these two limits, a right of sovereignty and a mechanism of discipline, which define, I believe, the arena in which power is exercised. But these two limits are so heterogeneous that they cannot possibly be reduced to each other. The powers of modern society are exercised through, on the basis of, and by virtue of, this very heterogeneity between a public right of sovereignty and a polymorphous disciplinary mechanism. This is not to suggest that there is on the one hand an explicit and scholarly system of right which is that of sovereignty, and, on the other hand, obscure and unspoken disciplines which carry out their shadowy operations in the depths, and thus constitute the bedrock of the great mechanism of power. In reality, the disciplines have their own discourse. They engender, for the reasons of which we spoke earlier, apparatuses of knowledge (*savoir*) and a multiplicity of new domains of understanding. They are extraordinarily inventive participants in the order of these knowledge-producing apparatuses. Disciplines are the bearers of a discourse, but this cannot be the discourse of right. The discourse of discipline has nothing in common with that of law, rule, or sovereign will. The disciplines may well be the carriers of a discourse that speaks of a rule, but a natural rule, a norm. The code they come to define is not that of law but that of normalization. Their reference is to a theoretical horizon which of necessity has nothing in common with the edifice of right. It is human science which constitutes their domain, and clinical knowledge their jurisprudence.

In short, what I have wanted to demonstrate in the course of the last few years is not the manner in which at the advance front of the exact sciences the uncertain, recalcitrant, confused dominion of human behavior has little by little been annexed to science: it is not through some advancement in the rationality of the exact sciences that the human sciences are gradually constituted. I believe that the process which has really rendered the discourse of the human sciences possible is the juxtaposition, the encounter between two lines of approach, two mechanisms, two absolutely heterogeneous types of discourse: on the one hand there is the reorganization of right that invests sovereignty, and on the other, the mechanics of the coercive forces whose exercise takes a disciplinary form. And I believe that in our own times power is exercised simultaneously through this right and these techniques and that these techniques and these discourses, to which the disciplines give rise invade the area of right so that the procedures of normalization come to be ever more constantly engaged in the colonization of those of law. I believe that all this can explain the global functioning of what I would call a *society of normalization*. I mean, more precisely, that disciplinary normalizations come into ever greater conflict with the juridical systems of sovereignty: their incompatibility with each other is ever more acutely felt and apparent; some kind of arbitrating discourse is made ever more necessary, a type of power and of knowledge that the sanctity of science would render neutral. It is precisely in the extension of medicine that we see, in some sense, not so much the linking as the perpetual exchange or encounter of mechanisms of discipline with the principle of right. The developments of medicine, the general medicalization of behaviors, conducts, discourses, desires, etc., take place at the point of intersection between the two heterogeneous levels of discipline and sovereignty. For this reason, against these usurpations by the disciplinary mechanisms, against this ascent of a power that is tied to scientific knowledge, we find that there is no solid recourse available to us today, such being our situation, except that which lies precisely in the return to a theory of right organized around sovereignty and articulated upon its ancient principle. When today one wants to object in some way to the disciplines and all the effects of power and knowledge that are linked to them, what is it that one does, concretely, in real life, what do[es] the Magistrates Union[2] or other similar institutions do, if not precisely appeal to this canon of right, this famous, formal right, that is said to be bourgeois, and which in reality is the right of sovereignty? But I believe that we find ourselves here in a kind of blind alley: it is not through recourse to sovereignty against discipline that the effects of disciplinary power can be limited, because sovereignty and disciplinary mechanisms are two absolutely integral constituents of the general mechanism of power in our society.

If one wants to look for a non-disciplinary form of power, or rather, to struggle against disciplines and disciplinary power, it is not toward the ancient right of sovereignty that one should turn, but toward the possibility of a new form of right, one which must indeed be anti-disciplinarian, but at the same time liberated from the principle of sovereignty. It is at this point that we once more come up against the notion of repression, whose use in this context I believe to be doubly unfortunate. On the one hand, it contains an obscure reference to a certain theory of sovereignty, the sovereignty of the sovereign rights of the individual, and on the other hand, its usage introduces a system of psychological reference points borrowed from the human sciences, that is to say, from discourses and practices that belong to the disciplinary realm. I believe that the notion of repression remains a juridical-disciplinary notion whatever the critical use one would make of it. To this extent the critical application of the notion of repression is found to be vitiated and nullified from the outset by the twofold juridical and disciplinary reference it contains to sovereignty on the one hand and to normalization on the other.

Notes

First appeared in 1972.
1. A deputy of the French Communist Party.
2. This Union, established after 1968, has adopted a radical line on civil rights, the law, and the prisons.

CHAPTER SIX

After the Masses

DICK HEBDIGE

FEW PEOPLE—whatever their political persuasion—looking at Britain in the 1980s would deny that we are living in new times. The crucial question is how far are the long-term global shifts in cultural, political and economic life mapped out under the heading of new times intrinsically connected to the rise of the Right? One way of opening up this question—if only to present a "worst case" scenario—is to see how these same shifts have been interpreted in recent debates on postmodernism.

The wide currency of this term over the last few years in Mediaville may alienate many readers. For some it may seem that the word has become too baggy or trendy or annexed by the Right to be of use. Others will protest that they never got the hang of modernism (or its relevance for the Left) let alone *post*modernism. After all, what have the design of buildings or pop videos or the fate of the novel or the current obsession with advertising, packaging and style got to do with the real political issues of the day? For others on the Left—perhaps those who are closer to the debates themselves—the resistance to the idea not just of postmodernism but more importantly of *postmodernity*—suggests a reaction against that sense of an ending that hangs over so much currently fashionable theorizing. After riding out all those arguments about post-industrialism and the end of ideology in the 1960s here we are again confronted with another version of apocalypse.

This refusal of apocalyptic thinking runs right to the core of what the contemporary Left's about. It's a matter of principle, identity and faith. If the multiple factions that make up the Left have any common identity then it is one which is rooted in a powerful sense of modernity as a condition in which all traditional "truths" and "absolute" values, all "natural" social roles and "essential" meanings are open to challenge and to change. If the Left has any unifying faith then it is the conviction that history is neither god-given nor predetermined but is there to be actively made and remade in a process of collective struggle by men and women freed from the chains of ignorance and fear. What can a theory of *post*modernism or *post*modernity have to say to people whose collective identity and political will are so deeply wedded to the sense of radical possibility opened up by modern times? To talk about the temporary fusion of the heady promises of modernity and capitalism is one thing. It's to say that the vanguard of the Left has been left behind for *now*. New times demand new strategies for change. On the other hand to use a term like "postmodernity" is to say that the motor of history has run down, that there is no united front along which the Left can advance, that there is no authority or rationality in accordance with which it can proceed. It is, in other words, to give up the ghost.

There is a great deal more at issue here than questions of "style." To appreciate just how much is at stake we have, from the start, to mark out a distinction between theories of post*modernism* which address a sense of crisis in the ways culture in the West is organized, produced and thought about, and those more general theories of post*modernity* which directly challenge the principles of hope, critique and practice on which Left politics have always been built. We may or may not care about the role of art and design in contemporary culture but we can't afford to ignore the larger crisis provoked by the severance—so evident throughout the world today, not just in "Thatcher's Britain"—of the link between modernity and progress. We have to think *through* that historic crisis even if we find it easier to reject the claim that history nowadays is finished, or that it is, as Jean Baudrillard puts it, a "toy" or a "game." A game what's more, that he insists the Left has lost.

The idea that "the dream is over" is hardly a new one—it forms one of the pressures against which socialism has always sought to make itself. But at the same time one of the ways in which socialism has been renewed in the past has been by actively engaging with those forces which have set out to consign it to the "rubbish heap of history." If the engagement with theories of postmodernity and postmodernism is to be fruitful—dialectical rather than defensive—then it has to be acknowledged from the start that such theories pose a challenge to the Left's ambition to "change the world" because they question the belief in rationality and progress which directs and underpins the Left's project(s). Those challenges have to be squarely faced if we are to move beyond them to understand the dynamics of new times.

Before looking at postmodernity, we have to consider the era it supposedly replaces. Marshall Berman sets out in his book *All That Is Solid Melts into Air* to provide a sketch of modern times by tracing out the connections between three terms. Firstly *modernization* refers to the economic, social and technological innovations associated with the rise of capitalism. Secondly *modernity* describes the radically transformed character of life under capitalism most clearly visible in the great European and American cities of the 19th and early 20th centuries. Lastly, there is *modernism*—the answering wave of experimental movements in the arts linked again to the capitalist metropolitan centers. Together these radical modernist innovations, from symbolism and cubism to surrealism and stream-of-consciousness writing, set out to articulate the experience of modernity. The terms of this engagement with modern life were always critical, whether modernists were rejecting "mass culture," negating bourgeois norms and values or seeking to align themselves with progressive social forces. In the case of the International Style of modern architecture and the Bauhaus ideals of industrial design (the so-called "machine aesthetic") the ambition was to merge with the modernization process itself in order literally to build a better world founded on rational principles (e.g., "form follows function").

But it's precisely this equation between modernity, progress and rationality that has itself been brought into question in the "postmodern" era. At the core of this question lies the "legitimation crisis." If modernity is a condition in which "all that is solid melts into air" then all the old institutions and centers of authority—from religion to royalty—which guaranteed stability and continuity in earlier epochs and more traditional societies are prone to crisis and contestation. If ideals like truth and justice are not underwritten by divine authority then how is authority to be guaranteed? If all values are flattened out beneath exchange then how are true and lasting values to be established? One of the quests within modernity has been to find ways of resisting this tendency towards the relativization of all values and claims to power by grounding knowledge and legitimating authority so that they are placed beyond question.

According to the French philosopher Jean-Francois Lyotard, this "legitimation crisis" has been solved through the invention of what he calls "the great meta-narratives" of the modern period. By this he means all those overarching belief systems originating in the Enlightenment—from the belief in rationality, science and causality to the faith in human emancipation, progress and the class struggle. These great stories have been used over what he calls the past "two sanguinary centuries" to legitimate everything from war, revolution, nuclear arsenals and concentration camps to social engineering, Taylorism, Fordist production models and the gulag. The collapse of faith in these meta-narratives heralds what Lyotard calls the "post-modern condition." None of the "centers of authority" legitimated by these collapsed meta-narratives—including that essential "holding operation," the modern nation-state—survives the transition into new times, at least as the latter are defined in postmodern theory.

What replaces them for the American Marxist critic, Fredric Jameson, is the universal "logic" of the market. For [Frederic] Jameson, the global spread of capital has meant that all such centers are either destroyed or have been made over and absorbed by the interlocking cultural and economic systems that make up "late capitalism." In the process the political and cultural maps of the modern period have been redrawn so that the old oppositions—science versus art, fact versus fiction, Left versus Right, high culture versus low culture, mass culture versus "progressive" modern art and so on—no longer hold. In the postmodern world no values prove "timeless," "authentic" or "oppositional" forever when absolutely everything from the price of pickled mushrooms on a Polish street corner to definitions of desirable art in the West moves with the market.

At the same time, the "radical" nature of modernism has been called into question in two ways. First, modern art is no longer marginal or oppositional: the "masterpieces" of the modern "tradition" now fetch astronomical prices at auctions and sit comfortably within the gallery system, and university and polytechnic arts curricula; TV ads routinely use all the shock effects of modern art. Second, as part of a process of critical review, the canon of High Modernism has been brought to book for its "Eurocentrism," its "masculinist" stress on transgression and transformation, its downgrading of everything that doesn't fall within its definition of what's important, women's art, domestic culture and reproduction, black and Third World art, "bourgeois" and "socialist" realism, peasant and working-class white, "mass" culture, middlebrow and high culture, nonmetropolitan culture, etc. Far from being "progressive," it's condemned for its partriarchal values, its aggressive change-the-world heroism, its colonialist plundering of "primitive" Third World art. But you don't even need the benefit of hindsight to see that any link between modernization, modernism and utopia is no longer tenable. That link has been dramatically broken—and not just in capitalist societies.

The violence that can flow from the fusion of centralized power structures, Fordist production models, aggressive modernization and a debased version of Modern Movement architectural principles is nowhere more apparent than in Romania today, where the seventy-year-old Ceauşescu is engaged in a village-leveling exercise described by the Helsinki Federation for Human Rights as "cultural genocide." The destruction of minority ethnic Hungarian and Saxon cultures tn Transylvania and the "rationalization" (eradication) of the informal peasant economy on which rural Romanians depend, are two of the consequences of Ceauşescu's transplantation of the inhabitants of over 7,000 villages to concrete "agroindustrial complexes," complete with huge communal kitchens and washrooms. Modernism here involves a tyrannical obliteration of difference. Nowhere is the Faustian link between a patriarchal gerontocracy and willed violence towards organically grown "archaic" cultural forms more clearly visible than in Ceauşescu's crazy plan to wrench "his" country into the Stalin era before he dies. As the rest of the Eastern bloc confronts the centripetal forces of *perestroika* and the public expression of formerly suppressed ethnic-cultural divisions and nationalist demands, Ceauşescu, the ailing "father," is attempting in the face of international opposition to exert absolute mastery over the future by turning Romania into a concentration camp.

The contention within a lot of postmodernism that today there is no center is not just a gesture of solidarity with these excluded, repressed or exterminated "others." It demands a review of priorities and a rethinking of terms like "representation" and "power" at so fundamental a level that any description of the crisis of the Left that doesn't take it seriously just will not be productive. But the contention also has specific ramifications at both the macro and the micro levels within theories of postmodernism and postmodernity. For Jameson it indicates the end of locality altogether as the multinational character of the late late show of capitalism reduces everything to its own image. The implication here is that we'll soon be able to watch "Dallas" or eat a Big Mac in any part of the inhabited world.

At the same time, the point where we "experience" all this and make sense of it as individuals has allegedly been made over too. The "sovereign sub-ject"—central to Enlightenment models of rationality, science and the indi-vidual—is itself "de-centered" from the throne of authority. It's de-centered in theory by the *new* "sciences"—psychoanalysis and Marxism. But in the 20th century it's also de-centered *practically* in the West by the rise of mass consumption and advertising. As the "consumption economy" has developed, so the value of commodities [has been] seen to derive less from the laws of economic exchange governing the market or from the ability of products to satisfy primary needs [than] from the way they function *culturally* as *signs* within coded systems of exchange.

This provides the key for the critique of the Marxist theory of value put forward by the French champion of postmodernity, Jean Baudrillard. For Baudrillard, the distinction between "real" and "false" needs upon which Marxist economics is based collapses as consumption becomes *primarily* about individuals and groups using commodities [as] a language to mark out taste and status *differences* between themselves. In his later work, commodi-ties and signs are seen to merge completely as the opposition between what things look like and what's really going on begins to dissolve in the "hyper-reality" of the media age. This process—what he calls "implosion of the real"—supposedly displaces all models of rational critique. It is no longer possible for us to see through the appearance of, for instance, a "free market" to the structuring "real relations" underneath (e.g., class conflict and the ex-propriation by capital of surplus value). Instead, signs begin increasingly to take on a life of their own, referring not to a real world outside themselves but to their own "reality"—the system that produces the signs.

It's at this point that Baudrillard grafts a global theory of postmodernity onto a global theory of cultural postmodernism to produce a scenario which is well and truly apocalyptic—"fatal," to use Baudrillard's word. In this world of surfaces TV takes over from the real as the place where real things happen only if they're screened (real things here include profits made on the screen[s] of computer terminals by dealers juggling prices on the international money and commodity futures markets). In such a thoroughly *imaged* universe—the world of Reagan-Gorbachev photocalls, Thatcher visits to Gdansk and HRH's *Vision of Britain*—"politics" becomes largely an adjunct of PR and showbiz even when the etiquette is breached (e.g., the attack on a newscaster on air by lesbian activists to publicize opposition to Clause 28). Rational cri-tique and the will to change the world are replaced by what he calls the "ec-stasy of communication"—a state characterized by "banal seduction" and "mindless fascination" where any kind of judgment—not just artistic but moral and political—becomes impossible.

Clearly a great deal more is at stake in the apocalypse laid out by Baudril-lard than a shift in the mode of production. But it's also clear that he offers a kind of picture of *some* of the changes that make up new times. However much we want to resist the chilly extremism of this kind of analysis, it's clear that the "information revolution" has implications far beyond the extension of financial services and the further diminution of our civil rights. The sheer volume and variety of information may conceal the fact that the shifts are qualitative as well as quantitative. One result of the print boom for instance, associated with desk-top publishing, Wapping and the end of hot-metal trade unionism, is that more and more publications compete for advertising reve-nue tied to increasingly fragmented and specialized markets. Manic compe-tition at the bottom end of the tabloid market has led editors to abandon the distinction between entertainment and information, as TV soap gossip crowds out "hard news" on the front pages. Although the tendency isn't new, in recent years it's been intensified to the point where hype creates its own "reality" so that some of the dailies now carry the "Aliens from Outer Space" stories pioneered in the notorious *Sunday Sport.*

What sense would an orthodox Left analysis make of this decline of stan-dards? It would probably begin by mentioning the circulation war, perhaps citing American precedents. It might go on to condemn the "Aliens Turned Our Son into an Olive" style of story as degraded entertainment, even as part of the ideology of authoritarian populism in which all "aliens" (gay men, the loony Left, black youths, the IRA, acid house fans, etc.), are defined as a threat to the "family of the nation," as part of the unassimilable enemy within. But such analyses would be inadequate insofar as they remain tied to an out-moded "economy of truth." They fail to acknowledge how far the ground has shifted. For what is also at stake in such mutations of the codes of journalism is the whole "information order" upon which meaningful debates over issues of this kind rely. The survival of the public realm—a forum of debate where conflicting interests and ideologies struggle to define reality—in turn depends upon the public's ability to discriminate *in the last analysis* between what is true and what isn't. If the generalized scepticism towards mainstream media reportage moves beyond issues of "fact" and interpretation—(what happened when, where and why and what does it mean?)—to question the line between truth and lies itself then the whole "economy of truth" collapses.

The idea of a verifiable information order, however precarious and shift-ing, however subject to negotiation and contestation by competing ideolo-gies, does not survive the transition to this version of new times. After all, it's not as if anybody is really being asked to believe in aliens. Instead they are being invited to relinquish the right to believe in the verifiability of public truths *per se*. Such a stretching of the codes of journalistic license beyond the limits established in the early days of the mass-circulation press may free the readers from any obligation to believe in the bourgeois myth of disinterested truth by offering itself as a kind of joke in which the reader is invited to participate (the "joke" is how low can we go?), but its potential dangers are also pretty clear: today aliens from Mars kidnap joggers, yesterday Ausch-witz didn't happen, tomorrow who cares what happens? Here the so-called "depthlessness" of the postmodern era extends beyond the integration of signs and commodities into salable "lifestyle packages," beyond the tendency of the media to feed more and more greedily off each other, to affect the very function and status of information itself. It may be that the Left will have to dig deep to find strategies capable of coping with the apparent "depthlessness" of new times versions of the "public realm."

It is easy to see why postmodernism has been characterised as an intellectual gloss for Thatcherism—an invitation issued by people who should know better to give up, lie back and enjoy. Yet in some of their founding premises and points of focus, theories of postmodernism don't offer a *description* of the dominant economic and cultural trends so very different from the territory mapped out on these pages as new times, though the analysis differs at a fundamental level. Some versions of postmodernism are patently fatalistic, even potentially fascistic, but the diverse currents and tendencies that theories of the "post" have sought to bind into and define have no intrinsic political belonging in themselves. On the one hand, in those circles where the politics of race and sexuality are taken seriously, critical postmodernism is identified with diversity and difference, a politics of contestation and change. On the other, in Baudrillard's "obscene" universe, postmodernity is associated with the annihilation of difference in the media age: the end of politics altogether.

For years *Marxism Today* has been arguing for a definition of the political as a "war of position" in which absolutely nothing is given or guaranteed. Such a "Marxism without guarantees" has already dispensed with Lyotard's "meta-narratives." Furthermore, the concentration in the work of people like Stuart Hall on the ways in which language has been used within contemporary British politics to actively construct—to *articulate*—"imaginary communities" clearly points a way forward beyond the impasse (or the armchair) in which so much of postmodern theory gets stuck. Thatcherism attempts to hegemonize the long-term movements described, though differently inflected, under the rubrics of new times and postmodernism within its project of "regressive modernization." There is nothing natural about the relationship between those forms and forces and that political will, just as there is nothing given or permanent about the "we" that Thatcherism has called into being.

This much is clear in recent debates over nationhood and national tradition. The struggle over the meaning of modernity, national identity and the past has offered a significant point of tension in Britain throughout the late 1980s—a point of tension which is there to be cracked open in the current controversy around the role of design and architecture in British life. Thatcherite definitions of "Britishness," national heritage and national pride have sought to align the "shape of the future" with a selective image of the past so that even the disruptions and upheavals of today's "communications revolution" are drawn into the charmed circle of national tradition through the analogy with the Industrial Revolution and the Victorian railway boom (the connection is especially pointed in London where the great 19th-century railway termini are being redeveloped as luxury hotels, leisure centers, office and shopping mall complexes). At the same time, within architecture where the term was first popularized, "postmodernism" has been used to describe developments as different in conception and appearance as the nostalgic, neo-Georgian retro-kitsch of Quinlan Terry, a planned 19-story gray, pink and red office [building] in the City of London and the "discreet" horizontal "ground-scrapers," huge, lateral, deep-plan dealing rooms located nearby, sometimes concealed behind the original facades of a block of "historic buildings." "Postmodernism" here has functioned largely as a cover for unrestrained development for profit. Some of the attacks on modernism (Terry's) are literally reactionary—*anti* rather than "post" modern. Some grow out of an allegedly populist challenge to the arrogance and authoritarianism of Modern Movement architecture while others use style and fashion rather than function as a metaphor for the shift out of Fordism into new times. It's significant that whereas the most celebrated examples of Modern Movement buildings tended to be office [buildings] rather than housing schemes, the examples of postmodernism most frequently cited in the architectural journals are supermarkets, shopping malls and leisure developments. In fact, the "postmodern city" may well be the product of what David Harvey calls "voodoo economics" where finance capital moves in to occupy the hollowed-out centers left by a declining manufacturing sector with the leisure, heritage and retail industries providing architectural light relief. To counter the argument that the culture of postmodernism heralds an entirely new epoch, it's worth considering the sober fact that some of the most feted examples of "modern" *and* "postmodern" architecture have been banks, from Mies van der Rohe's designs which helped to transform the skyline of Chicago's financial sector in the late 1930s to Richard Rogers' Lloyds building or Terence Farrell's designs for the revamped City of London.

What is clear is that in Britain the [high-rise building] has become a powerful symbol of a superseded socialist era. In the current debates, the [high-rise building]'s [figurative] collapse is used to point up the weaknesses of that other larger edifice—the postwar corporate state, with its mixed economy, its embattled health services, its strained, unlikely social and political consensus forged in the white heat of Harold Wilson's modernizing techno-jargon. The acquisition a few years back by Thatcher of a neo-Georgian Barratt home in an "executive estate" in Dulwich marks the ideological cut-off point from failed utopia to new realism, from council-house Britain to "enterprise culture," from stately-home and country-house conservatism to the tougher, "fairer" contours of the "property-owning democracy."

Yet beyond all the ideologizing, nobody—not even the architects—would claim that the original 1960s [high-rise buildings] were ever widely popular. There is a vast literature within sociology devoted to the Librium addiction and loss of community associated with Britain's "vertical streets." The enthusiastic responses to Prince Charles' vision of Britain as first and foremost a landscape to be conserved rather than designed testified to the strength of popular feeling on the issue. The affirmation within certain types of postmodernism of the particular against the general; the decorative, the "fantastic" and the "aspirational" against the "rational," the "formal" and the "academic"; the desirability of maintaining continuity with the past, the reverence for the "human scale," are all themes that can be articulated to a more imaginative and democratic, more innovative and pluralist version of socialism. In the words of Alexei Sayle: "No more living 200 feet in the air in a thing that looks like an off-set lathe or a baked bean canner."

Charles Jencks, the architect who pushed the term "postmodernism" to the center of architectural debate, stresses the importance of dialogue with clients, users and tradition/the past in the planning of new buildings. It is this assertion of the legitimacy of other people's desires that links postmodernism to a positive appraisal of new times. In new times the old hierarchical model of the expert standing Moses-like at the apex of a triangle and the masses laid out along the base waiting for deliverance collapses. The favored metaphors for intellectual activity in modernism were military (the revolutionary "vanguard," the artistic "avant-garde"), technical ("writers are the engineers of the soul"—Stalin), mechanical ("houses are machines for living"—Le Corbusier) and medical (the critic as "surgeon"). In postmodernism, ecological and organic metaphors predominate along with the softer model of the expert as facilitator and consultant. Postmodernism here has more value as one key to a pragmatic approach to consumer demands than as a global account of a "consumer economy" or as an insistence on any particular architectural style.

It's worth saying that within its own terms one of the more blatant paradoxes of Baudrillard's account of postmodernity is that it is itself a totalizing "meta-narrative"—one which makes the media, not the factory or class struggle or science, the "motivating" force —the literal *end* of history. According to Baudrillard the masses were an invention of the modern period: one of the myths used to legitimate Fordist projects as diverse as "the dictatorship of the proletariat," parliamentary democracy and selling soap powder. The decline of Fordism exposes the myth of the masses as an active force so completely that we live today—to quote the title of one of Baudrillard's books—literally "in the *shadow* of the silent majorities," so that all meanings "implode" into "the black hole" left by the masses' "disappearance." The "logic" of this position is as circular as it is solipsistic.

Postmodern pessimism of this kind is symptomatic of the crisis of a particular intellectual formation (male, white, European) shaped in the crucible of student politics in 1968. The "end of history" argument can be safely written off as the product of a bunker mentality spawned among a generation of liberally educated "critical" theorists by the disappointment that set in after the Road to Damascus radicalizations of 1968. Institutionally located intellectuals are marginalized at the best of times and are likely to feel even more redundant in the face of 1980s "new realism," "new vocationalism," and "enterprise culture." But the legacy of 1968 is, of course, itself contradictory. The student uprisings highlighted the decline of workerism, productivism and hierarchical, centralized party politics. But they also heralded the growing importance of cultural and identity politics, the politics of gender, race and sexuality, the ecology and autonomy movements. In the light of these new cultural and political forms and the emergent communities of interest attached to them, the pertinent question becomes not *has* history but rather exactly *whose* history is finished? Take, for instance, the relationship between postmodernism and feminism. While some postmodern pundits have tried to co-opt feminism, it's been a highly selective version of feminist theory that's been appropriated rather than the activism and historic aspirations that from the late 1960s onwards have brought together the various strands that make up the feminist movement. Some feminists have argued that postmodern theory merely involves male intellectuals claiming feminism for (the end of) history where history becomes little more than a long straight line of Great Male Thinkers rather than an uneven process of struggle which is concrete, open-ended and essentially collective. The story of the "legitimation crisis" begins to lose any overarching explanatory power in the face of that larger historical process. For if the value of particular ideas and accounts of the world is judged against the benchmark of history rather than philosophy then there are what Meaghan Morris calls other more important "guiding narratives" than the one Lyotard is promoting. Narratives like "making the world a better place for our children," "seeking social justice" are from this viewpoint more valuable than the postmodern lament for the end of history precisely because they are more likely to mobilize more people towards some version of ethical or socially responsible action.

What is of course so often forgotten in the hype surrounding postmodernism today is that there is a tradition of cultural socialism closer to home that is rooted in a similar skepticism towards the notion of the "masses." The late Raymond Williams always insisted that the "mass" was a category intellectuals tended to reserve contemptuously for other people, never for themselves. And if, after all is said and done, we still have need of meta-narratives then *The Long Revolution* may ultimately prove more *useful*, more progressive and empowering than the one that frames the theory of postmodernity because it acknowledges the fact that faith and idealism are themselves part of the historical process, vital constituents of the political *will*. It is also possible that something like a sociology of aspiration might grow out of the less totalizing approach to "ordinary people" that Williams recommends.

One of the features of post-Fordist production is the leading role given to market research, packaging and presentation. While it doesn't literally produce the social, it's nonetheless the case that marketing has provided the dominant and most pervasive classifications of "social types" in the 1980s (the yuppie is the most obvious example). We use these categories as a kind of social shorthand even if we are reluctant to find ourselves reflected in them. We live in a world and in bodies which are deeply scored by the power relations of race and class, sexuality and gender but we also live—whether or not we know it consciously—in a world of style-setters, innovators, sloanes, preppies, empty nesters (working couples with grown- up families), dinkies (dual-income-no-kids), casuals, sensibles, the constrained majority, and today's prime targets, the pre-teens and woofies (well-off-older-folk).

These are the types outlined in commercial lifestyling and "psycho-graphics"—forms of research which don't present descriptions of living, breathing individuals so much as hypothetical "analogues" of "aspirational clusters." In other words the new intensive but speculative forms of market research are designed to offer a social map of desire which can be used to determine where exactly which products should be "pitched" and "niched." All these types could no doubt be translated back into the old language (it would perhaps be relatively easy to return them to the axis of social class) but everything specific would be lost in the translation.

It is clear that such research methods and the marketing initiatives associated with them have been developed precisely to cut across the old social-sexual polarities. The parameters are designed to be transcultural and trans-national (the spread of "psychographics" in the UK is linked to the drive to go pan-European in preparation for 1992). We may find such forms of knowledge immoral, objectionable or sinister—a waste of time and resources which is unforgivable in a world where people are starving and in a country where people are still sleeping in the streets—but the fact is that they do actively create and sustain one *version* of the social. They depend for their success on the accurate outlining and anticipation (through observation and interviews with "target" subjects) not just of what new times (some) people think they want but of *what they'd like to be*. A sociology of aspiration might begin by combining the considerable *critical* and *diagnostic* resources available within existing versions of sociology and cultural studies with the *descriptive* and *predictive* knowledge available within the new intensive market research to get a more adequate picture of what *everybody* says they want and what they want to be in all its radical plurality. The challenge would, then, be to produce and distribute the required goods and services more efficiently and equitably than the opposition. Such a mix of traditional academic/social work and commercial/marketing knowledge functions would take the Left beyond the ghetto of "miserabilism" to which it is regularly consigned by the loony Right. Such a shift would require what certain forms of postmodernism recommend: a skepticism towards imposed general, "rational" solutions; a relaxation of the old critical and judgmental postures although it emphatically does not necessitate a retreat from first principles and primary objectives: a commitment to social justice, equality of opportunity and social welfare. The identity and faith on which Left politics have traditionally been founded remain in place. But beyond that a new kind of politics—as flexible and responsive to new demands and initiatives as the software that powers post-Fordist production—will have to be envisioned. It may well be that the two great collective identities through which the masses came together to "make history" in the last two hundred years—the first associated with nation, the second with class—are breaking down today in the overdeveloped world. But "emancipation narratives" are being written [a]round collectives other than the imaginary community of nation or the international brotherhood of socialist *man*. This is true even in popular culture and the "depthless" field of the media upon which Baudrillard operates.

Within the transfigured "public realm," established by transnational communications networks, new forms, both of alliance and contestation, are possible. One of the things ignored in the more "fatal" versions of new times is the binding power of the new transnational media systems: the power they have to move people not just to buy the products of the culture industries but to buy into networks that offer forms of community and alliance which can transcend the confines of class, race, gender, regional and national culture. Popular music offers many examples of this kind of bonding. Some of these "communities of affect" (rather than "communities of interest") are explicitly utopian. The simultaneously most spectacular yet most participatory examples to date of the kind of bonding made possible across transnational communications systems have been the televised events organized around Band Aid, Sport Aid, Live Aid and the Free Mandela movement. This is where you see the optimistic will in action. Televangelism is another less engaging example of this kind of mobilization specific to the media age.

Rather than "psychic autism" (Baudrillard) or "the waning of affect" (Jameson) such phenomena suggest the possibility of a new kind of politics existing primarily in and through the airwaves and organized around issues of universal moral concern. Such crusades are likely to be extended in the 1990s. Once again the desire to feel and to feel *connected* to a transitory mass of other people, to engage in transitory and *superficial* alliances of this kind is not intrinsically either good or bad. Instead it has to be *articulated*. Jimmy Swaggart managed to articulate the yearning for community and righteousness one way. Jerry Dammers, founder of the Two Tone movement and co-organizer of the Mandela concert, helped to direct the flow of similar desires in a radically different direction.

At the local level, the airwaves are there to be actively occupied (rather than passively tuned in to). In the UK, the use of music and style to articulate new ethnic identities underneath and against the monolithic version of "Britishness" available within Thatcherism has become one of the most remarkable (and marketable) aspects of cultural politics in the 1980s. Rap, house and funk music, for instance, are merely the latest in a long line of musics that have offered forms of community across the international black diaspora. At the same time they have literally plunged the fans back (through rhythms, lyrics and "quoted" snatches of speech from dead black leaders) into a version of black history and struggle in the New World—from slavery to civil rights to black power and the buppies—which may otherwise have lain silent and forgotten. Through sampling and citation, through rap and talkover, through mixing desks and on turntables, multi-ethnic musical traditions have been transformed and adapted on the ground to give a particular *modernist* voice and shape to a specifically black, British structure of feeling, in a place and at a time when the new Right has been implying that blackness and Britishness are, as Paul Gilroy puts it, mutually exclusive categories. In this way, the new syncretic or synthetic black British styles in the 1980s which rely on musical and sartorial cut-ups—mixes of sounds and images plundered from a range of ostensibly unrelated sources—form part of an ongoing process of active self-definition which is now being consciously extended by a new generation of black British independent film and video makers, writers, intellectuals and record producers.

Now young Britons of Asian origin have adopted similar strategies in the various styles associated with bhangra music which merges traditional Punjabi dance styles and rhythms with Indi-pop, black US and white GB funk, house and disco rhythms. Through the patterns of belonging and distancing established in these forms of cultural production, new forms of "British" identity become available which circulate along with the records themselves in the clubs and casette players and on the pirate radio stations. At a time when the integrity of the national culture is asserted against a common European identity, a genuinely cosmopolitan post-colonial space is opened up within and against "Englishness"—a set of identities available to all irrespective of their skin color, "rooted" in the airwaves. The process is by no means confined to black and Bengali subcultures. The "break-up" of imaginary Britishness can be heard too in the assertion of the Pogues' republicanism, in the Proclaimers' militant Celtic style. It's not just the "United" in the "United Kingdom" that is being broken down today. The rise of women singers and musicians like Yazz, Sade and Tanita Tikaram simultaneously challenge the monolithic sexism and heterosexism of 1960s and 1970s "rock" and racist notions of ethnic "belonging."

All these contradictory tendencies and possibilities could be described as part of the landscape of new times—a landscape which has yet to solidify, which is still to be made. They represent real challenges which cannot be written off as part of some linear global "logic" of postmodernism any more than they can be effectively framed within the old language of the Left. New political agendas and priorities are being forged on the ruins of the old and there seems little likelihood that a new set of universal values or objectives will emerge to bind us all together "beyond the fragments" into one progressive bloc. Meanwhile we shall have to watch for the significant points of tension in the various contradictory versions of "identity" offered to us rather than falling back into the positions traditionally reserved for the "radical" Left—the tension, for instance, between the new consumerism—the shop until you drop ethos—and the limits on consumption imposed by scarcity and ecological crisis, the tension between the competing demands of "meaningful" consumption and "responsible" citizenship. We shall have to go on placing ourselves and being placed in relation to a bewildering set of local/national/European/multi-national and international communities, interests and histories. And meanwhile we shall have to go on negotiating between the various fundamentalist demands for fixed identities and final truths and the modernist realization that identities are never fixed, that truths are never final.

But what's clear is that contrary to what Baudrillard says, there is absolutely nothing "fatal" or "finished" about new times. The task for the 1990s has to be how to rise to the challenge, how to abjure certain kinds of authority we might have laid claim to in the past, without losing sight of the longer-term objectives, how to articulate a new kind of socialism, how to make socialism, as Raymond Williams might have said, without the masses.

NOTE

First appeared in 1991.

REFERENCES

L. Appignanesi and G. Benninton (eds.), *Postmodernism*: ICA Documents 4, Institute of Contemporary Arts 1986.

J. Baudrillard, *For a Critique of the Political Economy of the Sign*, Telos 1981. *The Mirror of Production*, Telos 1979. *In the Shadow of the Silent Majorities*, Semiotext(e) 1984. *Simulations*, Semiotext(e) 1983. *America*, Verso 1988.

M. Poster (ed.), *Jean Baudrillard, Selected Writings*, Polity 1988.

M. Berman, *All That Is Solid Melts into Air*, Simon and Schuster 1983.

H. Foster (ed.), *Postmodern Culture*, Pluto 1985.

D. Harvey, *The Condition of Postmodernity*, Blackwell 1989.

J. F. Lyotard, *The Postmodern Condition; A Report on Knowledge*, Manchester University Press 1984.

M. Morris, *The Pirate's Fiancée: Feminism Reading Postmodernism*, Verso 1988.

R. Williams, *The Long Revolution*, Penguin 1963.

Family, Education, Photography

JUDITH WILLIAMSON

THE CRUCIAL importance of the family as an institution in maintaining the State is agreed upon by radical feminists and government ministers alike. Official recognition of its role was revealed in the proposed "Ministry of Marriage" some years back, but it has never been any secret that family life is the backbone of the nation. Its economic value to capitalism in providing both the unpaid maintenance of the labor force, and a floating pool of "reserve labor," i.e., women, has been well documented in Marxist and feminist writings. It also plays a direct ideological role in maintaining the status quo, through channeling the socialization of children into the accepted social structure, a role it shares with "education." These functions of the family show that it is intimately connected with what Gramsci calls "political society" or "the State."[1]

But what is contradictory about the *ideology* of the family is that it appears as the area of life most distant from the State, most "private" and entirely non-political. While this is by no means a new phenomenon, it is worth noting that a major Tory achievement in the years leading up to and after 1979 has been to imbue the family with an aura of independence and individualism in total opposition to the State, and particularly the Welfare State: so that while drawing heavily on the economic and social support of the family the government can manage to suggest that this burden is a gift of freedom, a seal of separateness from itself. The representation of the family as an autonomous emotional unit cuts across class and power relations to imply that we all share the same experience. It provides a common sexual and economic goal: images of family life hold out pleasure and leisure as the fulfillment of desires which, if not thus contained, could cause social chaos.

These images almost invariably take the form of photographs, and have done since the middle of the nineteenth century. However, photography is not just the means *through* which ideological representations are produced; like the family, it is an economic institution with its own structures and ideology. It is possible to distinguish three different production relationships in the area of photography and the family:

1. *The photograph as commodity in the "public" sphere:*
A photographer produces a photograph which is a commodity bought by a magazine, newspaper or advertising agency. It is "consumed" by us metaphorically, as

viewers, but we do not actually buy the image on, for example, a billboard. Often the photographs which are the commodities of greatest value in this market are of families, e.g., the Royal family, Cecil Parkinson's family, Sting visiting wife and new baby in hospital, etc. In this sphere families can *look* at representations not of themselves, but of other families they are encouraged to identify with themselves.

2. *The photograph as commodity in the "private" sphere:*
A photographer produces (usually in a studio) a photograph which is a commodity bought by the person/people photographed, mainly families (or would-be families, like engaged couples). In this sphere individual families can *buy* representations of themselves.

3. *The camera as commodity in the "private" sphere:*
When a photograph is taken by someone who is not a "photographer," i.e., an amateur, usually in a family, the photograph itself is not a salable commodity (unless it by chance shows something of public importance, or is a baby snap of a current pop-star, etc.). It is then the *camera* and *processing* which are the economic focus of the photographic industry; the value of photographs as commodities in the first two examples above is preserved through the clear ideological instructions in camera/processing advertisements about how and what to photograph. In this sphere families can *produce* representations of themselves.

I shall deal with the first category last, since public images of the family rely almost entirely on the styles and implications of the second two. Royal wedding photos differ only in scale from ordinary commissioned wedding photos (category 2); advertising images of happy families playing frisbee or eating picnics differ only in contrivance and technique from the arrangements of family leisure found in private albums (category 3). There is also another, somewhat different area—*Photography in "Education":* where on the one hand photos *not* sold as commodities take on the function of recording and monitoring, and on the other, photos of school groups, teams, or individual children become commodities sold to parents and other family relations. In this sphere photography occupies a position somewhere between the family album and criminal surveillance.

Perhaps the most influential family image in our culture has been that of the Madonna and child; father was absent long before he had to hold the camera. However, as the image of the family unit became secularized during the Renaissance, it became traditional for wealthy families to record and display their spiritual and material bonds through oil paintings of the entire family group; surrounded by land, possessions and, perhaps in a corner, a few discreet symbols of the mortality against which those possessions were shored. Only the upper classes could afford to commission such self-imagery; certainly poorer families *were* painted, but not at their own request. They featured as subjects for the more democratically minded artists who would, in this case, keep their pictures, not sell them to their poverty-stricken sitters.

(This tradition lingers on in documentary photography, where the poor, the foreign and the injured are still regarded as having no stake in the images they provide.)

This gap between those who could and could not afford to *own* pictures of themselves was dramatically narrowed by the advent of photographic portraiture in the mid-19th century. Early daguerreotypes had, like paintings, been unique and more expensive objects, but by the 1860s the possibility of photographic printing on paper brought this form of representation within the reach of the middle classes. Because at this stage photography was still a cumbersome affair, photographs were taken in the photographer's studio, which was furnished with a variety of props and backdrops, available equally to clients of all classes. It is sometimes quite difficult to tell the class of the stiffly posed Victorian couples leaning against classical pillars or standing in front of drapes, as they would be dressed in their best clothes and removed from their day-to-day surroundings.[2]

By the 1880s cameras were more mobile and could more easily enter the home space. Yet still the conventions of pose and setting were shared by working, middle and upper class alike. Queen Victoria was the first monarch to realize the marvelous ideological opportunities offered by photography and insisted on always being represented as a wife and mother, rather than a ruler. Photography played not merely an incidental but a central role in the development of the contemporary ideology of the family, in providing a form of representation which cut across classes, disguised social differences, and produced a sympathy of the exploited with their exploiters. It could make all families look more or less alike.

As the technology has become cheaper, the apparent democratization achieved in the *image* with Victorian photography, has now extended to the *means of production* of the image. Just as, in the last century, more people were able to own photographs, now more people are able to own cameras. Yet it is not entirely true to say that father (occasionally mother) has replaced the studio photographer. As cameras have become available on the mass market, the distinction between "professional" and "amateur" has been drawn more rigidly than ever before. Camera advertisements make quite clear that David Bailey or Don McCullin are allowed to take completely different kinds of pictures from us, even though the aspiring "amateur" may use the same equipment (and make his wife look ten years younger). This demarcation is important, because with the slipping of the means of production into civilian hands, as it were, it becomes all the more important to control the kinds of images produced. This is achieved through convention, advertising, and even the images you find on the covers of the little folder your negatives are returned in from the labs. It is quite clear that the spoils of a holiday abroad are meant to be snaps of children on beaches, rather than shots of foreign political events.

Family photographs today divide into two different types: the formal, of weddings, christenings, graduation and so on, where professional photo-

How to make your wife look 10 years younger.

Move up to the Fujica ST605 SLR. Immediately your photography's in a different class.

Its ultra-sophisticated lens (Fujinon 55mm f2.2), Silicon light meter and choice of three advanced focusing techniques enable you to control light to create exciting new effects.

You can shoot against the light. You can take photos in light that has other photographers safely tucked up in bed asleep. You can play around with lenses to get "mood" portraits in soft focus.

And you can be sure of perfect results. Every time.

Your dealer will be able to tell you more about all these advantages. And add a few of his own for good value.

He'll also tell you the price. You'll find it's not much to pay for a top quality camera with the world-wide reputation of Fuji behind it.

And as for a younger wife… Team your ST605 with Fuji film for true-to-life colour and crisp definition. Available in all popular sizes for prints and slides.

FUJI FILM Fujica widens your horizons.   Fujimex Limited, Faraday Road, Dorcan, Swindon, Wilts.   73

graphs are still frequently used, and the informal, of holidays and other leisure time. The formal are a record, a kind of proof that the traditional landmarks of life have been reached, and these pictures have much in common with early "posed" family photos. However, with the informal arrives a new element, never so highly developed as in contemporary family photographs: the necessity of "FUN."

In this modern "democratic" idea, just as in the earlier leveling notion of the *dignity* of the family, photography plays a formative role.[3] The "instant fun" offered by the Polaroid camera ad is both the fun *of* the picture, that process that takes place "before your eyes," and the fun *in* the picture, smiles and jolly moments frozen into one of those objects which create the systematic misrepresentation of childhood and family life. But it is as if the guarantee "before your eyes" ensured the very reality of the emotion pictured. The more transparent the process, the more indisputably real the content. And the dominant content, in home family photography, seems always to be pleasure. In earlier family images it seemed enough for the family members to be presented to the camera, to be *externally* documented; but now this is not enough, and *internal* states of constant delight are to be revealed on film. Fun must not only be had, it must be *seen* to have been had.

This raises the more psychoanalytic question of what is repressed in family photographs. Because besides being used externally as a unit of social cement, the family is also an extremely oppressive thing to be *in*. Photography erases this experience not only from the outside, in ads of happy, product-consuming families; it also erases it from within, as photos of angry parents, crying children or divorced spouses are selected for non-appearance in the

Actual image area 3¼" x 3¼"

SEE BEAUTIFUL SX-70 COLOUR PICTURES DEVELOP BEFORE YOUR EYES.

Press the electric button and out comes the picture…and the excitement starts. Deep brilliant SX-70 colours develop in minutes while everybody watches.

Polaroid's 2000 and 3000 instant picture cameras are two of the lowest-priced Polaroid cameras for SX-70 pictures. All exposures are automatic (even for flash).

And the SX-70 metallic dyes are among the most stable and resistant to fading ever known to photography. Polaroid colour pictures last.

Polaroid.
Instant fun, either way.

Actual print size 3¼" x 3¼"

OR BEAUTIFUL COLOUR PICTURES IN JUST 60 SECONDS.

Pass these beautiful colour pictures around just one minute after you take them. The fun is easy and inexpensive with Polaroid's Swinger instant picture cameras.

There are 5 models to choose from. They are all automatic and prices start surprisingly low …even for the Super Colour Swinger, which takes both colour and black and white instant pictures. All new Polaroid cameras are covered by our 3-year warranty.

And now you can save money on Polaroid instant film through our 50p-off promotion. Ask your dealer for details.

28   'Polaroid', 'SX-70' and 'Swinger' are registered trademarks of Polaroid Corporation, Cambridge, Mass. USA. Polaroid (UK) Ltd., Ashley Road, St. Albans, Herts. © Polaroid Corporation 1977

family album. It is of great significance within a family which photos are kept and which discarded, and also who takes photos of whom; and it is a fact not often thought worth commenting on that children are always the ones "taken" (though older children may own cameras). In the Kodak ad "Memories are made of this" it is father's hand that reaches for the camera in the foreground, to snap mother and the children who are unaware of his action. The ad

Memories are made of this.

stresses this with the barrier of the hedge, which makes father's photographic activity seem surreptitious, sneaky, almost voyeuristic.

But the important point is, *whose* memories are being made of this? It is by and large *parents'* memory that family photos represent, since parents took and selected the pictures. Yet children are offered a "memory" of their own childhoods, made up of images constructed entirely by others. The hegemony of one class over another in representing public history, which offers us "memories" of social life through TV and news photos, is paralleled in microcosm by this dominance of one version of family history, which represses much lived experience.

Yet as psychoanalysis has shown, nothing repressed ever disappears, and we may often be able to read in family photos "clues" to their repressed elements. Walter Benjamin says that "photography makes aware for the first time the optical unconscious, just as psychoanalysis discloses the instinctual

unconscious."[4] I would go further and say that the two are not only parallel; the "optical unconscious" may on occasion reveal the "instinctual unconscious." I discovered a personal example of this on examining old photographs that I found not in an album but loose in a drawer at my parents' house. To this day I have no memory of jealousy at my sister's birth when I was not yet two. Family mythology on the subject stated quite clearly that I had been a "good, grown-up girl" and welcomed the new baby from the start; I must have cottoned on that this was expected as I can remember nothing else. Yet I was struck not only by the undeniably anxious and ambiguous looks that I gave the baby in all early pictures, but by the surprising fact that we were virtually the same size, and I had not been a grown-up girl at all.

Most "education" goes hand in hand with families in repressing children and guiding them towards their niche in society; school and college photos reflect this with their family-like groupings. The school photo with the head in the center, staff clustered around, juniors cross-legged on the ground, prefects at the back, looks like the portrait of an extended Victorian dynasty. (Of course, the traditional way to defy the convention of the slowly-panning school photograph was to run around the back and appear twice.) However, most schools today have replaced or supplemented the giant school photo with individual photos not unlike studio shots, which are offered for sale to the child's parents. This shift reflects the trend from formal to more "personalized" family photography. The one moment in education careers still documented in traditional ritualistic form (like weddings) is graduation from college. Millions of students continue to hire gowns for this one day; their parents can have the photo which gives proof of their achievement.

All these kinds of photos merge with family photography. The one exception is the criminal type mug-shot usually taken on entry to the institution, so that staff can identify new students. But of course they are never really just "factual": haircut, clothes, expression, the way they write their names, all build up assumptions about students before we even meet them let alone get to know them. And the photographs required in applications, although ostensibly for identification only, are often known to affect choice of interviewees.

All the ideologies incorporated into domestic photography—democracy, choice, fun, leisure—are reproduced on a large scale in public photographs which, in modeling themselves on the family photograph's format, can more easily tap "family values." Any sensible politician will use a family photo rather than a mug-shot on their election hand-out. We can be relied on to sympathize with the family of the industrialist kidnapped by "terrorists," to share the excitement of royal weddings, and interest ourselves in the children of film stars. The *forms* of "private" photography are especially important in the public sphere to guarantee the intimacy and identification between audience and subject which a formal press-photograph could not achieve. Advertising also relies heavily on images of the family, the crucial consumers of domestic goods, although rather than following domestic photography it holds out aspirations of how families *should* look, act, and consume. These kinds of pictures make up the great bulk of advertising. But even the most unlikely campaigns will make use of the "family album" format to familiarize their product. My favorite is the ad for an American Express card which appears to have its own family/holiday album. This advertisement seems bizarre because nothing could be further removed in ideology than the family and giant banking corporations. Yet, returning to the discussion of the State, it is precisely this separation of the family from the political and economic interests it serves that gives it such ideological value; and photography, a process developed historically alongside the modern bourgeois family, has a large place in that value. Photography offers an important, enjoyable and potentially radical access to the means of producing self-images: but as long as those images remain bound by the ideology of the family, that potential will only occasionally or accidentally be realized.

NOTES

First appeared in 1986.

1. Gramsci, in the *Prison Notebooks*, describes "two major superstructural 'levels': the one that can be called 'civil society,' that is the ensemble of organisms commonly called 'private,' and that of 'political society' or 'the State.'" His distinction between the "hegemony" exercised by the dominant group in the former sphere, and the "direct domination" exercised by "juridical" government in the latter paves the way for Althusser's later differentiation between "Ideological State Apparatuses" and "Repressive State Apparatuses." While the family would usually be categorized as an "Ideological State Apparatus" in this schema, Gramsci's description of two "levels"

The Fairmont Family.
Of San Francisco, New Orleans and Dallas.

makes it possible to see that the family does also come under the exercise of "juridical government": it has a foot in both levels.

2. For some good examples of this, and a more detailed discussion of the history of family photographs, see Julia Hirsch, *Family Photographs: Content, Meaning and Effect.*

3. As Walter Benjamin has pointed out ("A Short History of Photography"), the "dignity" and "repose" that are part of the ideological aura of early photographs derive from the length of time necessary for successful photographic exposure. People had to stand very still as the light "struggled painfully out of darkness" onto the plate: thus technique and ideology were as inextricably linked as they are in today's "instant fun" Polaroid photography.

4. [Ibid.]

Culture / Power / HISTORY

Authority, (White) Power and the (Black) Critic; It's All Greek to Me

HENRY LOUIS GATES, JR.

For a language acts in divers ways, upon the spirit of a people;
even as the spirit of a people acts with a creative and
spiritualizing force upon a language.
—Alexander Crummell, *The Future of Africa*, 1860

Slowly but steadily, in the following years, a new vision began
gradually to replace the dream of political power—
a powerful movement, the rise of another ideal to guide
the unguided, another pillar of fire by night after a clouded day.
It was the idea of "book-learning"; the curiosity, born of
compulsory ignorance, to know and test the power of the
cabalistic letters of the white man, the longing to know.
Here at last seemed to have been discovered the mountain path
to Canaan; longer than the highway of Emancipation and law,
steep and rugged, but straight, leading to heights
high enough to overlook life.
—W. E. B. Du Bois, *The Souls of Black Folk*, 1903

The knowledge which would teach the white word was Greek
to his own flesh and blood . . . , and he could not articulate
the message of another people.
—W. E. B. Du Bois, *The Souls of Black Folk*, 1903

I

ALEXANDER CRUMMELL, a pioneering nineteenth-century Pan-Africanist, statesman, and missionary who spent the bulk of his creative years as an Anglican minister in Liberia, was also a pioneering intellectual and philosopher of language, founding the American Negro Academy in 1897 and serving as the intellectual godfather of W. E. B. Du Bois.[1] In his first annual address as president of the academy, delivered on 28 December 1898, Crummell selected as his topic "The Attitude of the American Mind toward the Negro Intellect."[2] Given the occasion of the first annual meeting of the great intellectuals of the race, he could not have chosen a more timely or appropriate topic.

Crummell wished to attack, he said, "the denial of intellectuality in the Negro; the assertion that he was not a human being, that he did not belong to the human race," assertions, he continued, which set out "to prove that the Negro was of a different species from the white man" (10). Crummell argues that the desire "to becloud and stamp out the intellect of the Negro" led to the enactment of "laws and statutes, closing the pages of every book printed to the eyes of Negroes; barring the doors of every school-room against them!" This, he concludes, "was the systematized method of the intellect of the South, to stamp out the brains of the Negro!"—a program which created an "almost Egyptian darkness [that] fell upon the mind of the race, throughout the whole land" (10). Crummell next shared with his audience a conversation which he had overheard in 1833 or 1834, when he was "an errand boy in the Anti-slavery office in New York City":

> On a certain occasion he [Crummell] heard a conversation between Secretary and two eminent lawyers from Boston—Samuel E. Sewell and David Lee Child. They had been to Washington on some legal business. While at the Capitol they happened to dine in the company of the great John C. Calhoun, then senator from South Carolina. It was a period of great ferment upon the question of Slavery, States' Rights, and Nullification; and consequently the Negro was the topic of conversation at the table. One of the utterances of Mr. Calhoun was to this effect—"That if he could find a Negro who knew the Greek syntax, he would then believe that the Negro was a human being and should be treated as a man." (10–11)

"Just think of the crude asininity," Crummell concluded rather generously, "of even a great man" (11).

For John C. Calhoun, then—who held during his lifetime the offices of U.S. congressman, secretary of war, vice-president, senator, and secretary of state and who stood firmly to his dying day a staunch advocate of states' rights and a symbol of an unreconstructed South—the person of African descent would never be a full member of the human community, fit to be anything more than a slave, until one individual black person—just one—demonstrated mastery of the subtleties of Greek syntax—of all things! Perhaps fearing that this goal would be too easily achieved, Calhoun later added mastery of the binomial theorem to his list of black herculean tasks.

The salient sign of the black person's humanity—indeed, the only sign for Calhoun—would be the mastering of the very essence of Western civilization, the very foundation of the complex fiction upon which white Western culture had been constructed, which turned out to be Greek syntax, of all things. It is highly likely that, for John C. Calhoun, "Greek syntax" was merely a hyperbolic figure of speech, a trope of virtual impossibility, the first to leap to mind during an impassioned debate over states' rights and the abolition of slavery. Calhoun, perhaps, felt driven to the hyperbolic mode because of the long racist tradition, in Western letters, of demanding that black people *prove* their full humanity, a tradition to which Calhoun was heir. We know this tradition all too well, marked as it is with the names of great intellectual Western racialists, among them Francis Bacon, David Hume, Immanuel Kant, Thomas Jefferson, and G. W. F. Hegel, to list only a few. Whereas each of these figures demanded that blacks write *poetry* to prove their humanity, Calhoun—writing in a post–Phillis Wheatley era—took refuge in, of all things, Greek syntax.

And, just as Phillis Wheatley's mistress and master had urged her to write poetry to refute racialists such as Hume and Kant, Calhoun's outrageous demand would not fall upon the deaf ears of the inarticulate intellectual inferior. In typical Afro-American fashion, a brilliant black intellectual accepted Calhoun's challenge, just as Wheatley had accepted a comparable challenge almost a century before. The anecdote that Crummell shared with his fellow black academicians, it turns out, was his shaping scene of instruction. For Crummell, Calhoun's challenge was his reason for jumping on a boat, sailing to England, and matriculating at Queens' College, Cambridge University, where he mastered, of all things, the intricacies of Greek syntax as part of the broader field of study in theology. Calhoun, we suspect, was not impressed.

But even after both John C. Calhoun and racial slavery had been long dead, Alexander Crummell never escaped the lesson he had learned as an errand boy at the "Anti-slavery" office. Crummell never stopped believing that mastering the master's tongue was the *sole* path to civilization and to intellectual freedom and social equality for the black person. It was the acquisition of Western "culture," he argued, that the black person "must claim as his rightful heritage, as a man: not stinted training, not a caste education, not," he concludes prophetically, "a Negro curriculum" (16). As he argues so passionately in his well-known speech, "The English Language in Liberia," which he delivered in 1860, the acquisition of the English language, along with the simultaneous acquisition of Christianity, is the wonderful sign of God's providence encoded in the nightmare of African enslavement in the racist wilderness of the New World:

The acquisition of [the English language] is elevation. It places the native man above his ignorant fellow, and gives him some of the dignity of civilization. New ideas are caught up, new habits formed, and superior and elevating wants are daily increased.[3]

Crummell accepted fully an argument central to the Enlightenment, that written and spoken language-use is the tangible sign of reason, and that it is the possession of reason which, as Francis Bacon put it in his *Novum Organon*, "made man a god to man." Crummell's first anonymous epigraph states this relation clearly:

Language, in connection with reason, to which it gives its proper activity, use, and ornament, raises man above the lower orders of animals, and in proportion as it is polished and refined, contributes greatly. . . to exalt one nation above another, in the scale of civilization and intellectual dignity. ("ELL," 8)

English, for Crummell, was "in proportion . . . polished and refined" in an *inverse* ratio as the African vernacular languages were tarnished and unrefined. And, while the fact that black people spoke English as a first language was "indicative of sorrowful history," a sign of "subjection and conquest," it was also "one of those ordinances of Providence, designed as a means for the introduction of new ideas into the language of a people; or to serve as a transitional step from low degradation to a higher and nobler civilization" ("ELL," 18).

English, for Crummell, was "the speech of Chaucer and Shakespeare, of Milton and Wordsworth, of Bacon and Burke, of Franklin and Webster," and its potential mastery was "this one item of compensation" that "the Almighty has bestowed upon us" in exchange for "the exile of our fathers from their African homes to America" ("ELL," 10). English was "a transforming agency, which is gradually subverting the native language of our tribes," he maintains with great approval, as the imperialistic forces of Great Britain "introduce trade and civilization, pioneer letters and culture, and prepare the way for the *English Language* and Religion." It is "this noble language," he concludes in the unmistakable air of triumph, that is "gradually lifting up and enlightening our heathen neighbors" ("ELL," 34, 32). In the English language are embodied "the noblest theories of liberty" and "the grandest ideas of humanity." By mastering the master's tongue, these great and grand ideas will become African ideas, because "ideas conserve men, and keep alive the vitality of nations. . . . With the noble tongue which Providence has given us, it will be difficult for us to be divorced from the spirit, which for centuries has been speaking through it" ("ELL," 51, 52).[4] "And this," Crummell proclaims, "is our language," and it is "upon the many treasures of this English tongue" that he has "dwell[ed] with delight" ("ELL," 29).

In direct and dark contrast to the splendor and wonders of the English language, Crummell pits the African vernacular languages.[5] "The refined and cultivated English language" is "alien alike from the speech of [our] sires and

the soil from whence they sprung." Let us, he continues, inquire "into the respective values of our native and acquired tongue. . . . The worth of our fathers' language, will, in this way, stand out in distinct comparison with the Anglo-Saxon, our acquired speech" ("ELL," 11, 19). Black vernacular languages,
for Crummell, embody "definite marks of inferiority connected with them all,
which place them at the widest distances from civilized languages." Crummell then lists these shared "marks of inferiority" of the black vernacular:

> Of this whole class of languages, it may be said, in the aggregate that (a) "They
> are," to use the words of Dr. Leighton Wilson, "harsh, abrupt, energetic, indis-
> tinct in enunciation, meagre in point of words, abound with inarticulate nasal and
> guttural sounds, possess but few inflections and grammatical forms, and are
> withal exceedingly difficult of acquisition." This is his description of the Grebo;
> but it may be taken, I think, as, on the whole, a correct description of the whole
> class of dialects which are entitled "Negro." (b) These languages, moreover, are
> characterized by lowness of ideas. As the speech of rude barbarians, they are
> marked by brutal and vindictive sentiments, and those principles which show a
> predominance of the animal propensities. (c) Again, they lack those ideas of vir-
> tue, of moral truth, and those distinctions of right and wrong with which we, all
> our life long, have been familiar. (d) Another marked feature of these languages
> is the absence of clear ideas of Justice, Law, Human Rights, and Governmental
> Order, which are so prominent and manifest in civilized countries. And (e)
> lastly—Those supernal truths of a personal, present Deity, of the moral govern-
> ment of God, of man's Immortality, of the Judgment, and of Everlasting Blessed-
> ness, which regulate the lives of Christians, are either entirely absent, or else
> exist, and are expressed in an obscure and distorted manner. ("ELL," 19–20)

So much for the black vernacular!

Any attempt even to render the master's discourse in our own black discourse is an egregious error, Crummell continues, because to do so is merely
to translate sublime utterances "in broken English—a miserable caricature of
their noble tongue" ("ELL," 50). Such was the case when English missionaries in the West Indies translated the Bible from the rich cadences of the King
James version into the "crude, mongrel, discordant jargon" of the black vernacular. No, translation just won't do, because "a language without its characteristic features, stamp, and spirit, is a lifeless and unmeaning thing." The
attempt to translate from English to the black vernacular is "so great a blun-
der" that we must abandon forever both indigenous African vernacular languages as well as the neo-African vernacular languages that our people have
produced in the New World. We must do so, concludes Crummell, because:

> All low, inferior, and barbarous tongues are, doubtless, but the lees and dregs
> of noble languages, which have gradually, as the soul of a nation has died out,
> sunk down to degradation and ruin. We must not suffer this decay on these
> shores, in this nation. We have been made, providentially, the deposit of a noble
> trust; and we should be proud to show our appreciation of it. Having come to the

heritage of this language we must cherish its spirit, as well as retain its letter. We must cultivate it among ourselves; we must strive to infuse its spirit among our reclaimed and aspiring natives. ("ELL," 50)

I cite the examples of John C. Calhoun and Alexander Crummell as metaphors of the relation between the critic of black literature and the broader, larger institution of literature. (However, lest anyone believe that the arguments of Calhoun, Kant, Jefferson, Hume, and Hegel have been relegated to their proper place in the garbage can of history, she or he need only recall the words of Japanese premier Nagasone a few months ago, when he remarked that America will *never* be the intellectual equal of Japan because of the presence of Chicanos, Puerto Ricans, and Blacks, whose presence lowers the country's collective IQ [!]—to which Ronald Reagan, when queried, replied that before responding he would need to see Nagasone's remarks "in context"!)

Calhoun and Crummell are my metaphors for acts of empowerment. Learning the master's tongue, for our generation of critics, has been an act of empowerment, whether that critical language be New Criticism, so-called humanism, structuralism, poststructuralism, Marxism, feminism, new historicism, or any other "ism" that I may have forgotten. Each of these critical discourses arises from a specific set of texts within the Western tradition. For the past decade, at least, many of us have busied ourselves with the necessary task of studying these movements in criticism, drawing upon their modes of reading to explicate the texts of our tradition.

This has been an exciting time for critics of Afro-American literature, producing perhaps not as much energy as did, say, the Harlem Renaissance or the Black Arts movement, but certainly producing as many critical essays and books about black literature, and yes, even jobs and courses in white English departments. Even with the institutionalization of the racism inherent in "Reagonomics" and with the death of Black Power, there have never been more jobs available in Afro-American literature in white colleges and universities than there are today, as even a cursory glance at the MLA Job List will attest (last year alone, thirty-seven such positions were advertised). In a few years, we shall at last have our very own Norton Anthology, a sure sign that the teaching of Afro-American literature has been institutionalized and will continue to be so, as only the existence of a well-marketed affordable anthology can do. Our pressing question now becomes this: In what languages shall we choose to speak, and write, our own criticisms? What are we now to do with the enabling masks of empowerment that we have donned as we have practiced one mode of white criticism or another?

II

Before considering these questions, it is useful to consider the resistance to (white) theory in the (black) tradition.[6] Unlike almost every other literary tradition, the Afro-American literary tradition was generated as a response to allegations that its authors did not and *could not* create "literature." Philosophers such as Hume, Kant, Jefferson, and Hegel seemed to decide that the presence of a written literature was the signal measure of the potential, innate "humanity" of all black people in Western cultures.

So insistent did these racist allegations prove to be, at least from the eighteenth to the early twentieth centuries, that it is fair to describe the subtext of the history of black letters as this urge to refute the claim that because blacks had no written traditions, they were bearers of an "inferior" culture. The relation between European and American critical theory, then, and the development of the African and Afro-American literary traditions, can readily be seen to have been ironic indeed. Even as late as 1911, when J. E. Casely-Hayford published *Ethiopia Unbound* (the "first" African novel), that pioneering author felt compelled to address this matter in the first two paragraphs of his text. "At the dawn of the twentieth century," the novel opens, "men of light and learning both in Europe and in America had not yet made up their minds as to what place to assign to the spiritual aspirations of the black man. Before this time," the narrative continues, "it had been discovered that the black man was not necessarily the missing link between man and ape. It has even been granted that for intellectual endowments he had nothing to be ashamed of in an *open* competition with the Aryan or any other type."[7] *Ethiopia Unbound*, it seems obvious, was concerned to "settle" the matter of black mental equality, which had remained something of an open question in European discourse for two hundred years. Concluding this curiously polemical exposition of three paragraphs, which precedes the introduction of the novel's protagonist, Casely-Hayford points to "the names of men like [W. E. B.] Du Bois, [Booker T.] Washington, [Wilmot E.] Blyden, [Paul Laurence] Dunbar, [Samuel] Coleridge-Taylor, and others" as *prima facie* evidence of the sheer saliency of what Carter G. Woodson once termed "the public [Negro] mind."[8] These were men, the narrative concludes, "who had distinguished themselves in the fields of activity and intellectuality," men who had demonstrated conclusively that the African's first cousin was indeed the European rather than the ape.

That the presence of a written literature could assume such large proportions in several Western cultures from the Enlightenment to this century is even more curious than is the fact that blacks themselves, as late as 1911, felt moved to respond to this stimulus, indeed, felt the need to speak the matter silent, to end the argument by producing literature. Few literary traditions have begun or been "sustained" by such a complex and curious relation to its criticism: allegations of an absence led directly to a presence, a literature often inextricably bound in a dialogue with its most scathing critics.[9]

Black literature, and its criticism, then, have been put to uses that were not primarily aesthetic; rather, they have formed part of a larger discourse on the nature of the black and his or her role in the order of things. The integral relation between theory and literary texts, therefore, which in other traditions has so very often been a sustaining relation, in our tradition has been an extraordinarily problematic one. The relations between theory, tradition, and integrity within the black literary tradition have not been, and perhaps cannot be, a straightforward matter.

Let us consider the etymology of the word "integrity," which I take to be the keyword implied in this matter. "Integrity" is a curious keyword to address in a period of bold and sometimes exhilarating speculation and experimentation, two other words which aptly characterize literary criticism in general, and Afro-American criticism in particular, at the present time. *Integritas*, the Latin origin of the English word, connotes wholeness, entireness, completeness, chastity, and purity, most of which are descriptive terms that made their way frequently into the writings of the American "New Critics," critics who seem not to have cared especially for, or about, the literature of Afro-Americans. Two of the most common definitions of "integrity" elaborate upon the sense of "wholeness" derived from the Latin original. Let me cite these here, as taken from the *Oxford English Dictionary*:

> 1. The condition of having no part or element taken away or wanting; undivided or unbroken state; material wholeness, completeness, entirety; something undivided; an integral whole. 2. The condition of not being marred or violated; unimpaired or uncorrupted condition; original perfect state; soundness.

It is the second definition of "integrity" (that is, connoting the absence of violation and corruption, the preservation of an initial wholeness or soundness) which I would like to consider in this deliberation on theory and integrity or, more precisely, upon that relationship which ideally should obtain between African or Afro-American literature and the theories we borrow, revise, or fabricate to account for the precise nature and shape of our literature and its "being" in the world.

Even though Houston Baker and I are often attacked for using theory and even though some black readers respond to our theories by remarking that "It's all Greek to me," it is probably true that critics of Afro-American literature (which [term], by the way, I employ as a less ethnocentric designation than "the Black Critic") are more concerned with the complex relation between literature and literary theory than we have ever been before. There are many reasons for this, not the least of which is our increasingly central role in "the profession," precisely when our colleagues in other literatures are engulfed in their own extensive debates about the intellectual merit of so very much theorizing. Theory, as a second-order reflection upon a primary gesture such as "literature," has *always* been viewed with deep mistrust and suspicion by those scholars who find it presumptuous and perhaps even decadent when criticism claims the right to stand, as discourse, on its own, as a parallel textual universe to literature. Theoretical texts breed other, equally "decadent," theoretical responses in a creative process that can be remarkably far removed from a poem or a novel.

For the critic of Afro-American literature this process is even more perilous, precisely because the largest part of contemporary literary "theory" derives from critics of Western European languages and literatures. Is the use of "theory" to write about Afro-American literature, we might ask rhetorically, merely another form of intellectual indenture, a form of mental servitude as pernicious in its intellectual implications as any other form of enslavement? This is the issue raised, for me at least, by the implied presence of the word "integrity" in this discussion. Does the propensity to theorize about a text or a literary tradition "mar," "violate," "impair," or "corrupt," the "soundness" of an "original perfect state" of a black text or of the black tradition? To argue the affirmative is to align one's position with the New Critical position that texts are "wholes" in the first place.

To be sure, this matter of criticism and integrity has a long and rather tortured history in black letters. It was David Hume, after all, who called Francis Williams, the Jamaican poet of Latin verse, "a parrot who merely speaks a few words plainly."[10] Phillis Wheatley has for far too long suffered from the spurious attacks of black and white critics alike for being the original *rara avis* of a school of so-called mockingbird poets, whose use and imitation of received European and American literary conventions has been regarded, simply put, as a corruption itself of a "purer" black expression, privileged somehow in black artistic forms such as the blues, signifying, the spirituals, and the Afro-American dance. Can we, as critics, escape a "mockingbird" relation to "theory," one destined to be derivative, often to the point of parody? Can we, moreover, escape the racism of so many critical theorists, from Hume and Kant through the Southern Agrarians and the Frankfurt School?

As I have argued elsewhere, there are complex historical reasons for the resistance to theory among critics of comparative black literature, which stem in part from healthy reactions against the marriage of logocentrism and ethnocentrism in much of post-Renaissance Western aesthetic discourse. Although there have been a few notable exceptions, theory as a subject of inquiry has only in the past decade begun to sneak into the discourse of Afro-American literature. The implicit racism of some of the Southern Agrarians who became the New Critics—not to mention Adorno's bizarre thoughts about something he calls "jazz"—did not serve to speed this process along at all. Sterling A. Brown has summed up the relation of the black tradition to the Western critical tradition: in response to Robert Penn Warren's line from "Pondy Woods" (1945), "Nigger, your breed ain't metaphysical," Brown replies, "Cracker, your breed ain't exegetical."[11]

No tradition is "naturally" metaphysical or exegetical, of course. Only recently have some scholars attempted to convince critics of black literature that the racism of the Western critical tradition is not a sufficient reason for us to fail to theorize about our own endeavor or even to make use of contemporary theoretical innovations when this seems either useful or appropriate. Perhaps predictably, a number of these attempts share a common concern with that which, in the received tradition of Afro-American criticism, has been most repressed: that is, with close readings of the text itself. This return of the repressed—the very language of the black text—has generated among our critics a new interest in theory. My charged advocacy of the relevance of

contemporary theory to reading Afro-American and African literature closely
has been designed as the prelude to the definition of principles of literary
criticism peculiar to the black literary traditions themselves, related to and
compatible with contemporary critical theory generally, yet "indelibly
black," as Robert Farris Thompson puts it.[12] All theory is text-specific, and
ours must be as well. Lest I be misunderstood, I have tried to work through
contemporary theories of literature *not* to "apply" them to black texts but
rather to *transform* by *translating* them into a new rhetorical realm. These
attempts have been successful in varying degrees; nevertheless, I have tried to
make them at all times interesting episodes in one critic's reflection on the
black "text milieu," by which he means "the tradition," and from which he
extracts his "canon."

It is only through this critical activity that the profession, in a world of
dramatically fluid relations of knowledge and power, and of the reemerging
presence of the tongues of Babel, can redefine itself away from a Eurocentric
notion of a hierarchial "canon" of texts, mostly white, Western, and male, and
encourage and sustain a truly comparative and pluralistic notion of the institution of literature. What all students of literature have in common is the art
of interpretation, even where we do not have in common the same texts. The
hegemony implicit in the phrase, "the Western tradition," primarily reflects
material relationships, and not so-called universal, transcendent, normative
judgments. Judgment is specific, both culturally and temporally. The sometimes vulgar nationalism implicit in would-be literary categories such as
"American Literature," or the not-so-latent imperialism implied by the vulgar
phrase "Commonwealth Literature," are extraliterary designations of control,
symbolic of material and concomitant political relations, rather than literary
ones. We, the scholars of our profession, must eschew these categories of
domination and ideology and insist upon the fundamental redefinition of
what it is to speak of "the canon."

Whether we realize it or not, each of us brings to a text an *implicit* theory of
literature, or even an unwitting hybrid of theories—a critical gumbo, as it
were. To become aware of contemporary theory is to become aware of one's
own presuppositions, those ideological and aesthetic assumptions that we
bring to a text unwittingly. It is incumbent upon us, those of us who respect
the sheer integrity of the black tradition, to turn to this very tradition to create
self-generated theories about the *black* literary endeavor. We must, above all,
respect the integrity of the separate traditions embodied in the black work of
art, by bringing to bear upon the explication of its meaning all the attention to
language that we may glean from developments in contemporary theory. By
the very process of "application," as it were, we recreate, through revision,
the critical theory at hand. As our familiarity with the black tradition and with
literary theory expands, we shall invent our own theories, as some of us have
begun to do—black, text-specific theories. We must learn to read a black text
within a black-formal cultural matrix.

I have tried to utilize contemporary theory to *defamiliarize* the texts of the black tradition, to create a distance between this black reader and our black texts, so that I may more readily *see* the formal workings of those texts. Wilhelm von Humboldt describes this phenomenon:

> Man lives with things mainly, even exclusively—since sentiment and action in him depend upon his mental representations—as they are conveyed to him by language. Through the same act by which he spins language out of himself he weaves himself into it, and every language draws a circle around the people to which it belongs, a circle that can only be transcended in so far as one at the same time enters another one.

I have turned to literary theory as a "second circle." I have done this to preserve the integrity of these texts, by trying to avoid confusing my experience as an Afro-American with the black act of language that defines a text. On the other hand, by learning to read a black text within a black formal cultural matrix, and explicating it with the principles of criticism at work in *both* the Euro-American and African-American traditions, I believe that we critics can produce richer structures of meaning than are possible otherwise.

This is the challenge facing the critic of black literature in the 1980s: not to shy away from white power—that is, literary theory; rather, to translate it into the black idiom, *renaming* principles of criticism where appropriate, but especially *naming* indigenous black principles of criticism and applying these to explicate our own texts. It is incumbent upon us to protect the integrity of our tradition by bringing to bear upon its criticism any tool of sensitivity to language that is appropriate. And what do I mean by "appropriate"? Simply this: *any* tool that enables the critic to explain the complex workings of the language of a text is an "appropriate" tool. For it is language itself, the black language of black texts, that expresses the distinctive quality of our literary tradition. A literary tradition, like an individual, is to a large extent defined by its past, its received traditions. We critics in the 1980s have the especial privilege of explicating the black tradition in ever closer detail. We shall not meet this challenge by remaining afraid of, or naive about, literary theory—that would only inflict upon our literary tradition the violation of the uninformed reading. We are the keepers of the black literary tradition. No matter what theories we seem to embrace, we have more in common with each other than we do with any other critic of any other literature. We write for each other, and for our own contemporary writers. This relation is a critical trust.

It is also a *political* trust. How can the demonstration that our texts sustain ever closer and more sophisticated readings *not* be political at a time in the academy when all sorts of so-called canonical critics mediate their racism through calls for "purity" of "the tradition," demands as implicitly racist as anything the Southern Agrarians said? How can the deconstruction, as it were, of the forms of racism itself (as carried out, for example, in a recent issue of *Critical Inquiry* by black and nonblack poststructuralists) not be political?[13] How can the use of literary analysis to explicate the racist social text in which we still find ourselves be anything *but* political? To be political, however, does not mean that I have to write at the level of diction of a Marvel comic book. No, my task—as I see it—is to help guarantee that black and so-called Third World literature is taught to black and Third World (and white) students by black and Third World (and white) professors in heretofore white mainstream departments of literature and to train university graduate and undergraduate students to think, to read, and even to *write* clearly, helping them to expose false uses of language, fraudulent claims and muddled arguments, propaganda and vicious lies, from all of which our people have suffered just as surely as we have from an economic order in which we were zeroes and a metaphysical order in which we were absences. These are the "values" that should be transmitted through black critical theory.

And, if only for the record, let me state clearly here that only a black person alienated from black language-use could fail to understand that we have been deconstructing white people's languages and discourses since that dreadful day in 1619 when we were marched off the boat in Virginia. Derrida did not invent deconstruction, *we* did! That is what the blues and signifying are all about. Ours must be a signifying, vernacular criticism, related to other critical theories, yet indelibly black, a critical theory of our own.

III

In the 9 December 1986 issue of the *Voice Literary Supplement*, in an essay entitled "Cult-Nats Meet Freaky-Deke," Greg Tate argues cogently and compellingly that:

> . . . black aestheticians need to develop a coherent criticism to communicate the complexities of our culture. There's no periodical on black cultural phenomena equivalent to The *Village Voice* or *Artforum*, no publication that provides journalism on black visual art, philosophy, economics, media, literature, linguistics, psychology, sexuality, spirituality, and pop culture. Though there are certainly black editors, journalists, and academics capable of producing such a journal, the disintegration of the black cultural nationalist movement and the brain-drain of black intellectuals to white institutions have destroyed the vociferous public dialogue that used to exist between them. (5)

While I would argue that *Sage, Calaloo*, and *BALF are* indeed fulfilling that function for academic critics, I am afraid that the truth of Tate's claim is irrefutable. But Tate's real and very important contribution to the future of black criticism is to be found in his most damning allegation. "What's unfortunate," he writes,

> is that while black artists have opened up the entire "text of blackness" for fun and games, not many black critics have produced writing as fecund, eclectic, and

freaky-deke as the art, let alone the culture, itself. For those who prefer exegesis with a polemical bent, just imagine how critics as fluent in black and Western culture as the postliberated artists could strike terror into that bastion of white supremacist thinking, the Western art [and literary] worlds. (5)

To which I can only say, echoing Shug in *The Color Purple*, "Amen. Amen." Only by reshaping the critical canon with our own voices in our own images can we meet Tate's challenge head-on.

Tate's challenge is a serious one because neither ideology nor criticism nor blackness can exist as an entity of itself, outside its forms or its texts. This is the central theme of *Invisible Man* and *Mumbo Jumbo*, for example. But how can we write or read the text of black theory? What language(s) do black people use to represent or to contain their critical or ideological positions? In what forms of language do we speak, or write, or *rewrite*? These are the issues at the heart of my essay.

Can we derive a valid, *integral* "black" text of criticism or ideology from borrowed or appropriated forms? That is, can an authentic black text emerge in the forms of language inherited from the master's class, whether that be, for instance, the realistic novel or poststructuralist theory? Can a black woman's text emerge authentically as borrowed, or "liberated," or revised, from the patriarchal forms of the slave narratives, on one hand, or from the white matriarchal forms of the sentimental novel, on the other, as Harriet Jacobs and Harriet Wilson attempted to do in *Incidents in the Life of a Slave Girl* (1861) and *Our Nig* (1859), respectively?

How much space is there between these two forms through which to maneuver, to maneuver without a certain preordained confinement or "garreting," such as that to which Valerie Smith alludes so pregnantly in her superb poststructuralist reading of Jacobs's *Incidents in the Life of a Slave Girl*?[14] Is to revise, in this sense, to exist within the confines of the garret, to extend the metaphor, only to learn to manipulate the representation of black structures of feeling between the cracks, the dark spaces, provided for us by the white masters? Can we write true texts of our ideological selves by appropriating the received forms of the oppressor—be that oppressor patriarchy or racism—forms in which we see no reflection of our own faces and through which we hear no true resonances of our own voices? Where lies the liberation in revision, where lies the ideological integrity of defining freedom in the modes and forms of difference charted so cogently by so many poststructuralist critics of black literature?

It is in these spaces, or garrets, of difference that black literature has dwelled. And while it is crucial to read closely these patterns of formal difference, it is incumbent upon us to understand that the quest was lost, in a major sense, before it had even begun, simply because the terms of our own self-representation have been provided by the master. Are our choices only to dwell either in the quicksand or in the garret of refutation, or negation, or revision? The ideological critique of revision must follow, for us as critics, our detailed and ever closer readings of these very modes of revision. It is not enough for us to show that these exist and to define them as satisfactory gestures of ideological independence. In this sense, our next set of concerns must be to address the black political signified, which is the cultural vision and the black critical language that underpin the search through literature and art for a profound reordering and humanizing of everyday existence. We must urge for our writers and critics the fullest and most ironic exploration of manner and matter, of content and form, of structure and sensibility so familiar and poignant to us in verbal and nonverbal black music—our most sublime forms of art—where ideology and art are one, whether we listen to Bessie Smith or to postmodern and poststructuralist Coltrane.

But what of the ideology of the black critical text? And what of our own critical discourse? In whose voices do we speak? Have we merely renamed terms received from the White Other? Just as we must urge that our writers meet . . . this challenge, we as critics must turn to our own peculiarly black structures of thought and feeling to develop our own language of criticism. We must do so by turning to the black vernacular, the language we use to speak to each other when no white people are around. My central argument is this: *black people theorize about their art and their lives in the black vernacular*. Unless we turn to the vernacular to ground our theories and modes of reading, we will surely sink in the mire of Nella Larsen's quicksand, remain alienated in the isolation of Harriet Jacobs's garret, or masked in the received stereotype of the Black Other helping Huck Honey to return to the raft again, singing "China Gate" with Nat King Cole under the Da Nang moon, standing with the Incredible Hulk as the monstrous double of mild-mannered, yet implicitly racist white people, or reflecting our balded heads in the shining flash of Mr. T's signifying gold chains.

IV

Before I return to John C. Calhoun and Alexander Crummell, those metaphors of progress, elevation, and intellectual equality with which I began my paper, let us consider another example of the black artist at the peculiar crossroads where the black world of letters meets the white. If mastering the forms of Western poetry to refute the racist logocentrism epitomized by Calhoun motivated Phillis Wheatley to break forever the silence of the black voice in the court of Western letters, and motivated Crummell to sail to Cambridge to master Greek syntax, how did Wole Soyinka respond to becoming the first black recipient of the Nobel Prize in Literature? The Nobel Prize, that sacred icon of Western intellectual and artistic attainment, many of us believed would be withheld from blacks for yet another century, and many of us consider to be another nuclear warhead dropped upon the last bastion of white racism—that is, their theories of our intellectual inferiority. Soyinka, born in Abeokuta, Nigeria, which Crummell had predicted to be one of the places in

West Africa at which the English language would reach perfection as spoken by black people ("ELL," 36), responded not as Crummell did to the racism that led [Crummel] to Cambridge, by extolling the virtues of the English language over the African vernacular languages, which [Crummell] thought to reflect the animal propensities of an inferior, barely human intellect. Instead, Soyinka recalled the irony that this single event in the history of black literature occurred while Nelson Mandela languishes in prison and while Western capitalism guarantees the survival and, indeed, the growth of the prison-house of apartheid. Dedicating his Laureate Speech to Nelson Mandela, Soyinka proceeded to attack the existence of apartheid and the complicity of the West in its continuation, as a nervous Swedish Academy shifted its weight uneasily.

Soyinka was most concerned to analyze the implications of African artistry and intellect being acknowledged before the white world, at long last, through this curious ritual called the Nobel Prize, endowed by the West's King of Dynamite and Weaponry. Soyinka refused to address his black audience; rather, he addressed his white auditors and, indeed, the racist intellectual tradition of Europe as exemplified by Hegel, Hume, Locke, Voltaire, Frobenius, Kant, and company, who "were unabashed theorists of racial superiority and denigrators of the African history and being."[15]

> The blacks of course are locked into an unambiguous condition: on this occasion I do not need to address *us*. We know, and we embrace our mission. It is the *other* that this precedent seizes the opportunity to address, and not merely those who live outside, on the fringes of conscience. . . .
>
> Some atavistic bug is at work here which defies all scientific explanation, an arrest in time within the evolutionary mandate of nature, which puts all human experience of learning to serious question! We have to ask ourselves then, what event can speak to such a breed of people? How do we reactivate that petrified cell which houses historic apprehension and developments? Is it possible perhaps that events, gatherings such as this might help? Dare we skirt the edge of hubris and say to them: Take a good look. Provide your response. In your anxiety to prove that this moment is not possible, you have killed, maimed, silenced, tortured, exiled, debased and dehumanized hundreds of thousands encased in this very skin, crowned with such hair, proudly content with their very being. ("NL," 8–9)

Soyinka's brilliant rhetorical gesture was to bring together an uncompromising renunciation of apartheid and a considered indictment of the racist tradition in Western letters that equates the possession of reason with the reflection of the voice and face of the master, a tradition that overwhelmed Alexander Crummell, standing as he did at a point of liminality between Western culture and African culture. Citing the work of Hume, Hegel, Montesquieu, and a host of others as "Dangerous for your racial self-esteem!" ("NL," 19), Soyinka marshaled a most impressive array of citations to chart the racist tradition in Western letters that would deny to the black world the particularity of its discourse, as typified for Soyinka by the sentiment of the expressionist Johannes Becher: "Negro tribes, fever, tuberculosis, venereal epidemics, intellectual psychic defects—I'll vanquish them" ("NL," 16). To underscore the failure of the Western intellectual to escape his or her own myopic racism in even the most sublime encounters with the Black Other, Soyinka compares Becher's exhortation with the commentary of Leo Frobenius upon encountering the most sacred, and most brilliantly rendered, bronze of the Yoruba people:

> And was it by coincidence that contemporaneously with this stirring manifesto, yet another German enthusiast, Leo Frobenius—with no claims whatever to being part of, or indeed having the least interest in the Expressionist movement, was able to visit Ile-Ife, the heartland and cradle of the Yoruba race and be profoundly stirred by an object of beauty, the product of the Yoruba mind and hand, a classic expression of that serene portion of the world resolution of that race. In his own words: "Before us stood a head of marvellous beauty, wonderfully cast in antique bronze, true to the life, incrusted with a patina of glorious dark green. This was, in very deed, the Olokun, Atlantic Africa's Poseidon." Yet listen to what he had to write about the very people whose handiwork had lifted him into these realms of universal sublimity: "Profoundly stirred, I stood for many minutes before the remnant of the erstwhile Lord and Ruler of the Empire of Atlantis. My companions were no less astounded. As though we had agreed to do so, we held our peace. Then I looked around and saw—the blacks—the circle of the sons of the 'venerable priest,' his Holiness the Oni's friends, and his intelligent officials. I was moved to silent melancholy at the thought that this assembly of degenerate and feeble-minded posterity should be the legitimate guardians of so much loveliness." A direct invitation to a free-for-all race for dispossession, justified on the grounds of the keeper's unworthiness, it recalls other schizophrenic conditions which are mother to, for instance, the far more lethal, dark mythopoeia of [the Nazis]. ("NL," 16–17)

"He is breaking an open door," one member of the Swedish Academy said to me while Soyinka spoke. "Why would he choose to indict apartheid at an historic moment such as this?" Soyinka chose to do so to remind the world that no black person can be truly free until we are all freed from even the *possibility* of racial oppression, and that even Nobel Prizes in Literature are useful only when [the] first black recipient reminds the world of that fact, and of the history of the use of race and reason as tropes of oppression in Western letters. As critics and artists, Soyinka argues, we must utilize the creative and critical tools at hand to stomp out racism. This is our first great task.

But what else contributes to the relation, then, between (white) power and the (black) critic? Soyinka's terms, and my title, might suggest that ours is the fate of perpetual negation, that we are doomed merely to "oppose," to serve within the academy as black signs of oppression to a political order in which we are the subjugated. We must oppose, of course, when opposition is called for. But our task is so very much more complex. Again, to define this task, I can do no better than to cite Soyinka: "And when we borrow an alien language to sculpt or paint in, we must begin by co-opting the entire properties of that language as correspondences to properties in our matrix of thought and expression."[16] Soyinka's own brilliant achievement in the drama is to have done just this, to have redefined the very concept of "tragedy" by producing a synthesis of African and European tragic forms. At all points, his "English" is Yoruba-informed, Yoruba-based. To assume that we can wear the masks, and speak the languages, of Western literary theory without accepting Soyinka's challenge is to accept, willingly, the intellectual equivalent of neocolonialism, placing ourselves in a relationship of discursive indenture.

It is the challenge of the black tradition to critique this relation of indenture, an indenture that obtains for our writers and for our critics. We must master, as even Jacques Derrida understands, how "to speak the other's language without renouncing [our] own."[17] When we attempt, by inversion, to appropriate "race" as a term for an essence—as did the negritude movement, for example ("We feel, therefore we are," as Leopold Senghor argued of the African)—we yield too much: in this case, *reason* as the basis of a shared humanity. Such gestures, as Anthony Appiah observes, are futile and dangerous because they further inscribe new and bizarre stereotypes.

How do we meet Soyinka's challenge in the discourse of criticism? The Western critical tradition has a canon, as the Western literary tradition does. I once thought it our most important gesture to *master* the canon of criticism, to *imitate* and *apply* it, but I now believe that we must turn to the black tradition itself to develop theories of criticism indigenous to our literatures. Alice Walker's revision of Rebecca Cox Jackson's parable of white interpretation (written in 1836) makes this point most tellingly. Jackson, a Shaker elder and black visionary, claimed like John Jea to have been taught to read by the Lord. She writes in her autobiography that she dreamed a white man came to her house to teach her how to *interpret* and understand the word of God, now that God had taught her to read:

> A white man took me by my right hand and led me on the north side of the room, where sat a square table. On it lay a book open. And he said to me, "Thou shalt be instructed in this book, from Genesis to Revelations." And then he took me on the west side, where stood a table. And it looked like the first. And said, "Yea, thou shalt be instructed from the beginning of creation to the end of time." And then he took me on the east side of the room also, where stood a table and book like the two first, and said, "I will instruct thee—yea, thou shall be instructed from the beginning of all things to the end of all things. Yea, thou shalt be well instructed. I will instruct."
>
> And then I awoke, and I saw him as plain as I did in my dream. And after that he taught me daily. And when I would be reading and come to a hard word, I would see him standing by my side and he would teach me the word right. And often, when I would be in meditation and looking into things which was hard to understand, I would find him by me, teaching and giving me understanding. And

oh, his labor and care which he had with me often caused me to weep bitterly, when I would see my great ignorance and the great trouble he had to make me understand eternal things. For I was so buried in the depth of the tradition of my forefathers, that it did seem as if I never could be dug up.[18]

In response to Jackson's relation of interpretive indenture to "a white man," Walker, in *The Color Purple*, records an exchange between Celie and Shug about turning away from "the old white man" which soon turns into a conversation about the elimination of "man" as a mediator between a woman and "everything":

You have to git man off your eyeball, before you can see anything a'tall.
   Man corrupt everything, say Shug. He on your box of grits, in your head, and all over the radio. He try to make you think he everywhere. Soon as you think he everywhere, you think he God. But he ain't. Whenever you trying to pray, and man plop himself on the other end of it, tell him to git lost, say Shug.[19]

Celie and Shug's omnipresent "man," of course, echoes the black tradition's synecdoche for the white power structure, "the man."

For non-Western, so-called noncanonical critics, getting the "man off your eyeball" means using the most sophisticated critical theories and methods available to reappropriate and redefine our own "colonial" discourses. We must use these theories and methods insofar as they are relevant to the study of our own literatures. The danger in doing so, however, is best put by Anthony Appiah in his definition of what he calls "the Naipaul fallacy":

It is not necessary to show that African literature is fundamentally the same as European literature in order to show that it can be treated with the same tools; . . . nor should we endorse a more sinister line. . . . : the post-colonial legacy which requires us to show that African literature is worthy of study precisely (but only) because it is fundamentally the same as European literature.[20]

We *must* not, Appiah concludes, ask "the reader to understand Africa by embedding it in European culture" ("S," 146).

We must, I believe, analyze the ways in which writing relates to race, how attitudes toward racial differences generate and structure literary texts by us *and* about us. We must determine how critical methods can effectively disclose the traces of ethnic differences in literature. But we must also understand how certain forms of difference and the *languages* we employ to define those supposed differences not only reinforce each other but tend to create and maintain each other. Similarly, and as important, we must analyze the language of contemporary criticism itself, recognizing especially that hermeneutic systems are not universal, color-blind, apolitical, or neutral. Whereas some critics wonder aloud, as Appiah notes, about such matters as whether or not "a structuralist poetics is inapplicable in Africa because structuralism is European" ("S," 145), the concern of the Third World critic should properly be to understand the ideological subtext that any critical theory reflects and embodies and the relation this subtext bears to the production of meaning. No critical theory—be it Marxism, feminism, poststructuralism, Kwame Nkrumah's "consciencism," or whatever—escapes the specificity of value and ideology, no matter how mediated it may be. To attempt to appropriate our own discourses by using Western critical theory uncritically is to substitute one mode of neocolonialism for another. To begin to do this in my own tradition, theorists have turned to the black vernacular tradition—to paraphrase Jackson, they have begun to dig into the depths of the tradition of our foreparents—to isolate the signifying black difference through which to theorize about the so-called discourse of the Other.

Even Crummell recognized that Western economic and political subjugation has inflicted upon us a desire to imitate, to please, to refashion our public discursive images of our black selves after that of the colonizer: "He will part," Crummell, with great satisfaction, concludes of the colonized African, "at any moment, with the crude uncouth utterances of his native tongue, for that other higher language, which brings with its utterance, wealth and gratification" ("ELL," 34–35). This, it seems to me, is the trap, the tragic lure, to which those who believe that critical theory is a color-blind, universal discourse or a culturally neutral tool like a hammer or a screwdriver have unwittingly succumbed. And by succumbing to this mistake, these critics fail to accept the wonderful opportunity offered to our generation of critics as heirs to the Black Arts movement, the great achievement of which, as Greg Tate correctly concludes, was to define a "black cultural difference" and "produce a post-liberated black aesthetic [which is] responsible for the degree to which contemporary black artists and intellectuals feel themselves heirs to a culture every bit as def [*sic*] as classical Western civilization. This cultural confidence," he concludes, "has freed up more black artists to do work as wonderfully absurdist as black life itself."[21] As Tate concludes, where is the black critical theory as great as this greatest black art? Our criticism is destined merely to be derivative, to be a pale shadow, of the white master's critical discourse, until we become confident enough to speak in our own black languages as we theorize about the black critical endeavor.

We must redefine "theory" itself from within our own black cultures, refusing to grant the racist premise that theory is something that white people do, so that we are doomed to imitate our white colleagues, like reverse black minstrel critics done up in whiteface. We are all heirs to critical theory, but we black critics are heir to the black vernacular critical tradition as well. Our task now is to invent and employ our own critical theory, to assume our own propositions, and to stand within the academy as politically responsible and responsive parts of a social and cultural African-American whole. Again, Soyinka's words about our relation to the black tradition are relevant here:

> That world which is so conveniently traduced by Apartheid thought is of course that which I so wholeheartedly embrace—and this is my choice—among several options—of the significance of my presence here. It is a world which is so

self-sufficient, so replete in all aspects of its productivity, so confident in itself and in its destiny that it experiences no fear in reaching out to others and in responding to the reach of others. It is the hearthstone of our creative existence. It constitutes the prism of our world perception and this means that our sight need not be and has never been permanently turned inwards. If it were, we could not so easily understand the enemy on our doorstep, nor understand how to obtain the means to disarm it. When this society which is Apartheid South Africa indulges from time to time in appeals to the outside world that it represents the last bastion of civilization against the hordes of barbarism from its North, we can even afford an indulgent smile. It is sufficient, imagines this state, to raise the spectre of a few renegade African leaders, psychopaths and robber barons who[m] we ourselves are victims of—whom we denounce before the world and overthrow when we are able—this Apartheid society insists to the world that its picture of the future is the reality which only its policies can erase. This is a continent which only destroys, it proclaims, it is peopled by a race which has never contributed anything positive to the world's pool of knowledge. A vacuum, that will suck into its insatiable maw the entire fruits of centuries of European civilization, then spew out the resulting mush with contempt. How strange that a society which claims to represent this endangered face of progress should itself be locked in centuries-old fantasies, blithely unaware of, or indifferent to the fact that it is the last, institutionally functioning product of archaic articles of faith in Euro-Judaic thought. ("NL," 11–12)

As deconstruction and other poststructuralisms or even an aracial Marxism, and other "articles of faith in Euro-Judaic thought" exhaust themselves in a self-willed racial never-never land in which we see no true reflections of our black faces and hear no echoes of our black voices, let us—at long last—master the critical traditions and languages of Africa and Afro-America. Even as we continue to reach out to others in the critical canon, let us be confident in our own black tradition and in their compelling strength to sustain systems of critical thought as yet dormant and unexplicated. We must, in the truest sense, turn inward even as we turn outward to redefine every institution in this profession—the English Institute, the MLA, the School of Criticism, what have you—in our own images. We must not succumb, as did Alexander Crummell, to the tragic lure of white power, the mistake of accepting the empowering language of white critical theory as "universal" or as our own language, the mistake of confusing the enabling mask of theory with our own black faces. Each of us has, in some literal or figurative manner, boarded on a ship and sailed to a metaphorical Cambridge, seeking to master the master's tools, and to outwit this racist master by compensating for a presupposed lack. In my own instance, being quite literal-minded, I booked passage some fourteen years ago on the QE II! And much of my early work reflects this desire to outwit the master by trying to speak his language as fluently as he. Now, we must, at last, don the empowering mask of blackness and talk *that* talk, the language of black difference. While it is true that we must, as Du

Bois said so long ago, "know and test the power of the cabalistic letters of the white man," we must also know and test the dark secrets of a black and hermetic discursive universe that awaits its disclosure through the black arts of interpretation. For the future of theory, in the remainder of this century, is black, indeed.

NOTES

First appeared in 1987.

1. Du Bois acknowledges Crummell's influence in a moving essay in *The Souls of Black Folk* (Chicago: A. C. McClung & Co., 1903), see chapter 12, "Of Alexander Crummell."

2. Alexander Crummell, "The Attitude of the American Mind toward the Negro Intellect," *The American Negro Academy, Occasional Papers, no. 3* (Washington, D.C.: The Academy, 1898), 8–19; subsequent citations from this work will be given parenthetically in the text.

3. Crummell, "The English Language in Liberia," in *The Future of Africa* (New York: Charles Scribner, 1862), 35; subsequent citations from this work, abbreviated "ELL," will be given parenthetically in the text.

4. Crummell is here echoing Emerson's dictate about the necessity of black people's producing written "ideas" because "ideas only save races"; see Emerson's speech "Emancipation in the West Indies," *The Complete Essays and Other Writings of Ralph Waldo Emerson* (New York: Modern Library, 1940 [1844]).

5. Despite his sustained and energetic effort to utilize the acquisition of English as the saving grace of African enslavement, it is only fair to note that Crummell is not unaware of the terrible irony in his argument. As he admits,

> ... I would not have you to suppose that I forget the loss which has accompanied all this gain. ... No! I do not forget that to give our small fraction of the race the advantages I have alluded to, a whole continent has been brought to ruin; the ocean has been peopled with victims; whole tribes of men have been destroyed; nations on the threshold of civilization reduced to barbarism; and generation upon generation of our sires brutalized! No, my remarks, at best, are discordant; and I avoid collateral themes in order to preserve as much unity as possible, while endeavoring to set forth the worth and value of the English Language. ("ELL," 30)

6. See Paul de Man, "The Resistance to Theory," *Yale French Studies*, no. 63 (1982): 3–20. More extensive versions of this section of my essay appear in my "Criticism in the Jungle," in *Black Literature and Literary Theory*, ed. Henry Louis Gates, Jr. (New York: Methuen, 1984), 1–24, and "Writing 'Race' and the Difference It Makes," *Critical Inquiry* 12, no. 1 (Autumn 1985): 1–20.

7. J. E. Casely-Hayford, *Ethiopia Unbound: Studies in Race Emancipation* (London: Cass, 1911), 1–2; . . . .

8. Carter G. Woodson, introduction, *The Mind of the Negro as Reflected in Letters Written during the Crisis, 1800–1860* (New York: Negro Univ. Press, 1969), v.

9. I have traced the history and theory of this critical debate in my *Black Letters and the Enlightenment*, forthcoming from Oxford University Press.

10. David Hume, "Of National Characters," in *The Philosophical Works*, ed. Thomas Hill Green and Thomas Hodge Grose (Darmstadt, 1964), 3:252 n.1.

11. Sterling A. Brown, lecture, Yale University, 17 April 1979.

12. Robert Farris Thompson, *Indelibly Black: Essays on African and Afro-American Art* (forthcoming).

13. See *Critical Inquiry* 12, no. 1 (Autumn 1985).

14. Valerie Smith, " 'Loopholes of Retreat': Architecture and Ideology in Harriet Jacobs's *Incidents in the Life of a Slave* [*Girl*]," paper presented at the 1985 American Studies Association meeting, San Diego.

15. Wole Soyinka, "Nobel Lecture, 1986: This Past Must Address Its Present," 10 December 1986, 10; subsequent citations from this work, abbreviated "NL," will be given parenthetically in the text.

16. Soyinka, cited in "Nigeria: The New Culture," *New York Post*, 17 February 1987.

17. Jacques Derrida, "The Last Word in Racism," in *"Race," Writing, and Difference*, ed. Henry Louis Gates, Jr. (Chicago: University of Chicago Press, 1986), 333.

18. Rebecca Cox Jackson, "A Dream of Three Books and a Holy One," *Gifts of Power: The Writings of Rebecca Jackson, Black Visionary, Shaker Eldress*, ed. Jean McMahon Humex (Amherst, Mass.: The University of Massachusetts Press, 1981), 146–147.

19. Alice Walker, *The Color Purple* (New York: Harcourt, Brace, Jovanovich, 1982), 179.

20. Anthony Appiah, "Strictures on Structures: The Prospects for a Structuralist Poetics of African Fiction," in *Black Literature and Literary Theory*, 146, 145; subsequent citations from this work, abbreviated as "S," will be given parenthetically in the text.

21. Greg Tate, "Cult-Nats Meet Freaky-Deke," *Voice Literary Supplement*, 9 December 1986, 5.

Women, Class and Sexual Differences in the 1830s and 1840s: Some Reflections on the Writing of a Feminist History

SALLY ALEXANDER

It is impossible ever to govern subjects rightly, without
knowing as well what they really are as what they only seem;
which the *Men* can never be supposed to do, while they labor
to force *Women* to live in constant masquerade.
—Sophia, *Women Not Inferior to Man*, 1739

This desire of being always woman is the very consciousness
that degrades the sex. Excepting with a lover, I must repeat
with emphasis, a former observation,—it would be well
if they were only agreeable or rational companions.
—Mary Wollstonecraft, *A Vindication of the Rights
of Woman*, 1792

Throughout history, people have knocked their heads against
the riddle of the nature of femininity—. . . . Nor will you
have escaped worrying over this problem—those of you who
are men; to those of you who are women this will not apply—
you are yourselves the problem.
—Sigmund Freud, Lecture on Femininity, 1933,
Standard Edition, vol. xxii

For a long time I have hesitated to write a book on woman.
The subject is irritating, especially to women; and it is not
new. . . . The voluminous nonsense uttered during the last
century seems to have done little to illuminate the problem.
After all, is there a problem? And if so, what is it?
Are there women, really? . . . One wonders if women still
exist, if they will always exist, whether or not it is desirable
that they should, what place they occupy in this world,
what their place should be.
—Simone de Beauvoir, *The Second Sex*, 1949

The Problem: Woman, a Historical and Political Category

The problem: woman, [and] the riddle: femininity have a capricious but nevertheless a political history. [They are c]apricious because they surface at different moments among different social milieux, within diverse political movements; and [have] a history in the sense that the social conditions and political status of women have undergone changes which may be traced, and with them some of the shifts in the meanings of femininity. As we become acquainted with the historical range and diversity of women's political status and social roles, the enigma itself occupies a different place. It is removed [from] history to some other realm beyond the reach of social analysis and political theory. Since there can be no aspect of the human condition which is not social where could that other place be?

If the meaning of femininity, and the political implications of Womanhood have at moments in the past three hundred years been contested, then it must be that what they represent is not some universal and eternal essence of woman, but the difficulty of the sexual relation itself between women and men which is always a social ordering, and one where the unconscious and its conflicting drives and desires press most urgently on conscious behavior, where political thought, though most capable of producing principles of equality and justice in its delineations of the proper relations between the sexes, nevertheless cannot always anticipate or circumscribe the urgency of those conflicts as they are lived.

Feminism, the conscious political movement of women, has been since the seventeenth century the principal contender in the struggles for the reorganization of sexual difference and division, and hence the social meaning of womanhood. If feminism's underlying demand is for women's full inclusion in humanity (whether that inclusion is strategically posed in terms of equal rights, socialism, or millenarianism) then the dilemma for a feminist political strategy may be summed up in the tension between the plea for equality and the assertion of sexual difference. If the sexes are different, then how may that difference (and all that it implies for the relative needs and desires of women and men) be represented throughout culture, without the sex that is different becoming subordinated?

History offers many symptoms of this difficulty, from the sixteenth century Royal Edicts, which prohibited women's public gossip, to the nineteenth century House of Commons references to women as "the sex" or feminism as the "shrieking sisterhood." Whether dismissed as a "monstrous regiment," "set of devils," or a "menace to the Labour movement" (the phrases are those of John Knox, John Keats and G. D. H. Cole respectively), feminism both arouses sexual antagonisms and invokes a threat which cannot be explained with reference to the demands of the women's movements—nothing if not reasonable in themselves. By suggesting that what both feminism and femininity stand for is not Woman—who, like Man, is no more or less than human—but the social organization of sexual difference and division, I am refusing to abandon femininity to an enigma/mystery beyond history. But then the problem becomes how to write a history of women and feminism which engages with those issues.

"A History of Our Own"

It is difficult to remember now how there could have been such a gust of masculine laughter at the 1969 Ruskin History Workshop when a number of [we] women asked for a meeting of those present who might be interested in working on "Women's History." I do remember the bewilderment and indignation we felt as we walked away from the conference to plan another of our own. It seemed to be the word—Woman—which produced the laughter. Why? Those plans became the first National Women's Liberation conference held at Ruskin College, Oxford in early 1970 (an event which wiped the smile off the male students' faces). The television room had been taken over by the crèche (run by men), and the college was swarming with women, women, and women. Student Union meetings for weeks afterwards rang with incoherent but passionate antagonism to the Women's Conference, focusing on the violations of students' freedoms that it had been imposed. The different implications, it seems, of women's liberation were lived vividly, though differently, for some men and hundreds of women that weekend. So my interest in women's history coincided with the beginning of my own education as an intellectual at a trade union college (I was a student at Ruskin from 1969–70) and the emergence of the Women's Liberation Movement from the late 1960s. The dichotomies—Women and Labor, Sex and Class, Feminism and Socialism have been the intimate inhabitants of both my psyche and my intellectual work (if the two can be separated) as they have been for many women of my political generation.

Intellectual Feminism

In the early 1970s socialist-feminists struggled to transform those dichotomies into political and theoretical relationships through campaigns and study groups. We diligently appraised and attempted to secure for our own purposes some of the traditions of Marxist thought, appropriating the concepts of political economy, historical and dialectical materialism and assessing their revolutionary practices through a feminist lens. If I ask what was/is the relationship between class struggle and the sexual division of labor, then historical materialism's focus on the mode of production is illuminating and suggestive. It imaginatively speculates on labor both as a form of activity which involves a relationship between Man and Nature, and as a system of social relations between women and men. But if the categories of political economy can sometimes reveal the operations of the labor market convincingly, the political traditions of Marxism have had little to say about feminism or the needs and aspirations of women; while historical materialism, by identifying class struggle as the motor of history pushes the questions of sexual divisions and difference to the periphery of the historical process. Whether posited as objects of analysis, or included as part of the narrative, they can be present in Marxist—and most labor—history, only as digressions from the real subject of history—class struggle; and their theoretical status is subservient to the study of modes of production.

If feminism has been only one of the detonators of "crisis" in Marxist thought and practice it has been the most insistently subversive because it will not give up its wish to speak in the name of women; of women's experience, subjectivity, and sexuality. "A history of our own," "a language of our own," "the right to determine our own sexuality," these were the distinctive themes of rebellion for the Women's Liberation Movement in the early 1970s. We were asking the impossible perhaps. As a feminist I was (and still am) under the spell of those wishes, while as a historian [I was] writing and thinking under the shadow of a labor history which silences them. How can women speak and think creatively within Marxism when they can neither enter the narrative flow as fully as they wish, nor imagine that there might be other subjectivities present in history than those of class (for to imagine that is to transgress the laws of historical materialism)? This is a difficulty to which I shall return.

Other intellectual traditions and ways of thinking about women, sexual divisions, and feminism pushed the categories Women and Labor, Sex and Class, Feminism and Socialism apart in my mind, refusing any analogy between them, or any mutual set of determinations and effects. The discovery of histories of women written by earlier generations of feminists showed how women's experience has to be remembered anew with each resurgence of feminist consciousness; between times it scarcely leaves a trace. Why this recurring amnesia, and why the attenuated feminist voice?

Radical feminism (from the United States; British radical feminist history surfaced later in the decade), offered a breathtakingly audacious understanding of the relations between the sexes in history. Sexual divisions prefigure those of class was the message that Shulamith Firestone and Kate Millett flung at a male dominated intellectual world; patriarchy the concept which they restored to the center of debates around social formations and social relations between the sexes.[1]

Since the seventeenth century feminists have rallied against the tyranny of men, male power, male domination and in the idiom of the 1970s, sexism. But those categories, while retaining a polemic conviction, I believe, have to be transcended too in any full history of women or feminism. Ironically radical feminism writes women's subjectivity and active agency out of history as effectively as any Marxism. Little girls become women because of what male dominated institutions tell and compel them to do. History is simply one long death knell of women's independent activity and consciousness. There were witches but men killed them; women were sensual, erotic, and adventurous but men used and abused them; women loved each other, but men forbade that love to be spoken; women were wives and mothers, but only because men wanted them to be; women were workers but men seized their skills, etc., etc. Men have much to answer for, but the envy and fears and desires of one sex can't carry all the determinations of history. If they can, then we are again in a world where women's identity, action, speech, and desires are all explained in terms of something else, in this case, the male psyche. Women are subordinated and silenced because they live in a world shaped in the interests of and dominated by men. Only a political revolution of women could ever destroy male power if it is conceived as so absolute in its effects.

But the writings and campaigns of previous feminisms exhibit contradictions and difficulties internal to the thoughts of both individual feminists, and the movements for which they claimed to speak, that cannot be reduced to the tyranny of men. As the vindicator of women's rights, Mary Wollstonecraft, for instance, did not absolve women from culpability in their own history; she castigated the coquetry of women of the leisured classes, condemned their feeble development of reason and virtue, their excess of sensibility, their false modesty. All this she attributed to an education which fitted women exclusively for marriage and the pleasures of men. But reading her letters and novels brings the irresistible recognition that she could diatribe so thoroughly against the thrall of men's authority and desires over women's lives, because she herself fell so violently and seemingly arbitrarily a prey to them herself. Do we reject the authenticity of those conflicting desires because men have placed them there for us? And then, how do we explain divisions within the women's movement itself in the mid-nineteenth century?

Just two examples: in the 1870s the suffrage campaign refused to endorse publicly the Ladies' National Association's Campaign against the Contagious Diseases Acts. Josephine Butler and the "grave and educated ladies" who reached out to their "fallen sisters" acquiesced in this suffragist silence, a denial as profound as any repudiation of a common sisterhood of women that came from outside the women's movement.[2] The suffragists' decision was made for reasons of political expediency. The second example indicates deeper tensions and divisions within the women's movement on the same questions: the identity or nature of woman, and the political representation of sexual difference.

The coalescence of feminist organizations broke up with the partial achievement of "Votes for Women" in 1918. From 1917 the largest suffragist organization, The National Union of Societies for Equal Citizenship (formerly named the National Union of Suffragist Societies), had been debating political priorities, culminating in Eleanor Rathbone's attempt to place the endowment of motherhood and birth control as the new unifying aims in 1924. Eleanor Rathbone argued that what distinguished women from men was motherhood; from maternity the natural feminine dispositions flowed and should be acknowledged in the economic policies and social provisions demanded by the women's movement.[3] "We must," she argued in a Presidential speech to NUSEC early in the 1920s,

> demand what we want for women, not because it is what men have got, but because it is what women need to fulfill the potentialities of their own natures and to adjust themselves to the circumstances of their own lives.

But any projection of motherhood into the political arena had always been strongly opposed by those who, led by Millicent Garrett Fawcett, had always maintained that to emphasize sexual difference, or women's "maternal function," would jeopardize their claims for equality. The theme of this disagreement was insistent: equality or difference, and if difference, then how could that difference be represented within politics without its being used to submerge women in domesticity, to deny them the full fruits of equality—by justifying their economic dependence and political subjection? The extent of sisterhood, the political implications of womanhood have proved as elusive and divisive within the women's movement as within the government, political parties or the male dominated labor movement in the past 150 years.

Every moment of dissonance and disagreement within feminism, as well as between women and men, demands recovering and disentangling—demands a historical reading. Neither Marxism nor radical feminism yet offers a history which can grasp the issues that feminism both stands for and raises. If Marxism persistently avoids sexual antagonism by relegating sexual difference to a natural world, then radical feminism conceives of women as shaped literally by men's desires. Histories of femininity and feminism have temporalities of their own—apart from those of class or men. The political narratives of feminism are as diverse and fractured as the vocabulary of individual rights and egalitarian aspiration itself is, when it surfaces now among the ascendant bourgeoisie in eighteenth-century Britain, now among the English Jacobins in the 1790s, among the Owenites and Unitarians in the 1820s and '40s, and in Victorian Britain, accumulating an intensity of grievance and yearning among women from very different social and political milieux.

The emergence of a mass feminist politics is most often attributed to the effects of the industrial revolution and the ideological hegemony of the bourgeoisie.[4] The former, by separating work and home, the latter by instilling ideas of domesticity among the working classes, allocated women and men to the private and public domains respectively. But we come closer to the terrain of feminist grievance and capture a decisive moment in its political temporality if we examine the forms of working class politics themselves in the 1830s and 1840s, and their language of demand and aspiration. If the working class emerged as a political category in those years (remembering its long history of gestation) then Woman emerged as a social problem. The emergence was simultaneous, the roots of grievance and their political representation different.

Feminist Consciousness and Class Struggle

Feminism as a self-conscious political movement appears when women, or some women in the name of their sex, distinguish themselves and their needs, from those of their male kin within families, communities, and class. Feminism's protest is always posed in terms of women's perceptions of themselves and their status in relation to men. From a litany of their discontents feminism gathers an identity of women, and formulates the demands and aspirations that will transform the social relations/conditions in which women and men will live. Whatever the starting point of its dissatisfactions—lack of education, men's property [rights] over women in marriage, "domestic drudgery," the prohibitions on female labor, the double standard of sexual morality, exclusion from the franchise—feminists from the seventeenth century have refused to concede that relationships between the sexes belong outside history in any conception of the natural world, which is where philosophers, poets, or Marxist historians, until provoked, have been content to abandon or place them. Feminism looks outward at the social forms of sexual division and the uneven destinies that claim the two sexes, but the critical look becomes an enquiry into the self and sexual difference and asks "What am I [as] a woman, and how am I different from a man?" No social relationship is left unturned, if only by implication, in this endeavor.

Feminism's return to the individual subject in its attempt to distinguish woman as a social category from man is one clue to some of its moments of emergence. There must be available a language of the individual political subject—a language which articulates the dissemination of the political order through the individual's identification with (and subjection to) its law. Some seventeenth century Protestant sects which proposed the unmediated communion between the Soul and God and dissolved the family in the community of all believers enabled women to claim an equal right with men to "preach and prophecy," for the "soul knows no distinction of sex,"[5] and in the eighteenth and nineteenth centuries feminism seized on the language of democratic rights within both liberal and utopian political discourse. But for the individual voice of a "Sophia" or Mary Wollstonecraft to become a movement there had to be not only feminine discontent but also a widespread yearning for another way of life. Before a language of rebellion can pass into general speech it must appeal to the imagination of a wide social group. Thus feminism appears at moments of industrial and political dislocation when disparate social groups are struggling to "find a voice" in the new emerging order, when seemingly stable forms of social organization are tumbling down, as in the English and French revolutions and in the 1830s and '40s.[6]

In speaking of the self and sexual difference feminism is at its most disturbing. Sexuality, intimacy, divergent conceptions of need are evoked and haunt the Marxist historian with the specters of bourgeois individualism, gossip, and the crumbling of working class unity. Ten years of women's history has calmed immediate fears. Few labor historians now hesitate to write of women's work, to mention the family or note the absence of women from some forms of political life. Working class "experience" has been stretched—though the political significance of those worlds beyond the workplace, alehouse, clubroom, union branch meeting are still argued about.[7] But if we are to pursue the history of women's experience and of feminism there can be no retreat from a closer inquiry into subjectivity and sexual identity. For if feminism insists on the political significance of the female subject and on the urgent need to reorganize sexual difference and division, it is to convey a more generous conception of human consciousness and its effects at the levels of popular resistance, collective identifications, and forms of political address and organization.

Social Being: Consciousness or Subjectivity?

The focus on the self and sexual difference throws into disarray the smooth elision assumed within Marxist thought between social being, consciousness and politics. Two distinctions are drawn: between material and mental life and true and false consciousness. Mental life flows from material conditions. Social being is determined above all by class position—location within the relations of production. Consciousness and politics, all mental conceptions spring from the material forces and relations of production and so reflect those class origins.[8] Collective class consciousness is the recognition of the shared experience of exploitation, and working class politics its expression, which in its most advanced form is revolutionary socialism. Thus there are graduated levels of consciousness (from spontaneous to political) before the historic destiny of the working class can be realized.[9] When historical materialism is compressed in this way into a series of laws, they are abandoned only at the risk of jettisoning the dynamics of history.

Let a more skilled philosopher unravel the polarities: material/mental; true/false; cause/effect. Here I only want to point to the absence of the individual sexually differentiated subject in Marxism. The question marks hover over social being, and how it is experienced—by women and by men.

"Experience" of class, even if shared and fully recognized, does not, as Edward Thompson and others have suggested, produce a shared and even consciousness.[10] Class is not only a diverse (geographically, from industry to industry, etc.) and divisive (skilled/unskilled; male/female labor, etc.) "experience," but that experience itself is given a different meaning. For Marxists, meaning is produced through ideologies. The bourgeoisie as the dominant class has control over the relations and the forces of production and therefore the production of ideologies, which mask the reality of social being to the working class. Thus ideologies serve the interest of antagonistic classes.

Debates within Marxism which attempt to release ideology from its economic/material base are inexhaustible. Engels and Lenin have been perhaps the sternest advocates of the grip of the base on the superstructure; Gramsci and Mao Tse-Tung elaborat[ed] on the continuum and flux of ideas among the people, the tenacity of traditions, and the irrepressible capacity of the human consciousness to produce forms of communal order and ways of thinking independent of the sway of hegemonic ideologies. But if we step aside from these debates to ask not how are ideologies produced, but how, in Juliet Mitchell's phrase, do "we live as ideas," then we enter the realm of social being and experience along another path—the path of subjectivity and sexual identity.[11] Against Marxism's claims that the determining social relationship is between wage labor and capital, exploiter and exploited, proletarian and capitalist, feminism insists on the recognition that subjective identity is also constructed as masculine or feminine, placing the individual as husband or wife, mother or father, son or daughter, and so on. And these subjectivities travel both into political language and forms of political action, where they may be severed from class or class interests, indeed may be at odds with them.

In order to place subjectivity and sexual difference firmly at the center of my research and historical writing I draw on the psychoanalytic account of the unconscious and sexuality. Psychoanalysis offers a reading of sexual difference rooted not in the sexual division of labor (which nevertheless organizes that difference), nor within nature, but through the unconscious and language. This poses the issue of psychic reality—a reality which like Marx's concepts of commodity fetishism and exploitation, will not be encountered through empirical observation. Psychoanalysis allows for a rich elaboration of subjectivity, identification and desire—essentially the psychic processes which give a political movement its emotional power.

The French psychoanalyst Jacques Lacan's re-emphasis on the part played by language—the symbolic order—in the production of meaning, and unconscious fantasy in the construction of subjectivity, has been taken up by some feminists because it retrieves sexual difference from the seemingly obvious "anatomy is destiny." Perhaps this needs further elaboration. Those who prefer to move straight to the political language of working class movements in the 1830s and '40s should skip this following (selective) exegesis.

Subjectivity, Sexual Difference, and Language

For Lacan the acquisition of subjectivity and sexual identity are a simultaneous and always precarious process which occurs as the human infant enters language; that is as s/he is spoken to and about and as s/he learns to speak. The human animal is born into language and comes into being through its terms.[12] Or, to put it another way, language, which pre-exists the infant, identifies us first as boy/girl, daughter/son. Language orders masculinity and femininity; they are positions which shift between and within discourses. The infant takes up these positions and moves between them as s/he journeys through the oedipal trauma, which marks the entry into human culture for every infant. The infant is compelled to acknowledge the significance of sexual difference through the presence or absence of the phallus—the primary and privileged sign of sexual difference. Neither little boys nor little girls possess the phallus; they are placed in a different relationship to it through the threat of castration and prohibition, which have different implications for femininity (lack) and masculinity (loss). The relationship to the phallus is mediated through fantasy; recognition of loss/lack, absence/presence is prefigured from birth as the infant differentiates itself from others—the absence/presence of the desired object (breast/mother); the look and speech of others. Fantasy fills the void left by the absent object. Castration and prohibition represent human law, within which every infant has to take up a place, initially as masculine or feminine, and never without a struggle. A struggle, because it is around these moments—absence/loss, pleasure/unpleasure—that the libidinal organization of need, demand, and desire is shaped.[13]

Subjectivity, and with it sexual identity, is constructed through a process of differentiation, division and splitting, and is best understood as a process which is always in the making, is never finished or complete. In this sense, the unified coherent subject presented in language is always a fiction, and so susceptible to disruption by the unconscious (or in collision with an alternative concept of the self in language). Everyday speech with its discontinuities, hesitations, contradictions, indicates on the one hand the process itself, and on the other, the difficulty the individual subject has in aligning her- or himself within the linguistic order, since there are as many different orders as there are discourses to structure them and always the possibility of more. [This] difficulty . . . is underlined for the little girl/woman by the impossibility for her of taking up a positive or powerful place in a culture which privileges masculinity and therefore men. Subjectivity and sexual identity are always achieved with difficulty, and the achievement is always precarious. The unpredictable effects of that achievement remain inaccessible to conscious thought in the repressed wishes to be one with the other, to belong to the other sex, as well as envy of and desire for the other sex. Both subjectivity and sexual identity are therefore unstable and involve antagonism and conflict in their very construction. Antagonism and instability are lived out not only within the individual psyche and its history, they mediate all social relations between women and men; they prefigure and cohabit with class antagonisms, and, as the history of feminism demonstrates, may well disrupt class solidarities.

Post-Saussarian linguistics' nonreferential theory of language and insistence on the arbitrary nature of the sign mark these instabilities. Meaning is produced through the chain of signifiers—the way words are strung together and organized into narratives, analysis, systems of thought—and may be gleaned from the study of those, rather than from reference to the objects and phenomena which they only designate, leaving them always open to dispute and redefinition[14] ([a] salutary, if familiar, reminder to the historian that historical reconstruction of the past is always through interpretation of the sources, which serve [as] memory-traces for the psychoanalyst, as the primary sources from which and over which we impose our own interpretations and causalities). There is no relation of sex, Lacan cautions us (meaning no natural relation: no relation that can be read off from anatomy, biology, or the demands of procreation) except, I would emphasize, as it is articulated in language.

It is partly because feminism inquires into the self in its concern to distinguish woman from man as a social category, and because of one of the points of that return has been a dissatisfaction with historical materialism's privileging of class (narrowly defined) as the determining social experience, economic relation and agency of political change, that the limits of Marxist history's notion of social being, consciousness and politics, and the articulations between them are so clearly revealed. Feminist history has to emancipate itself from class as the organizing principle of history, the privileged signifier of social relations and their political representations.

Marxism and other sociological theories of social being are resistant to any psychology which could be read as proposing a universal human nature. If they allow for a human nature at all it is one that is produced by the environment (shadows of the Enlightenment). The subjectivity of psychoanalysis does not . . . imply a universal human nature [either;] it suggests that some forms of mental functioning—the unconscious, fantasy, memory, etc.—seem to be so. Subjectivity in this account is neither universal nor ahistorical. First structured through relations of absence and loss, pleasure and unpleasure, difference and division, these are simultaneous with the social naming and placing among kin, community, school, class which are always historically specific.

Why open up history to the unconscious? But historians are as familiar as the analyst, poet, philosopher, everyone in their daily lives, with the power of the imaginary: dreams, fantasy, desire, fear, envy, pleasure. Historians of pre-industrial society have fewer inhibitions about speaking of myth, ritual, magic and their significance in human organization. Perhaps the fear that . . . introducing the unconscious and fantasy into social history is to open a Pandora's box, to deny the rationale of political and social life, is stalled by the distance of pre-industrial societies from our own. Against these reservations, I only suggest that the persistent problem of femininity and the presence of feminism indicate that the box is already wide open.

It is not my intention to reconstruct the individual unconscious, or individual subjectivity (which may be glimpsed nevertheless by the historian through autobiography, memory, or speech). [I] merely [wish] to emphasize that the symbolic sets the terms within which any social group must position itself [in order to] conceive of a new social order, and that the symbolic has a life of its own. And secondly, that human subjectivity shapes, as it is itself shaped by, political practice and language—it leaves its imprint there.

There are just one or two further thoughts to leave in the mind of the reader before turning to the working class politics of the 1830s and '40s.

Histories of all mass movements in the epoch of industrial capitalism reveal the power of language—oratory, polemic, propaganda—to both capture the allegiance of the constituency addressed, and to formulate social visions, to translate need and desire into demand. Insofar as the political vision is in combat with the present rule of law, then the question of strategy, how that law is to be encountered and negotiated, will depend on the relative balance of visionary aspiration and concrete political demand within a political move- ment. The strength of desire in utopian visions of transcendence means that there is little room for negotiation within government, law, or any of the ex- isting domains of authority. We may glean an insight into the mentality of transcendence from Lacan's exploration of desire, which is predicated on ab- sence/loss, is always in excess of demand, and is produced through language. The desire for harmony, a world free from conflict, is—like the unified sub- ject—a wish whose realization is elusive, though a wish that compels. Since even utopian visions, when translated into living communities, must impose their own moralities and laws, they too become open to challenge from those who wish to disobey, or to imagine another order. What happens when the visionaries become the lawmakers?

Both feminism and psychoanalysis suggest (in different ways), and history appears to confirm their findings, that antagonism between the sexes is an unavoidable aspect of the acquisition of sexual identity, and one that can be explained neither by anatomy nor environment alone. If antagonism is always latent, it is possible that history offers no final resolution, only the constant reshaping, reorganizing of the symbolization of difference, and the sexual division of labor. The questions for the historians of feminism are why at some moments does sexual difference and division take on a political signifi- cance—which elements in the organization are politicized, what are the terms of negotiation, and between whom?

Radicalism and Women

Humble Petition of the Poor Spinners. . . . Sheweth, that the Business of Spinning, in all its branches, hath ever been, time out of mind, the peculiar employment of women; insomuch that every single woman is called in law a Spinster . . . that this employment above all others is suited to the condition and circumstances of the Female Poor; inasmuch as not only single women, but married ones also, can be employed in it consistently with the necessary cares of their families; for, the business being carried on in their own houses, they can at any time leave when the care of their families requires their attendance, and can re-assume the work when family duty permits it; nay they can, in many instances, carry on their work and perform their domestic duty at the same time; particularly in the case of attending a sick husband or child, or an aging parent.
—*Humble Petition of the Poor Spinners*, Leicester, 1788

Now the doctrine of the Free-trader is, that no law is given—
no responsibility is incurred! That wealth cannot . . . be misapplied. . . .
The Free-trader, therefore, laughs at the idea of Christian laws interfering
with him. He rejects the interposition of the Almighty; he is an independent
agent. He cannot be a Christian. Every Christian believes that man has
fallen from perfection, that he is selfish, covetous, and that he needs the
unerring teaching of the Almighty. The Christian must require that all human
law shall be founded on the laws revealed in the
Word of Truth.
The Christian will never forget, the Free-trader will never remember, that the
head and eye must never be permitted to invade the rights of the hands
and the feet. The Christian knows that society is one compact body, each
individual member being dependent on the rest, each requiring the protection
of all. The Free-trader on the contrary, persuades himself that each member
is a separate piece of independence, an isolated self.
—Richard Oastler, 1847

We do not hesitate to say, that the tone of mind and thought which has
overthrown authority and violated every code human and divine abroad,
and fostered chartism and rebellion at home is the same which
has also written *Jane Eyre.*
—*Quarterly Review*, 1849

If we turn to the 1830s and '40s with these reflections in mind and ask the question [W]hy were some women able to speak of their rights to sexual and economic independence and to deliberate on the formation of the new morality and social order within Owenism and not within contemporary movements of similar class composition undergoing similar experiences of industrial dislocation[?], then the focus on subjectivity and language is suggestive.

The Short-time Committees from the 1820s, Anti–Poor Law struggles, Owenism and Chartism in the 1830s and '40s involved women; speaking for the poor, the working classes, the unenfranchised, the dispossessed, they included both sexes and all generations. But if we listen more closely to the common elements in their analysis of discontent and language of aspiration we discover firstly that women could only speak as active subjects at selective moments, and within the community. Men spoke in the first person for the community as a whole when appealing to public opinion; while political demand, communal rights, distribution and dispensation of the law [were] a dialogue of negotiation between the men of the communities and the ruling class—"capitalists and lawgivers." And secondly, the place in the vision of the new social order that these movements afforded women was founded on the conceptions of the sexual division of labor, property, laws of inheritance and the relative "capacities" and status of women and men within marriage prevalent among rural and urban industrial communities from the eighteenth century which had never scrupulously observed the principle of equality between the sexes. Sexual difference was intimately bound up in notions of labor, property and kin in popular radical thought, and [on] their respective organization women's access to knowledge, skill, and independent political subjectivity depended.

When whole communities rebelled against punitive legislation, or the depredation of customary rights, against unemployment or starvation—as they did in different parts of the country through the Factory Movement, Anti–Poor Law campaigns and Chartism—then women rioted, attended public assemblies and processions, formed committees, though women and men were often segregated. In active resistance against proletarianization the political subject was the community and radical rhetoric addressed wives as well as husbands, mothers as well as fathers, female and child labor as well as male. Nevertheless, whenever community resistance was formally organized into democratically elected committees with powers to negotiate with employers, justices of the peace, government representatives, then men were in the forefront and the spokesmen of those committees. Women were excluded from these forms of public speech not through the separation of workshop and home (though their increasing distance did underlie the "separate spheres" emphasis of nineteenth century feminist thought, and the different forms of political and industrial organizations of women and men in the second half of the nineteenth century)[;] they had been excluded from formal political organization and conceptions of the individual legal, political, and economic subject since the end of the seventeenth century.[15]

The legal, political, and economic subject in radical popular speech reaching back to the seventeenth century Levellers was the propertied individual, and the propertied individual was always masculine—whether head of household, skilled tradesman, or artisan whose property was his labor, or the evocation of the Freeborn Briton. Early nineteenth century radicalism did not so much refer to the "experience" of the dispossessed communities as draw on the rules of association, the idiom and rhetoric of the leaders of their struggles: the small master craftsmen, the displaced domestic worker, the artisan and mechanic, the skilled factory operatives. [These were m]en with a long history of trade association, for whom custom and status as well as skill determined the level of wages, length of the working day, entry to a trade, etc., for whom the collective wisdom and knowledge of their skill was lodged in the custom and practice of the workshop, and whose authority and control extended through apprenticeship rules to their children and other kin. Skilled men outlining the grievances that fueled the factory reform movements in the textile districts from the 1820s to the 1840s, the several attempts at general unions, spoke of being "robbed" or "disinherited" of the right to practice their trade; of the "slavery" of the mills; of their resistance to becoming the "hired servants" of the "new breed of employer." The vocabulary of grievance is similar among the tailors, shoemakers, and cabinet-makers in London resisting the "sweating and puffing" system; and it stretches back to the small master clothiers in the North and West of England who gave evidence to the 1806 Royal Commission on the Woollen Industry, Britain's first and major capitalized industry, and one which employed a majority of women and children through the seventeenth and eighteenth centuries. In the minds of these different groups of male workers their status as fathers and heads of families was indelibly associated with their independence through "honorable" labor and property in skill, which identification with a trade gave them.[16]

It was as fathers and heads of household that the radical artisan[s] spoke of the loss of parental control and authority over kin, the predatory sexual freedom of the mills, the destruction of "habits and morals." Despair and anger still reverberate through the speeches, petitions and addresses to the public, the employers, the people, or Parliament, at the destruction of a whole way of life wrought by the "despots of capital," the factory, the workhouse, or "class legislation." But it was the anger of men threatened in their whole being with loss of skill, sexual and economic authority. John Doherty, mule-spinner, radical, factory reformer, trade unionist, commenting on the manufacturer who advertised in a Glasgow newspaper for women to work in his mills:

> [I]f he could not find in his heart to employ, and pay men for doing his work, he should look out for women whose morals are already corrupted, instead of those whose lives are yet pure and spotless. For everyone will admit, that to place persons of both sexes, of fifteen or sixteen years indiscriminately together, and put them in receipt of 12s and 16s a week, which is entirely at their own disposal, without education and before their habits are fixed, and their reason sufficiently mature to controul [*sic*] their passions and restrain their appetites . . . such persons will [not] grow up as chaste, moral and obedient to their parents, as if they had still not remained under the salutary restraint of parental controul [*sic*]. If the practice were to become general, of employing girls and boys instead of men, it could place the son and daughter of fifteen, at the head of the family, to whose whims and caprices the father must bend and succumb, or in many cases starve.[17]

Popular Political Economy

John Doherty and his contemporaries resisted "capitalists and lawmakers" as deeply because they usurped "parental controul" as for any change in the work process. Underlying this resistance were the two themes which spanned all visions of a new social order, whether for a General Union of the trades, social regeneration, cooperative communities, or the Charter: labor, as the producer of wealth and knowledge, should receive its just reward; and kinship was the natural and proper relation of morality, authority and law.

The labor theory of value expounded in radical political economy assigned neither labor nor responsible parenthood exclusively to men. Thomas

Hodgskin, philosophical anarchist, stated only that labor's share of wealth should provide the

> necessaries and conveniences required for the support of the labourer and his family; or that quantity which is necessary to enable the labourers one with another, to subsist and to perpetuate their race without either increase or diminution.

Skilled labor is the laborer's knowledge, and "the time necessary to acquire a knowledge of any species of skilled labour ... is, in many cases, several years." Hodgskin describes the "most important operation" in the accumulation and transmission of knowledge and skill—the parent's work in rearing and educating the children:

> The labor of the parents produces and purchases, with what they receive as wages, all the food and the clothing which the rising generation of labourers use, while they are learning those arts by means of which they will hereafter produce all the wealth of society. For the rearing and educating of all future labourers (of course I do not mean *book* education, which is the smallest and least useful part of all which they have to learn) their parents have no stock stored up beyond their own practical skill. Under the strong influence of natural affections and parental love, they prepare by their toils, continually day after day, and year after year, through all the long period of infancy and childhood of their offspring, those future labourers who are to succeed to their toils and their hard fare, but who will inherit their productive power, and be what they now are, the main pillars of the social edifice.[18]

Food, clothing, knowledge, love and labor are equally the possessions and gifts of both parents, and theirs equally to pass on to their children. But this was the world as it should be. Utopian thinkers expunged from their vocabulary any privileged relation between men and either skill, or inheritance. But if there was in small rural manufacturing communities or urban crafts and trades, a community of skill and knowledge within families, it was not transmitted in public speech—whether the discourse of bargain and polemic with employers and government, or popular propaganda—as it wasn't in formal organizations of the trades and communities. Masculine privilege was embedded in popular conceptions of both skilled labor and authority, and inheritance was through male and not female kin.

Women simply could not speak within these terms. From the mid-eighteenth century, though women were drawn into the informal and intermittent trade associations, they received full authority to practice their craft only through male kin: father, husband, or if a widow, through ... eldest son or principal journeyman. Skilled men's unions throughout the nineteenth century excluded women, and the wage "sufficient to support a wife and children" was the father's and not the mother's. There was reciprocity between the respective "capacities" of women and men when considered as husbands and wives within a domestic system of industry. But somehow there slips into the discourse of men as they defend or expound that system, an estimation of women as wives, workers, and mothers which belies full equality of status. Wives of wool-combers, weavers, cobblers, tailors and all skilled men or small masters "assisted" their husbands in their trades, besides fulfilling their household duties; with their husbands they "brought up the children to a trade," until the age of thirteen or fourteen when the child came under the proper supervision of his father or male relative (which girls seldom did). If women's work was mentioned it was described as an "inferior" sort of work, always with the implication that it required less skill and strength, or even that such a task as picking or burling was done by "inferior people, women, and children," as one witness explained to the 1806 Royal Commission on the Woollen Industry.[19]

A woman's skill resided in the household and her property in the virtue of her person. Separated from the home, her family and domestic occupations, or outside the bonds of matrimony, a woman was assured of neither skill nor virtue.

Engels touched the nerve in his ferocious indictment of industrial capitalism in 1844. Describing in dramatic rhetoric the destruction of the family by the factory system he alights—as did all his contemporaries—on the evil effects of the wife's employment at the mill:

> In many cases the family is not wholly dissolved by the employment of the wife, but turned upside down. The wife supports the family, the husband sits at home, tends the children, sweeps the room and cooks . . . in Manchester alone many hundred such men could be cited, *condemned to domestic occupations*. It is easy to imagine the wrath aroused among the working-men by this reversal of all relations within the family, while other social conditions remain unchanged. (my italics)

So much for the equal status of women's work. Engels' saving grace, from the point of view of the feminist, is the final clause. And he redeems himself forever, as he continues, in some confusion, to argue that if

> this condition which unsexes the man and takes from the woman all womanliness without being able to bestow upon the man true womanliness, or the woman true manliness—this condition which degrades, in the most shameful way, both sexes, and through them, Humanity . . . then, so total a reversal of the position of the sexes can have come to pass only because the sexes have been placed in a false position from the beginning. If the reign of the wife over the husband, as inevitably brought about by the factory system is inhuman, the pristine rule of the husband over the wife must have been inhuman too.[20]

"The reign of the wife over the husband as inevitably brought about by the factory system"—the "condition which unsexes the man"—underlined all the polemic and rhetoric deployed by working class movements against the "new breed of employers," the "capitalist lords and despots." Those who have studied the literature of grievance in the history of the industrial revolution, are familiar with the lament of skilled men threatened with the loss of skill and knowledge by the factory or the sweatshop, and made anxious about the destruction of the family and the home by the competition of the wives and children.[21] The motivation was not in any simple sense class-war, nor the pursuit of economic self-interest, nor even (at least not in every case?) the conscious desire to dominate their women—but to posit a vision of the social organization of labor centered around kin and the household which permitted natural affections and love as well as skill to flow simultaneously from domestic and working life; which allowed for a continuing dialogue between "masters and men"; and which enabled the "natural differences and capacities" of the sexes to determine the division of labor between wife and husband, male and female laborer. This was a language of grievance which embraced moral and sexual orders as well as economic discontents—social preoccupations which became severed in political demands within the labor movement (but not the feminist) in the later nineteenth century.[22] In the early nineteenth century this vision was posed again and again by the representatives of the working class as a mode of industrial organization which had once been there, that was natural and that was being wantonly destroyed by capital and the government.

We come closer to grasping the reason for the emergence of a feminist voice within Owenism and not within other working class movements (or not in a sustained form) if we consider briefly their political diagnosis and strategy, and secondly their different social visions and the implications of these for the nature and place of women and men.

The People's Charter

"Fellow Country Women," the Female Political Union of Newcastle upon Tyne declared in 1843,

> we entreat you to join us to help the cause of freedom, justice, and honesty and truth, to drive poverty and ignorance from our land, and establish happy homes, true religion, righteous government, and good laws.[23]

The plea could have been made by Parson Bull, the belligerent enemy of the new Poor Law and its implementation in the North of England at the end of the 1830s, Richard Oastler, Tory Radical and "King" of the factory operative and starving hand-loom weaver (whose motto was "The Altar, the Throne, and the Hearth"), or any one of the many radical men active in those campaigns. Chartism was a mass movement of women as well as men which united all those movements against "bad laws and unjust legislators." Richard Pilling's defense speech at his trial in Lancaster in 1843 on a charge of seditious conspiracy, reveals the overlapping of grievance and aspirations in those struggles.

> Suppose, gentlemen of the jury, you were obliged to subsist on the paltry pittance given to us in the shape of wages, and had a wife and six helpless children . . . to

support, how would you feel? Though you were to confine me to a dungeon I should not submit to it. I have a nervous wife—a good wife—a dear wife—a wife that I love and cherish, and I have done everything that I could in the way of resisting reductions in wages, that I might keep her and my children from the workhouse, for I detest parish relief. It is wages I want. I want to be independent of every man and that is the principle of every man in this court . . . it has been a wage question with me. And I do say that if Mr. O'Connor has made it a chartist question he has done wonders to make it extend through England, Ireland, and Scotland. But it was always a wage question, and ten hours bill with me.[24]

The women of Newcastle did not demand independence; their interests were those of their "fathers, husbands and brothers," and their place was in the home, from which they had been torn by poverty and the "scorn of the rich" who, "not content with despising our feelings, . . . demand the control of our thoughts and wants." The People's Charter mobilized the whole of the laboring population behind its demand for universal suffrage, and, at moments, shopkeepers and tradesmen, as well as humanitarian philanthropists, thought it deleted women from that universality,

> lest the false estimate man entertains of this half of the human family may cause his ignorance and prejudice to be enlisted to retard the progress of his own freedom.

Those women who acquiesced in their exclusion did so because they shared the social visions of their men. "Love of God, and hatred of wrong" compelled the women of Newcastle to "assist" their men to have the "Charter (made) into a law and emancipate the white slaves of England."[25] Dorothy Thompson has documented women's participation in Chartism (as well as its ambivalence on the question of women's suffrage):

> [Women] joined in protests and action against the police, the established Church, the exploitation of employers and the encroachments of the state. They articulated their grievances sometimes in general political terms, basing their case on appeals to former laws and natural rights, sometimes in ethical or religious terms, appealing to the Bible for the legitimation of protest.[26]

It was these last—natural rights and Biblical Law—which together with the evocation of a golden age always prove insecure foundations for equality between the sexes.

The Golden Age: The Law of Nature and the Law of God

Chartism appealed for a return to a golden age, or at least to an imagined Eden before 1832 "invaded" the civil liberties of the people (in Disraeli's and Oastler's phrase), introducing "class legislation," and before the factory system reduced the working classes to slavery and impoverishment. For Chartists the association of the working classes was one which clung to a hope of industrial organization rooted in the household and kinship, and based on the land. The appeal to the land always evokes, when it recurs in popular ideologies, a lost and more egalitarian past, one closer to natural sources of affection, feeling and community. The place of women in that evocation seldom escapes submission. The tendency is—and I'm oversimplifying—to place women closer to nature and the animal world, distancing them from human law and knowledge. Somehow women are placed under a different law from men because of their natural function and capacity. Men become the natural protectors and defenders of women, whose place is in the home, with their children, providing those comforts—which to quote the Newcastle women again—"our hearts told us should greet our husbands after their fatiguing labors." Women's exclusion from independent political subjectivity is then a consequence of their different capacity and place. Valued for their household skills and domestic virtue as a part of the family under the protection of men, independence is almost inconceivable. The tendency is present even in R. J. Richardson's ardent advocacy of women's equal right to the suffrage in 1840, where natural differences between the sexes are given as a divine imperative. Surveying women's labor to substantiate that right, he fumed against "money-grabbers" and "slave-drivers" who forced women into employment in fields, mines, and mills, and found only in weaving the ideal occupation for women:

> In hand-loom weaving, it is no uncommon thing to see in a weaver's cottage under the window on the ground floor, a loom at which the weaver's wife is employed at the same time she is surveying her domestic affairs; for instance, she will leave her loom, peel potatoes for dinner, put them on the fire, then return to her loom; should the child cry in its cradle, she will stop, leave her loom, give it the breast, or a plaything, or get it to sleep, and return to her loom again, and so on alternately the day through.

There are two kinds of women in Richardson's text: the gentle, domestic persons of his imagination, "those tender creatures we call ours"; and those to whom he spoke in their many different workplaces, who listened patiently as he regaled them on the inappropriate nature of their employment, its defilement of their femininity:

> This is the work of men . . . and you ought not to perform it: your places are in your homes; your labours are your domestic duties; your interests in the welfare of your families, and not in slaving thus for the accumulation of the wealth of others, whose slaves you seem willing to be; for shame on you! go seek husbands, those of you who have them not, and make them toil for you; and those of you who have husbands and families, go home and minister to their domestic comforts.

I suspect most replied as the women of the printfields in Leven, Dumbartonshire that

> they were conscious that they were not in their proper places; but that, as they had no voice in making the laws they could not help their degraded position.

Richardson's principle and concluding point was that women should be allowed to intervene in political affairs because "I believe God ordained women 'to temper men,'" and that

> when we consider that it is to women we owe our existence, that we receive from her our earliest thoughts and bias of our minds—that we are indebted to her for all that makes life a blessing—would it not be unwise, ungrateful and inhuman in man to deny them every advantage they can possess in society?[27]

Such a highlighting of sexual difference cannot help but to undermine the demand for political equality between women and men, especially when that difference is given a divine authorization.

Christian humanitarianism—of all denominations—distinguished the emotional fervor of much popular oratory and polemic. The law of the Bible was employed to defend the rights and liberties of the working man against the "Church, the Throne and the Aristocracy," who would "rob the poor man" not only of his liberty but also of "his wife and of his children."[28] The social vision of the Chartists met the political and economic critique of Whiggery and Utilitarianism expounded by the Tory democrats. The meeting point was women: the protection of the rights of the "weakest and most defenceless, the widow and the fatherless"; a social order in which each person had her or his special place, and the appeal to a benevolent Constitution whose executive exercised political power with responsibility, always with care for the freedoms and liberties and rights of the people—a people for whom only men could speak publicly.

A New Moral World

Owenism differed from radicalism in the possibilities it offered women. Determinedly secular, Owenism envisaged a new science of human nature and promised to revolutionize emotions and feelings as well as labor and law. Since environment[,] not God or nature[,] made character, environment could be changed. There was nothing natural in the sexual division of labor, nor in the "despotic" rule of wives by their husbands. The confinement of women to "domestic drudgery" was an unjust usurpation of human freedom and female capacity (the difference between the radicals and the Owenites echoes the quarrel between Rousseau and Mary Wollstonecraft). The only natural aspect of the relation between the sexes was the flow of sensuality, the "sacred pleasures of the flesh," about which, as Barbara Taylor drily points out, female Owenites were more circumspect on the whole (except those fleeing tyrannical husbands or living the life of the "liberated libido") than men. The Owenites imagined a whole New Moral World. Theirs was a vocabulary of transcendence[,] not negotiation; there was neither a longing to return to a golden past, nor any submission to the natural laws of the market. Owenism reached out for new social forms which would displace industrial competitive society with cooperative modes of work, egalitarian communities, a reformed marriage and a new religion of reason and universal love. As Barbara Taylor has so ably and eloquently argued, utopian socialism promised the liberation of all humanity at once, of all human relations and social institutions.[29] Egalitarian and democratic in spirit if not always in practice, some women found a voice for their discontents and desires as women there. It was a vision of progress and a renewed humanity; a language of community and cooperation which only sometimes foundered on the democratic rights of the individual.

A new science of human nature, a new moral world, these were more fertile soil for feminism—the independent voice of women demanding equality with men and their full inclusion in humanity—than the natural order and natural difference. And Owenism's version of transcendence (anticipating the millenarianism of the later nineteenth century women's suffrage movement) invited some women to imagine a full emancipation, for it was partly through negotiation with existing law and government that equality or reciprocity between women and men within working class movements—or their public political discourses—collapsed.

Natural differences between the sexes could easily slip into a relation of inequality between women and men as the possibility of a domestic system of industry, with a family of laborers and household economy, faded, and with that fading the dialogue between masters and men, who sometimes addressed each other as "men, as husbands, as fathers, as friends and Christians," hardened into the confrontations between capital and labor. Symptomatic of the changing class relations is the changing value and status of "female labor" as it moved in and out of the home, and in and out of those modes of address. The equivocation of political discourse of working class movements on the questions of "female labor" is illustrated by John Doherty's prevarications. Imprisoned for obstructing the use of female "knobsticks" to break a strike of spinners in Glasgow in 1818, a leader of the mule spinners through the 1820s and early '30s, he opposed the "cotton lords'" use of female labor to undercut the men. Men's resistance to women spinners—justified on grounds of their lesser strength and skill—was part of the struggle against machinery and an attempt to retain a notion of apprenticeship, which, as Doherty conceded to the Select Committee [inquiring] into the Combinations of Workmen in 1838, did not "exist formally, but it does frightfully to the workman." And Doherty suggests to the same Committee that men's monopoly in mule spinning (except in Glasgow where there had been strikes for equal pay) should be extended to the wheel (prevalent in Manchester). He agreed that women's employment in the mills had a "bad effect on morals and domestic habits," and that the greater strength required on wheels in Manchester would "shortly put women out." On the other hand, Doherty, a humanitarian and Owenite, as well as a trades unionist, addressing the London tailors in an article in May 1834, both condemned the "dastardly strategem" of hiring female labor to replace the men, and urged on the tailors that this undercutting would not be possible if they themselves [would] acknowledge "the natural equality of women; include them in all your schemes of improvement, and raise them as high in the sense of scale and independence as yourselves."[30] But natural difference fitted ill with "natural equality."

Male Fears and Female Labor

The spectacle of female labor aroused the deepest fears among many different sectors of public opinion in the mid-nineteenth century—alerted as they were by a prolific and diverse literature to the "condition of England" question. The disintegration and demoralization of the working class family in the midst of economic growth and imperial power haunted social consciences among both the Whigs and Tories as they pondered the possibility of social revolution. This fusion of anxiety is less surprising when we remember that what women stood for was not simply domestic virtue and household skills, but sexual ordering itself. If men represented—to such different groups as radical artisans, Tory democrats, utilitarian legislators—labor, then what women represented first of all was sexuality—which, if not harnessed to re-production threatened sexual anarchy and chaos (epithets applied to both the prostitute and the militant feminist in Victorian England). Men's desire to confine women to their proper place must be understood—at least in part—as a desire to (legally) control and (morally) order sexuality. Women's capacity to bear children—if infused with divine sanction—makes her one with God in creating life. "It is bad enough if you corrupt the man," Lord Shaftesbury declared to a silent House of Commons as he introduced the bill banning women's underground work in the mines, "but if you corrupt the woman, you poison the waters of life at the very fountain."[31] It was the power of this thought that eventually persuaded even such die-hard opponents of the Ten-Hour Day as Peel to, if not relent, at least adhere to the principle of protection of women. The *Northern Star* put their case on female labor in the mines rather more bluntly:

> Keep them at home to look after their families, decrease the pressure on the labor market and there is then some chance of a higher rate of wages being enforced.[32]

Through the history of wage labor female labor has meant cheap labor to working class men, and the threat of cheap labor sets sexual antagonism, always latent between women and men, into livid activity at the workplace and in the unions. Reorganization of the labor process produced continual shifts in the sexual division of labor, provoking anxiety about the destruction of the home and family which were imprinted in the language of popular resistance since the late eighteenth century. There is a sense in which the vocabulary and rhetoric of the radical artisan evoked a memory of a past that was never there—except in aspiration. It nevertheless retains a powerful hold over the political imagination of the labor movement, bequeathing a vocabulary of loss and nostalgia to working class struggle. The appeal to the family, home and hearth and women's place beside it is its conservative edge—though the yearning for harmony and for sources of emotional satisfaction for which they stand are more tenacious. The labor theory of value remains alive in the labor movement, too, lending weight to men's demands for a family wage. But except when held within egalitarian principles of community and equal rights of women and men in marriage, the notion of the family wrapped up in that theory was (and is) inimical to the "full and complete" emancipation of women. For whereas for men the threat of cheap labor means *loss* of employment, status and skill, to women workers their cheapness represents *lack* of independence, status and skill. Feminism's demand for work, training, and economic independence has always unnerved the male dominated labor movement, while "lack" of those things permeates the idiom of nineteenth century feminism. Ironically what women lacked became one of the defining features of femininity, and on the shop-floor, in the unions and working class political parties this lack could become politically divisive. In fact, women's special needs received short shrift in the labor movement, whether femininity was defined positively as motherhood, or negatively as lack. The former produced demands for birth control, family endowment, easier divorce—which never received more than a lukewarm reception in the labor movement as a whole until the late 1930s; and the latter produced the demands for equal pay, equal right to skill and training, to which men's response was always the reassertion of their status as breadwinners for the family.

I am not suggesting that the public speech of skilled men as they addressed their employers, the public, or the government, was the only form of popular discourse. That communities imposed their own moral laws, as well as conceptions of the value of women's and men's different social skills and responsibilities is certain. And women themselves often spoke of a different reality. But we capture only fragments of those customs. Many of them were conveyed through oral traditions destroyed (if not altogether lost or forgotten) by the swell in population, movements into the towns, destruction of crafts and dismantlement of apprenticeship rules, wage controls, etc. What we are witnessing from a distance is the uneven erosion of local cultures and the submergence of political order which through representative government gradually (and unwillingly) drew the individual into a contract with national government. The process was uneven and did not immediately replace other forms of communal relations of power and law, but increasingly came to dominate all public political discourse as the Parliamentary legislature became more intrusive and claimed to be the seat of representative democracy.

Whatever their intentions, the Chartists by deleting women, the factory reformers by submitting to the principle of protection of women, and every working class custom, insofar as it refused an equal status to women within the class, placed women in a different relationship to the state than men.[33] Women fell under the protection of their fathers, husbands, or Parliament and were denied an independent political subjectivity. When feminism emerged as a self-conscious and sometimes mass political movement of women in the nineteenth century it was to demand economic independence and the full rights and duties of citizenship—to combat the exclusion of women from a "common humanity" and women's lack of masculine privilege. Women's protest gathered force until nothing less than the "whole world of labour" and nothing short of Womanhood suffrage would satisfy the most radical feminists. Both women and the working class emerged in the 1840s, two universal social and political categories which demanded universal rights and liberties in, as Ethel Snowden, feminist and socialist, carefully phrased it—"all those matters of their common humanity where sex does not enter and impose an impassible barrier."[34] But if there is nothing "impassible" about the social ordering of sexual difference, representing difference as a relation of equality in language through political culture was—and remains—elusive.

NOTES

First appeared in 1983.

1. Shulamith Firestone, *The Dialectics of Sex*, London 1971. Kate Millett, *Sexual Politics*, New York 1970. For a survey of feminist theories of patriarchy, see Veronica Beechey, "On Patriarchy," *Feminist Review*, no. 3, 1979, pp. 66–83. For a disagreement among feminist historians, see Sheila Rowbotham, Sally Alexander, Barbara Taylor, "Debate on Patriarchy," ed. Raphael Samuel, *People's History and Socialist Theory*, London 1983.

2. For an account of the LNA's campaign, see Judith R. Walkowitz, *Prostitution and Victorian Society: Women, Class, and the State*, Cambridge 1980, part II. For its effects among women and the Women's Movement, Ray Strachey, *The Cause*, 1928, Virago reprint 1978, pp. 196–198.

3. Eleanor Rathbone, *Milestones*, London 1929, p. 28.

4. Histories of the suffrage movement pursue a fairly straightforward narrative of the achievement of women's suffrage. The more comprehensive theories focus on the intellectual components of women's thought, and the class composition of the feminists. There is a general consensus: the former derives from Protestant individualism, Enlightenment thought and philanthropy; and the feminists were overwhelmingly middle class (e.g. Richard Evans, *The Feminists*, London 1977; Olive Banks, *Faces of Feminism*, Oxford 1981). Feminism's middle class character has led to its neglect by socialist historians. A valuable exception is Juliet Mitchell, "Women and Equality," in eds. J. Mitchell and A. Oakley, *The Rights and Wrongs of Women*, Pelican 1976, pp. 379–399. No recent histories of British feminism have surpassed two classic studies: Ray Strachey's *The Cause*, 1928, and Sylvia Pankhurst's *The Suffragette Movement*, 1931, both reprinted by Virago. Written by protagonists in the Cause, both view the study as a struggle in human progress. Ray Strachey, a liberal/socialist, gives a brief but comprehensive survey of the Women's Movement from the mid-nineteenth [century] to the 1920s. Despite Sylvia Pankhurst's tendency to shape her narrative around the achievements of her family (beginning with her father), *The Suffragette Movement* is nevertheless a mine of information on the early radical feminist, socialist, and labor movements, is full of fascinating thumbnail portraits and packed with analysis. The reader is swept along by the messianic vision of the author, the elements of idealism, sacrifice, and martyrdom that characterized the "Cause."

5. Keith Thomas, "Women and the Civil War Sects," *Past and Present*, no. 13, 1958, pp. 42–57. Christopher Hill, *The World Turned Upside Down*, London 1972, chapter 15.

6. For a feminist reading of the GNCTU, Barbara Taylor, *Eve and the New Jerusalem*, London 1983, chapter 4.

7. For a recent example of that "stretching," Ellen Ross, "Survival Networks: Women's Neighbourhood Sharing in London before World War One," *HWJ*, Spring 1983, issue 15, pp. 4–28.

8. Karl Marx, "Preface to a Contribution to the Critique of Political Economy," Marx and Engels, *Selected Works*, [reprint] London 1970, pp. 180–85, is the most succinct statement.

9. V. I. Lenin, *What Is to Be Done*, [reprint] Moscow 1969.

10. E. P. Thompson, *The Making of the English Working Class*, Pelican, 1968. The Preface.

11. Juliet Mitchell, *Psychoanalysis and Feminism*, London 1974, Introduction p. xv.

12. Juliet Mitchell's Introduction in, eds. J. Mitchell and J. Rose, *Feminine Sexuality, Jacques Lacan and the École Freudienne*, London 1983, p. 5.

13. Juliet Mitchell's and Jacqueline Rose's introductions to *Feminine Sexuality* are lucid accounts of Lacan's project. J. Mitchell's *Psychoanalysis and Feminism* parts 1 and 2 give a careful reading of Freud's account of the acquisition of femininity. The most useful essay on fantasy is Jean Laplanche and J.-B. Pontalis, "Fantasy and the Origins of Sexuality," *International Journal of Psychoanalysis*, vol. 49, 1968, Part 1, pp. 1–17. Sigmund Freud, *Femininity* (1933), Standard Edition, Vol. XXII, pp. 112–135, though controversial among feminists, is still—for me—both riveting and convincing. For aspects of that controversy, Elizabeth Wilson, "Psychoanalysis: Psychic Law and Order," *Feminist Review*, No. 8, Summer 1981, pp. 63–78, and J. Rose, "Femininity and Its Discontents," *Feminist Review*, No. 14, Summer 1983, pp. 5–21.

14. The use I make of Lacan's Freud, and the significance of language in the production of meaning and the construction of the subject are my own responsibility. Useful essays are Jacques Lacan, "The Function and Field of Speech and Language in Psychoanalysis," and "The Agency of the Letter in the Unconscious or Reason Since Freud," *Écrits*, London 1980, pp. 30–113, 146–78. E. Benveniste, *Problems in General Linguistics*, Miami chs. 19, 20, and 22. Ferdinand de Saussure, *Course on General Linguistics*, London 1981.

15. I am only speaking of the *public* political speech of these movements. While these do not and cannot convey less accessible forms of popular consciousness, many of which transmitted through oral conditions, myth, ritual, etc., have been lost or forgotten, public political discourse nevertheless indicates some incidents of popular identification. Dorothy Thompson's essay, "Women in Nineteenth-Century Radical Politics," in eds. J. Mitchell and A. Oakley, *The Rights and Wrongs of Women*, Pelican, 1976, pp. 112–38, has shaped discussion around women's participation in working class movements in the first half of the nineteenth century. Lin Shaw, "Women in Working Class Politics in Norwich," paper given to the Feminist History Group, London, December 1979, covered forms and content of working class politics in detail and related their decline to the changing local political and industrial structure of Norwich in the second half of the nineteenth century.

16. See for example the many reports on the Handloom Weavers and industrial populations in the 1830s and '40s. And in particular, Report and Minutes of Evidence of the Select Committee on the State of the Woollen Manufacture in England, P.P. 1806, vol. 3, and Report from the Select Committee to Examine Petitions from Hand-Loom Weavers, P.P. 1834, vol. 10.

17. R. G. Kirby, A. E. Musson, *The Voice of the People, John Doherty, 1798–1854*, Manchester 1975, p. 73. Neil J. Smelser's *Social Change in the Industrial Revolution*,

London 1979 ed. is often criticized by historians for its dense methodology, mechanistic model of change, and specific inaccuracies. The central hypothesis, however, that operatives grew restless as kinship ties were severed in the reorganization of the labor process is suggestive in the context of this essay. Jane Humphries in "Class Struggle and the Persistence of the Working-Class Family," *Cambridge Journal of Economics*, 1977, 1, pp. 241–58, and ["]Protective Legislation, the Capitalist State and Working Class Men: The Case of the 1842 Mines Regulation Act," *Feminist Review*, No. 19, Spring 1982, argues that the resilience of the working class family stems in part from men's defense of "an institution which affects their standard of living, class cohesion and ability to wage the class struggle."

18. Thomas Hodgskin, *Labour Defended against the Claims of Capital*, 1825, reprinted London 1922, pp. 31, 48, 50.

19. Lin Shaw describes the Norwich weaver's political economy (drawn from Hodgskin) as including the demand for a wage to support a wife and three children. Adam Smith, *The Wealth of Nations*, [reprint] Chicago ed. 1976, pp. 76–77, suggests the "husband and wife together" must earn sufficient [income] to raise four children, on the expectation that two will die, but implies that the woman's wage will only have to support herself. Smith's political economy was approved by radical working men; it was the infusion of Malthusianism into political economy that provoked hostility. For a discussion of the "family wage" in the transition from from manufacture to modern industry see Sally Alexander, *Women's Work in Nineteenth Century London*, London 1983, pp. 20–32. For women's exclusion from skill and workmen's organizations, Ivy Pinchbeck, *Women Workers and the Industrial Revolution 1750–1850*, London 1969, pp. 126–27; for examples of women weaving with husbands, fathers, etc., A. P. Wadsworth and J. DeLacy Mann, *The Cotton Trade and Industrial Lancaster 1600–1780*, Manchester 1965, pp. 332, 336. For women in the early textile unions, Wadsworth and Mann, Chapter 18; H. A. Turner, *Trade Union Growth Structure and Policy*, London 1962, parts II, III, and IV. For the masculine language and character of the early Trade Unions, A. Aspinall, *The Early English Trade Unions*, London 1949.

20. F. Engels, *The Condition of the Working Class in 1844*, in K. Marx and F. Engels, *On Britain*, [reprint] Moscow 1962, pp. 177–79.

21. For example, the skilled tailor speaking to Henry Mayhew quoted in S. Alexander, *Women's Work in Nineteenth Century London*, pp. 31–32.

22. Michael Ignatieff, "Marxism and Classic Political Economy," in ed. R. Samuel, *People's History and Social Theory*, London 1981, pp. 344–52, describes the similar narrowing of preoccupations as political economy became an economic science in the mid-nineteenth century.

23. "Address of the Female Political Union of Newcastle upon Tyne to their Fellow Countrywomen," in ed. D. Thompson, *The Early Chartists*, London 1971, p. 130.

24. Richard Pilling's Defence, from the *[Trial] of Fergus O'Connor and 58 Other Chartists on a Charge of Seditious Conspiracy at Lancaster*, 1843, ed. F. O'Connor. I'm grateful to Eileen Yeo for this reference.

25. Address of the Female [Political] Union, *The Early Chartists*, II, 128–29. For a fuller discussion of the political language of Chartism, Gareth Stedman Jones, "The Language of Chartism," ed. James Epstein and D. Thompson, *The Chartist Experience*, London 1972, pp. 3–58. The wording of the 1838 Charter is worth quoting in full: "Among the suggestions we received for improving this Charter, is one for embracing women among the possession of the franchise. Against this reasonable proposition we have no just arguments to adduce, but only to express our fears of entertain-

ing it, lest the false estimate man entertains of this half of the human family may cause his ignorance and prejudice to be enlisted to retard the progress of his own freedom. And therefore, we deem it far better to lay down just principles, and look forward to the rational improvement of society, than to entertain propositions which may retard the measure we wish to promote." *Address of the Working Man's Association to the Radical Reformers of Great Britain and Ireland*, London 1838, p. 9. Whether the false estimate is attributed to their fellow working men, or their representatives in Parliament is not clear.

26. D. Thompson, "Women in Nineteenth Century Radical Politics," p. 131.

27. Extract from R. J. Richardson, "The Rights of Woman" in *The Early Chartists*, pp. 115–36.

28. Cecil Driver, *Tory Radical, The Life of Richard Oastler*, Oxford 1946, p. 434 but see whole of chapter 32 for Oastler's Tory democracy.

29. Barbara Taylor, "Lords of Creation," *New Statesman*, 7 March 1980, pp. 361–62, and G. Stedman Jones, "Utopian Socialism Reconsidered," unpub. ms. 1979, B. Taylor, *Eve and the New Jerusalem*, Ch. 2 for a discussion of Owenite ideas on the position of women.

30. Minutes of Evidence, Select Committee on Combinations of Workmen, P.P. 1838, Vol. 8, p. 263; *The Voice of the People*, p. 299, and passim.

31. Quoted in Pinchbeck, *Women Workers*, p. 267.

32. Angela John, *By the Sweat of Their Brow, Women Workers at Victorian Coal Mines*, London 1981, p. 57. Those for and against the Factory Acts did not divide along party lines. By the 1840s, there was universal agreement that female labor should be protected; the argument in Parliament was how best that intervention should be made. Samuel Kydd (pseud. Alfred), *The History of the Factory Movement*, London 1857, is the most interesting discussion of contemporary political opinion as it divided between those who interpreted the laws of nature and revelations with benevolence (e.g. pp. 117, 118, and 208) and those who feared the dangers of intervening in the freedom of labor, and all opinion in between (esp. ch. 15).

33. Intentions are blurred, but whereas the workingmen delegates from the factory districts celebrated their victory in 1847 with the following resolution: "That we are deeply thankful to Almighty God for the success which has on all occasions attended our efforts in this sacred cause, and especially for the final result of all our labours, by which the working classes are now put in possession of their long-sought-for-measure—The Ten Hours Bill" their friends in Parliament reaffirmed their hopes that the increased leisure won would be used for "mental and moral improvement" and especially that the female factory operatives would promote and improve their "domestic habits." *The Ten Hours Advocate*, ed. Philip Grant, for the Lancaster Short-Time Committee, 1846–47, pp. 300–301.

34. Ethel Snowden, *The Feminist Movement*, London n.d. (1911), p. 258.

Nations, Publics, and Political Cultures: Placing Habermas in the Nineteenth Century

GEOFF ELEY

By "the public sphere" we mean first of all a realm of our
social life in which something approaching public opinion can
be formed. Access is guaranteed to all citizens. A portion of
the public sphere comes into being in every conversation in
which private individuals assemble to form a public body.
They then behave neither like business nor professional people
transacting private affairs, nor like members of a constitutional
order subject to the legal constraints of a state bureaucracy.
Citizens behave as a public body when they confer in an
unrestricted fashion—that is, with the guarantee of freedom of
assembly and association and the freedom to express and
publish their opinions—about matters of general interest.
In a large public body this kind of communication requires
specific means for transmitting information and influencing
those who receive it. Today newspapers and magazines,
radio and TV are the media of the public sphere. We speak of
the political public sphere in contrast, for instance, to the
literary one, when public discussion deals with objects
connected to the activity of the state. Although state activity is
so to speak the executor, it is not a part of it. . . . Only when
the exercise of political control is effectively subordinated to
the democratic demand that information be accessible
to the public, does the political public sphere win an
institutionalized influence over the government through
the instrument of law-making bodies.[1]

IN THIS summary statement Habermas reveals perhaps better than in the book itself how far his conception of the public sphere amounts to an ideal of critical liberalism which remains historically unattained. History provides only distorted realizations, both at the inception of the public sphere (when the participant public was effectively limited to the bourgeoisie) and with the later transformations (which removed this "bourgeois ideal" of informed and rational communication still further from any general or universal implementation). *Strukturwandel der Öffentlichkeit* rests on an immanent critique, in which Habermas confronts the liberal ideal of the reasoning public with the reality of its own particularism and long-term disempowerment. From a vantage point in the late 1950s the main direction of Habermas's perspective was, not surprisingly, pessimistic—"etching an unforgettable portrait of a degraded public life, in which the substance of liberal democracy is voided in a combination of plebiscitary manipulation and privatized apathy, as any collectivity of citizenry disintegrates."[2] But the book was not just a story of decay. It remains a careful exploration of a particular historical moment, in which certain possibilities for human emancipation were unlocked—possibilities which for Habermas were ordered around the "central idea of communicatively generated rationality," which then became the leitmotif of his own life's work.[3]

In a nutshell, the public sphere means "a sphere which mediates between society and state, in which the public organizes itself as the bearer of public opinion." Historically, its growth occurred in the later eighteenth century with the widening of political participation and the crystalizing of citizenship ideals. It eventuated from the struggle against absolutism (or in the British case, from the struggle for a strengthening of constitutional monarchy), and aimed at transforming arbitrary authority into rational authority, subject to the scrutiny of a citizenry organized into a public body under the law. It was identified most obviously with the demand for representative government and a liberal constitution, and more broadly with the basic civil freedoms before the law (speech, press, assembly, association, no arrest without trial, and so on). But Habermas was less interested in this more familiar process of overt political change. More fundamentally, the public sphere presumed the prior transformation of social relations, their condensation into new institutional arrangements, and the generation of new social, cultural, and political discourse around this changing environment. Conscious and programmatic *political* impulses emerged most strongly where such underlying processes were reshaping the overall context of social communication. The public sphere presupposed this larger accumulation of sociocultural change. It was linked to the growth of urban culture—metropolitan and provincial—as the novel arena of a locally organized public life (meeting houses, concert halls, theaters, opera houses, lecture halls, museums), to a new infrastructure of social communication (the press, publishing companies, and other literary media; the rise of a reading public via reading and language societies; subscription publishing and lending libraries; improved transportation; and adapted centers of sociability like coffeehouses, taverns, and clubs), and to a new universe of voluntary association.

In other words, the public sphere derives only partly from the conscious demands of reformers and their articulation into government. Indeed, the latter were as much an effect of its emergence as a cause. Socially, the public sphere was the manifest consequence of a much deeper and long-term process of societal transformation—that Habermas locates between the late Middle Ages and the eighteenth century as a trade-driven transition from feudalism to capitalism in which the capital accumulation resulting from long-distance commerce plays the key role and for which the mercantilist policies of the later seventeenth and eighteenth centuries were the midwife. The category of the public was the unintended consequence of long-run socioeconomic change—eventually precipitated by the aspirations of a successful and self-conscious bourgeoisie, whose economic functions and social standing implied a cumulative agenda of desirable innovation. Habermas postulates a causal homology of culture and economics in this sense, growing from "*the traffic in commodities and news* created by early capitalist long-distance trade" (p. 15). On the one hand, commercialization undermined the old basis of the household economy, reoriented productive activity "toward a commodity market that had expanded under public direction and supervision," and reconstituted state/society relations on the basis of a new distinction between the private and the public; on the other hand, the flow of international news attendant on the growth of trading networks generated a new category of public knowledge and information, particularly in the context of the seventeenth-century wars and intensified competition among "nations" in the mercantilist sense, which led to a new medium of formal exchange and the invention of the press. This model of change, in which both new cultural possibilities and new political forms appear as the excrescence of an accumulating structural transformation, might be applied to a range of phenomena normally associated with industrialization or the developmental process. Thus in very general terms, the nineteenth-century growth of local government owed much to improvised grappling with the problems of an urbanizing society (poverty, policing, amenities like lighting and sewage, commercial licensing, revenue creation, and so on), to the extent of the local state's being actually *constituted* by the practical associational initiatives of a new citizenry in the making—but as the unintended, rolling effect of structurally invited interventions, as opposed to the strategic result of a coherent design.

Ultimately, though, Habermas is less interested in the realized political dimension of the public sphere—that is, the particular political histories of the late eighteenth and earlier nineteenth centuries—than in abstracting a strong ideal against which later forms of the public sphere can be set. His own vantage point—as the legatee of the Frankfurt School, who resumed their critique of mass culture at the height of the Christian Democratic state and the postwar boom, at a low ebb of socialist and democratic prospects—is crucial to an understanding of the book's motivating problematic. Habermas affirmed the critique of the present (the consciousness industry, the commodification of culture, the manipulation and manipulability of the masses), while he specifically retrieved the past (the Enlightenment as the founding moment of modernity). By contrast with Horkheimer and Adorno, he upheld the Enlightenment's progressive tradition. Thus his model of the public sphere has an avowedly double function: as Hohendahl says, "It provides a paradigm for analyzing historical change, while also serving as a normative category for political critique."[4] Arguably, it is the latter that really drives the analysis. Moreover, while the public sphere argument is clearly crucial to politics in the full democratic sense (as the enlargement of human emancipation), its main thrust is anterior to politics of the parliamentary or institutional kind. For Habermas, the parliamentary stands of a Fox were less important than the larger context of rational and unrestricted discourse from which they had grown and which they could presuppose. The faculty of "publicness" begins with reading, thought, and discussion, with reasonable exchange among equals, and it is this ideal that really focuses Habermas's interest. It resided in the act of discussion and the process of exchange:

> The truly free market is that of cultural discourse itself, within, of course, certain normative regulations; . . . What is said derives its legitimacy neither from itself as message nor from the social title of the utterer, but from its conformity as a statement with a certain paradigm of reason inscribed in the very event of saying.[5]

It is perhaps unclear how far Habermas believes his ideal of rational communication, with its concomitant of free and equal participation, to have been actually realized in the classical liberal model of *Öffentlichkeit*. Sometimes he acknowledges the class and property-bound basis of participation, but not to the extent of compromising his basic historical claim. However, the model also postulates a "structural transformation of the public sphere," and as suggested above, the narrowing of the ideal's possibilities over the longer run forms the main starting point of the book. Particularly from the last third of the nineteenth century, the growing contradictions of a capitalist society—the passage of competitive into monopoly or organized capitalism, the regulation of social conflicts by the state, and the fragmentation of the rational public into an arena of competing interests—serve to erode the independence of public opinion and undermine the legitimacy of its institutions. In the cultural sphere proper, from the arts to the press and the mass entertainment industry, the processes of commercialization and rationalization have increasingly targeted the individual consumer while eliminating the mediating contexts of reception and rational discussion, particularly in the new age of the electronic mass media. In this way the classic basis of the public sphere—a clear distinction between public good and private interest, the principled demarcation of state and society, and the constitutive role of a participant citizenry, defining public policy and its parameters through reasoned exchange, free of domination—disappears. The relations between state and society are reordered, to the advantage of the former and the detriment of a "free" political life.

Now, the strengths and weaknesses of Habermas's work on the public sphere have been much discussed (though mainly in the German-speaking rather than the English-speaking world, it should be said), not least in the papers and sessions of the present conference that precede my own.[6] A certain amount of overlap is inevitable, and I certainly would not want to discuss the historical dimensions of the argument in isolation from its theoretical value. But I want to confine myself to a series of comments which confront Habermas's work with a corpus of intervening historical writing (not all of it by historians), which sometimes confirms, sometimes extends, and sometimes undermines his argument. These concern (1) a wide variety of literatures that confirm the usefulness of the core concept of the public sphere, (2) the question of gender and the implications of women's history and feminist theory, (3) the state and politics in the strict sense, and (4) the problem of popular culture.

THE FINDINGS OF SOCIAL HISTORY

The value of the Habermasian perspective has been fundamentally borne out by recent social history in a variety of fields. On rereading the book (after originally discovering it in my own case in the early 1970s and then systematically engaging with it in the later part of that decade) it is striking to see how securely and imaginatively the argument is historically grounded, given the thinness of the literature available at the time. In this respect I am very struck by the affinity with the work of Raymond Williams, on whose argument in *Culture and Society, 1780–1950* (London, 1958) Habermas draws extensively in the early part of the book. The form of the argumentation is very similar to that of Williams (e.g., the whole introductory discussion culminating in the treatment of the shift in the meanings of the terms for "public" in English, German, and French between the late seventeenth and late eighteenth centuries—pp. 1–26). The very method—of moving from the "world of letters" to the structure of society—is characteristic of Williams's project in his early work. The later stage of Habermas's argument about the public sphere's transformation and degeneration (e.g., Ch. 18: "From a Culture-Debating Public to a Culture-Consuming Public," or Ch. 20: "From the Journalism of Private Men of Letters to the Public Consumer Services of the Mass Media") anticipates the broad historical argument of *The Long Revolution* (London, 1961), and *Communications* (Harmondsworth, 1962), in which Williams developed his ideas about the long-term decline in the forms and degree of popular access and control in the area of culture. On the other hand, Williams's subsequent work on mass media has always maintained a strong affirmative stance on the democratic potentials of new communications technologies (see especially his *Television: Technology and Cultural Form* [London, 1974], or the chapter on "Culture and Technology" in *The Year 2000* [New York, 1983], pp. 128–52), and his view of film, radio, TV, popular fiction, popular music, and so on is far removed from the Frankfurt School's critique of mass culture and popular taste via the notion of commodity fetishism—a critique that it is unclear whether, and how far, Habermas himself would share. Incidentally, rather remarkably there is no entry for "public" in Williams's *Keywords: A Vocabulary of Culture and Society* (London, 1976; revised and expanded ed., 1983).[7]

Moving from Habermas's general approach and mode of argument to areas of research that fall concretely or empirically within the public sphere framework, I wish to mention a number of examples, which certainly don't exhaust the contexts in which Habermas's idea could be embodied, but which are those most familiar to me. These are as follows:

- A large amount of eighteenth-century British social history, mainly associated with the influence of J. H. Plumb, but also including a range of urban history, which effectively fills in the framework Habermas proposed without (so far as I know) being explicitly aware of it.[8]

- A similar literature on popular liberalism in Britain, concentrated in the period of Gladstone between the 1860s and 1890s, but with some anticipation earlier in the nineteenth century in the politics and moral campaigning of provincial religious Dissent.[9]

- A less plentiful literature on the social context of liberalism in Germany, running from the social history of the Enlightenment to the period of unification in the 1860s.[10]

- A disparate literature on political socialization and political mobilization in peasant societies, partly in social history, partly in sociology, and to a lesser extent in anthropology. The breaking down of parochial identities and the entry of rural societies into national political cultures—or the nationalization of the peasantry, as it might be called—is in one dimension the creation of local public spheres and their articulation with a national cultural and political arena. The literature on rural politics and peasant mobilization in nineteenth-century France is especially interesting from this point of view.[11]

- An equally disparate literature in the sociology of communications, focused on the history of the press and other media, the rise of a reading public, popular literacy, and mass communications. As already mentioned above, the work of Raymond Williams is especially central here, together with a considerable body of work in British cultural studies, much of it filtered through the British reception of Gramsci. But another fundamental point of departure is the classic work of Karl Deutsch, *Nationalism and Social Communication: An Inquiry into the Foundations of Nationality* (Cambridge, Mass., 1966; orig. ed. 1954), which has been most imaginatively taken up by the Czech historian Miroslav Hroch for a systematic analysis of the emergence of nationalities in the nineteenth century. In practice, in large parts of southern and eastern Europe in the later nineteenth century (and in the extra-European colonial world in the twentieth century) the emergence of nationality (i.e., the growth of a public for nationalist discourse) was simultaneously the emergence of a public sphere. This codetermination makes a large body of literature on nationalism relevant to the historical discussion of Habermas's idea.[12]

What all of these literatures have in common is a focus on voluntary association and associational life as the main medium for the definition of public commitments. If we take one of the above arguments about the public sphere's conditions of existence seriously—that it presumed the prior transformation of social relations and took clearest shape where the overall context of social communication was being institutionally reformed—there are good grounds for taking voluntary association as a main indicator of social progress in Habermas's sense. In fact, Habermas treats this subject himself to some extent by noting the importance of reading and literary societies to the new public aspirations. But the confluence of these older eighteenth-century associations (reading societies, patriotic clubs, political discussion circles, freemasonry, other secret societies) with more specific political ambitions during the era of the French Revolution, and with the desire for social prestige on the part of the emergent bourgeoisie, also produced a more visible push for social leadership and domination. Thus throughout Germany in the early decades of the nineteenth century the urban and small-town bourgeoisie crystalized their nascent claims to social primacy by forming themselves into an exclusive social club, usually called something like Harmony, Concordia, Ressource, or Union. A club of this kind was the matrix for the formation of a local elite. It acquired its own buildings, recruited only the most prestigious pillars of local society (who might number some thirty businessmen, merchants, lawyers, doctors, and civil servants in a local population of some 6,000 at the start of the century), admitted new members only by careful election, offered a wide range of social facilities (including the reading room), and organized balls, concerts, banquets, and lectures. It was the obvious center of political discussion, and generated a variety of philanthropic, charitable, and recreational activities in the community at large. Thus in Heilbronn in southwest Germany, the Harmony had its own building with club rooms, reading rooms, library, and a surrounding park called the Shareholders' Garden. It was the center of a fine web of informally organized activity radiating into the local social scene. Indeed, the visible performance of civic duties was vital to a notable's moral authority in the town, whether by sitting on charitable or philanthropic committees, improving public amenities, patronizing the arts, promoting education, organizing public festivals, or commemorating great events.[13]

Such associational initiatives were fundamental to the formation of a bourgeois civil society (*bürgerliche Gesellschaft*) in nineteenth-century Germany, in ways that are intimated and assumed in Habermas's text, but which perhaps lack the necessary concrete elaboration for the nineteenth century. Put simply, voluntary association was in principle the logical form of bourgeois emancipation and bourgeois self-affirmation. This was true in three strong ways. First, the ideal and practice of association were explicitly hostile, by both organization and intent, to older principles of corporate organization, which ascribed social place by hereditary and legal estate. By contrast, the new principle of association offered an alternative means of expressing opinion and forming taste, which defined an independent *public* space beyond the legal prescriptions of status and behavior of the monarchical and/or absolutist state. It is central to Habermas's conception of the public sphere in this sense. Second, sociologically, associationism reflected the growing strength and density of the social, personal, and family ties among the educated and propertied bourgeoisie (*Bildung und Besitz*). It described a public arena where the dominance of the bourgeoisie would naturally run. It was the constitutive organizational form of a new force for cultural and political change, namely, the natural social power and self-consciously civilized values of a bourgeoisie starting to see itself as a general or universal class. Third, voluntary association was the primary context of expression for bourgeois aspirations to the general leadership of nineteenth-century society. It provided the theatrical scaffolding for the nineteenth-century bourgeois drama. In this context the underlying principles of bourgeois life—economic, social, moral—were publicly acted out and consciously institutionalized into a model for the other classes, particularly the petty bourgeoisie and the working class, who became the objects of philanthropic support and cultural edification.[14]

Now, the treatment of this theme in nineteenth-century German historiography is rather truncated, mainly because the liberal ideal of emancipation (to which the arguments from voluntary association and the public sphere are hitched) is usually thought to have been decisively blocked by the 1860s and 1870s: if liberalism in Bismarckian and Wilhelmine Germany was such a broken reed, historians see little point in studying the emancipatory purposes of local associational life. If the main story was of decline and degeneration (of liberalism and the public sphere), then the value of looking at the associational arena tends to fall.[15] We can find stronger coverage of such matters, therefore, in a national historiography where the unity of the bourgeoisie's social progress and liberal political success has remained intact in historians' understanding, namely, that of Britain.

For many years J. H. Plumb's *The Growth of Political Stability in England, 1675–1725* (London, 1967) was one of the few texts keeping open a broader and more developed approach to eighteenth-century British politics, as opposed to the narrow interest-based conception of high politics that had come to dominate the field in general. In the intervening two decades Plumb himself published a series of essays that carried this further and explored the cultural changes that allowed something like a free political life to begin to take shape. Though the shadow of a theory barely darkens his pages, Plumb's contributions fall interestingly within the framework Habermas lays out, concerning things like the growth of a reading public, the commercialization of leisure, expanding educational provision, the transition from private to public entertainment, and the general spread of such trends from the capital to the provinces. In effect, this amounted to the gradual coherence of a self-conscious middle-class public, which wore its provincialism less as an embarrassment than as an expression of buoyant creativity.[16]

Moreover, Plumb has inspired a wider body of work, for which John Brewer's study of politics in the 1760s is a splendid example. While Brewer tackles the structure of politics in general, his most important chapters concern the impact of extraparliamentary activity on the parliamentary arena. His chapter on the press covers the entire institutional fabric of public debate in the 1760s, including the nature of literacy, media of publication (newspapers, periodicals, pamphlets, squibs, handbills, songs), the complexities of literary production (as in the seasonality and varied media of circulation), the discrepancies between circulation and actual readership, the role of "bridging" ("the transmission of printed information in traditional oral forms," as in ballads), the social universe of coffeehouse and club, and the spread of postal and turnpike communications. He adds an analysis of the ritual and symbolic content of crowd behavior during the Wilkite manifestations that deepens George Rudé's classic treatment and tells us much about the nascent forms of a new popular politics. When combined with the substantive treatments of mid-century radicalism and its transformations (particularly via the impact of the American radicals), these discussions present "an alternative structure of politics," which in the conjunctures of the 1780s and 1790s had major democratic and oppositional implications. How far the "alternative structure" coincided, organizationally, sociologically, and ideologically, with the emergence of the public sphere described by Habermas is a moot question (which I will return to in the section "Popular Culture and the Public Sphere"). But for present purposes, we may simply note the detailed embodiment of a novel notion of the "public."[17]

John Money's study of the West Midlands, likewise influenced by Plumb, makes a related contribution. Money is concerned with the transition from a rural to a mainly urban-industrial society and with the cultural adaptations that managed to contain much of the potential for social conflict in the new manufacturing center of Birmingham. He suggests that Birmingham's social, economic, and political integration within the wider county community of Warwick was strengthened rather than fractured by the experience of urban growth, and between the 1760s and 1790s this cultural resilience allowed a new sense of regional identity to form. This claim is explored through careful analyses of the local notables—Birmingham merchants and manufacturers— who both kept their links with the county landowners via projects like the Birmingham General Hospital and societies like the Bean Club and the masonic lodges, and defined a separate identity vis-à-vis London and the other regions. Naturally, the process of regional development was not without tensions, and Money devotes much space to the unfolding of religious and other ideological disagreements, and to the emergence of a more popular radicalism. But in the end neither the hostilities of Anglicanism and Dissent nor the pressure for reform nor the promise of Jacobinism were strong enough to tear the fabric of regional community.[18]

More than anything else, Money's book is a study of regional political culture. With Brewer, he shares an intimate knowledge of the structure of public discourse in the chosen period—not just the press, but the public spectacle of music and the stage, the associational milieu of "taverns, coffee-houses and clubs," and the literary world of "printing, publishing and popular instruction"—what Money calls "the means of communication and the creation of opinion." It becomes clear from this kind of analysis that the origins of an independent political life—i.e., a public sphere in Habermas's sense—must be sought in this wider domain of cultural activity, from which a self-confident middle class began to emerge. The foundations were laid before Brewer's and Money's period between the 1680s and 1760s in what has been called an "English urban renaissance," when the growth of towns; new patterns of personal consumption; expanding demand for services, professions, and luxury trades; and the commercialization of leisure all combined to stimulate a new culture of organized recreation, public display, improved amenities, and urban aesthetics.[19] But the political consequences of this process could flourish only in the later part of the eighteenth century, with the commercialization that produced "the birth of a consumer society" and the growing differentiation and self-consciousness of "the middling sort or bourgeoisie" (the "men of moveable property, members of professions, tradesmen and shopkeepers," who comprised some "million of the nation's nearly seven million" inhabitants and who strove for independent space between the "client economy" of the aristocracy and the real dependence of the laboring poor).[20]

Money shows how this flourishing could happen in very practical ways. First, the extension of formal culture to the provinces presupposed public places in which performances and concerts could be held. Hence the phenomenon of the assembly room built by private subscription, where the social elite could meet for balls, music, lectures, and theater, what Plumb calls a "transitional stage between private and fully public entertainment."[21] Such assemblies were sustained by associational action, which in Birmingham extended from the freemasons and other secret circles, to an elite formation like the Bean Club, or equally exclusive intellectual groups like the Lunar Society and reading societies. From this crystalized a wider sense of cultural and political identity, for which the building of the Birmingham General Hospital between 1765 and 1779 by private subscription was the archetypal case. The Hospital's triennial music festivals established themselves as major occasions for the gathering of the West Midlands' leading families, playing a key part in attracting patronage and realizing the town's cultural ambitions.[22] Second, new networks of communication seem especially important, not just because the press and a reading public ease the exchange of information and ideas, but in the larger sense of providing a new institutional context for political action. Money stresses the canal building of the last third of the century, which had an enormous effect in solidifying the new regional and eventually national identities. The floating of a canal scheme entailed an entire repertoire of political initiatives (the creation of new regional political networks, deliberate cultivation of public opinion, participation within the national parliamentary institutions, widespread lobbying of the affected private and public interests), which eventually culminated in the call for a more rational public authority to expedite the whole unwieldy process. This last was key, for to avoid the duplication of projects and an anarchy of particularistic interests, there developed an urgent need to rationalize the activity, and this was increasingly done by reference to some larger "national interest." As Money says, such conflicts became best handled by an appeal to Parliament "as mediator between the public interest on the one hand and private property and enterprise on the other."[23] In the related area of road building such resolution was achieved by inventing the institution of the turnpike trust. As a third case I cite the abortive General Chamber of Manufacturers of Great Britain, formed between 1785 and 1787 as a short-lived response to some of the government's fiscal measures. Though indifferently successful outside the West Midlands and Manchester, this further solidified regional networks and simultaneously oriented them toward national institutions, both existing (Parliament) and notional (a national market).

Now, illustrative analysis of this kind, which puts Habermas's idea to work, can be easily duplicated, because the formation of political culture in this sense has been a fundamental dimension of the capitalist developmental process (except, one should immediately say, where the latter has been imposed from above or without by authoritarian vanguards in situations of extreme societal "backwardness"). But how are we to judge Habermas's idea in its light? The basic point is clear enough, namely, the relationship of the new liberal values of the later eighteenth and early nineteenth centuries to definite developmental processes of class formation and social growth (the transition from feudalism to capitalism, as Habermas describes it, with the concomitant rise of the bourgeoisie). For Brewer no less than for Habermas, a particular ideological structure or cultural formation (liberalism, the ideal of emancipation grounded in rational communication, the Enlightenment discourse of freedom) is the complex effect of a socioeconomic developmental process (the transition from feudalism to capitalism, the rise of capitalism, commercialization, the birth of a consumer society), mediated via the novel institutional structures of the public sphere.[24] At one level Habermas shows how the genesis of the liberal tradition can be grounded in a particular social history, and analyses such as Brewer's or Money's are an excellent concretizing of that project.

On the other hand, what are the problems? Basically, Habermas confines his discussion too much to the bourgeoisie. In his preface Habermas does specifically limit himself to "the *liberal* model of the bourgeois public sphere" (p. xviii) on the grounds of its dominance, distinguishing it from both "the plebeian public sphere" associated with the Jacobin phase of the French

Revolution, which later manifested itself in Chartism and the anarchist strains of the continental labor movement, and "the plebiscitary-acclamatory form of regimented public sphere characterizing dictatorships in highly developed industrial societies" (by which he presumably means fascism). The reference to these alternative forms is too cryptic to allow any sensible speculation about what Habermas means in detail, but he does describe the plebeian version as being "suppressed in the historical process" and in any case "oriented toward the intentions of the bourgeois public sphere" (and therefore a dependent variant). I will be returning to this point again below. But here I want to stress the *variable* origins of *Öffentlichkeit*. The virtue of "publicness" could materialize other than by the intellectual transactions of a polite and literate bourgeois milieu. Despite the best efforts of the latter precisely to appropriate such a function to itself and to establish exclusive claims on the practice of reason, "private people putting reason to use" (Habermas, p. xviii) could also be found elsewhere. In this respect we can make three important points:

1. The liberal desideratum of reasoned exchange also became available for nonbourgeois subaltern groups, whether the radical intelligentsia of Jacobinism and its successors or wide sections of social classes like the peasantry or the working class. Whether in literary (the production and circulation/diffusion of ideas) or political terms (the adoption of constitutions and liberties under the law), the global ideological climate encouraged peasant and working-class voices to strive for the same emancipatory language. That is, the positive values of the liberal public sphere quickly acquired broader democratic resonance, with the resulting emergence of impressive popular movements, each with its own distinctive movement cultures (i.e., form of public sphere). It's open to question how far these were simply derivative of the liberal model (as Habermas argues) and how far they possessed their own dynamics of emergence and peculiar forms of internal life. There is enough evidence from the literature on Owenism, Chartism, and British popular politics and on the forms of political sociability in the French countryside to take this argument seriously.[25] Some recent writing has stressed Chartism's confinement in an inherited political framework and its indebtedness to a given language of political opposition, it is true.[26] But we can see such a movement as in one sense "a child of the eighteenth century" (Habermas, p. xviii), and therefore bound by a dominant model, and at the same time acknowledge its historical specificity and autonomous forms of expression. In particular, Habermas's oppositions of "educated/uneducated" and "literate/illiterate" simply don't work, because (as we shall see) the liberal public sphere was faced at the very moment of its appearance by not only a "plebeian" public that was disabled and easily suppressed, but also a radical one that was combative *and* highly literate.

2. Because of the international impact of the French Revolution, the liberal political ideal encapsulated by the concept of the public sphere was made available in many parts of Europe way ahead of the long-run social transformations, which in western Europe form the starting point of Habermas's argument. All

over east-central and southern Europe, and frequently representing little more than themselves, small groups of intellectuals responded to the French Revolution and its legacy by lodging their own claims to nationhood. The French experience bequeathed a political vocabulary in which such new aspirations could be engaged, a structured ideological discourse of rights and self-government into which such emergent intelligentsias might naturally insert themselves. The encounter with revolutionary France induced conscious reflection not only on the circumstances of political dependence in which such societies invariably found themselves, but also on the associated handicaps of socioeconomic backwardness. Indeed, the radical departures of the French Revolution not only gave sympathetic intellectuals in more "backward" societies a new political language for articulating their own aspirations, it also allowed them to conceptualize their situations as "backwardness" to begin with. It interpellated them in that sense via the new forms of nationalist political address. Armed with the new political consciousness, they then set about constituting a national public sphere in all the ways discussed above—from literary societies, subscription networks, the press, and a national reading public, to the gymnastic and sharpshooter clubs, and the popular reading rooms that carried the activity into the countryside—but with the crucial differences: it was stimulated from the outside rather than being the spontaneous outgrowth of indigenous social development, in response to backwardness rather than progress; and it was consciously expansive rather than narrowly restrictive, oriented toward proselytizing among the people rather than closing ranks against them.[27]

3. It is important to acknowledge the existence of *competing* publics, not just later in the nineteenth century, when Habermas presents the fragmentation of the classical liberal model of *Öffentlichkeit*, but at every stage in the history of the public sphere, and, indeed, from the very beginning. I've argued immediately above in (1) and (2) that emancipatory activity meeting Habermas's criteria could originate in ways that seem not to be encompassed in his classical model (in popular peasant and working-class movements, and in nationalist activity). His conception is needlessly restrictive in other ways too. He *both* idealizes its bourgeois character (by neglecting the ways in which its elitism blocked and consciously repressed possibilities of broader participation/emancipation) *and* ignores alternative sources of an emancipatory impulse in popular radical traditions (such as the dissenting traditions studied by Edward Thompson and Christopher Hill).[28] By subsuming all possibilities into his "liberal model of the bourgeois public sphere," Habermas misses this diversity. More to the point, he misses the extent to which the public sphere was always constituted by conflict. The emergence of a bourgeois public was never defined solely by the struggle against absolutism and traditional authority, but necessarily addressed the problem of popular containment as well. The classic model was already being subverted at the point of its formation, as the actions of subordinate classes threatened to redefine the meaning and extent of the "citizenry." And who is to say that the discourse of the London Corresponding Society was any less "rational" than that of, say, the Birmingham Lunar Society (let alone the Birmingham Bean

Club)? Consequently, the "public sphere" makes more sense as the structured setting where cultural and ideological contest or negotiation among a variety of publics takes place, rather than as the spontaneous and class-specific achievement of the bourgeoisie in some sufficient sense. I will return to this point again below.

GENDER AND THE PUBLIC SPHERE

So far I have considered Habermas's idea mainly in its own terms, by elaborating on what I take to be his conception of bourgeois culture and seeing how the latter might be concretized by using bodies of recent work in social history; and I have begun to indicate some of the ways in which his limitation of the public sphere model to the bourgeoisie starts to become problematic in this light. In fact, Habermas's idea works best as the organizing category of a specifically liberal view of the transition to the modern world and of the ideal bases on which political and intellectual life should be conducted. But his model of how reason in this sense is attained—of a "subjectivity originating in the interiority of the conjugal family" (p. 51), becoming conscious first of itself and then of a wider domain of communicative human relations, traveling into a larger associational arena (book clubs, reading societies, salons, etc.) of literary-intellectual exchange and rational-critical debate, and then replicating itself in a political public sphere of property owners—is an extremely idealized abstraction from the political cultures that actually took shape at the end of the eighteenth and start of the nineteenth century. At one level this is a familiar historian's complaint: "reality" was more "complicated" than that (and too complicated for *any* theory to be adequate, it is often implied); and indeed, the kind of associational initiatives discussed above were certainly subject to a messier set of particular causalities than Habermas appears to allow, at least for the purposes of his immediate theorization. But this is not just a matter of "the facts" and getting them straight. The formation of Birmingham's later eighteenth century associational networks, or the creation of an elite club in early-nineteenth-century German small towns, or the creation of literary societies in mid-nineteenth century Bohemia all involved questions of *interest*, *prestige*, and *power*, as well as those of rational communication. The public sphere in its classical liberal/bourgeois guise was partial and narrowly based in that sense, and was constituted from a field of conflict, contested meanings, and exclusion.

The most consistent of these exclusions—preceding and outlasting, for instance, the calling into question of the public sphere's boundaries on the criterion of class—is based on gender. Nancy Fraser has done an excellent job of facing Habermas's basic categories of social analysis—the systematically integrated domains of the economy and state, and the socially integrated domains of the lifeworld (namely, the private sphere of the family and the public sphere of citizenship), where each constitutes a distinct action context (of functionally driven transactions secured via the media of money and power; and of value-driven interactions focused on intersubjective consensus), corresponding to processes of material and symbolic reproduction, respectively— with the "gender subtext" that runs continuously through these separations. As she says, in Habermas's theory the economic and state systems are simultaneously "disengaged or detached from the lifeworld" and then "related to and embedded in it"; the systems have to be situated "*within* the lifeworld . . . in a context of everyday meanings and norms," and for this purpose the lifeworld "gets differentiated into two spheres that provide appropriate complementary environments for the two sytems"—namely, "the 'private sphere' or modern, restricted, nuclear family . . . linked to the (official) economic system" via the medium of monetary exchange; and "the 'public sphere' or space of political participation, debate, and opinion formation . . . linked to the state-administrative system" via the exchange medium of power. To cut a long and extremely careful critique short, Fraser concludes that the addition of the gender perspective cuts through the structure of distinctions Habermas maintains:

> Once the gender-blindness of Habermas's model is overcome, however, all these connections come into view. It then becomes clear that feminine and masculine gender identity run like pink and blue threads through the areas of paid work, state administration and citizenship as well as through the domain of familial and sexual relations. This is to say that gender identity is lived out in all arenas of life. It is one (if not the) "medium of exchange" among all of them, a basic element of the social glue that binds them to one another.[29]

I want to take this basic feminist critique as understood, and confine myself to a few general observations about the directions of some recent historical work. First, an accumulating tradition of feminist critique has shown how far modern political thought is highly gendered in its basic structures, particularly in the context of the Enlightenment and the French Revolution, when the key elements of liberal and democratic discourse were originally formed. Thus the constitutive moment of modern political understanding was itself constituted by newly conceived or rearranged assumptions about woman and man: this was not only registered in the practical achievements of constitutions, legal codes, and political mobilization and their forms of justification, but also ordered the higher philosophical discourse around the universals of reason, law, and nature, grounding it in an ideologically constructed system of differences in gender. The elaboration of this system was complex, and need not concern us in detail here. Without questioning the continuity of women's oppression in earlier periods and societies, there is a strong case for seeing the form of women's exclusion from political participation and civil rights as the historically specific consequence of processes that worked themselves out in the context of the French Revolution. The new category of the "public man" and his "virtue" was constructed via a series of oppositions to "femininity," which both mobilized older conceptions of domesticity and women's place and rationalized them into a formal claim concerning women's "nature." At the most fundamental level, particular constructions of "womanness" defined the quality of being a "man," so that the *natural* identification of sexuality and desire with the feminine allowed the *social* and *political* construction of masculinity. In the rhetoric of the 1780s and 1790s reason was counterposed conventionally to "femininity, if by the latter we mean (as contemporaries did) pleasure, play, eroticism, artifice, style, politesse, refined facades, and particularity."[30] Given this mannered frivolity, women were to be silenced to allow masculine speech—in the language of reason— full rein.

Thus the absence of women from the political realm "has not been a chance occurrence, nor merely a symptom of the regrettable persistence of archaic patriarchies," but a specific product of the French Revolutionary era. In addition to the other radical departures of that time, modern politics was also constituted "*as* a relation of gender."[31] Moreover, the very breakthrough to new systems of constitutional legality—in which social relations were reordered by conceptions of right, citizenship, and property, and by new definitions of the public and the private—necessarily forced the issue of woman's place, because the codification of participation allowed—indeed, required—conceptions of gender difference to be brought into play. As Landes says, this occurred via "a specific, highly gendered bourgeois male discourse that depended on women's domesticity and the silencing of 'public' women, of the aristocratic and popular classes"; and "the collapse of the older patriarchy gave way to a more pervasive *gendering* of the public sphere."[32] This obviously has major implications for Habermas's argument. He is certainly not unaware of the exclusion of women from the nineteenth-century polities or of the patriarchal nature of the eighteenth- and nineteenth-century family (see, e.g., pp. 43–56, 132). But these matters are assimilated to his general notion of the widening discrepancy between ideal and reality in the nineteenth-century history of the public sphere, and the major ambiguity at the center of Habermas's thinking (the abstraction of an ideal of communicative rationality from historical appearances that were always already imperfect in its terms) lessens the force of the recognition. In fact, the critique of women's subordination can proceed at two levels. On the one hand, there is the synthetic attack on patriarchy as a continuous figure of European political thought from Hobbes through Locke to the Enlightenment and beyond. Women are essentially confined within the household. "Within this sphere, women's functions of child-bearing, child-rearing and maintaining the household are deemed to correspond to their unreason, disorderliness and 'closeness' to nature. Women and the domestic sphere are viewed as inferior to the male-dominated 'public' world of civil society and its culture, property, social power, reason and freedom."[33] But on the other hand, the beauty of Landes's analysis is to have shown how this pattern of subordination was reformulated and recharged in the midst of the major political cataclysm—the

French Revolution—through which the ideal of human emancipation was otherwise radically enlarged. In other words, Habermas's model of rational communication was not just vitiated by persisting patriarchal structures of an older sort; the very inception of the public sphere was itself shaped by a new exclusionary ideology directed at women. As Carol Pateman puts it:

> In a world presented as conventional, contractual and universal, women's civil position is ascriptive, defined by the natural particularity of being women; patriarchal subordination is socially and legally upheld throughout civil life, in production and citizenship as well as in the family. Thus to explore the subjection of women is also to explore the fraternity of men.[34]

Second, the story of associational activity may also be retold in gendered terms—i.e., by highlighting the exclusionary treatment of women, not just as an additive retrieval of a previously neglected aspect, but as an insight that fundamentally reconstructs our sense of the whole. Again, simply invoking traditional patriarchal structures to explain the exclusion of women from politics is perhaps too easy: as Catherine Hall says, middle-class *men* had not been involved in the English political process before the late eighteenth and early nineteenth centuries, and given the general radicalism of the road that led to 1832, the marginalization of middle-class women from this process— i.e., why the attack on traditional values stopped short of patriarchy—needs some specific explanation.[35] In supplying the latter, Davidoff and Hall have stressed *both* the constitutive importance of gender (i.e., the historically specific structuring of sexual difference) in the ordering of the middle-class social world (via particular structures of family and domesticity, and particular styles of consumption) *and* the reciprocal interactions between this private sphere and the public sphere of associational life and politics, in which the latter both reflected and actively reproduced the gendered distinctions of class identity generated between home and work.[36] At a time of enormous socio-economic and political disorder (from the 1790s to the 1840s), "middle-class farmers, manufacturers, merchants and professionals ... , critical of many aspects of aristocratic privilege and power, sought to translate their increasing economic weight into a moral and cultural authority ... not only within their own communities and boundaries, but in relation to other classes"; and they did so via the same associational trajectory (from informal family/ friendship/religious/business networks, through clubs and coffeehouses, to public voluntary associations of a philanthropic-cum-charitable, scientific/ cultural/educational, business/professional/property-related, and political-campaigning kind), which I have argued carried Habermas's public sphere concretely into existence. But—and this is the point to note here—this activity strictly demarcated the roles of men and women via a mobile repertoire of ideologies and practices, which consistently assigned women to a nonpolitical private sphere, "having at most a supportive role to play in the rapidly expanding political world of their fathers, husbands and brothers."[37] Davidoff and Hall present this gendering of the public sphere in a remarkable richness of detail. It is salutary to substitute their summary description for the characterization of the associational context of the public sphere unfolded above:

> Middle-class men's claims for new forms of manliness found one of their most powerful expressions in formal associations. The informal, convivial culture of eighteenth-century merchants, traders and farmers was gradually superseded by the age of societies. Men organized themselves in myriad ways, promoting their economic interests, providing soup kitchens for the poor, cultivating the arts, reaching into populated urban areas and rural outposts. This network of association redefined civil society, creating new arenas of social power and constructing a formidable base for middle-class men. Their societies provided opportunities for the public demonstration of middle-class weight and responsibility; the newspaper reports of their events, the public rituals and ceremonials designed for their occasions, the new forms of public architecture linked to their causes. The experience of such associations increased the confidence of middle-class men and contributed to their claims for political power, as heads of households, representing their wives, children, servants and other dependents. This public world was consistently organized in gendered ways and had little space for women. Indeed, middle-class women in the second half of the nineteenth century focused many of their efforts on attempting to conquer the bastions of this public world, a world which had been created by the fathers and grandfathers.[38]

Third, this separation of spheres—between the masculine realm of public activity and the feminine realm of the home, which certainly didn't preclude (and was finely articulated with) relations of interconnectedness between business/occupation and household, and engendered a particular conception of the public and the private for the emergent nineteenth-century middle class[39]—was replicated in the situation of the working class. In most of the early democratic movements of the late eighteenth and early nineteenth centuries, with the significant exception of the followers of Owen, Fourier, and some other utopian socialists, popular sovereignty was basically a male preserve. Chartism in Britain, as the strongest and most impressive of these movements, is a good example, because the famous Six Points for the democratization of the constitution drawn up in 1837–1838 expressly excluded votes for women. While individual Chartists raised the issue intermittently thereafter, the enduring consensus (shared by the movement's women no less than the men) was that female suffrage deserved a low priority. This was even clearer elsewhere in movements of peasants, shopkeepers, and artisans, where democratic aspirations were practically linked to the economics of small-scale household production and to a sexual division of labor in which women had a significant but subordinate place. By the end of the nineteenth century European socialist parties had certainly put women's political rights into their programs. But it's worth recalling how little female suffrage had actually progressed before 1914, with women enjoying the vote only in parts of the North American West and just four of today's parliamentary states—

New Zealand (1893), Australia (1903), Finland (1906), and Norway (1913)—interestingly all of them frontier states in one way or another.

The reasons for such entrenched discrimination were naturally complex, but ultimately had to do with ideas about the "naturalness" of woman's place and the proper social ordering of sexual difference. Women had no autonomous political standing in the prevailing theories of government and representation. As Sally Alexander says: "The legal, economic and political subject in radical popular speech reaching back to the seventeenth-century Levellers, was the propertied individual, and the propertied individual was always masculine—whether head of household, skilled tradesman or artisan whose property was his labor." Inscribed in the political language of radical democracy were definite notions of masculinity and femininity organized around a clear distinction between the *public world* and a *domestic-cum-communal sphere*, where patriarchal "notions of labor, property and kin" structured—and limited—"women's access to acknowledge, skill and independent political subjectivity." Women were highly active in Chartism and other radical agitations of the early nineteenth century. But when they spoke, they did so within the walls of the embattled popular community itself. It fell to men to speak to the outside world "in the first person for the community as a whole." *Public* discourse in the full sense, involving the whole field of popular socioeconomic discontents, campaigns for civil freedoms, struggles over the law, and the demand for the vote, was closed to women. It was conducted as "a dialogue of negotiation between the men of the communities and the ruling class—'capitalists and lawgivers.'"[40]

For the various groups of radical working men—"the small master craftsmen, the displaced domestic worker, the artisan and mechanic, the skilled factory operatives," who provided the backbone of Chartism and the related movements—the integrity of the household was constitutive for political identity; and whatever complementarities and reciprocities there may have been between men and women in the household division of labor, as a system of domestic authority the family was centered on masculine privilege. Thus in voicing their anger against the advance of capitalist industry, which undermined their skills and pulled their wives and children into the factory, radical artisans were also defending their own sexual and economic regime in the family. In their minds "their status as fathers and heads of families was indelibly associated with their independence through 'honorable' labor and property in skill, which identification with a trade gave them." Women, by contrast, had no access to such independence. In their own right they were excluded from most trades and could practice a craft only by virtue of their male kin. Usually, they "assisted" the latter. Her "skill" was in the household, her "property in the virtue of her person." But "separated from the home, her family and domestic occupations, or outside the bonds of matrimony, a woman was assured of neither." Logically enough, a woman's political identity was subsumed in that of the man, and it was no accident that the rare proponents of female suffrage among the Chartists also limited their advocacy to "spinsters and widows," because wives and husbands were simply deemed to be one.[41]

This thinking was easily adapted to the changed circumstances of industrialization. The manner of the adjustment was already signaled by the calls for "protective" laws that became especially clamorous in the 1830s and 1840s: demanding the protection of women and children against the degrading and brutalizing effects of work in the new mills, they also reflected the desire for an idealized notion of family, hearth, and home, where benign patriarchy and healthy parental authority ordered the household economy by the "natural differences and capacities" of women and men. When wives and children were forced into the factory by the unemployment or depressed earning power of the husband-father, this natural order was upset. To this dissolution of moral roles—the "unsexing of the man," in Engels' phrase—were then added the effects of women's cheap labor, whose increasing utilization by the new capitalists spelled a loss of jobs, status, and skill for the skilled man. Whatever the real basis of these fears, this fusion of economic and ideological anxieties—resistance to the capitalist reorganization of industry, and the desire to quarantine the family's moral regime—proved a potent combination for those categories of skilled workers strong enough actually to secure a strong bargaining position for themselves.[42] In the new prosperity and greater political stability in British society after 1850, such groups of workers were able to come into their own.

The result was a recharged domestic ideology of masculine privilege, whose realistic attainment was now confined to those groups of skilled workingmen able to support a wife and children on the strength of their own earning power alone. The nature of the labor market for most men—involving the irregularity, casualness, and seasonality of most unskilled and much skilled employment, with the connected difficulties of low, irregular wages and weak organization—ensured that male earnings had to be supplemented by whatever income the wife and the rest of the family could produce, usually in casual, sweated, or home-based employment or in the locally based informal economy. Measured by the rest of the working class, therefore, the position of the skilled craftsman able to keep his wife in domesticated nonemployment was becoming an extremely privileged one—not just in relation to women, but in relation to the mass of unskilled males too. Trade unionism before the 1890s was virtually predicated on this system of exclusion, and the new ideal of the "family wage" was a principal mechanism separating the small elite of trade-unionized craftsmen from the mass of ordinary workers. But not only did it strengthen the material advantages enjoyed by the craft elite. It also postulated a normative definition of women's employment as something exceptional and undesirable, and delivered ideological justifications for "keeping women in their place"—or, at least, for not according their interests the same priority as male workers' in trade union terms—that proved persuasive far outside the ranks of the labor aristocrats themselves and became a pervasive feature of working-class attitudes towards women's political status. Thus it was a paradox of socialist politics before 1914 that parties which were in many ways the staunchest advocates of women's rights in the political arena had also originated in the activism of skilled workers who practiced the worst systems of craft exclusiveness against women—both in immediate terms and in terms of the larger social discrimination/subordination they implied. As we know from the scholarship of the last two decades, the socialist tradition's official supportiveness for women's rights usually concealed a practical indifference to giving them genuine priority in the movement's agitation. More basically, such political neglect was linked to attitudes and practices deeply embedded in the material conditions of working-class everyday life, at work, in the neighborhood, and at home. Behind the labor movement's neglect of women's issues were historically transmitted patterns of masculinist behavior and belief which trade unionists and left-wing politicians were consistently unwilling to challenge.[43]

I can best express the relevance of this to the discussion of the public sphere by considering the relationship of the private and the public. The specification of a public sphere necessarily implies the existence of another sphere that's private, and by contrast with what Habermas sometimes implies, as Fraser has argued, the boundaries between these two domains are not fast but permeable. The discussion here is also complicated by the recent revival of theorizing around "civil society": as John Keane reminds us, in the eighteenth and nineteenth centuries the state/civil society couplet was operated by political theorists in a rich variety of ways; we might add that such diversity is compounded by the difficulties of distinguishing the autonomies of the private realm in these traditions (e.g., where does the economic belong in this three-way schema of state/civil society/private sphere; how far is morality the vector of an interventionism that transcends all three; how do we deal with subjectivity?); and it is by no means clear how Habermas's theory of the public sphere fits with this older tradition of thought.[44] But allowing for this diversity of meanings, it may be useful to remind ourselves in a simplified way of the varying definition the public realm may be given. Is this a purely "political" matter in the narrower sense of government and public administration, for instance, or should the legitimate reach of political intervention extend to other more "private" spheres like the economy, recreation, the family, sexuality, and interpersonal relations? Broadly speaking, there have been probably three main answers within the classical left-wing tradition:

- A *pure democratic* one, stressing the political rights of democracy and based in a clear separation of the public from the private sphere, in which the constitution guarantees strong rights of autonomy to the latter through civil freedoms, freedom of conscience and religion, property rights, rights of privacy, and so on
- A *socialist* one, in which the public sphere of democracy becomes extended to the economy through nationalization, the growth of the public sector, trade unionism, the welfare state and other forms of socialized public provision

in the areas of health care, social insurance, education, recreation, and so on

- A *utopian* one, in which democracy becomes radically extended to social relations as a whole, including large areas of personal life, domestic living arrangements, and child raising, usually in the form of some kind of communitarianism

In the period since 1968 we may add a fourth version of this relationship between the public and the private, which subjects each of the above to searching critique, and that is the *feminist* one. Aside from facing the earlier versions with the need to address the interests/aspirations of women as well as men, the feminist version brings the principle of democracy to the center of the private sphere in a qualitatively different way. It systematically politicizes the personal dimension of social relations in a way that transforms the public/ private distinction—in terms of family, sexuality, self, and subjectivity. Obviously, contemporary feminism is not without its antecedents. Thus the utopian socialists of the 1830s and 1840s had politicized the personal sphere in ways that seem strikingly radical when set against the staider preoccupations of the later nineteenth-century socialist tradition. Strong notions of women's reproductive rights and liberated sexuality could also be found on the margins of the left between the 1880s and 1914, and more extensively in the cultural radicalism of 1917–1923. But it is only really in the last third of the twentieth century that the gendered characteristics of the classical public sphere have been properly opened to critique—by elaborating theories of sexuality and subjectivity, identifying ideologies of motherhood, confronting the sexual division of labor in households, and developing a critique of the family as such. As Pateman says:

> The meaning of "civil society". . . has been constructed through the exclusion of women and all that we symbolize. . . . To create a properly democratic society, which includes women as full citizens, it is necessary to deconstruct and reassemble our understanding of the body politic. This task extends from the dismantling of the patriarchal separation of private and public, to a transformation of our individuality and sexual identities as feminine and masculine beings. These identities now stand opposed, part of the multifaceted expression of the patriarchal dichotomy between reason and desire. The most profound and complex problem for political theory and practice is how the two bodies of humankind and feminine and masculine individuality can be fully incorporated into political life. How can the present of patriarchal domination, opposition and duality be transformed into a future of autonomous, democratic differentiation?[45]

State Formation and the Public Sphere

Despite the richness—empirically and imaginatively—of Habermas's account of the formation of (West) European political culture in the eighteenth and early nineteenth centuries, there is little discussion of the state per se or of specific political histories, at least in the senses we've become familiar with during the last two decades, whether via the state-theoretical literatures generated/provoked by Marxists in the 1970s or in the more heterogeneous work on state formation, which was already under way when Habermas conceived his book in the 1950s and early 1960s (most obviously associated with the influence of the Committee on Comparative Politics of the U.S. Social Science Research Council set up in 1954). At the same time, while this omission is significant (in that it has a necessary bearing on how the overall problematic of modern political development is constructed/implied in Habermas's text), Habermas's purpose was different and legitimately specific, concerned, as we have seen, with the "free space" of society rather than a state-centered approach to public authority or political development. He also has lots to say with relevance to the latter, particularly in his extensive and very interesting discussions of the law. Moreover, if we consider the major contributions to the historical discussion of comparative political development produced since the late 1960s (most of them by nonhistorians in the professional sense, incidentally), they have remarkably little to say to the questions of the public sphere and political culture formation raised by Habermas. These works include the writings of Barrington Moore, Jr., and Charles Tilly, both of whom pioneered the turn by U.S. sociology to history in this area; Immanuel Wallerstein's studies of the "modern world-system," Perry Anderson's of absolutism, and Theda Skocpol's of "states and social revolutions"; and the more recent and differently accented projects of Anthony Giddens and Michael Mann. Wallerstein is only secondarily concerned with political, as opposed to economic, history; Anderson deals with state and society relations, but for an earlier period and at a level of generality that makes it hard to engage with Habermas's questions (the latter will in any case be more pertinent to the next installment of Anderson's project, namely, the comparative analysis of bourgeois revolutions); Skocpol focuses rather stolidly on the state in the narrower sense, as a central nexus of government institutions. Tilly's work on collective action and state formation brings us closer to political culture, but deals with "the extractive and repressive activities of states" rather than the cultural and ideological ones. Barrington Moore poses the problem of comparative political development through the gross interactions of social forces ("lord and peasant in the making of the modern world"), and has little directly to say about the structure of states, the shaping of a public sphere, or the contribution of urban classes. Neither Mann nor Giddens has anything to say about the public sphere in the sense discussed by this paper; the former's forthcoming second volume may well treat this theme directly, but the latter's discussion of "Class, Sovereignty and Citizenship" is bizarrely perfunctory and deals with the subject under an entirely "administrative" perspective.[46] Each of these otherwise extremely interesting works pays little attention to political culture, to the wider impact of the state in society and the modalities of popular consent and opposition, or to the social processes from which political activity ultimately derived. From this point of view, Habermas's translation of the discussion onto a sociocultural terrain, particularly for its time, represents a welcome shift of perspective and might well have found greater resonance in the literature on state formation than it has.

As a view of political development, though, Habermas's framework has a number of drawbacks, some of which have already been mentioned. For one thing, by using a model of communicative rationality to mark the rise of liberalism and the constitutionalizing of arbitrary authority, and by stressing the transition to a more interventionist state under advanced capitalism, he strongly implies a *weak* state during the classical public sphere's period of initial formation. But it is unclear how the boundaries between state and society are to be drawn from Habermas's analysis of this period. Was the liberal state really so uninterested in regulating the private sphere or so noninterventionist in the resolution of social and political conflict? Habermas is very good on the legal reforms necessary to promote and ratify the changing bases of property, and as Karl Polanyi always insisted, the road to laissez-faire was paved in state intervention. The same was true of sociocultural and political, no less than of economic freedoms: to deregulate society, and confirm a protected space for the public, an entire regulative program was required.[47] Secondly, and in a similar vein, Habermas's argument idealizes the element of rational discourse in the formation of the public sphere, and neglects the extent to which its institutions were founded on sectionalism, exclusiveness, and repression. In eighteenth-century Britain parliamentary liberty and the rule of law were inseparable from the attack on customary rights, popular liberties, and nascent radical democracy, as Edward Thompson's work has so eloquently reminded us.[48] As I suggested above, the participants in the bourgeois public always faced two ways in this sense—forward in confrontation with the old aristocratic and royal authorities, but also backward against the popular/plebeian elements already in pursuit. We can't grasp the ambiguities of the liberal departure—the consolidation of the classical public sphere in the period, say, between 1760 and 1850—without acknowledging the fragility of the liberal commitments and the element of contestation in this sense. It's only by extending Habermas's idea in this direction—toward the *wider* public domain, where authority is not only constituted as rational and legitimate, but where its terms may also be contested and modified (and occasionally overthrown) by society's subaltern groups—that we can accommodate the complexity.

For this purpose, I want to suggest, an additional concept may be introduced, namely, Antonio Gramsci's idea of "hegemony." Some basic awareness of this is now fairly extensive, but, while there is now no shortage of careful critical exegesis around Gramsci's own intentions, the wider usage can be ill-informed and glib, and it is important to clarify the purposes the idea is meant to serve. It is worth beginning with Gwyn A. Williams's useful definition, which was also the form in which most of us first encountered the concept before the more extensive translation and discussion of Gramsci's thought in the 1970s: hegemony signifies "an order in which a certain way of life and thought is dominant, in which one concept of reality is diffused throughout society in all its institutional and private manifestations, informing with its spirit all taste, morality, customs, religious and political principles, and all social relations, particularly in their intellectual and moral connotation."[49] Now, this is fine as far as it goes, but it can also license a number of misconceptions, so several points need to be made in elaboration. First, "hegemony" should not be used interchangeably with "ideology" or "ideological domination" *tout court* in a perspective stressing the "manipulations" or "social control" deliberately exercised by a ruling class. As Raymond Williams says in the course of a brilliant exposition: hegemony comprises "not only the conscious system of ideas and beliefs [i.e., 'ideology' in a commonly accepted sense] but the whole lived social process as practically organized by specific dominant meanings and values," "a sense of reality for most people in the society, a sense of absolute because experienced reality beyond which it is very difficult for most members of the society to move, in most areas of their lives." Hegemony should be seen

> as in effect a saturation of the whole process of living—not only of political or economic activity, nor only of manifest social activity, but of the whole substance of lived identities and relationships, to such a depth that the pressures and limits of what can ultimately be seen as a specific economic, political and cultural system seem to most of us the pressures and limits of simple experience and common sense. Hegemony is then not only the articulate upper level of "ideology," nor are its forms of control only those ordinarily seen as "manipulation" or "indoctrination." It is the whole body of practices and expectations, over the whole of living: our senses and assignments of energy, or shaping perceptions of ourselves and our world.[50]

This sense of completeness and externally structured experience, of "the wholeness of the process" by which a given social order holds together and acquires its legitimacy, is the most obvious feature of Gramsci's idea.[51]

Second, however, Gramsci's idea of hegemony was not a "totalitarian" concept (contrary to some of the older commentaries of the 1950s and 1960s, such as H. Stuart Hughes, *Consciousness and Society* [New York, 1958], pp. 96–104). In fact, he used it carefully to distinguish elements of pluralism and competition, of persuasion and consent, from the more repressive and coercive forms of rule and the conventional process of governing in the administrative sense. Though he takes careful note of direct interventions by the state against society to suppress opposition, to contain dissent, and to manipulate educational, religious, and other ideological apparatuses for the production of popular compliance, therefore, Gramsci expressly links hegemony to a domain of public life (which he calls "civil society," but which might also be called the "public sphere") that is relatively independent of such controls, and hence makes its achievement a far more contingent process. To establish its supremacy, in Gramsci's view, a dominant class must not only *impose* its rule via the state, it must also demonstrate its claims to "intellectual and moral leadership," and this requires the arts of persuasion, a continuous labor of creative ideological intervention. The capacity "to articulate different visions of the world in such a way that their potential antagonism is neutralized," rather than simply suppressing those visions beneath "a uniform conception of the world," is the essence of hegemony in Gramsci's sense.[52] But by the same virtue, hegemony is also susceptible to change and negotiation—not just because it involves the pursuit of consent under conditions of pluralism (however limited), but also because this process nonetheless operates through social relations of dominance and subordination structured by class inequality, and therefore involves contradictory and opposing interests.

Third, therefore, hegemony is characterized by uncertainty, impermanence, and contradiction. As I put it with Keith Nield on an earlier occasion, hegemony "is not a fixed and immutable *condition*, more or less permanent until totally displaced by determined revolutionary action, but is an institutionally negotiable *process* in which the social and political forces of contest, breakdown and transformation are constantly in play."[53] In this sense, hegemony is always in the process of construction, because bringing the process to closure would entail either a utopia of social harmony or the replacement of hegemonic by coercive rule. Hegemony is always open to modification, and under specific circumstances may be more radically transformed or even (though not very often) break down altogether. Thus civil society provides opportunities for *contesting* as well as *securing* the legitimacy of the system. More than anything else, then, hegemony has "to be won, secured, constantly defended." It requires "a struggle to win over the dominated classes in which any 'resolution' involves both *limits* (compromises) and *systematic contradictions*."[54] The dominance of a given social group has to be continually renegotiated in accordance with the fluctuating economic, cultural, and political strengths of the subordinate classes.

Gramsci's distinction between "hegemonic" and "coercive" forms of rule is also operated historically. That is, developed capitalist polities whose legitimacy rests on a fairly stable "equilibrium of hegemonic and coercive institutions" are directly contrasted with an older type of state that lacks this vital reciprocity with civil society:

> In the ancient and medieval state alike, centralization, whether political-territorial or social . . . was minimal. The state was, in a certain sense, a mechanical bloc of social groups. . . . The modern state substitutes for the mechanical bloc of social groups their subordination to the active hegemony of the directive and dominant group, hence abolishes certain autonomies, which nevertheless are reborn in other forms, as parties, trade unions, cultural associations.[55]

The passage from one type of state to another presupposes processes of social change that allow new political ambitions to be crystallized. For Gramsci, the latter consist of three moments: the growth of corporate solidarities; their organization into a larger class collectivity; and their translation onto the highest political plane of "universal" interest. With the development of the last of these aspirations, the process of hegemonic construction may be said to have begun, with the growth of a new "national-popular" dimension to public life, and a new claim to "intellectual and moral leadership" in the society as a whole. It is in the context of such a history that the institutional landscape of civil society gradually takes shape. In a now famous and much-quoted passage, Gramsci hinted at the comparative possibilities of this approach:

> In Russia the state was everything, civil society was primordial and gelatinous; in the West there was a proper relation between state and civil society, and when the state trembled a sturdy structure of civil society was at once revealed. The state was only an outer ditch, behind which there stood a powerful system of fortresses and earthworks.[56]

For Gramsci, this contrast was specifically a way of explaining the success of the Bolsheviks in the Russian Revolution, which simultaneously illustrated the fundamentally different strategy required of the Left in Western Europe, where the greater complexity of the social fabric, the liberal traditions of citizenship and constitutionalism, and the functioning pluralism of the political system meant that power was diffused more intangibly through a wide variety of nonofficial practices and organizations, as opposed to being physically embodied in a central core of state institutions in the capital city: if in Russia the backwardness of civil society left the state an isolated citadel, which could then be stormed, in the West the structures of existing society were far more complex, requiring a long-term war of position on the part of a revolutionary opposition, and not the insurrectionary war of movement. For our purposes, nineteenth-century Russia provides an excellent counterexample for the growth of the public sphere. It displayed the absence of all those processes—particularly the emancipatory impulse of free associational initiative, which under Tsarism was precluded by a combination of social backwardness and repressive state authority—which Habermas's concept of *Öffentlichkeit* presupposed.

POPULAR CULTURE AND THE PUBLIC SPHERE

Of course, for Gramsci civil society was not quite the neutral context for the emergence of rational political discourse in the ideal and abstract sense intended by Habermas. As I have argued, it was an arena of contested meanings, in which different—and opposing—publics maneuvered for space, and from which certain "publics" (women, subordinate nationalities, popular classes like the urban poor, the working class, and the peasantry) may have been excluded altogether. Moreover, this element of contest was not just a matter of coexistence, in which such alternative publics participated in a tolerant pluralism of tendencies and groupings; such competition also occurred in class-divided societies structured by inequality, and consequently questions of domination and subordination—power, in its economic, social, cultural, and political dimensions—were also involved. That being so, hegemony—as the harnessing of public life to the interests of one particular group, i.e., a social bloc ordered around the dominant classes—had to be systematically worked at, whether consciously and programmatically (as in the early stages of such a process of hegemonic construction) or increasingly as the "natural" and unreflected administration or reproduction of a given way of doing things. *Intellectuals* in Gramsci's schema—as a broadened social category, including journalists, party officials, teachers, priests, lawyers, technicians, and other professionals, as well as writers, professors, and intellectuals in the narrower conventional sense—were the functionaries of this process.

I want to explore this element of conflict—the fractured and contested character of the public sphere—by looking again at the latter's constitutive moment as Habermas presents it in the later eighteenth century in Britain and I want to do so by drawing on the extremely interesting work of Gunther Lottes, who (by contrast with most of the Anglo-American work on the subject) is familiar with Habermas's framework and, indeed, uses it to develop his argument.[57] Lottes's book is a reworking of a key part of Edward Thompson's *Making of the English Working Class* and revolves around a careful analysis of the emergence of a radical intelligentsia and its relationship to a plebeian public in later-eighteenth-century England, conducted in two stages. During the first, in the 1770s and 1780s, radical intellectuals postulated a regeneration of the constitution through popular education and parliamentary reform. The corruption and besetting factionalism of the governing system were to be challenged by an extraparliamentary campaign of public enlightenment. At this stage, Lottes argues, the links between intelligentsia and public were external rather than organic, asserted at the level of principle and propaganda, but not yet consummated through new forms of communication or structures of popular participation. Moreover, this earlier intelligentsia was recruited from the upper reaches of society, from three overlapping groups of notables (*Honoratioren*): landowners, merchants, and other prosperous businessmen, whose intellectual pursuits presumed (though not complacently) the material security of their social position; representatives of the academic professions, mainly lawyers and Nonconformist clergy; and the literati and writers in the narrower sense, newly constituted as a separate profession by the emergent literary marketplace. Their activity was loosely structured around London's coffeehouse society, in the discussion circles and debating clubs typified by the Robin Hood Society, the Speculative Society, or the Debating Society in Coachmakers' Hall. If anything, the provincial counterparts were more ramified and vital, certainly in the major centers of Manchester and Birmingham. At the political apex was the Society for Constitutional Information, founded in 1780, which remained the principal forum of the radical intelligentsia until the launching of the London Corresponding Society (LCS) in 1792. Thus far, it may be thought, Lottes's account fits very nicely into Habermas's framework, and adds further to the illustrative materials provided by Brewer, Money, and others discussed earlier. But the subsequent unfolding of his argument is more subversive.

At one level, the reform movement of the 1780s, which was expressly committed to the creation of an extraparliamentary public, broke the existing frame of legitimate politics. By seeking to educate the general populace into citizenship, the pre-Jacobin radicals raised the issue of universal manhood suffrage and broke "with the previously uncontested dogma of political theory that property alone justified a claim to political participation."[58] Yet at the same time, the Society for Constitutional Information made no attempt at direct popular mobilization. This, the open agitation of the masses within a new practice of participatory democracy, occurred only with the *second* of Lottes's two stages, that of the English Jacobinism proper. As the organizing instance of the new activity, the LCS then had two distinguishing features. By comparison with the earlier radicals its leadership was drawn more broadly from the less prestigious and established circles of the intelligentsia—not only recognized intellectuals like the merchant's son Maurice Margarot, the Unitarian minister Jeremiah Joyce, or the lawyers Felix Vaughan, John Frost, and John Martin, but also "not yet arrived or declassed marginal existences of the London literary-publicistic scene" like John Gale Jones, Joseph Gerrald, William Hodgson, the Binns brothers (John and Benjamin), or John Thelwall ("the prototype of the literatus from a modest background who tried vainly for years to find a foothold in the London artistic and literary scene"), the numerous small publishers and book dealers, and the "first representatives of an artisan intelligentsia" like the shoemaker Thomas Hardy, the silversmith John Baxter, the hatter Richard Hodgson, or the tailor Francis Place.[59] Then second, this new Jacobin intelligentsia set out deliberately to mobilize the masses, by carrying the work of political education into the turbulent reaches of the plebeian culture itself.

Thus the key to the LCS's originality was its relationship to the ebullient but essentially prepolitical culture of the urban masses, what Lottes calls "the socio-cultural and institutional context of the politicization of the petty and sub-bourgeois strata."[60] In adopting the democratic principle of "members unlimited," the LCS committed itself not only to a program of popular participation, but also to a "confrontation with the traditional plebeian culture," of which it was certainly no uncritical admirer. As Lottes says, "The Jacobin ideal of the independent, well-informed and disciplined citizen arriving at decisions via enlightened and free discussion stood in crass contradiction with the forms of communication and political action characteristic of the plebeian culture."[61] In other words, riot, revelry, and rough music were to be replaced by the political modalities of the pamphlet, committee room, resolution, and petition, supplemented where necessary by the disciplined democracy of an orderly open-air demonstration. The most valuable parts of Lottes's account are those exploring the practicalites of this departure—in the meticulous constitutionalism of the LCS, in the creation of an atmosphere for rational political discussion, in the radicals' critique of the "mob," and in the details of their "enlightenment praxis." A new "plebeian public sphere" (*plebejische Öffentlichkeit*) emerged from these endeavors, nourished on the intense political didacticism of the LCS sections, a rich diet of pamphlets, tracts, and political magazines, and the theatrical pedagogy of Thelwall's Political Lectures. Unlike the radicals of the 1780s, the Jacobins entered into a *direct* relationship with their putative public, and unlike conventional parliamentarians, they did so in a nonmanipulative and nondemagogic way.

This was the real significance of the popular radicalism of the 1790s in Britain. It was more than a mere stage in the long-term movement toward parliamentary reform between the 1760s and 1832, and more than a mere epiphenomenon of the deeper trend toward extraparliamentary "association." It was also more than the founding moment of the nineteenth-century labor movement (which was how it was mainly presented in the older labor history and allied accounts). It was a specific attempt—defined by the global context of the "Atlantic Revolution," the national dynamics of the movement for parliamentary reform, the complex sociology of the English intelligentsia, and the political economy of the London and provincial handicrafts—to educate the masses into citizenship. It should be viewed as "partly the achievement and partly the continuing expression of a comprehensive effort at enlightenment and education, aimed at bringing the urban stratum of small tradesmen and artisans to the point where they could articulate their social and political discontent no longer in the pre-political protest rituals of the traditional plebeian culture, but instead in a political movement with firm organization, a middle and long-term strategy, and a theoretically grounded program."[62] As such, it was as much the "end product of the bourgeois enlightenment of the eighteenth century" as it was the herald of the nineteenth-century working-class movement. As Albert Goodwin, another historian of the English Jacobinism, puts it, the tradesmen, shopkeepers, and mechanics addressed by the LCS were to be educated into political knowledge not just to ensure "their more effective participation in politics," but "to rid society of the turbulence and disorder which was then often inseparable from the ventilation of popular grievances."[63]

At the same time, there were definite limits to the English Jacobins' possible achievement. For one thing the advanced democracy of the LCS *presumed* the very maturity and sophistication it was meant to *create*. The goals of political pedagogy were hard to reconcile with the competing demands of effective organization, creative leadership, and maximum participation of the members—what Lottes calls "the triangular tension of organizational effectiveness, fundamental democratic consciousness at the grass roots, and educational mission"[64]—particularly when government repression was stepped up after 1793. Moreover, tactically it was hard to confront the "backwardness" of the popular culture too intransigently without beginning to compromise the resonance of the radical propaganda and undermining the movement's basic democratic legitimacy. The Jacobins were also confined in a

different direction by the tenacity of the dominant eighteenth-century opposi-
tionist ideology—a potent combination of "Country" ideology and natural
rights thinking—which stressed the degeneration of an originally healthy
constitution and raised serious obstacles to the adoption of Tom Paine's
more radical break with the English constitutional tradition. In this respect,
the Jacobin radicals remained dependent on the intellectual legacy of the
1780s, and most of their distinctive achievements (e.g., Thelwall's social as
opposed to his political theory) were well within the limits of this earlier
tradition.[65]

Lottes's account nicely brings together the points I've been trying to make
(although it should be said straight away that his discussion remains as gender blind as Habermas's own). On the one hand, the actual pursuit of communicative rationality via the modalities of the public sphere at the end of the
eighteenth century reveals a far richer social history than Habermas's conception of a specifically bourgeois emancipation allows; on the other hand,
Habermas's concentration on *Öffentlichkeit* as a specifically *bourgeois* category subsumes forms of popular democratic mobilization that were always
already present as contending and subversive alternatives to the classical liberal organization of civil society in which Habermas's ideal of the public
sphere is confined. From a vantage point in 1989, when the French Revolution is being divested of its radical democratic and popular progressive content, and discussion of the latter returned to certain Cold War simplicities of
the 1950s (as "the origins of totalitarian democracy"), apparently without serious dispute, it is no unimportant matter to point to the foreshortening of
Habermas's conception in this respect. (Of course, this is *not* to convict
Jürgen Habermas himself of the same ideological syndrome but merely to
identify a difficulty that needs clarification.) My four headings of discussion—the findings of current social history, the problem of gender, processes
of state formation, and the question of popular politics—are not the only ones
under which Habermas's work could be considered historically. A more extensive discussion of nineteenth-century nationalist movements, or the literature on communications, or the question of popular/mass culture in the
Frankfurt School's notation, would all have been interesting candidates for
inclusion. More fundamentally, perhaps, the "linguistic turn" and the "new
cultural history" could also be used to cast Habermas's work in an interesting
critical light, as Habermas's own recent engagement with the legacy of Foucault has already made clear. In particular, the claim to *rational* discourse,
certainly in the social and gendered exclusiveness desired by the late-eighteenth-century bourgeoisie, was simultaneously a claim to *power* in Foucault's sense, and given the extent of Foucault's influence during the last decade, a whole other discussion might have been developed around this insight.
To repeat: none of this diminishes the value and interest of Habermas's original intervention, particularly given its timing three decades ago. My purpose
has not been to dismiss the latter, but to indicate some of the ways in which it
needs to be clarified and extended.

NOTES

First appeared in 1992.

1. Jürgen Habermas, "The Public Sphere," *New German Critique* 3 (1974): 49. Habermas originally developed his argument, of course, in *Strukturwandel der Öffent-lichkeit* (Neuwied, 1962). The page references in parentheses in my text are to the page proofs of the new English edition.

2. Perry Anderson and Peter Dews, in their interview with Habermas, "A Philoso-phico-Political Profile," in Peter Dews, ed., *Autonomy and Solidarity: Interviews with Jürgen Habermas* (London, 1986), p. 178.

3. Rick Roderick, *Habermas and the Foundations of Critical Theory* (New York, 1986), p. 43.

4. Peter U. Hohendahl, "Critical Theory, Public Sphere and Culture: Jürgen Haber-mas and his Critics," *New German Critique* 16 (1979): 92.

5. Terry Eagleton, *The Function of Criticism: From "The Spectator" to Post-Structuralism* (London, 1984), p. 15.

6. Given the close attention to Habermas's work in the 1970s and 1980s, it is inter-esting that this, his first major work, which established both his reputation and endur-ing theoretical interests, has only now received its translation, and indeed, the general ignorance and neglect of its significance in the English-speaking world is rather re-markable. Peter Hohendahl is something of an exception in this respect. Aside from the commentary cited in note 4 above, he also introduced Habermas's work in *New German Critique* 3 (1974): 45–48, and applied it in "Prolegomena to a History of Literary Criticism," *New German Critique* 11 (1977): 151–163. See also his *Literatur und Oeffentlichkeit* (Munich, 1974) and *The Institution of Criticism* (Ithaca, 1982). Discussion of *Strukturwandel* is strikingly absent from the main English language commentaries on Habermas's work: Thomas McCarthy, *The Critical Theory of Jürgen Habermas* (Cambridge, Mass., 1978); David Held, *Introduction to Critical Theory* (Berkeley, 1980); Rick Roderick, *Habermas and the Foundations of Critical Theory*; Anthony Giddens, "Jürgen Habermas," in Quentin Skinner, ed., *The Return of Grand Theory in the Human Sciences* (Cambridge, 1985), pp. 121–139; John B. Thompson and David Held, eds., *Habermas: Critical Debates* (Cambridge, Mass., 1982). This is perhaps most striking of all in John Keane, *Public Life and Late Capi-talism: Toward a Socialist Theory of Democracy* (Cambridge, 1984), a work avow-edly inspired by a reading of Habermas, but which remarkably manages not to discuss directly or at any length the intellectual context and historical validity of *Strukturwan-del* itself. The same is true of Keane's recent two volumes on the current discourse of civil society, which fail to pose the relevance of Habermas's pioneering analysis to the terms of that discussion. See John Keane, *Democracy and Civil Society* (London, 1988), and Keane ed., *Civil Society and the State: New European Perspectives* (Lon-don, 1988). In this respect, Joan B. Landes, *Women and the Public Sphere in the Age of the French Revolution* (Ithaca, 1988), is an equally striking exception. See also Richard Sennett, *The Fall of Public Man: On the Social Psychology of Capitalism* (New York, 1976).

7. There is an entry for "Private," but even this doesn't deal with the public/private distinction. See Raymond Williams, *Keywords: A Vocabulary of Culture and Society*, revised ed. (New York, 1983), pp. 242–243. For a similar, but immensely more gran-diose project, with its place in a very different national intellectual tradition, see Otto

Brunner, Werner Conze, and Reinhart Koselleck, eds., *Geschichtliche Grundbegriffe*, 5 vols. (Stuttgart, 1972–1989); and for a succinct introduction to this project, see Keith Tribe, "The *Geschichtliche Grundbegriffe* Project: From History of Ideas to Conceptual History," *Comparative Studies in Society and History* 31 (January 1989): 180–184.

8. See the following: J. H. Plumb, "The Public, Literature, and the Arts in the Eighteenth Century," in Michael R. Marrus, ed., *The Emergence of Leisure* (New York, 1974), pp. 11–37; Plumb, *The Commercialization of Leisure* (Reading, 1973); Plumb, "The New World of Childhood in Eighteenth-Century England," *Past and Present* 67 (May 1975): 64–95; Neil McKendrick, John Brewer, and J. H. Plumb, *The Birth of a Consumer Society: The Commercialization of Eighteenth-Century England* (Bloomington, 1982); P. J. Corfield, *The Impact of English Towns, 1700–1800* (Oxford, 1982); Peter Clark and Paul Slack, eds., *Crisis and Order in English Towns, 1500–1700* (London, 1972); Peter Clark, ed., *Country Towns in Pre-Industrial England* (Leicester, 1981); Peter Borsay, "The English Urban Renaissance: The Development of Provincial Urban Culture, c. 1680–c. 1760," *Social History* 5 (May 1977): 581–603; Borsay, "Culture, Status, and the English Urban Landscape," *History* 67 (1982): 1–12; Borsay, "The Rise of the Promenade: The Social and Cultural Use of Space in the English Provincial Town, c. 1660–1800," *British Journal of Eighteenth-Century Studies* 9 (1986): 125–140; Angus McInnes, "The Emergence of a Leisure Town: Shrewsbury 1660–1760," *Past and Present* 120 (August 1988): 53–87; John Brewer, *Party Ideology and Popular Politics at the Accession of George III* (Cambridge, 1976); Brewer, "English Radicalism in the Age of George III," in J. G. A. Pocock, ed., *Three British Revolutions: 1641, 1688, 1776* (Princeton, 1980), pp. 265–288; Linda Colley, *In Defiance of Oligarchy: The Tory Party, 1714–1760* (Cambridge, 1982); Colley, "Whose Nation? Class and National Consciousness in Britain 1750–1830," *Past and Present* 113 (November 1986): 97–117; John Money, *Experience and Identity: Birmingham and the West Midlands 1760–1800* (Montreal, 1977); Nicholas Rogers, "The Urban Opposition to Whig Oligarchy, 1720–60," in Margaret Jacob and James Jacob, eds., *The Origins of Anglo-American Radicalism* (London, 1984), pp. 132–148.

9. The classic account is John Vincent, *The Formation of the British Liberal Party 1857–68* (Harmondsworth, 1972). Patricia Hollis, ed., *Pressure from Without* (London, 1974), is a good introduction to British liberalism's associational world at midcentury, while Eileen Yeo and Stephen Yeo, eds., *Popular Culture and Class Conflict 1590–1914* (Brighton, 1981), opens a window on its relationship to popular culture. See also the essays on "Animals and the State," "Religion and Recreation," "Traditions of Respectability," and "Philanthropy and the Victorians," in Brian Harrison, *Peaceable Kingdom: Stability and Change in Modern Britain* (Oxford, 1982), pp. 82–259, which (despite the book's overall complacency) remain fundamental to this subject. A sense of the earlier-nineteenth-century ambience can be had from two collections of the antislavery movement, Christine Bolt and Seymour Drescher, eds., *Anti-Slavery, Religion, and Reform: Essays in Memory of Roger Anstey* (Folkestone, 1980), and David Eltis and James Walvin, eds., *The Abolition of the Atlantic Slave Trade: Origins and Effects in Europe, Africa, and the Americas* (Madison, 1981). Monographs on particular associations and places are legion. Stephen Yeo's *Religion and Voluntary Associations in Crisis* (London, 1976) on Reading is the most unruly but also the most interesting. For an excellent view of the whole Gladstonian show in motion, see Paul McHugh, *Prostitution and Victorian Social Reform* (London, 1980).

10. The best introduction to the social context of the Enlightenment is via the work of Franklin Kopitzsch: "Die Aufklärung in Deutschland: Zu ihren Leistungen, Grenzen und Wirkungen," *Archiv für Sozialgeschichte* 23 (1983): 1–21 (with an excellent guide to the wider bibliography); *Grundzüge einer Sozialgeschichte der Aufklärung in Hamburg und Altona*, 2 vols. (Hamburg, 1982); Kopitzsch, ed., *Aufklärung, Absolutismus und Bürgertum in Deutschland: Zwölf Aufsätze* (Munich, 1976). More generally, see Otto Dann, "Die Anfänge politischer Vereinsbildung in Deutschland," in Ulrich Engelhardt, Volker Sellin, and Horst Stuke, eds., *Soziale Bewegung und politische Verfassung: Beiträge zur Geschichte der modernen Welt* (Stuttgart, 1976), pp. 197–232; Dann, ed., *Lesegesellschaften und bürgerliche Emanzipation: Ein europäischer Vergleich* (Munich, 1981); Rolf Engelsing, *Analphabetentum und Lektüre: Zur Sozialgeschichte des Lesens in Deutschland zwischen feudaler und industrieller Gesellschaft* (Stuttgart, 1973); Engelsing, *Der Bürger als Leser: Lesergeschichte in Deutschland 1500–1800* (Stuttgart, 1974); Thomas Nipperdey, "Verein als soziale Struktur in Deutschland im späten 18. und frühen 19. Jahrhundert," in *Gesellschaft, Kultur, Theorie* (Göttingen, 1976), pp. 174–205; Dieter Düding, *Organisierter gesellschaftlicher Nationalismus in Deutschland (1808–1847): Bedeutung und Funktion der Turner- und Sängervereine für die deutsche National-bewegung* (Munich, 1984); Gert Zang, ed., *Provinzialisierung einer Region: Regionale Unterentwicklung und liberale Politik in der Stadt und im Kreis Konstanz im 19. Jahrhundert: Untersuchungen zur Entstehung der bürgerlichen Gesellschaft in der Provinz* (Frankfurt, 1978); Geoff Eley, *Reshaping the German Right: Radical Nationalism and Political Change after Bismarck* (London and New Haven, 1980); Rudy Koshar, *Social Life, Local Politics, and Nazism: Marburg, 1880–1935* (Chapel Hill, 1986), esp. pp. 91–125.

11. The *Journal of Peasant Studies* is the best general guide to this literature, but for access to the discussion of a particular region see Grant Evans, "Sources of Peasant Consciousness in South-East Asia: A Survey," *Social History*, 12 (1987), pp. 193–211. For the French literature see Peter McPhee, "Recent Writing on Rural Society and Politics in France, 1789–1900," *Comparative Studies in Society and History* 30 (1988): 750–752; Edward Berenson, "Politics and the French Peasantry: The Debate Continues," *Social History* 12 (1987): 213–229; Ted W. Margadant, "Tradition and Modernity in Rural France during the Nineteenth Century," *Journal of Modern History* 56 (1984): 667–697.

12. See Miroslav Hroch, *Social Preconditions of National Revival in Europe: A Comparative Analysis of the Social Composition of Patriotic Groups among the Smaller European Nations* (Cambridge, 1985), a combined and revised edition of two earlier books in German (1968) and Czech (1971), which enjoyed some subterranean influence in the English-speaking world by the later 1970s, mainly through the occasional writings on nationalism of Eric Hobsbawm. See also Tom Nairn, *The Break-Up of Britain: Crisis and Neo-Nationalism* (London, 1977, revised ed. 1981). For an introduction to cultural studies, see Richard Johnson, "What Is Cultural Studies Anyway?" *Social Text* 10 (1986/1987): 38–80; and Stuart Hall, "Cultural Studies and the Center: Some Problematics and Problems," in Hall et al., eds., *Culture, Media, Language* (London, 1980), pp. 25–48. For relevant work in communications, see James Curran, Michael Gurevitch, and Janet Woollacott, eds., *Mass Communication and Society* (London, 1977); George Boyce, James Curran, and Pauline Wingate, eds., *Newspaper History from the Seventeenth Century to the Present Day* (London, 1978); Harry Christian, ed., *The Sociology of Journalism and the Press*, Sociological Review Mon-

ograph 29 (Keele, 1980); Michael Gurevitch, Tony Bennett, James Curran, and Janet Woollacott, eds., *Culture, Society and the Media* (London, 1982). For Raymond Williams, see esp. *Marxism and Literature* (Oxford, 1977), and *Culture* (London, 1981). For Gramsci, see Geoff Eley, "Reading Gramsci in English: Observations on the Reception of Antonio Gramsci in the English-Speaking World, 1957–82," *European History Quarterly* 14 (1984): 441–477. Work on Eastern Europe may be approached through Gale Stokes, "The Social Origins of East European Politics," *East European Politics and Societies* 1 (1987): 30–74, and Stokes (ed.), *Nationalism in the Balkans: An Annotated Bibliography* (New York, 1984). For other regions, see Tom Garvin, "The Anatomy of a Nationalist Revolution: Ireland, 1858–1928," *Comparative Studies in Society and History* 28 (1986): 468–501; Samuel Clark and James S. Donnelly, eds., *Irish Peasants: Violence and Political Unrest, 1780–1914* (Madison, 1983); Rosalind Mitchison, ed., *The Roots of Nationalism: Studies in Northern Europe* (Edinburgh, 1980).

13. See Eley, *Reshaping the German Right*, pp. 32ff., 150ff. The Heilbronn example comes from Theodor Heuss, *Preludes to Life: Early Memoirs* (London, 1955), pp. 34f. Otherwise, see the basic literature cited in note 10 above, esp. Dann, "Anfange politischer Vereinsbildung," and Nipperdey, "Verein als soziale Struktur."

14. The best analyses are by David Blackbourn, "The Discreet Charm of the Bourgeoisie: Reappraising German History in the Nineteenth Century," in Blackbourn and Geoff Eley, *The Peculiarities of German History: Bourgeois Society and Politics in Nineteenth-Century Germany* (Oxford, 1984), pp. 159–192; and "Politics as Theatre: Metaphors of the Stage in German History, 1848–1933," in Blackbourn, *Populists and Patricians: Essays in Modern German History* (London, 1987), pp. 246–264. In its cultural dimensions, Blackbourn's is *the* classic Habermasian analysis. See also H. Barmeyer, "Zum Wandel des Verhältnisses vom Staat und Gesellschaft: Die soziale Funktion von historischen Vereinen und Denkmalsbewegung in der Zeit liberaler bürgerlicher Öffentlichkeit," *Westfälische Forschungen* 29 (1978–1979): 125.

15. Blackbourn and Eley, *Peculiarities of German History*, was written to contest this tradition of explanation. In the second half of the 1980s Jürgen Kocka began to revisit the latter in cultural terms, while leaving the political argument about the weakness of liberalism intact; there has also been remarkably little attention to *Vereine* (voluntary associations) under the auspices of Kocka's project. See the following: Kocka, ed., *Bürger und Bürgerlichkeit im 19. Jahrhundert* (Göttingen, 1987); Kocka, ed., *Arbeiter und Bürger im 19. Jahrhundert: Variante ihres Verhältnisses im europäischen Vergleich* (Munich, 1986); Kocka, ed., *Bürgertum im 19. Jahrhundert: Deutschland im europäischen Vergleich*, 3 vols. (Munich, 1988); Ute Frevert, ed., *Bürgerinnen und Bürger: Geschlechterverhältnisse im 19. Jahrhundert* (Göttingen, 1988); Dieter Langewiesche, ed., *Liberalismus im 19. Jahrhundert: Deutschland im europäischen Vergleich* (Göttingen, 1988); Hannes Siegrist, ed., *Bürgerliche Berufe: Beiträge zur Sozialgeschichte der Professionen, freien Berufe und Akademiker im internationalen Vergleich* (Göttingen, 1988). With the exception of the second of these titles (which issued from a conference organized by Kocka at the *Historische Kolleg* in Munich in June 1984), this activity was focused on a year-long research project at the Center of Inter-disciplinary Research at Bielefeld University in 1986–1987. In addition, twelve meetings of the *Arbeitskreis für moderne Sozialgeschichte* under the direction of Werner Conze were devoted to the theme of *Bildungsbürgertum* during 1980–1987. See Conze and Kocka, eds., *Bildungsbürgertum im 19. Jahrhundert* (Stuttgart, 1985). Three further volumes from these meetings are planned.

16. See the works by Plumb cited in note 8 above.

17. See Brewer, *Party Ideology and Popular Politics*, and "Commercialization and Politics," in McKendrick, Brewer, and Plumb, *Birth of a Consumer Society*, pp. 197–262.

18. See Money, *Experience and Identity*.

19. See the works by Borsay cited in note 8 above.

20. Brewer, "Commercialization and Politics," p. 197.

21. Plumb, "The Public, Literature, and the Arts," p. 32.

22. Here, see Borsay, "English Urban Renaissance," pp. 590–593, for the growth of towns as a new type of social center. He picks out four main instances: health resorts (Bath, Tunbridge, Scarborough, Buxton, Harrogate, Cheltenham); county towns and other administrative centers (diocesan centers like Lichfield or other legal centers like Preston, Lancashire, for the Duchy Courts); "travel towns" such as Stamford; and new industrial towns (Birmingham, Manchester, Liverpool, and Bristol). For a dissenting view, see McInnes, "Emergence of a Leisure Town," which adds to Borsay's picture rather than supplanting it.

23. Money, *Experience and Identity*, p. 29.

24. However, Habermas is silent on the grand question of causality, i.e., the specific causal mechanisms/relationships between, on the one hand, the longer-term processes of social development and, on the other, hand the emergence of specific ideologies, traditions of thought, and cultural patterns, or between each of these and specific political events (whether on the global scale of the French Revolution or the smaller scale of local political conflicts). The question of the bourgeoisie's collective agency is not faced. For my own attempt to pose this question (if hardly to answer it), see Geoff Eley, "In Search of the Bourgeois Revolution: The Particularities of German History," *Political Power and Social Theory* 7 (1988): 105–133.

25. I have made this argument for Britain in Geoff Eley, "Rethinking the Political: Social History and Political Culture in Eighteenth- and Nineteenth-Century Britain," *Archiv für Sozialgeschichte*, 21 (1981): esp. 438–457, and in a reworked form in "Edward Thompson, Social History and Political Culture: The Making of a Working-Class Public, 1780–1850," in Harvey J. Kaye and Keith McClelland, eds., *E. P. Thompson: Critical Debates* (Cambridge, 1990), pp. 12–49. Some of the most suggestive contributions to this theme have been by Eileen Yeo: "Robert Owen and Radical Culture," in Sidney Pollard and John Salt, eds., *Robert Owen: Prophet of the Poor* (London, 1971), pp. 104ff.; "Christianity in Chartist Struggle 1838–1842," *Past and Present* 91 (1981): 99–139; and "Some Practices and Problems of Chartist Democracy," in James Epstein and Dorothy Thompson, eds., *The Chartist Experience: Studies in Working-Class Radicalism and Culture, 1830–1860* (London, 1982), pp. 345–380. See also James Epstein, "Some Organizational and Cultural Aspects of the Chartist Movement in Nottingham," ibid., pp. 221–268; and Barbara Taylor, *Eve and the New Jerusalem: Socialism and Feminism in the Nineteenth Century* (New York, 1983). For the wider literature on the political sociability of the French peasantry, see the essays by McPhee, Berenson, and Margadant cited in note 11 above. In particular, see Maurice Agulhon, *The Republic in the Village: The People of the Var from the French Revolution to the Second Republic* (Cambridge, 1982); Edward Berenson, *Populist Religion and Left-Wing Politics in France, 1832–52* (Princeton, 1984); and Peter McPhee, "On Rural Politics in Nineteenth-Century France: The Example of Rodes, 1789–1851," *Comparative Studies in Society and History* 23 (1981): 248–277.

26. Gareth Stedman Jones, "Rethinking Chartism," in Stedman Jones, *Languages of Class: Studies in English Working-Class History 1832–1982* (Cambridge, 1983), pp. 90–178.

27. See Geoff Eley, "Nationalism and Social History," *Social History* 6 (1981): 83–107, and Eley, "Remapping the Nation: War, Revolutionary Upheaval, and State Formation in Eastern Europe, 1914–1923," in Peter J. Potichnyj and Howard Aster, eds., *Ukrainian–Jewish Relations in Historical Perspective* (Edmonton, 1988), pp. 220–230.

28. The classic sources, of course, are Edward Thompson, *The Making of the English Working Class* (London, 1963), pp. 17–185, and Christopher Hill, *The World Turned Upside Down* (London, 1972). Also see the more recent following works by Hill: *The Experience of Defeat: Milton and Some Contemporaries* (London, 1984); *Turbulent, Seditious and Factious People: John Bunyan and His Church* (Oxford, 1988); and "Why Bother about the Muggletonians?" in Hill, Barry Reay, and William Lamont, *The World of the Muggletonians* (London, 1983), pp. 6–22. See also Lamont, "The Muggletonians, 1652–1979: A 'Vertical Approach,'" *Past and Present* 99 (1983): 22–40, and the subsequent debate between Hill and Lamont, ibid., 104 (1984): 153–163. For some general commentary, see Barry Reay, "The World Turned Upside Down: A Retrospect," in Geoff Eley and William Hunt, eds., *Reviving the English Revolution. Reflections and Elaborations on the Work of Christopher Hill* (London, 1988), pp. 53–71.

29. Nancy Fraser, "What's Critical about Critical Theory? The Case of Habermas and Gender," in Seyla Benhabib and Drucilla Cornell, eds., *Feminism as Critique* (Minneapolis, 1987), pp. 31–55. The quotations are from pp. 41, 45.

30. Landes, *Women and the Public Sphere*, p. 46. Landes explains this opposition to a great extent by a counterreaction against the public role of aristocratic women in the salons of the ancien regime, which then generalized its hostility to the "unnatural" prominence of women in public life and made femininity a general repository for the vices that republican virtue would overcome.

31. Ibid., p. 204.

32. Ibid., p. 2.

33. John Keane, Introduction, in Keane, ed., *Civil Society and the State*, p. 21.

34. Carole Pateman, "The Fraternal Social Contract," ibid., p. 121. See also Pateman's book, *The Sexual Contract* (Cambridge, 1988); Landes, *Women and the Public Sphere*; Jean Bethke Elshtain, *Public Man, Private Woman: Women in Social and Political Thought* (Princeton, 1981); Ellen Kennedy and Susan Mendus, eds., *Women in Western Political Philosophy: Kant to Nietzsche* (New York, 1987); and the brilliant discussions scattered through Dorinda Outram, *The Body and the French Revolution: Sex, Class, and Political Culture* (London and New Haven, 1989). For a dissentient view, see Sylvana Tomaselli, "The Enlightenment Debate on Women," *History Workshop Journal* 20 (1985): 101–124.

35. Catherine Hall, "Private Persons versus Public Someones: Class, Gender and Politics in England, 1780–1850," in Carolyn Steedman, Cathy Urwin, and Valerie Walkerdine, eds., *Language, Gender and Childhood* (London, 1985), p. 11.

36. The approach is much more nuanced than can be described here. See in particular the definition of consumption (heavily influenced by the current discourse of the British intellectual left) as a way of integrating the "private" sphere of "the family and women's labour" into a Marxist discussion of production and social reproduction:

And yet, the creation of the private sphere has been central to the elaboration of consumer demand, so essential to the expansion and accumulation process which characterizes modern societies. The recent work which has analyzed consumption as a process of "cultural production," looks not only at its role in reproduction but also at the creation of need and the ways in which particular desires and pleasures come to define social identities and to be represented as cultural products. This approach has necessarily emphasized the gender dimension. Furthermore, consumption is instrumental in forming and maintaining status, the "relational" element of class, the continual claim and counter-claim to recognition and legitimation. Gender classification is always an important element in the positioning of groups and individuals and the competition for resources which takes place at every level of society. Women, in their association with consumption, are often seen as creators as well as the bearers of status.

See Leonore Davidoff and Catherine Hall, *Family Fortunes: Men and Women of the English Middle Class, 1780–1850* (London, 1987), p. 29f.

37. Hall, "Private Persons versus Public Someones," p. 11.

38. Davidoff and Hall, *Family Fortunes*, p. 416.

39. Davidoff and Hall are excellent on the complex imbrication of family and economics in the late-eighteenth/early-nineteenth-century English middle class. See ibid., pp. 195–315.

40. Sally Alexander, "Women, Class and Sexual Differences in the 1830s and 1840s: Some Reflections on the Writing of a Feminist History," *History Workshop Journal* 17 (1984): 136, 137, 139. The quotations that follow have the same source.

41. See Dorothy Thompson, *The Chartists: Popular Politics in the Industrial Revolution* (New York, 1984), p. 125, which cites pamphlets by the Manchester Chartist Reginald John Richardson and the London Chartist John Watkins to this effect.

42. Alexander is very good on this. Capitalist transformation of the work process and the concomitant dissolution of existing family controls reflected "the two themes which spurred all visions of a new social order" in the first half of the nineteenth century in Britain—namely, the idea that "labour, as the producer of wealth and knowledge, should receive its just reward" and the belief that "kinship was the natural and proper relation of morality, authority and law." See "Women, Class and Sexual Differences," p. 138. Engels' phrase is taken from *The Condition of the Working Class in 1844*, in Karl Marx and Friedrich Engels, *On Britain* (Moscow, 1962), p. 179.

43. There is a useful discussion of this point in Richard J. Evans, "Politics and the Family: Social Democracy and the Working-Class Family in Theory and Practice before 1914," in Evans and W. R. Lee, eds., *The German Family: Essays on the Social History of the Family in Nineteenth- and Twentieth-Century Germany* (London, 1981), pp. 256–288.

44. See Keane, "Remembering the Dead: Civil Society and the State from Hobbes to Marx and Beyond," in *Democracy and Civil Society*, esp. pp. 35f.

45. Pateman, "The Fraternal Social Contract," p. 123.

46. See Immanuel Wallerstein, *The Modern World System*, vol. 1: *Capitalist Agriculture and the Origins of the European World-Economy in the Sixteenth Century* (New York, 1974); vol. 2: *Mercantilism and the Consolidation of the European World-Economy, 1600–1750* (New York, 1980); and vol. 3: *The Second Era of Great Expansion of the Capitalist World-Economy, 1730–1840s* (San Diego, 1989); Perry Anderson, *Lineages of the Absolutist State* (London, 1974); Charles Tilly, ed., *The Formation of National States in Western Europe* (Princeton, 1975); Theda Skocpol,

States and Social Revolutions: A Comparative Analysis of France, Russia, and China (Cambridge, 1979); Barrington Moore, Jr., *Social Origins of Dictatorship and Democracy* (Boston, 1966); Michael Mann, *The Sources of Social Power*, vol. 1: *A History of Power from the Beginning to A.D. 1760* (Cambridge, 1986); Anthony Giddens, *The Nation-State and Violence*, vol. 2 of *A Contemporary Critique of Historical Materialism* (Berkeley, 1987), pp. 198–221.

47. See Karl Polanyi, *The Great Transformation: The Political and Economic Origins of Our Time* (Boston, 1944), esp. pp. 139ff.; and Fred Block and Margaret R. Somers, "Beyond the Economistic Fallacy: The Holistic Social Science of Karl Polanyi," in Theda Skocpol, ed., *Vision and Method in Historical Sociology* (Cambridge, 1984), esp. pp. 52–62. The paraphrase of Polanyi is really Peggy Somers's.

48. See esp. the following works of Edward Thompson: "The Moral Economy of the English Crowd in the Eighteenth Century," *Past and Present* 50 (1971): 76–131; "Patrician Society, Plebeian Culture," *Journal of Social History* 7 (1973–1974): 382–405; *Whigs and Hunters: The Origin of the Black Act* (Harmondsworth, 1975); "Eighteenth-Century English Society: Class Struggle without Class?" *Social History* 3 (1978): 133–166. I have commented on this aspect of Thompson's work in "Rethinking the Political," pp. 432ff.

49. Gwyn A. Williams, "The Concept of 'Egemonia' in the Thought of Antonio Gramsci: Some Notes in Interpretation," *Journal of the History of Ideas* 21 (1960): 587.

50. Williams, *Marxism and Literature*, pp. 109f.

51. Ibid., p. 108.

52. Ernesto Laclau, *Politics and Ideology in Marxist Theory* (London, 1977), p. 161.

53. Geoff Eley and Keith Nield, "Why Does Social History Ignore Politics?" *Social History* 5 (1980): 269.

54. Stuart Hall, Bob Lumley, and Gregor McLennan, "Politics and Ideology: Gramsci," in *On Ideolology* Working Papers in Cultural Studies, 10 (Birmingham, 1977), p. 68.

55. Antonio Gramsci, *Selections from the Prison Notebooks* (London, 1971), p. 54. The earlier quoted phrase, "equilibrium . . . ," comes from Eric J. Hobsbawm, "The Great Gramsci," *New York Review of Books* 21, no. 5 (April 1974): 42.

56. Gramsci, *Selections from the Prison Notebooks*, p. 238.

57. Günther Lottes, *Politische Aufklärung und plebejisches Publikum: Zur Theorie und Praxis des englischen Radikalismus im späten 18. Jahrhundert* (Munich, 1979).

58. Ibid., p. 14.

59. Ibid., pp. 223ff.

60. Ibid., p. 109.

61. Ibid., p. 337.

62. Ibid., p. 14.

63. Albert Goodwin, *The Friends of Liberty* (London, 1979), p. 157.

64. Lottes, *Politische Aufklärung*, p. 337.

65. Ibid., pp. 263–334.

The Prose of Counter-Insurgency

RANAJIT GUHA

I

WHEN A peasant rose in revolt at any time or place under the Raj, he did so necessarily and explicitly in violation of a series of codes which defined his very existence as a member of that colonial, and still largely semi-feudal society. For his subalternity was materialized by the structure of property, institutionalized by law, sanctified by religion and made tolerable—and even desirable—by tradition. To rebel was indeed to destroy many of those familiar signs which he had learned to read and manipulate in order to extract a meaning out of the harsh world around him and live with it. The risk in "turning things upside down" under these conditions was indeed so great that he could hardly afford to engage in such a project in a state of absent-mindedness.

There is nothing in the primary sources of historical evidence to suggest anything other than this. These give the lie to the myth, retailed so often by careless and impressionistic writing on the subject, of peasant insurrections being purely spontaneous and unpremeditated affairs. The truth is quite to the contrary. It would be difficult to cite an uprising on any significant scale that was not in fact preceded either by less militant types of mobilization when other means had been tried and found wanting or by parley among its principals seriously to weigh the pros and cons of any recourse to arms. In events so very different from each other in context, character, and the composition of participants as the Rangpur *dhing* against Debi Sinha (1783), the Barasat *bidroha* led by Titu Mir (1831), the Santal *hool* (1855) and the "blue mutiny" of 1860 the protagonists in each case had tried out petitions, deputations or other forms of supplication before actually declaring war on their oppressors.[1] Again, the revolts of the Kol (1832), the Santal and the Munda (1899–1900) as well as the Rangpur *dhing* and the jacqueries in Allahabad and Ghazipur districts during the Sepoy Rebellion of 1857–58 (to name only two out of many instances in that remarkable series) had all been inaugurated by plan and in some cases protracted consultations among the representatives of the local peasant masses.[2] Indeed there is hardly an instance of the peasantry, whether the cautious and earthy villagers of the plains or the supposedly more volatile *adivasis* of the upland tracts, stumbling or drifting into rebellion. They had far too much at stake and would not launch into it except as a deliberate, even if desperate, way out of an intolerable condition of existence. Insurgency, in other words, was a motivated and conscious undertaking on the part of the rural masses.

Yet this consciousness seems to have received little notice in the literature on the subject. Historiography has been content to deal with the peasant rebel merely as an empirical person or member of a class, but not as an entity whose will and reason constituted the praxis called rebellion. The omission is indeed dyed into most narratives by metaphors assimilating peasant revolts to natural phenomena: they break out like thunderstorms, heave like earthquakes, spread like wildfires, infect like epidemics. In other words, when the proverbial clod of earth turns, this is a matter to be explained in terms of natural history. Even when this historiography is pushed to the point of producing an explanation in rather more human terms it will do so by assuming an identity of nature and culture, a hallmark, presumably, of a very low state of civilization and exemplified in "those periodical outbursts of crime and lawlessness to which all wild tribes are subject," as the first historian of the Chuar rebellion put it.[3] Alternatively, an explanation will be sought in an enumeration of causes—of, say, factors of economic and political deprivation which do not relate at all to the peasant's consciousness or do so negatively—triggering off rebellion as a sort of reflex action, that is, as an instinctive and almost mindless response to physical suffering of one kind or another (e.g., hunger, torture, forced labor, etc.) or as a passive reaction to some initiative of his superordinate enemy. Either way insurgency is regarded as *external* to the peasant's consciousness and Cause is made to stand in as a phantom surrogate for Reason, the logic of that consciousness.

II

How did historiography come to acquire this particular blind spot and never find a cure? For an answer one could start by having a close look at its constituting elements and examine those cuts, seams and stitches—those cobbling marks—which tell us about the material it is made of and the manner of its absorption into the fabric of writing.

The corpus of historical writings on peasant insurgency in colonial India is made up of three types of discourse. These may be described as *primary*, *secondary* and *tertiary* according to the order of their appearance in time and their filiation. Each of these is differentiated from the other two by the degree of its formal and/or acknowledged (as opposed to real and/or tacit) identification with an official point of view, by the measure of its distance from the event to which it refers and by the ratio of the distributive and integrative components in its narrative.

To begin with primary discourse, it is almost without exception official in character—official in a broad sense of the term. That is, it originated not only with bureaucrats, soldiers, sleuths and others directly employed by the government, but also with those in the non-official sector who were symbiotically related to the Raj, such as planters, missionaries, traders, technicians and so on among the whites and landlords, moneylenders, etc. among the natives. It was official also insofar as it was meant primarily for administrative use—for the information of government, for action on its part and for the determination of its policy. Even when it incorporated statements emanating from "the other side," from the insurgents or their allies, for instance, as it often did by way of direct or indirect reporting in the body of official correspondence or even more characteristically as "enclosures" to the latter, this was done only as a part of an argument prompted by administrative concern. In other words, whatever its particular form—and there was indeed an amazing variety ranging from the exordial letter, telegram, dispatch and communique, to the terminal summary, report, judgment and proclamation—its production and circulation were both necessarily contingent on reasons of State.

Yet another of the distinctive features of this type of discourse is its immediacy. This derived from two conditions: first, that statements of this class were written either concurrently with or soon after the event, and second, that this was done by the participants concerned, a "participant" being defined for this purpose in the broad sense of a contemporary involved in the event either in action or indirectly as an onlooker. This would exclude of course that genre of retrospective writing in which, as in some memoirs, an event and its recall are separated by a considerable hiatus, but would still leave a massive documentation—"primary sources" as it is known in the trade—to speak to the historian with a sort of ancestral voice and make him feel closer to his subject.

The two specimens quoted below are fairly representative of this type. One of these relates to the Barasat uprising of 1831 and the other to the Santal rebellion of 1855.

TEXT 1[4]

To the Deputy Adjutant General of the Army

Sir,

Authentic information having reached Government that a body of *Fanatic Insurgents* are now committing *the most daring and wanton atrocities on the Inhabitants* of the Country in the neighbourhood of Tippy in the Magistracy of Baraset and have set at defiance and repulsed the utmost force that the local Civil Authority could assemble for their apprehension, I am directed by the Hon'ble Vice President in the Council to request that you will without delay Communicate to the General Officer Commanding the Presidency Division the orders of Government that one Complete Battalion of Native Infantry from Barrackpore and two Six Pounders manned with the necessary compliment [*sic*] of Golundaze from Dum Dum, the whole under the Command of a Field Officer of judgement and decision, be immediately directed to proceed and rendezvous at Baraset when they will be joined by 1 Havildar and 12 Troopers of the 3rd Regiment of Light Cavalry now forming the escort of the Hon'ble the Vice President.

2nd. The Magistrate will meet the Officer Commanding the Detachment at Barraset and will afford the necessary information for his guidance relative to the position of the Insurgents; but without having any authority to interfere in such Military operations as the Commanding Officer of the Detachments may deem expedient, for the purpose of routing or seizing or in the event of resistance destroying those who persevere in *defying the authority of the State* and *disturbing the public tranquility*.

3rd. It is concluded that the service will not be of such a protracted nature as to require a larger supply of ammunition than may be carried in Pouch and in two Tumbrils for the Guns, and that no difficulties will occur respecting carriage. In the contrary event any aid needed will be furnished.

4th. The Magistrate will be directed to give every assistance regarding supplies and other requisites for the Troops.

Council Chamber   I am & ca
10th November 1831   (Sd.) Wm. Casement Coll.
                                                 Secy. to Govt. Mily. Dept.

TEXT 2[5]

From W. C. Taylor Esqre.
To F. S. Mudge Esqre.
    Dated 7th July 1855

My dear Mudge,

There is a great gathering of Sontals 4 or 5000 men at a place about 8 miles off and I understand that they are all well armed with Bows and arrows, Tulwars, Spears & ca. and that *it is their intention to attack all the Europeans round and plunder and murder them. The cause of all this is that one of their Gods is supposed to have taken the Flesh and to have made his appearance at some place near this, and that it is his intention to reign as a King over all this part of India, and has ordered the Sontals to collect and put to death all the Europeans and influential Natives round. As this is the nearest point to the gathering I suppose it will be first attacked* and think it would be best for you to send notice to the authorities at Berhampore and ask for military aid as *it is not at all a nice look out being murdered* and as far as I can make out this is a *rather serious affair*.

Sreecond   Yours & ca
7th July 1855   /Signed/W. C. Taylor

Nothing could be more immediate than these texts. Written as soon as these events were acknowledged as rebellion by those who had the most to fear from it, they are among the very first records we have on them in the collections of the India Office Library and the West Bengal State Archives. As the evidence on the 1831 *bidroha* shows,[6] it was not until 10 November that the Calcutta authorities came to recognize the violence reported from the Barasat region for what it was—a full-blooded insurrection led by Titu Mir and his men. Colonel Casement's letter identifies for us that moment when the hitherto unknown leader of a local peasantry entered the lists against the Raj and thereby making his way into history. The date of the other document, too, commemorates a beginning—that of the Santal *hool*. It was on that very day, 7 July 1855, that the assassination of Mahesh daroga following an encounter between his police and peasants gathered at Bhagnadihi detonated the uprising. The report was loud enough to register in that note scribbled in obvious alarm at Sreecond by a European employee of the East India Railway for the benefit of his colleague and the *sarkar*. Again, these are words that convey as directly as possible the impact of a peasant revolt on its enemies in its first sanguinary hours.

III

None of this instantaneousness percolates through to the next level—that of the secondary discourse. The latter draws on primary discourse as *matériel* but transforms it at the same time. To contrast the two types one could think of the first as historiography in a raw, primordial state or as an embryo yet to be articulated into an organism with discrete limbs, and the second as the processed product, however crude the processing, a duly constituted if infant discourse.

The difference is quite obviously a function of time. In the chronology of this particular corpus the secondary follows the primary at a distance and opens up a perspective to turn an event into history in the perception not only of those outside it but of the participants as well. It was thus that Mark Thornhill, Magistrate of Mathura during the summer of 1857 when a mutiny of the Treasury Guard sparked off jacqueries all over the district, was to reflect on the altered status of his own narrative, in which he figured as a protagonist himself. Introducing his well-known memoirs, *The Personal Adventures and Experiences of a Magistrate during the Rise, Progress, and Suppression of the Indian Mutiny* (London, 1884) twenty-seven years after the event he wrote:

> After the suppression of the Indian Mutiny, I commenced to write an account of my adventures. . . . [B]y the time my narrative was completed, the then interest of the public in the subject was exhausted. Years have since passed, and an interest of another kind has arisen. The events of that time have become history, and to that history my story may prove a contribution. . . . I have therefore resolved to publish my narrative. . . .

Shorn of contemporaneity a discourse is thus recovered as an element of the past and classified as history. This change, aspectual as well as categorial, sites it at the very intersection of colonialism and historiography, endowing it with a duplex character linked at the same time to a system of power and the particular manner of its representation.

Its authorship is in itself witness to this intersection and Thornhill was by no means the only administrator turned historian. He was indeed one of many officials, civilian and military, who wrote retrospectively on popular disturbances in rural India under the Raj. Their statements, taken together, fall into two classes. First, there were those which were based on the writers' own experience as participants. Memoirs of one kind or another, these were written either at considerable delay after the events narrated or almost concurrently with them but intended, unlike primary discourse, for a public readership. The latter, an important distinction, shows how the colonialist mind managed to serve Clio and counter-insurgency at the same time so that the presumed neutrality of one could have hardly been left unaffected by the passion of the other, a point to which we shall soon return. Reminiscences of both kinds abound in the literature on the Mutiny, which dealt with the violence of the peasantry (especially in the North Western Provinces and central India) no less than with that of the sepoys. Accounts such as Thornhill's, written long after the event, were matched by near contemporary ones such as Dunlop's *Service and Adventure with Khakee Ressallah* or *Meerut Volunteer Horse during the Mutinies of 1857–58* (London, 1858) and Edwards' *Personal Adventures during the Indian Rebellion in Rohilcund, Futtehghur, and Oudh* (London, 1858) to mention only two out of a vast outcrop intended to cater for a public who could not have enough of tales of horror and glory.

The other class of writings to qualify as secondary discourse is also the work of administrators. They, too, addressed themselves to a predominantly non-official readership but on themes not directly related to their own experience. Their work includes some of the most widely used and highly esteemed accounts of peasant uprisings written either as monographs on particular events, such as Jamini Mohan Ghosh's on the Sannyasi-and-Faqir disturbances and J. C. Price's on the Chuar Rebellion, or as statements included in more comprehensive histories like W. W. Hunter's story of the Santal *hool* in *The Annals of Rural Bengal*. Apart from these there were those distinguished contributions made by some of the best minds in the Civil Service to the historical chapters of the *District Gazetteers*. Altogether they constitute a substantial body of writing which enjoys much authority with all students of the subject and there is hardly any historiography at the next, that is, tertiary, level of discourse that does not rely on these for sustenance.

The prestige of this genre is to no mean extent due to the aura of impartiality it has about it. By keeping their narrative firmly beyond the pale of personal involvement these authors managed, if only by implication, to confer on it a semblance of truth. As officials they were carriers of the will of the state, no doubt. But since they wrote about a past in which they did not figure as functionaries themselves, their statements are taken to be more authentic and less biased than those of their opposite numbers, whose accounts, based on reminiscences, were necessarily contaminated by their intervention in rural disturbances as agents of the Raj. By contrast the former are believed to have approached the narrated events from the outside. As observers separated clinically from the site and subject of diagnosis they are supposed to have found for their discourse a niche in that realm of perfect neutrality—the realm of History—over which the Aorist and the Third person preside.

IV

How valid is this claim to neutrality? For an answer we may not take any bias for granted in this class of historical work from the mere fact of its origin with authors committed to colonialism. To take that as self-evident would be to deny historiography the possibility of acknowledging its own inadequacies and thus defeat the purpose of the present exercise. As should be clear from what follows, it is precisely by refusing to *prove* what appears as obvious that historians of peasant insurgency remain trapped—in the obvious. Criticism must therefore start not by naming a bias but by examining the components of the discourse, vehicle of all ideology, for the manner in which these might have combined to describe any particular figure of the past.

The components of both types of discourse and their varieties discussed so far are what we shall call segments. Made up of the same linguistic material, that is strings of words of varying lengths, they are of two kinds which may be designated, according to their function, as indicative and interpretative. A gross differentiation, this is meant to assign to them, within a given text, the role respectively of reporting and explaining. This however does not imply their mutual segregation. On the contrary they are often found embedded in each other not merely as a matter of fact but of necessity.

One can see in *Texts 1* and *2* how such imbrication works. In both of them the straight print stands for the indicative segments and the italics for the interpretative. Laid out according to no particular pattern in either of these letters they interpenetrate and sustain each other in order to give the documents their meaning, and in the process endow some of the strings with an ambiguity that is inevitably lost in this particular manner of typographical representation. However, the rough outline of a division of functions between the two classes emerges even from this schema—the indicative stating (that is reporting) the actual and anticipated actions of the rebels and their enemies, and the interpretative commenting on them in order to understand (that is to explain) their significance.

The difference between them corresponds to that between the two basic components of any historical discourse which, following Roland Barthes' terminology, we shall call *functions* and *indices*.[7] The former are segments that make up the linear sequence of a narrative. Contiguous, they operate in a relation of solidarity in the sense of mutually implying each other and add up to increasingly larger strings which combine to produce the aggregative statement. The latter may thus be regarded as a sum of micro-sequences to each of which, however important or otherwise, it should be possible to assign names by a metalinguistic operation using terms that may or may not belong to the text under consideration. It is thus that the functions of a folktale have been named by Bremond, after Propp, as *Fraud, Betrayal, Struggle, Contract,* etc. and those of a triviality such as the offer of a cigarette in a James Bond story designated by Barthes as *offering, accepting, lighting,* and *smoking.* One may perhaps take a cue from this procedure to define a historical statement as a discourse with a name subsuming a given number of named sequences. Hence it should be possible to speak of a hypothetical narrative called "The Insurrection of Titu Mir" made up of a number of sequences including *Text 1* quoted above.

Let us give this document a name and call it, say, *Calcutta Council Acts.* (Alternatives such as *Outbreak of Violence* or *Army Called Up* should also do and be analyzable in terms corresponding to, though not identical with, those which follow.) In broad terms the message *Calcutta Council Acts* (C) in our text can be read as a combination of two groups of sequences called *alarm* (a) and *intervention* (b), each of which is made up of a pair of segments—the former of *insurrection breaks out* (a′) and *information received* (a″) and the latter of *decision to call up army* (b′) and *order issued* (b″), one of the constituents in each pair being represented in its turn by yet another linked series— (a′) by *atrocities committed* (a_1) and *authority defied* (a_2), and (b″) by *infantry to proceed* (b_1), *artillery to support* (b_2) and *magistrate to co-operate* (b_3). In other words the narrative in this document can be written up in three equivalent steps so that

$$C = (a + b) \qquad\qquad (I)$$
$$= (a′ + a″) + (b′ + b″) \qquad\qquad (II)$$
$$= (a_1 + a_2) + a″ + b′ + (b_1 + b_2 + b_3). \quad (III)$$

It should be clear from this arrangement that not all the elements of step II can be expressed in micro-sequences of the same order. Hence we are left at step III with a concatenation in which segments drawn from different levels of the discourse are imbricated to constitute a roughly hewn and uneven structure. Insofar as functional units of the lowest denomination like these are what a narrative has as its syntagmatic relata its course can never be smooth. The hiatus between the loosely cobbled segments is necessarily charged with uncertainty, with "moments of risk," and every micro-sequence terminates by opening up alternative possibilities only one of which is picked up by the next sequence as it carries on with the story. "Du Pont, Bond's future partner, offers him a light from the lighter but Bond refuses; the meaning of this bifurcation is that Bond instinctively fears a booby-trapped gadget."[8] What Barthes identifies thus as "bifurcation" in fiction, has its parallels in historical discourse as well. The alleged commitment of atrocities (a_1) in that official dispatch of 1831 cancels out the belief in the peaceful propagation of Titu's new doctrine which had already been known to the authorities but ignored so far as inconsequential. The expression, *authority defied* (a_2), which refers to the rebels having "set at defiance and repulsed the utmost force that the local

Civil Authority could assemble for their apprehension," has as its other if unstated term his efforts to persuade the Government by petition and deputation to offer redress for the grievances of his co-religionists. And so on. Each of these elementary functional units thus implies a node which has not quite materialized into an actual development, a sort of zero sign by means of which the narrative affirms its tension. And [it is] precisely because history as the verbal representation by man of his own past is by its very nature so full of hazard, so replete indeed with the verisimilitude of sharply differentiated choices, that it never ceases to excite. The historical discourse is the world's oldest thriller.

V

Sequential analysis thus shows a narrative to be a concatenation of not so closely aligned functional units. The latter are dissociative in their operation and emphasize the analytic rather than the synthetic aspect of a discourse. As such they are not what, by themselves, generate its meaning. Just as the sense of a word (e.g. "man") is not fractionally represented in each of the letters (e.g. M, A, N) which make up its graphic image nor of a phrase (e.g. "once upon a time") in its constituting words taken separately, so also the individual segments of a discourse cannot on their own tell us what it signifies. Meaning in each instance is the work of a process of integration which complements that of sequential articulation. As Benveniste has put it, in any language "it is dissociation which divulges to us its formal constitution and integration its signifying units."[9]

This is true of the language of history as well. The integrative operation is carried out in its discourse by the other class of basic narrative units, that is, *indices*. A necessary and indispensable correlate of *functions*, they are distinguished from the latter in some important respects:

> Indices, because of the vertical nature of their relations are truly semantic units: unlike "functions" . . . they refer to a signified, not to an "operation." The ratification of indices is "higher ups" . . . a paradigmatic ratification. That of functions, by contrast, is always "further on," is a syntagmatic ratification. *Functions* and *indices* thus overlay another classic distinction: functions involve metonymic relata, indices metaphoric relata; the former correspond to a functionality of doing, the latter to a funtionality of being.[10]

The vertical intervention of indices in a discourse is possible because of the disruption of its linearity by a process corresponding to dystaxia in the behavior of many natural languages. Bally who has studied this phenomenon in much detail finds that one of several conditions of its occurrence in French is "when parts of the same sign are separated" so that the expression, "elle a pardonné" taken in the negative, is splintered and reassembled as "elle *ne nous a jamais plus pardonné*."[11] Similarly the simple predictive in Bengali "shé jābé" can be rewritten by the insertion of an interrogative or a string of negative conditionals between the two words to produce respectively "shé *ki* jabé" and "shé *na hoy na* jabé."

In a historical narrative, too, it is a process of "distension and expansion" of its syntagm which helps paradigmatic elements to infiltrate and reconstitute its discrete segments into a meaningful whole. It is precisely thus that the coordination of the metonymic and metaphorical axes is brought about in a statement and the necessary interaction of its functions and indices actualized. However these units are not distributed in equal proportions in all texts: some have a greater incidence of one kind than of the other. As a result a discourse could be either predominantly metonymic or metaphorical depending on whether a significantly larger number of its components are syntagmatically ratified or paradigmatically.[12] Our *Text 1* is of the first type. One can see the formidable and apparently impenetrable array of its metonymic relata in step III of the sequential analysis given above. Here at last we have the perfect authentication of the idiot's view of history as one damn'd thing after another: *rising—information—decision —order*. However, a closer look at the text can detect chinks which have allowed "comment," to worm its way through the plate armor of "fact." The italicized expressions are witness to this paradigmatic intervention and indeed its measure. Indices, they play the role of *adjectives* or *epithets* as opposed to verbs which, to speak in terms of homology between sentence and narrative, is the role of functions.[13] Working intimately together with the latter they make the dispatch into more than a mere register of happenings and help to inscribe into it a meaning, an interpretation so that the protagonists emerge from it not as peasants but as "*Insurgents*," not as Musalman but as "*fanatic*"; their action, not as resistance to the tyranny of the rural elite but as "*the most daring and wanton atrocities on the inhabitants*"; their project, not as a revolt against zamindari but as "*defying the authority of the State*," not as a search for an alternative order in which the peace of the countryside would not be violated by the officially condoned anarchy of semi-feudal landlordism but as, "*disturbing the public tranquility*."

If the intervention of indices "substitutes meaning for the straightforward copy of the events recounted,"[14] in a text so charged with metonymy as the one discussed above, it may be trusted to do so to an even greater degree in discourses which are predominantly metaphorical. This should be evident from *Text 2* where the element of comment, italicized by us, largely outweighs that of report. If the latter is represented as a concatenation of three functional sequences, namely, *armed Santals gathering*, *authorities to be alerted*, and *military aid requested*, it can be seen how the first of these has been separated from the rest by the insertion of a large chunk of explanatory material and how the others are, too, enveloped and sealed off by comment. The latter is inspired by the fear that Sreecond being "*the nearest point to the gathering . . . will be first attacked*" and of course "*it is not at all a nice look out being murdered*." Notice, however, that this fear justifies itself *politically*, that is, by imputing to the Santals an "*intention to attack . . . plunder . . . and put to death all the Europeans and influential Natives*" so that "*one of their Gods*" in human form may "*reign as a King over all this part of India.*" Thus, this document is not neutral in its attitude to the events witnessed, and put up as "evidence" before the court of history it can hardly be expected to testify with impartiality. On the contrary it is the voice of committed colonialism. It has already made a choice between the prospect of Santal self-rule in Damin-i-Koh and the continuation of the British Raj and identifies what is allegedly good for the promotion of one as fearsome and catastrophic for the other—as "*a rather serious affair.*" In other words the indices in this discourse—as well as in the one discussed above—introduce us to a particular code so constituted that for each of its signs we have an antonym, a counter-message, in another code. To borrow a binary representation made famous by Mao Tse-Tung,[15] the reading, "*It's terrible!*" for any element in one must show up in the other as "*It's fine!*" for a corresponding element and vice versa. To put this clash of codes graphically one can arrange the indices italicized below of *Texts 1* and *2* in a matrix called "TERRIBLE" (in conformity to the adjectival attribute of units of this class) in such a way as to indicate their mapping into the implied, though unstated terms (given in straight types) of a corresponding matrix "FINE."

TERRIBLE	FINE
Insurgents	peasants
Fanatic	Islamic puritan
daring and wanton atrocities on the Inhabitants	resistance to oppression
defying the authority of the State	revolt against zamindari
disturbing the public tranquility	struggle for a better order
intention to attack, etc.	intention to punish oppressors
one of their Gods to reign as a King	Santal self-rule

What comes out of the interplay of these mutually implied but opposed matrices is that our texts are not the record of observations uncontaminated by bias, judgment and opinion. On the contrary, they speak of a total complicity. For if the expressions in the right-hand column taken together may be said to stand for insurgency, the code which contains all signifiers of the subaltern practice of "turning things upside down" and the consciousness that informs it, then the other column must stand for its opposite, that is, counter-insurgency. The antagonism between the two is irreducible and there is nothing in this to leave room for neutrality. Hence these documents make no sense except in terms of a code of pacification which, under the Raj, was a complex of coercive intervention by the State and its protégés, the native elite, with arms and words. Representatives of the primary type of discourse in the historiography of peasant revolts, these are specimens of the prose of counter-insurgency.

VI

How far does secondary discourse too share in such commitment? Is it possible for it to speak any other prose than that of a counter-insurgency? Those narratives of this category in which their authors figure among the protagonists are of course suspect almost by definition, and the presence of the grammatical first person in these must be acknowledged as a sign of complicity. The question however is whether the loss of objectivity on this account is adequately made up by the consistent use of the aorist in such writings. For as Benveniste observes, the historical utterance admits of three variations of the past tense—that is, the aorist, the imperfect and the pluperfect, and of course the present is altogether excluded.[16] This condition is indeed satisfied by reminiscences separated by a long enough hiatus from the events concerned. What has to be found out therefore is the extent to which the force of the preterit corrects the bias caused by the absence of the third person.

Mark Thornhill's memoirs of the Mutiny provide us with a text in which the author looks back at a series of events he had experienced twenty-seven years ago. "The events of that time" had "turned into history," and he intends, as he says in the extract quoted above, to make a contribution "to that history," and thus produce what we have defined as a particular kind of secondary discourse. The difference inscribed in it by that interval is perhaps best grasped by comparing it with some samples of primary discourse we have on the same subject from the same author. Two of these[17] may be read together as a record of his perception of what happened at the Mathura sadar station and the surrounding countryside between 14 May and 3 June 1857. Written by him donning the district magistrate's topee and addressed to his superiors—one on 5 June 1857, that is, within forty-eight hours of the terminal date of the period under discussion, and the other on 10 August 1858 when the events were still within vivid recall as a very recent past—these letters coincide in scope with that of the narrative covering the same three weeks in the first ninety pages of his book written nearly three decades later, donning the historian's hat.

The letters are both predominantly metonymic in character. Originating as they did almost from within the related experience itself they are necessarily foreshortened and tell the reader in breathless sequences about some of the happenings of that extraordinary summer. The syntagm thus takes on a semblance of factuality with hardly any room in it for comment. Yet here again the welding of the functional units can be seen, on close inspection, to be less solid than at first sight. Embedded in them there are indices revealing the anxieties of the local custodian of law and order ("the state of the district generally is such as to *defy all control*"; "the *law* is at a *standstill*"), his fears ("*very alarming* rumours of the approach of the rebel army"), his moral disapprobation of the activities of the armed villagers ("the disturbances in the district . . . increasing . . . in . . . *enormity*"), his appreciation by contrast of the native collaborators hostile to the insurgents ("... the Seths' house ... *received us most kindly*"). Indices such as these are ideological birthmarks displayed prominently on much of this type of material relating to peasant revolts. Indeed, taken together with some other relevant textual features— e.g., the abrupt mode of address in these documents so revealing of the shock and terror generated by the *émeute*—they accuse all such allegedly "objective" evidence on the militancy of the rural masses to have been tainted at its source by the prejudice and partisan outlook of their enemies. If historians fail to take notice of these telltale signs branded on the staple of their trade, that is a fact which must be explained in terms of the optics of a colonialist historiography rather than construed in favor of the presumed objectivity of their "primary sources."

There is nothing immediate or abrupt about the corresponding secondary discourse. On the contrary it has various perspectives built into it to give it a depth in time and following from this temporal determination, its meaning. Compare for instance the narration of events in the two versions for any particular day—for, say, 14 May 1857 at the very beginning of our three-week period. Written up in a very short paragraph of fifty-seven words in Thornhill's letter of 10 August 1858 this can be represented fully in four pithy segments without any significant loss of message: *mutineers approaching*; *information received from Gurgaon*; *confirmed by Europeans north of the district*; *women and non-combatants sent off to Agra*. Since the account starts, for all practical purposes, with this entry, there are no exordia to serve as its context, giving this instant takeoff the sense, as we have noticed, of a total surprise. In the book however that same instant is provided with a background spread over four and a half months and three pages (pp. 1–3). All of this time and space is devoted to some carefully chosen details of the author's life and experience in the period preceding the Mutiny. These are truly *significant*. As indices they prepare the reader for what is to come and help him to *understand* the happenings of 14 May and after, when these enter into the narrative at staggered stages. Thus the mysterious circulation of chapatis in January and the silent but expressive concern on the part of the narrator's brother, a high official, over a telegram received at Agra on 12 May conveying the still unconfirmed news of the Meerut uprising, portend the developments two days later at his own district headquarters. Again the trivia about his "large income and great authority," his house, horses, servants, "a chest full of silver plate, which stood in the hall and ... a great store of Cashmere shawls, pearls, and diamonds" all help to index, by contrast, the holocaust which was soon to reduce his authority to nothing, and turn his servants into rebels, his house into a shambles, his property into booty for the plundering poor of town and country. By anticipating the narrated events thus, if only by implication, secondary discourse destroys the entropy of the first, its raw material. Henceforth there will be nothing in the story that can be said to be altogether unexpected.

This effect is the work of the so-called "organization shifters"[18] which help the author to superimpose a temporality of his own on that of his theme, that is "to 'dechronologize' the historical thread and restore, if only by way of reminiscence or nostalgia, a Time at once complex, parametric, and non-linear . . . braiding the chronology of the subject-matter with that of the language-act which reports it." In the present instance the "braiding" consists not only in fitting an evocative context to the bare sequence related in that short paragraph of his letter. The shifters disrupt the syntagm twice to insert in the breach, on both occasions, a moment of authorial time suspended between the two poles of "waiting," a figure ideally constituted to allow the play of digressions, asides and parentheses forming loops and zigzags in a story-line and adding thereby to its depth. Thus, waiting for news about the movements of the mutineers he reflects on the peace of the early evening at the sadar station and strays from his account to tell us in violation of the historiographical canon of tense and person: "The scene was simple and full of the repose of Eastern life. In the times that followed it often recurred to my memory." And, again, waiting later on for transport to take away the evacuees gathered in his drawing room, he withdraws from that particular night for the duration of a few words to comment: "It was a beautiful room, brightly lighted, gay with flowers. It was the last time I thus saw it, and so it remains impressed upon my memory."

How far does the operation of these shifters help to correct the bias resulting from the writer's intervention in the first person? Not much by this showing. For each of the indices wedged into the narrative represents a principled choice between the terms of a paradigmatic opposition. Between the authority of the head of the district and its defiance by the armed masses, between the habitual servility of his menials and their assertion of self-respect as rebels, between the insignia of his wealth and power (e.g., gold, horses, shawls, bungalow) and their appropriation or destruction by the subaltern crowds, the author, hardly differentiated from the administrator that he was twenty-seven years ago, consistently chooses the former. Nostalgia makes the choice all the more eloquent—a recall of what is thought to be "fine," such as a peaceful evening or an elegant room, emphasizing by contrast the "terrible" aspects of popular violence directed against the Raj. Quite clearly there is a logic to this preference. It affirms itself by negating a series of inversions which, combined with other signs of the same order, constitute a code of insurgency. The pattern of the historian's choice, identical with the magistrate's, conforms thus to a counter-code, the code of counter-insurgency.

VII

If the neutralizing effect of the aorist fails thus to prevail over the subjectivity of the protagonist as narrator in this particular genre of secondary discourse, how does the balance of tense and person stand in the other kind of writing within the same category? One can see two distinct idioms at work here, both identified with the standpoint of colonialism but unlike each other in expressing it. The cruder variety is well exemplified in *The Chuar Rebellion of 1799* by J. C. Price. Written long after the event, in 1874, it was obviously meant by the author, Settlement Officer of Midnapur at the time, to serve as a straightforward historical account with no particular administrative end in view. He addressed it to "the casual reader" as well as to any "future Collector of Midnapore," hoping to share with both "that keen interest which I have felt as I have read the old Midnapore records."[19] But the author's "delight . . . experienced in pouring over these papers" seems to have produced a text almost indistinguishable from the primary discourse used as its source. The latter is, for one thing, conspicuous by its sheer physical presence. Over a fifth of that half of the book which deals specifically with the events of 1799 is made up of direct quotations from those records and another large part [consists] of barely modified extracts. More important for us, however, is the evidence we have of the author's identification of his own sentiments with those of that small group of whites who were reaping the whirlwind produced by the wind of a violently disruptive change the Company's Government had sown in the south-western corder of Bengal. Only the fear of the beleaguered officials at Midnapur station in 1799 turns seventy-five years later into that genocidal hatred characteristic of a genre of post-Mutiny British writing. "The disinclination of the authorities, civil or military, to proceed in person to help to quell the disturbances is most striking," he writes shaming his compatriots and then goes on to brag:

> In these days of breech-loaders half a dozen Europeans would have been a match for twenty times their number of Chuars. Of course with the imperfect nature of the weapons of that day it could not be expected that Europeans would fruitlessly rush into danger, but I should have expected that the European officers of the station would have in some instances at least courted and met an attack in person and repulsed their assailants. I wonder that no one European officer, civilian or military, with the exception of perhaps Lieutenant Gill, owned to that sensation of joyous excitement most young men feel now-a-days in field sports, or in any pursuit where there is an element of danger. I think most of us, had we lived in 1799, would have counted it better sport had we bagged a marauding Chuar reeking with blood and spoils, than the largest bear that the Midnapore jungles can produce.[20]

Quite clearly the author's separation from his subject matter and the difference between the time of the event and that of its narration here have done little to inspire objectivity in him. His passion is apparently of the same order as that of the British soldier who wrote on the eve of the sack of Delhi in 1857: "I most sincerely trust that the order given when we attack Delhi will be . . . 'Kill every one; no quarter is to be given.' "[22] The historian's attitude to rebels is in this instance indistinguishable from that of the State—the attitude of the hunter to his quarry. Regarded thus an insurgent is not a subject of understanding or interpretation but of extermination, and the discourse of history, far from being neutral, serves directly to instigate official violence.

There were, however, other writers working within the same genre who are also known to have expressed themselves in a less sanguinary idiom. They are perhaps best represented by W. W. Hunter and his account of the Santal insurrection of 1855 in *The Annals of Rural Bengal*. It is, in many respects, a remarkable text. Written within a decade of the Mutiny and twelve years of the *hool*,[22] it has none of that revanchist and racist overtone common to a good deal of Anglo-Indian literature of the period. Indeed the author treats the enemies of the Raj not only with consideration but with respect although they had wiped it off from three eastern districts in a matter of weeks and held out for five months against the combined power of the colonial army and its newly acquired auxiliaries—railways and the "electric telegraph." One of the first modern exercises in the historiography of Indian peasant revolts, it situates the uprising in a cultural and socio-economic context, analyzes its causes, and draws on local records and contemporary accounts for evidence about its progress and eventual suppression. Here, to all appearances, we have that classic instance of the author's own bias and opinion dissolving under the operation of the past tense and the grammatical third person. Here, perhaps, historical discourse has come to its own and realized that ideal of an "apersonal . . . mode of narrative . . . designed to wipe out the presence of the speaker"?[23]

This semblance of objectivity, of the want of any obviously demonstrable bias, has, however, nothing to do with "facts speaking for themselves" in a state of pure metonymy unsullied by comment. On the contrary the text is packed with comment. One has to compare it with something like the near contemporary article on this subject in *Calcutta Review* (1856) or even K. K. Datta's history of the *hool* written long after its suppression to realize how little there is in it of the details of what actually happened.[24] Indeed the narration of the event occupies in the book only about 7 percent of the chapter which builds up climactically toward it, and somewhat less than 50 per cent of the print devoted specifically to this topic within that chapter. The syntagm is broken up again and again by dystaxia and interpretation filters through to assemble the segments into a meaningful whole of a primarily metaphorical character. The consequence of this operation that is most relevant for our purpose here is the way in which it distributes the paradigmatic relata along an axis of historical continuity between a "before" and an "after," forelengthening it with a context and extending it into a perspective. The representation of insurgency ends up thus by having its moment intercalated between its past and future so that the particular values of one and the other are rubbed into the event to give it the meaning specific to it.

VIII

To turn first to the context, two-thirds of the chapter which culminates in the history of the insurrection is taken up with an inaugural account of what may be called the natural history of its protagonists. An essay in ethnography this deals with the physical traits, language, traditions, myths, religion, rituals, habitat, environment, hunting and agricultural practices, social organization and communal government of the Santals of the Birbhum region. There are many details here which index the coming conflict as one of contraries, as between the noble savage of the hills and mean exploiters from the plains—references to [the former's] personal dignity ("He does not abase himself to the ground like the rural Hindu"; the Santal woman is "ignorant of the shrinking squeamishness of the Hindu female," etc.) implying the contrast with his would-be reduction to servitude by Hindu moneylenders, his honesty ("Unlike the Hindu, he never thinks of making money by a stranger, scrupulously avoids all topics of business, and feels pained if payment is pressed upon him for the milk and fruit which his wife brings out") [implying the contrast] with the greed and fraud of the alien traders and landlords leading eventually to the insurrection, his aloofness ("The Santals live as much apart as possible from the Hindus") [implying the contrast] with the *diku*'s intrusion into his life and territory and the holocaust which inevitably followed.

The indices give the uprising not only a moral dimension and the values of a just war, but also a depth in time. The latter is realized by the operation of diachronic markers in the text—an imaginary past by creation myths (appropriate for an enterprise taken up on the Thakur's advice) and a real but remote past (befitting a revolt steeped in tradition) by the sherds of prehistory in ritual and speech with the Santals' ceremony of "Purifying for the Dead" mentioned, for instance, as the trace of "a faint remembrance of the far-off time when they dwelt beside the great rivers" and their language as "that intangible record on which a nation's past is graven more deeply than on brass tablets or rock inscriptions."

Moving closer to the event the author provides it with a recent past covering roughly a period of sixty years of "direct administration" in the area. The moral and temporal aspects of the narrative merge here in the figure of an irreconcilable contradiction. On the one hand there were, according to Hunter, a series of beneficial measures introduced by the government—the Decennial Settlement helping to expand the area under cultivation and induce the Santals, since 1792, to hire themselves out as agricultural laborers; the setting up, in 1832, of an enclosure ringed off by masonry pillars where they could colonize virgin land and jungle without fear of harassment from hostile tribes; the development of "English enterprise" in Bengal in the form of indigo factories for which "the Santal immigrants afforded a population of day-laborers"; and last but not the least of bonanzas, their absorption by thousands into labor gangs for the construction of railways across that region in 1854. But there were, on the other hand, two sets of factors which combined to undo all the good resulting from colonial rule, namely, the exploitation and oppression of the Santals by greedy and fraudulent Hindu landlords, moneylenders and traders, and the failure of the local administration, its police and the courts to protect them or redress the wrongs they suffered.

IX

This emphasis on contradiction serves an obviously interpretative purpose for the author. It makes it possible for him to locate the cause of the uprising in a failure of the Raj to make its ameliorative aspects prevail over the still lingering defects and shortcomings in its exercise of authority. The account of the event therefore fits directly into the objective stated at the beginning of the chapter, that is, to interest not only the scholar "in these lapsed races" but the statesman as well. "The Indian statesman will discover," he had written there referring euphemistically to the makers of British policy in India, "that these Children of the Forest are . . . amenable to the same reclaiming influences as other men, and that upon their capacity for civilisation the future extension of English enterprise in Bengal in a large measure depends." It is this concern for "reclamation" (shorthand for accelerating the transformation of the tribal peasantry into wage labor and harnessing them to characteristically colonialist projects for the exploitation of Indian resources) which explains the mixture of firmness and "understanding" in Hunter's attitude to the rebellion. A liberal-imperialist he regarded it both as a menace to the stability of the Raj and as a useful critique of its far from perfect administration. So while he censured the government of the day for not declaring Marital Law soon enough in order to cut down the *hool* at its inception, he was careful to differentiate himself from those of his compatriots who wanted to punish the entire Santal community for the crime of its rebels and deport overseas the population of the districts involved. A genuinely far-sighted imperialist he looked forward to the day when the tribe, like many other aboriginal peoples of the subcontinent, would demonstrate its "capacity for civilization" by acting as an inexhaustible source of cheap labor power.

This vision is inscribed into the perspective with which the narration ends. Blaming the outbreak of the *hool* squarely on that "cheap and practical administration" which paid no heed to the Santals' complaints and concentrated on tax collection alone it goes on to catalogue the somewhat illusory benefits of "the more exact system that was introduced after the revolt" to keep the power of the usurers over debtors within the limits of the law, check the use of false weights and measures in retail trade, and ensure the right of bonded laborers to choose freedom by desertion or change of employers. But more than administrative reform it was "English enterprise" again which radically contributed to the welfare of the tribe. The railways "completely changed the relation of labor to capital" and did away with that "natural reason for slavery—to wit, the absence of a wage-fund for free workmen." The demand for plantation labor in the Assam tea-districts "was destined still further to improve the position of the Santals" and so was the stimulus for indenturing coolies for the Mauritius and the Caribbeans. It was thus that the tribal peasant prospered thanks to the development of a vast subcontinental and overseas labor market within the British Empire. In the Assam tea gardens "his whole family gets employment, and every additional child, instead of being the means of increasing his poverty, becomes a source of wealth," while the coolies returned from Africa or the West Indies "at the expiry of their contracts with savings averaging £20 sterling, a sum sufficient to set up a Santal as a considerable proprietor in his own village."

Many of these so-called improvements were, as we know now looking back at them across a century, the result of sheer wishful thinking or so ephemeral as not to have mattered at all. The connection between usury and bonded labor continued all through British rule well into independent India. The freedom of the labor market was seriously restricted by the want of competition between British and indigenous capital. The employment of tribal families on tea plantations became a source of cynical exploitation of the labor of women and children. The advantages of mobility and contractuality were canceled out by irregularities in the process of recruitment and the manipulation of the contrary factors of economic dependence and social differentiation by *arkatis*. The system of indenturing helped rather less to liberate servile labor than to develop a sort of second serfdom, and so on.

Yet this vision which never materialized offers an insight into the character of this type of discourse. The perspective it inspired amounted in effect to a testament of faith in colonialism. The *hool* was assimilated there to the career of the Raj and the militant enterprise of a tribal peasantry to free themselves from the triple yoke of *sarkari*, *sahukari* and *zamindari* to "English enterprise"—the infrastructure of Empire. Hence the objective stated at the beginning of the account could be reiterated toward the end with the author saying that he had written at least "partly for the instruction which their [the Santals'] recent history furnishes as to the proper method of dealing with the aboriginal races." The suppression of local peasant revolts was a part of this method, but it was incorporated now in a broader strategy designed to tackle the economic problems of imperial politics. "These are the problems," says Hunter in concluding the chapter, "which the Indian statesmen during the next fifty years will be called upon to solve. Their predecessors have given civilization to India; it will be their duty to render that civilisation at once beneficial to the natives and safe for ourselves." In other words this historiography was assigned to a role in a political process that would ensure the security of the Raj by a combination of force to crush rebellion when it occurred and reform to preempt it by wrenching the tribal peasantry out of their rural bases and distributing them as cheap labor power for British capital to exploit in India and abroad. The overtly aggressive and nervous prose of counter-insurgency born of the worries of the early colonial days came thus to adopt in this genre of historical writing the firm but benign, authoritarian but understanding idiom of a mature and self-assured imperialism.

X

How is it that even the more liberal type of secondary discourse is unable thus to extricate itself from the code of counter-insurgency? With all the advantage he has of writing in the third person and addressing a distinct past the official turned historian is still far from being impartial where official interests are concerned. His sympathies for the peasants' sufferings and his understanding of what goaded them to revolt, do not, when the crunch comes, prevent him from siding with law and order and justifying the transfer of the campaign against the *hool* from civilian to military hands in order to crush it completely and quickly. And as discussed above, his partisanship over the outcome of the rebellion is matched by his commitment to the aims and interests of the regime. The discourse of history, hardly distinguished from policy, ends up by absorbing the concerns and objectives of the latter.

In this affinity with policy historiography reveals its character as a form of *colonialist knowledge*. That is, it derives directly from that knowledge which the bourgeoisie had used in the period of their ascendancy to interpret the world in order to master it and establish their hegemony over Western societies, but turned into an instrument of national oppression as they began to acquire for themselves "a place in the sun." It was thus that political science which had defined the ideal of citizenship for European nation-states was used in colonial India to set up institutions and frame laws designed specifically to generate a mitigated and second-class citizenship. Political economy which had developed in Europe as a critique of feudalism was made to promote a neo-feudal landlordism in India. Historiography, too, adapted itself to the relations of power under the Raj and was harnessed more and more to the service of the state.

It was thanks to this connection and a good deal of talent to back it up that historical writing on themes of the colonial period shaped up as a highly coded discourse. Operating within the framework of a many-sided affirmation of British rule in the subcontinent it assumed the function of representing the recent past of its people as "England's Work in India." A discourse of power in its own right it had each of its moments displayed as a triumph, that is, as the most favorable upshot of a number of conflicting possibilities for the regime at any particular time. In its mature form, therefore, as in Hunter's *Annals*, continuity figures as one of its necessary and cardinal aspects. Unlike primary discourse it cannot afford to be foreshortened and without a sequel. The event does not constitute its sole content, but is the middle term between a beginning which serves as a context and an end which is at the same time a perspective linked to the next sequence. The only element that is constant in this ongoing series is the Empire and the policies needed to safeguard and perpetuate it.

Functioning as he does within this code Hunter with all the goodwill so solemnly announced in his dedicatory note ("These pages . . . have little to say touching the governing race. My business is with the people") writes up the history of a popular struggle as one in which the real subject is not the people but, indeed, "the governing race" institutionalized as the Raj. Like any other narrative of this kind his account of the *hool*, too, is there to celebrate a continuity—that of British power in India. The statement of causes and reforms is no more than a structural requirement for this continuum providing it respectively with context and perspective. These serve admirably to register the event as a datum in the life-story of the Empire, but do nothing to illuminate that consciousness which is called insurgency. The rebel has no place in this history as the subject of rebellion.

XI

There is nothing in tertiary discourse to make up for this absence. Farthest removed in time from the events which it has for its theme it always looks at them in the third person. It is the work of non-official writers in most cases or of former officials no longer under any professional obligation or constraint to represent the standpoint of the government. If it happens to carry an official view at all this is only because the author has chosen it of his own will rather than based on administrative involvement. There are indeed some historical works which actually show such a preference and are unable to speak in a voice other than that of the custodians of law and order—an instance of tertiary discourse reverting to that state of crude identification with the regime so characteristic of primary discourse.

But there are other and very different idioms within this genre ranging from liberal to left. The latter is particularly important as perhaps the most influential and prolific of all the many varieties of tertiary discourse. We owe it to some of the best studies on Indian peasant insurgency and more and more of these are coming out all the time as evidence both of a growing academic interest in the subject and the relevance that the subaltern movements of the past have to contemporary tensions in our part of the world. This literature is distinguished by its effort to break away from the code of counter-insurgency. It adopts the insurgent's point of view and regards, with him, as "fine" what the other side calls "terrible," and vice versa. It leaves the reader in no doubt that it wants the rebels and not their enemies to win. Here, unlike in secondary discourse of the liberal-imperialist type, recognition of the wrongs done to the peasants leads directly to support for their struggle to seek redress by arms.

Yet these two types, so very different from and contrary to each other in ideological orientation, have much else that is common between them. Take for instance that remarkable contribution of radical scholarship, Suprakash Ray's *Bharater Krishak-bidroha O Ganatantrik Samgram*[25] and compare its account of the Santal uprising of 1855 with Hunter's. The texts echo each other as narratives. Ray's, being the later work, has all the advantage of drawing on more recent research such as Datta's, and thus being more informed. But much of what it has to say about the inauguration and development of the *hool* is taken—in fact, quoted directly—from Hunter's *Annals*.[26] And both the authors rely on the *Calcutta Review* (1856) article for much of their evidence. There is thus little in the description of this particular event which differs significantly between the secondary and tertiary types of discourse.

Nor is there much to distinguish between the two in terms of their admiration for the courage of the rebels and their abhorrence of the genocidal operations mounted by the counter-insurgency forces. In fact, on both these points Ray reproduces *in extenso* Hunter's testimony, gathered first-hand from officers directly involved in the campaign, that the Santals "did not understand yielding," while for the army, "it was not war . . . it was execution."[27] The sympathy expressed for the enemies of the Raj in the radical tertiary discourse is matched fully by that in the colonialist secondary discourse. Indeed, for both, the *hool* was an eminently just struggle—an evaluation derived from their mutual concurrence about the factors which had provoked it. Wicked landlords, extortionate usurers, dishonest traders, venal police, irresponsible officials and partisan processes of law—all figure with equal prominence in both the accounts. Both the historians draw on the evidence recorded on this subject in the *Calcutta Review* essay, and for much of his information about Santal indebtedness and bond slavery, about moneylenders' and landlords' oppression and administrative connivance at all this Ray relies heavily again on Hunter, as witness the extracts quoted liberally from the latter's work.[28]

However, causality is used by the two writers to develop entirely different perspectives. The statement of causes has the same part to play in Hunter's account as in any other narrative of the secondary type—that is, an essential aspect of the discourse of counter-insurgency. In this respect his *Annals* belongs to a tradition of colonialist historiography which, for this particular event, is typically exemplified by that racist and vindicative essay, "The Sonthal Rebellion." There the obviously knowledgeable but tough-minded official ascribes the uprising, as Hunter does, to banias' fraud, mahajani transaction, zamindari despotism and sarkari inefficiency. In much the same vein Thornhill's *Personal Adventures* accounts for the rural uprisings of the period of the Mutiny in Uttar Pradesh quite clearly by the breakdown in traditional agrarian relations consequent on the advent of British rule. O'Malley identifies the root of the Pabna *bidroha* of 1873 in rack-renting by landlords, and the Deccan Riots Commission [identifies] that of the disturbances of 1875 in the exploitation of the Kunbi peasantry by alien moneylenders in Poona and Ahmednagar districts.[29] One could go on adding many other events and texts to this list. The spirit of all these is well represented in the following extract from the *Judicial Department Resolutions* of 22 November 1831 on the subject of the insurrection led by Titu Mir:

> The serious nature of the late disturbances in the district of Baraset renders it an
> object of paramount importance that the *cause* which gave rise to them should be
> fully *investigated* in order that the motives which activated the insurgents may be
> rightly *understood* and such measures adopted as may be deemed expedient *to*
> *prevent a recurrence of similar disorders.*[30]

That sums it up. To know the cause of a phenomenon is already a step
taken in the direction of controlling it. To *investigate* and thereby *understand*
the cause of rural disturbances is an aid to measures "deemed expedient *to*
prevent a recurrence of similar disorders." To that end the correspondent of
the *Calcutta Review* (1856) recommended "that condign retribution,"
namely, "that they [the Santals] should be surrounded and hunted up everywhere . . . that they should be compelled, by force, if need be, to return to the
Damin-i-koh, and to the wasted country in Bhaugulpore and Beerbhoom, to
rebuild the ruined villages, restore the desolate fields to cultivation, open
roads, and advance general public works; and do this under watch and guard
. . . and that this state of things should be continued, until they are completely
tranquillized, and reconciled to their allegiance."[31] The gentler alternative put
forward by Hunter was, as we have seen, a combination of Martial Law to
suppress an ongoing revolt and measures to follow it up by "English enterprise" in order (as his compatriot had suggested) to absorb the unruly peasantry as a cheap labor force in agriculture and public works for the benefit
respectively of the same *dikus* and railway and roadwork engineers against
whom they had taken up arms. With all their variation in tone, however, both
the prescriptions to "make . . . rebellion impossible by the elevation of the
Sonthals"[32]—indeed, all colonialist solutions arrived at by the casual explanation of our peasant uprisings—were grist to a historiography committed to
assimilating them to the transcendental Destiny of the British Empire.

XII

Causality serves to hitch the *hool* to a rather different kind of Destiny in
Ray's account. But the latter goes through the same steps as Hunter's—that
is, *context-event-perspective* ranged along a historical continuum—to arrive
there. There are some obvious parallelisms in the way the event acquires a
context in the two works. Both start off with prehistory (treated more briefly
by Ray than Hunter) and follow it up with a survey of the more recent past
since 1790 when the tribe first came into contact with the regime. It is there
that the cause of the insurrection lies for both—but with a difference. For
Hunter the disturbances originated in a local malignance in an otherwise
healthy body—the failure of a district administration to act up to the then
emerging ideal of the Raj as the *ma-baap* of the peasantry and protect them
from the tyranny of wicked elements within the native society itself. For Ray
it was the very presence of British power in India which had goaded the San-

tals to revolt, for their enemies the landlords and moneylenders owed their authority and indeed their existence to the new arrangements in landed property introduced by the colonial government and the accelerated development of a money economy under its impact. The rising constituted, therefore, a critique not only of a local administration but of colonialism itself. Indeed he uses Hunter's own evidence to arrive at that very different, indeed contrary, conclusion:

> It is clearly proved by Hunter's own statement that the responsibility for the extreme misery of the Santals lies with the English administrative system taken as a whole together with the zamindars and mahajans. For it was the English administrative system which had created zamindars and mahajans in order to satisfy its own need for exploitation and government, and helped them directly and indirectly by offering its protection and patronage.[33]

With colonialism, that is, the Raj as a system and in its entirety (rather than any of its local malfunctions) identified thus as the prime cause of rebellion, its outcome acquires radically different values in the two texts. While Hunter is explicit in his preference of a victory in favor of the regime, Ray is equally so in favor of the rebels. And corresponding to this each has a perspective which stands out in sharp contrast to that of the other. It is for Hunter the consolidation of British rule based on a reformed administration which no longer incites jacqueries by its failure to protect *adivasis* from native exploiters, but transforms them into an abundant and mobile labor force readily and profitably employed by Indian landlords and "English enterprise." For Ray the event is "the precursor of the great rebellion" of 1857 and a vital link in a protracted struggle of the Indian people in general and peasants and workers in particular against foreign as well as indigenous oppressors. The armed insurrection of the Santals, he says, has indicated a way to the Indian people. "That particular way has, thanks to the great rebellion of 1857, developed into the broad highway of India's struggle for freedom. That highway extends into the twentieth century. The Indian peasantry are on their march along that very highway."[34] In fitting the *hool* thus to a perspective of continuing struggle of the rural masses the author draws on a well-established tradition of radical historiography, as witness, for instance, the following extract from a pamphlet which had a wide readership in left political circles nearly thirty years ago:

> The din of the actual battles of the insurrection has died down. But its echoes have kept on vibrating through the years, growing louder and louder as more peasants joined in the fight. The clarion call that summoned the Santhals to battle . . . was to be heard in other parts of the country at the time of the Indigo Strike of 1860, the Pabna and Bogra Uprising of 1872, the Maratha Peasant Rising in Poona and Ahmednagar in 1875–76. It was finally to merge in the massive demand of the peasantry all over the country for an end to zamindari and moneylending oppression. . . . Glory to the immortal Santhals who . . . showed the path

to battle! The banner of militant struggle has since then passed from hand to hand over the length and breadth of India.[35]

The power of such assimilative thinking about the history of peasant insurgency is further illustrated by the concluding words of an essay written by a veteran of the peasant movement and published by the Pashchimbanga Pradeshik Krishak Sabha on the eve of the centenary of the Santal revolt. Thus,

> The flames of the fire kindled by the peasant martyrs of the Santal insurrection a hundred years ago had spread to many regions all over India. Those flames could be seen burning in the indigo cultivators' rebellion in Bengal (1860), in the uprising of the raiyats of Pabna and Bogra (1872), in that of the Maratha peasantry of the Deccan (1875–76). The same fire was kindled again and again in the course of the Moplah peasant revolts of Malabar. That fire has not been extinguished yet, it is still burning in the hearts of the Indian peasants. . . .[36]

The purpose of such tertiary discourse is quite clearly to try and retrieve the history of insurgency from that continuum which is designed to assimilate every jacquerie to "England's Work in India" and arrange it along the alternative axis of a protracted campaign for freedom and socialism. However, as with colonialist historiography, this, too, amounts to an act of appropriation which excludes the rebel as the conscious subject of his own history and incorporates the latter as only a contingent element in another history with another subject. Just as it is not the rebel but the Raj which is the real subject of secondary discourse and the Indian bourgeoisie that of tertiary discourse of the History-of-the-Freedom-Struggle genre, so is an *abstraction* called Worker-and-Peasant, *an ideal rather than the real historical personality of the insurgent*, made to replace him in the type of literature discussed above.

To say this is of course not to deny the political importance of such appropriation. Since every struggle for power by the historically ascendant classes in any epoch involves a bid to acquire a tradition, it is entirely in the fitness of things that the revolutionary movements in India should lay a claim to, among others, the Santal rebellion of 1855 as a part of their heritage. But however noble the cause and instrument of such appropriation, it leads to the mediation of the insurgent's consciousness by the historian's—that is, of a past consciousness by one conditioned by the present. The distortion which follows necessarily and inevitably from this process is a function of that hiatus between event-time and discourse-time which makes the verbal representation of the past less than accurate in the best of cases. And since the discourse is, in this particular instance, one about properties of the mind—about attitudes, beliefs, ideas, etc., rather than about externalities which are easier to identify and describe, the task of representation is made even more complicated than usual.

There is nothing that historiography can do to eliminate such distortion altogether, for the latter is built into its optics. What it can do, however, is to acknowledge such distortion as parametric—as a datum which determines the form of the exercise itself, and to stop pretending that it can *fully* grasp a past consciousness and reconstitute it. Then and only then might the distance between the latter and the historian's perception of it be reduced significantly enough to amount to a close approximation which is the best one could hope for. The gap as it stands at the moment is indeed so wide that there is much more than an irreducible degree of error in the existing literature on this point. Even a brief look at some of the discourses on the 1855 insurrection should bear this out.

XIII

Religiosity was, by all accounts, central to the *hool*. The notion of power which inspired it was made up of such ideas and expressed in such words and acts as were explicitly religious in character. It was not that power was a content wrapped up in a form external to it called religion. It was a matter of both being inseparably collapsed as the signified and its signifier (*vagarthaviva samprktau*) in the language of that massive violence. Hence the attribution of the rising to a divine command rather than to any particular grievance; the enactment of rituals both before (e.g., propitiatory ceremonies to ward off the apocalypse of the Primeval Serpents—Lag and Lagini, the distribution of *tel-sindur*, etc.) and during the uprising (e.g., worshiping the goddess Durga, bathing in the Ganges, etc.); the generation and circulation of myth in its characteristic vehicle—rumor (e.g., about the advent of "the exterminating angel" incarnated as a buffalo, the birth of a prodigious hero to a virgin, etc.).[37] The evidence is both unequivocal and ample on this point. The statements we have from the leading protagonists and their followers are all emphatic and indeed insistent on this aspect of their struggle, as should be obvious even from the few extracts of source material reproduced below in the Appendix. In sum, it is not possible to speak of insurgency in this case except as a religious consciousness—except, that is, as a massive demonstration of self-estrangement (to borrow Marx's term for the very essence of religiosity) which made the rebels look upon their project as predicated on a will other than their own: "Kanoo and Seedoo Manjee are not fighting. The Thacoor himself will fight."[38]

How authentically has this been represented in historical discourse? It was identified in official correspondence at the time as a case of "fanaticism." The insurrection was three months old and still going strong when J. R. Ward, a Special Commissioner and one of the most important administrators in the Birbhum region, wrote in some desperation to his superiors in Calcutta, "I have been unable to trace the insurrection in Beerbhoom to any thing but *fanaticism*." The idiom he used to describe the phenomenon was typical of the shocked and culturally arrogant response of nineteenth-century colonialism to any radical movement inspired by a non-Christian doctrine among a subject population: "These Sonthals have been led to join in the rebellion

under a persuasion which is clearly traceable to their brethren in Bhaugulpore, that an Almighty & inspired Being appeared as the redeemer of their
Caste & their *ignorance & superstition* was easily worked into a *religious
frenzy* which has stopped at nothing."[39] That idiom occurs also in the *Calcutta Review* article. There the Santal is acknowledged as "an eminently religious man" and his revolt as a parallel of other historical occasions when
"*the fanatical spirit of religious superstition*" had been "swayed to
strengthen and help forward a quarrel already ready to burst and based on
other grounds."[40] However, the author gives this identification a significantly
different slant from that in the report quoted above. There an incomprehend-
ing Ward, caught in the blast of the *hool*, appears to have been impressed
with the spontaneity of "a religious frenzy which . . . stopped at nothing." By
contrast the article written after the regime had recovered its self-confidence,
thanks to the search-and-burn campaign in the disturbed tracts, interprets religiosity as a propagandist ruse used by the leaders to sustain the morale of
the rebels. Referring, for instance, to the messianic rumors in circulation it
says, "All these absurdities were no doubt *devised* to keep up the courage of
the numerous rabble."[41] Nothing could be more elitist. The insurgents are
regarded here as a mindless "rabble" devoid of a will of their own and easily
manipulated by their chiefs.

But elitism such as this is not a feature of colonialist historiography alone.
Tertiary discourse of the radical variety, too, exhibits the same disdain for the
political consciousness of the peasant masses when it is mediated by religiosity. For a sample let us turn to Ray's account of the rising again. He quotes
the following lines from the *Calcutta Review* article in a somewhat inaccurate
but still clearly recognizable translation:

> Seedoo and Kanoo were at night seated in their home, revolving many things . . .
> a bit of paper fell on Seedoo's head, and suddenly the Thakoor (god) appeared
> before the astonished gaze of Seedoo and Kanoo; he was like a white man though
> dressed in the native style; on each hand he had ten fingers; he held a white book,
> and wrote therein; the book and with it 20 pieces of paper . . . he presented to the
> brothers; ascended upwards, and disappeared. Another bit of paper fell on
> Seedoo's head, and then came two men . . . hinted to them the purport of
> Thakoor's order, and they likewise vanished. But there was not merely one appa-
> rition of the sublime Thakoor; each day in the week for some short period, did he
> make known his presence to his favourite apostles. . . . In the silvery pages of the
> book, and upon the white leaves of the single scraps of paper, were words writ-
> ten; these were afterwards deciphered by literate Sonthals, able to read and inter-
> pret; but their meaning had already been sufficiently indicated to the two
> leaders.[42]

With some minor changes of detail (inevitable in a living folklore) this is
indeed a fairly authentic account of the visions the two Santal leaders believed they had had. Their statements, reproduced in part in the Appendix
(Extracts 3 and 4), bear this out. These, incidentally, were not public pro-

nouncements meant to impress their followers. Unlike "The Thacoor's Perwannah" (Appendix: Extract 2), intended to make their views known to the authorities before the uprising, these were the words of captives facing execution. Addressed to hostile interrogators in military encampments they could have little use as propaganda. Uttered by men of a tribe which, according to all accounts, had not yet learned to lie,[43] these represented the truth and nothing but the truth for their speakers. But that is not what Ray would credit them with. What figures as a mere insinuation in the *Calcutta Review* is raised to the status of an elaborate propaganda device in his introductory remarks on the passage cited above. Thus:

> Both Sidu and Kanu knew that the slogan (*dhwani*) which would have the most effect among the *backward* Santals, was one that was religious. Therefore, *in order to inspire* the Santals to struggle they *spread* the word about God's directive in favour of launching such a struggle. The story *invented* (*kalpita*) by them is as follows.[44]

There is little that is different here from what the colonialist writer had to say about the presumed backwardness of the Santal peasantry, the manipulative designs of their leaders and the uses of religion as the means of such manipulation. Indeed, on each of these points Ray does better and is by far the more explicit of the two authors in attributing a gross lie and downright deception to the rebel chiefs without any evidence at all. The invention is all his own and testifies to the failure of a shallow radicalism to conceptualize insurgent mentality except in terms of an unadulterated secularism. Unable to grasp religiosity as the central modality of peasant consciousness in colonial India he is shy to acknowledge its mediation of the peasant's idea of power and all the resultant contradictions. He is obliged therefore to rationalize the ambiguities of rebel politics by assigning a worldly consciousness to the leaders and an otherworldly one to their followers making of the latter innocent dupes of crafty men armed with all the tricks of a modern Indian politician out to solicit rural votes. Where this lands the historian can be seen even more clearly in the projection of this thesis to a study of the Birsaite *ulgulan* in Ray's subsequent work. He writes,

> In order to propagate this religious doctrine of his Birsa adopted *a new device* (*kaushal*)—just as Sidu, the Santal leader, had done on the eve of the Santal rebellion of 1885. Birsa knew that the Kol were a *very backward* people and were full of *religious superstition* as a result of Hindu-Brahmanical and Christian missionary propaganda amongst them over a long period. Therefore, it would not do to avoid the question of religion if the Kol people were to be liberated from those wicked religious influences and drawn into the path of rebellion. Rather, in order to overcome the evil influences of Hindu and Christian religions, it would be necessary to spread his new religious faith among them in the name of that very God of theirs, and to introduce new rules. *To this end, recourse had to be had to falsehood, if necessary, in the interests of the people.*

Birsa *spread* the word that he had received this new religion of his from the chief deity of the Mundas, Sing Bonga, himself.[45]

Thus the radical historian is driven by the logic of his own incomprehension to attribute a deliberate falsehood to one of the greatest of our rebels. The ideology of that mighty *ulgulan* is nothing but pure fabrication for him. And he is not alone in his misreading of insurgent consciousness. Baskay echoes him almost word for word in describing the Santal leader's claim to divine support for the *hool* as propaganda meant "to inspire the Santals to rise in revolt."[46] Formulations such as these have their foil in other writings of the same genre which solve the riddle of religious thinking among the Santal rebels by ignoring it altogether. A reader who has Natarajan's and Rasul's once influential essays as his only source of information about the insurrection of 1855, would hardly suspect any religiosity at all in that great event. It is represented there *exclusively* in its secular aspects. This attitude is of course not confined to the authors discussed in this essay. The same mixture of myopia and downright refusal to look at the evidence that is there, characterizes a great deal more of the existing literature on the subject.

XIV

Why is tertiary discourse, even of the radical variety, so reluctant to come to terms with the religious element in rebel consciousness? Because it is still trapped in the paradigm which inspired the ideologically contrary, because colonialist, discourse of the primary and secondary types. It follows, in each case, from a refusal to acknowledge the insurgent as the subject of his own history. For once a peasant rebellion has been assimilated to the career of the Raj, the Nation or the People, it becomes easy for the historian to abdicate the responsibility he has of exploring and describing the consciousness specific to that rebellion and be content to ascribe it to a transcendental consciousness. In operative terms, this means denying a will to the mass of the rebels themselves and representing them merely as instruments of some other will. It is thus that in colonialist historiography insurgency is seen as the articulation of a pure spontaneity pitted against the will of the State as embodied in the Raj. If any consciousness is attributed at all to the rebels, it is only a few of their leaders—more often than not some individual members or small groups of the gentry—who are credited with it. Again, in bourgeois-nationalist historiography it is an elite consciousness which is read into all peasant movements as their motive force. This had led to such grotesqueries as the characterization of the Indigo Rebellion of 1860 as "the first non-violent mass movement"[47] and generally of all the popular struggles in rural India during the first hundred and twenty-five years of British rule as the spiritual harbinger of the Indian National Congress.

In much the same way the specificity of rebel consciousness had eluded radical historiography as well. This has been so because it is impaled on a concept of peasant revolts as a succession of events ranged along a direct line of descent—as a heritage, as it is often called—in which all the constituents have the same pedigree and replicate each other in their commitment to the highest ideals of liberty, equality and fraternity. In this ahistorical view of the history of insurgency all moments of consciousness are assimilated to the ultimate and highest moment of the series—indeed to an Ideal Consciousness. A historiography devoted to its pursuit (even when that is done, regrettably, in the name of Marxism) is ill-equipped to cope with contradictions which are indeed the stuff history is made of. Since the Ideal is supposed to be one hundred per cent secular in character, the devotee tends to look away when confronted with the evidence of religiosity as if the latter did not exist or explain it away as a clever but well-intentioned fraud perpetrated by enlightened leaders on their moronic followers—all done, of course, "in the interests of the people"! Hence, the rich material of myths, rituals, rumors, hopes for a Golden Age and fears of an imminent End of the World, all of which speaks of the self-alienation of the rebel, is wasted on this abstract and sterile discourse. It can do little to illuminate that combination of sectarianism and militancy which is so important a feature of our rural history. The ambiguity of such phenomena, witnessed during the Tebhaga movement in Dinajpur, as Muslim peasants coming to the Kisan Sabha "sometimes inscribing a hammer or a sickle on the Muslim League flag" and young maulavis "reciting melodious verse from the Koran" at village meetings as "they condemned the jotedari system and the practice of charging high interest rates"[48] will be beyond its grasp. The swift transformation of class struggle into communal strife and vice versa in our countryside evokes from it either some well-contrived apology or a simple gesture of embarrassment, but no real explanation.

However, it is not only the religious element in rebel consciousness which this historiography fails to comprehend. The specificity of a rural insurrection is expressed in terms of many other contradictions as well. These, too, are missed out. Blinded by the glare of a perfect and immaculate consciousness the historian sees nothing, for instance, but solidarity in rebel behavior and fails to notice its Other, namely, betrayal. Committed inflexibly to the notion of insurgency as a generalized movement, he underestimates the power of the brakes put on it by localism and territoriality. Convinced that mobilization for a rural uprising flows exclusively from an overall elite authority, he tends to disregard the operation of many other authorities within the primordial relations of a rural community. A prisoner of empty abstractions, tertiary discourse, even of the radical kind, has thus distanced itself from the prose of counter-insurgency only by a declaration of sentiment so far. It has still to go a long way before it can prove that the insurgent can rely on its performance to recover his place in history.

APPENDIX

Extract 1

I came to plunder . . . Sidoo and Kaloo [Kanhu] declared themselves Rajas &
[said] they would plunder the whole country and take possession of it—they
said also, no one can stop us for it is the order of the Takoor. On this account
we have all come with them.

Source: *JP*, 19 July 1855: Balai Majhi's Statement (14 July 1855).

Extract 2

The Thacoor has descended in the house of Seedoo Manjee, Kanoo Manjee,
Bhyrub and Chand, at Bhugnudihee in Pergunnah Kunjeala. The Thakoor in
person is conversing with them, he has descended from Heaven, he is conversing with Kanoor and Seedoo, The Sahibs and the white Soldiers will
fight. Kanoo and Seedoo Manjee are not fighting. The Thacoor himself will
fight. Therefore you Sahibs and Soldiers fight with the Thacoor himself
Mother Ganges will come to the Thacoor's (assistance) Fire will rain from
Heaven. If you are satisfied with the Thacoor then you must go to the other
side of the Ganges. The Thacoor has ordered the Sonthals that for a bulluck
plough 1 anna is to be paid for revenue. Buffalo plough 2 annas The reign of
Truth has begun True justice will be administered He who does not speak the
truth will not be allowed to remain on the Earth. The Mahajuns have committed a great sin The Sahibs and the amlah have made everything bad, in this
the Sahibs have sinned greatly.

Those who tell things to the Magistrate and those who investigate cases for
him, take 70 or 80 R.s. with great oppression in this the Sahibs have sinned.
On this account the Thacoor has ordered me saying that the country is not the
Sahibs. . . .

P.S. If you Sahibs agree, then you must remain on the other side of the
Ganges, and if you dont agree you cant remain on that side of the river, I will
rain fire and all the Sahibs will be killed by the hand of God in person and
Sahibs if you fight with muskets the Sonthal will not be hit by the bullets and
the Thacoor will give your Elephants and horses of his own accord to the
Sonthals . . . if you fight with the Sonthals two days will be as one day and
two nights as one night. This is the order of the Thacoor.

Source: *JP*, 4 October 1855: "The Thacoor's Perwannah" ("dated 10 Saon
1262").

Extract 3

Then the Manjees & Purgunnaits assembled in my Verandah, & we consulted
for 2 months, "that Pontet & Mohesh Dutt don't listen to our complaints & no

one acts as our Father & Mother" then a God descended from heaven in the form of a cartwheel & said to me "Kill Pontet & the Darogah & the Mahajuns & then you will have justice & a Father & Mother"; then the Thacoor went back to the heavens; after this 2 men like Bengallees came into my Verhandah; they each had six fingers half a piece of paper fell on my head before the Thacoor came & half fell afterwards. I could not read but Chand & Seheree & a Dhome read it, they said "The Thacoor has written to you to fight the Mahajens & then you will have justice." . . .

Source: *JP*, 8 November 1855: "Examination of Sedoo Sonthal late Thacoor."

Extract 4

In Bysack the God descended in my house I sent a perwannah to the Burra Sahib at Calcutta. . . . I wrote that the Thacoor had come to my house & was conversing with me & had told all the Sonthals that they were to be under the charge of me & that I was to pay all the revenue to Government & was to oppress no one & the zamindars & Mahajans were committing great oppression taking 20 pice for one & that I was to place them at a distance from the sonthals & if they do not go away to fight with them.

Ishwar was a white man with only a dootee & chudder he sat on the ground like a Sahib he wrote on this bit of paper. He gave me 4 papers but afterwards presented 16 more. The thacoor had 5 fingers on each hand. I did not see him in the day I saw him only in the night. The sonthals then assembled at my house to see the thacoor.

[At Maheshpur] the troops came & we had a fight . . . afterwards seeing that men on our side were falling we both turned twice on them & once drove them away, then I made poojah . . . & then a great many balls came & Seedoo & I were both wounded. The thacoor had said "water will come out of the muskets" but my troops committed some crime therefore the thacoors prediction[s] were not fulfilled about 80 sonthals were killed.

All the blank papers fell from heaven & the book in which all the pages are blank also fell from heaven.

Source: *JP*, 20 December 1855: "Examination of Kanoo Sonthal."

NOTES

First appeared in 1983.
Abbreviations used in the footnotes:
BC Board's Collections, India Office Records (London)
JC Fort William Judicial Consultations in *BC*
JP Judicial Proceedings, West Bengal State Archives (Calcutta)
MDS *Maharaja Derby Sinha* (Nashipur Raj Estate, 1914)

1. The instances are far too numerous to cite. For some of these see *MDS*, pp. 46–7, 48–9 on the Rangpur *dhing*; *BC* 54222: Metcalfe & Blunt to Court Directors (10 April 1832), paras. 14–15 on the Barasat uprising; W. W. Hunter, *Annals of Rural Bengal* (7th edition; London, 1897), pp. 237–8, and *JP*, 4 Oct. 1855: "The Thacoor's Perwannah" for the Santal *hool* C. E. Buckland, *Bengal under the Lieutenant-Governors*, vol. I (Calcutta, 1901), p. 192 for the "blue mutiny."

2. See, for instance, *MDS*, pp. 579–80; *Freedom Struggle in Uttar Pradesh*, vol. IV (Lucknow, 1959), pp. 284–5, 549.

3. J. C. Price, *The Chuar Rebellion of 1799*, p. cl. The edition of the work used in this essay is the one printed in A. Mitra (ed.), *District Handbooks: Midnapur* (Alipore, 1953), Appendix IV.

4. *BC* 54222: *JC*, 22 Nov. 1831: "Extract from the Proceedings of the Honorable the Vice President in Council in the Military Department under date the 10th November 1831." Emphasis added.

5. *JP*, 19 July 1855: Enclosure to letter from the Magistrate of Murshidabad, dated 11 July 1855. Emphasis added.

6. Thus, *BC* 54222: *JC*, 3 Apr. 1832: Alexander to Barwell (28 Nov. 1831).

7. My debt to Roland Barthes for many of the analytic terms and procedures used in this section and generally throughout this essay should be far too obvious to all familiar with his "Structural Analysis of Narratives" and "The Struggle with the Angel" in Barthes, *Image-Music-Text* (Glasgow, 1977), pp. 79–141, and "Historical Discourse" in M. Lane (ed.), *Structuralism, A Reader* (London, 1970), pp. 145–55, to require detailed reference except where I quote directly from this literature.

8. Barthes, *Images-Music-Text*, p. 102.

9. Émile Benveniste, *Problèmes de linguistique générale, I* (Paris, 1966), p. 126. The original, "la dissociation nous livre la constitution formelle; l'intégration nous livre des unités signifiantes," has been rendered somewhat differently and I feel, less happily, in the English translation of the work, *Problems in General Linguistics* (Florida, 1971), p. 107.

10. Barthes, *Image-Music-Text*, p. 93.

11. Charles Bally, *Linguistique Générale et Linguistique Française* (Berne, 1965), p. 144.

12. Barthes, *Elements of Semiology* (London, 1967), p. 60.

13. Barthes, *Image-Music-Text*, p. 128.

14. Ibid, p. 119.

15. *Selected Works of Mao Tse-Tung*, vol. I (Peking, 1967), pp. 26–7.

16. Benveniste, [*Problèmes*], p. 239.

17. [Mark Thornhill], *Freedom Struggle in Uttar Pradesh*, vol. V, pp. 685–92.

18. For Roman Jakobson's exposition of this key concept, see his *Selected Writings, 2: Word and Language* (The Hague and Paris, 1871), pp. 130–47. Barthes develops the notion of organization shifters in his essay "Historical Discourse," pp. 146–8. All extracts quoted in this paragraph are taken from that essay unless otherwise mentioned.

19. Price, [*Chuar Rebellion*], p. clx.

20. Ibid.

21. Reginald G. Wilberforce, *An Unrecorded Chapter of the Indian Mutiny* (2nd edition; London, 1894), pp. 76–7.

22. It appears from a note in this work that parts of it were written in 1866. The

dedication bears the date 4 March 1868. All our references to this work in quotation or otherwise are to Chapter IV of the seventh edition (London, 1897) unless otherwise stated.

23. Barthes, *Image-Music-Text*, p. 112.

24. Anon., "The Sonthal Rebellion," *Calcutta Review* (1856), pp. 223–64; K. K. Datta, "The Santal Insurrection of 1855–57," in *Anti-British Plots and Movements before 1857* (Meerut, 1970), pp. 43–152.

25. [Suprakash Ray, *Bharater Krishak-bidroha O Ganatantrik Samgram*], Vol. I (Calcutta, 1966), Ch. 13.

26. For these see ibid., pp. 323, 325, 327, 328.

27. Ibid., p. 337; Hunter, [*Annals*], pp. 247–9.

28. Ray, [*Bharater Krishak-bidroha*], pp. 316–19.

29. Anon., [*Sonthal Rebellion*], pp. 238–41; Thornhill, [*Freedom Struggle*], pp. 33–5; L. S. S. O'Malley, *Bengal District Gazetteers: Pabna* (Calcutta, 1923), p. 25; *Report of the Commission Appointed in India to Inquire into the Causes of the Riots Which Took Place in the Year 1875 in the Poona and Ahmednagar Districts of the Bombay Presidency* (London, 1878), *passim*.

30. *BC* 54222; *JC*, 22 Nov. 1831 (no. 91). Emphasis added.

31. Anon., [*Sonthal Rebellion*], pp. 263–4.

32. Ibid., p. 263.

33. Ray, [*Bharater Krishak-bidroha*], p. 318.

34. Ibid., p. 340.

35. L. Natarajan, *Peasant Uprisings in India, 1850–1900* (Bombay, 1853), pp. 31–2.

36. Abdulla Rasul, *Saontal Bidroher Amar Kahini* (Calcutta, 1954), p. 24.

37. The instances are far too numerous to cite in an essay of this size, but for some samples see *Mare Hapram Ko Reak Katha*, Ch. 79, in A. Mitra (ed.), *District Handbooks: Bankura* (Calcutta, 1953).

38. Appendix: Extract 2.

39. *JP*, 8 Nov. 1855: Ward to Government of Bengal (13 Oct. 1855). Emphasis added.

40. Anon., [*Sonthal Rebellion*], p. 243. Emphasis added.

41. Ibid., p. 246. Emphasis added.

42. Ibid., pp. 243–4. Ray, [*Bharater Krishak-bidroha*], pp. 321–2.

43. This is generally accepted. See, for instance, Sherwill's observation about the truth being "sacred" to the Santals, "offering in this respect a bright example to their lying neighbours, the Bengalis." *Geographical and Statistical Report of the District Bhaugulpoor* (Calcutta, 1854), p. 32.

44. Ray, [*Bharater Krishak-bidroha*], p. 321. Emphasis added.

45. Ray, *Bharater Baiplabik Samgramer Itihas*, vol. II (Calcutta, 1970), p. 95. Emphasis added. The sentence italicized by us in the quoted passage reads as follows in the Bengali original: "*Eijanyo prayojan hoiley jatir svarthey mithyar asroy grahan karitey hoibey.*"

46. Dhirendranath Baskay, *Saontal Ganasamgramer Itihas* (Calcutta, 1976), p. 66.

47. Jogesh Chandra Bagal (ed.), *Peasant Revolution in Bengal* (Calcutta, 1853), p. 5.

48. Sunil Sen, *Agrarian Struggle in Bengal, 1946–47* (New Delhi, 1972), p. 49.

GLOSSARY

adivasi — Autochthonous population; member of a scheduled tribe.

amla — Landlord's managerial staff.

arkati — A recruiter of labor for plantations, roadworks, railways, etc.

bakasht — Land originally cultivated by tenants but "resumed" by landlords on the ground of non-payment of rent and let out again usually though not always to share-croppers;—*malik*: lit. under the owner's cultivation.

baksheesh, bakshish — Gratuity; tip.

bandh — Mud bank built for flood control.

bataidar — Sharecropper.

batta — Commission.

begar — Forced labor.

benami — Land fraudulently held under a fictious name.

bhoodan — Lit. gift of land; name of a movement initiated by Vinoba Bhave in the wake of the Telengana peasant uprising to persuade landlords to part voluntarily with one-sixth of their estates for distribution among the landless villagers.

bidroha — Uprising; rebellion.

chaukidar, chowkidar — Village watchman; locally appointed member of auxiliary police force.

cutcherry — Landlord's estate office.

daroga — Sub-inspector of police.

dhing — Word for disturbance, uprising, etc. in a dialect of northern Bengal.

diara — Alluvial land gained by recession of a river.

diku — Foreigner; outsider.

diwan — Manager of a landlord's estate.

gramdan — Gift made of an entire village as part of the land distribution movement inspired by Vinoba Bhave's "sarvodaya" doctrine.

hool — Uprising, disturbance. Used often to describe the Santal insurrection of 1855.

inqalab zindabad — "Long live revolution": words often chanted in the course of militant demonstrations.

jila — District.

kari — Archer.

karori — Revenue collector.

katcha seer — Unit of weight amounting approximately to 900 grams.

khadi — Fabric made of hand-spun yarn and used mostly for wear as a sign of commitment to the nationalist cause.

kisan — Cultivator; farmer; peasant; agricultural worker.

kotha — Small plot of land given to an attached or bonded laborer in lieu of cash wages.

kutcherry — See *cutcherry*.

larai — Fight; struggle.

ma-baap — Lit. mother and father. A term often used to represent the relation between the peasants and superordinate elite authorities as one between children and parents.

makai khet — Maize field.

mansab — A rank in the bureaucracy of the Mughal State.

mustajir — A revenue-farmer in Mughal India.

padyatra — Ritual walk for a cause practiced on a large scale during the *bhoodan* (q.v.) movement.

paik — Foot-soldier.

prakhand — Community Development Block.

rabi — Winter crop such as wheat, gram, etc. in Bihar.

raiyat, ryot — Tenant cultivator.

sadar — Small town serving as the headquarters of district administration in colonial India.

sardar — Chief; leader.

salami — Commission.

thana — Police station: its jurisdiction; the building where it is located.

thanadar — A local military commander in Mughal India.

tola — Hamlet.

vāgarthāviva samprktau — Lit. "blended like word and meaning." A phrase used by Kalidasa in *Raghuvamsam*.

waqai-navis — News reporter.

Theory in Anthropology since the Sixties

SHERRY B. ORTNER

EVERY YEAR, around the time of the meetings of the American Anthropological Association, the *New York Times* asks a Big Name anthropologist to contribute an op-ed piece on the state of the field. These pieces tend to take a rather gloomy view. A few years ago, for example, Marvin Harris suggested that anthropology was being taken over by mystics, religious fanatics, and California cultists; that the meetings were dominated by panels on shamanism, witchcraft, and "abnormal phenomena"; and that "scientific papers based on empirical studies" had been willfully excluded from the program (Harris 1978). More recently, in a more sober tone, Eric Wolf suggested that the field of anthropology is coming apart. The sub-fields (and sub-sub-fields) are increasingly pursuing their specialized interests, losing contact with each other and with the whole. There is no longer a shared discourse, a shared set of terms to which all practitioners address themselves, a shared language we all, however idiosyncratically, speak (Wolf 1980).

The state of affairs does seem much as Wolf describes it. The field appears to be a thing of shreds and patches, of individuals and small coteries pursuing disjunctive investigations and talking mainly to themselves. We do not even hear stirring arguments any more. Although anthropology was never actually unified in the sense of adopting a single shared paradigm, there was at least a period when there were a few large categories of theoretical affiliation, a set of identifiable camps or schools, and a few simple epithets one could hurl at one's opponents. Now there appears to be an apathy of spirit even at this level. We no longer call each other names. We are no longer sure of how the sides are to be drawn up, and of where we would place ourselves if we could identify the sides.

Yet as anthropologists we can recognize in all of this the classic symptoms of liminality—confusion of categories, expressions of chaos and antistructure. And we know that such disorder may be the breeding ground for a new and perhaps better order. Indeed, if one scrutinizes the present more closely, one may even discern within it the shape of the new order to come. That is what I propose to do in this article. I will argue that a new key symbol of theoretical orientation is emerging, which may be labeled "practice" (or "action" or "praxis"). This is neither a theory nor a method in itself, but rather, as I said, a symbol, in the name of which a variety of theories and methods are being developed. In order to understand the significance of this trend, however, we must go back at least twenty years and see where we started from, and how we got to where we are now.

Before launching this enterprise it is important to specify its nature. This essay will be primarily concerned with the *relations* between various theoretical schools or approaches, both within periods of time, and across time. No single approach will be exhaustively outlined or discussed in itself; rather, various themes or dimensions of each will be highlighted insofar as they relate to the larger trends of thought with which I am concerned. Every anthropologist will probably find his or her favorite school oversimplified, if not outright distorted, insofar as I have chosen to emphasize features that do not correspond to what are normally taken, among the practitioners, to be its most important theoretical features. Thus readers seeking more exhaustive discussions of particular approaches, and/or discussions pursued from a point of view more interior to the approaches, will have to seek elsewhere. The concern here, again, is with elucidating relations.

THE SIXTIES: SYMBOL, NATURE, STRUCTURE

Although there is always some arbitrariness in choosing a starting point for any historical discussion, I have decided to begin in the early 1960s. For one thing, that is when *I* started in the field, and since I generally assume the importance of seeing any system, at least in part, from the actor's point of view, I might as well unite theory and practice from the outset. It is thus fully acknowledged that this discussion proceeds not from some hypothetical external point, but from the perspective of this particular actor moving through anthropology between 1960 and the present.

But actors always wish to claim universality for their particular experiences and interpretations. I would further suggest then that, in some relatively objective sense, there was in fact a major set of revolutions in anthropological theory, beginning in the early sixties. Indeed it appears that such revisionist upheaval was characteristic of many other fields in that era. In literary criticism, for example,

> by the 1960's a volatile mixture of linguistics, psychoanalysis and semiotics, structuralism, Marxist theory and reception aesthetics had begun to replace the older moral humanism. The literary text tended to move towards the status of phenomenon: a socio-psycho-culturo-linguistic and ideological event, arising from the offered competencies of language, the available taxonomies of narrative order, the permutations of genre, the sociological options of structural formation, the ideological constraints of the infra-structure.... [There was a] broad and contentious revisionist perception. (Bradbury 1981:137)

In anthropology at the close of the fifties, the theoretical *bricoleur*'s kit consisted of three major, and somewhat exhausted, paradigms—British structural-functionalism (descended from A. R. Radcliffe-Brown and Bronislaw

Malinowski), American cultural and psychocultural anthropology (descended from Margaret Mead, Ruth Benedict, et al.), and American evolutionist anthropology (centered around Leslie White and Julian Steward, and having strong affiliations with archaeology). Yet it was also during the fifties that certain actors and cohorts central to our story were trained in each of these areas. They emerged at the beginning of the sixties with aggressive ideas about how to strengthen the paradigms of their mentors and ancestors, as well as with, apparently, much more combative stances vis-à-vis the other schools. It was this combination of new ideas and intellectual aggressiveness that launched the three movements with which this account begins: symbolic anthropology, cultural ecology, and structuralism.

Symbolic Anthropology

"Symbolic anthropology" as a label was never used by any of its main proponents in the formative period—say, 1963–66. Rather it was a shorthand tag (probably invented by the opposition), an umbrella for a number of rather diverse trends. Two of its major variants appear to have been independently invented, one by Clifford Geertz and his colleagues at the University of Chicago, and the other by Victor Turner at Cornell.[1] The important differences between the Geertzians and the Turnerians are probably not fully appreciated by those outside the symbolic anthropology scene. Whereas Geertz was primarily influenced by Max Weber (via Talcott Parsons), Turner was primarily influenced by Emile Durkheim. Further, Geertz clearly represents a transformation upon the earlier American anthropology concerned mainly with the operations of "culture," while Turner represents a transformation upon the earlier British anthropology concerned mainly with the operations of "society."

Geertz's most radical theoretical move (1973b) was to argue that culture is not something locked inside people's heads, but rather is embodied in public symbols, symbols through which the members of a society communicate their worldview, value-orientations, ethos, and all the rest to one another, to future generations—and to anthropologists. With this formulation, Geertz gave the hitherto elusive concept of culture a relatively fixed locus, and a degree of objectivity, that it did not have before. The focus on symbols was for Geertz and many others heuristically liberating: it told them where to find what they wanted to study. Yet the point about symbols was that they were ultimately vehicles for meanings; the study of symbols as such was never an end in itself. Thus, on the one hand, Geertzians[2] have never been particularly interested in distinguishing and cataloguing the varieties of symbolic types (signals, signs, icons, indexes, et cetera—see, in contrast, Singer 1980); nor, on the other hand (and in contrast with Turner to whom we will get in a moment), have they been particularly interested in the ways in which symbols perform certain practical operations in the social process—heal people through curing rites, turn boys and girls into men and women through initiation, kill people through sorcery—and so forth. Geertzians do not ignore these practical social effects, but such operations have not been their primary focus of interest. Rather, the focus of Geertzian anthropology has consistently been the question of how symbols shape the ways social actors see, feel, and think about the world, or, in other words, how symbols operate as vehicles of "culture."

It is further worth noting, in anticipation of the discussion of structuralism, that Geertz's heart has always been more with the "ethos" side of culture than with the "worldview," more with the affective and stylistic dimensions than with the cognitive. While of course it is very difficult (not to say unproductive and ultimately wrong-headed) to separate the two too sharply, it is nonetheless possible to distinguish an emphasis on one or the other side. For Geertz, then (as for Benedict, especially, before him), even the most cognitive or intellectual of cultural systems—say, the Balinese calendars—are analyzed not (only) to lay bare a set of cognitive ordering principles, but (especially) to understand how the Balinese way of chopping up time stamps their sense of self, of social relations, and of conduct with a particular culturally distinctive flavor, an ethos (1973e).[3]

The other major contribution of the Geertzian framework was the insistence on studying culture "from the actor's point of view" (e.g., 1975). Again, this does not imply that we must get "into people's heads." What it means, very simply, is that culture is a product of acting social beings trying to make sense of the world in which they find themselves, and if *we* are to make sense of a culture, we must situate ourselves in the position from which it was constructed. Culture is not some abstractly ordered system, deriving its logic from hidden structural principles, or from special symbols that provide the "keys" to its coherence. Its logic—the principles of relations that obtain among its elements—derives rather from the logic or organization of action, from people operating within certain institutional orders, interpreting their situations in order to act coherently within them (1973d). It may be noted here, however, that while the actor-centered perspective is fundamental to Geertz's framework, it is not systematically elaborated: Geertz did not develop a theory of action or practice as such. He did, however, firmly plant the actor at the center of his model, and much of the later practice-centered work builds on a Geertzian (or Geertzo-Weberian) base, as we shall see.

The other major figure in the Chicago school of symbolic anthropology has been David Schneider. Schneider, like Geertz, was a product of Parsons, and he, too, concentrated primarily on refining the culture concept. But his efforts went toward understanding the *internal logic* of systems of symbols and meanings, by way of a notion of "core symbols," and also by way of ideas akin to Claude Lévi-Strauss's concept of structure (e.g., 1968, 1977). Indeed, although Geertz prominently used the phrase "cultural *system*" (emphasis added), he never paid much attention to the systemic aspects of culture, and it was Schneider who developed this side of the problem much more fully. Schneider in his own work cut culture off from social action much more radically than Geertz did. Yet, perhaps precisely because social action ("practice," "praxis") was so radically separated from "culture" in Schneider's work, he and some of his students were among the earliest of the symbolic anthropologists to see practice itself as a problem (Barnett 1977; Dolgin, Kemnitzer, and Schneider 1977).

Victor Turner, finally, comes out of quite a different intellectual background. He was trained in the Max Gluckman variant of British structural-functionalism, which was influenced by Marxism, and which stressed that the normal state of society is not one of solidarity and harmonious integration of parts, but rather one of conflict and contradiction. Thus, the analytic question was not, as for the straight line descendants of Durkheim, how solidarity is fine-tuned, reinforced, and intensified, but rather how it is constructed and maintained in the first place over and above the conflicts and contradictions that constitute the normal state of affairs. To the American reader, this may appear to be only a minor variant on the basic functionalist project, since for both schools the emphasis is on the maintenance of integration, and specifically on the maintenance of the integration of "society" —actors, groups, the social whole—as opposed to "culture." But Gluckman and his students (including Turner) believed their differences from the mainstream to be quite deep. Moreover, they always constituted a minority within the British establishment. This background may account in part for Turner's originality vis-à-vis his compatriots, leading ultimately to his independently inventing his own brand of an explicitly symbolic anthropology.

Despite the relative novelty of Turner's move to symbols, however, there is in his work a deep continuity with British social anthropological concerns, and, as a result, profound differences between Turnerian and Geertzian symbolic anthropology. For Turner, symbols are of interest not as vehicles of, and analytic windows onto, "culture"—the integrated ethos and worldview of a society—but as what might be called operators in the social process, things that, when put together in certain arrangements in certain contexts (especially rituals), produce essentially social transformations. Thus, symbols in Ndembu curing or initiation or hunting rituals are investigated for the ways in which they move actors from one status to another, resolve social contradictions, and wed actors to the categories and norms of their society (1967). Along the way toward these rather traditional structural-functional goals, however, Turner identified or elaborated upon certain ritual mechanisms, and some of the concepts he developed have become indispensable parts of the vocabulary of ritual analysis—liminality, marginality, antistructure, communitas, and so forth (1967, 1969).[4]

Turner and the Chicago symbolic anthropologists did not so much conflict with one another as simply, for the most part, talk past one another. Yet the Turnerians[5] added an important, and characteristically British, dimension to the field of symbolic anthropology as a whole, a sense of the *pragmatics* of symbols. They investigated in much more detail than Geertz, Schneider, et al., the "effectiveness of symbols," the question of how symbols actually do what all symbolic anthropologists claim they do: operate as active forces in the social process (see also Lévi-Strauss 1963; Tambiah 1968; Lewis 1977; Fernandez 1974).

In retrospect, one may say that symbolic anthropology had a number of significant limitations. I refer not to the charges that it was unscientific, mystical, literary, soft-headed, and the like leveled at it by practitioners of cultural ecology (see below). Rather, one may point to symbolic anthropology's lack, especially in its American form, of a systematic sociology; its underdeveloped sense of the politics of culture; and its lack of curiosity concerning the production and maintenance of symbolic systems. These points will be discussed more fully in the course of this article.

Cultural Ecology[6]

Cultural ecology represented a new synthesis of, and a further development upon, the materialist evolutionism of Leslie White (1943, 1949), Julian Steward (1953, 1955), and V. Gordon Childe (1942). Its roots go back to Lewis Henry Morgan and E. B. Tylor in the nineteenth century, and ultimately back to Marx and Engels, although many of the 1950s evolutionists, for understandable political reasons, were not encouraged to emphasize the Marxist connection.[7]

White had been investigating what came to be labeled "general evolution," or the evolution of culture-in-general, in terms of stages of social complexity and technological advancement. These stages were subsequently refined by Elman Service (1958), and by Marshall Sahlins and Elman Service (1960), into the famous bands-tribes-chiefdoms-states scheme. The evolutionary mechanisms in White's framework derived from more or less fortuitous events: technological inventions that allowed for the greater "capture of energy," and population growth (and perhaps warfare and conquest) that stimulated the development of more complex forms of social/political organization and coordination. Steward (1953) attacked both the focus on the evolution of culture-in-general (as opposed to specific cultures), and the lack of a more systematically operative evolutionary mechanism. Instead, he emphasized that specific cultures evolve their specific forms in the process of adapting to specific environmental conditions, and that the apparent uniformity of evolutionary stages is actually a matter of similar adaptations to similar natural conditions in different parts of the world.

If the idea that culture was embodied in public, observable symbols was the key to the liberation of symbolic anthropology from earlier American cultural anthropology, the concept that played a similar role in cultural ecology was "adaptation." (See Alland 1975 for a summary.) Just as Geertz had trumpeted that the study of culture as embodied in symbols removed the problem of getting inside people's heads, so Sahlins proclaimed the focus on adaptation to environmental factors as the way around such amorphous factors as cultural *gestalten* and historical dialectics (1964). There was a large-scale rejection of the study of the inner workings of both culture in the American sense and society in the British sense. Internal dynamics were seen as hard to measure, and even harder to choose among for purposes of assigning causal primacy, whereas external factors of natural and social environment were amenable to treatment as fixed, measurable, "independent variables:"

> For decades, centuries now, intellectual battle has been given over which sector of culture is the decisive one for change. Many have entered the lists under banners diverse. Curiously, few seem to fall. Leslie White champions technological growth as the sector most responsible for cultural evolution; Julian Huxley, with many others, sees "man's view of destiny" as the deciding force; the mode of production and the class struggle are still very much in contention. Different as they are, these positions agree in one respect, that the impulse to development is generated from within. . . . The case for internal causes of development may be bolstered by pointing to a mechanism, such as the Hegelian dialectic, or it may rest more insecurely on an argument from logic. . . . In any event, an unreal and vulnerable assumption is always there, that cultures are closed systems. . . . It is precisely on this point that cultural ecology offers a new perspective. . . . [I]t shifts attention to the relation between inside and outside; it envisions as the mainspring of the evolutionary movement the interchange between culture and environment. Now which view shall prevail is not to be decided on a sheet of paper. . . . But if adaptation wins over inner dynamism, it will be for certain intrinsic and obvious strengths. Adaptation is real, naturalistic, anchored to those historic contexts of cultures that inner dynamism ignores. (Sahlins 1964:135– 136)[8]

The Sahlins and Service version of cultural ecology, which was also adhered to by the mainstream of the archaeology wing of anthropology, was still fundamentally evolutionist. The primary use of the adaptation concept was in explaining the development, maintenance, and transformation of social forms. But there was another variant of cultural ecology, which developed slightly later, and which came to dominate the materialist wing in the sixties. Its position, expressed most forcefully by Marvin Harris (e.g., 1966) and perhaps most elegantly by Roy Rappaport (1967), drew heavily on systems theory. It shifted the analytic focus away from evolution, and toward explaining the existence of particular bits of particular cultures in terms of the adaptive or system-maintaining functions of those bits. Thus, the Maring *kaiko* ritual prevented the degradation of the natural environment (Rappaport 1967), the Kwakiutl potlatch maintained a balance of food distribution over tribal segments (Piddocke 1969), and the sacredness of the cow in India protected a vital link in the agricultural food chain (Harris 1966). In these studies, the interest has shifted from how the environment stimulates (or prevents) the development of social and cultural forms, to the question of the ways in which social and cultural forms function to maintain an existing relationship with the environment. It was these latter sorts of studies that came to represent cultural ecology as a whole in the sixties.

One would have had to be particularly out of touch with anthropological theory at the time not to have been aware of the acrimonious debate between the cultural ecologists and the symbolic anthropologists. Whereas the cultural ecologists considered the symbolic anthropologists to be fuzzy-headed mentalists, involved in unscientific and unverifiable flights of subjective interpretation, the symbolic anthropologists considered cultural ecology to be involved with mindless and sterile scientism, counting calories and measuring rainfall, and willfully ignoring the one truth that anthropology had presumably established by that time: that culture mediates all human behavior. The Manichaean struggle between "materialism" and "idealism," "hard" and "soft" approaches, interpretive "emics" and explanatory "etics," dominated the field for a good part of the decade of the sixties, and in some quarters well into the seventies.

That most of us thought and wrote in terms of such oppositions may be partly rooted in more pervasive schemes of Western thought: subjective/objective, nature/culture, mind/body, and so on. The practice of fieldwork itself may further contribute to such thinking, based as it is on the paradoxical injunction to participate and observe at one and the same time. It may be then that this sort of polarized construction of the intellectual landscape in anthropology is too deeply motivated, by both cultural categories and the forms of practice of the trade, to be completely eliminated. But the emic/etic struggle of the sixties had a number of unfortunate effects, not the least of which was the prevention of adequate self-criticism on both sides of the fence. Both schools could luxuriate in the faults of the other, and not inspect their own houses for serious weaknesses. In fact, both sides were weak not only in being unable to handle what the other side did (the symbolic anthropologists in renouncing all claims to "explanation," the cultural ecologists in losing sight of the frames of meaning within which human action takes place); both were also weak in what neither of them did, which was much of any systematic sociology.[9]

Indeed, from the point of view of British social anthropology, the whole American struggle was quite meaningless, since it seemed to leave out the necessary central term of all proper anthropological discussion: society. Where were the social groups, social relationships, social structures, social institutions, that mediate *both* the ways in which people think ("culture") *and* the ways in which people experience and act upon their environment? But this set of questions could not be answered (had anybody bothered to ask them) in terms of British social anthropological categories, because the British were having their own intellectual upheavals, to which we will return in due course.

Structuralism

Structuralism, the more-or-less single-handed invention of Claude Lévi-Strauss, was the only genuinely new paradigm to be developed in the sixties. One might even say that it is the only genuinely original social science paradigm (and humanities [paradigm,] too, for that matter) to be developed in the twentieth century. Drawing on linguistics and communication theory, and considering himself influenced by both Marx and Freud, Lévi-Strauss argued that the seemingly bewildering variety of social and cultural phenomena could be rendered intelligible by demonstrating the shared relationships of those phenomena to a few simple underlying principles. He sought to establish the universal grammar of culture, the ways in which units of cultural discourse are created (by the principle of binary opposition), and the rules according to which the units (pairs of opposed terms) are arranged and combined to produce the actual cultural productions (myths, marriage rules, totemic clan arrangements, and the like) that anthropologists record. Cultures are primarily systems of classification, as well as the sets of institutional and intellectual productions built upon those systems of classification and performing further operations upon them. One of the most important secondary operations of culture in relation to its own taxonomies is precisely to mediate or reconcile the oppositions which are the bases of those taxonomies in the first place.

In practice, structural analysis consists of sifting out the basic sets of oppositions that underlie some complex cultural phenomenon—a myth, a ritual, a marriage system—and of showing the ways in which the phenomenon in question is both an expression of those contrasts and a reworking of them, thereby producing a culturally meaningful statement of, or reflection upon, order. Even without the full analysis of a myth or ritual, however, the sheer enumeration of the important sets of oppositions in a culture is taken to be a useful enterprise because it reveals the axes of thought, and the limits of the thinkable, within that and related cultures (e.g., Needham 1973b). But the fullest demonstration of the power of structural analysis is seen in Lévi-Strauss's four-volume study, *Mythologiques* (1964–71). Here the method allows the ordering of data both on a vast scale (including most of indigenous South America, and parts of native North America as well), and also in terms of explicating myriad tiny details—why the jaguar covers his mouth when he laughs, or why honey metaphors are used to describe the escape of game animals. The combination of wide scope and minute detail is what lends the work its great power.

Much has been made of the point that Lévi-Strauss ultimately grounds the structures he discerns beneath society and culture in the structure of the mind. Both the point itself, and the criticism of it, are perhaps somewhat irrelevant for anthropologists. It seems incontrovertible that all humans, and all cultures, classify. This suggests in turn an innate mental propensity of some sort, but it does not mean that any particular scheme of classification is inevitable, [any] more than the fact that all humans eat motivates some universal system of food categories.

The enduring contribution of Lévi-Straussian structuralism lies in the perception that luxuriant variety, even apparent randomness, may have a deeper unity and systematicity, derived from the operation of a small number of underlying principles. It is in this sense that Lévi-Strauss claims affinity with

Marx and Freud, who similarly argue that beneath the surface proliferation of forms, a few relatively simple and relatively uniform mechanisms are operating (DeGeorge and DeGeorge 1972). Such a perception, in turn, allows us to distinguish much more clearly between simple transformations, which operate within a given structure, and real change, revolution if you will, in which the structure itself is transformed. Thus, despite the naturalistic or biologistic base of structuralism, and despite Lévi-Strauss's personal predilection for considering that *plus ça change, plus c'est la même chose*, the theory has always had important implications for a much more historical and/or evolutionary anthropology than that practiced by the master. The work of Louis Dumont in particular has developed some of these evolutionary implications in analyzing the structure of the Indian caste system, and in articulating some of the profound structural changes involved in the transition from caste to class (1965, 1970; see also Goldman 1970, Barnett 1977, Sahlins 1981).[10]

Structuralism was never all that popular among American anthropologists. Although it was seen at first (mostly by the cultural ecologists) as a variant of symbolic anthropology, its central assumptions were in fact rather distant from those of the symbolic anthropologists (with the partial exception of the Schneiderians). There were a number of reasons for this, which can be only very briefly sketched: (1) the very pure cognitive emphasis of Lévi-Strauss's notion of meaning, as against the Americans' interest in ethos and values; (2) Lévi-Strauss's rather austere emphasis on arbitrariness of meaning (all meaning is established by contrasts, nothing carries any meaning in itself), as against the Americans' interest in relations between the *forms* of symbolic constructs and the *contents* for which they are vehicles;[11] and (3) the explicitly abstract locus of structures, divorced in every way from the actions and intentions of actors, as against the symbolic anthropologists' fairly consistent, if variably defined, actor-centrism (again, Schneider is a partial exception to this point). For all these reasons, and probably more, structuralism was not as much embraced by American symbolic anthropologists as might have appeared likely at first glance.[12] It was granted what might be called fictive kinship status, largely because of its tendency to focus on some of the same domains that symbolic anthropologists took as their own—myth, ritual, etiquette, and so forth.

The main impact of structuralism outside of France was in England, among some of the more adventurous British social anthropologists (see especially Leach 1966). Lévi-Strauss and the British were in fact more truly kin to one another, born of two lines of descent from Durkheim. In any event, structuralism in the British context underwent a number of important transformations. Avoiding the question of mind, and of universal structures, British anthropologists primarily applied structural analysis to particular societies and particular cosmologies (e.g., Leach 1966, 1969; Needham 1973a; Yalman 1969; the point also applies to Dumont [1970] in France). They also focused in more detail on the process of mediation of oppositions, and produced a number of quite original ruminations upon anomaly and antistructure, especially Mary

Douglas's *Purity and Danger* (see also Turner 1967, 1969; Leach 1964; Tambiah 1969).

However, there was also an important way in which many of the British purged structuralism of one of its more radical features—the eradication of the Durkheimian distinction between the social "base" and the cultural "reflection" of it. Lévi-Strauss had claimed that if mythic structures paralleled social structures, it was not because myth reflected society, but because both myth and social organization shared a common underlying structure. Many of the British structuralists (Rodney Needham is the major exception), on the other hand, went back to a position more in the tradition of Durkheim and Marcel Mauss, and considered myth and ritual as reflecting and resolving "at the symbolic level" oppositions taken to be fundamentally social.[13] As long as British structuralism was confined to the study of myth and ritual, then, it was possible for it to fit nicely into British anthropology without having a very profound effect upon it. It became their version of cultural or symbolic anthropology, their theory of superstructure. It was only later, when a structural (i.e., structural-Marxist) eye was turned on the British concept of social structure itself, that the sparks began to fly.

In a number of fields—linguistics, philosophy, history—there was a strong reaction against structuralism by the early seventies. Two interrelated features—the denial of the relevance of an intentional subject in the social and cultural process, and the denial of any significant impact of history or "event" upon structure—were felt to be particularly problematic, not to say unacceptable. Scholars began to elaborate alternative models, in which both agents and events played a more active role. These models did not, however, get much play in anthropology until the late seventies, and they will be discussed in the final section of the essay. In anthropology during most of that decade, structuralism itself, with all its flaws (and virtues), became the basis of one of the dominant schools of theory, structural Marxism. We move now to that decade.

THE SEVENTIES: MARX

The anthropology of the 1970s was much more obviously and transparently tied to real-world events than that of the preceding period. Starting in the late 1960s, in both the United States and France (less so in England), radical social movements emerged on a vast scale. First came the counterculture, then the antiwar movement, and then, just a bit later, the women's movement: these movements not only affected the academic world, they originated in good part within it. *Everything* that was part of the existing order was questioned and criticized. In anthropology, the earliest critiques took the form of denouncing the historical links between anthropology on the one hand, and colonialism and imperialism on the other (e.g., Asad 1973, Hymes 1974). But this merely scratched the surface. The issue quickly moved to the deeper question of the nature of our theoretical frameworks, and especially the degree to which they embody and carry forward the assumptions of bourgeois Western culture.

The rallying symbol of the new criticism, and of the theoretical alternatives offered to replace the old models, was Marx. Of all the great nineteenth-century antecedents of modern social science, Marx had been conspicuously absent from the mainstream theoretical repertoire. Parsons's *Structure of Social Action*, one of the sacred texts of the Harvard-trained symbolic anthropologists, surveyed the thought of Durkheim and Weber, and of two economic theorists, Alfred Marshall and Vilfredo Pareto, whose main significance in that context seemed to be that they were Not Marx. The British, including both the symbolic anthropologists and the structuralists, were still firmly embedded in Durkheim. Lévi-Strauss claimed to have been influenced by Marx, but it took a while for anyone to figure out what he meant by that. Even the cultural ecolog[ists], the only self-proclaimed materialists of the sixties, hardly invoked Marx at all; indeed Marvin Harris specifically repudiated him (1968). One does not need to be an especially subtle analyst of the ideological aspects of intellectual history to realize that the absence of a significant Marxist influence before the seventies was just as much a reflex of real-world politics as was the emergence of a strong Marxist influence in the seventies.

There were at least two distinct Marxist schools of anthropological theory: structural Marxism, developed mainly in France and England, and political economy, which emerged first in the United States, and later in England as well. There was also a movement that might be called cultural Marxism, worked out largely in historical and literary studies, but this was not picked up by anthropologists until recently, and will be addressed in the final section of the essay.

Structural Marxism

Structural Marxism was the only one of the schools developed entirely within the field of anthropology, and probably for that reason was also the earliest in its impact. Within it, Marx was used to attack and/or rethink, or at the very least to expand, virtually every theoretical scheme on the landscape—symbolic anthropology, cultural ecology, British social anthropology, and structuralism itself. Structural Marxism constituted a would-be total intellectual revolution, and if it did not succeed in establishing itself as the only alternative to everything else we had, it certainly succeeded in shaking up most of the received wisdom. This is not to say that it was necessarily the actual writings of the structural Marxists themselves (e.g., Althusser 1971; Godelier 1977; Terray 1972; Sahlins 1972; Friedman 1975) that had this effect; it was simply that structural Marxism was the original force within anthropology for promulgating and legitimating "Marx," "Marxism," and "critical inquiry" in the discourse of the field as a whole (see also Diamond 1979).

The specific advance of structural Marxism over its antecedent forms of materialist anthropology lay in its locating the determinative forces not in the natural environment and/or in technology, but specifically within certain structures of social relations. Ecological considerations were not excluded, but they were encompassed by and subordinated to the analysis of the social, and especially political, organization of production. Cultural ecology was thus attacked as "vulgar materialism," reinforcing rather than undoing the classical capitalist fetishization of "things," the domination of subjects by objects rather than by the social relations embodied in, and symbolized by, those objects (see especially Friedman 1974). The critical social relations in question, referred to as the mode(s) of production, are not to be confused with the surface organization of social relations traditionally studied by British social anthropologists—lineages, clans, moieties, and all the rest. These surface forms of what the British called "social structure" are seen as native *models* of social organization that have been bought by anthropologists as the real thing, but that actually mask, or at least only partially correspond to, the hidden asymmetrical relations of production that are driving the system. Here, then, was situated the critique of traditional British social anthropology (see especially Bloch 1971, 1974, 1977; Terray 1975).

In addition to critiquing and revising both cultural ecology and British social anthropology, structural Marxists turned their attention to cultural phenomena. Unlike the cultural ecologists, the structural Marxists did not dismiss cultural beliefs and native categories as irrelevant to the real or objective operations of society, nor, alternatively, did they set about to show that apparently irrational cultural beliefs, such as the sacred cow, actually had practical adaptive functions. Just as the New Left in the real world took cultural issues (life style, consciousness) more seriously than the Old Left had done, so the structural Marxists allocated to cultural phenomena (beliefs, values, classifications) at least one central function in their model of the social process. Specifically, culture was converted to "ideology," and considered from the point of view of its role in social reproduction: legitimating the existing order, mediating contradictions in the base, and mystifying the sources of exploitation and inequality in the system (O'Laughlin 1974; Bloch 1977; Godelier 1977).

One of the virtues of structural Marxism, then, was that there was a place for everything in its scheme. Refusing to see inquiries into material relations and into "ideology" as opposed enterprises, its practitioners established a model in which the two "levels" were related to one another via a core of social/political/economic processes. In this sense, they offered an explicit mediation between the "materialist" and "idealist" camps of sixties anthropology. The mediation was rather mechanical, as we will discuss in a moment, but it was there.

More important, to my mind, the structural Marxists put a relatively powerful sociology back into the picture. They cross-fertilized British social anthropological categories with Marxist ones, and produced an expanded model of social organization ("mode of production") which they then proceeded to apply systematically to particular cases. Whereas other Marxisms emphasized relations of political/economic organization ("production") almost exclusively, the structural Marxists were, after all, anthropologists, trained to pay attention to kinship, descent, marriage, exchange, domestic organization, and the like. They thus included these elements within their considerations of political and economic relations (often giving them a more Marxist ring by calling them "relations of reproduction") and the total effect was to produce rich and complex pictures of the social process in specific cases. Given the relative paucity, mentioned earlier, of detailed sociological analysis in the various sixties schools, this was an important contribution.

All this having been said, one may nonetheless recognize that structural Marxism had a number of problems. For one thing, the narrowing of the culture concept to "ideology," which had the powerful effect of allowing analysts to connect cultural conceptions to specific structures of social relations, was too extreme, and posed the problem of relating ideology back to more general conceptions of culture. For another, the tendency to see culture/ideology largely in terms of mystification gave most of the cultural or ideological studies in this school a decided functionalist flavor, since the upshot of these analyses was to show how myth, ritual, taboo, or whatever maintained the status quo. Finally, and most seriously, although structural Marxists offered a way of mediating the material and ideological "levels," they did not actually challenge the notion that such levels are analytically distinguishable in the first place. Thus despite criticizing the Durkheimian (and Parsonian) notion of "the social" as the "base" of the system, they merely offered a deeper and allegedly more real and objective "base." And despite attempting to discover more important functions for the "superstructure" (or despite claiming that what is base and what is superstructure varies culturally and/or historically, or even occasionally and rather vaguely that the superstructure is part of the base) they continued to reproduce the idea that it is useful to maintain such a set of analytic boxes.

In this sense, it may be seen that structural Marxism was still very much rooted in the sixties. While it injected a healthy dose of sociology into the earlier scheme of categories, and while this sociology was itself relatively originally conceived, the basic pigeonholes of sixties thought were not radically revised. Further, unlike the political economy school and other more recent approaches to be discussed shortly, structural Marxism was largely nonhistorical, a factor which, again, tied it to earlier forms of anthropology. Indeed one may guess that it was in part this comfortable mix of old categories and assumptions wrapped up in a new critical rhetoric that made structural Marxism so appealing in its day. It was in many ways the perfect vehicle for academics who had been trained in an earlier era, but who, in the seventies, were feeling the pull of critical thought and action that was exploding all around them.

Political Economy

The political economy school has taken its inspiration primarily from world-systems and underdevelopment theories in political sociology (Wallerstein 1976; Gunder Frank 1967). In contrast to structural Marxism, which focused largely, in the manner of conventional anthropological studies, on relatively discrete societies or cultures, the political economists have shifted the focus to large-scale regional political/economic systems (e.g., Hart 1982). Insofar as they have attempted to combine this focus with traditional fieldwork in specific communities or microregions, their research has generally taken the form of studying the effects of capitalist penetration upon those communities (e.g., *American Ethnologist* 1978; Schneider and Schneider 1976). The emphasis on the impact of external forces, and on the ways in which societies change or evolve largely in adaptation to such impact, ties the political economy school in certain ways to the cultural ecology of the sixties, and indeed many of its current practitioners were trained in that school (e.g., Ross 1980). But whereas for sixties cultural ecolog[ists], often studying relatively "primitive" societies, the important external forces were those of the natural environment, for the seventies political economists, generally studying "peasants," the important external forces are those of the state and the capitalist world system.

At the level of theory, the political economists differ from their cultural ecology forebears partly in showing a greater willingness to incorporate cultural or symbolic issues into their inquiries (e.g., Schneider 1978; Riegelhaupt 1978). Specifically, their work tends to focus on symbols involved in the development of class or group identity, in the context of political/economic struggles of one sort or another. The political economy school thus overlaps with the burgeoning "ethnicity" industry, although the literature in the latter field is too vast and too amorphous for me to do more than nod to here. In any event, the willingness of the political economists to pay attention, in however circumscribed fashion, to symbolic processes, is part of the general relaxation of the old materialism/idealism wars of the sixties.

The emphasis of this school upon larger regional processes is also salutary, at least up to a point. Anthropologists do have a tendency to treat societies, even villages, as if they were islands unto themselves, with little sense of the larger systems of relations in which these units are embedded. The occasional work (e.g., Edmund Leach's *Political Systems of Highland Burma*) that has viewed societies in larger regional context has been something of an unclassifiable (if admired) freak. To ignore the fact that peasants are part of states, and that even "primitive" societies and communities are invariably involved in wider systems of exchanges of all sorts, is to seriously distort the data, and it is the virtue of the political economists that they remind us of this.

Finally, the political economists must be given leading credit for stressing very strongly the importance of history for anthropological study. They are not the first to have done so, nor are they the only ones doing so now, and I will say more about anthropology's rapprochement with history in the conclusions of this essay. Nonetheless, it is certainly the members of this school who appear the most committed to a fully historical anthropology, and who are producing sustained and systematic work grounded in this commitment.

On the negative side of the ledger, we may complain first that the political economy model is too economic, too strictly materialist. One hears a lot about wages, the market, the cash nexus, economic exploitation, underdevelopment, and so forth, but not enough about the relations of power, domination, manipulation, control, and the like which those economic relations play into, and which for actors constitute much of the experienced pain of economic injustice. Political economy, in other words, is not political enough.

My main objection, however, is located deeper in the theoretical model of political economy. Specifically, I find the capitalism-centered view of the world questionable, to say the least, especially for anthropology. At the core of the model is the assumption that virtually everything we study has already been touched ("penetrated") by the capitalist world system, and that therefore much of what we see in our fieldwork and describe in our monographs must be understood as having been shaped in response to that system. Perhaps this is true for European peasants, but even here one would want at least to leave the question open. When we get even further from the "center," however, the assumption becomes very problematic indeed. A society, even a village, has its own structure and history, and this must be as much part of the analysis as its relations with the larger context within which it operates. (See Joel Kahn [1980] for a more balanced view.)

The problems derived from the capitalism-centered worldview also affect the political economists' view of history. History is often treated as something that arrives, like a ship, from outside the society in question. Thus we do not get the history *of* that society, but the impact of (our) history *on* that society. The accounts produced from such a perspective are often quite unsatisfactory in terms of traditional anthropological concerns: the actual organization and culture of the society in question. Traditional studies of course had their own problems with respect to history. They often presented us with a thin chapter on "historical background" at the beginning and an inadequate chapter on "social change" at the end. The political economy study inverts this relationship, but only to create the inverse problem.

The political economists, moreover, tend to situate themselves more on the ship of (capitalist) history than on the shore. They say in effect that we can never know what the other system, in its unique, "traditional," aspects, really looked like anyway. By realizing that much of what we see as tradition is in fact a response to Western impact, so the argument goes, we not only get a more accurate picture of what is going on, but we acknowledge at the same time the pernicious effects of our own system upon others. Such a view is also present, but in modes of anger and/or despair rather than pragmatism, in a number of recent works that question philosophically whether we can ever truly know the "other"—Edward Said's *Orientalism* is the prime example (see also Rabinow 1977; Crapanzano 1980; Riesman 1977).

To such a position we can only respond: Try. The effort is as important as the results, in terms of both our theories and our practices. The attempt to view other systems from ground level is the basis, perhaps the only basis, of anthropology's distinctive contribution to the human sciences. It is our capacity, largely developed in fieldwork, to take the perspective of the folks on the shore, that allows us to learn anything at all—even in our own culture—beyond what we already know. (Indeed, as more and more anthropologists are doing fieldwork in Western cultures, including the United States, the importance of maintaining a capacity to see otherness, even next door, becomes more and more acute.) Further, it is our location "on the ground" that puts us in a position to see people not simply as passive reactors to and enactors of some "system," but as active agents and subjects of their own history.

In concluding this section, I must confess that my placement of the political economy school in the seventies is something of an ideological move. In fact political economy is very much alive and well in the eighties, and it will probably thrive for some time. My periodization is thus, like that of all histories, only partly related to real time. I have included political economy and structural Marxism within this period/category because both schools continue to share a set of assumptions distinct from what I wish to emphasize for the anthropology of the eighties. Specifically, both assume, together with earlier anthropologies, that human action and historical process are almost entirely structurally or systemically determined. Whether it be the hidden hand of structure or the juggernaut of capitalism that is seen as the agent of society/history, it is certainly not in any central way real people doing real things. These are precisely the views from which at least some anthropologists, as well as practitioners in many other fields, appear to be struggling to break free as we move into the present decade.

INTO THE EIGHTIES: PRACTICE

I began this article by noting the apparent accuracy of Wolf's remarks to the effect that the field of anthropology is disintegrating, even granting the low degree of integration it had in the past. I also suggested that one could find scattered over the landscape the elements of a new trend that seems to be gathering force and coherence. In this final section I call attention to this new trend, sketch it, and subject it to a preliminary critique.

For the past several years, there has been growing interest in analysis focused through one or another of a bundle of interrelated terms: practice, praxis, action, interaction, activity, experience, performance. A second, and closely related, bundle of terms focuses on the doer of all that doing: agent, actor, person, self, individual, subject.

In some fields, movement in this direction began relatively early in the seventies, some of it in direct reaction to structuralism. In linguistics, for example, there was an early rejection of structural linguistics and a strong move to view language as communication and performance (e.g., Bauman and Sherzer 1974; Cole and Morgan 1975). In anthropology, too, there were scattered calls for a more action based approach. In France, Pierre Bourdieu published his *Outline of a Theory of Practice* in 1972. In the United States, Geertz attacked both hypercoherent studies of symbolic systems (many of them inspired by his own programmatic papers) and what he saw as the sterile formalism of structuralism, calling instead for anthropologists to see "human behavior . . . as . . . symbolic action" (1973a:10; see also Dolgin, Kemnitzer, and Schneider 1977; Wagner 1975; T. Turner 1969). In England, there was a minority wing that criticized traditional views of "social structure" not from the point of view of structural Marxism, but from the perspective of individual choice and decision making (e.g., Kapferer 1976).[14]

For much of the seventies, however, the structural Marxists and, later, the political economists, remained dominant, at least within anthropology. For them, social and cultural phenomena were to be explained largely by being referred to systemic/structural mechanisms of one sort or another. It was only in the late seventies that the hegemony of structural Marxism, if not that of political economy, began to wane. An English translation of Bourdieu's book was published in 1978, and it was at about that time that the calls for a more practice-oriented approach became increasingly audible. Here is a sampler:

> The instruments of reasoning are changing and society is less and less represented as an elaborate machine or a quasi-organism than as a serious game, a sidewalk drama, or a behavioral text. (Geertz 1980a:168)

> We need to watch these systems [of kinship] in action, to study tactics and strategy, not merely the rules of the game. (Barnes 1980:301)

> [G]ender conceptions in any society are to be understood as functioning aspects of a cultural system through which actors manipulate, interpret, legitimize, and reproduce the patterns . . . that order their social world. (Collier and Rosaldo 1981:311)[15]

> What do actors want and how can they get it? (Ortner 1981:366)

> If structural/semiotic analysis is to be extended to general anthropology on the model of its pertinence to "language," then what is lost is not merely history and change, but practice—human action in the world. Some might think that what is lost is what anthropology is all about. (Sahlins 1981:6)

As was the case with the strong revisionist trend in the sixties, the present movement appears much broader than the field of anthropology alone. In linguistics, Alton Becker, in a much-cited article, has emphasized issues of text building over and against reification of The Text (1979). In sociology, symbolic interactionism and other forms of so-called microsociology appear to be attracting new attention,[16] and Anthony Giddens has dubbed the relationship between structure and "agency" one of the "central problems" of modern social theory (1979). In history, E. P. Thompson has railed against theorists (every[one] from Parsonians to Stalinists) who treat "history as a 'process without a subject' [and] concur in the eviction from history of human agency" (1978:79). In literary studies, Raymond Williams insists that literature must be treated as the product of particular practices, and accuses those who abstract literature from practice of performing "an extraordinary ideological feat" (1977:46). If we push further—and here we skirt dangerous ground—we might even see the whole sociobiology movement as part of this general trend, insofar as it shifts the evolutionary mechanism from random mutation to intentional choice on the part of actors seeking to maximize reproductive success. (I should probably say, right here and not in a footnote, that I have a range of very strong objections to sociobiology. Nonetheless, I do not think it is too far-fetched to see its emergence as part of the broad movement to which I am drawing attention here.)

The practice approach is diverse, and I will not attempt to compare and contrast its many strands. Rather I will select for discussion a number of works that seem to share a common orientation within the larger set, an orientation that seems to me particularly promising. I do not wish to canonize any single one of these works, nor do I wish to provide a label for the subset and endow it with more reality than it has. What I do here is more like beginning to develop a photograph, to coax a latent form into something recognizable.

We may begin by contrasting, in a general way, this (subset of) newer practice-oriented work with certain more established approaches, especially with symbolic interactionism in sociology (Blumer 1962; Goffman 1959; see also Berreman 1962, and more recently Gregor 1977 in anthropology) and with what was called transactionalism in anthropology (Kapferer 1976, Marriott 1976, Goody 1978, Barth 1966, Bailey 1969). The first point to note is that these approaches were elaborated in opposition to the dominant, essentially Parsonian/Durkheimian, view of the world as ordered by rules and norms.[17] Recognizing that institutional organization and cultural patterning exist, the symbolic interactionists and transactionalists nonetheless sought to minimize or bracket the relevance of these phenomena for understanding social life:

> From the standpoint of symbolic interaction, social organization is a framework inside of which acting units develop their actions. Structural features, such as "culture," "social systems," "social stratification," or "social roles," set conditions for their action but do not determine their action. (Blumer 1962:152)

The newer practice theorists, on the other hand, share a view that "the system" (in a variety of senses to be discussed below) does in fact have very powerful, even "determining," effect upon human action and the shape of events. Their interest in the study of action and interaction is thus not a matter of denying or minimizing this point, but expresses rather an urgent need to understand where "the system" comes from—how it is produced and reproduced, and how it may have changed in the past or be changed in the future. As Giddens argues in his important recent book (1979), the study of practice is not an antagonistic alternative to the study of systems or structures, but a necessary complement to it.

The other major aspect of the newer practice orientation, differentiating it significantly from earlier interactionist and transactionalist approaches, resides in a palpable Marxist influence carrying through from the seventies.

Partly this is visible in the way in which things like culture and/or structure are viewed. That is, although the newer practice theorists share with sixties anthropology a strong sense of the shaping power of culture/structure, this shaping power is viewed rather darkly, as a matter of "constraint," "hegemony," and "symbolic domination." We will come back to this position in greater detail later. More generally, the Marxist influence is to be seen in the assumption that the most important forms of action or interaction for analytic purposes are those which take place in asymmetrical or dominated relations, that it is these forms of action or interaction that best explain the shape of any given system at any given time. Whether it is a matter of focusing directly on interaction (even "struggle") between asymmetrically related actors, or whether it is more broadly a matter of defining actors (whatever they are doing) in terms of roles and statuses derived from asymmetrical relations in which they participate, the approach tends to highlight social asymmetry as the most important dimension of both action and structure.

Not all current practice work manifests the Marxist influence. Some of it— like symbolic interactionism and transactionalism themselves—is more in the spirit of Adam Smith. The members of the subset with which I am concerned, however, implicitly or explicitly share at least the critical flavor of seventies anthropology, if not a systematic allegiance to Marxist theory per se.

Yet to speak of a Marxist influence in all of this is actually to obscure an important aspect of what is going on: an interpenetration, almost a merger, between Marxist and Weberian frameworks. In the sixties, the opposition between Marx and Weber, as "materialist" and "idealist," had been emphasized. The practice theorists, in contrast, draw on a set of writers who interpret the Marxist corpus in such a way as to render it quite compatible with Weber's views. As Weber put the actor at the center of his model, so these writers emphasize issues of human praxis in Marx. As Weber subsumed the economic within the political, so these writers encompass economic exploitation within political domination. And as Weber was centrally concerned with ethos and consciousness, so these writers stress similar issues within Marx's work. Choosing Marx over Weber as one's theorist of reference is a tactical move of a certain sort. In reality, the theoretical framework involved is about equally indebted to both. (On theory, see Giddens 1971; Williams 1976; Avineri 1971; Ollman 1971; Bauman 1973; Habermas 1973; Goldmann 1977. For substantive case analyses in this Weberian-Marxist vein, see Thompson 1966; Williams 1973; Genovese 1976.)

I will proceed to explicate and evaluate the "new practice" position by way of posing a series of questions: What is it that a practice approach seeks to explain? What is practice? How is it motivated? And what sorts of analytic relationships are postulated in the model? Let me emphasize very strongly that I do not offer here a coherent theory of practice. I merely sort out and discuss, in a very preliminary fashion, some of the central axes of such a theory.

What Is Being Explained?

As previously indicated, modern practice theory seeks to explain the relationship(s) that obtain between human action, on the one hand, and some global entity which we may call "the system," on the other. Questions concerning these relationships may go in either direction—the impact of the system on practice, and the impact of practice on the system. How these processes work will be taken up below. Here we must say a few words about the nature of "the system."

In two recent works in anthropology that explicitly attempt to elaborate a practice-based model (Bourdieu 1978 [1972]; and Sahlins 1981), the authors nominally take a French structuralist view of the system (patterns of relations between categories, and of relations between relations). In fact, however, both Bourdieu's *habitus* and Sahlins's "cosmological dramas" behave in many ways like the American concept of culture, combining elements of ethos, affect, and value with more strictly cognitive schemes of classification. The choice of a French or an American perspective on the system does have certain consequences for the shape of the analysis as a whole, but we will not pursue these here. The point is that practice anthropologists assume that society and history are not simply sums of ad hoc responses and adaptations to particular stimuli, but are governed by organizational and evaluative schemes. It is these (embodied, of course, within institutional, symbolic, and material forms) that constitute the system.

The system, further, is not broken up into units like base and superstructure, or society and culture, but is rather a relatively seamless whole. An institution—say, a marriage system—is at once a system of social relations, economic arrangements, political processes, cultural categories, norms, values, ideals, emotional patterns, and so on and on. No attempt is made to sort these components into levels and to assign primacy to one or the other level. Nor, for example, is marriage as a whole assigned to "society," while religion is assigned to "culture." A practice approach has no need to break the system into artificial chunks like base and superstructure (and to argue over which determines which), since the analytic effort is not to explain one chunk of the system by referring it to another chunk, but rather to explain the system as an integral whole (which is not to say a harmoniously integrated one) by referring it to practice.

But if the system is an integral whole, at the same time all of its parts or dimensions do not have equal analytic significance. At the core of the system, both forming it and deforming it, are the specific realities of asymmetry, inequality, and domination in a given time and place. Raymond Williams, a Marxist literary/cultural historian, sums up both the insistence upon holism and the privileged position of domination characteristic of this view. Picking up Antonio Gramsci's term "hegemony" as his label for the system, he argues that "hegemony" is a concept which at once includes and goes beyond two powerful earlier concepts: that of "culture" as a "whole social process," in which men define and shape their whole lives; and that of "ideology" in any of its Marxist senses, in which a system of meanings and values is the expression or projection of a particular class interest.

"Hegemony" goes beyond "culture" in its insistence on relating the "whole social process" to specific distributions of power and influence. To say that men define and shape their whole lives is true only in abstraction. In any actual society there are specific inequalities in means and therefore in capacity to realize this process. . . . Gramsci therefore introduces the necessary recognition of dominance and subordination in what has still, however, to be recognized as a whole process.

It is in just this recognition of the *wholeness* of the process that the concept of "hegemony" goes beyond "ideology." What is decisive is not only the conscious system of ideas and beliefs, but the whole lived social process as practically organized by specific and dominant meanings and values. . . .

[Hegemony] is in the strongest sense a "culture," but a culture which has also to be seen as the lived dominance and subordination of particular classes. (Williams 1977:108–109, 110)

What a practice theory seeks to explain, then, is the genesis, reproduction, and change of form and meaning of a given social/cultural whole, defined in—more or less—this sense.

What Is Practice?

In principle, the answer to this question is almost unlimited: anything people do. Given the centrality of domination in the model, however, the most significant forms of practice are those with intentional or unintentional political implications. Then again, almost anything people do has such implications. So the study of practice is after all the study of all forms of human action, but from a particular—political—angle.

Beyond this general point, further distinctions may be introduced. There is first of all the question of what are taken to be the acting units. Most practice anthropology to date takes these units to be individual actors, whether actual historical individuals, or social types ("women," "commoners," "workers," "junior siblings," et cetera). The analyst takes these people and their doings as the reference point for understanding a particular unfolding of events, and/ or for understanding the processes involved in the reproduction or change of some set of structural features. In contrast to a large body of work in the field of history, there has been relatively little done in anthropology on concerted collective action (but see Wolf 1969; Friedrich 1970; Blu 1980; see also the literature on cargo cults, especially Worsley 1968). Even in studies of collective action, however, the collectivity is handled methodologically as a single subject. We shall be discussing, throughout this section, some of the problems that arise from the essential individualism of most current forms of practice theory.

A second set of questions concerns the temporal organization of action. Some authors (Bourdieu is an example) treat action in terms of relatively ad hoc decision making, and/or relatively short-term "moves." Others suggest, even if they do not develop the point, that human beings act within plans or programs that are always more long range than any single move, and indeed that most moves are intelligible only within the context of these larger plans (Sahlins [1981] implies this, as do Ortner [1981] and Collier and Rosaldo [1981]; for an older example, see Hart and Pilling [1960]). Many such plans are culturally provided (the normative life cycle, for example), but many others must be constructed by actors themselves. Even projects generated ("creatively") by actors, however, tend to take stereotyped forms, insofar as the constraints and the resources of the system are relatively constant for actors in similar positions. In any event, an emphasis on larger "projects" rather than particular "moves" underlines the point that action itself *has* (developmental) structure, as well as operating *in*, and in relation *to*, structure.

Finally, there is the question of the kinds of action taken to be analytically central to the current approach. Everyone seems to agree in opposing a Parsonian or Saussurian view in which action is seen as sheer en-actment or execution of rules and norms (Bourdieu 1978; Sahlins 1981; Giddens 1979). Moreover, everyone seems also to agree that a kind of romantic or heroic "voluntarism," emphasizing the freedom and relatively unrestricted inventiveness of actors, will not do either (e.g., Thompson 1978). What is left, then, is a view of action largely in terms of pragmatic choice and decision making, and/or active calculating and strategizing. I will have more to say about the strategic model in the next section, when I discuss the views of motivation entailed in practice theory. Here, however, I wish to question whether the critique of en-actment or execution may not have gone too far. Indeed, despite the attacks on Parsons by Bourdieu and Giddens, both recognize the central role of highly patterned and routinized behavior in systemic reproduction. It is precisely in those areas of life—especially in the so-called domestic domain—where action proceeds with little reflection, that much of the conservatism of a system tends to be located. Either because practice theorists wish to emphasize the activeness and intentionality of action, or because of a growing interest in change as against reproduction, or both, the degree to which actors really do simply enact norms because "that was the way of our ancestors" may be unduly undervalued.

What Motivates Action?

A theory of practice requires some sort of theory of motivation. At the moment, the dominant theory of motivation in practice anthropology is derived from interest theory. The model is that of an essentially individualistic, and somewhat aggressive, actor, self-interested, rational, pragmatic, and perhaps with a maximizing orientation as well. What actors do, it is assumed, is rationally go after what they want, and what they want is what is materially and politically useful for them within the context of their cultural and historical situations.

Interest theory has been raked over the coals many times before. Here it is sufficient simply to note a few points that have particular relevance for anthropological studies of practice.

Insofar as interest theory is, even if it pretends not to be, a psychological theory, it is clearly far too narrow. In particular, although pragmatic rationality is certainly one aspect of motivation, it is never the only one, and not always even the dominant one. To accord it the status of exclusive motivating force is to exclude from the analytic discourse a whole range of emotional terms—need, fear, suffering, desire, and others—that must surely be part of motivation.

Unfortunately, anthropologists have generally found that actors with too much psychological plumbing are hard to handle methodologically, and practice theorists are no exception. There is, however, a growing body of literature which explores the variable construction of self, person, emotion, and motive in cross-cultural perspective (e.g., M. Rosaldo 1980, 1981; Friedrich 1977; Geertz 1973a, 1975; Singer 1980; Kirkpatrick 1977; Guemple 1972). The growth of this body of work is itself part of the larger trend toward an interest in elaborating an actor-centered paradigm, as is the fact that the subfield of psychological anthropology seems to be enjoying something of a renaissance (e.g., Paul 1982; Kracke 1978; Levy 1973). One may hope for some cross-fertilization between the more sociologically oriented practice accounts, with their relatively denatured views of motive, and some of these more richly textured accounts of emotion and motivation.

If interest theory assumes too much rationality on the part of actors, it also assumes too much activeness. The idea that actors are always pressing claims, pursuing goals, advancing purposes, and the like may simply be an overly energetic (and overly political) view of how and why people act. We may recall here the distinction, underscored by Geertz, between interest theory and strain theory (1973c). If actors in interest theory are always actively striving for gains, actors in strain theory are seen as experiencing the complexities of their situations and attempting to solve problems posed by those situations. It follows from these points that the strain perspective places greater emphasis on the analysis of the system itself, the forces in play upon actors, as a way of understanding where actors, as we say, are coming from. In particular, a system is analyzed with the aim of revealing the sorts of binds it creates for actors, the sorts of burdens it places upon them, and so on. This analysis, in turn, provides much of the context for understanding actors' motives, and the kinds of projects they construct for dealing with their situations (see also Ortner 1975, 1978).

While strain theory does not rectify the psychological shortcomings of interest theory, it does at least make for a more systematic exploration of the social forces shaping motives than interest theory does. Indeed, one may say that strain theory is a theory of the social, as opposed to psychological, production of "interests," the latter being seen less as direct expressions of utility and advantage for actors, and more as images of solutions to experienced stresses and problems.

Finally, an interest approach tends to go hand in hand with seeing action in terms of short-term tactical "moves" rather than long-term developmental "projects." From a tactical point of view, actors seek particular gains, whereas from a developmental point of view, actors are seen as involved in relatively far-reaching transformations of their states of being—of their relationships with things, persons, and self. We may say, in the spirit of Gramsci, that action in a developmental or "projects" perspective is more a matter of "becoming" than of "getting" (1957). Intrinsic to this latter perspective is a sense of motive and action as shaped not only by problems being solved, and gains being sought, but by images and ideals of what constitutes goodness—in people, in relationships, and in conditions of life.

It is a peculiarity of interest theory that it is shared across a broad spectrum of analysts, Marxist and non-Marxist, "old" and "new" practice theorists. The popularity and durability of the perspective, despite numerous attacks and criticisms, suggest that especially deep changes in our own practices will be required if anything is to be dislodged in this area.

The Nature of Interactions between Practice and the System

1. How does the system shape practice? Anthropologists—American ones, anyway—have for the most part long agreed that culture shapes, guides, and even to some extent dictates behavior. In the sixties, Geertz elaborated some of the important mechanisms involved in this process, and it seems to me that most modern practice theorists, including those who write in Marxist and/or structuralist terms, hold an essentially Geertzian view. But there are certain changes of emphasis, derived from the centrality of domination within the practice framework. For one thing, as noted earlier, the emphasis has shifted from what culture allows and enables people to see, feel, and do, to what it restricts and inhibits them from seeing, feeling, and doing. Further, although it is agreed that culture powerfully constitutes the reality that actors live in, this reality is looked upon with critical eyes: why this one and not some other? And what sorts of alternatives are people being dis-abled from seeing?

It is important to note that this view is at least partly distinct from a view of culture as mystification. In a mystification view, culture (= "ideology") tells lies about the realities of people's lives, and the analytic problem is to understand how people come to believe these lies (e.g., Bloch 1977). In the approach under discussion here, however, there is only one reality, and it is culturally constituted from top to bottom. The problem is not that of the system telling lies about some extrasystemic "reality," but of why the system as a whole has a certain configuration, and of why and how it excludes alternative possible configurations.

In any event, in terms of the specific question of how the system constrains practice, the emphasis tends to be laid on essentially cultural and psychological mechanisms: mechanisms of the formation and transformation of "consciousness." Although constraints of material and political sorts, including force, are fully acknowledged, there seems to be general agreement that action is constrained most deeply and systematically by the ways in which culture controls the definitions of the world for actors, limits their conceptual tools, and restricts their emotional repertoires. Culture becomes part of the self. Speaking of the sense of honor among the Kabyle, for example, Bourdieu says:

> [H]onour is a permanent disposition, embedded in the agents' very bodies in the form of mental dispositions, schemes of perception and thought, extremely general in their application, such as those which divide up the world in accordance with the oppositions between the male and the female, east and west, future and past, top and bottom, right and left, etc., and also, at a deeper level, in the form of bodily postures and stances, ways of standing, sitting, looking, speaking, or walking. What is called the sense of honour is nothing other than the cultivated disposition, inscribed in the body schema and the schemes of thought. (1978:15)

In a similar vein, Foucault says of the discourse of "perversions":

> The machinery of power that focuses on this whole alien strain did not aim to suppress it, but rather to give it an analytical, visible, and permanent reality: it was implanted in bodies, slipped in beneath modes of conduct, made into a principle of classification and intelligibility, established as a *raison d'être* and a natural order of disorder. . . . The strategy behind this dissemination was to strew reality with them and incorporate them into the individual. (1980:44)

Thus insofar as domination is as much a matter of cultural and psychological processes as of material and political ones, it operates by shaping actors' dispositions such that, in the extreme case, "the agents' aspirations have the same limits as the objective conditions of which they are the product" (Bourdieu 1978:166; see also Rabinow 1975; Barnett and Silverman 1979; Rabinow and Sullivan 1979).

At the same time, however, those authors who emphasize cultural domination also place important limits on the scope and depth of cultural controls. The extreme case is never reached, and often never even approached. Thus while accepting the view of culture as powerfully constraining, they argue that hegemony is always more fragile than it appears, and never as total as it (or as traditional cultural anthropology) would claim. The reasons given for this state of affairs are various, and relate directly to the ways in which the different authors conceptualize systemic change. This brings us to our final set of questions.

2. How does practice shape the system? There are really two considerations here—how practice reproduces the system, and how the system may be changed by practice. A unified theory of practice should ideally be able to account for both within a single framework. At the moment, however, it is clear that a focus on reproduction tends to produce a rather different picture from a focus on change, and we will thus take these issues separately.

Beginning with reproduction, there is of course a long tradition in anthropology of asking how it is that norms, values, and conceptual schemes get reproduced by and for actors. Prior to the sixties, at least in American anthropology, emphasis was laid upon socialization practices as the primary agents of this process. In England, however, the influence of the Durkheimian paradigm generated an emphasis on ritual. It was through the enactment of rituals of various kinds that actors were seen as coming to be wedded to the norms and values of their culture, and/or to be purged, at least temporarily, of whatever dissident sentiments they might harbor (e.g., Gluckman 1955; V. Turner 1969; Beidelman 1966). The ritual focus, or what might be called the focus on extraordinary practice, became even stronger in the sixties and seventies. American symbolic anthropologists took up the view that ritual was one of the primary matrices for the reproduction of consciousness (Geertz 1973b; Ortner 1978), even if they dissented from certain aspects of the British approach. The structural Marxists, too, placed great weight on the power of ritual to mediate social structural contradictions and mystify the workings of the system. Ritual in fact is a form of practice—people *do* it—and to study the reproduction of consciousness, mystified or otherwise, in the processes of ritual behavior is to study at least one way in which practice reproduces the system.

The newer practice approaches, by contrast, place greater emphasis on the practices of ordinary living. Although these were not by any means ignored in earlier work, they assume greater prominence here. Thus despite his stress on the highly intentionalized moments of practice, Bourdieu also pays close attention to the little routines people enact, again and again, in working, eating, sleeping, and relaxing, as well as the little scenarios of etiquette they play out again and again in social interaction. All of these routines and scenarios are predicated upon, and embody within themselves, the fundamental notions of temporal, spatial, and social ordering that underlie and organize the system as a whole. In enacting these routines, actors not only continue to be shaped by the underlying organizational principles involved, but continually re-endorse those principles in the world of public observation and discourse.

One question lurking behind all of this is whether in fact *all* practice, everything everybody does, embodies and hence reproduces the assumptions of the system. There is actually a profound philosophic issue here: how, if actors are fully cultural beings, they could ever do anything that does not in some way carry forward core cultural assumptions. On the more mundane level, the question comes down to whether divergent or nonnormative practices are simply variations upon basic cultural themes, or whether they actually imply alternative modes of social and cultural being.

These two formulations are grounded in two quite different models of systemic change. One is the classic Marxist model, in which the divisions of labor and the asymmetries of political relations create, in effect, incipient countercultures within the dominant system. At least some of the practices and modes of consciousness of dominated groups "escape" the prevailing hegemony. Change comes about as a result of class struggle in which formerly dominated groups succeed to power and institute a new hegemony based on their own distinctive ways of seeing and organizing the world.

There are a variety of problems with this model that I will not review here. I will simply note that it appears to overstate the differences of conceptual, as opposed to tactical, orientations between classes or other asymmetrically related entities. The model seems to work best when class differences are also, historically, cultural differences, as in cases of colonialism and imperialism (e.g., Taussig 1980). It works less well for many other sorts of cases with which anthropologists typically deal—culturally homogeneous systems in which inequities and asymmetries of various kinds (based on gender, age, or kinship, for example) are inseparable from complementarities and reciprocities that are equally real and equally strongly felt.

Recently, Marshall Sahlins has offered a model which derives systemic change from changes in practices in a rather different way. Sahlins argues that radical change need not be equated with the coming to power of groups with alternative visions of the world. He emphasizes instead the importance of changes of meaning of existing relations.

In a nutshell, Sahlins argues that people in different social positions have different "interests" (a term Sahlins worries over, and uses in an extended sense), and they act accordingly. This does not in itself imply either conflict or struggle, nor does it imply that people with different interests hold radically different views of the world. It does imply, however, that they will seek to enhance their respective positions when opportunities arise, although they will do so by means traditionally available to people in their positions. Change comes about when traditional strategies, which assume traditional patterns of relations (e.g., between chiefs and commoners, or between men and women), are deployed in relation to novel phenomena (e.g., the arrival of Captain Cook in Hawaii) which do not respond to those strategies in traditional ways. This change of context, this refractoriness of the real world to traditional expectations, calls into question both the strategies of practice and the nature of the relationships which they presuppose:

> [T]he pragmatics had its own dynamics: relationships that defeated both intention and convention. The complex of exchanges that developed between Hawaiians and Europeans . . . brought the former into uncharacteristic conditions of internal conflict and contradiction. Their differential connections with Europeans

thereby endowed their own relationships to each other with novel functional content. This is structural transformation. The values acquired in practice return to structure as new relationships between its categories. (Sahlins 1981:50)

Sahlins's model is appealing in a number of ways. As already noted, he does not equate divergence of interest with an almost countercultural formation, and is thus not forced to see change in terms of actual replacement of groups (although there is some of this, eventually, in the Hawaiian case, too). Further, in arguing that change may come about largely through (abortive) attempts to apply traditional interpretations and practices, his model unites mechanisms of reproduction and transformation. Change, as he says, is failed reproduction. And finally, in stressing changes of *meaning* as an essentially revolutionary process, he renders revolution itself less extraordinary (if no less dramatic, in its own way) than the standard models would have it.

One may nonetheless register a few quibbles. For one thing, Sahlins is still struggling with the interest perspective. He confronts it briefly, and he offers a formula that attempts to soften some of its more ethnocentric qualities, but he does not really grapple with the full range of thought and feeling that moves actors to act, and to act in complex ways.

Further, one may suggest that Sahlins makes change appear a bit too easy. Of course the book is short, and the model only sketched. Moreover, the relative "openness" of any given system, and of different types of systems, is probably empirically variable (see, e.g., Yenogoyan 1979). Nonetheless, Sahlins notes only in passing the many mechanisms that tend, in the normal course of events, to hold a system in place despite what appear to be important changes in practices. The moves to maintain the status quo by those who have vested interests are perhaps the least of these, and in any event they may backfire or produce unintended novel results. More important is the sort of "drag" introduced into the system by the fact that, as a result of enculturation, actors embody the system as well as living within it (see Bourdieu 1978). But mature actors are not all that flexible. An adequate model of the capacity of practice to revise structure must thus in all probability encompass a long-term, two- or three-generation developmental framework.

A related point derives from the fact that much of systemic reproduction takes place via the routinized activities and intimate interactions of domestic life. To the degree that domestic life is insulated from the wider social sphere (a degree generally much greater than is the case in Polynesia), important practices—of gender relations and child socialization—remain relatively untouched, and the transmission of novel meanings, values, and categorical relations to succeeding generations may be hindered. At the very least, what gets transmitted may be significantly—and conservatively—modified.

In short, there are probably far more linkages, and far more possibilities of slippage, in the route leading back from practice to structure than Sahlins's relatively smooth account allows for. Nonetheless, if the course of structural change is more difficult than he makes it appear, Sahlins presents a convincing account of how it may be easier than some would claim.

I close this final section with two reservations beyond those already expressed. The first concerns the centrality of domination within the contemporary practice framework, or at least within that segment of it upon which we have focused here. I am as persuaded as many of the authors that to penetrate into the workings of asymmetrical social relations is to penetrate to the heart of much of what is going on in any given system. I am equally convinced, however, that such an enterprise, taken by itself, is one-sided. Patterns of cooperation, reciprocity, and solidarity constitute the other side of the coin of social being. In this post-seventies context, views of the social in terms of sharing, exchange, and moral obligation—in David Schneider's famous phrase, "diffuse, enduring solidarity"—are treated largely as ideology. Often of course they *are* ideological. Yet a Hobbesian view of social life is surely as biased as one that harks back to Rousseau. An adequate model must encompass the full set.

My second point is not so much a critical reservation as a kind of fingering of an irony at the core of the practice model. The irony, although some may not feel it as such, is this: that although actors' intentions are accorded central place in the model, yet major social change does not for the most part come about as an *intended* consequence of action. Change is largely a by-product, an *un*intended consequence of action, however rational action may have been. Setting out to conceive children with superior mana by sleeping with British sailors, Hawaiian women became agents of the spirit of capitalism in their society. Setting out to preserve structure and reduce anomaly by killing a "god" who was really Captain Cook, the Hawaiians put in motion a train of events that ultimately brought down their gods, their chiefs, and their world as they knew it. To say that society and history are products of human action is true, but only in a certain ironic sense. They are rarely the products the actors themselves set out to make.[18]

CONCLUSIONS AND PROSPECTS

It has not been my intention, as I said earlier, to give an exhaustive account of any single school of anthropological thought over the last two decades. Rather I have been concerned with the relations between various intellectual trends in the field, within and across time. Nor has this been, as is surely obvious, a wholly disinterested inquiry. The strands of thought I have chosen to emphasize are those which I see as being most important in bringing the field to a certain position today, and my representations concerning where we are today are themselves clearly selective.

Much of what has been said in this essay can be subsumed within Peter Berger and Thomas Luckmann's little epigram: "Society is a human product.

Society is an objective reality. Man [*sic*] is a social product" (1967:61). Most prior anthropologies have emphasized the second component of this set: society (or culture) has been regarded as an objective reality in some form or another, with its own dynamics divorced in large part from human agency. The American cultural and psychocultural anthropologists, in addition, have emphasized the third component, the ways in which society and culture shape personality, consciousness, ways of seeing and feeling. But until very recently, little effort has been put toward understanding how society and culture themselves are produced and reproduced through human intention and action. It is around this question, as I see it, that eighties anthropology is beginning to take shape, while at the same time maintaining—ideally—a sense of the truths of the other two perspectives.

I have thus taken practice as the key symbol of eighties anthropology. I am aware, however, that many would have chosen a different key symbol: history. Around this term cluster notions of time, process, duration, reproduction, change, development, evolution, transformation (see Cohn 1981). Rather than seeing the theoretical shift in the field as a move from structures and systems to persons and practices, it might thus be seen as a shift from static, synchronic analyses to diachronic, processual ones. Viewing the shift in this way, the practice approach comprises only one wing of the move to diachrony, emphasizing microdevelopmental processes—transactions, projects, careers, developmental cycles, and the like.

The other wing of the move to diachrony is macroprocessual or macrohistorical, and itself comprises at least two trends. On the one side, there is the political economy school already discussed, which attempts to understand change in the small-scale societies typically studied by anthropologists by relating that change to large-scale historical developments (especially colonialism and capitalist expansion) external to the societies in question. On the other, there is a more ethnographic sort of historical investigation, which pays greater attention to the internal developmental dynamics of particular societies over time. External impingements are taken into account, but there is greater effort to delineate forces of both stability and change at work within a given system, as well as the social and cultural filters operating to select and/ or reinterpret whatever may be coming in from outside (e.g., Geertz 1980b; Blu 1980; R. Rosaldo 1980; Wallace 1980;. Sahlins 1981; Ortner 1989; Kelly 1985).

Anthropology's rapprochement with history is in my view an extremely important development for the field as a whole. If I have chosen in this essay not to emphasize it, it is only because, at the moment, the trend is too broad. It covers, rather than reveals, important distinctions. Insofar as history is being amalgamated with virtually every kind of anthropological work, it offers a pseudointegration of the field which fails to address some of the deeper problems. As argued in this essay, those deeper problems were generated by the very successes of systems and structuralist approaches, which established the reality of the thinglike nature of society, but which failed to ask, in any systematic way, where the thing comes from and how it might change.

To answer these questions with the word "history" is to avoid them, if by history is meant largely a chain of external events to which people react. History is not simply something that happens to people, but something they make—within, of course, the very powerful constraints of the system within which they are operating. A practice approach attempts to see this making, whether in the past or in the present, whether in the creation of novelty or in the reproduction of the same old thing. Rather than fetishizing history, a practice approach offers, or at least promises, a model that implicitly unifies both historical and anthropological studies.[19]

There have, of course, been attempts to put human agency back in the picture before. These attempts, however, yielded either too much or too little to the systems/structures perspective. In the case of Parsons's "general theory of action," action was seen almost purely as en-actment of the rules and roles of the system. In the cases of symbolic interactionism and transactionalism, systemic constraints were minimized, the system itself being viewed as a relatively unordered reservoir of "resources" that actors draw upon in constructing their strategies. The modern versions of practice theory, on the other hand, appear unique in accepting all three sides of the Berger and Luckmann triangle: that society is a system, that the system is powerfully constraining, and yet that the system can be made and unmade through human action and interaction.

All of which is not to say either that the practice perspective represents the end of the intellectual dialectic or that it is perfect. I have touched upon many of its defects in the present essay. Like any theory, it is a product of its times. Once, practice had the romantic aura of voluntarism—"man," as the saying went, "makes himself." Now practice has qualities related to the hard times of today: pragmatism, maximization of advantage, "every man," as the saying goes, "for himself." Such a view seems natural in the context of the failure of many of the social movements of the sixties and seventies, and in the context of a disastrous economy and a heated up nuclear threat. Yet however realistic it may appear at the moment, such a view is as skewed as voluntarism itself. A lot of work remains to be done.

NOTES

First appeared in 1984.

1. For the discussion of the sixties and the seventies, I will for the most part invoke only the most representative figures and works. In an article of this length, many interesting developments must be bypassed. One important figure of this period who gets left by the wayside is Gregory Bateson (e.g., 1972), who, though himself clearly a powerful and original thinker, never really founded a major school in anthropology.

2. E.g., Ortner 1975; M. Rosaldo 1980; Blu 1980; Meeker 1979; Rosen 1978.

3. If culture itself had been an elusive phenomenon, one may say that Geertz has pursued the most elusive part of it, the ethos. It may also be suggested that this, among other things, accounts for his continuing and broad-based appeal. Perhaps the majority of students who go into anthropology, and almost certainly the majority of nonanthropologists who are fascinated by our field, are drawn to it because they have been struck at some point in their experience by the "otherness" of another culture, which we would call its ethos. Geertz's work provides one of the very few handles for grasping that otherness.

4. Another point of contrast between Turner and Geertz is that Turner's concept of meaning, at least in those early works that launched his approach, is largely referential. Meanings are things that symbols point to or refer to, like "matriliny" or "blood." Geertz, on the other hand, is primarily concerned with what might be called Meaning, with a capital M—the purpose, or point, or larger significance of things. Thus he quotes Northrop Frye: "You wouldn't go to *Macbeth* to learn about the history of Scotland—you go to it to learn what a man feels like after he's gained a kingdom and lost his soul" (Geertz 1973f:450).

5. E.g., Munn 1969; Myerhoff 1974; Moore and Myerhoff 1975; Babcock 1978.

6. This section is partly based on readings, partly on semiformal interviews with Conrad P. Kottak and Roy A. Rappaport, and partly on general discussions with Raymond C. Kelly. Absolution is extended to all of the informants.

7. White and Childe were fairly explicit about the Marxist influence on their work.

8. This was the programmatic position. In practice, Sahlins did pay a good deal of attention to internal social dynamics.

9. The early Turner is a partial exception to this point, but most of his successors are not.

10. Dumont is another of those figures who deserve more space than can be afforded here.

11. This is not to imply that American symbolic anthropologists deny the doctrine of arbitrariness of symbols. But they do insist that the choice of a particular symbolic form among several possible, equally arbitrary, symbols for the same conception, is not only not arbitrary, but has important implications that must be investigated.

12. James Boon (e.g., 1972) has devoted a fair amount of effort to reconciling Lévi-Strauss and/or Schneider on the one side, with Geertz on the other. The outcome is generally heavily in favor of structuralism. (See also Boon and Schneider 1974.)

13. Lévi-Strauss himself moved from a Durkheim/Mauss position in "La Geste d'Asdiwal" (1967) to the more radical structuralist position in *Mythologiques*. It is no accident that Leach, or whoever made the decision, chose to present "La Geste d'Asdiwal" as the lead essay in the British collection, *The Structural Study of Myth and Totemism* (1967).

14. The transactionalist tradition in British anthropology may of course be traced back further.

15. I would argue, if I had more space, that feminist anthropology is one of the primary contexts in which a practice approach has been developing. The Collier and Rosaldo (1981) article is a good example. See also Ortner (1981).

16. Mayer Zald, personal communication, at the Social Science History Seminar (University of Michigan), 1982.

17. Parsons and his colleagues gave the term "action" central place in their scheme (1962 [1951]), but what they meant by this was essentially *en*-actment of rules and

norms. Bourdieu, Giddens, and others have pointed this out, and have cast their arguments in part against this position.

18. Michel Foucault, whose later work (1979 and 1980) is certainly part of the current practice trend, and who is making an impact in at least some quarters of anthropology, has put this point nicely: "People know what they do; they frequently know why they do what they do; but what they don't know is what they do does" (quoted in Dreyfus and Rabinow 1982:187). I regret having been unable to incorporate Foucault into the discussions of this section. In particular, he has been struggling against some of the ramifications of the individualism at the heart of much of practice theory, although he has wound up tying himself into other knots—such as "intentionality without a subject, [and] a strategy without a strategist" (ibid.)—in the process.

19. It might be objected that the political economists themselves put practice in a central position in their model. As external events impinge, actors in a given society react and attempt to deal with those impingements. The problem here is that action is primarily re-action. The reader might object in turn that re-action is central to Sahlins's model too. But the point in Sahlins is that the nature of the reaction is shaped as much by internal dynamics as by the nature of the external events.

References

Alland, Alex. 1975. "Adaptation," in *Annual Review of Anthropology*, 4. Palo Alto: Annual Reviews, Inc.

Althusser, Louis. 1971. *Lenin and Philosophy*, Ben Brewster, trans. New York and London: Monthly Review Press.

American Ethnologist. 1978. Special issue on Political Economy (5:3).

Asad, Talal, ed. 1973. *Anthropology and the Colonial Encounter*. London: Ithaca Press.

Avineri, Shlomo. 1971. *The Social and Political Thought of Karl Marx*. Cambridge: Cambridge University Press.

Babcock, Barbara, ed. 1978. *The Reversible World: Symbolic Inversion in Art and Society*. Ithaca, New York: Cornell University Press.

Bailey, F. G. 1969. *Strategems and Spoils*. New York: Schocken.

Barnes, J. A. 1980. "Kinship Studies: Some Impressions on the Current State of Play." *Man*, 14:2, 293–303.

Barnett, Steve. 1977. "Identity Choice and Caste Ideology," in *Symbolic Anthropology*, J. Dolgin, D. Kemnitzer, and D. Schneider, eds. New York: Columbia University Press.

Barnett, Steve, and Silverman, Martin G. 1979. *Ideology and Everyday Life*. Ann Arbor: University of Michigan Press.

Barth, Fredrik. 1966. "Models of Social Organization." Royal Anthropological Institute of Great Britain and Ireland, Occasional Papers 23.

Bateson, Gregory. 1972. *Steps to an Ecology of Mind*. New York: Ballantine Books.

Bauman, Richard, and Sherzer, Joel, eds. 1974. *Explorations in the Ethnography of Speaking*. Cambridge: Cambridge University Press.

Bauman, Zygmund. 1973. *Culture as Praxis*. London and Boston: Routledge and Kegan Paul.

Becker, A. L. 1979. "Text-Building, Epistemology, and Aesthetics in Japanese Shadow Theater," in *The Imagination of Reality*, A. L. Becker and A. A. Yengoyan, eds. Norwood, New Jersey: Ablex.

Beidelman, Thomas. 1966. "Swazi Royal Ritual." *Africa*, 36:4, 373–405.

Berger, Peter, and Luckmann, Thomas. 1967. *The Social Construction of Reality*. Garden City, New York: Doubleday.

Berreman, Gerald. 1962. *Behind Many Masks: Ethnography and Impression Management in a Himalayan Village*. Monograph 4. Ithaca, New York: Society for Applied Anthropology.

Bloch, Maurice. 1971. "The Moral and Tactical Meaning of Kinship Terms." *Man*, 6:1, 79–87.

———. 1974. "The Long Term and the Short Term: The Economic and Political Significance of the Morality of Kinship," in *The Character of Kinship*, J. Goody, ed. Cambridge: Cambridge University Press.

———. 1977. "The Disconnection between Power and Rank as a Process." *Archives Européene de Sociologie*, 18:107–48.

Blu, Karen. 1980. *The Lumbee Problem: The Making of an American Indian People*. Cambridge: Cambridge University Press.

Blumer, Herbert. 1962. "Society as Symbolic Interaction," in *Human Behavior and Social Processes*, A. M. Rose, ed. Boston: Houghton Mifflin.

Boon, James A. 1972. "Further Operations of 'Culture' in Anthropology: A Synthesis of and for Debate." *Social Science Quarterly*, 52 (September), 221–52.

Boon, James A., and Schneider, David M. 1974. "Kinship vis-à-vis Myth: Contrasts in Lévi-Strauss' Approach to Cross-cultural Comparison." *American Anthropologist*, 76:4, 794–817.

Bourdieu, Pierre. 1978 [1972]. *Outline of a Theory of Practice*, Richard Nice, trans. Cambridge: Cambridge University Press.

Bradbury, Malcolm. 1981. Comment on "Modern Literary Theory: Its Place in Teaching." *Times Literary Supplement* (6 February), 137.

Childe, V. Gordon. 1942. *What Happened in History*. New York: Penguin.

Cohn, Bernard S. 1981. "Anthropology and History in the 1980's." *Journal of Interdisciplinary History*, 12:2, 227–52.

Cole, P., and Morgan, J., eds. 1975. *Syntax and Semantics 3: Speech Acts*. New York: Academic Press.

Collier, Jane, and Rosaldo, Michelle Z. 1981. "Politics and Gender in Simple Societies," in *Sexual Meanings: The Cultural Construction of Gender and Sexuality*, Sherry B. Ortner and Harriet Whitehead, eds. Cambridge and New York: Cambridge University Press.

Crapanzano, Vincent. 1980. *Tuhami: Portrait of a Moroccan*. Chicago: University of Chicago Press.

DeGeorge, Richard, and DeGeorge, Fernande, eds. 1972. *The Structuralists from Marx to Lévi-Strauss*. Garden City, New York: Doubleday.

Diamond, Stanley, ed. 1979. *Toward a Marxist Anthropology*. The Hague: Mouton.

Dolgin, J., Kemnitzer, D., and Schneider, D. M. 1977. "As People Express Their Lives, So They Are . . . " in their *Symbolic Anthropology*. New York: Columbia University Press.

Douglas, Mary. 1966. *Purity and Danger*. New York: Frederick A. Praeger.

Dreyfus, Hubert L., and Rabinow, Paul. 1982. *Michel Foucault: Beyond Structuralism and Hermeneutics*. Chicago: University of Chicago Press.

Dumont, Louis. 1965. "The Modern Conception of the Individual: Notes on Its Genesis." *Contributions to Indian Sociology*, 8:1, 13–61.

———. 1970. *Homo Hierarchicus: An Essay on the Caste System*, M. Sainsbury, trans. Chicago: University of Chicago Press.

Fernandez, James. 1974. "The Mission of Metaphor in Expressive Culture." *Current Anthropology*, 15:2, 119–45.

Firth, Raymond. 1963 [1951]. *Elements of Social Organization*. Boston: Beacon Press.

Foucault, Michel. 1979. *Discipline and Punish: The Birth of the Prison*, Alan Sheridan, trans. New York: Random House.

———. 1980. *The History of Sexuality*. Volume I, Robert Hurley, trans. New York: Vintage.

Friedman, Jonathan. 1974. "Marxism, Structuralism, and Vulgar Materialism." *Man*, n.s. 9:3, 444–69.

——. 1975. "Tribes, States and Transformations," in *Marxist Analyses and Social Anthropology*, M. Bloch, ed. New York: John Wiley and Sons.

Friedrich, Paul. 1970. *Agrarian Revolt in a Mexican Village*. Englewood Cliffs, New Jersey: Prentice-Hall.

———. 1977. "Sanity and the Myth of Honor: The Problem of Achilles." *Ethos*, 5.3, 281–305.

Geertz, Clifford. 1973. *The Interpretation of Cultures*. New York: Basic Books.

———. 1973a. "Thick Description: Toward an Interpretive Theory of Culture," in Geertz, *Interpretation of Cultures*.

———. 1973b. "Religion as a Cultural System," in Geertz, *Interpretation of Cultures*.

———. 1973c. "Ideology as a Cultural System," in Geertz, *Interpretation of Cultures*.

———. 1973d. "The Cerebral Savage: On the Work of Claude Lévi-Strauss," in Geertz, *Interpretation of Cultures*.

———. 1973e. "Person, Time and Conduct in Bali," in Geertz, *Interpretation of Cultures*.

———. 1973f. "Deep Play: Notes on the Balinese Cockfight," in Geertz, *Interpretation of Cultures*.

———. 1975. "On the Nature of Anthropological Understanding." *American Scientist*, 63:1, 47–53.

———. 1980a. "Blurred Genres: The Refiguration of Social Thought." *The American Scholar*, 49:2, 165–79.

———. 1980b. *Negara: The Theater-State in Nineteenth Century Bali*. Princeton: Princeton University Press.

Genovese, Eugene D. 1976. *Roll, Jordan, Roll: The World the Slaves Made*. New York: Random House.

Giddens, Anthony. 1971. *Capitalism and Modern Social Theory*. Cambridge: Cambridge University Press.

———. 1979. *Central Problems in Social Theory: Action, Structure and Contradiction in Social Analysis*. Cambridge: Cambridge University Press.

Gluckman, Max. 1955. *Custom and Conflict in Africa*. Glencoe, Illinois: The Free Press.

Godelier, Maurice. 1977. *Perspectives in Marxist Anthropology*, Robert Brain, trans. Cambridge: Cambridge University Press.

Goffman, Erving. 1959. *The Presentation of Self in Everyday Life*. Garden City, New York: Doubleday.

Goldman, Irving. 1970. *Ancient Polynesian Society*. Chicago: University of Chicago Press.

Goldmann, Lucien. 1977. *Cultural Creation in Modern Society*, Bart Grahl, trans. Oxford: Basil Blackwell.

Goody, Esther N., ed. 1978. *Questions and Politeness: Strategies in Social Interaction*, New York: Cambridge University Press.

Gramsci, Antonio. 1957. *The Modern Prince and Other Writings*, Louis Marks, trans. New York: International Publishers.

Gregor, Thomas. 1977. *Mehinaku: The Drama of Daily Life in a Brazilian Indian Village*. Chicago: University of Chicago Press.

Guemple, Lee. 1972. Panel on "Cultural Basis of Social Relations: Kinship, Person, and Actor." Annual Meetings of the American Anthropological Association, Toronto.

Gunder Frank, André. 1967. *Capitalism and Underdevelopment in Latin America*. New York and London: Monthly Review Press.

Habermas, Jurgen. 1973. *Theory and Practice*, John Viertel, trans. Boston: Beacon Press.

Harris, Marvin. 1966. "The Cultural Ecology of India's Sacred Cattle." *Current Anthropology*, 7:1, 51–64.

———. 1968. *The Rise of Anthropological Theory*. New York: Crowell.

———. 1978. "No End of Messiahs." *New York Times* (26 November), sec. 4, p. 21.

Hart, Keith. 1982. *The Development of Commercial Agriculture in West Africa*. Cambridge: Cambridge University Press.

Hart, C. W. M., and Pilling, Arnold R. 1960. *The Tiwi of North Australia*. New York: Holt, Rinehart, Winston.

Hymes, Dell, ed. 1974. *Reinventing Anthropology*. New York: Vintage.

Kahn, Joel S. 1980. *Minangkabau Social Formations: Indonesian Peasants and the World Economy*. Cambridge: Cambridge University Press.

Kapferer, Bruce, ed. 1976. *Transaction and Meaning: Directions in the Anthropology of Exchange and Human Behavior*. Philadelphia: ISHI Publications.

Kelly, Raymond. 1985. *The Nuer Conquest: The Structure and Development of an Expansionist System*. Ann Arbor: University of Michigan Press.

Kirkpatrick, John T. 1977. "Person, Hierarchy, and Autonomy in Traditional Yapese Theory," in *Symbolic Anthropology*, Dolgin, Kemnitzer, and Schneider, eds.

Kracke, Waud H. 1978. *Force and Persuasion: Leadership in an Amazonian Society*. Chicago: University of Chicago Press.

Leach, Edmund. 1954. *Political Systems of Highland Burma*. Boston: Beacon Press.

———. 1960. "The Sinhalese of the Dry Zone of Northern Ceylon," in *Social Structure in Southeast Asia*, G. P. Murdock, ed. London: Tavistock.

———. 1964. "Anthropological Aspects of Language: Animal Categories and Verbal Abuse," in *New Directions in the Study of Language*, E. H. Lenneberg, ed. Cambridge: MIT Press.

———. 1966. *Rethinking Anthropology*. London School of Economics Monographs on Social Anthropology, no. 22. New York: Humanities Press.

———. 1969. *Genesis as Myth and Other Essays*. London: Jonathan Cape.

Leach, Edmund, ed. 1967. *The Structural Study of Myth and Totemism*. London: Tavistock.

Lévi-Strauss, Claude. 1963. "The Effectiveness of Symbols," in his *Structural Anthropology*, C. Jacobson and B. G. Schoepf, trans. New York: Basic Books.

————. 1964–71. *Mythologiques (Introduction to a Science of Mythology)*. 4 vols. Paris: Plon.

————. 1967. "La Geste d'Asdiwal," in *Structural Study of Myth and Totemism*, Leach, ed.

Levy, Robert. 1973. *Tahitians: Mind and Experience in the Society Islands*. Chicago: University of Chicago Press.

Lewis, Gilbert. 1977. "A Mother's Brother to a Sister's Son," in *Symbols and Sentiments*, I. Lewis, ed. London: Academic Press.

Marriott, McKim. 1976. "Hindu Transactions: Diversity without Dualism," in *Transaction and Meaning*, Kapferer, ed.

Meeker, Michael E. 1979. *Literature and Violence in North Arabia*. Cambridge: Cambridge University Press.

Moore, Sally Falk, and Myerhoff, Barbara G., eds. 1975. *Symbols and Politics in Communal Ideology*, Ithaca, New York: Cornell University Press.

Munn, Nancy. 1969. "The Effectiveness of Symbols in Murngin Rite and Myth," in *Forms of Symbolic Action*, R. Spencer, ed. Seattle: University of Washington Press.

Myerhoff, Barbara G. 1974. *Peyote Hunt: The Sacred Journey of the Huichol Indians*. Ithaca, New York: Cornell University Press.

Needham, Rodney. 1973a. "The Left Hand of the Mugwe: An Analytical Note on the Structure of Meru Symbolism," in *Right and Left*, Needham, ed.

Needham, Rodney, ed. 1973b. *Right and Left: Essays on Dual Symbolic Classification*. Chicago: University of Chicago Press.

O'Laughlin, Bridget. 1974. "Mediation of a Contradiction: Why Mbum Women Do Not Eat Chicken," in *Woman, Culture and Society*, M. Rosaldo and L. Lamphere, eds. Stanford: Stanford University Press.

Ollman, Bertell. 1971. *Alienation: Marx's Conception of Man in Capitalist Society*. Cambridge: Cambridge University Press.

Ortner, Sherry B. 1975. "Gods' Bodies, Gods' Food: A Symbolic Analysis of a Sherpa Ritual," in *The Interpretation of Symbolism*, R. Willis, ed. London: Malaby Press.

————. 1978. *Sherpas through their Rituals*. Cambridge: Cambridge University Press.

————. 1981. "Gender and Sexuality in Hierarchical Societies: The Case of Polynesia and Some Comparative Implications," in *Sexual Meanings*, S. Ortner and H. Whitehead, eds. Cambridge: Cambridge University Press.

————. 1989. *High Religion: A Cultural and Political History of Sherpa Buddhism*. Princeton: Princeton University Press.

Parsons, Talcott. 1949 [1937]. *The Structure of Social Action*. New York: The Free Press of Glencoe.

Parsons, Talcott, and Shils, Edward A., eds. 1962 [1951]. *Toward a General Theory of Action*. New York: Harper and Row.

Paul, Robert A. 1982. *The Tibetan Symbolic World: Psychoanalytic Explorations*. Chicago: University of Chicago Press.

Piddocke, Stuart. 1969. "The Potlatch System of the Southern Kwakiutl: A New Perspective," in *Environment and Cultural Behavior*, A. P. Vayda, ed. Austin: University of Texas Press.

Rabinow, Paul. 1975. *Symbolic Domination: Cultural Form and Historical Change in Morocco*. Chicago: University of Chicago Press.

————. 1977. *Reflections on Fieldwork in Morocco*. Berkeley: University of California Press.

Rabinow, Paul, and Sullivan, William M. 1979. "The Interpretive Turn: Emergence of an Approach," in their *Interpretive Social Science: A Reader*. Berkeley: University of California Press.

Rappaport, Roy A. 1967. *Pigs for the Ancestors*. New Haven: Yale University Press.

Riegelhaupt, Joyce. 1978. "The Revolt of Maria da Fonte: Peasants, 'Women,' and the State." Manuscript.

Riesman, Paul. 1977. *Freedom in Fulani Social Life: An Introspective Ethnography*. Chicago: University of Chicago Press.

Rosaldo, Michelle Z. 1980. *Knowledge and Passion: Ilongot Notions of Self and Social Life*. Cambridge: Cambridge University Press.

———. 1981. "Towards an Anthropology of Self and Feeling." Manuscript.

Rosaldo, Renato. 1980. *Ilongot Headhunting, 1883–1974*. Stanford: Stanford University Press.

Rosen, Lawrence. 1978. "The Negotiation of Reality: Male-Female Relations in Sefrou, Morocco," in *Women in the Muslim World*, L. Beck and N. Keddie, eds. Cambridge: Harvard University Press.

Ross, Eric B., ed. 1980. *Beyond the Myth of Culture: Essays in Cultural Materialism*, New York and London: Academic Press.

Sahlins, Marshall, 1964. "Culture and Environment," in *Horizons of Anthropology*, S. Tax, ed. Chicago: Aldine.

———. 1972. *Stone Age Economics*. Chicago: Aldine.

———. 1981. *Historical Metaphors and Mythical Realities: Structure in the Early History of the Sandwich Islands Kingdom*. Ann Arbor: University of Michigan Press.

Sahlins, Marshall, and Service, Elman R., eds. 1960. *Evolution and Culture*. Ann Arbor: University of Michigan Press.

Said, Edward W. 1979. *Orientalism*. New York: Vintage.

Schneider, David M. 1968. *American Kinship: A Cultural Account*, Englewood Cliffs, New Jersey: Prentice-Hall.

———. 1977. "Kinship, Nationality, and Religion in American Culture: Toward a Definition of Kinship," in *Symbolic Anthropology*, Dolgin, Kemnitzer, and Schneider, eds.

Schneider, Jane. 1978. "Peacocks and Penguins: The Political Economy of European Cloth and Colors," *American Ethnologist*, 5:3, 413–47.

Schneider, Jane, and Schneider, Peter. 1976. *Culture and Political Economy in Western Sicily*. New York: Academic Press.

Service, Elman, R. 1958. *Profiles in Ethnology*, New York: Harper and Row.

Singer, Milton. 1980. "Signs of the Self: An Exploration in Semiotic Anthropology," *American Anthropologist*, 82:3, 485–507.

Steward, Julian H. 1953. "Evolution and Process," in *Anthropology Today*, A. L. Kroeber, ed. Chicago: University of Chicago Press.

———. 1955. *Theory of Culture Change*. Urbana: University of Illinois Press.

Tambiah, Stanley J. 1968. "The Magical Power of Words." *Man*, n.s. 3:2, 175–208.

———. 1969. "Animals Are Good to Think and Good to Prohibit." *Ethnology*, 8:4, 423–59.

Taussig, Michael T. 1980. *The Devil and Commodity Fetishism in South America*. Chapel Hill: University of North Carolina Press.

Terray, Emmanuel. 1972. *Marxism and "Primitive" Societies*, Mary Klopper, trans. New York: Monthly Review Press.

————. 1975. "Classes and Class Consciousness in the Abron Kingdom of Gyaman," in *Marxist Analyses and Social Anthropology*, M. Bloch, ed. New York: John Wiley and Sons.

Thompson, E. P. 1966. *The Making of the English Working Class*. New York: Vintage.

————. 1978. *The Poverty of Theory and Other Essays*. New York: Monthly Review Press.

Turner, Terence S. 1969. "Oedipus: Time and Structure in Narrative Form," in *Forms of Symbolic Action*, R. Spencer, ed. Seattle: University of Washington Press.

Turner, Victor. 1967. *The Forest of Symbols*. Ithaca, New York: Cornell University Press.

————. 1969. *The Ritual Process*. Chicago: Aldine.

Wagner, Roy. 1975. *The Invention of Culture*. Chicago: University of Chicago Press.

Wallace, Anthony F. C. 1980. *Rockdale: The Growth of an American Village in the Early Industrial Revolution*. New York: W. W. Norton.

Wallerstein, Emmanuel. 1976. *The Modern World System*. New York: Academic Press.

White, Leslie A. 1943. "Energy and the Evolution of Culture." *American Anthropologist*, 45:3, 335–56.

————. 1949. *The Science of Culture*. New York: Farrar Straus.

Williams, Raymond. 1973. *The Country and the City*. New York: Oxford University Press.

————. 1976. *Keywords: A Vocabulary of Culture and Society*. New York: Oxford University Press.

————. 1977. *Marxism and Literature*. Oxford: Oxford University Press.

Wolf, Eric R. 1969. *Peasant Wars of the Twentieth Century*. New York: Harper and Row.

————. 1980. "They Divide and Subdivide and Call it Anthropology." *New York Times* (30 November), Ideas and Trends Section, p. E9.

Worsley, Peter. 1968. *The Trumpet Shall Sound: A Study of "Cargo" Cults in Melanesia*. New York: Schocken.

Yalman, Nur. 1969. "The Structure of Sinhalese Healing Rituals," in *Forms of Symbolic Action*, R. Spencer, ed. Seattle: University of Washington Press.

Yengoyan, A. A. 1979. "Cultural Forms and a Theory of Constraints," in *The Imagination of Reality*, A. L. Becker and A. A. Yengoyan, eds. Norwood, New Jersey: Ablex.

Cosmologies of Capitalism: The Trans-Pacific Sector of "The World System"

MARSHALL SAHLINS

DEVELOP-MAN ECONOMICS

On 20 November 1839, the Revd. John Williams of the London Missionary Society was killed shortly after landing at Dillon's Bay, Eromanga, one of the New Hebrides islands (now Vanuatu). Already famous as "the Apostle of Polynesia," Williams was abruptly translated to martyrdom by certain Melanesians, purportedly in blind revenge for outrages earlier inflicted on them by White sandalwood traders. Or so runs the pious description of the event which, like calling it "murder" or them "savages," characteristically inscribes the actions of islanders in the notions of Westerners. The historiographic tradition of such incidents has since improved, but not to the extent of ridding itself of the Christian virtue of understanding the Melanesians on the grounds that it was not them who cast the first stone. As if they could have no reasons or violence of their own devising. Never mind that the indigenous meaning of Williams' death—in its ceremonial details strangely reminiscent of the fall of Captain Cook at Hawaii—never mind that the local meaning seems to have been nothing less than deicide.[1] In almost all the European accounts of these events the islanders have nothing to do but to react to the determining presence of the foreigner. The explanatory principle, as Dorothy Shineberg says, is that "there must be a White man behind every brown" (1967: 214).[2]

Of course I invoke the missionary's fate in a metaphoric way: in order to join the anthropological chorus of protest against the idea that the global expansion of Western capitalism, or the World System so-called, has made the colonized and "peripheral" peoples the passive objects of their own history and not its authors, and through tributary economic relations has turned their cultures likewise into adulterated goods. In *Europe and the People without History*, Eric Wolf is compelled to argue that attention must be paid to these people, that they are in fact historical beings, somebody more than "victims and silent witnesses" of their own subjugation (1982: x). Wolf was moved to say so because in the headier days of World System theory it had seemed that there was nothing left for anthropology to do but the global ethnography of capitalism. Anthropology would be manifest destiny. For other societies were regarded as no longer possessing their own "laws of motion"; nor was there any "structure" or "system" to them, except as given by Western-capitalist domination.[3] Yet such ideas, are they not the academic form of the same domination? As though the West, having materially invaded the lives of others, would not intellectually deny them any cultural integrity. World System theory becomes the super-structural expression of the very imperialism it despises—the self-consciousness of the World System itself.

Yet why is it that in Wolf's magisterial book the same kind of thing happens? One searches here in vain for a sustained analysis of how local peoples attempt to organize what is afflicting them in their own cultural terms. Wolf invites us to see the Mundurucu and the Meo as historic agents, but what he actually shows is how they "were drawn into the larger system to suffer its impact and become *its* agents" (1982: 23; my emphasis). An evident problem is Wolf's nostalgia for the Marxist-utilist theory favored by many world systematists. I mean the idea of culture as a reflex of the "mode of production," a set of social appearances taken on by material forces that somehow possess their own instrumental rationality and necessity.[4] From this comes the contradiction that neutralizes all the anthropological good intentions. On one hand, Wolf argues for the people's active historic role, which must mean the way they shape the material circumstances laid on them according to their own conceptions; while on the other hand, he advocates a cultural theory that supposes the people's conceptions are a function of their material circumstances.

But we need to take more seriously Marx's understanding of production as the appropriation of nature within and through a determinate form of society. It follows that a mode of production itself will specify no cultural order unless and until its own order as production is culturally specified. Production, Marx wrote, is the reproduction of "a definite mode of life" (Marx & Engels, 1965: 32). A system of production is the relative form of an absolute necessity, a particular historical way of meeting human requirements. Hence the people's cultural assumption of external conditions that they do not create and cannot escape is the very principle of their historic action. Constructed in relation to the forces of nature—and typically also in relation to pressures of other societies—every cultural scheme known to history has been the product of just this pragmatic predicament. Not to suggest, then, that we ignore the modern juggernaut, but that its historical course be viewed as a cultural process. Western capitalism has loosed on the world enormous forces of production, coercion and destruction. Yet precisely because they cannot be resisted, the relations and goods of the larger system also take on meaningful places in local schemes of things. In the event, the historical changes in local society are also continuous with the superseded cultural scheme, even as the new state of affairs acquires a cultural coherence of a distinct kind. So we shall have to examine how indigenous peoples struggle to integrate their experience of the world system in something that is logically and ontologically more inclusive: their own system of the world.

The problem is how to avoid the usual reduction of the intercultural encounter to a kind of physics on one side or a teleology on the other. I mean the

common perception of the global economy simply and mechanically as material forces, and the corollary descriptions of local histories as unrelieved
chronicles of cultural corruption. True that within a century of Captain
Cook's "discovery" of the Sandwich Islands, American entrepreneurs were
seizing the land and making the Hawaiians into a rural proletariat. But not
true that the course of Hawaiian history since 1778 was governed by this
outcome or that it consisted merely in the replacement of Polynesian by bourgeois relations. The Islands, on the contrary, had seen a significant period of
indigenous development, when the ruling chiefs appropriated Western commodities to their own hegemonic projects—which is also to say, to traditional
conceptions of their own divinity. If thereafter Hawaii rapidly succumbed to
imperialist pressures, it was precisely because the effects of foreign commerce were amplified by its encompassment in a Polynesian competition for
celestial powers. This happens over and over in modern world history: the
capitalist forces are realized in other forms and finalities, in exotic cultural
logics far removed from the native-European commodity fetishism (cf. Simmons, 1988).[5] Hence, the World System is not a physics of proportionate
relationships between economic "impacts" and cultural "reactions." The specific effects of the global-material forces depend on the various ways they are
mediated in local cultural schemes.

Rather than a planetary physics this is a *history* of world capitalism—
which, moreover, in a double fashion will testify to the authenticity of other
modes of existence. First by the fact that modern global order has been decisively shaped by the so-called peripheral peoples, by these diverse ways they
have culturally articulated what was happening to them. Second, and despite
the terrible losses that have been suffered, the diversity is not dead; it persists
in the wake of Western domination. Indeed, respectable scholars now argue
that modern world history since c. 1860 has been marked by the simultaneous
development of global integration and local differentiation.[6] For a long time
anthropologists and historians were taken in by a certain mystique of Western
domination: the conceit that the world expansion of capitalism brings all
other cultural history to an end. It would be wiser, as John Kelly suggests, to
add the concept of "post-Westernism" to the current post-modernist vogue
for postisms (Kelly, 1988).[7]

But I mean to focus here on an earlier stage, from the mid-eighteenth to the
mid-nineteenth century, with a view toward illustrating how the peoples of
the Pacific islands and the adjacent Asian and American mainlands reciprocally shaped the "impact" of capitalism and thereby the course of world history. In part the title "Cosmologies of Capitalism" comes from the observation that often in the islands, in a sort of Neolithic homage to the Industrial
Revolution, Western goods and even persons have been incorporated as indigenous powers. European commodities here appear as signs of divine benefits and mythic bestowals, negotiated in ceremonial exchanges and displays
that are also customary sacrifices.[8] Hence, the local interests in certain European goods which, by a motivated logic of the concrete, could be assimilated

to indigenous ideas of social "valuables" or sacred kinds. In contrast to relatively limited markets in means of production or short-term booms in muskets and other means of destruction, European traders in the Pacific often found this demand for luxe insatiable (Fisher 1977; Sahlins, 1990; Salisbury, 1962; Shineberg, 1967).

Notice that from the point of view of the indigenous people, the exploitation by the world system may well be an enrichment of the local system. Even as there is net transfer of labor power to the metropole through unequal exchange rates, the hinterland peoples are acquiring more goods of extraordinary social value with less effort than they ever could in the days of their ancestors. There follow the greatest feasts, exchanges and sing-sings that ever happened (cf. Gregory, 1982; Lederman, 1986; Strathern, 1979). And as this means the greatest accumulation of divine benefits cum human social powers, the whole process is a *development* in the cultural terms of the people concerned.

It is not "backwardness"—except from a Western-bourgeois perspective. Nor is it just "conservatism." Surely there is a cultural continuity. But continuity is not the same thing as immobility; indeed *the strongest continuity may consist in the logic of the cultural change.* "Neo-traditional development" might be the appropriate term, given the evident paradoxes in harnessing custom to commerce. But I prefer the improvised neo-Melanesian I overheard at the University of South Pacific, where the insertion of the English "development" in a pidgin sentence came out sounding (to me) like "develop-man." From the point of view of what the people consider worthy of human beings, this is indeed *develop-man.* It is a cultural self-realization on a material scale and in material forms never before known, yet not for all that the simple penetration of capitalist-market relations. Of course the dependence on the world economy, which has its own reasons and progress, can render the local develop-man vulnerable over the longer run. But again, destiny is not history. Nor is it always tragedy. Anthropologists tell of some spectacular forms of indigenous cultural change turning into modes of political resistance—in the name of cultural persistence.[9]

So in response to various develop-man impulses, Western merchants searching the Pacific for exchange-value were forced to accede to local demands for prestige-value. But this was ultimately because of certain Chinese prestige values, to which the whole of world commerce was held hostage. Ever since the opening of direct trade with the West in the earlier sixteenth century, the Chinese had been vastly unimpressed with European manufactures, even with the latter-day wonders of the Industrial Revolution, and were taking little but precious silver in return for their own goods. Moreover, during the eighteenth century, this Chinese allergy to Western commodities was coupled to a rapidly growing craving for tea in Britain and her English-speaking colonies, which resulted in a flood of silver toward the Orient—with reverberating effects on the mines of Potosi and thus on the African slave trade.[10] As is well known, Britain was able to overcome the unfavorable trade balance it contracted from its tea habit only by inflicting an even greater addiction on the Chinese in the form of opium imported from India: an illegal traffic backed up in 1839 by an infamous war. Having few such resources to push nor much silver, the Americans and Australians roamed the Pacific for products acceptable to China. Hence the maritime fur trade of Northwest America (in which the Americans followed the British) and the commerce in sandalwood and trepang in South Sea islands. Shineberg notes that although the Australians "were fond of expiating on the superstitious nature of the Chinese who would buy sandalwood at high prices to burn before their altars," considering their own balance of trade, "the colonial tea-drinking habit was no less quaint" (1967: 6). Add in the tobacco and the luxury goods the islanders were content to receive for their part in all this and the Pacific trade proves, as Shineberg says, "that human frailty knows no race" (1967: 151).

Stated more positively and anthropologically, this is also the most general argument of my paper. The general idea is that the world system is the rational expression of relative cultural logics, that is, in the terms of exchange-value. A system of cultural differences organized as division of labor, it is a global market in human frailties, where they all can be gainfully transacted in a common pecuniary medium. Just as Galileo thought that mathematics was the language of the physical world, so the bourgeoisie have been pleased to believe that the cultural universe is reducible to a discourse of price—despite the fact that other peoples would resist the one idea and the other by populating their existence with other considerations. Fetishism, then, is the custom of the capitalist world economy, since it precisely translates these real-historic cosmologies and ontologies, these various relations of persons and systems of objects, into the terms of a cost-benefit analysis: a simple chrematistic pidgin-language, by means of which we are also able to acquire social-science understandings at bargain rates. Of course, the capacity to reduce social properties to market values is exactly what allows capitalism to master the cultural order. Yet at least sometimes the same capacity makes the world capitalism the slave to local concepts of status, means of labor control and preferences in goods which it has no will to obliterate, inasmuch as it would not be profitable. A history of the world system, therefore, must discover the culture mystified in the capitalism. As a famous historical theater of Western exploration, the Pacific seems a good place to start.

CHINA TRADE

Nous ne plierons jamais cette nation à nos goûts & à nos idées.
—Cibot, 1782a: 267

In September 1793, George Lord Viscount Macartney, the envoy of the Western Ocean barbarian ruler George III, having come to present tributes to the Celestial Emperor and to be "turned toward civilization" by the imperial virtue—or in his own view, Ambassador Plenipotentiary and Extraordinary of his Britannic Majesty, instructed to establish diplomatic relations with China with a view toward liberalizing the Canton trade while opening new markets for British manufacturers, some fine examples of which he was carrying as presents to the Ch'ien-lung Emperor on the occasion of his eighty-third birthday—in September 1793, then, Macartney received the imperial reply to his King's message. Addressed to a subject lord, this famous edict reads in part:

> We, by the Grace of Heaven, Emperor, instruct the King of England to take note of our charge.
>
> Although your country, O King, lies in the far oceans, yet inclining your heart towards civilization you have specially sent an envoy respectfully to present a state message, and sailing the seas he has come to our Court to kotow and to present congratulations for the Imperial birthday, and also to present local products, thereby showing your sincerity.
>
> We have perused the text of your state message and the wording expresses your earnestness. From it your sincere humility and obedience can clearly be seen. . . .
>
> The Celestial Empire, ruling all within the four seas [i.e., the world], simply concentrates on carrying out the affairs of Government properly, and does not value rare and precious things. . . . In fact, the virtue and power of the celestial Dynasty has penetrated afar to the myriad kingdoms, which have come to render homage, and so all kinds of precious things from "over mountain and sea" have been collected here, things which your chief envoy and others have seen for themselves. Nonetheless we have never valued ingenious articles, nor do we have the slightest need for your country's manufactures. (Cranmer-Byng, 1962: 337, 340)[11]

It has been said of the Ch'ien-lung edict (by no less than Bertrand Russell) that China cannot be understood until this document has ceased to seem absurd (Cranmer-Byng, 1957–8: 182). I would not claim to dispel the strangeness; on the contrary, I begin by generalizing it.

The Ch'ien-lung Emperor was not the first or the last ruler of the Celestial Kingdom to dismiss Western things. In 1816, his successor, in refusing to see another English ambassador (Lord Amherst), expressed the same imperial indifference: "My dynasty attaches no value to products from abroad; your nation's cunningly wrought and strange wares do not appeal to me in the least" (Malone, 1934: 173). Nor was the disinterest in European goods a sentiment of Manchu emperors only. It had been going on since the previous Ming dynasty, upwards of 300 years, and as concerns the British ever since 1699, when the Honorable East India Company established itself at Canton. From the beginning the company was embarrassed for want of any English goods to put into the trade.[12] Besides, the traffic was increasingly controlled and harassed by Chinese regulations. By the mid–eighteenth century it had settled into the classic arrangements of an insulated "port-of-trade" (cf. Polanyi et

al., 1957). British shipping was limited to Canton, where the Company's su-
percargoes were required to treat exclusively with licensed Chinese merchants—who passed along the numerous duties and extortions of lower and
higher imperial officials as irksome charges on the terms of exchange. The
Westerners were also quarantined socially and not greatly appreciated culturally. Dermigny summarizes the situation of European merchants at Canton:

> Relegated to their 300 meters of quay, a simple guichet on the flank of this
> enormous China through which passed silver and merchandise only, but by no
> means language or ideas, they [the Europeans] remained nearly completely mar-
> ginal to a civilization which they gave up all hope of understanding. To the con-
> tempt manifested for them as Barbarians they would respond with a redoubled
> contempt for the barbarian country that China was in their eyes. (Dermigny,
> 1964, v. 2: 512)[13]

Still, the English had put up with it to get silks, nankeens, and porcelains,
and then more and more because of tea. By the middle eighteenth century
tea-drinking in Britain had diffused to all social classes and become, as Lord
Macartney said, not simply "an indispensable luxury" like other Chinoiserie,
but "an indispensable necessity of life" (Cranmer-Byng, 1962: 212). Were
England to be suddenly deprived of tea, observed the secretary of the Macartney mission, Sir George Staunton, the effect would be a national "calam-
ity" (1799, v. 1: 12). Yet historically speaking tea had appeared in Britain
only yesterday, around 1650 (Milburn, 1813, v. 2: 527ff; Repplier, 1932;
Ukers, 1935). The first tea brought in by the East India Company amounted to
143 lbs. 8 oz. in 1669. By the 1740s, however, the Company's annual imports
were running over 2,000,000 lbs., and by 1800 over 20,000,000 lbs. (Morse,
1966; Pritchard, 1929).[14] So, if the Chinese Emperor's status as the Son of
Heaven was entailed in his contempt for foreign-barbarian manufactures, on
the British side, in their own cosmic scheme, "tea was . . . the god to which
everything else was sacrificed" (Pritchard, 1936: 163).

Notably sacrificed were the famous British woolens, offered up on the
Canton market at significant losses in order to finance the purchase of teas.
(This must be the origin of the [New York] garment industry joke to the effect
that they made up their losses in volume—the tea, of course, bringing super-
profits in Britain.) During the last decade of the eighteenth century the dump-
ing of woolens increased substantially, which helped reduce silver expenditures (Pritchard, 1929: 155). In 1820 the Directors of the Company reported
they had sustained a net loss of £1,685,103 on British products over the past
twenty-three years, due to "'forcing the trade beyond the demand'" (Morse,
1966, v. 1:75).[15] By now the Industrial Revolution was well under way, and
apart from the woolens manufacturers the producers and merchants of steel
and iron goods, of ships and marine equipment, and of cotton textiles were all
clamoring for the opening of new markets—especially the cotton kings, after
the freeing of the Arkwright patent in 1785 caused a crisis of overproduction.
The clamor was one good reason why the Government decided on the Mac-

artney mission—which cost the East India Company another £78,000. Yet no more after the mission than before were the Chinese merchants willing to take risks on these sundry British goods.[16] The one thing always acceptable was silver coin. On the Westerners' part, however, this continuous drain of treasure was not at all to their mercantilist liking.

Until the early 1800s, or for nearly three centuries, China was the tomb of European silver—from which none ever returned. Over 150 million in Spanish dollars thus disappeared into the Celestial Kingdom during the eighteenth century alone. Soon the British (although not the Americans and other Westerners) would be clear of this problem, due not only to woolen imports but especially to the private "Country Trade" in Indian opium and raw cotton, operating under license from the East India Company. Credit procedures allowed the Company to put the Canton returns of the Country Trade to its own account. Still, during the 250 years before the First Opium War (1839–42) an estimated 350 millions (*reals*) in silver bullion were imported by Western merchants into China (Mancall, 1984: 100). And although Europe's Asian trade was thus clearly complementary to its American trade—whence came the silver that bought the tea that John Bull drank—Wallerstein finds the whole affair "strange indeed," considering Europe's "passionate hoarding of bullion," and proposes to exclude it from the capitalist world system, apparently because it was organized on Asian terms (1974: 330; but see Astell, 1982: 89–90).

These terms were evident not only in the Ch'ien-lung Emperor's reply to George III but in nearly every incident of the Macartney mission, which is why I focus attention on it.[17] Sent to "negotiate" a treaty, as he conceived between equal sovereigns of independent states, Lord Macartney came face-to-face—at that by special grace, as he should have been face-to-ground—with the Unique Man whose benevolent rule was the sole means of order in the human world. His Lordship, who wanted to impress the Chinese Court with the powers of his own civilization, represented as the extension of the virtues of his own king, was received by the Supreme Lord whose own virtue (*te*) was the condition of the possibility of any civilization whatsoever. With such universal power there could be no question of treating or negotiating, but only of submitting or "coming to be transformed." This means transformed to culture from the undifferentiated and disordered state of barbarism that the English shared, in such outer realms as Europe, with the wildest monstrosities of nature. Through his sacrificial offices and the example of his sage behavior, through the virtue of his person as diffused by the conduct of his officials, the Son of Heaven uniquely mediated between humanity and the transcendent celestial source of earthly welfare. His were classical powers of hierarchy: inclusive politically, as they were total culturally.[18]

In the ancient imperial tradition, the founder of the dynasty, recipient of a renewed Mandate of Heaven, promulgates a new calendar, new weights and measures, and a new musical scale. He thus institutes human time and space, economy and harmony—all as the extension of the imperial person: "'His voice was the standard of sounds,' a famous Han historian writes of the legendary founder of the Hsia dynasty, 'his body was the standard of measures of length.' He could thus determine the Numbers which serve to regulate Time and Space, as well as the Music which creates the universal harmony" (Granet, 1930: 16). The first Manchu emperor did not hesitate to employ a Jesuit astronomer to formulate the dynasty's calendrical system (Fu, 1966, f. 1: 3–4; Spence, 1980: 3f). Nor did he or his successors neglect to harmonize the occupations of mankind with the Heavenly passage of the seasons: by the correct sacrifices, of course; but also by the exclusive distribution on New Year's Day of the annual calendar—counterfeit of which was a penal offense and falsification a capital crime.[19] Such gifts of time were among the benefits barbarians could receive in return for submitting tributes, along with the seals to affix to their own dated edicts, patents of office and noble ranks in the Chinese system, valuable presents from the emperor, and often the right to trade for Chinese goods.[20]

Trade fits into the tribute system, normally as the sequitur, since the "tribute system" in its most general sense referred to the material mode of integration into civilization. Barbarians' tributes were signs of the force of attraction of the imperial virtue, objectifications of the Emperor's civilizing powers. "The kings of former times," relates an official Ming document, "cultivated their own refinement and virtue in order to subdue persons at a distance, whereupon the barbarians (of the east and north) came to Court to have audience" (in Fairbank, 1942: 132). Thus the following perception of the Carolingian empire, from a Ch'ing period account:

> During the middle of the T'ang Dynasty [AD 618–906], Charlemagne, a wise and learned man, gifted with civil and military talents, became Emperor of the Germans and the French. His fame and virtue spread far afield, and all the barbarians submitted to him. (in Schurmann & Schell, 1967: 123)

The tributes of the barbarians were obligatorily special products of their own countries. Hence in certain symbolic respects the more bizarre they were, the better: as signifying at once the inclusiveness of the imperial virtue, its capacity to encompass a universal diversity, and the emperor's ability to order the fluctuations of the world beyond the Chinese pale by the control of its monsters and its wonders (cf. Mancall, 1984: 16). Consider this flowery encomium penned in 1419 by a Confucian literatus in celebration of the arrival of a tributary giraffe, that is, a "unicorn" *(ch'i-lin)*:

> When the virtue of the Imperial Ruler above reaches the Great Purity, below reaches the Great Stillness, and in between reaches the Myriad Spirits, then a *ch'i-lin* [giraffe] appears. . . . It is also said: when the virtue of the Ruler penetrates into the dark waters of chaos and his transforming influence reaches out to all living beings, then a *ch'i-lin* appears. (in Walker, 1956: 24)

Rendered principally at the Winter solstice and the Emperor's birthday, the barbarians' tributes were in this way connected with world rebirths, securing for them the material benefits of the Ruler's intercession with Heaven. Prosperity was entailed also in the valuable presents received by the tribute emissary from the Emperor, showing that the latter knew how to "cherish men who come from afar." Again trade was part of the same set of conceptions: officially regarded as a "boon" granted to the barbarians, as Fairbank explains, "the necessary means of their sharing in the bounty of China" (1942: 139). So Lord Macartney's intention to liberalize trade by offering birthday presents to the Emperor was not unintelligible to the Chinese, or at least lent itself to a working misunderstanding.[21] Nor would such conceptions imply Chinese disinterest in trade or preclude its functional uses in politics or profits. In the long history of the Chinese frontiers, most famously in the north, commerce was often an instrument of policy: whether encouraged as part of a forward policy of expansion, or permitted in an effort to neutralize a barbarian threat (cf. Lattimore, 1940; Fairbank & Teng, 1941).

As I say, such structures appear as events in the chronicles of the Macartney mission. But I can only just refer, for example, to His Lordship's refusal to ko-tow before the Emperor, of which perhaps too much has already been made in an Orientalist vein (cf. Pritchard, 1943). Enough to note that Macartney, insisting that one should distinguish between the homage of tributary princes and the respects of "a great and independent sovereign" such as his own, proposed that he would go through with the ko-tow if a Chinese official of equal rank would do the same before a portrait of George III (Cranmer-Byng, 1962: 100, 119, *et passim*). This proposal, said the Imperial Court documents, "showed ignorance" (Cranmer-Byng, 1957–58: 156–8). Again, there is Macartney's repeated desire to get down to the business of negotiating, once the embassy had been ceremoniously received by the Emperor and the gifts exchanged. The desire was never fulfilled because so far as the Chinese were concerned, the business was already finished—the ceremonies *were* the business (Cranmer-Byng, 1962: 137, 148; cf. Hivea, 1986). Here it seems relevant to note that during the first fifty years of the East India Company's existence in China, it had not a single (Western) employee who could speak Chinese (Pritchard, 1929: 39). The so-called astronomer of the Macartney mission, Dr. Dinwiddie, complained repeatedly about the inability of the English to understand what was going on. "'With what countenance will Lord Macartney return to Europe after his shameful treatment?' he asks. 'No apology will satisfy. We go home—are asked what we have done. Our answer— we could not speak to the people'" (Proudfoot, 1968: 87, cf. p. 71).[22]

However, Lord Macartney was aware that the banners flying on the fleet of Chinese river junks carrying him toward Peking read "The English Ambassador bringing tribute to the Emperor of China." He knew, but he diplomatically chose to ignore it, as a tactic in the sustained counter-argument the British were also making in the language of goods. As they understood, the so-called tributes were "specimens of the best British manufacture, and all the late inventions for adding to the conveniences and comforts of social life," carefully selected to answer to "the double purpose of gratifying those to whom they were presented, and exciting a more general demand for the purchase of similar articles" (Staunton, 1799, v. 2: 23).[23] So in the several incidents where the distinction was explicitly drawn between "presents" (what the British were calling them) and "tributes" (what the Chinese called them), one could never guess what the cunning Occidentals were really thinking. Their "presents" were really *samples* of their wares. Even beyond that they were *examples* of industrial ingenuity, designed to signify the "superiority" of British civilization and the majesty of George III. Including instruments for scientific experiments, a globe with the tracks of Captain Cook's discoveries, handsome carriages and sword blades that could cut through iron without losing their edge, these presents, as Sir George Staunton put it, had been carefully chosen to "denote" the progress of Western science and to "convey information" to the Emperor (ibid., p. 243). "'It was meant to surprise the Chinese with the power, learning and ingenuity of the British people,' says Dinwiddie, 'for which purpose a splendid assortment of astronomical and scientific apparatus were among the presents to his Celestial Majesty'"—this included a planetarium that had taken thirty years to make,—"'and was allowed to be the most wonderful piece of mechanism ever emanating from human hands'" (Proudfoot, 1868: 26). To the British, then, their presents were self-evident signs of an industrial logic of the concrete: the signs of "our preeminence" (Cranmer-Byng, 1962: 191). They were supposed to communicate a whole political, intellectual and moral culture (Hivea, 1986: 135f). Yet if ever anyone carried coals to Newcastle, it was British people carrying signs of civilization to the Chinese.

In his journal, Macartney is repeatedly indignant at the mandarins' refusal to be mortified. But from the mandarins' perspective if the "presents" were indeed "tributes," expressing the barbarians' sincere desire to turn to civilization, manifestly they could not be superior to things Chinese. At best, they were what they should be: rare and strange exotica from an outer world where categories were crossed, blurred, inverted and confused. So were the British "presents" interpreted, Staunton learned, on the streets of Peking:

> Among the stories that caught, at this moment, the imagination of the people, the arrival of the Embassy was said to furnish no inconsiderable share. The presents brought by it to the Emperor, were asserted to include whatever was rare in other countries, or not known before to the Chinese. Of the animals that were brought, it was gravely mentioned, that there was an elephant the size of a monkey, and as fierce as a lion, and a cock that fed on charcoal. Everything was supposed to vary from what had been seen in Pekin before, and to possess qualities different from what had been there experienced in the same substances. (Staunton, 1799, v. 2: 21; cf. Cranmer-Byng, 1962: 114; Proudfoot, 1868: 51).[24]

In a wonderful Orientalist text written some half-century later, the English sinologist Thomas Meadows explains that Chinese people, beholding such a technical marvel as an English ship, simply do not get the message that the country in which it was produced "*must*" be inhabited by an energetic and rich population "free to enjoy the fruits of its own labour," that it "*must*" have a powerful government, good laws "and be altogether in a high state of civilization" (1847: 235; Meadows sounds like a modern functionalist archaeologist, although not more mistaken). The Chinese will allow, he adds, that the English can do some extraordinary things, but so do elephants and other wild beasts. Indeed Dinwiddie recorded just this kind of contemporary reaction to the Macartney mission, including the Chinese failure to appreciate the native Western theory of the systematic relation between technology and civilization:

> Their prejudices are invincible. Ask them whether the contrivers and makers of such curious and elegant machinery must not be men of understanding, and superior persons. They answer—"These are curious things, but what are their use? Do the Europeans understand the art of Government as equally polished?" (Proudfoot, 1868: 50)

All this helps explain Lord Macartney's failure to induce a general demand for British goods: why, for example, he did not get the Chinese to throw away their chopsticks, as he was convinced they would when he demonstrated the "conveniency" of Sheffield knives, forks and spoons (Cranmer-Byng, 1962: 225–6).[25]

As it happened, when the Emperor told Lord Macartney he had no need of Britain's ingenious devices, he was not lying. He had them all, and in greater magnificence than ever Macartney could offer, though he kept them notably in his outlying hunting parks and summer palaces, Jehol beyond the Great Wall, where he received the English ambassador; and the "Garden of Perfect Brilliance," Yuan Ming Yuan, also outside Peking. If here the Emperor displayed his universality, his inclusion of the barbarians, it was at a distance from the Chinese harmonies that contrastively set off the capital and the Middle Kingdom as a whole. This symbolic contrast, I mean to show, is a key to the imperial trade policies.[26]

At Jehol where the Emperor hunted were stored untold riches from the lands of barbarians—who were likewise hunted and collected. In numerous pavilions decorated with scenes of the Emperor's progresses and imperial feats of the chase (in which the Emperor was "always seen at full gallop shooting wild beasts with arrows" [Staunton, 1799, v. 2, 82]) Lord Macartney was able to see for himself

> every kind of European toys and sing-songs; with spheres, orreries, clocks, and musical automatons of such exquisite workmanship, and in such profusion, that our presents must shrink from the comparison and "hide their diminished heads." And yet I am told that the fine things we have seen are far exceeded by others of the same kind in the apartments of the ladies and in the European repository at Yuan-ming Yuan. (Cranmer-Byng, 1962: 125–6)

The English never did see the "European repository": the impressive set of palaces in the Italianate baroque style at Yuan Ming Yuan, designed for the

Emperor by Jesuit missionaries and cluttered with all sorts of European wealth. A French missionary who had viewed these palaces found it "incredible how rich this sovereign is in curiosities and magnificent objects of all kinds from the Occident" (in Malone, 1934: 160).[27] Yet the foreign treasures were only part of an assemblage that aimed to make the imperial retreats complete with every imaginable creation of nature as well as of humanity. As Granet says, even things that no collector could find nevertheless figured there, sculpted or drawn: it was a universal collection of "evocative singularities" (Granet, 1968: 274). Such diversity was directly linked to the ruler's power. Indeed if the Ch'ien-lung Emperor made Jehol a museum of his prowess, it was in the tradition of the original conqueror Ch'in Shih Huang-ti (reign: 221–210 B.C.), who "in order to enjoy all his victories at once and in detail," had as many palaces built in his grandiose gardens as he had destroyed principalities, each edifice reproducing the residence of a defeated ruler (Cibot, 1782b; cf. Yang, 1974: 168).

The synthesis of diversity and conquest made these imperial retreats perfect microcosms. They represented the whole world as the work of the Emperor and within his power. "All the beasts of the air, of the water, of the earth thronged in his fish ponds and his parks. No species was wanting in his botanic gardens; the waves of his lakes could be seen breaking against the distant lands in which could be recognized the mysterious Isles of the immortals" (Granet, 1930: 394). Written of the great emperor Wu of Han, the description summarizes just as well Lord Macartney's wide-eyed account of the East Garden of the Ch'ien-lung Emperor at Jehol (Cranmer-Byng, 1962: 124ff; cf. Malone, 1928).[28] For the Manchu emperor, one would only need to add the condensed collections of human life: the villages and monasteries, libraries and temples, as well as peasant fields of every crop. The libraries housed exhaustive collections of knowledge, the results of a search initiated by the Emperor in 1771 for the most rare and valuable books of the realm (Guy, 1987). Yet merely by contemplating his garden the sage king could cultivate his powers of rule, since in such a setting meditation amounted to the absorption of the universe.[29] At Yuan Ming Yuan, there was even a miniature walled town with streets, squares, temples, marketplaces, shops and civic buildings (see acompanying plate). If at Versailles Marie Antoinette played the shepherdess in pastoral idylls, at Yuan Ming Yuan the Empress, women of the Court and the Emperor dressed up as city dwellers to join a throng of eunuchs, themselves impersonating merchants, artisans, peddlers, porters, soldiers and even pickpockets, in scenes that reproduced "all the hurly-burly, the comings and goings, and even the swindling of the big cities" (Attiret, 1843 [1743]: 790).

The Jesuit painter Attiret, to whom we owe this eighteenth-century description, goes on to contrast the apparent disarray of the summer gardens with the balanced arrangements of the imperial palace at Peking. The "beautiful order" of the latter he likens to our Western notions of symmetry and

She Wei Ch'eng in Yuan Ming Yuan. Street flanked by shops leading toward a gate in
the background. From Siren 1949; original painting by T'ang Tai and Shen Yuan,
Bibliotheque Nationale, Paris.

uniformity, where nothing is without parallels, nothing displaced, but everything responds exactly to what is *en face* and counterposed to it (see accompanying plate). In Yuan Ming Yuan, however, there reigns a "beautiful disorder," which could even be called an "anti-symmetry." Chinese sources
confirm that the apparent disorder—while avoiding submission to "a symmetry even more tiresome than it is cold and monotonous"—is again meant to
imitate nature (Cibot, 1782b: 318). The linked connotations of natural heterogeneity and imperial power are resumed by Attiret's observation that not one
of the pastoral pavilions resembled another; instead, "one would say that each
is made according to the ideas and model of some foreign country" (1843:
791). Extending even to the smallest architectural details, the diversity repeatedly evokes from the Jesuit artist the sense of a human mastery of a universal plenitude: "Not until I came here had I seen doors and windows with
such a variety of form and figure: round, oval, square, polygons of all kinds;
or in the form of fans, flowers, vases, birds, beasts, fishes—in short, in every
regular or irregular shape" (1843: 792). Yet it is remarkable, comments
Granet, that when the Chinese have welcomed "legends or techniques,

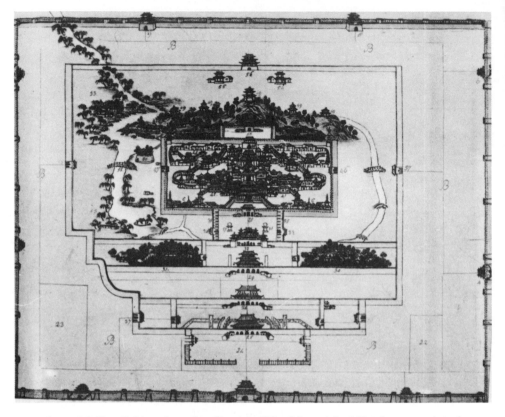

Imperial City, Peking, from the album (v. IV) of the original Dutch manuscript of
A. E. van Braam, *Memoriaal wegens de ambassade der Nederlandsche
Oost-Indische Compagnie voor denKyzer van China in de jaren 1794/95*,
as reproduced in Duyvendak 1938 (facing p. 46).

jongleries or ideas tinged with exoticism, they have never admitted these in
the house." Since ancient times an elegant system of classification has
reigned over such domestic habitations, a balanced order of things Chinese.
Whereas in the parks reserved "to their hunts, their *fetes*, their games," the
rulers receive "everything that is brought to them: ideas or gods, exotic or
new, astrologers, poets and clowns" (Granet, 1968: 295–6).[30] And, one might
add, English lords and their curious gifts, such as the fine carriages Macartney brought, which were never used but instead consigned to an undignified
place in one of the rococo palaces at Yuan Ming Yuan (Barrow, 1805: 145;
Swinhoe, 1861: 331).[31]

   The point I want to make is that these imperial gardens and hunting lodges
signified a cultural politics, encompassing an economics that was likewise
inclusive and exclusive and could thus adapt appropriately to the practical
situation. The opposition between the emperor's countryside and the imperial

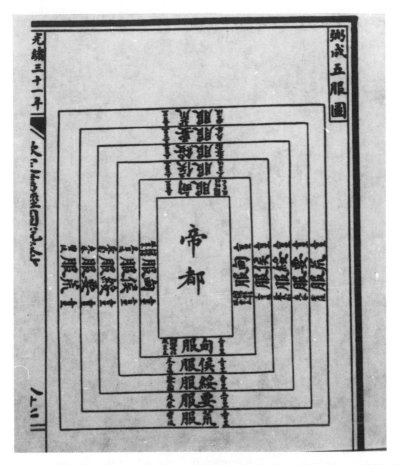

Traditional conception of the radiation of Chinese civilization (Needham, 1959: 502).
Proceeding outwards from the metropolitan center, Needham writes, "we have, in
concentric rectangles, (a) the royal domains, (b) the lands of the tributary feudal
princes and lords, (c) the 'zone of pacification,' i.e. the marches, where Chinese
civilization was in the course of adoption, (d) the zone of allied barbarians,
(e) the zone of cultureless savagery."

city recapitulated a whole cosmography of civilization—sometimes called
"the inner-outer separation" (Wang, 1968)—which the Chinese have represented also in other ways. Needham reproduces an ancient Chinese plan of
the world, laid out as a series of inclusive squares surrounding a central royal
domain (see accompanying figure). Extending outward from the royal center,
the epitome of a structured order, are barbarian zones of decreasing civilization and pacification, ending in the far reaches of a "cultureless savagery"
(Needham, 1959: 502). By setting China apart while at the same time making
it the central source of world order, this theory of civilization lends itself

equally to projects of imperial expansion and cultural withdrawal, to heg-emonic inclusions or xenophobic exclusions, according to the contingencies of the situation.

This may well be a normal dynastic cycle, including the pendulation between a forward economic policy and a period of xenophobic retreat, coin-ciding with a territorial expansion that ultimately reveals the limits and weak-nesses of the Chinese imperium. For the dynastic conquests in ascendant phases would encourage just those processes Lattimore identifies as sources of decline, notably the development of gentry power and mercantile wealth (Lattimore, 1940). Diverting revenues from the central government and im-posing ruin on the peasantry, the rise of these private powers issues in a crisis of the imperial regime. The government proves less and less able to cope with the twinned menaces of domestic uprising and barbarian incursion which now appear, the unwanted offspring of its own successes. Hence the close correlation between the achievement of world empire and the inauguration of a political economy of exclusion, by contrast to an earlier, inclusive relation to the barbarian periphery when the new dynasty was proving its claim to the Mandate of Heaven.

Sinologists have made this argument for the Ming period (Fletcher, 1968) as well as for the Ch'ing dynasty at issue here (Dermigny, 1964, v. 2: 468f, see especially 487–95). The spectacular expansion of Ming under the Yung-lo Emperor (reign: 1403–34) is well known, especially the great voyages of the eunuch admiral Cheng-ho which ran China's writ from East Africa to the East Indies. In huge armadas, with personnel running into the tens of thou-sands, Cheng-ho sailed as far as the Persian Gulf and African coast, "collect-ing vassals like souvenirs" (Cameron, 1970: 124; Lo, 1958; Needham, 1971: 487f; Fairbank, 1942: 40–1; Dermigny, 1964, v. 1: 300f). By contrast the later Ming saw a radical decline in foreign tributary embassies, together with an imperial disinterest in foreign trade—just when the Europeans came in (Fairbank & Teng, 1941).[32] A similar withdrawal had marked the later T'ang dynasty (post–eighth century), when strict trade restrictions were imposed in the name of the ethical integrity of the Middle Kingdom. Yet a century before Chinese noblemen dressed *à la Turque* were camping out in felt tents on the streets of Peking. In the earlier "fullness of T'ang" a passion for the exotic in every shape and form—from green-eyed Inner Asian dancing girls to the san-dalwood of India or the spices of the Moluccas—had gripped all classes of Chinese society (Schafer, 1963).[33] Still, this kind of oscillation, as Joseph Fletcher observes of the comparable Ming cycle, entailed no change in the Chinese theory of Empire. The inclusive and exclusive policies were alterna-tive practical modalities of the same concept of hierarchy. In later Ming, Fletcher writes, the emperors

> began to fulfill their mandate more passively. More and more, China stood aloof, disdained trade, and viewed the acceptance of Central Asian tribute as a conces-sion; nevertheless, it would be a distortion to regard the early Ming explorations

simply as the events of an isolated episode. That the Ming tried to draw the world closer during the early history of the dynasty and not afterwards reflects the Ming's early strength and its later weakness. It does not reflect a change of doctrine or an abdication of the emperor's world supremacy. The early initiative and later withdrawal occurred within the context of the same institutions and imperial claims. The foreign expeditions and diplomatic concessions of the Hung-wu and Yung-lo periods represent Ming values in a period of strength, while the antiforeignism and anticommercialism of the later Ming are their expression in a period of weakness. (Fletcher, 1968: 215; cf. Dermigny, 1964, v. 1: 296)

We see how inadequate is the idea of Chinese "self-sufficiency" which Western scholars have been repeating tautologically and for too long to explain Ming and Ch'ing indifference to European commodities (Cranmer-Byng, 1962: 12; Fairbank, 1942: 139; Greenberg, 1951: 5). Even in the earlier Ch'ing there had been more than traces of a revived commercial cycle, complemented by the interest of the long-ruling K'ang Hsi Emperor (reign: 1662–1722) in European arts and sciences (Mancall, 1984: 60–3, 85f; Spence, 1975; Pritchard, 1929: 104ff; Wills, 1979). But now there were new factors in play, including the Manchu failure to control a developing private trade in the southeast, in which also were engaged barbarian forces of an unprecedented kind (cf. Fu, 1966: 122–3; Fairbank & Teng, 1941). Outside the orbit of Chinese civilization, these Western forces were eccentric to its tempos. Unlike the traditional frontier peoples and vassals, the Europeans could never be controlled or bought off (cf. Lattimore, 1940). Indeed, their demands on China generally augmented over time, according to their own entrepreneurial rhythms. The Manchu dynasts found Western silver quite useful for their own world-system projects. But during the rule of the Ch'ien-lung Emperor, precisely at the greatest extent of Manchu conquests and the height of the imperial powers, the Son of Heaven preferred to satisfy his interest in things foreign through the contemplation of his own gardens. From what he saw there, he could always be sure of his world-constituting virtue.

THE SANDWICH ISLANDS

While the Celestial Emperor had no need of British manufacturers, the kings and would-be kings of the Sandwich Islands, by reason of their own heavenly status, could not get enough. Nor was their avidity confined to European material goods, which they considered generally superior to their own; they wanted the identity of the European great, whose names and habits they adopted as signs of their own dignity. By 1793, the same year the Ch'ien-lung Emperor commended the tributary English king for showing him the proper reverence, the three most powerful Hawaiian rulers had been pleased to name their sons and heirs "King George" (Bell, 1929 I(5):64).[34] An agent of the American Fur company describes the Honolulu sporting scene in 1812:

At the race course I observed Billy Pitt, George Washington and Billy Cobbet walking together in the most familiar manner, and apparently engaged in confidential conversation; while in the center of another group, Charley Fox, Thomas Jefferson, James Madison, Bonnepart [*sic*] and Tom Paine were seen on equally friendly terms with each other. (Cox, 1832: 144)

Within the decade the Hawaiian "Billy Pitt," a.k.a. Kalanimoku, [would] indeed be "Prime Minister" of a unified Sandwich Islands kingdom, with his classifactory brothers "Cox" Ke'eaumoku and "John Adams" Kuakini respectively ruling as the governors of Maui and Hawai'i Island.

Clearly these foreigners by whom Hawaiian ruling chiefs took consciousness of themselves were not unruly barbarians from the margins of the earth. Rather, they came from the sky beyond the horizon: from the mythical Kahiki, the celestial and overseas homelands of gods, sacred chiefs and cultural good things. Like the royal ancestors who brought thence foods, rites, tabus—the means of human life and the distinctions of social order—the White men or *Haole* were perceived as bearers of powers civilizing and divine (cf. Sahlins, 1981, 1985). Well into the nineteenth century the history of the Islands was shaped by this correlation between foreign and Polynesian powers-that-be.

From the time of Cook, who was searching [for] a northwest passage to the Orient, Westerners had come to Hawaii because of the China trade. But nearly everything in the intercultural encounter was the opposite to their Chinese experience. Macartney had refused to kowtow to the Chinese Emperor, as it would impugn the dignity of his own King; whereas, when Cook first stepped ashore at Kaua'i Island the Hawaiians promptly prostrated before him, as they did for those high chiefs whom they called *akua*, "gods" (Malo, 1951:54). And if the great Hawaiian chiefs competed to distinguish themselves by taking on European identities, it was because unlike the Celestial Emperor, the Unique Man, they confronted each other as perpetual rivals who in their own divinity were virtual doubles (cf. Valeri, 1972, 1981; Sahlins, 1985b).

Traditionally Hawaiian ruling chiefs had vied for ancestry and tabu status by strategic marriages with noble women and violent sacrifices of royal adversaries. Such exploits could represent in social practice the theory of sovereignty encoded in myth and enacted in annual rite: theory of usurpation by the upstart warrior, who is archetypally a stranger, and whose victory over the god or king of ancient lineage involves also the seizure of his predecessor's sacred wife. The realm of the political, then, appears as a practical version of the cosmological: a transposition of the Polynesian scheme of the appropriation of the bearing earth (= the sacred wife) from the god (= the reigning king) by and for humankind (= the usurper-warrior). But as thus transposed to practice, the competition for divine honors becomes permanent and indecisive. By virtue of a long history of strategic intermarriages, contending chiefs are all able to trace their lineage one way or another (i.e., bilaterally) to the same godly sources. Genealogy turns into an argument rather than an entitlement. And a kind of entropy appears in the system of rank, a tendency to move toward an undifferentiated state, for by some line of descent or another an ambitious chief could pretend to seniority over political rivals who on similar grounds supposed themselves superior to him. In traditional times a chief rich in lands and followers could always hope to turn such assets into a legitimate claim of distinction. Thus the role assumed by the late eighteenth-century visitations of Kahiki: in analogous ways the chiefs searched [for] distinction in the relations and goods of Western commerce. The whole of this history seems epitomized by an incident of 1793, when the soon-conqueror of archipelago Kamehameha formally greeted the British commander Vancouver while clad in a fine Chinese dressing gown which he considered "the most valuable garment in his wardrobe" as his predecessor (Kalaniopu'u) had received it as a present from Captain Cook (Manby, 1929: 40).[35]

However, the report of certain Americans alongside English and Frenchmen among the *tout* Honolulu of 1812 reflects an important shift in the international order of the trans-Pacific commerce. By the turn of the nineteenth century, Yankee entrepreneurs had captured the Northwest Coast–Canton fur trade, the possibilities of which were originally disclosed by Cook's third voyage, and initially exploited by British shipping.[36] Cut off from the British West Indies after the Revolution, the merchants of the fledgling United States had turned to the markets of the Far East. The problem was that they had precious little silver to offer for Chinese goods. "To find something saleable in Canton was the riddle of the China trade," Samuel Eliot Morison observes, but "Boston and Salem solved it" (1961: 46).[37] Morison perhaps exaggerates, inasmuch as Pacific sea-otter pelts and other fine furs never yielded the Americans more than about one-sixth of the funds they needed to pay for Chinese goods (Pitkin, 1835: 245f). The rest had to be covered in specie, such as they got from the neutral carrying trade in Europe during the French Revolutionary and Napoleonic wars.[38] This continuing silver drain gave American traders an equally persistent interest in products of Pacific islanders that could fit the categories of Chinese consumers.

Thus the search for sandalwood, such as the Chinese had been importing from India and the Indies since the T'ang dynasty for use in noble architecture, fine objets d'art and to disseminate the whiff of an increasingly influential Buddhism. As incense and in image, "the divinely sweet odour of the sandal expressed to the senses the antidemonic properties concealed within its godlike body" (Schafer, 1963: 137). A thousand years later, by virtue of powers undreamed of in this philosophy, the properties concealed in sandalwood trees of the New Hebrides, Hawaii and the Fiji Islands, used to drive out Chinese demons, could thereby be transformed into teas that in turn generated pecuniary returns to American entrepreneurs at whatever the cost to whom it might concern.

In Hawaii the sandalwood trade superseded an earlier commerce in "refreshments" that had already made the Islands "a great caravansary" on the

Northwest Coast–Canton fur trade route (Fleurieu in Bradley, 1968: 22). The strategic location of the group was one reason for the refreshment trade. Another was the superior ability of Hawaiian chiefs, by comparison to the Northwest Indians, to supply provisions to the shipping (Howay, 1930). I say "chiefs" because (as I have elsewhere documented), they took main control of this trade, using traditional privileges such as their tabuing-powers to organize it in their own interests (cf. Sahlins, 1981). Suffice it here to note that the chiefs were able to impose their own demands: at once on Westerners for armaments; and on the Hawaiian people for labor and produce, largely unpaid. By 1810 the Hawaii Island ruler Kamehameha, through a superior access to European trade—grounded in a privileged relation to the manes of Captain Cook—had unified the group in a conquest kingdom. Hawaiian sandalwood was about to become the staple commercial interest of the Islands. To American merchants it became even more interesting around 1820, as returns declined in the maritime fur trade. Whereas in Hawaii, the sandalwood trade literally enriched the customary conflicts between the king and ranking chiefs, which more and more appeared as demonstrations of indigenous mana in the most appropriate forms of foreign wealth. The rivalries became so serious that *Haole* inside-dopesters were predicting a partition of the kingdom among "the grandees" after Kamehameha's death, a kind of decentralization that had also happened before (Whitman, 1979: 89; Chamisso, 1981: 431–2; Rocquefeuil, 1823, v. 2: 342f; cf. Sahlins, 1972: 144f). But as it happened now, the King died in 1819, thus bringing the Polynesian political cycle into conjunction with an equally characteristic capitalist economic cycle—and launching the Hawaiian great on their brilliant careers of conspicuous consumption.

America in 1818–19 was in the grip of a financial crisis. Among New England merchants the shortage of specie put a premium on Hawaiian sandalwood as a means of carrying on a China trade. The Americans thereupon

> descended upon the islands in a swarm, bringing with them everything from pins, scissors, clothing, and kitchen utensils to carriages, billiard tables, house frames, and sailing ships, and doing their utmost to keep the speculating spirit at a fever heat among the Hawaiian chiefs. And the chiefs were not slow about buying; if they had no sandalwood at hand to pay for the goods, they gave promissory notes. (Kuykendall 1968: 69)

They were not slow about buying—only about paying. Contemporary documents give the impression of an *opera bouffe* staged in naive tropical settings richly furnished from an international division of labor: these huge Polynesian notables covered in variegated costumes of fine Chinese silk and English broadcloth, being hauled through the dusty lanes of Honolulu in pony chaises or wheelbarrows by straining menials clad in loincloths, or playing at scenes of European dining in thatched houses at teak tables set with English silver and crystal—with all the good things imported on the never-never. Whereas the common people enter only as supporting characters: arduous work, given the sheer bulk of the ruling chiefs. Although many of the chiefs were now professing Christians, they would never learn to mortify their own flesh. The family that *de facto* governed the Islands after Kamehameha's death (the Ka'ahumanu people) included five brothers and sisters weighing in at contemporary estimates of 250 to 350 lbs (Bloxam, Narrative 15, 28 May 1825; Dampier, 1971: 48). Signifying the control of land, food and people, and the means of their productivity—all godlike powers—fat was beautiful in the Hawaiian system. But in recompense for the prolonged labor of working sandalwood, the underlying people were only poorly fed, or not fed at all; nor did they share in the commercial returns. Their labor was exacted as a kind of ground rent due to the chiefly "lord of the land" (*haku'aina*; cf. Mathison, 1825: 384–5).

Meanwhile the elite consumption fever was being fueled by two intersecting systems of rivalry: on one side, the American merchants competing with each other for custom; on the other, the Hawaiian chiefs with the custom of competing with each other.[39] And all the while the traders were undercutting one another—as by advancing ever more elegant goods while denigrating their competitors'—they were appealing to the chiefs' emulative spirit of self-regard. As the Hawaiian historian says: "The chiefs were all bent at this time at securing honors for themselves" (Kamakau, 1961: 265). By the close of 1821, the King and chiefs are reported to own "Ten large and elegant Brigs, besides a large number of Sloops & Schooners, all of which they have purchased from Americans" (USCD, Jones: 31 Dec. 1821). This includes *Cleopatra's Barge*, a luxuriously fitted and leaky vessel sent out by a Boston firm to dazzle the local nobility, which King Liholiho (Kamehameha II) agreed to buy for $90,000 in sandalwood—that the firm's Honolulu agent Bullard could not collect (Bullard, Letters). Still, Bullard reported optimistically to Boston: "If you want to know how religion stands at the Islands, I can tell you; all sects are tolerated and the King worships the Barge" (ibid., 1 Nov. 1821).

By this time in fact the King had formally abolished the old religion, yet he and the other ruling chiefs continued to testify to a divinity of ancient memory in their own nature. Hence their appropriation of Western distinctions between "plain" and "fancy" goods, and their appreciation especially for those fineries whose luster, reflecting a celestial brilliance, accorded with their received ideas of aristocratic flash. "Send out articles of a showy kind," the merchant John C. Jones wrote to his suppliers (ML: 9 Mar 1823); "everything new and elegant will sell at a profit, coarse articles are of no use" (ibid., 31 May 1823); "fine cloth would have commanded any price" (10 Oct. 1822).[40] Trade goods were glorious artificial extensions of sacred chiefly bodies already stretched to their organic limits. Indeed, just as in the case of the chiefs' avoirdupois, all their indulgences seemed designed to magnify their persons, including the expenditures on the large corps of domestic retainers kept to minister to their bodily wants and pleasures (Steward, 1930: 138; Corney, 1896: 105; Judd, 1966: 21). The chief's retinue was like a superbeing, its numerous members functioning to sustain the one life with which all were identified. At the same time, given the traditional indeterminacies of chiefly honors, the entropy of the ranking system, each chief was bent on proving in the new medium of commercial prowess that he was equal to and better than, the same as and different from, the others. The elite economy was an arena of differentiation, where invidious distinctions were played out between the powers-that-be and those that only would-be.

Thus certain other characteristics of this Polynesian market: the endless pursuit of novelty, the rage for the latest Boston fashions, and the hoarding of foreign goods taken as signs and projections of the "civilized" person. Another trader writes to his Boston suppliers that having sold fifteen bedsteads he had exhausted the Honolulu market since "they are all alike." He adds that "your best silks are but little wanted" because stuff of the same kind had come out before in a competitor's ship, "and they [the Hawaiians] want such patterns as they have never seen before" (Hunnewell, Letters: 30 Dec. 1829). This pursuit of individual distinction had been running strong since Kamehameha's death—"Everyone that comes brings better and better goods, and such as they have not seen will sell when common ones will not" (Bullard, Letters: 4 July 1821). And precisely as the commercial goods contributed to personal distinction, they were not at all destined for general distribution. They were ostentatiously hoarded up, a conspicuous thesaurization: amassed even to the point of waste, as if any depletion of the accumulated foreign goods were the sign of a personal diminishment. The chiefs were disinclined to make any inroads on their stocks-in-hand, even when needed for some ceremonial purpose. They preferred then to buy more of what they already had in abundance:

> These people have an incurable reluctance to part with anything they have stored away. There is now an immense amount of property stowed away in cases & dirty houses which is rotting away, but which the chiefs will not take out of their repositories even to use themselves. The King [Liholiho] some time ago was in want of duck [cloth] when it was scarce & bought a few bolts at a very high price, when at the same time he had two or three hundred bolts which was stored away rotting. (Hammatt Journal: 18 Aug. 1823)

Related to production by such interests of consumption, the Hawaiian nobility soon showed themselves unable to compete with advancing capitalist modes of exploiting the Islands' resources. As Adam Smith said: "It seldom happens that a great proprietor is a great improver" (*Weal. Nat.* III. 2). The ruling chiefs had a greater ability to accumulate goods than they had to make others pay for them. Even were they inclined to productive investments, all they had were commercial debts—which the common people lost interest in working off by forced labor perhaps faster than they were losing the population numbers to do so. The chiefs, too, were dying out: a mortality that is usually taken as the reason they gave the authority over to White men. But the explanation reverses matters. The chiefs were obsolete as a ruling class, and simply failed to make use of available social means of reproducing themselves as such.[41] In a similar situation of misfortune the Kwakiutl Indians recruited women and commoner men to noble positions, thereby sustaining the celebrated "potlatch" system for nearly two centuries. And if the Kwakiutl chief had no daughter by whose marriage he could transfer ancestral names and privileges, and thus constitute enduring alliances with other lineages, he could marry off his son's left side or else make someone a wife out of his own left foot (Boas, 1966: 55).

THE KWAKIUTL

The early contact histories of British Columbia and the Sandwich Islands are linked by the same European names—Cook and Vancouver, Portlock and Dixon, Meares, Colnett, Ebenezer Townsend, Peter Corney—but the relationship the Kwakiutl fashioned with such Westerners, then and later, was different from the Hawaiian experience. This much was the same: for the Indians, too, wealth and power were traditionally obtained from beyond society, and especially from sea and sky; so in analogous ways certain Western commodities were subsumed as indigenous values. Still, to mention only the most striking difference, the Kwakiutl acquired cosmic powers not by consuming the riches of the market economy, as though to inflate their own persons, but by ostentatiously giving goods away, in a manner that signified the incorporation of other people.

Western commerce had made possible a spectacular process of development on the Northwest Coast, the elaboration of the famous potlatch system (cf. Boas, 1897, 1921, 1930, 1935, 1966).[42] Ceremonial and aesthetic as well as political, this was a total cultural development that for over 15 years resisted the equally broad assault of Western imperialism, whether in the form of Christian missionaries, legal sanctions of the Canadian government, or the relations of capitalist production in the lumber, fishing, canning and prostitution industries. The Kwakiutl could not be faulted for their aptitudes as wage workers, or even as entrepreneurs, but White men often wrung their hands about what the Indians did with their earnings, which was to pile up Hudson's Bay blankets and other bizarre stuff for colossal giveaways.[43] In 1881 the first Indian Agent sent a report of the "apathetic state" of the Kwakiutl, from which he "must endeavor to lift them"; their apathy, as he described it, consisted of being "surrounded with boxes of property all ready for the potlatch" (Codere, 1950: 82). Summarizing an extensive study of such official documents, Codere writes:

> Throughout the years, the Kwakiutl are described as industrious but not progressive; as measuring up to almost any standard of enterprise, skillfulness, adaptability and productivity, but as failing to possess these premium qualities in relation to the proper goals, or to be inspired to them by the proper motivations. It is

as though Kwakiutl were able to exploit the new culture to their own ends. . . . (ibid., p. 8; cf. Fisher, 1977)

Potlatches involving Hudson's Bay blankets escalated after the establishment of Fort Rupert in 1849, reaching a high of 33,000 in one affair of 1933, but including such expenditures as 200 silver bracelets, 7,000 brass bracelets and 240 washbasins in an 1895 distribution, and more recently the likes of sewing machines, gramophones, watches and pool tables (ibid., pp. 90–1; Codere, 1961: 464). The blankets replaced the worked skins of various animals and cedar bark robes distributed on analogous occasions (although in smaller quantities) in earlier times. Distinctions of rank formerly made by different types of skins were no longer so signified, a change that seems correlated with the participation of commoners and women in positions traditionally reserved to the nobility. But I draw attention especially to the contrast between this standardization of the main commercial-prestige good, the Hudson's Bay blanket, and the differentiating consumption of the Hawaiian elite, who always demanded "such patterns as they have never seen before"—with no intention either of lavishing their riches on others. Whereas, by giving trade blankets to others, the Kwakiutl testified to different sacred powers.

Hunters on the sea and land, the Indians lived by inflicting death.[44] They reproduced human life by killing sentient beings whom they considered to be, underneath their animal skins or guises, persons like themselves. Animals are of common origin with humanity, part of the same universal society. Indeed the lives of people and game or fish are interdependent: for if the animals willingly give themselves to the Indians, it is because the Indians know how to assure the rebirth of their prey through the ritual respects they accord the remains—a cycle of reincarnation that typically passes through a human phase when the animal is consumed as food. Arcane beliefs perhaps, but they were critical to the fur trade and potlatch. As a distribution of worked animal skins donned by the recipients as robes, the potlatch is exactly the same kind of ritual reincarnation staged as a social event.[45] Recall that animals are humans under the skin. Hence the distribution of skins as blankets recreates the animal victims in living human form: moreover, in large numbers and in a respectful way, as worked-up and cultural goods. Of course in the fur trade the animal skins had to be given up. But what, other than their own total modes of production and reproduction, could compel the Indians to take stripped woolen blankets as "economic" equivalents?

Hudson's Bay blankets had yet other powers concealed in their unassuming appearance. In potlatches they were given away by chiefs to validate their privileges and add greatness to their names. The blankets represented the chief's attainments in *nawalak*, a generalized life-giving power which myth tells can kill enemies effortlessly, restore the dead to life and accomplish miracles of hunting and wealth-getting (cf. Goldman, 1975; Dullabaun, 1979). Just so, the gifts are said to "swallow" the recipients who are chiefs of other lineages (*numayam*) and tribes. At issue are certain powers of inclusion: an attempt at hierarchy, which is also the transcending of social boundaries.

For precisely by translation into the common medium of blankets, the unique ancestral privileges (*tlogwe*) of the different Kwakiutl lineages could be matched and compared—that is, as the generic *nawalak* (cf. Dullabaun, 1979). Each lineage begins with a distinct and inalienable stock of privileges bestowed by the founder. In the typical narrative, a specific animal descends from the heavens to a particular place on the beach, takes off his animal mask and becomes the human ancestor. The mask itself is one of these permanent lineage treasures, as are certain totem poles, house posts, carved boxes, feast dishes and the names that confer given place and precedence in the pan-Kwakiutl potlatch order. Means and signs of the lineage's existence, creators of food and riches, these "precious things," as Marcel Mauss observed, "have in themselves a productive virtue" (1966: 220–1). Indeed the chief who possesses them recreates himself as the ancestor, and thus crossing the space between present and past, man and spirit, he is able to traverse the paradigmatic boundary of life and death.[46]

This, the heroic overcoming of death, is the Kwakiutl mode of cultural production. Of course it describes hunting, which not only brings life out of death but, as animals are basically human, courts the risks of a *cannibalisme generalise* (cf. Walens, 1981: 101). Yet in the same way Kwakiutl shamanism, warfare, trade, marriages, or the ceremonies of the winter solstice are so many analogous and interrelated projects of derring-do, involving the capture of powerful forces beyond society and their transformation into beneficent sources of human existence.[47] Likewise, Kwakiutl politics: the chiefs increased the "weight" of their inherited names by appropriating privileges from other lineages and tribes—external powers they could ultimately validate by potlatch-distributions that again subordinated ("swallowed") the names and claims of rival-others. Dullabaun summarizes these homologies in the Kwakiutl negotiations of power:

> Power must be acquired . . . The mode of acquisition always involves crossing some kind of categorical boundary. So, for example, one leaves the beach (where the villages are located) and goes deep into the forest to acquire a treasure. Or one travels a long distance over the sea to acquire powers through marriage from these distant fathers-in-law. The most radical kind of boundary crossing (and hence the source of the most valued power) occurs when a person (an initiate in the winter ceremonial) imitates his patron spirit and in so doing becomes the spirit (i.e., takes the spirit's name and powers). (Dullabaun, 1979: 49)

Transactions of power involved a second fund of privileges (*tlogwe*), mostly like the original lineage treasures except that they were alienable, as indeed they had been obtained in heroic encounters of the ancestors with spirits of the sea or forest. The most important acquired privileges were rights to the winter ceremonial performances in which such ancestral feats were reenacted—in a context where lineage boundaries were also transcended: by the organization of larger communities along the lines of ritual societies. Negotiations of acquired privileges were thus the decisive moves of tribal politics. And family histories were chronicles of the victories thus achieved in marriage and war. The chiefs gained treasures from noble fathers-in-law in marriage—as the so-called payment of the marriage debt, which followed the bride—and in war through the right of the slayer to seize the ceremonial honors of his victim. Once again involving the appropriation of powers across a social boundary, the one and the other are humanized versions of the deeds of legendary heroes in the spiritual outer realms. The son-in-law stands to his father-in-law as the warrior to his victim—or as the hero to his patron spirit.[48] So Kwakiutl say of marriage, "The chiefs make war upon the princess of the tribes" (Boas, 1966: 53; 1935: 65n.). The object of an ambitious chief was to marry the daughters of all the others. For these others, the alliance with a powerful chief, on whom one bestowed further privileges, was indeed a practical alternative to battle.[49] Whereas for the rising chief, the attendance of numerous relatives at the potlatches following on his marital conquests "showed you were a prominent, you were a big man, and you were related to all the different tribes. That's what it meant" (Spradley, 1969: 247). And as a result of the chief's marriages, his descendants could boast in family histories: "Therefore I am full of names and privileges. And therefore I have many chiefs and ancestors all over the world" (Boas, 1921: 844).

Notice the incorporative phrasing: marriage appropriates new ancestors; it includes the powers of other lineages in one's own. It remains only to demonstrate the heritage in potlatch, thereby turning the incorporation of ancestors into the encompassment of contemporaries. And need one demonstrate here that the blankets which will thus transcend the boundaries between groups and combine them in a higher order, embody in their own production these same social qualities? Or better, they incorporate the same qualities in a stronger form, since Hudson's Bay blankets are the product of the successive negotiations of life and death in the hunt, Indian and foreigner in trade.[50] Representing in this way generic powers (*nawalak*), the blankets, counted and distributed, make it possible to compare on a scale of greatness chiefly names and lineage privileges (*tlogwe*) that are otherwise incommensurable. Each lineage has its own unique powers, unrelated in origin to the others: the gift of an independent ancestor, associated with a particular territory. In this respect the cosmology of Kwakiutl politics is the converse of the Hawaiian. In Hawaii the sacred ancestral powers are ultimately one, united by common descent in a universal genealogy. Accordingly, the political problem to which Hawaiian chiefs devoted herculean efforts of consumption during the sandalwood trade was how to differentiate their sacred claims. If they were obsessed with fashionable differences in Western goods, it was in order to make qualitative distinctions out of their quantitative gradations in standing. Whereas the Indians wanted more and more of the same good, a standardized sign of universal powers, which when publicly distributed made quantitative comparisons of their qualitative differences.[51] The expansion of capitalist trade opened new vistas of social greatness to Kwakiutl chiefs, and withal a spectacular process of local develop-man.[52]

CONCLUSION: TEA AND OTHER GOODS TO THINK

Things like this had initially happened all around the Pacific because of that god Tea to whom the British were prepared to sacrifice "everything else," especially everything that belonged to other people. Or the historian might have said "the goddess Tea," insofar as its rituals were touted in the eighteenth century as domesticating and its virtues as non-intoxicating, properties that contrasted with its more masculine rivals for popular consumption: beer, ale and gin.[53] One readily grasps the function of tea as delivering a docile and effective working class into the maws of the developing capitalism. But if the spread of the tea-habit were to be studied seriously, one might suppose that here no less than elsewhere the practical function is a situational mode of a native scheme of cosmic proportions. Certainly it involves some peculiar Western ideas of the person as an imperfect creature of need and desire, whose whole earthly existence can be reduced to the pursuit of bodily pleasure and the avoidance of pain. A theological tragedy of long standing, this description of the human condition became a philosophical creed in the seventeenth century and then the everyday fare of the eighteenth—as witness the rapid dissemination of what Sidney Mintz has called "drug foods" among the European popular classes (Mintz, 1985). The development of modern Western "civilization" has depended on an enormous soft-drug culture, at least as a condition of tolerability, marked by the daily general consumption of such substances as tea, coffee, chocolate, tobacco and sugar—a list without much redeeming nutritious value.

If these opiates became rituals of the people—or indeed like religion they made bearable the earthly existence of fallen man—was it not because people were condemned to continuous misery by their insatiable bodily needs? Such had been the tragic Western sense of human nature at least since Augustine. Man is fated to a life that is penal not only because it is mortal, but because he is alone in a natural world that "does not make good what it promises; it is a liar and deceiveth" (in Deane, 1963: 45). Its deception consists in the impossibility of satisfying human lusts, notably the avarice for temporal goods. Man therefore never ceases hoping in this world, and never attains what he hopes for. Pursuing one thing after another, he finds "nothing remains permanently . . . his needs are so multiplied that he cannot find the one thing needful, a single and unchangeable nature" (ibid.). Only the state, law and morality—imperfect earthly reflections of the heavenly city—have kept this society of self-regarding men from dissolving into a war of each against all: described by Augustine in the same way that Hobbes, more than a thousand years later, [would] characterize the natural state. But by the seventeenth century, the Augustinian values were on the way to being overthrown. The earthly underside of man, with all its attendant miseries, was about to become a moral virtue. Or at least, in Locke's whiggish reading of the penalties of the Original Sin, human suffering was the beneficent gift of Providence—as "the great spur to human industry."[54]

So by the time of Adam Smith, every person's permanent misery—that is, scarcity and need—had become the premise of economic wisdom and the source of national welfare. The social and moral sublimation of temporal desires had indeed been dissolved by an oncoming capitalism. What for Augustine was slavery, the human bondage to bodily desires, was in the bourgeois view the essential human freedom. Man became the pleasure-pain machine invented by Hobbes and favored by the Enlightenment *philosophes*: a creature that moves to those things that do him his own good, and away from things that do him evil—motions to-wards and from-wards that were supposed to comprehend the entire universe of human behavior. The new rationality was based on an exquisite sensitivity to pleasure and pain, especially to pain, which is at once more enduring than pleasure and the condition of its possibility. But then, the capitalist economy had made a supreme fetish of human needs in the sense that needs, which are always social and objective in character, had to be assumed as subjective experiences of bodily affliction.

Whereas Asia in the eighteenth century entered into the consciousness of Europe as a cure. Land of spices and drugs, of the preservers of food and life, the Orient, as Dermigny says, presented to Europe not merely a spectacle dazzling to the eye but a presence that insinuated itself into the whole body. "What it procured for a sick and sinful Europe—sick no doubt because it was sinful—were means for restoring health: remedies" (Dermigny, 1964, v. 1: 18).[55]

So whatever the pain, "have a cup'a tea, everything'll be all right." Interesting that like coffee and chocolate, tea was not sweetened in its country of origin, though in the West all these drinks were taken with sugar from the time of their introduction. It is as if the sweetened bitterness of the beverage represented to the taste the kind of transformation it could effect in one's moral existence. And perhaps nothing better demonstrates the social genesis of these magical effects than the fact that in Britain tea soon took on psychological values far removed from its chemical properties. After all, it contains caffeine and was early advertised as a stimulant (Repplier, 1932: 5–6). Now Englishmen regularly drink tea to calm their nerves. But it would take another lecture—the Frazer lecture—to catalogue all the powers ascribed to this brew by her devotees. Truly she is a goddess worthy of the sacrifices the world has made for her.

NOTES

First appeared in 1988.

1. On Williams's death and various explanations thereof, see Turner (1861: 490), Robertson (1902: 56–9), Prout (1843: 388f.), Murray (1862:179, 195–6, 206–8) and Shineberg (1967: 205–7). Among the apparent parallels to Cook's death at Hawaii— apart from the manner in which Williams was collectively mobbed after he was drowned in shallow water—was the missionary's reported intrusion in the great annual feast (*nisekar*). From all reports, this was a solstitial event analogous to the Hawaiian Makahiki, also marked by sham battles and an interdiction of war (cf.

Humphreys, 1926: 180–1). As other Europeans, moreover, Williams was locally categorized as *Nobu*, the name of the lost creator-god at Eromanga, again analogous to the
Hawaiian Lono, of whom Cook was an avatar (cf. Capell, 1938: 72–3). It is said that
Williams's body was traded to some nearby people in exchange for pigs for the annual
feast, although his companion, a certain Harris, was eaten directly. On the ritual dimensions of Cook's death, see Sahlins (1985).

2. Langridge voices the common wisdom of the "martyrdom," to the effect that
"the tragic occurrence was due almost entirely to the evil deeds of white men preceding his [Williams's] visit" (1934: 15). Shineberg doubts it, noting that the last major
violence at Eromanga consisted of attacks by Hawaiians on local people across the
island from Dillon's Bay some nine years before Williams's death (cf. Bennet, 1832).
Shineberg's comments on Eurocentric explanations such as Langridge's are worth repeating in full:

> The retaliation-only theory fits perfectly into the concept of the passive role of the Melane-
> sian in culture contact, for it implies that there must be a white man behind every brown.
> Only in response to European action is the islander seen to act. He may not take the initia-
> tive: he may not have his own independent good reasons for killing Europeans—motives
> emanating from his own desires and customs—but must wait for the European to offend
> him. (Shineberg, 1967: 214)

3. "The multiple cultures, the multiple 'traditions' that have flourished within the
space-time boundaries of historical capitalism, have been no more primordial than the
multiple institutional frameworks. They are largely the creations of the modern world,
part of its ideological scaffolding" (Wallerstein, 1983: 76; cf. Frank, 1966: 19).

4. Consider Wallerstein's idea of "cultures" (i.e., "ideas, values, science, art, religion, language, passion, and color") as "the ways in which people clothe their politico-
economic interests and drives in order to express them, hide them, extend them in
space and time, and preserve their memory" (1980: 65).

5. The most striking examples concern the ways Western commodities are indigen-
ized in other cultural logics. Thus Lederman reports from the New Guinea Highlands:
"The Mendi we know do not see these objects in the same way as we see them: their
purposes supplied for us. . . . In our objects, they perceive multiple possibilities for
satisfying needs the manufacturers never imagined" (1986: 5). The report is echoed in
a recent ethnohistory of the Cree: "most technical innovations adopted by Indians
were modified to fit their existing perceptions and social system, and many European
goods were employed in Indian culture for purposes other than those for which they
were produced in Europe" (Thistle, 1986: 35).

6. See the cogent discussion of the modern development of cultural difference in
Bright and Geyer (in press). There is a parallel in the classic World System theory,
especially as it applies (or does not apply) to China. The theory holds, on one hand,
that the empire of capital is inconsistent with political hegemony: world empire would
impose considerations and interests of other kinds on bourgeois enterprise. Hence the
escape of capital from the political framework of the state has been necessary to the
development of the modern world economy (Wallerstein, 1974: 127; cf. Mancall,
1984: 67). On the other hand, if the World System does not constitute a unified world
society, it does suppose a system of autonomous states to bear the costs, as well as a
set of complementary local differences in products, demands and labor-forms. Hence
local differentiation is a condition of global integration, and vice versa. Of course,
all this would be as true in the era of industrial capitalism as in mercantile capitalism.

7. The "mystique of Western domination" encompasses a whole series of related propositions, ranging in value from absurd to false, and including: (1) that before the expansion of the West other peoples had lived and developed "in isolation"—which just means that *we* weren't there; (2) that the historic adaptations they were compelled to make to one another do not count as such, for everything then was "pristine" and "indigenous"; (3) that their interaction with the West however has been a qualitatively different process; since (4) European power uniquely destroys the ancient harmonies and coherence of these exotic cultures; and (5) in the process of their "acculturation" or assimilation to the West their own cultural distinctiveness is irreversibly extinguished.

8. In the earlier decades of European contact, Hawaiians called such things as watches and astronomical instruments *akua*, just as Maori called them *alua* or Fijians deemed various European wonders *kalou*. All these Polynesian terms are usually glossed as "god." See note 1 (above) on the inclusion of foreign persons in such categories.

9. Cf. Lederman, 1986a: 12; Codere, 1950: 81f. For a number of examples of the develop-man phenomenon, see the volume on *Affluence and Cultural Survival* edited by Salisbury and Tooker (1984). Trigger's analysis of the development of the Huron confederacy in the sixteenth and early seventeenth centuries is particularly pertinent. This was a total develop-man process in which the political evolution was complemented by an increase in the extent and volume of trade, growth of craft production and enrichment of ritual life. "The new social order," Trigger observes, "was based on an expanded application of principles that must already have been present and applied in embryonic form in Huron society in prehistoric times and, in this sense, is traditional" (1984: 22). No doubt the cognate League of the Iroquois could be understood from this vantage (cf. Hunt, 1960) —not to forget all the Plains Indian cultures as historically known.

10. Already in the latter sixteenth century, when New World production of silver was booming, "a prime beneficiary of this Potosi-led boom was Ming China" (Axtell, 1982: 72). As Antonia de Morga "explained in his informative discussion of trade in Manila at this time, the Chinese accepted only silver for their products, 'for they do not like gold, nor any other goods in exchange, nor do they carry any to China' " (ibid., pp. 75–6; cf. Spate, 1979). On silver imports to China in the eighteenth century see Pritchard (1929; 1936) or Dermigny (1964).

11. The Emperor's edict summarily rejects all the requests Lord Macartney had hoped to "negotiate," reminding the English king that: "You, O King, should simply act in conformity with our wishes by strengthening your loyalty and swearing perpetual obedience so as to ensure that your country may share the blessings of peace" (ibid., p. 340). To mark the presentation of British tributes, the Ch'ien-lung Emperor also composed a poem, which further explicates the theory of his world-constituting virtue:

> Now England is paying homage . . .
> My Ancestors' merit and virtue must have reached their distant shores.
>
> Though their tribute is commonplace, my heart approves sincerely.
> Curios and the boasted ingenuity of their devices I prize not.
> Though what they bring is meagre, yet,
> In my kindness to men from afar I make generous return,
> Wanting to preserve my good health and power.

(Ibid., p. x)

12. The great historian of this trade, H. B. Morse, writes: "as early as 1700, there were experienced the two embarrassments which beset the East India Company during its two centuries of trade to China—the difficulty of providing any English products the Chinese would buy, and the strain of providing the silver the Chinese demanded" (1966, v. 1: 113).

13. Sir George Staunton, secretary of the Macartney embassy, characterized the Canton trade arrangements of the Chinese as, "The ancient prejudices against all strangers . . . reduced into a system, supported on the fullest confidence in the perfect state of their own civilization; and the comparative barbarism of every other nation" (1799, v. 1: 8). Besides Morse (1966; 1971) and Dermigny (1964), general descriptions of the Canton system in the eighteenth century may be found in the works of Pritchard (1929; 1936), Greenberg (1951), Fairbank (1969) and Mancall (1984).

14. Nor do these figures accurately chart British consumption since for some years prior to the Commutation Act of 1784, which drastically reduced import duties on teas, more was being smuggled into the country from the continent than was legally imported by the Company. The Act reduced duties from c. 119 percent to 12½ percent—and thereby crippled the trade of all other Western nations at Canton. The American trade, however, was just beginning and soon would have good success. For comparative figures for this period, see Milburn (1813, v. 2: 486). Dermigny gives an indication of the increase in tea exports from China as carried by merchants of all countries: from an average 1,530,275 *livres marc* in 1719–24, to 44,858,000 *livres marc* in 1827–33 (1964, v. 1: 74n.).

15. Neither opium nor tea, but rather woolens were the true drug on the Canton market. In the years 1775–95, the Company's average annual losses on woolens were calculated at 5.6 percent, but the Company's average annual profit during this period was 28 percent on investment, and for tea alone, 31.4 percent (Pritchard, 1936: 157, 166).

16. Company records for 1786 indicate that: "'The Patterns of Norwich, Manchester & Hallifax Stuffs have been shewn to the [Chinese] Merchants, but it is not their opinion that any of them will answer for this Market: the Cotton Stuffs are too expensive, & the Chinese manufacture a variety of different kinds which tho' not so elegant are better adapted to their modes of dress'" (Morse, 1966, v. 2: 120).

17. The present account of the Macartney embassy is drawn from Lord Macartney's own journal (Cranmer-Byng, 1962) as well as the chronicles of Staunton (1799), Dinwiddie (Proudfoot, 1868), Alexander (MS), Barrow (1805) and Anderson (1795), the official Chinese correspondence (Cranmer-Byng, 1957–8), the East India Company instructions (Pritchard, 1938), and pertinent correspondence from missionaries in China (Pritchard, 1935). The English journals are not of equal value or probity; that of Barrow is particularly suspect (cf. Proudfoot, 1868: 44n., 52). An excellent analysis of the Macartney embassy is developed in James Hivea's recent dissertation (1986), to which I am much indebted. On aspects of the Chinese imperium discussed here in connection with the Macartney mission, see especially Fairbank (1942, 1968, 1971), Fairbank & Teng (1941), Granet (1930, 1968), Mancall (1984), Franke (1967), de-Bary, Chan & Watson (1960), Spence (1975) and Wakeman (1970).

18. "One fact signals the privileged place that the Chinese give to Politics. For them, the history of the World does not begin before that of Civilization. It does not start with a narrative of creation or cosmological speculations. It is joined from the beginning with the biography of the Sovereign" (Granet, 1968: 283).

19. "Sole master of the Calendar and by virtue of this prime mover of the whole Chinese territory, such appears, in the tradition of the Han, the Son of Heaven"

(Granet, 1930: 382). On the Emperor's grand sacrifices in Ch'ing times, see Zito (1984).

20. In 1660 the Russian Tsar, according to official Chinese court records,

> sent another Embassy to bring a memorial and to present tribute. In the memorial he [the Tsar] did not follow our calendar, but dated it 1165, and called himself a Great Khan with many boastful words. This memorial was sent to the princes and ministers for deliberation.
> They argued: "We should expel his embassy and refuse his tribute." (Fu, 1966, v. 1: 24)

The Emperor overruled this opinion, and said that the Russians should be feasted by the Board of Rites and given presents—as signs of the imperial tolerance—but denied an imperial audience. In 1676, another Russian envoy, although received by the Emperor, was then not recognized and dismissed, according to official records, for failure to kowtow (ibid., pp. 49–50).

21. In granting permission for the Macartney Embassy to enter the country, the Ch'ien-lung Emperor observed that in their request the British had properly expressed "'the highest reverence (*gong*), obedience (*shun*), earnestness (*gin*) and faithfulness (*zhi*),' as well as 'the sincerity of facing toward transformation'" (Hivea, 1986: 265).

22. Previous to the Macartney mission there had been only two Chinese speakers in the Company's service, both now departed from the scene (Pritchard, 1938: 497n). I would not, however, make too much of the English shows of "ignorance" in regard to the Chinese imperium or Chinese custom. It is clear from Macartney's private and even more from Staunton's published account that they were well aware of the Chinese conception of the Emperor's sovereignty, for indeed their intent was to deny it, break it down, and substitute their own. Thus Staunton knew that the Chinese subjects of the Emperor considered he "virtually rules the world," that they "scarcely distinguish the relations or duties of other nations or individuals to him from their own, which are, indeed, unbounded" (1799, v. 2: 25). Staunton also knew the difference between reciprocity and hierarchy in the relations between states, and the Chinese view of such matters: "Such were the avowed or affected notions entertained by the Chinese government, of the superiority or independence of the empire, that no transaction with foreigners was admissible to it on the ground of reciprocal benefit, but as a grace and condescension from the former to the latter" (ibid., p. 72; cf. Pritchard, 1935: 50).

23. The instructions issued to Lord Macartney by the Home Secretary Henry Dundas remind him that:

> The Directors of the East India Company, who have ordered one of their ships to accompany the Embassy, have shipped on board a great variety of articles of British goods not for the purpose of Sale, but to be dispersed and distributed by you in most likely manner to excite a taste for and establish the use of such articles in China. (Morse, 1966, v. 2: 240; cf. Pritchard, 1935: 222)

Moreover, while Macartney was in China, he sent the ship-of-war that also accompanied him, the *Lion* (Sir Erasmus Gower) to Japan, the Philippines, Borneo and the Celebes, to prepare for a visit from the mission, the instructions to Gower in the case of Borneo saying:

> Nothing would be more desirable, or more consistent with the general object of the mission, than any fair and peaceable endeavour to spread the use of British manufactures throughout every part of Asia, from whence any valuable return might be made to Europe, which was eminently the case of Borneo. (cited in Staunton, 1799, v. 1: 253)

24. And although Macartney was pleased to believe that he had dispelled the Chinese idea of the English as barbarians by the example of his own civilized conduct, his journal suggests that in popular quarters the Embassy enjoyed a reputation for cannibalism—the same as attributed to the Portuguese in the early sixteenth century. "A Chinese boy," Macartney writes, "who was appointed to wait upon young George Staunton [son of Sir George] would not for a long time trust himself to sleep in the house with our European servants, being afraid, he said, that they would eat him" (Cranmer-Byng, 1962: 226; cf. Pranke, 1967: 27f).

25. The persistence of Western perspectives on such matters is demonstrated by the mid-twentieth century echo of Meadows' remarks about the English ship in the comments of Cranmer-Byng, editor of the Macartney journal: "All the scientific apparatus which Macartney took with him, all the obvious superiority of the H.M.S. *Lion*, a 64-guy ship, over the Manchu war junks, was wasted on these men" (Cranmer-Byng, 1962: 36). But then, in another context, Fairbank cites Meadows' observation in regard to Chinese people who had had no opportunity of knowing Westerners:

> I do not recollect conversing with one, and I have conversed with many, whose previous notions of us were not analogous to those we entertain of savages. They were always surprised, not to say astonished, to learn that we have surnames, and understand the family distinctions of father, brother, wife, sister, etc.; in short that we live otherwise than as a herd of cattle. (in Fairbank, 1969: 19)

26. On the imperial retreats of Yuan Ming Yuan and Jehol, see Malone (1934), Siren (1949), Hedin (1933), Danby (1950) and M'Ghee (1862: 203ff.). These retreats are notably located northwest (Yuan Ming Yuan) and north (Jehol) of Peking, thus in more sinister ritual directions (cf. Zito, 1984); the European palaces at Yuan Ming Yuan, of which mention is made below, were likewise at the northern border of this summer palace complex.

27. Père Bourgeois goes on to say:

> You ask me if the Emperor has any Venetian and French glass. Thirty years ago he already had so many pieces that, not knowing where to put them, he had a quantity of the first grade broken up to make window panes for his European buildings. . . . [The] hall which he had made new for the tapestries . . . of Gobelins, which the French court sent in 1767 . . . 70 feet long and of good width . . . is so full of machines that one can hardly move about in it. Some of these machines have cost two or three hundred thousand francs, for the work on them is exquisite and they are enriched with innumerable precious stones. (Ibid.)

28. For a description of the Emperor Wu's famous Shang-lin garden which captures all the symbolism in an appropriate poetic form, see the chapter on Ssu-ma Hsiang-na in Ssu-ma Ch'ien's history (Watson, 1961, v. 2: 297–321). The poem, "Sir Fantasy," is a political drama in which the wonders of the Son of Heaven's garden encompass the descriptions of the parks of lesser lords, whose own rivalry is likewise represented in competing celebrations of the scale and variety of their pleasure-retreats. Cibot records that the successors of the Emperor Wu through the seventh century similarly "attempted to assemble everything that was scarce, dispersed and scattered here and there over the most immense regions . . . within their gardens everything was collected, like an abridgement of the universe" (1782b: 310).

29. The Ch'ien-lung Emperor recounted how his father, at Yuan Ming Yuan, "to appreciate the hard work of the farmers and mulberry growers . . . had fields, and barns, and plots of vegetables, by which he understood the importance of rain and

sunshine for the crops. The wind among the pines and the moon over the water entered his breast, inspiring thoughts of beauty" (in Malone, 1934: 64).

30. Wakeman draws attention also to the contrast between the "meanders . . . and carefully chosen grotesqueries" of the Summer Palace and the "formality" of the Forbidden City (1970: 8). For Wakeman, it is the contrast, as it were, of the king's two bodies: his private and public personae. However, the argument here is that these are complementary aspects of the same imperium, involving also the contrasts of civilization and nature, Chinese and barbarian, passive and active rule, peace and war, expression and acquisition of virtue, and more. The seasonal movements between the palace and the retreats, as well as the different modes of imperial behavior in each, would clearly contribute to a richer elucidation of the theory of rule.

31. Many of Macartney's presents to the Ch'ien-lung Emperor remained at Yuan Ming Yuan until 1860 when an Anglo-French expeditionary force commanded by Lord Elgin—son of the one who took all the marbles—pillaged and burned the priceless Summer Palace, thus finally proving the "preeminence" of European civilization by one of the greatest acts of vandalism in history.

32. Using Watanabe's study (1975) of Ming tributes, one may construct a graphic representation of the decline in foreign-tributary relations in the last half of the dynasty:

	Number of Tributary Missions to China	
	Years 1368–1505	Years 1506–1643
By land	611	145
By ocean	355	7

Mutatis mutandis, it is all as in the Sung dynasty's official history:

"The *te* of T'ang having declined, the [missions] of distant *hung-fu* areas did not come." Then, with Sung unification, foreign countries came from all directions in response to the dynasty's awe-inspiring majesty and virtue (*wei-te*). (Wang, 1968: 47)

33. Schafer notes:

The Chinese taste for the exotic permeated every social class and every part of daily life: Iranian, Indian and Turkish figures and decorations appeared on every kind of household object. The vogue for foreign clothes, foreign food and foreign music was especially prevalent in the eighth century, but no part of the T'ang era was free from it. (1963: 28)

34. On the efforts of the Hawai'i Island King Kamehameha (later conqueror of the Archipelago) to "live like King George" in the early 1790s, see Sahlins (1981: 30). This work and others (Sahlins, 1985a; Kirch & Sahlins, 1992) can be consulted for greater detail in events of Hawaiian history discussed here. Unfortunately the present necessity of providing comparative materials from Hawaii involves the double academic fault of repeating myself in a too-condensed way.

35. Since Cook did not see China and such a present is not mentioned in the chronicles of his voyage, Kamehameha's story seems unlikely, except that fur traders such as Meares and Colnett were perceived by Hawaiians as connected to Cook and perhaps one of these brought the Chinese gown to the Islands.

36. For American participation in the Canton market during the maritime fur trade and subsequent periods see Latourette (1917), Morse (1966), and Pitkin (1935), and for the particular impact on Hawaii, Bradley (1968) and Morgan (1948). The British fur traders included Indian "Country Traders" (cf. Meares, 1790). The fact that the Indian Country trade in opium and raw cotton at Canton was well on the way to resolving the problem of British silver expenditures probably made it easier for the Americans to displace the British on the Northwest Coast. In the first decade of the nineteenth century the Americans also extended their operations to sealing off the California coast and the Falklands. A sense of the shifting presence of British and Americans in the Pacific at this time can be had from a sample of the shipping in the Hawaiian Islands (based on Judd & Lind, 1974). In the years 1786–99, British ships outnumbered Americans in the Islands by a ratio of 6:5; whereas, in the period 1800–10, Americans took a 19:1 lead (cf. Howay, 1930: 4).

37. Of all commodities, Latourette writes, specie was, "the one which the United States could least spare at that time. They had no silver or gold mines of importance. What came into the country was largely smuggled in from the Spanish colonies and was greatly needed to pay European bills. Specie was consequently hard to obtain for such luxuries as China goods, and when secured, much popular irritation was felt at its use for such a purpose" (Latourette, 1917: 28).

38. Americans were in the neutral carrying trade until the Jeffersonian embargo of 1808–9; thereafter the European trade was resumed but with an altered set of markets. The War of 1812–14 also reduced American trade in the Pacific and China (cf. Pitkin, 1835: 302).

39. "Till now," goes the characteristic complaint of a *Haole* merchant about his competitors' trading practices, "I never knew the rascality of mankind, everyone here is ready to cut his neighbor's throat, truth is never spoken, treachery is the order of the day. I am disgusted with my fellow [White] man" (J. C. Jones, ML: 6 July 1821).

40. The instructions on appropriate Boston cargoes for the Hawaii trade that Jones was sending to the firm of Marshall and Wildes, amounting to a current catalogue of Polynesian splendours, are an interesting example of the way the indigenous conception of *mana* shaped the course of capitalist profit. The catalogue ranges from "superfine broadcloth & cassimere" or domestic tablecloths, writing desks and trunks covered with red leather, to the steamboat for which "the King and Pitt would give any price." "You'd be surprised how fast these people are advancing toward civilization," Jones writes, telling how just the other day Mr. Pitt asked for three gold-adorned carriages (ML: 31 May 1823). The carriages were of the general type Macartney had brought to China, but which left the Emperor and court unimpressed.

41. Cf. The Minutes of the Hawaiian Council of Nobles during the Session of 1845, where an ennoblement procedure was discussed and adopted (AH/Leg. Journ.).

42. On Kwakiutl potlatching and cosmology, apart from Boas' classical descriptions, I have relied heavily on the interpretive accounts of Goldman (1975), Dullabaun (1979) and Walens (1981), as well as the studies of Codere (1950, 1957, 1967), Drucker & Heizer (1967) and Barnett (1938). An important study of analogous ideas among Nelson Island Eskimos by Fienup-Riordan (1983) has also been most useful.

43. "The Coast Indian demonstrated a comprehension of the economic values of the day. But what did he do when he was paid off after his season of industry? Did he spend his hard-won earnings for things regarded as beneficial and progressive by Victorian standards? Did he invest them sagaciously for future benefit? He did not. He blew the works in a potlatch" (Drucker & Heizer 1967: 28).

44. "The Kwakiutl universe," comments Walens, "is predicated on a single, fundamental assumption: that the universe is a place where some beings are eaten by other beings and where it is the role of some beings to die so that other beings may feed on them and live" (Walens, 1981: 12).

45. And perhaps the more necessary inasmuch as certain animals used for skins, among them sea otter and deer, were customarily not eaten by Kwakiutl; cf. Walens, 1981: 135–6.

46. "To cross what should be an absolute divide and return safely is an exceptional feat confined to the exceptional person who has been chosen or accepted by the spirits" (Goldman, 1975: 100).

47. In the Winter ceremonial (which was also a time of heightened potlatch activity) the benefits are diffused to the collectivity and the cosmos itself: through the recapture of chiefly initiates who had been abducted and possessed by various spirits of the wild, in ritual dramas that thus recapitulated heroic ancestral feats of mythic time. As the journeys of the initiates endowed them with spiritual powers, so their successful reincorporation into the community restored the year itself to life, that is, brought it back from the darkness and death of the solstice (Goldman, 1975: 98f.). Moreover, the principal initiate, the *hamatsa* dancer, victim of a great cannibal spirit, survives and transcends the cannibal proclivities he ritually demonstrates on his return from the wild. Slowly he is reborn and restored into the human community: proof of man's ability to overcome the generalized cannibalism by which he lives. Here it is notable that (impersonated) animal spirits help in the restoration of the *hamatsa* dancer, which thus seems to show the continued willingness of the animals to give their own flesh— on the condition of certain ritual sacrifices of human flesh.

48. Dullabaun explains:

A man becomes his spirit (takes his name) and obtains the spirit's treasures that enable him to catch game, i.e., obtain food. The son-in-law takes the name of his father-in-law and catches the game (the wife). Marriage and war are parallels in this respect: when a man captures another in war, he takes the captive's name, any dances that he owns, and his body (which is consumed). In marriage, the son-in-law takes names and dances as well as blankets, animal skins and food. These latter are consumed, burned or more typically, given away. (Dullabaun, 1979: 87–8)

49. In his excellent autobiographical account, the Kwakiutl leader James Sewid tells how his father's father was given a daughter in marriage by a certain Bella Coola chief, whose own people had previously attacked Sewid's grandfather's people. So the Bella Coola chief "let him marry his daughter so he [Sewid's grandfather] could get all their masks and songs so he wouldn't attack their villages" (Spradley, 1969: 200; for the mythical analogue, see Boas, 1966: 53).

50. Just as marriage negotiations take on the guise of war expeditions, an early notice of trade between a group of Tsimashian and a party of Vancouver's people indicates that the Indians ritually donned war regalia for the purpose of the exchange (Vancouver, 1801, v. 4: 133f.; cf. Gunther, 1972).

51. Codere remarks on the traditional disposition of Kwakiutl to produce goods in standardized forms, as it were, a preadaptation that allowed them to appreciate certain possibilities of the Industrial Revolution:

The habituation to standardized and pluralized manufactured objects was carried over into the new economic situation in their acquisition of European manufactures. One of the most interesting features of the potlatch was the distribution of great numbers of manufactured goods of the same category. (Codere, 1950: 18)

52. We need not enter the lists of recent debate about whether the protocol of 658 potlatch names among Southern Kwakiutl was put together after the construction of Fort Rupert in 1849 or had already existed in 1760. Goldman (1975) argues the latter position against Codere (1950) and Drucker & Heizer (1967), who have sought to document the post-contact development of the Southern Kwakiutl confederation. For present purposes it is enough to note, first, that the expansion of warfare, intertribal marriage alliances and feasting beginning in the late eighteenth century set the Kwakiutl in a political field that ran far beyond the writ of their own lineage-based potlatch protocol (the 658 names). Second, many of these relations, as manifested in potlatches, aimed at hierarchical inclusions, which cannot be said for the protocol list of 658 names. As Goldman shows (1975: 27–8), the so-called ranking of these names supposed no principle of logic or hierarchical order. The order was presumed to have been established by fiat in a mythical or an early-human time, and consisted merely of a precedence list—which seems to have been used differently on occasions of different kinds (cf. Drucker & Heizer, 1967). Unlike *nawalak* and the implication of incorporation in the potlatch system, there is nothing here of a rank *principle*.

53. "The tea-pot was a household god, a homely, companionable little god, fitting into every circumstance of life, and always bringing some definite measure of content" (Repplier, 1932: 40).

54. *Essay Concerning Human Understanding*, II. x. 6.

55. Nor were the curative powers of the Orient restricted to the physical body alone. Fascinated also by the vision of an immense and well-governed Chinese empire, the philosophers passed easily to exotic prescriptions for the body politic. A country "that furnishes remedies for the health of the body" could also become "the exemplary empire for the order of societies" (ibid.).

BIBLIOGRAPHY

Abbreviations

AH/Leg. Journ.	Legislative Journals of the Hawaiian Kingdom. Archives of Hawaii. Honolulu.
ML	Marshall Letters: "Copies of letters rec'd from the Sandwich Islands & Canton," by Josiah Marshall, 1820–32. Houghton Library, Harvard University (Ms Am W/63F).
USCD	Dispatches from United States Consuls in Honolulu, Vol. 1. Microfilm (M-144) of original at U.S. National Archives, Washington D.C.

Alexander, W. (MS) "Journal of a Voyage to Pekin in China on board the Hindustan EIM which accompanied Lord Macartney on his Embassy to the Emperor," Add. MSS. 35, 174. British Museum.

Anderson, A. (1795) *A Narrative of the British Embassy to China, in the Years 1792, 1793 and 1794*. London: J. Debrett.

Attiret, le Père (1843 [1743]) "Lettre du Père Attiret," in M. L. Aimé-Martin (ed.),

Lettres édifiantes et curieuses, Vol. 3, pp. 786–95. Paris: Société du Panthéon Littéraire.

Axtell, W. S. (1982) "International bullion flows and the Chinese economy *circa* 1530–1650," *Past & Present*, 95, 68–90.

Barnett, H. G. (1938) "The nature of the potlatch," *American Anthropologist*, 40, 349–58.

Barrow, J. (1805) *Travels in China*. . . . Philadelphia: W. F. McLaughlin.

Bell, E. (1929–30) "Log of the Chatham," *Honolulu Mercury,* I(4), 7–26; I(5), 55–69; I(6), 76–96; II(1), 80–91; II(2), 119–29.

Bennett, G. (1832) "Account of the Islands Erromanga and Tanna, New Hebrides Group," *The Asiatic Journal*, 3 (n.s.), 119–31.

Bloxam, R. R. (MS) "A Narrative of a Voyage to the Sandwich Islands in H.M.S. Blonde. 1824–1825–1826," (MS 4255). National Library of Australia.

Boas, F. (1920) "The Social Organization of the Kwakiutl," *American Anthropologist*, 22, 111–26.

——— (1921) *Ethnology of the Kwakiutl,* Parts I and II. Bureau of American Ethnology, Report No. 35.

——— (1930) *The Religion of the Kwakiutl Indians*, Part II. Columbia University Contributions to Anthropology, Vol. 10.

——— (1935) *Kwakiutl Culture as Reflected in Mythology*. Memoirs of the American Folklore Society, Vol. 28.

——— (1966) *Kwakiutl Ethnography*, ed. H. Codere. Chicago: University of Chicago Press.

Bradley, H. W. (1968 [1943]) *The American Frontier in Hawaii*. Gloucester, Mass: Peter Smith (reissue of 1943 edition).

Bright, C. & Geyer, M. (In press) "For a Unified History of the World in the 20th Century," *Radical History Review*.

Bullard, C. B. (Letters) "Letterbook of Charles B. Bullard, Supercargo for Bryant and Sturgis at the Hawaiian Islands and Canton, March 20, 1821–July 11, 1823." Typescript copy at the Hawaiian Mission Children's Society Library, Honolulu.

Cameron, N. (1970) *Barbarians and Mandarins*. New York: Weatherhill.

Capell, A. (1938) "The Stratification of afterworld beliefs in the New Hebrides," *Folklore*, 49, 51–84.

Chamisso, A. von (1981) *Voyage autour du monde*. Paris: Le Sycomore.

Cibot, le Père (1782a) "Notice sur les objets de commerce à importer en Chine," *Mémoires concernant l'histoire, les sciences, les arts, les moeurs, les usages, etc. des Chinois par les missionaires de Pe-kin*, Vol. 8, pp. 267–70. Paris: Nejon.

——— (1782b) "Essai sur les jardins de plaisance des Chinois," in *Mémoires concernant l'histoire, les sciences, les arts, les moeurs, les usages, etc. des Chinois par les missionaires de Pe-kin*, Vol. 8, pp. 301–26. Paris: Nejon.

Codere, H. (1950) *Fighting with property: a study of Kwakiutl potlatching and warfare 1792–1930*. Monographs of the American Ethnological Society, 18, New York: J. J. Augustin.

——— (1957) "Kwakiutl Society: Rank without Class," *American Anthropologist*, 59, 473–86.

———(1961) "Kwakiutl," in *Perspectives in American Indian Culture Change*, E. H. Spicer (ed.), pp. 431–516. Chicago: University of Chicago Press.

Corney, P. (1896) *Voyages in the northern Pacific: Narrative of several trading voyages from 1813 to 1818*. . . . Honolulu: Thrum.

Cox, R. (1832) *Adventures on the Columbia River*. New York: Harper.

Cranmer-Byng, J. L. (1957–8) "Lord Macartney's Embassy to Peking in 1793 (From Official Chinese Documents)," *Journal of Oriental Studies*, I, 117–86.

—— (1962) *An Embassy to China: Being the Journal Kept by Lord Macartney During his Embassy to the Emperor Ch'ien-lung 1793–1794*. London: Longmans.

Dampier, R. (1971) *To the Sandwich Islands on H.M.S. Blonde*, P. K. Joerger (ed.). Honolulu: University of Hawaii Press.

Danby, H. (1950) *The Garden of Perfect Brightness*. Chicago: Regenery.

de Bary, W., Chan, W.-T. & Watson, B. (eds.) (1960) *Sources of Chinese Tradition*. New York: Columbia University Press.

Deane, H. (1963) *The Political and Social Ideas of St. Augustine*, New York: Columbia University Press.

Dermigny, L. (1964) *La Chine et L'Occident: Le commerce à Canton au XVIIIth siècle*, 3 vols. Paris: S.E.V.P.E.N.

Drucker, P. & Heizer, R. F. (1967) *To Make My Name Good: A Reexamination of the Southern Kwakiutl Potlatch*. Berkeley: University of California Press.

Dullabaun, M. A. (1979) "Being, value and supernatural power: a reinterpretation of Kwakiutl exchange." MA Thesis in Anthropology, University of Chicago.

Dumont, L. (1977) *From Mandeville to Marx*. Chicago: University of Chicago Press.

—— (1986) *Essays on Individualism*. Chicago: University of Chicago Press.

Duyvendak, J. J. L. (1938) "The Last Dutch Embassy to the Chinese Court (1794–1795)," *T'oung Pao Archives*, 34, 1–137.

Fairbank, J. K. (1942) "Tributary trade and China's relations with the West," *Far Eastern Quarterly*, I, 129–149.

—— (1969) *Trade and Diplomacy on the China Coast*. Stanford: Stanford University Press.

—— (1971) *The United States and China*, 3rd edition. Cambridge, Mass.: Harvard University Press.

Fairbank, J. K. (ed.) (1968) *The Chinese World Order*. Cambridge, Mass.: Harvard University Press.

Fairbank, J. K. & Teng, S. Y. (1941) "On the Ch'ing Tributary System," *Harvard Journal of Asian Studies*, 6, 135–246.

Fienup-Riordan, A. (1983) *The Nelson Island Eskimo*. Anchorage: Alaska Pacific University Press.

Fisher, R. (1977) *Contact and Conflict: Indian-European Relations in British Columbia, 1774–1890*. Vancouver: University of British Columbia Press.

Fletcher, J. F. (1968) "China and Central Asia, 1368–1884," in J. K. Fairbank (ed.), *The Chinese World View*, pp. 206–24. Cambridge, Mass.: Harvard University Press.

Frank, A. G. (1966) "The development of underdevelopment," *Monthly Review*, 18, 17–31.

Franke, W. (1967) *China and the West*. Columbia: University of South Carolina.

Fu, L.-S. (1966) *A Documentary Chronicle of Sino-Western Relations (1644–1820)*, 2 vols. Tucson: The University of Arizona Press.

Goldman, I. (1975) *The Mouth of Heaven*. New York: John Wiley.

Granet, M. (1930) *Chinese Civilization*. London: Kegan Paul, Trench, Trubner & Co.

—— (1968) *La pensée chinoise*. Paris: Editions Albin Michel. [Reprint of 1934 edition, La Renaissance du Livre.]

Greenberg, M. ([1951] n.d.) *British Trade and the Opening of China 1800–1842*. New

York: Monthly Review Press. (Reprint of Cambridge University Press edition, 1951.)

Gregory, C. A. (1982) *Gifts and Commodities*. New York: Academic Press.

Gunther, E. (1972) *Indian Life on the Northwest Coast of North America: As Seen by the Early Explorers and Fur Traders During the Last Decades of the Eighteenth Century*. Chicago: University of Chicago Press.

Guy, R. K. (1987) *The Emperor's Four Treasuries: Scholars and the State in the Late Ch'ien-lung Era*. Cambridge, Mass.: Council on East Asian Studies, Harvard University.

Hedin, S. (1933) *Jehol: City of Emperors*. New York: Dutton.

Hivea, J. (1986) *Guest Ritual and Interdomainal Relations in the Late Qing*. Dissertation submitted to the Faculty of the Division of the Humanities, Dept. of History, University of Chicago.

Howay, F. W. (1930) "Early relations between the Hawaiian islands and the Northwest Coast," in A. P. Taylor & R. S. Kuykendall (eds.), *The Hawaiian Islands . . . Captain Cook Sesquicentennial Celebration*, pp. 11–38. Honolulu: Archives of Hawaii.

———— (1930–4) "A list of trading vessels in the maritime fur trade, 1795 . . . to . . . 1825." *The Transactions of the Royal Society of Canada*, Third Series, Section 2, 24, 111–34; 25, 117–49; 26, 43–86; 27, 119–47; 28, 11–49.

Humphreys, C. B. (1926) *The Southern New Hebrides*. Cambridge: Cambridge University Press.

Hunnewell, J. (Letters) "Papers of James Hunnewell," Vol. 29a, Baker Library, Harvard School of Business.

Hunt, G. T. (1960) *The Wars of the Iroquois*. Madison: The University of Wisconsin Press.

Judd, B. & Lind, H. Y. (1974) *Voyages to Hawaii before 1860*. Honolulu: The University Press of Hawaii for Hawaiian Mission Children's Society.

Judd, L. F. (1966), *Honolulu: Sketches of Life in the Hawaiian Islands from 1828 to 1861*. Chicago: Lakeside Press.

Kamakau, S. M. (1961) *Ruling Chiefs of Hawaii*. Honolulu: Kamehameha Schools Press.

Kelly, J. D. (1988) *Bhakti and the Spirit of Capitalism in Fiji*. Dissertation submitted for the degree of Doctor of Philosophy in Anthropology. University of Chicago.

Kirch, P. & Sahlins, M. (1992) Anahulu: The Anthropology of History in the Kingdom of Hawaii. Chicago: University of Chicago Press.

Kuykendall, R. S. (1968) *The Hawaiian Kingdom*, Vol. I *1778–1854*. Honolulu: University of Hawaii Press.

Langridge, A. K. (1934) *The Conquest of Cannibal Tanna*. London: Hodder and Stoughton.

Latourette, K. S. (1919) "The history of early relations between the United States and China, 1784–1844," *Transactions of the Connecticut Academy of Arts and Sciences*, 22, 1–209.

Lattimore, O. (1940) *Inner Asian Frontiers of China*. New York: American Geographical Society.

Lederman, R. (1986a) "Changing Times in Mendi: Notes towards Writing Highland New Guinea History," *Ethnohistory*, 33, 1–30.

———— (1986b) *What Gifts Engender*. Cambridge: Cambridge University Press.

Lo J.-P. (1958) "The Decline of the Early Ming Navy," *Oriens Extremus*, 5, 149–68.

Malone, C. B. (1934) *History of the Peking Summer Palaces under the Ch'ing Dynasty*. Illinois Studies in the Social Sciences Vol. 21, Nos. 1–2.

Manby, T. (1929) "Journal of Vancouver's Voyage to the Pacific Ocean (1791–1793)," *Honolulu Mercury*, I(2), 33–45.

Mancall, M. (1984) *China at the Center*. New York: The Free Press.

Marx, K. & Engels, F. ([reprint] 1965) *The German Ideology*. London: Lawrence and Wishart.

Mathison, G. F. (1825) *Narrative of a Visit to Brazil, Chile, Peru and the Sandwich Islands during the Years 1821 and 1822*. London: Knight.

Mauss, M. (1966) *Sociologie et Anthropologie*. Paris: Presses Universitaires de France.

Meadows, T. T. (1847) *Desultory Notes on the Government and People of China.* . . . London: W. H. Allen.

M'Ghee, R. J. L. (1862) *How We Got to Pekin: A Narrative of the Campaign in China of 1860*. London: Bentley.

Meares, J. (1790) *Voyages made in the Years 1788 and 1789, from China to the Northwest Coast of America, to which are Prefixed an Introductory Narrative of a Voyage Performed in 1786, from Bengal, in the Ship Nootka*. London: Logographic Press.

Milburn, W. (1813) *Oriental Commerce* . . . , 2 vols. London: Black, Parry & Co.

Mintz, S. (1985) *Sweetness and Power*. New York: Viking Penguin.

Morgan, T. (1948) *Hawaii. A Century of Economic Change 1778–1876*. Cambridge Mass.: Harvard University Press.

Morison, S. E. (1961) *The Maritime History of Massachusetts, 1783–1860*. Boston: Houghton Mifflin (Sentry).

Morse, H. B. (1966) *The Chronicles of the East India Company Trading to China 1635–1834*, 4 vols. Taipei: Ch'eng-Wen Publishing Company.

Murray, A. W. (1862) *Missions in Western Polynesia*. London: John Snow.

Needham, J. (1959) *Science and Civilisation in China*, Vol. 3. Cambridge: Cambridge University Press.

———— (1971) *Science and Civilisation in China*, Vol. 5. Cambridge: Cambridge University Press.

Pitkin, T. (1835) *A Statistical View of the Commerce of the United States of America*. New Haven: Durrie & Peck.

Polanyi, K., Arensberg, C. M. & Pearson, H. W. (eds.) (1957) *Trade and Market in the Early Empires*. Glencoe: The Free Press.

Pritchard, E. T. (1929) *Anglo-Chinese Relations During the Seventeenth and Eighteenth Centuries*. University of Illinois Studies in the Social Sciences, 17 (Nos. 1–2).

———— (1935) "Letters from Missionaries at Peking relating to the Macartney Embassy (1793–1803)," *T'oung Pao*, 31, 1–57.

———— (1936) "The crucial years of early Anglo-Chinese relations," *Research Studies of the State College of Washington*, 4(3–4), 95–442.

———— (1938) "Instructions of the East India Company to Lord Macartney on His Embassy to China and His Reports to the Company, 1792–4," *The Journal of the Royal Asiatic Society for 1938*, 201–30, 374–96, 493–509.

———— (1943) "The Kotow in the Macartney Embassy to China in 1793," *Far Eastern Quarterly*, 2, 163–201.

Proudfoot, W. J. (1868) *Biographical Memoir of James Dinwiddie, L.L.D., Astronomer in the British Embassy to China, 1792, '3, '4.* . . . Liverpool: Edward Howell.

Prout, E. (1843) *Memoir of the Life of the Rev. John Williams*. New York: Allen, Morrill and Wardwell.

Repplier, A. (1932) *To Think of Tea!* Boston: Houghton Mifflin.

Robertson, H. A. (1902) *The Martyr Isle Erromanga*. New York: A. C. Armstrong and Son.

Rocquefeuil, C. de (1823) *Journal d'un voyage autour du monde, pendant les années 1816, 1817, 1818, et 1819*, 2 vols. Paris: Lebel.

Sahlins, M. (1972) *Stone Age Economics*. Chicago: Aldine.

—— (1981) *Historical Metaphors and Mythical Realities*. Michigan: University of Michigan Press for the Association for Social Anthropology in Oceania.

—— (1985a) *Islands of History*. Chicago: University of Chicago Press.

—— (1985b) "Hierarchy and Humanity in Polynesia," in Hooper, A. and J. Huntsman (eds.), *Transformations of Polynesian Culture,* pp. 195–217. Auckland: The Polynesian Society.

—— (1990) "The Political Economy of Grandeur in Hawaii from 1810 to 1830," in Emiko Ohnuki-Tierney (ed.), *Culture Through Time: Anthropological Approaches*. Stanford: Stanford University Press.

Salisbury, R. (1962) *From Stone to Steel.* Cambridge: Cambridge University Press.

Salisbury, R. F. & Tooker, E. (eds.) (1984) *Affluence and Society*. 1981 Proceedings of the American Ethnological Society. Washington, D.C.: The American Ethnological Society.

Schafer, E. H. (1963) *The Golden Peaches of Samarkand*. Berkeley: The University of California Press.

Schurmann, F. & Schell, O. (eds.) (1967) *Imperial China*. New York: Vintage Books.

Shineberg, D. (1967) *They Came for Sandalwood: A Study of the Sandalwood Trade in the South-West Pacific 1830–1865*. Melbourne: Melbourne University Press.

Simmons, W. S. (1988) "Culture Theory in Contemporary Ethnohistory," *Ethnohistory*, 35, 1–14.

Siren, O. (1949) *Gardens of China*. New York: Ronald Press.

Spate, O. H. K. (1979) *The Spanish Lake*. Minneapolis: University of Minnesota Press.

Spence, J. D. (1975) *Emperor of China: Self-Portrait of K'ang-hsi*. New York: Vintage Books.

—— (1980) *To Change China: Western Advisors in China 1620–1960*. Harmondsworth: Penguin.

Spradley, J. P. (ed.) (1969) *Guests Never Leave Hungry: The Autobiography of James Sewid, a Kwakiutl Indian*. New Haven: Yale University Press.

Staunton, G. (1799) *An Authentic Account of an Embassy from the King of Great Britain to the Emperor of China*, 2 vols. Philadelphia: Campbell.

Stewart, C. S. (1830) *Journal of a residence in the Sandwich Islands, during the years 1823, 1824, and 1825. . . .* Third edition. London: H. Fisher, Son, & P. Jackson.

Strathern, A. (1979) "Gender, Ideology and Money in Mt. Hagen," *Man*, 14, 530–48.

Swinhoe, R. (1961) *Narrative of the North China Campaign of 1860*. London: Smith, Elder & Co.

Thistle, P. C. (1986) *Indian-European Trade Relations in the Lower Saskatchewan River Region to 1840*. Winnipeg: The University of Manitoba Press, Manitoba Studies in Native History, No. 11.

Turner, G. (1861) *Nineteen Years in Polynesia*. London: Snow.

Trigeer, B. G. (1984) "The Road to Affluence: A Reassessment of Early Huron Responses to European Contact," in R. F. Salisbury and E. Tooker (eds.), *Affluence and Society*, pp. 12–25. Washington, D.C.: The American Ethnological Society.

Ukers, W. H. (1935) *All About Tea*, 2 vols. New York: The Tea and Coffee Trade Journal Co.

Valeri, V. (1972) "Le fonctionnement du système des rangs à Hawaii, *L'Homme*, 12, 29–66.

—— (1981) "Pouvoir des dieux, rire des hommes," *Anthropologie et Société*, 5(3), 11–34.

Vancouver, G. (1801) *A Voyage of Discovery in the North Pacific Ocean . . . in the Years 1790, 1791, 1792, 1793, 1794, and 1795*, new edition, 5 vols. London: Stockdale.

Wakeman, F., Jr. (1970) "High Ch'ing: 1683–1839," in J. B. Crowley (ed.), *Modern East Asia*, pp. 1–28. New York: Harcourt, Brace & World.

Walens, S. (1981) *Feasting with Cannibals*. Princeton: Princeton University Press.

Walker, R. (1956) *China and the West: Cultural Collision*. New Haven: Far Eastern Publications, Yale University, Sinological Series, No. 5.

Wallerstein, I. (1974/1980) *The Modern World System*, 2 vols. New York: Academic Press.

—— (1983) *Historical Capitalism*. Thetford, Norfolk: Thetford Press.

Wang, G.-W. (1968) "Early Ming Relations with Southeast Asia: A Background Essay," in J. K. Fairbank (ed.), *The Chinese World Order*, pp. 34–62. Cambridge: Harvard University Press.

Watanabe, H. (1975) "An Index of the Embassies and Tribute Missions from Islamic Countries to Ming China (1368–1466) as Recorded in the *Ming Shih-lu* Classified According to Geographic Area," *Memoirs of the Research Department of the Tajo Bunko*, 33, 285–374.

Watson, B. (ed. & trans.) (1961), *Records of the Grand Historian of China* [Ssu-ma Ch'ien], 2 vols. New York: Columbia University Press.

Whitman, J. B. (1979) *An Account of the Sandwich Islands: The Hawaiian Journal of John B. Whitman, 1813–1835*, John Dominis Holt (ed.). Honolulu and Salem: Topgallant and Peabody Museum of Salem.

Wills, J. E., Jr. (1979) "Maritime China from Wang Chih to Shih Lang: Themes in Peripheral History," in Jonathan D. Spence and J. E. Wills, Jr. (eds.), *From Ming to Ch'ing*, pp. 204–38. New Haven: Yale University Press.

Wolf, E. R. (1982) *Europe and the People without History*. Berkeley: University of California Press.

Yang, H.-Y. & Yang, G. (eds.) (1974) *Records of the Historian, Written by Szuma Chien*. Trans. by Yang Hsien-yi and Gladys Yang. Hong Kong: The Commercial Press.

Yang, L.-S. (1968) "Historical Notes on the Chinese World Order," in J. K. Fairbank (ed.), *The Chinese World Order*, pp. 20–33. Cambridge: Harvard University Press.

Zito, A. R. (1984) "Re-presenting Sacrifice: Cosmology and the Editing of Texts," *Ch'ing-shi Wen-ti*, 5(2), 47–78.

CULTURE / Power / History

Living to Tell: Madonna's Resurrection of the Fleshly

SUSAN McCLARY

A GREAT DEAL of ink has been spilled in the debate over pop star Madonna's visual image and the narratives she has enacted for music video. Almost every response in the spectrum has been registered, ranging from unambiguous characterizations of her as "a porn queen in heat"[1] or "the kind of woman who comes into your room at three A.M. and sucks your life out,"[2] to formulations that view her as a kind of organic feminist whose image "enables girls to see that the meanings of feminine sexuality can be in their control, can be made in their interests, and that their subjectivities are not necessarily totally determined by the dominant patriarchy."[3]

What most reactions to Madonna share, however, is an automatic dismissal of her music as irrelevant. The scorn with which her ostensible artistic focus has been trivialized, treated as a conventional backdrop to her visual appearance, often is breathtaking. For example, John Fiske's complex and sympathetic discussion of the struggle over meaning surrounding Madonna begins, "Most critics have nothing good to say about her music, but they have a lot to say about her image."[4] He then goes on to say a lot about her image, and he, too, has nothing whatsoever to say about the music. E. Ann Kaplan's detailed readings of Madonna's music videos likewise push the music to the side and treat the videos strictly through the techniques of film criticism.[5]

This paper will concentrate on Madonna, the musician. First, I will locate her within a history of gender relationships in the music world: I hope to demonstrate that Madonna has served as a lightning rod to make only slightly more perceptible the kinds of double binds always presented to a woman who attempts to enter Western music. Second, I will turn to her music and examine some of the ways she operates within a persistently repressive discourse to create liberatory musical images. Finally I will present a brief discussion of the music videos "Open Your Heart" and "Like a Prayer," in which I consider the interactions between musical and visual components.

Throughout this paper, I will be writing of Madonna in a way that assigns considerable credit and responsibility to her as a creator of texts. To be sure, the products ascribed to Madonna are the result of complex collaborative processes involving the input of co-writers, co-producers, studio musicians, video directors, technicians, marketing specialists, and so forth. As is the case in most pop, there is no single originary genius for this music.

Yet the testimonies of co-workers and interviewers indicate that Madonna is very much in control of almost every dimension of her media persona and her career. Even though certain components of songs or videos are contributed by other artists, she has won and fiercely maintains the right to decide finally what will be released under her name. It may be that Madonna is best understood as head of a corporation that produces images of her self-representation rather than as the spontaneous, "authentic" artist of rock mythology. But a puppet she's not. As she puts it, "People have this idea that if you're sexual and beautiful and provocative, then there's nothing else you could possibly offer. People have always had that image about women. And while it might have seemed like I was behaving in a stereotypical way, at the same time, I was also masterminding it. I was in control of everything I was doing, and I think that when people realized that, it confused them."[6]

I am stressing Madonna's agency in her own self-representation in part because there is such a powerful tendency for her agency to be erased completely—for her to be seen as just a mindless doll fulfilling the male fantasies of anonymous puppeteers. This particular strategy for dismissing Madonna has always seemed odd to me because the fantasies she enacts are not very successful at being male fantasies, if that is their objective. They often inspire discomfort and anxiety among men who wish to read her as a genuine "Boy Toy."[7] And I am rather amused when men who are otherwise not conspicuously concerned with feminist issues attack Madonna for setting the cause of women back twenty years, especially because so many girls and women (some of them feminist theorists, including even Betty Friedan)[8] perceive her music and videos as articulating a whole new set of possible feminine subject positions. Furthermore, her spirited, self-confident statements in interviews (several of which are sprinkled liberally throughout this paper) tend to lend support to the interpretations of female fans.

Yet Madonna's agency is not hers alone: even if she wrote everything she performs all by herself, it would still be important to remember that her music and personae are produced within a variety of social discursive practices. Her style is assembled from the musics of many different genres, and her visual images draw upon the conventions of female representation that circulate in film, advertisements, and stage shows. Indeed, in order to be as effective as she unquestionably is, she has to speak intelligibly to the cultural experiences and perceptions of her audience. Her voices are credible precisely because they engage so provocatively with ongoing cultural conversations about gender, power, and pleasure.

Moreover, as will be demonstrated throughout this paper, Madonna's art itself repeatedly deconstructs the traditional notion of the unified subject with finite ego boundaries. Her pieces explore—sometimes playfully, sometimes seriously—various ways of constituting identities that refuse stability, that remain fluid, that resist definition. This tendency in her work has become increasingly pronounced; for instance, in her recent controversial video "Express Yourself" (which borrows its imagery from Fritz Lang's *Metropolis*), she slips in and out of every subject position offered within the video's narrative context (including those of the cat and the tyrannical master of industry), refusing more than ever to deliver the security of a clear, unambiguous message or an "authentic" self.

Thus I do not want to suggest that she (of all artists) is a solitary creator who ultimately determines fixed meanings for her pieces. But I will focus on how a woman artist can make a difference within discourse. To strip Madonna of all conscious intention in her work is to reduce her once again to a voiceless, powerless bimbo. In a world in which many people assert that she (along with most other women artists) can't have meant what one sees and hears because she isn't smart enough, claims of intentionality, agency, and authorship become extremely important strategically.

WOMEN AS PRODUCERS OF MUSIC

Although there are some notable exceptions, women have traditionally been barred from participating in Western music. The barriers that have prevented them from participation have occasionally been formal: in the seventeenth century there were even papal edicts proscribing women's musical education.[9] More often, however, women are discouraged from considering themselves as potential musicians through more subtle means. As macho rock star David Lee Roth (rarely accused of being an ardent feminist) observes, "What if a little girl picked up a guitar and said 'I wanna be a rock star'? Nine times out of ten her parents would never allow her to do it. We don't have so many lead guitar women, not because women don't have the ability to play the instrument, but because they're kept locked up, taught to be something else. I don't appreciate that."[10]

Women have, of course, been discouraged from writing or painting as well, and feminist scholars in literary and art history have already made the barriers hindering women in those areas familiar. But there are additional factors that make female participation in music still riskier than in either literature or the visual arts. First, the charismatic performance of one's music is often crucial to its promotion and transmission. Whether Liszt in his matinee-idol piano recitals, Elvis on the "Ed Sullivan Show," or the aforementioned David Lee Roth, the composer-performer often relies heavily on manipulating audience response through his enactments of sexual power and desire.[11]

However, for a man to enact his sexuality is not the same as for a woman: Throughout Western history, women musicians have usually been assumed to be publicly available, have had to fight hard against pressures to yield, or have accepted the granting of sexual favors as one of the prices of having a career. The seventeenth-century composer Barbara Strozzi—one of the very few women to compete successfully in elite music composition—may have been forced by her agent-pimp of a father to pose for a bare-breasted publicity portrait as part of his plan for launching her career.[12] Women on the stage are viewed as sexual commodities regardless of their appearance or seriousness. Brahms pleaded with the aging Clara Schumann (provocatively dressed, to be sure, in widow's weeds) to leave off her immodest composition and concertizing.[13] One of Madonna's principal accomplishments is that she brings this hypocrisy to the surface and problematizes it.

Second, musical discourse has been carefully guarded from female participation in part because of its ability to articulate patterns of desire. Music is an extremely powerful medium, all the more so because most listeners have little rational control over the way it influences them. The mind/body split that has plagued Western culture for centuries shows up most paradoxically in attitudes toward music: The most cerebral, nonmaterial of media is at the same time the medium most capable of engaging the body. This confusion over whether music belongs with mind or with body is intensified when the fundamental binary opposition of masculine/feminine is mapped onto it.[14] To the very large extent that mind is defined as masculine and body as feminine in Western culture, music is always in danger of being perceived as a feminine (or effeminate) enterprise altogether.[15] And one of the means of asserting masculine control over the medium is by denying the very possibility of participation by women. For how can an enterprise be feminine if actual women are excluded?

Women are not, of course, entirely absent from traditional music spectacle: Women characters may even be highlighted as stars in operas. But opera, like the other genres of Western music, is an almost exclusively male domain in that men write both libretti and music, direct the stage action, and interpret the scores. Thus it is not surprising that operas tend to articulate and reinforce precisely the sexual politics just described. The proceedings are controlled by a discourse organized in accordance with masculine interests—a discourse that offers up the female as spectacle while guaranteeing that she will not step out of line. Sometimes desire is articulated by the male character while the passive, domesticated female acquiesces. In such instances, the potential violence of male domination is not necessarily in evidence: The piece seems to unfold in accordance with the "natural" (read: patriarchal) sexual hierarchy.

But a kind of desire-dread-purge mechanism prevails in operas in which the tables are turned and a passive male encounters a strong, sexually aggressive female character. In operas such as *Carmen*, *Lulu*, or *Salome*, the "victimized male" who has been aroused by the temptress finally must kill her in order to reinstate social order.[16] Even in so-called absolute music (instrumental music in which there is no explicit extramusical or programmatic component), the themes conventionally designated as "feminine" must be domesticated or eradicated for the sake of narrative closure.[17]

The ways in which fear of female sexuality and anxiety over the body are inscribed in the Western music tradition are obviously very relevant for the would-be (wannabe?) woman musician. First, women are located within the discourse in a position of both desire and dread—as that which must reveal that it is controlled by the male or which must be purged as intolerable. Many male attacks on Madonna unself-consciously locate their terror in the fact that she is not under masculine control. Like Carmen or Lulu, she invokes the body and feminine sexuality; but unlike them, she refuses to be framed by a structure that will push her back into submission or annihilation. Madonna interprets the problem as follows: "I think for the most part men have always been the aggressors sexually. Through time immemorial they've always been in control. So I think sex is equated with power in a way, and that's scary in a way. It's scary for men that women would have that power, and I think it's scary for women to have that power—or to have that power and be sexy at the same time."[18]

Second, the particular popular discourse within which Madonna works— that of dance—is the genre of music most closely associated with physical motion. The mind/body–masculine/feminine problem places dance decisively on the side of the feminine body rather than with the objective "masculine" intellect. It is for this reason that dance music in general usually is dismissed by music critics—even by "serious" rock critics. Recall the hysterical scorn heaped upon disco when it emerged—and also recall that disco was the music that underwrote the gay movement, black urban clubs, *Saturday Night Fever*'s images of working-class leisure, and other contexts that did not conform to the cherished ideal of (white, male, heterosexual, middle-class) rebel rock.[19] Similar dismissals of dance music can be found throughout the critical history of Western "serious" music. To the extent that the appeal is to physicality rather than abstracted listening, dance music is often trivialized at the same time that its power to distract and arouse is regarded with anxiety.[20]

Madonna works out of a discursive tradition that operates according to premises somewhat different from those of mainstream Western music. Her musical affiliations are with African-American music, with a culture that places great value on dance and physical engagement in music. It also is a culture that has always had prominent female participants: There are no white equivalents of Bessie Smith or Aretha Franklin, women who sing powerfully of both the spiritual and the erotic without the punitive, misogynist frame of European culture.[21] In critiquing Madonna's music, Dave Marsh (usually a defender of Madonna) once wrote: "A white Deniece Williams we don't need."[22] But perhaps that is precisely what we *do* need: a white woman musician who can create images of desire without the demand within the discourse itself that she be destroyed.

Madonna's Music

Madonna writes or co-writes most of her own material. Her first album was made up principally of her tunes. She surrendered some of the writing responsibility on *Like a Virgin* (interestingly, two of the songs that earned her so much notoriety—"Material Girl" and "Like a Virgin"—were written by men). But in her third album, *True Blue*, she is credited (along with her principal collaborators, Patrick Leonard and Stephen Bray) with co-production and with the co-writing of everything except "Papa Don't Preach." She co-wrote and co-produced (with Leonard Bray and Prince) all of the songs on her most recent album, *Like a Prayer*. It is quite rare for women singers to contribute so much to the composition of their materials, and it is almost unheard of for them to acquire the skills required for production. Indeed, very few performers of either sex attain sufficient prestige and power within the recording business to be able to demand that kind of artistic control.

Madonna's music is deceptively simple. On one level, it is very good dance music: inevitably compelling grooves, great energy. It is important to keep in mind that before she even presented her scandalous video images to the public, she had attracted a sizable following among the discerning participants of the black and gay disco scenes through her music alone. She remains one of the few white artists (along with George Michael) who regularly show up on the black charts.

Her music deliberately aims at a wide popular audience rather than at those who pride themselves on their elite aesthetic discrimination. Her enormous commercial success is often held against her, as evidence that she plays for the lowest common denominator that she prostitutes her art (and, by extension, herself).[23] Moreover, the fact that her music appeals to masses of young girls is usually taken as proof that the music has absolutely no substance, for females in our culture are generally thought to be incapable of understanding music on even a rudimentary level. But surely Madonna's power as a figure in cultural politics is linked to her ability to galvanize that particular audience—among others.[24]

To create music within a male-defined domain is a treacherous task. As some women composers of so-called serious or experimental music are discovering, many of the forms and conventional procedures of presumably value-free music are saturated with hidden patriarchal narratives, images, agendas.[25] The options available to a woman musician in rock music are especially constrictive, for this musical discourse is typically characterized by its phallic backbeat. It is possible to try to downplay that beat, to attempt to defuse its energy, but this strategy often results in music that sounds enervated or stereotypically "feminine." It is also possible to appropriate the phallic energy of rock and to demonstrate (as Chrissie Hynde, Joan Jett, or Lita Ford do so very well) that boys don't have any corner on that market. But that beat can always threaten to overwhelm: witness Janet Jackson's containment by producers Jimmy Jam and Terry Lewis in (ironically) her song "Control."

Madonna's means of negotiating for a voice in rock resemble very much the strategies of her visual constructions; that is, she evokes a whole range of conventional signifiers and then causes them to rub up against each other in ways that are open to a variety of divergent readings, many of them potentially empowering to girls and women. She offers musical structures that promise narrative closure and at the same time resist or subvert them. A traditional energy flow is managed—which is why to many ears the whole complex seems always already absorbed—but that flow is subtly redirected.

The most obvious of her strategies is irony: the irony of the little-girl voice in "Like a Virgin" or of fifties girl-group sentiment in "True Blue." Like her play with the signs of famous temptresses, bustiers, and pouts, her engagement with traditional musical signs of childish vulnerability projects her knowledge that this is what the patriarchy expects of her and also her awareness that this fantasy is ludicrous. Her unsupervised parody destroys a much-treasured male illusion: Even as she sings "True blue, baby, I love you," she becomes a disconcerting figure—the woman who knows too much, who is not at all the blank virginal slate she pretends to present. But to her female audience, her impersonation of these musical types is received with delight as a knowing wink, a gesture of empowerment.[26]

Madonna's engagement with images of the past is not always to be understood as parody, however. Some of the historical figures she impersonates are victims of traditions in opera and popular culture that demand death as the price for sexuality.[27] Principal among the victims she invokes are Carmen and Marilyn Monroe, both highly desired, sexual women who were simultaneously idolized and castigated and finally sacrificed to patriarchal standards of behavior. It is in her explicit acknowledgment of the traditional fate of artistic women who dare be erotic and yet in her refusal to fall likewise a victim that Madonna becomes far more serious about what have been referred to as "sign crimes."[28] If the strategy of appropriating and redefining conventional codes is the same in these more serious pieces as in the "True Blue" parody, the stakes are much, much higher.

An Aside on Narrative Schemas in Western Music

In order to account for the radical quality of the music in "Live to Tell" (and, later, "Like a Prayer"), I must undertake a detour back into the assumptions that guarantee the tonal narratives of the masculine canon since the seventeenth century. Tonal music is narratively conceived at least to the extent that the original key area—the tonic—also serves as the final goal. Tonal structures are organized teleologically, with the illusion of unitary identity promised at the end of each piece. But in order for pieces to have any narrative content, they must depart from the tonic and enact an adventure in which other key areas are visited (often theorists say "conquered") and in which the certainty of tonal identity is at least temporarily suspended. Otherwise there is no plot. Yet with the exception of a few pieces in the nineteenth and early twentieth centuries that deliberately call into question the premise of this narrative schema, the outcome—the inevitable return to tonic—is always known in advance. To the extent that "Other" keys stand in the way of unitary identity, they must finally be subdued for the sake of narrative closure.[29] They serve as moments both of desire (because without the apparent longing to approach these other keys, there is only stagnation) and of dread (because they threaten identity).

Such narratives can easily be observed in nineteenth-century symphonies, in which lyrical "feminine" themes are encountered and then annexed (for the sake of closure and generic convention) to the key of the "masculine" theme. The more seductive or traumatic the encounter with the Other, the more violent the "necessary" heroic reaction. Beethoven's symphonies are especially telling in this regard: In the "Eroica," an unprecedented level of dissonant bashing seems "required" to maintain thematic, rhythmic, and tonal identity. The struggle appears justified in the end, however, when we get to hear the uninterrupted transcendence of the theme in its tonic homeland.[30] In the Ninth Symphony, in which identity is marked as far more tentative, the violence levels are even higher. The arcadian third movement (a rare moment in which Beethoven permits dialogue and freedom of movement without the suggestion of overt anxiety) is self-consciously obliterated by the crashing dissonance introducing the finale's "Ode to Joy" [*sic*].[31] Such musical procedures correspond to narratives of desire and dread in literature of the time, the most celebrated of which is Faust's horror of being absorbed into Gretchen's world and his "need" to wrench himself free of her—even though it means her death—in order to continue his heroic, transcendental quest for identity.[32]

Most popular music avoids this schema, for songs typically are contented with the sustaining of harmonic identity. There is usually no implied Other within these musical procedures, no structural obstacle or threat to overcome. However, all that is required to transform these stable procedures into narratives is for a detail to be problematized—to be construed as Other and as an obstacle to the configuration defined as Self or identity. In such songs, time becomes organized around the expectation of intensified conflict, climax, and eventual resolution. They adopt, in other words, the same desire-dread-purge sequence that characterizes the narratives of so much classical music and literature.

Rock songs that work on the basis of this sequence can be found from Led Zeppelin to the recent hit, The Cult's "Fire Woman [you're to blame]." I will discuss as examples a couple of songs by the Heavy Metal band Whitesnake. Several of Whitesnake's songs quite clearly enact within the music the excitement of interacting with the area of the Other (personified in their videos by Tawny Kitaen as temptress) and yet the horror of being sucked in by that area, which precipitates and justifies outbreaks of violence for the sake of identity consolidation.

"Here I Go Again" defines the sixth degree of the scale as the moment of desire and yet of potential entrapment.[33] The choice of that scale degree is not accidental: There is a strong gravitational tendency in tonal music for six (a relatively weak position, sometimes referred to as "feminine") to resolve down to five, which belongs to the ("masculine") tonic triad. In pop as in classical music procedures, the tonic is rather boring by itself, and lingering on the sixth degree can create a delicious tension. However, if six threatens to take over, then identity may be lost. In "Here I Go Again," so-called deceptive cadences on the sixth degree repeatedly rob the piece of certainty yet create precisely the sense of nostalgic longing that characterizes the song. Its spectacularly enacted "climax" occurs only after a prolonged episode in which the harmony seems paralyzed on the "feminine" modal degrees, and the violence of the climax permits the return to the progressions that define quintessential masculine cadential control. The piece concludes, however, not with certainty but with a fade; and in the video, the fade is accompanied by images of a devouring Kitaen hauling lead singer David Coverdale over into the back seat of the car he is driving. This is what happens, apparently, when the purge is unsuccessful.

In "Still of the Night," the threat is far more intense, both musically and theatrically. At the end of the first verse (on the words "in the still of night"), Coverdale strains upward—both vocally and physically, as though in orgasm—to hold onto the sixth degree before returning decisively to tonic control. The second time through, however, both the heroic Coverdale and the harmony get trapped for what seems an interminable duration in that position, which has been so carefully defined as that of desire. The energy drains away, the musical and physical gestures mime impotence, and Kitaen struts about striking menacing poses. For a long time, there seems to be no possibility of escape or return. When the musical energy finally manages to extricate itself from the abyss, the rest of the piece is concerned with attempting violently to purge the contaminating element. In the video, this eradication sequence is dramatized visually as Kitaen is dragged off and tossed into a paddy wagon marked "Sex Police."

What we have here—in the abstract symphony as well as these particular Metal fantasies—is the playing out in music of a classic schema of Western masculine subjectivity. This schema has become quite familiar in recent years as it has been discovered and theorized by many different kinds of researchers in various disciplines, including psychoanalysts, feminists, and cultural critics. For instance, film and literary theorist Teresa de Lauretis describes the pattern thus:

> In the mythical text, then, the hero must be male regardless of the gender or the character, because the obstacle, whatever its personification (sphinx or dragon, sorceress or villain), is morphologically female—and indeed, simply, the womb, the earth, the space of his movement. As he crosses the boundary and "penetrates" the other space, the mythical subject is constructed as human being and as male: he is the active principle of culture, the establisher of distinction, the creator of differences. Female is what is not susceptible to transformation, to life or death: she (it) is an element of plot-space, a topos, a resistance, matrix and matter.[34]

Likewise, John Fiske has written about how this schema informs the narrative conventions of popular episodic television shows such as "Magnum P.I.":

Like all ideological constructs, masculinity is constantly under threat—it can never rest on its laurels. The threats come internally from its insecure bases in the rejection of the mother (and the guilt that this inspires) and the suppression of the feminine, and externally from social forces, which may vary from the rise of the women's movement to the way that the organization of work denies many men the independence and power that their masculinity requires. Thus masculinity has to be constantly reachieved, rewon. This constant need to reachieve masculinity is one of the underlying reasons for the popularity of the frequent televisual display of male performance.[35]

This schema underlies virtually all of our cultural texts; it is inscribed and transmitted in literature, art, philosophy, theology. And, as we have seen, a great deal of music, too, is organized in accordance with this pattern: Indeed, music without words (so-called absolute music) is especially prone to relying on it, treating it as though it were a design dictated by natural or metaphysical law. But it is one thing to be aware of this scheme and its implications as an analyst and theorist. It is quite another to take the formal procedures conventionally inscribed within these discourses and to cause them to tell another story, especially if one finds oneself always already cast by society in the position of the Other rather than that of the "universal" (i.e., masculine) Self.

"LIVE TO TELL" AS COUNTERNARRATIVE

In the stage show performance of "Live to Tell," the backdrop of the stage is filled with a huge projection of Madonna as Monroe—the quintessential female victim of commercial culture. The instrumental introduction sets up a bass pedal on D, performed by an inert synthesizer sonority utterly lacking in warmth. Over the pedal, a series of bleak open fifths mechanically mark the pulses of the metric order as though they were inevitable. This stark image alternates with an energetic pattern that emerges suddenly in the area of the relative major, F. The second sound-image differs from the opening sonority in part because the major key is semiotically associated with hope. Moreover, the bass is active rather than static, and it resists the apparent inevitability of the opening meter by anticipating slightly each of its changes. It seems to possess freedom of motion. However, just as this passage seems on the brink of establishing F major as the principal point of reference, it is recontained by the clanging fifths and the empty pedal on D. A traditional reading would understand D (with its pedal and fifths) as fundamental—as that which defines identity—and F major as the "feminine" region which—even if it offers the illusion of hope, escape, and freedom—must be contained and finally purged for the sake of satisfactory closure.[36]

When she begins singing the verse, Madonna temporarily steps outside of this dichotomy of D-versus-F to sing over a new pedal on C. As she sings, her voice repeatedly falls lethargically back to the void of the C pedal, as though she cannot overcome the gravitational pull it and the meter exert. Her text suggests that she has a weighty, long-buried "tale to tell," and her language ("I was not ready for the fall," "the writing on the wall") resonates with biblical references. If she as a woman is necessarily identified as the Other, as she who is held responsible for "the Fall," how is she to enter into narrative? How to step into a musical procedure in which the choices are already so loaded?

With the chorus ("a man can tell a thousand lies"), she opts for the warmer major key of F, her momentum picks up, and she begins to sound as though she will establish this more affirmative region as her tonic or point of reference. However, to close in this second region—conventionally the "feminine" position—is to accept as identity the patriarchal definition of femininity. Moreover, to the extent that F major is not the opening key, to cadence here is to choose fantasy; for while this key is reassuring and nurturing, it is not "reality" as the piece defines it initially. And formal convention would dictate that this second key area must eventually be absorbed and purged. Thus closure here is revealed as perilous. At the last moment before the implied cadence ("it will burn inside of *me*"), she holds to a pitch incompatible with harmonic closure. The age-old contrapuntal norm would dictate that her melodic pitch (once again the sixth degree, the image of desire in the White-snake piece) must resolve down to conform with the bass. Instead, her melodic pitch and the harmonic backdrop hold in a stand-off until the bass—not the melody—moves to conform to the melody's (that is, to *her*) will.

The pitch cadenced on, however, is D; and while it defies immediate closure, it also strikes the common tone that permits the pitiless pedal of the beginning to return. As before, Madonna steps outside the dilemma to C for a verse in which she wearily comments on her subjective knowledge of beauty, warmth, truth, light even in the face of this apparent no-win situation. But eventually she must rejoin the world in which she has to engage with the choice between F and D, and once again she works to avoid closure in either.

Finally, after this escape-recontainment process has occurred a couple of times, the bottom suddenly drops out. It sounds as though the piece has ended in the foreordained defeat of the victim—she who is offered only the second-position slot in the narrative schema. In her live performance, at this point Madonna sinks to the floor and lies motionless for what seems an interminable length of time. There is silence except for the low, lifeless synthesizer drone on D. For someone like myself who is used to this scenario as the inevitable end of my heroines, witnessing this moment from a performer who has been so brash, so bursting with erotic energy and animation, is bitter indeed. But then she rises from the floor, bearing with her the ghosts of all those victims—Marilyn most explicitly, but also Carmen, bare-breasted Barbara Strozzi, and all the others who were purged for the sake of social order and narrative closure—and begins singing again.

In order to take charge of the narrative procedure, Madonna begins to oscillate strategically between the two tonal poles on D and F. As she sings "If I ran away, I'd never have the strength," she sings over a bass that moves up and down indecisively between D and A (mediant of F, but dominant of D), suggesting a blurred region in which both keys cohabit. When the opening dilemma returns, she prevents the recontainment gesture of the fifths by anticipating their rhythmic moment of reentry and jumping in to interpose the F major refrain instead. So long as she manages thus to switch back and forth, she can determine the musical discourse. To settle for an option—either option—is to accept a lie, for it is flexibility in identity rather than unitary definition that permits her to "live to tell." The piece ends not with definitive closure but with a fade. As long as we can hear her, she continues to fluctuate.

This extraordinary song finally is not about unambiguous triumph: Triumph would be easy to simulate, since this is what tonal pieces conventionally do. Yet given the premises of this song, triumphant closure would be impossible to believe. Moreover, it would merely reproduce the structure of oppression that informs narrative convention. Rather, it is about staying in motion for the sake of survival, resisting closure wherever it lies in wait.[37]

By thus creating songs that refuse to choose between identity and Other, that invoke and then reject the very terms of this schema of narrative organization, Madonna is engaged in rewriting some very fundamental levels of Western thought. In "Live to Tell," the two clear regions of the traditional narrative schema seem to be implied. Semiotically, the unyielding fifths are "masculine," the lyrical, energetic refrain "feminine," and the early part of the piece reveals that the fifths are formally designed to contain the excess and relative freedom of the refrain. But to the extent that identification with the feminine moment in the narrative spells death, the piece cannot embrace this space as reality without losing strategic control. Thus the singer risks resisting identification with "her own" area, even if it means repeated encounters with that which would contain her. In a sense, she sets up residence on the moments of the harmonic context that fluctuate between desire and dread on the one hand and resolution on the other. Rather than deciding for the sake of secure identity (a move that would lapse back into the narrative of masculine subjectivity), she inhabits both and thus refuses closure.

Formulations such as this are all the more remarkable because the ideological implications of musical narratives are only now beginning to be analyzed by cultural critics. The fact that some of Madonna's music enacts models of organization that correspond to formulations of critics such as Teresa de Lauretis need not suggest that Madonna is a connoisseur of critical theory. Yet to the extent that de Lauretis and Madonna inhabit the same historical world and grapple with the same kinds of problems with respect to feminine identity, their similarities are not entirely coincidental either. And Madonna is as much an expert in the arena of musical signification as de Lauretis is in theoretical discourse. It seems clear that she has grasped the assumptions embedded within these basic musical mechanisms and is audaciously redirecting them.

It must be conceded that male musicians could construct forms along these lines if they wanted to do so—there is nothing essentially feminine about what Madonna is doing in this piece.[38] But most men would not perceive that there was a problem in the standard narrative, would not enact struggles that involve resistance to purging the alien element. The strategies of Madonna's songs are those of one who has radically conflicting subject positions—one who has been taught to cheer for resolutions in cultural narratives, but who also realizes that she is of the sort that typically gets purged for the sake of that resolution. Madonna's refusal of definition (which infuriates many a critic) goes beyond the paradox of her name, her persona, her visual imagery. It also produces brave new musical procedures.

MUSIC AND MUSIC VIDEO: "OPEN YOUR HEART"

Having thus been converted to Madonna as a musician who dares to create liberatory visions, I find the necessity of reading her music videos all the more urgent. Visual images seem to speak much louder than music—at least critics of Madonna's videos have found it difficult to notice the music, given the provocative nature of the pictures. Yet it is generally accepted that music in film covertly directs the affective responses of viewers far more than they know. I would suggest that the *music* in music videos is largely responsible for the narrative continuity and the affective quality in the resultant work, even if it is the visual images we remember concretely.[39]

I was acquainted with the song "Open Your Heart" long before I saw the video attached to it. While affectively much more upbeat than "Live to Tell," the musical imagery of "Open Your Heart" shares many of its resistant qualities: Up against the shimmering, pulsating energy of the backup, Madonna avoids conforming to the beat; and, at cadences, she subverts expected points of arrival. But unlike [the play with closure] in "Live to Tell," in which resistance indicates sheer survival, the play with closure in "Open Your Heart" creates the image of open-ended jouissance—an erotic energy that continually escapes containment.

By contrast, the video of "Open Your Heart" begins not in a visual field of open erotic joy but rather in the confined environment of a peepshow. Madonna sings the song from the center of a carousel that revolves to display her to the gazes of customers peering safely from their cubicles. Here she becomes Marlene Dietrich in *The Blue Angel*, her usually exuberant motion restrained to what she is able to accomplish with her only prop: a stationary chair. At one point in the first segment of the video, she is filmed dancing; but the camera is almost still, and her motions are confined to the small range the static camera can take in.

This confinement is especially noteworthy given the extraordinary exhilaration of the music: The tension between the visual and musical dimensions of the video is extremely unsettling. Only when she disappears from the carousel and reappears to run away from her patriarchal boss with the young boy do the music and visuals begin to be compatible. In other words, two very different narrative strata are present in the video: that of the relatively consistent jouissance in the music versus that of the transformation from patriarchal puppet to androgynous kid in the visuals.

Like many of Madonna's strategies, the one she attempts in this video is quite audacious. For instance, the peepshow situation is shot so that the leering patrons are rendered pathetic and grotesque, while she alone lays claim to subjectivity: Thus, the usual power relationship between the voyeuristic male gaze and object is here destabilized. Likewise, the young boy's game of impersonating the femme fatale and Madonna's transvestism at the end both refuse essentialist gender categories and turn sexual identity into a kind of play. Still, the video is risky, because for all those who have reduced her to "a porn queen in heat," there she is: embodying that image to the max. Those features of the video that resist a reductive reading of this sort—the non-fit of the music, the power inversions, the narrative of escape to androgyny—can easily be overlooked. This is, of course, always the peril of attempting to deconstruct pornographic images: It becomes necessary to invoke the image in order to perform the deconstruction, but, once presented, the image is in fact there in all its glory.

In this video, Madonna confronts the most pernicious of her stereotypes and then attempts to channel it into a very different realm: a realm where the feminine erotic need not be the object of the patriarchal gaze, where its energy can motivate play and nonsexual pleasure. The end of this video is as tenuous as the transcendent pitch in "Live to Tell": it speaks not of certainty but of horizons, of possibilities, of the hope of survival within available discursive practices.

POSTSCRIPT: "LIKE A PRAYER"

These themes—survival, pleasure, resistance to closure—are re-engaged most dramatically in Madonna's recent song and video, "Like a Prayer." In contrast to the relationship between sight and sound in "Open Your Heart," the tensions she is putting into play in this music video are virtually all audible within the music itself, prior to the visual images. Moreover, many of the tensions that always have surrounded her personae are here made explicit.

The central dichotomy she inevitably invokes is that of the virgin and the whore.[40] Her name (actually, fortuitously, her given name: Madonna Louise Veronica Ciccone), her apparently casual flaunting of crucifixes and rosary beads as accessories, and her overtly erotic dress and behavior have consistently thrown into confusion the terms of that standard binary opposition; but what precisely she means by this play of signs has never been obvious. Indeed, many critics have taken her use of religious imagery to be a prime example of what Fredric Jameson calls "blank pastiche": The symbols are seen as detached from their traditional contexts and thus as ceasing to signify.[41] However, Madonna's insistence on the codes of Catholic iconography has always at least potentially engaged with the sedimented memory of that tradition, even if only negatively—as blasphemy. In "Like a Prayer," the religious connotations of her entire project are reactivated and reinterpreted. But although this set of issues is finally foregrounded, her treatment of these highly sensitive themes is quite unexpected and, as it turns out, highly controversial.

The song draws upon two very different semiotic codes associated with two very different forms of Christianity: Catholicism and the black Gospel church. These codes would seem at first glance to be incompatible. But Madonna is tapping into a tradition of Catholicism that has long been suppressed: that of the female mystics such as St. Teresa who claimed to have experienced mystical union with Christ.[42] In St. Teresa's writings, religious ecstasy is described through images of sexual ecstasy, for the intensity of her relationship with the deity could only be expressed verbally to other human beings through metaphors of submission, penetration, even orgasm. In the seventeenth century, composers of sacred music freely borrowed images of desire and eroticism from the steamy operatic stage for purposes of their devotionals and worship services, for these experiences were thought to be relevant to the new forms of personalized faith encouraged by both the Reformation and Counter-Reformation.[43]

After the seventeenth century, this strain of religious erotic imagery was purged from mainstream Christian denominations, only to reemerge occasionally during moments of intense emotional revivalism. Certain forms of charismatic fundamentalism since the eighteenth century have employed erotic imagery for purposes of inducing personalized meditation or even trance states and speaking in tongues. Both Bach's pietistic bride-and-groom duets (see Cantata 140) and Jerry Lee Lewis's evangelical rock 'n' roll ("Whole Lot of Shakin' Goin' On") testify to this phenomenon. However, the semiotic connections between religious and sexual ecstasy are most consistently apparent in the black Gospel churches. Throughout its history (as preserved on recordings), Gospel has freely borrowed musical and poetic styles from the secular music of its day. Witness, for instance, the mergers with jazz, blues, funk, and rap evident on present-day Gospel radio stations or, for that matter, the entire career of Aretha Franklin. Moreover, the Gospel church continually produces new generations of black pop musicians whose music is fueled by the fervent energy of that spiritual context.

"Like a Prayer" opens with an invocation of stereotyped mystical Catholicism: with the halo of a wordless (heavenly) choir and the fundamental accompaniment of a "timeless" pipe organ as she sings of how "Life is a mystery." But with the words "When you call my name" (when, in other words, she is hailed as a new kind of subject), Madonna breaks into ecstatic, funky, Gospel-flavored dance music. These two moments are distinguished for narrative purposes through the same harmonic contrast between D and F as in

"Live to Tell." What seems to be a struggle between mystical timelessness on D minor and exuberant, physical celebration on F major ensues. This time, however, she is not afraid to embrace F as tonic, especially when halfway through, on the words "your voice can take me there," she lands decisively on that pitch.

But D does not disappear entirely—it re-enters for a long, rather sinister return of the beginning material in the middle of the song. Eventually, however, the music is channeled back to F major for more celebration. Gradually D comes to serve only for "deceptive" cadences. Traditionally, deceptive cadences spell disappointment, a jarring intervention at the promised moment of identity. But in "Like a Prayer," they provide the means of avoiding closure and maintaining the dance. Finally, in the long, ecstatic coda to the song, F and D at cadences become in a sense interchangeable: No longer self and Other, they become two flickering moments in a flexible identity that embraces them both, that remains constant only insofar as both continue to be equally present.

This is similar to the strategy of "Live to Tell," except that here the music itself does not involve the suggestion of threatened annihilation. But the controversial video released with the album sets up something like the external threats of containment articulated in "Live to Tell." The video is organized in terms of an inside and an outside. Outside the church is the world of Ku Klux Klan cross-burnings, of rape and murder, of racist authority. One of the most striking moments in the video occurs when Madonna dances provocatively in front of the burning crosses, aggressively defying those who burn crosses to contain her and her sexuality as well. And, indeed, Madonna has testified to having planned originally to present an even more extreme scenario: "I had all these ideas about me running away with the black guy and both of us getting shot by the KKK."[44] Video director Mary Lambert says of the segment with the burning crosses: "That's an ecstatic vision. The cross is a cautionary symbol and Madonna's performance throughout has been tortured and emotional. The inference of Ku Klux Klan racism is there, but the burning cross is an older symbol than the Klan. Saints had it. It symbolizes the wrath of God."[45]

But inside the church is the possibility of community, love, faith, and interracial bonding. The references to Catholic mysticism and the black Gospel church are made explicit in the visuals, with a heady mixture of a miraculously weeping statue, the stigmata, the St. Teresa–like union between the saint and the believer, and the highly physical musical performance by the Andrae Crouch Choir. Within the security of the church, difference can be overcome and the boundless joy of the music can become reality.[46] As in "Live to Tell," this song is about survival rather than simple triumph. And it is about the possibility of creating musical and visual narratives that celebrate multiple rather than unitary identities, that are concerned with ecstatic continuation rather than with purging and containment.[47]

CONCLUSION

With a very few exceptions, women composers of "serious" music are not even beginning to address issues such as these: they are, for the most part, still trying to pass for men.[48] In a world in which the safe options are denying gender difference or restricting the expression of the feminine erotic to all-women contexts, Madonna's counternarratives of female heterosexual desire are remarkable. That she manages to outrage those who would have her conform and to delight those who are still trying to puzzle out their own future options within patriarchal society indicates that her strategies are more or less successful.

I am not prepared to say that she is the only—or even the best—model for the future. But the intelligence with which she zeroes in on the fundamental gender tensions in culture and the courage with which she takes them on deserve much greater credit than she usually is given. If Madonna does, in fact, "live to tell" (that is, survive as a viable cultural force), an extraordinarily powerful reflex action of patriarchy will have been successfully challenged.[49]

NOTES

First appeared in 1990.

1. J. D. Considine, "That Girl: Madonna Rolls across America," *BUZZ* 2, no. 11 (September 1987): 17: "According to the PMRC's Susan Baker, in fact, Madonna taught little girls how to act 'like a porn queen in heat.'" E. Ann Kaplan refers to her image as a combination of bordello queen and bag lady. See *Rocking around the Clock: Music Television, Postmodernism, and Consumer Culture* (New York: Methuen, 1987), p. 126.

2. Mile Miles, music editor of the *Boston Phoenix*, as quoted in Dave Marsh, "Girls Can't Do What the Guys Do: Madonna's Physical Attraction," in *The First Rock & Roll Confidential Report* (New York: Pantheon, 1985), p. 161. Compare the imagery in Considine, "That Girl," p. 16: "By some accounts—particularly a notorious *Rolling Stone* profile—Madonna slept her way to the top, sucking her boyfriends dry, then moving on to the next influential male." Both Marsh and Considine refute this image, but it is a fascinating one that combines the predatory sexuality of the vampire and succubus with the servile masochism of female character in *Deep Throat*.

3. John Fiske, "British Cultural Studies and Television," in *Channels of Discourse*, ed. Robert C. Allen (Chapel Hill: University of North Carolina Press, 1987), p. 279.

4. Ibid., p. 270.

5. See Kaplan, *Rocking around the Clock*, especially pp. 115–27; and "Feminist Criticism and Television," *Channels of Discourse*, pp. 211–53.

6. Mikal Gilmore, "The Madonna Mystique," *Rolling Stone*, September 10, 1987, p. 87. I wish to thank Ann Dunne for this citation.

7. In his interview with Madonna in *Rolling Stone*, March 28, 1989, Bill Zehme says: "Maybe you noticed this already, but a number of songs on the new album [*Like*

a Prayer] have sort of antimale themes." Her response: "[*Surprised*] Well, gee, I never thought of that. This album definitely does have a very strong feminine point of view. Hmmm. I've had some painful experiences with men in my life, just as I've had some incredible experiences. Maybe I'm representing more of the former than the latter. I certainly don't hate men. No, no, no! Couldn't live without them!" (p. 180). Madonna is caught typically in a double bind in which she is chastised at the same time for being a passive doll and for being an aggressive man-hater. See again the citations in n. 1.

8. On a special MTV broadcast called "Taboo Videos" (March 26, 1988), Betty Friedan states in an interview: "I tell you, Madonna—in contrast to the image of women that you saw on MTV—at least she had spirit, she had guts, she had vitality. She was in control of her own sexuality and her life. She was a relatively good role model, compared with what else you saw."

9. Jane Bowers, "Women Composers in Italy, 1566–1700," in *Women Making Music: The Western Art Tradition 1150–1950*, ed. Jane Bowers and Judith Tick (Urbana: University of Illinois Press, 1986), pp. 139–40: "On 4 May 1686 Pope Innocent XI issued an edict which declared that 'music is completely injurious to the modesty that is proper for the [female] sex, because they become distracted from the matters and occupations most proper for them.' Therefore, 'no unmarried woman, married woman, or widow of any rank, status, condition, even those who for reasons of education or anything else are living in convents or conservatories, under any pretext, even to learn music in order to practice it in those convents, may learn to sing from men, either laymen or clerics or regular clergy, no matter if they are in any way related to them, and to play any sort of musical instrument.' "

An especially shocking report of the silencing of women performers is presented in Anthony Newcomb, *The Madrigal at Ferrara, 1579–1597* (Princeton: Princeton University Press, 1980). The court at Ferrara had an ensemble with three women virtuoso singers who became internationally famous. Duke Alfonso of Ferrara had the "three ladies" sing for Duke Guglielmo of Mantua and expected the latter to "praise them to the skies." "Instead, speaking loudly enough to be heard both by the ladies and by the Duchesses who were present [Duke Guglielmo] burst forth, 'ladies are very impressive indeed—in fact, I would rather be an ass than a lady.' And with this he rose and made everyone else do so as well, thus putting an end to the singing" (p. 24).

See also the examinations of the restrictions placed on women as musicians and performers in Richard Leppert, *Music and Image: Domesticity, Ideology and Sociocultural Formation in Eighteenth-century England* (Cambridge: Cambridge University Press, 1988); and Julia Kosa, "Music and References to Music in *Godey's Lady's Book*, 1830–77" (Ph.D. dissertation, University of Minnesota, 1988).

10. David Lee Roth, cited in Marsh, "Girls Can't Do," p. 165. I might add that this is a far more liberal attitude than that of most academic musicians.

11. This is not always an option socially available to male performers, however. The staged enactment of masculine sensuality is problematic in Western culture, in which patriarchal rules of propriety dictate that excess be projected onto women in spectacles. Thus Liszt, Elvis, and Roth can be understood as effective in part because of their transgressive behaviors. This distinction in permissible activities in music theater can be traced back to the beginnings of opera in the seventeenth century. See my "Constructons of Gender in the Dramatic Works of Monteverdi," *Cambridge Opera Journal* 1, no. 3 (1989): 203–23. See also Robert Walser, "Running with the Devil: Power, Gender and Madness in Heavy Metal Music" (Ph. D. dissertation, University of Minnesota, forthcoming).

12. Ellen Rosand, "The Voice of Barbara Strozzi," in *Women Making Music*, p. 185. See also Anthony Newcomb, "Courtesans, Muses, or Musicians? Professional Women Musicians in Sixteenth-Century Italy," in *Women Making Music*, pp. 90–115. For more on the role of Renaissance courtesans in cultural production, see Ann Rosalind Jones, "City Women and Their Audiences: Louise Labé and Veronica France," in *Rewriting the Renaissance: The Discourses of Sexual Difference in Early Modern Europe*, ed. Margaret W. Ferguson, Maureen Quilligan, and Nancy J. Vickers (Chicago: University of Chicago Press, 1986), pp. 299–316.

13. See the excerpts from Clara's diary entries and her correspondences with Robert Schumann and Brahms in Carol Neuls-Bates, ed., *Women in Music: An Anthology of Source Readings from the Middle Ages to the Present* (New York: Harper and Row, Publishers, 1982), pp. 92–108; and Nancy B. Reich, *Clara Schumann: The Artist and the Woman* (Ithaca: Cornell University Press, 1985). *Women in Music* contains many other documents revealing how women have been discouraged from participating in music and how certain of them persisted to become productive composers nonetheless.

14. For examinations of how the mind/body split intersects with gender in Western culture, see Genevieve Lloyd, *The Man of Reason: "Male" and "Female" in Western Philosophy* (Minneapolis: University of Minnesota Press, 1984); Susan Bordo, "The Cartesian Masculinization of Thought," *Signs* 11, no. 3 (1986): 439–56; and Evelyn Fox Keller, *Reflections on Gender and Science* (New Haven: Yale University Press, 1985).

For discussions of how these slipping binary oppositions inform music, see Geraldine Finn, "Music, Masculinity and the Silencing of Women," in *New Musicology*, ed. John Shepherd (New York: Routledge, forthcoming), and my "Agenda for a Feminist Criticism of Music," *Canadian University Music Review*, forthcoming.

15. This binary opposition is not, of course, entirely stable. Imagination, for instance, is an attribute of the mind, though it was defined as "feminine" during the Enlightenment and consequently becomes a site of contestation in early Romanticism. See Jochen Schulte-Sasse, "Imagination and Modernity: Or the Taming of the Human Mind," *Cultural Critique* 5 (Winter 1986–87): 23–48. Likewise, the nineteenth-century concept of "genius" itself was understood as having a necessary "feminine" component, although actual women were explicitly barred from this category. See Christine Battersby, *Gender and Genius* (London: Women's Press, 1989).

The common association of music with effeminacy is only now being examined in musicology. See Leppert, *Music and Image*; Linda Austern, "'Alluring the Auditorie to Effeminacie': Music and the English Renaissance Idea of the Feminine," paper presented at the American Musicological Society Meeting, Baltimore (November 1988); and Jeffrey Kallberg, "Genre and Gender: The Nocturne and Women's History," unpublished paper; Maynard Solomon, "Charles Ives: Some Questions of Veracity," *Journal of the American Musicological Society* 40 (1987): 466–69. Solomon writes: "He [Ives] is both drawn to music and repelled by it. 'As a boy [I was] partially ashamed of music,' he recalled—'an entirely wrong attitude but it was strong—most boys in American country towns, I think felt the same. . . . And there may be something in it. Hasn't music always been too much an emasculated art?' To ward off such feelings, Ives would eradicate the traces of the 'soft-bodied' and the 'decadent' in his work, perhaps employing the techniques of modernism to conceal the atmospheric, lyrical, yielding strata which often underlie his first ideas" (p. 467).

16. See Catherine Clément, *Opera or the Undoing of Women*, trans. Betsy Wing (Minneapolis: University of Minnesota Press, 1988), and my "Sexual Politics in Classical Music" and "Excess and Frame: The Musical Representation of Madwomen," in my *Feminine Endings: Music, Gender, Sexuality* (Minneapolis: University of Minnesota Press, forthcoming).

17. See my "Sexual Politics."

18. Quoted in Gilmore, "The Madonna Mystique," p. 87. Musicologist Leo Treitler recently has discussed the Madonna character in the film *Desperately Seeking Susan* while re-examining the politics of representation in Berg's opera *Lulu*. See "The Lulu Character and the Character of Lulu," *Music and the Historical Imagination* (Cambridge, Mass.: Harvard University Press, 1989), pp. 272–75.

19. See Richard Dyer, "In Defense of Disco," in *On Record: Rock, Pop, and the Written Word*, ed. Simon Frith and Andrew Goodwin (New York: Pantheon Press, 1990), pp. 410–18.

20. See, for instance, Theodor W. Adorno's hysterical denouncements of jazz in "Perennial Fashion—Jazz," in *Prisms*, trans. Samuel Weber and Shierry Weber (Cambridge, Mass.: MIT Press, 1981), pp. 121–32: "They [jazz fans] call themselves 'jitterbugs,' bugs which carry out reflex movements, performers of their own ecstasy" (p. 128); and "the aim of jazz is the mechanical reproduction of a regressive moment, a castration symbolism. 'Give up your masculinity, let yourself be castrated,' the eunuchlike sound of the jazz band both mocks and proclaims, 'and you will be rewarded, accepted into a fraternity which shares the mystery of impotence with you, a mystery revealed at the moment of the initiation rite'" (p. 129).

21. However, I have often encountered hostile reactions on the part of white middle-class listeners to Aretha Franklin's frank sensuality, even when (particularly when) it is manifested in her sacred recordings, such as "Amazing Grace." The argument is that women performers ought not to exhibit signs of sexual pleasure, for this invariably makes them displays for male consumption. See the discussion in John Shepherd, "Music and Male Hegemony," in *Music and Society: The Politics of Composition, Performance and Reception*, ed. Richard Leppert and Susan McClary (Cambridge: Cambridge University Press, 1987), pp. 170–72.

22. Marsh, "Girls Can't Do," p. 162.

23. See Mary Harron's harsh and cynical critique of rock's commercialism in general and Madonna in particular in "McRock: Pop as a Commodity," in *Facing the Music*, ed. Simon Frith (New York: Pantheon Books, 1988), pp. 173–220. At the conclusion of a reading of Madonna's "Open Your Heart" video, Harron writes: "The message is that our girl [Madonna] may sell sexuality, but she is free" (p. 218). See also Leslie Savan, "Desperately Selling Soda," *Village Voice*, March 14, 1989, p. 47, which critiques Madonna's decision to make a commercial for Pepsi. Ironically, when her video to "Like a Prayer" (discussed later in this paper) was released the day after the first broadcast of the commercial, Pepsi was pressured to withdraw the advertisement, for which it had paid record-high fees. Madonna had thus maintained her artistic control, even in what had appeared to be a monumental sell-out.

24. See the discussion of the responses to Madonna of young girls in Fiske, "British Cultural Studies," pp. 269–83. See also the report of responses of young Japanese fans in Gilmore, "The Madonna Mystique," p. 38. Madonna's response: "But mainly I think they feel that most of my music is really, really positive, and I think they appreciate that, particularly the women. I think I stand for everything that they're really taught

to not be, so maybe I provide them with a little bit of encouragement." Considine, "That Girl," quotes her as saying, "Children always understand. They have open minds. They have built-in shit detectors" (p. 17).

25. See my "Getting Down Off the Beanstalk: The Presence of a Woman's Voice in Janika Vandervelde's *Genesis II*," [in my] *Feminine Endings*.

26. "There is also a sense of pleasure, at least for me and perhaps a large number of other women, in Madonna's defiant look or gaze. In 'Lucky Star' at one point in the dance sequence Madonna dances side on to the camera, looking provocative. For an instant we glimpse her tongue: the expectation is that she is about to lick her lips in a sexual invitation. The expectation is denied and Madonna appears to tuck her tongue back into her cheek. This, it seems, is how most of her dancing and grovelling in front of the camera is meant to be taken. She is setting up the sexual idolization of women. For a woman who has experienced this victimization, this setup is most enjoyable and pleasurable, while the male position of voyeur is displaced into uncertainty." Robyn Blair, quoted in Fiske, "British Cultural Studies," p. 283.

27. For the ways women performers have been seen as inviting tragic lives, see Robyn Archer and Diana Simmonds, *A Star Is Torn* (New York: E. P. Dutton, 1986); Gloria Steinem, *Marilyn* (New York: Henry Holt and Company, 1986). For an analysis of Hitchcock's punishments of sexual women, see Tania Modleski, *The Women Who Knew Too Much: Hitchcock and Feminist Theory* (New York: Methuen, 1988). For treatments of these issues in classical music, see my "Sexual Politics" and "The Undoing of Opera: Toward a Feminist Criticism of Music," foreword to Clément, *Opera*, pp. ix–xviii.

28. In Gilmore, "Madonna Mystique," Madonna states: "I do feel something for Marilyn Monroe. A sympathy. Because in those days, you were really a slave to the whole Hollywood machinery, and unless you had the strength to pull yourself out of it, you were just trapped. I think she didn't know what she was getting herself into and simply made herself vulnerable, and I feel a bond with that. I've certainly felt that at times—I've felt an invasion of privacy and all that—but I'm determined never to let it get me down. Marilyn Monroe was a victim, and I'm not. That's why there's really no comparison." The term "sign crimes" is from Arthur Kroker and David Cook, *The Postmodern Scene: Excremental Culture and Hyper-Aesthetics* (New York: St. Martin's Press, 1986), p. 21.

29. For more on how tonal music produces narrative meaning, see my "Pitches, Expression, Ideology: An Exercise in Mediation," *Enclitic* 7 (Spring, 1983): 76–85; "The Blasphemy of Talking Politics during Bach Year," in *Music and Society*, pp. 13–62; and "A Musical Dialectic from the Enlightenment: Mozart's Piano Concerto in G Major, K. 453, Movement 2," *Cultural Critique* 4 (Fall 1986): 129–69.

30. For an excellent narrative account of the *Eroica*, see Philip Downs, "Beethoven's 'New Way' and the Eroica," in *The Creative World of Beethoven*, ed. Paul Henry Lang (New York: W. W. Norton and Company, 1970), pp. 83–102. Downs's interpretation is not inflected, however, by concerns of gender or "extramusical" notions of alterity.

31. For another reading of the Ninth Symphony, see Leo Treitler, "History, Criticism, and Beethoven's Ninth Symphony" and "To Worship That Celestial Sound: Motives for Analysis," in *Music and the Historical Imagination*, pp. 19–66.

32. Leslie Fiedler argues that this narrative convention likewise informs American male literature. See *Love and Death in the American Novel*, rev. ed. (New York: Stein

and Day, 1982), and *What Was Literature? Class Culture and Mass Culture* (New York: Simon and Schuster, 1982). For a superb theoretical discussion of these issues in literature, see Teresa de Lauretis, "Desire in Narrative," in *Alice Doesn't* (Bloomington: Indiana University Press, 1984), pp. 103–57.

33. In this and subsequent readings of pieces, I will occasionally refer to particular pitches and pitch relationships to ground my argument in material evidence. However, my prose throughout is designed to be accessible to these who are not acquainted with music jargon. If you listen to the songs, you should be able to hear the details to which I refer quite easily. Both songs are on the album *Whitesnake* (Geffen Records, 1987).

34. Teresa de Lauretis, "The Violence of Rhetoric; Considerations on Representation and Gender," in *Technologies of Gender* (Bloomington: Indiana University Press, 1987), pp. 43–44.

35. Fiske, "British Cultural Studies," p. 262. For more on constructions of masculine subjectivity, see Arthur Brian, *Masculinity and Power* (London: Basil Blackwell, 1989), and Klaus Theweleit, *Male Fantasies*, I and II, trans. Stephen Conway, Erica Carter, and Chris Turner (Minneapolis: University of Minnesota Press, 1987 and 1989). I owe my knowledge of and interest in Metal to Rob Walser. I wish to thank him for permitting me to see his "Forging Masculinity: Heavy Metal Sounds and Images of Gender," forthcoming in *Sound and Vision*, ed. Simon Frith, Andrew Goodwin, and Lawrence Grossberg.

36. Compare, for example, the opening movement of Schubert's Unfinished Symphony, in which the tune we all know and love is in the second position and is accordingly quashed. George Michael's "Hand to Mouth" (in the *Faith* album) is a good example of the same imperatives at work in popular music. In both the Schubert and Michael, the pretty tune represents illusion up against harsh reality. I wish to thank Rob Walser for bringing the Michael song to my attention.

37. This strategy of always staying in motion is advocated in Teresa de Lauretis, "The Technology of Gender," in *Technologies of Gender*, especially pp. 25–26. See also Denise Riley, *"Am I That Name?"*: *Feminism and the Category of "Women" in History* (Minneapolis: University of Minnesota Press, 1988); and Kaja Silverman, "Fragments of a Fashionable Discourse," in *Studies in Entertainment: Critical Approaches to Mass Culture*, ed. Tania Modleski (Bloomington: Indiana University Press, 1986), pp. 150–51. I discuss Laurie Anderson's "O Superman" or "Langue d'Amour" in terms of these strategies in "This Is Not a Story My People Tell: Time and Space According to Laurie Anderson," *Discourse*, forthcoming.

38. Some of the so-called Minimalist composers, such as Philip Glass and Steve Reich, also have called the conventions of tonal closure into question, as did Debussy at an earlier moment. See my "Music and Postmodernism," *Contemporary Music Review*, forthcoming.

39. Andrew Goodwin advances a similar argument in "Music Video in the (Post) Modern World," *Screen* 18 (Summer 1987): 39–42.

40. In the souvenir program book from her 1987 tour, Madonna is quoted as saying: "Madonna is my real name. It means a lot of things. It means virgin, mother, mother of earth. Someone who is very pure and innocent but someone who's very strong." Needless to say, this is not how the name has always been received.

41. For a cynical interpretation, see Steve Anderson, "Forgive Me, Father," *Village Voice*, April 4, 1989, p 68: "Madonna snags vanguard attention while pitching critics into fierce Barthesian discussions about her belt buckles. Certainly she's an empire

of signs, but the trick behind the crucifixes, opera gloves, tulle, chains, and the recent rosary-bead girdle is that they lead only back to themselves, representing *nothing*."

But see also the complex discussion in Fiske, "British Cultural Studies," pp. 275–76, who quotes Madonna as saying, "I have always carried around a few rosaries with me. One day I decided to wear [one] as a necklace. Everything I do is sort of tongue in cheek. It's a strong blend—a beautiful sort of symbolism, the idea of someone suffering, which is what Jesus Christ on a crucifix stands for, and then not taking it seriously. Seeing it as an icon with no religiousness attached. It isn't sacrilegious for me." Fiske concludes that "her use of religious iconography is neither religious nor sacrilegious. She intends to free it from this ideological opposition and to enjoy it, use it, for the meanings and pleasure that it has for her and *not* for those of the dominant ideology and its simplistic binary thinking."

42. For excellent discussions of the Catholic tradition of female saints and erotic imagery, see Caroline Walker Bynum, "The Female Body and Religious Practice in the Later Middle Ages," in *Zone: Fragments for a History of the Human Body*, ed. Michael Feher et al. (New York: Zone, 1989), pp. 160–219, and Julia Kristeva, *Tales of Love*, trans. Leon S. Roudiez (New York: Columbia University Press, 1987), especially pp. 83–100 and 297–317.

This association is in line with many of Madonna's statements concerning Catholicism, such as her claim that "nuns are sexy" (Fiske, "British Cultural Studies," p. 275). However, she need not be aware of St. Teresa in order for these kinds of combinations of the sacred and erotic to occur to her. Once again, her experiences as a woman in this culture mesh in certain ways with the traditional symbolism of holy submission in Christianity, and thus her metaphors of spirituality are similar in many ways to St. Teresa's. She also intends to create this collision in the song and video. In Armond White, "The Wrath of Madonna," *Millimeter* (June 1989): 31, Mary Lambert (director of the "Like a Prayer" video) states: "Madonna and I always work together on a concept. We both felt the song was about sexual and religious ecstasy." The black statue in the church is identified as St. Martin de Porres. I wish to thank Vaughn Ormseth for bringing this article to my attention.

43. See the many settings of texts from the Song of Songs by composers such as Alessandro Grandi or Heinrich Schütz. The sacred erotic likewise influenced the literary and visual arts. See Bernini's sculpture of or Richard Crashaw's poem concerning St. Teresa. I am at the moment writing a book, *Power and Desire in Seventeenth-Century Music*, which examines this phenomenon.

44. Quoted in Liz Smith's column, *San Francisco Chronicle*, April 19, 1989, p. E1. I wish to thank Greil Marcus for bringing this to my attention. Lydia Hamessley first pointed out to me the significance of inside and outside in the organization of the video.

45. White, "The Wrath of Madonna," p. 31.

46. For an excellent discussion of the political strength of the music, rhetoric, and community of the black church today, see the interview of Cornel West by Anders Stephanson in *Universal Abandon? The Politics of Postmodernism*, ed. Andrew Ross (Minneapolis: University of Minnesota Press, 1988), pp. 277–86. Madonna speaks briefly about her identification with black culture in Zehme, "Madonna," p. 58.

47. For another sympathetic discussion of the politics of this video, see Dave Marsh, "Acts of Contrition," *Rock & Roll Confidential* 67 (May 1989): 1–2.

48. See my "Getting Down Off the Beanstalk."

49. A version of this paper was first presented for the conference Feminism and Mass Culture at SUNY-Buffalo (March 1988). I wish to thank Nancy Armstrong, Rey Chow, George Lipsitz, and Robert Walser for their valuable suggestions as I was revising the paper for publication.

Ritual and Resistance:
Subversion as a Social Fact

NICHOLAS B. DIRKS

There is subversion, no end of subversion,

only not for us.

ANTHROPOLOGY AND HISTORY

The social history of modern India has developed side by side with anthropology. In anthropology, as in social science more generally, "order" has typically been the chief ordering principle of discourse. When anthropology puts particular emphasis on order, it sanctifies it with the adjective "ritual." Ritual is not only principally about order, it is often the domain in which our sociological conception of society is properly realized. In this view, social relations are displayed and renewed and the hierarchical forms underlying social relations confirmed and strengthened by ritual.

While social historians of areas outside of South Asia (or other third world areas in anthropologyland) have worked in greater autonomy from anthropology, they have recently turned to anthropology to enable them to understand many aspects of social life that had not been addressed by political or intellectual history, and later proved equally intractable to the quantitative methods of early social history. In both cases, social historians have consumed anthropological theories and rubrics too uncritically, little realizing that interdisciplinary collaboration should leave neither of the constituent disciplines untouched. In this paper, I focus on everyday forms of resistance, critiquing both anthropological assumptions about ritual and historical reifications of these assumptions. In taking "ritual" as my subject, I also argue that too often the combination of the key terms "everyday" and "resistance" leads us to look for new arenas where resistance takes place, rather than also realizing that many more "traditional" arenas are also brimming with resistance. Finally, I seek to suggest that our old theories of either "ritual" or "resistance" are not all that are at risk in this enterprise; also at risk are the underlying presuppositions of order that undergird and normalize most historical or social scientific writing.

RITUAL AS A SOCIAL FACT

"Ritual" is a term that sanctifies and marks off a space and a time of special significance. Ritual may be part of everyday life, but it is fundamentally opposed to "the everyday." Anthropologists have typically identified ritual as a moment and an arena in which meaning is cathected and crystalized, in which social experience is distilled and displayed. As summarized by Geertz, Durkheim and Robertson-Smith set the terms of anthropological discourse on ritual by emphasizing the manner in which ritual "reinforce[s] the traditional social ties between individuals. . . . [T]he social structure of a group is strengthened and perpetuated through the ritualistic or mythic symbolization of the underlying social values upon which it rests."[1] Rituals are thus seen as embodying the essence of culture, "as dramatizing the basic myths and visions of reality, the basic values and moral truths, upon which . . . [the] world rests."[2] This is not to say that anthropologists have always treated ritual as static. In her important book on ritual in Nepal, Ortner (showing Geertz's influence) clarifies that while she says that rituals "dramatize basic assumptions of fact and value in the culture," she is, in fact, coding a more complex assertion, namely, that "such 'fundamental assumptions' are actually constructed, or reconstructed, and their fundamentality reestablished, in the course of the rituals themselves."[3] Nonetheless, as her more recent work indicates,[4] this earlier clarification reflected a particular moment in anthropology, when Durkheimian assumptions about meaning and ritual were being reevaluated but left basically unchallenged. Ritual might have been viewed as a process that was profoundly integrated into the complex and shifting social worlds of anthropological subjects, but ritual was still the principal site of cultural construction, and the study of culture was fundamentally about shared meanings and social values.

Some years later, when summarizing theoretical developments in anthropology since the sixties, Ortner[5] noted that ritual had been shifted from center stage by new concerns in anthropology with practice and everyday life. This new call to practice has been part of a general move away from traditional subjects, such as kinship and ritual, or at least away from traditional approaches to these subjects. Rituals were often seen as opposed to the everyday character of experience, even though it has been increasingly conceded that everyday life is highly ritualized. Pierre Bourdieu, the chief theoretical advocate of practice as a new focus for anthropology, critiqued the normative character of most social theory, in which meaning is analyzed as if it could be abstracted from the everyday contexts of production, reproduction, and strategic manipulation. Bourdieu argued that it was only by attending to the actual practice of rituals, such as gift giving—the contexts in which gifts were given, the multiple interests behind giving and receiving, the sequencing and timing of gifts and countergifts, as well as the differential nature of things given—that it would be possible to break away from the standard anthropological interpretation of social action and meaning. Nonetheless, even calls for practice-oriented anthropologies from such theorists as Bourdieu confirm the residual centrality of the cultural: in Bourdieu's theoretical proposals, "capital" is now modified by the adjective "symbolic."[6]

In recent years, as social history has become increasingly anthropologized, historians have appropriated ritual as a subject and employed anthropological perspectives on ritual. William Sewell invoked a Geertzian conception of ritual to demonstrate that ritual performances—in his particular story, rituals that employed old regime forms in postrevolutionary contexts—were used to symbolically mark and socially solidify the emerging communities of labor in late eighteenth- and early nineteenth-century France.[7] More commonly, Turner, Van Gennep, and Gluckman, rather than Geertz, have been cited when historians have attempted to analyze ritual. (Geertz has been used by historians principally for his semiotic theory of culture, not for his gentle critique of functionalist analyses of ritual.)[8] Following these anthropological authors, historians have typically been interested in such rituals as the carnival or the charivari, in rites of inversion or status reversal. Some historians have accepted the functionalist undergirding of anthropological writing about these rituals, concurring at least to some extent that rituals, in Gluckman's terms, "obviously include a protest against the established order" but "are intended to preserve and strengthen the established order."[9] As Natalie Davis puts it, rituals "are ultimately sources of order and stability in a hierarchical society. They can clarify the structure by the process of reversing it. They can provide an expression of, and a safety valve for, conflicts within the system. They can correct and relieve the system when it has become authoritarian. But, so it is argued, they do not question the basic order of the society itself. They can renew the system, but they cannot change it."[10] From a textual perspective, Stephen Greenblatt has recognized that the anxiety about royal authority induced by Shakespeare in such plays as *Richard II* and *Henry V* serves only to enhance the power of authority; as he says, "actions that should have the effect of radically undermining authority turn out to be the props of that authority."[11]

Nevertheless, many historians have recognized in the ritual of carnival something more than this, seizing on the prepolitical elements of class struggle and contestation, concentrating on the unsettling and disorderly aspects of the periodic inversion. In so doing, they usually have had to suspend the teleological framing they might have preferred to record as critics of the social order; rituals rarely became highly politicized, and often did lapse back into the social orders that produced them, whether or not that social order was reinforced or slightly shaken as a result. Subversion was either contained or transformed into order.

In literary studies, which since the translation of Bakhtin's extraordinary book on Rabelais in 1968 have become even more carnivalesque than social history, the relation between periodic disorder and subversion on the one hand and order and containment on the other has been widely debated. Terry

Eagleton is one of many critics of Bakhtin who think that Bakhtin's celebration of the political potential and meaning of the carnival is misguided:

> Indeed carnival is so vivaciously celebrated that the necessary political criticism is almost too obvious to make. Carnival, after all, is a *licensed* affair in every sense, a permissable rupture of hegemony, a contained popular blow-off as disturbing and relatively ineffectual as a revolutionary work of art. As Shakespeare's Olivia remarks, there is no slander in an allowed fool.[12]

Be that as it may, it is striking how frequently violent social clashes apparently coincided with carnival. And, while carnival was always licensed, not all that happened during carnival was similarly licensed. Carnival was socially dangerous, semiotically demystifying, and culturally disrespectful, even though it often confirmed authority, renewed social relations, and was rarely either politicized or progressive.[13]

In all these debates the question of whether ritual can occasion, or serve as the occasion for, resistance is read in terms of one specific form of ritual and one particular kind of resistance. We hear only about the carnival or the charivari, about rituals that involve reversal and inversion, not about rituals that are about power and authority of both secular and sacred kinds. And we evaluate the politics of ritual only in terms of a discourse on resistance that seeks out contestatory and confrontational upsurges by the lower classes. It is perhaps no accident that Natalie Davis was less affected by these discursive blinkers than many of her contemporaries since her most critical discussion of the carnival concerns the status of women who could not participate in public and politicized moments of confrontation, consigned as they were to the private, the domestic, and the particular. Thus a concern with gender has led some writers to a critique of the virile assumptions underlying most writings on resistance.[14]

Recent writing on everyday resistance has moved away from concentrating only on clearly "political" moments and movements, but the definition of everyday experience typically excludes such activities as ritual. For example, James Scott, who has made an important and eloquent plea for the study of everyday forms of peasant resistance, ignores the possibility that ritual could constitute an important site of resistance.[15] This is partly because of his basic economistic preoccupations and partly because he is suspicious of ritual. In his long and rich book, he makes only two brief references to rituals of status reversal, otherwise referring to ritual as constitutive of community. Scott exemplifies the way that many writers concerned with resistance accept with little modification the Durkheimian foundations of social scientific conceptions of ritual. Alf Ludtke, who has exemplified the concerns of a number of German historians in relation to the recovery of the everyday experience of the working class, has also ignored the possible importance of ritual.[16]

Meanwhile, anthropologists have continued to be interested in ritual, though only rarely in its resistance possibilities. An important exception has been Jean Comaroff, an anthropologist who has worked among the Tshidi of southern Africa and who (like Ortner) was clearly deeply influenced by the practice theory of Bourdieu. Comaroff has written about the repressed and oppressed tensions of the violently established and violently maintained hegemony in South Africa. She found that

> while awareness of oppression obviously runs deep, reaction may appear erratic, diffuse, and difficult to characterize. It is here that we must look beyond the conventionally explicit domains of "political action" and "consciousness"; for, when expressions of dissent are prevented from attaining the level of open discourse, a subtle but systematic breach of authoritative cultural codes might make a statement of protest which, by virtue of being rooted in a shared structural predicament and experience of dispossession, conveys an unambiguous message.[17]

Comaroff goes on specifically to argue that ritual constitutes one of these unconventional domains, suggesting that "ritual provides an appropriate medium through which the values and structures of a contradictory world may be addressed and manipulated." Comaroff thus sees the syncretistic ritual and religious movements that have accompanied capitalist penetration into the third world as "purposive attempt[s] to defy the authority of the hegemonic order." Indeed, she argues that "such exercises do more than just express revolt; they are also more than mere acts of self-representation. Rather, they are at once both expressive and pragmatic, for they aim to change the real world by inducing transformations in the world of symbol and rite."[18] It is this mode of situating ritual practice, belief, and symbolism in a political world of hegemony and struggle—a world in which representation itself is one of the most contested resources—which I follow in this paper.

But I also seek to go further, starting with a more basic premise. I will not evaluate ritual practice on the basis of whether or not it aims to change the "real world," however much it may lack self-consciousness. Rather, I will look at traditional village rituals in India that appear to have the effect of restoring social relations and upholding relations of authority, both within the village and between it and the larger political unit of the kingdom or state. I will seek to determine if the way in which order and disorder have been narrativized as basic components of these rituals enables us to recognize and understand the multiple foci and forms of disorder as I encountered them—for anthropologists have viewed ritual not merely as a sociological mechanism for the production of order, but also as a cosmological and symbolic site for the containment of chaos and the regeneration of the world (as we, or they, know it).

Elsewhere I have argued that current anthropological writing on ritual underplays, both at the level of kingdoms or large political units and at the level of village rituals and festivals, the social fact that ritual constitutes a tremendously important arena for the cultural construction of authority and the dramatic display of the social lineaments of power.[19] Although I presented examples of conflict, I saw conflict largely as a product of the breakdown of authority under colonialism. Here, I shall argue that precisely because of the centrality of authority to the ritual process, ritual has always been a crucial site of struggle, involving both claims about authority and struggles against (and within) it. By historicizing the study of ritual, we can see that while rituals provide critical moments for the definition of collectivities and the articulation of rank and power, they often occasion more conflict than consensus, and that each consensus is provisional, as much a social moment of liminality in which all relations of power (and powerlessness) are up for grabs as a time for the reconstitution and celebration of a highly political (and thus disorderly) ritual order. Resistance to authority can be seen to occur precisely when and where it is least expected.

THE FESTIVAL OF AIYANAR

The ritual I will focus on is crucial here because although it is only one of several village rituals, it is the one that inaugurates all other village rituals, often setting the calendrical and cosmological agenda for the yearly ritual cycle. The festival of Aiyanar, called the *kutirai etuppu*, was also critical in that it vividly reflected and displayed the hierarchical relations within the village, with the village headman, or *ampalam*, as the ostensive center of these relations. The priests for this ritual, who were also the potters (Velars) who made the clay horses that were consecrated in the central ritual action, had to obtain permission from the ampalam in order to begin making the clay horses. The ampalam was the host for the festival, and his emblems were as important in the procession as the clay horses themselves; the ampalam received the first honors, which he then distributed to the other members of the village at the conclusion of the ritual. In short, the ampalam represented the totality of the village, in a rite that was seen and said by some to celebrate and regenerate the village itself.

When I was in the "field"—for me, the little kingdom of Pudukkottai, one of the largest of the little kingdoms in the early modern period of the Tamil-speaking region of southern India, and under the British Raj, the only princely state in the Tamil country—it took little time to realize that Aiyanar was a critical deity, and the yearly festival in his honor a crucial festival, in local ritual life. Village elders and headmen would regularly take me to their own shrine of Aiyanar as the most important stop on the village tour. They would tell me all about their village festival—how it was famous for miles around, how I would be able to observe and recognize the political centrality of the headman, that I should definitely plan to return to their village on the occasion of the festival. Clearly ritual was important, and clearly this was the social ritual par excellence, at least in the postindependence days of a post-royal kingdom. During the course of my fieldwork, I attended and took extensive notes on about twelve of these festivals in different villages throughout the state. Because of my interest in local social relations and structures of authority, I was drawn into this festival, which became a chief focus of my ethnographic research.

There was one festival in particular that I looked forward to attending. The village headman had been an especially rewarding informant, and spent many hours telling me about the complex details of social organization in his village and his *natu*, the territorial unit that was coterminous with the settlement zone of his subcaste group (also called "natu") of Kallars, the royal caste in Pudukkottai. He was a patriarch of classic proportions. He told me about the festival of Aiyanar with the care and comprehension of a radio cricket commentator, and as the festival neared, he even visited my house in town on two occasions to submit to further questions and my tape recorder. I was told exactly when the festival would begin, and we agreed that I would arrive soon after dusk, to participate in the final preparations, which would culminate in the commencement of the festival around midnight (like many other rituals, the festival went on through the night). When the festival was still a week away, I expected a formal visit from the headman to invite me as an honored outside guest, but when he failed to turn up, I assumed that he was unable to come because he was enmeshed in the myriad preparations for the festival. On the appointed evening I drove my motorcycle the requisite thirty-five miles across potholed tarmac and dusty bullock cart tracks, only to arrive in a village that was virtually dark, with no visible evidence of any approaching festivities. The village headman looked dismayed and surprised as I rolled up on my motorcycle, though less dismayed than me, since I heard, as I switched off my engine, the unmistakable hiss of a rapidly deflating tire, the devastating effect of a large acacia thorn's union with my nonradial tire. The headman told me that the festival had been called off, and that he had hoped I would have guessed this since he had not come with the formal invitation. In any case, he said, he could not have come to tell me that there would be no festival, since this would have been inauspicious, and would have made it even more unlikely than it already was that the festival could take place. But this admirable foresight had not turned things around. The festival could not be organized: a long-standing factional dispute in the village was not, in the end, resolved, and the festival became yet another casualty of this dispute. My immediate concern, apart from the fact that my tire was flat and I was not carrying a spare, was that I had lost a brilliant opportunity to match theory, narrative, and practice, to follow up the story of a festival that I had been tracking industriously over the preceding weeks and months. But as my host instructed his son and assorted relatives to hitch up the bullock cart to arrange for my long and bumpy transport back to town, my disappointment yielded to bewilderment—for I learned that the festival on which I had garnered such exquisite detail had not taken place for seven years, and that no one in the village had any genuine expectation that it would take place this year.

Most fieldwork stories can be allegorized. We begin with calm self-confidence, our initial assumptions and convictions still unchecked by the chaotic realities and serendipities of the field. We then find ourselves in some disastrous predicament, which in unsettling us (and sometimes our informants), enables us to cross the fault line of cultural difference, to familiarize ourselves with the concerns and logics of new social terrains, to achieve new forms of communion with our anthropological subjects, to attain wisdom. In fact, at the time I was simply seriously annoyed. Nevertheless, I tell my story here to suggest that although I had been aware of the extent to which the festivals of Aiyanar gave rise to conflict and dispute at the time, it was only then, and increasingly over the years since, that I changed the way I thought about ritual. I began to realize the extent to which this story illustrates the flip side of my concern with how village rituals reflected and displayed political authority and political relations. I had begun thinking about Aiyanar by using his festival to attack Dumont's notion (which he developed in a number of places, notably in an important article on the festival of Aiyanar in Tamil Nadu)[20] that religion and ritual always encompass politics and power. I argued that the festival, far from revealing the transcendence of a religious domain and the uncontested supremacy of Brahmanic persons and principles, was in large part about the intersections of power and social relations in the village, locality, and kingdom. The royal symbolism of Aiyanar, the ritual centrality of kingship, and the local power of the headmen were all confirmed and displayed by the ritual process. But having established the political character and referents of the festival, I still found it difficult to come to terms with the facts that these festivals were always sites for struggle and contestation, that speech about the festivals reflected concerns about ritual order and auspiciousness that were part of a another ritual order, different from that of the ritual event itself, and that even when the ritual event did not happen, it was as significant as when it did. I came to realize that the nonevent of the called-off ritual was not, in fact, a nonevent, after all.

During the rest of my fieldwork, I learned that many of the other great events of ritual calendars were similar nonevents. The festivals of Aiyanar did not happen almost as often as they did. Moreover, when they happened, they did not always include everyone in the village, or result in the village communal harmony that I had previously assumed; indeed, this communal harmony was disturbed not only along the so-called traditional lines of caste or faction but along developing class lines as well. I also learned that while at one level, the festival was about the reestablishment of control over disorder of a threatening nature, it was also about the range of possibilities that existed precisely at the moment of maximal contact between order and disorder. But it is now time to backtrack to the festival itself, before we allow it, as it did that night for me, to deconstruct itself.

In Pudukkottai, Aiyanar was often the principal village deity, though some villages include temples of Aiyanar in which the village deity was said to be a goddess. According to most of my informants, the most significant feature of Aiyanar was his role as the protector. He was more specifically called the protection deity, the protector of boundaries, and the one who protected those who took refuge with him. Aiyanar's shrines were always located on the periphery of the village, in order best to protect the village from outside predation, as well as from the forces of danger that lurked in the forests and wastelands just outside the zone of village civilization. The kutirai etuppu festival (the installation of the ceramic horses) began a month before the main festival day. The head of the potters (Velars), the community that made the terra-cotta offerings and often acted as principal priests for Aiyanar, would take a handful of clay (*pitiman*) from the village tank. The pitiman was placed in a brass plate and handed to the village ampalam, who then returned it to the Velars, along with the ritual dues. The ampalam had to make this gift, signifying his permission for the festival to begin, to entitle the Velars to proceed with the preparation of the offerings. The gift was made in part in the form of *puja*, the blessed return of a gift that was first offered to the superior being. The central position of the ampalam was thus enunciated and displayed at the moment of the festival's inauguration.

Throughout the festival itself, though each one varied in details, the role of the ampalam was particularly conspicuous, and as important as that of the deity. The festival began and ended at his house, the central locus of all village gatherings. There, the first ritual action of the festival had taken place a month earlier, when the ampalam returned the pitiman to the head of the Velars. Similarly, the first ritual action of the festival day was often the puja performed to the ampalam's family deity, with the gift adorned with the emblems that represented and encapsulated the family's heritage. Granted by the Raja, and passed from generation to generation within the family, these emblems now symbolized that this festival was sponsored by the village ampalam, a festival at once personal and public, the private puja of the ampalam's family and the public performance of the entire village.

The central action of the festival was a procession from the ampalam's house to the temple of Aiyanar on the outskirts of town. Crowds of villagers accompanied the terra-cotta horses that were to be installed before the shrine of Aiyanar. At the temple a "Sanskritic" *naivedya* (offering) was made to Aiyanar, at the conclusion of which a goat was sacrificed to the subsidiary deities Karuppar and Muni. Much has been made of the fact that when the goat sacrifice is conducted, a curtain is drawn before the shrine of Aiyanar, who is vegetarian and to be protected from the sight of bloodshed. The sacrifice is carried out immediately in front of the shrine, though ostensibly to a different deity altogether.

In Dumont's well-known analysis of this festival, he places too much importance on the opposition of purity and impurity (deducing from diet that Aiyanar is principally modeled on the Brahman, even though in behavior and legend Aiyanar is far more like the king) and on his contention that Aiyanar's relation to other village deities reflects the encompassment of the political by the religious. The kingly aspects of the deity and the critical role of the ampalam are either ignored or subordinated to a secondary importance. Dumont's failure to provide a fully satisfactory analysis of Aiyanar and his festival is part of his larger refusal to grant that a king can, in certain contexts, encompass and incorporate the divine, the Brahmanic, as well as the social and political constituents of caste solidarity and warrior strength. In the village, where the king was represented by the ampalam, the festival at once elevated the ampalam and his political authority, displayed the ampalam's relation to the king, effected an identity between the latter and the village, and produced, through the celebration of a festival on behalf of a god who so dramatically exemplified the royal function, the conditions under which the village could be victorious against the forces of evil and danger.

But this is not the whole story. It is precisely the political permeability of ritual that makes possible a succession of contested performances, readings, and tellings. In India, kingship had been the dominant trope for the political, but far from the only one. As I stated at the beginning, the festival of Aiyanar frequently did not happen, or occasioned everything from violent dispute to multiple celebration, as in one village where three separate village festivals took place under the leadership of three rival castes and their factional affiliates.

For example, in the early 1920s in Tiruvappur, a village close to Pudukkottai town and made up mostly of Kallars, weavers, and service castes, the Velars petitioned that they were under no compunction to receive the pitiman from the village headman. They insisted that since the headman's *inam* (benefice) lands did not carry the stipulation that he should give the pitiman, there was no other authoritiative basis for the claim that the pitiman could be given only by the headman. The headman in turn petitioned the government that the performance of the festival without his permission, granted through the pitiman, was an infringement of his hereditary right, as proved by the fact that his family had been granted inam lands with the specific injunction to conduct the ordinary pujas and other festivals in the temples of Aiyanar in Tiruvappur. Both petitions employed the same colonial bureaucratic logic, giving inams (and the authority of local headmen) a rational legal basis they had not had in precolonial times.

For the Diwan's assistant, the Diwan Peishkar, the resolution of the case rested first on the proper interpretation of the significance of the grant of pitiman. His inquiries, in line with my own more recent ones, led him to decide quite correctly that the grant of pitiman signified far more than the intended cooperation of the nattars (elders): "If it signifies mere cooperation without the slightest tinge of authority or idea of special privilege the villagers would not have objected to the continuance of the system. On the other hand, the grant of pitiman is considered to be a grant of permission by the nattars to conduct the kutirai etuppu. Both the nattars and the artisans view it in this light and it is why the former are unwilling to lose the privilege and the latter anxious to discontinue the system." He then had to decide whether this privilege could be sustained under the bureaucratic terms of service implied by the wording of the inam grant, which was vague enough to accommodate both the intepretation put forward in the petition and the one in the counterpetition. The Diwan Peishkar investigated customs in other temples of Aiyanar to determine precedent, only to find that each case differed, hardly the stuff of precedent. To further complicate matters, the Diwan Peishkar felt that he had to determine whether the dispute concerned the hereditary privileges of the headmen as traditional caste headman or, in a deliberately alienating bureaucratic move, as state functionaries.

The Brahmanical Diwan Peishkar was also troubled by his belief that religion was an individual concern, and that all devotees should be able to commission the Velars to make horses for them without the intervention of the Nattar. Such control over the individual vows of others seemed to him "revolting to a devotee's sense of honour and reason." The Diwan Peishkar recommended that the Nattars be allowed to commission the installation of clay horses on their own behalf, but not on the behalf of others. The separation of the individual rights of Nattars from their right to commission clay horses on behalf of the entire village only made sense, however, in terms of a newly formulated bureaucratic conception of religion, since the individual vows of devotees would have been encompassed by the social fact that the festival, even when contested, was a village festival. The Diwan Peishkar's recommendation struck at the core of the headman's objections, since he saw his privilege as an enactment of his authoritative position in the village temple and, indeed, in the village at large. But in the invention of an autonomous domain and logic of religion, the underlying social issues were ignored. The struggle between the service and dominant groups was a struggle over authority, and thus had its most visible and important expression in the Aiyanar ritual, which itself resisted bureaucratic appropriation by the new Brahman-British religious sensibility (though it succumbed to the bureaucratic definition of the *inam*).

As it turned out, the Diwan was less zealous than the Diwan Peishkar to upset the local structure of authoritative relations in Tiruvappur. He recommended that the Nattars continue to be vested with the right to give the pitiman. He did, however, insist that the Nattars had to signify their permission by giving back the pitiman immediately and routinely, thus heading off the mischievous possibility that they might abuse their right, a sacred trust. "Authority" was defended in name, but was undermined by the attempts of the bureaucratic establishment to make religion an individual and private rather than a social and public affair. Although this did not allay all the concerns of the petitioners, they had at least been able to use the language of bureaucratic control to make an important formal complaint.

Indeed, Tiruvappur had been the scene of many similar disputes at least as early as 1885. At one point, the local Paraiyars ("untouchables") had asserted themselves against the ampalam by refusing to beat drums outside the temple. In another instance, the Velars had resisted the authoritative claims of the Kallar headman, denying his privilege to carry the scythe used for the ritual slaughter and present it to the Velars, who actually did the cutting. On one occasion they had even refused, in their role as priests, to offer *pracatam* (the transubstantiated offering) from Aiyanar to the ampalam. Like his 1920s counterpart, the Diwan had upheld the rights of the ampalams, at the same trying to rationalize the exercise of these rights.

Many similar disputes took place, but only a few of them leaked into official view, usually because the disputes were dealt with in summary (and no doubt brutal) fashion by the dominant groups. So although these files alerted me to a record of contention, it was only in towns close to the court, and also in bigger towns and temples, such as those studied by Appadurai and Breckenridge,[21] that ritual was a clearly contentious affair in the historical record. Many of these disputes concerned the distribution of honors and pracatam in temples and locked a dominant lineage and its headman in fervent dispute with each other; otherwise, the disputes were usually buried by the dominant group (which had to seek no higher authority). Thus, when Appadurai and Breckenridge proposed that ritual in south India involved conflict, they proposed a radically new sense of the kinds of resources over which conflict developed, but referred for the most part to factional forms of conflict. In the Indian context, however, factional dispute has been the only acceptable form of social conflict. I am arguing here that conflict took place between social groups at all levels of the social hierarchy, and that conflict is always present in the basic structures of Indian social organization. Indeed, as I suggested above, I only realized the range (and subtlety) of dispute and contestation through a combination of ethnographic accident and historical investigation.

There were many other instances in which ritual turned out to be a core arena for resistance, particularly for groups, such as artisans and "untouchables," who could resist by simply withholding their services. The closest thing to a municipal strike in the history of Pudukkottai town took place in the early 1930s, when the untouchables protested the establishment of a municipal crematorium by withholding their ritual funeral services from all their patron groups. The municipality backed down in short order because of the consternation of one high-caste family after another, who felt they were dishonoring their dead. And Kathleen Gough has vividly documented the breakdown of village ritual in rural Tanjavur, where untouchable groups, fired in part by the growth of a local communist movement, have increasingly withheld their ritual services from village festivals.[22] But Gough's assertion that village rituals would not recover from the effects of recent change and growing class consciousness has not been sustained by the experience of the last thirty years. In fact, village rituals continue to be important precisely because of their association with conflict.

Although village rituals were clearly sites for struggle between elite groups and their factions over who was in charge, this, too, was only part of the story. Rituals were generalizable sites for struggle of all kinds, including—as my earlier story suggests—the struggle between discourse and event, between what could be said and what could be done. Ritual was a discursive and practical field in which a great deal was at stake and a great deal was up for grabs. But when conflict developed in ritual, it always made the ritual a site for appropriation as well as for struggle. The headman of the darkened, quiet village had appropriated the interpretive function of a ritual that he always knew would not take place; the absence of any actual event was an embarrassment only when I pressed my curiosity and showed up without the proper invitation. The Brahman administrators of Pudukkottai appropriated the dispute for their own purposes, of undermining the religious authority of rural Kallar elites and implementing new colonial standards for the evaluation of religious activity and the establishment of religion within a newly created domain of civil society. Anthropologists have appropriated ritual to advocate the religious dimensions, character, and force of the social, which in the case of Dumont's transformation of Durkheim, is located in a world of religiously validated hierarchy. These appropriations are all examples of the way ritual has become central to the field of power relations in southern India. But these same appropriations have never fully succeeded in containing the power of ritual, as they have always been checked by the profoundly subversive character of traditional ritual practice (at least as I observed, and didn't observe, it in southern India)—for not only did ritual discourse and ritual practice operate at angles to each other, both discourse and practice were open to a multiplicity of contesting and resisting agencies, even when these agencies were themselves constituted by (or in relation to) the concealed agencies of colonial hegemony.

Possession and Danger

I have so far completely ignored one of the most important but also complex sources of agency and action in the festival of Aiyanar. I do not mean the symbolism surrounding the lord Aiyanar himself, but rather his incarnation in the form of the *camiyatis*, the people in the village who during the course of the festival were routinely possessed by the lord Aiyanar. Possession was an absolutely critical part of this and other village festivals in the south, and aside from the goat sacrifice and the feast, it was the most charged event in village ritual practice.

In one fairly typical festival that took place in a village near Pudukkottai town, all but one of the people who were to be possessed by Aiyanar were members of the dominant Kallar caste. Though the ampalam was the central character, as the festival unfolded attention was increasingly focused on the camiyatis. Initially chosen for possessing special spiritual powers, the five Kallars were the hereditary camiyatis who participated in the festival each year. They walked immediately behind the drum-beating Paraiyars. Not yet in full trance, the camiyatis began to show signs of possession as they walked on to the beat of the drums, their bodies sporadically quivering at the touch of Aiyanar, who was shortly to enter into them. The procession walked straight to the small temple to Aiyanar, which, like all others, was on the borders of the village. The people who had come in the procession, led by the ampalam and the camiyatis, then worshiped the subsidiary deities, Karuppar and Muni. The camiyatis then picked up bags of ash and began walking back to the village, accompanied by the Paraiyars. As they walked through the village, the women of each house came towards them and poured water over their feet to cool them. The camiyatis blessed the women with the ash they carried. We walked through the Kallar section of town by way of the ampalam's house, to the Velar settlement on the eastern side of the village. There, the procession was welcomed by the playing of festival music by the pipers of a nearby temple and the explosions of firecrackers. The five Kallar camiyatis stood before the newly decorated terra-cotta horses, soon to be installed in front of the Aiyanar shrine.

A Paraiyar from a nearby village came forward and carefully dressed the camiyatis in special clothes. The Paraiyar wore a garland made of silver balls, his head was wrapped with a red cloth, his chest was draped with multicolored strands of cloth, a new towel was tied around his waist, and garlands of bells were wrapped around him. His face was painted with vermilion and sandalwood paste. This Paraiyar was called the *munnoti*, the leader, the one who went first. In a few minutes he became possessed on his own, to the music of the drums and horn (*nadaswaram*). He began to jump wildly when the incense and camphor smoke was shown to him, and he stared fixedly at the sky. He suddenly leapt into the crowd, snatched the ampalam's spear, and began to beat the ground with it. He was jumping and running around and through the crowd, all the while circumambulating the six figures. The ampalam then came up to him, garlanded him, and smeared sacred ash on his forehead, after which the ampalam was finally able to retrieve his spear. After this, the munnoti led the other camiyatis into states of possession. Someone whispered in my ear that the munnoti was the burning lamp that lights other lamps. Full possession was achieved when the munnoti held the camphor up to the other camiyatis, one by one.

Now that all the camiyatis were fully possessed, the procession was ready to commence. The Paraiyars went first, followed at some distance by the pipers, and then by the munnoti and the five Kallar camiyatis; next came the terra-cotta offerings sponsored by the village, followed by the smaller offerings of individual villagers. Behind them walked the ampalam, surrounded by many of his kinsmen. As the procession moved around the village, on its way back to the temple of Aiyanar, villagers came up to the camiyatis to be blessed, often asking questions about the future. The camiyatis frequently stopped to make prophetic statements either in response to specific questions or about general problems afflicting the village. When we reached the temple, the eyes of the terra-cotta figures were opened with the blood of a cock, sacrificed by the munnoti (who was then given the cock). The terra-cotta animals were then installed in front of the temple. A grand puja was held to Aiyanar. The Velar priests offered tamarind rice, broke coconuts, and then held up the flame in an act of worship, after which they offered the sacred ash to the worshipers. Then the priests left Aiyanar's shrine, pulling its curtains closed.

Shortly thereafter, a goat was sacrificed by one of the camiyatis to Karuppar, and after this, the ampalam distributed the pracatam from both pujas to the constituent groups in the village. One by one, the camiyatis drifted away, each to be relieved of the extraordinary privilege and exhaustion of the possession. The festival ended with much feasting, and an all-night dramatic performance.

It is clear that possession was a central part of the ritual drama. But what was possession all about—what did possession signify? Most of the literature on possession deals with the nasty kind, when it is the devil rather than the lord who has taken up residence within a mortal. But the munnoti is the exorcist's opposite—a man whose skill and power is precisely to induce possession rather than rid us of it. But this, too, is an extraordinary form of power, and one that has many dangers. It is significant that for this role an "untouchable" is chosen; while all the regular camiyatis are of the dominant Kallar caste, the one person who makes their possession possible could never be invited into their houses or be allowed to dine with them. And his power was not completely contained by hierarchy, for there were moments of real fear when he seized the ampalam's spear and began dancing wildly about; the fear of Aiyanar was clearly enhanced by his choice of this unruly Paraiyar as his principal vehicle and agent. And the Paraiyar appeared to contain not only the full ferocity of Aiyanar, but also the contradictions of Aiyanar's multiple symbolism and the festival's ritual connotations. For when the Paraiyar seized the spear, he simultaneously signaled its potential appropriation and confirmed (and perhaps enhanced) the spear's (and the ampalam's) centrality and power.

When, a few days after the festival, I went to visit the Paraiyar in his nearby hamlet, the contrast was difficult to fathom. It was midafternoon, and the Paraiyar was sleeping off the effects of a morning spent consuming a huge amount of arrack. The Paraiyar combined in his person an exaggerated deference and a smoldering bitterness. On the one hand, he acted as though he were deeply honored that I should visit him; that he failed to recognize me for a moment or two seemed due more to drink than to any difficulty remembering my presence in the festival through the daze of his own possession. On the other hand, he took great pleasure in puncturing my illusions about the festival. He told me that there was a rival festival in the village hosted by Konars (shepherds), and as he spoke, he almost laughed at the hollow claims of the Kallar headmen, who could no longer control an inferior caste group. Thus the very man who played such a critical ritual role in the festival clearly had a good measure of contempt for his patrons. And his patrons were no longer masters of the only game in town.

Thus perhaps we can appreciate rather more the level of danger encoded in the ritual seizure by the Paraiyar of the ampalam's spear, the subtextual presence of contest and disorder. And the seizure was not the only moment of danger, not the only reason why containment was a live issue throughout the festival. Aiyanar was clearly hard to handle, and those possessed by him had to negotiate a delicate balance between playacting and overacting. I was repeatedly told that the possession was real, that it took people many years to learn how to accept the visitation of the lord, that it required the supervision of a man of special powers both to learn and to do, and that after a spell of possession, it would take days and sometimes weeks for the possessed person to return fully to normal, exhausted and shaken by the experience. And I was told that if a camiyati turned out not to be really possessed, merely playacting, he would be ridiculed and excluded thereafter from the festival and its proceedings. After all, the festival was critical to the well-being of the village, and if Aiyanar was misrepresented by an imposter, then the festival might fail, and certainly the advice handed down by the lord to the anxious and enquiring villagers would be spurious. There were also times when possession could prove too much; the camiyati was called the vessel, and when this vessel could not contain the concentrated power of the lord, it might crack. In such instances, the camiyati would not recover from possession, he would stay deranged and disturbed, and then there would be need of an exorcist.

It is possible to account for all of this with a traditional view of ritual. Van Gennep was keenly aware of the danger and disorder that was part of ritual, and built this into his explanation of liminality and ritual transformation.[23] But his theory has a tendency to contain danger too readily, too automatically, and to assume that disorder is ultimately epiphenomenal. I would propose here that possession was a form of ritual practice that was genuinely dangerous and always already subversive. Part of the subversiveness had to do with what we have already considered, the constant possibility of conflict, fission, paralysis, and hermeneutic, if not agonistic, explosion. But the subversiveness had also to do with the politics of representation and misrepresention, as did the implosions of power, inherent in both the role of the headman and that of the camiyatis.

The festival was a powerful spectacle in large part because of the dramatic role of the possessed camiyatis. The festival seemed to me at times, particularly since I attended many different festivals in different villages, like theater. Victor Turner has already observed this, using the term "ritual drama," by which he meant that ritual could be analyzed as though it were an unfolding drama, with the participants as actors who engaged in the unseen forces of life through the vicarious agencies of ritualistic enactment.[24] But if what I witnessed was theater to the participants, it was very different from what has come to be accepted as theater in the West. As Stephen Greenblatt notes, "[T]he theatre elicits from us complicity rather than belief."[25] But in rural southern India, there were elements of both complicity and belief; there were roles and masquerades depended on far more than skillful artifice and conceit. Further, there was the possibility that something could go wrong, and this provided an urgency and unpredictability to the drama that makes Turner's phrase seem both too dramatic and vaguely sacrilegious. One of the inescapable implications of the camiyati's predicament, the risk that possession could be inauthentic, was that all agency and all representation—authority itself—in the ritual was at risk as well. Identity was most fragile at the moment of its transformation and multiple reference. And the risk that the possessed might be faking it no doubt raised the possibility that the headman, whose authority and connections with the king were both celebrated and renewed in the festival, might also be faking it. After all, everyone knew, even though I had not yet been told, that the headman claimed a sovereignty over the entire village that was not granted by the rival shepherds. It was the compelling, contestable, and dangerous components of the ritual drama that also raised the stakes. The spectators did not simply gaze; they vied with one another to participate more actively and more centrally in the festival, to interlocute the camiyatis, to see the cutting of the goat, and to collect and consume the *prasada*—the transubstantiated return—of the lord.

I have given just a few illustrations to suggest what I might mean by the subversive nature of ritual practice and discourse. I will close with one last observation. Each ritual event is patterned activity, to be sure, but it is also invented anew as it happens. When I witnessed one festival, there was frequent confusion about what was to be done. At one point, a participant in the festival leaned over toward me, realizing that I had seen many similar festivals, and asked me what I thought they should do next. At the time, I thought that I was already intruding too much on the authenticity of the ritual event, and that to offer an opinion—and I did have one—would be to cross the fragile threshold of legitimate participation implied in the oxymoronic motto of anthropology: participant observation. But I was wrong, for the authenticity of the event was inscribed in its performance, not in some time- and custom-sanctioned version of the ritual. And the authenticity of Aiyanar's festival, in particular, was inscribed in its uncertainty and its contestability—even when it didn't actually take place.

ANTHROPOLOGY AND AIYANAR

I have argued that the festival of Aiyanar is about (and provides opportunities for) resistance precisely because it is also about the display and achievement of power. My reading of the ritual challenges both general anthropological assumptions about ritual and, more specifically, Louis Dumont's sense of Aiyanar's conformance to his more general theory about caste and the ideology of hierarchy. My reading also challenges a more political interpretation of the festival by Christopher Fuller in his tightly argued essay, "The Hindu Pantheon and the Legitimation of Hierarchy."[26] Fuller finds, contrary to the expectation that high forms of religion might best legitimate existing social hierarchies, that "south Indian Hinduism's substantialist representation of Sanskritic deities does not legitimate relationships of inequality at all."[27] In fact, the religious sensibility surrounding the Sanskritic deities simply denies altogether the necessity of inferiors for superiors, thus eliding any reference to social hierarchy. However, Fuller extends Dumont's argument about Aiyanar, suggesting that the "burden of legitimating caste hierarchy is instead left to village deities."[28] While Fuller argues that village deities resist "the ideal world of Brahmanical superiority through absolute independence," they do so "relationally in the idiom of hierarchy." Indeed, village deities symbolize the "continued inferiority and dependence" of the low castes.[29]

Fuller bases his argument on the structural relations of symbolic transactions in village rituals, specifically, on the relational definition of village deities and the clearly marked distinction between vegetarian forms of puja and animal forms of sacrifice. He sees high and low forms of local deities symbolically correlated with high and low forms of worship, forms associated not only with diet but also with procedures of worship. He then assumes that these high and low forms, which ritually and symbolically seem mutually interdependent, correlate with high and low forms of caste, thus legitimating the caste structure through ritual practice.

Fuller is not unaware of the possibility that popular religion can embody political resistance, and carefully contrasts his interpretation of Aiyanar with Genovese's reconstruction of the role of resistance in the religious life of American slaves. Whereas American slaves could transform "Christianity from a religion which, in the eyes of white slaveholders, legitimated slavery into a fount of resistance to it"[30] through identifying Jesus with Moses, Fuller can imagine no similar possibility of transformation or resistance in south Indian village religion. Not only does Fuller imagine the caste system to be fundamentally immutable, he writes as though the symbolic correlations between high and low deities on the one hand and high and low castes on the other presupposed an acceptance of the structure of hierarchy. His interpretation is possible not only because he leaves the problematic relationship between king and Brahman in the person of Aiyanar aside but also because he accepts Dumont's account of the ritual performance, devoid of any contradiction, disorder, or contest.

I would suggest that Fuller's reading is partial not only because he uncritically accepts a Dumontian interpretation of caste but also because he employs a notion of ritual predicated on certain fixed assumptions about order and power. This is true despite an admirable attempt to consider the social implications of ritual practice, for he correctly sees ritual as embedded in societal relations and social meanings. However, the social categories that appear to be inscribed in the ritual order of things do not entail an acceptance of hierarchy.

In fact, the curious relationship of Brahman and king in the figure of Aiyanar, and the precarious balance between "high" and "low" forms—village and forest, power and possession, nonviolence and violence, vegetarian and nonvegetarian, among others—would suggest a very different reading of the ritual and its social meanings. To the extent that the categories of "high" and "low" are constructed anew in any given ritual setting, we must be attentive as well to the contests over authority and power that take place around and through ritual means and idioms. We need not make Genevese's case that ritual is a fount of outright resistance in order to find struggle, disorder, and appropriations from below taking place through, and within, ritual practice. Certainly, in the south Indian case, the relations between Brahmans and Kallars (members of the royal caste in Pudukkottai) or between Kallars and Paraiyars (remember the munnoti's expertise and precedence in divine possession) are not nearly as unproblematic as assumed in Fuller's, not to mention Dumont's, analysis. Not only are caste identities and relations deeply politicized, they are contested throughout the field of ritual practice; all symbolic correlations within the ritual domain and between it and the social are opened to doubt, question, contest, and appropriation. Because of the open and disorderly character of the ritual process, ritual is one of the primary arenas in which politics takes place.

RITUAL DISORDER AND ORDER

As we increasingly, and from differing perspectives, examine ordinary life, the fixtures of ordinariness thus give way to fractures, and we see that struggle is everywhere, even where it is least dramatic, and least visible.[31] Even in the heart of anthropology, ritual now seems to be as much about contest and struggle as about power and order. Struggle becomes visible where previously we could not see it, a trope for a critical vision of the world. Consensus is no longer assumed unless proven otherwise; even more unsettling for our social science, rebellion and resistance can no longer be identified through traditional indices of the extraordinary. The ordinary and the extraordinary trade places.

We should reflect briefly on the potential epistemological implications of finding resistance, rebellion, or disorder, everywhere. In most of our social scientific thinking, order is presented as a universal human need, an expression of reason and the basis of the social. Order thus becomes naturalized, while all that produces and is produced by disorder becomes marginalized as extraordinary and unnatural. When naturalized, order is an ideological tool, which works to suppress or contain disorder and subversion.

Ironically, many current understandings of discursive domination (following Foucault) or hegemony (following Gramsci) are at least in part informed by notions of order that seem antipathetic to the posture of critique, for our notions of power appear both totalizing and a priori. "Power" is virtually synonomous with order, even though as used currently, the term implies a critical stance on order. Thus in denaturalizing order, we must also denaturalize power, attending to its own fissures and dispersals. In turn, we should not see resistance as a pure counterpart to power, for there are dangers in reifying our concepts of struggle. But if order can be seen as an effect of power rather than its condition, then resistance, too, can be freed from the (teleological) requirement that it establish a new order in order to be recognized as significant.

Power need not be seen as either a cause or a first principle. Power is, rather, a relation, or, more precisely, an endless series of relations, characterized—we now emphasize—by struggle. Although struggle may always, as Foucault suggests, be interior to power, it (as our current preoccupation) can seriously subvert our normal assumptions, about both power and order.[32]

The festival of Aiyanar is about power and disorder, about order and resistance. For at the same time that the power of the deity and the headman are displayed, this power is distributed to others and opened to potential contestation. At the same time that the ritual order of precedence among groups in the village is rehearsed and inscribed in the structures of worship, the resistance of subordinate or factional groups, and the resistance of multiple interpretations, can be effectively deployed. At the same time that representation, in discourse or event, makes ritual claims about order, representation itself becomes the object of struggle. At the same time that worship transforms disorder into order, disorder becomes available for the spirits of the dead and the spirit of unrest. Ritual now appears not only as a powerful way to produce the reality effect of the natural, but also as a way to contest and even appropriate that reality itself. For ritual—like the anthropological concept of culture itself—is not always principally about order, and it does not always contain the disorder of things.

Notes

I am grateful to my colleagues in history and anthropology at the University of Michigan for their comments in seminars when I delivered this paper. I am also particularly indebted to Val Daniel, Geoff Eley, Steven Mullaney, Gyan Prakash, and Sherry Ortner. The opening epigraph is Stephen Greenblatt's transformation of Kafka; see Greenblatt, *Shakespearean Negotiations* (Berkeley: University of California Press, 1988), 65.

1. Clifford Geertz, *The Interpretation of Cultures* (New York: Basic Books, 1973), 142.

2. Sherry Ortner, characterizing Milton Singer's views, in Ortner, *Sherpas through Their Rituals* (Cambridge: Cambridge University Press, 1978), 1.

3. Ibid., 2.

4. Ortner, *High Religion* (Princeton, N.J.: Princeton University Press, 1989).

5. Ortner, "Theory in Anthropology since the Sixties," *Comparative Studies in Society and History* 26, 1 (1984).

6. Pierre Bourdieu, *Outline of a Theory of Practice,* translated by Richard Nice (Cambridge: Cambridge University Press, 1982).

7. William Sewell, *Work and Revolution in France* (Cambridge: Cambridge University Press, 1980).

8. See Stuart Clark, "French Historians and Early Modern Popular culture," *Past and Present,* no. 100 (1983); and Hans Medick, "Missionaries in the Row Boat? Ethnological Ways of Knowing as a Challenge to Social History," *Comparative Studies in Society and History* 29, no. 1 (1987).

9. Max Gluckman, *Custom and Conflict in Africa* (Oxford: Blackwell Press, 1965), 109.

10. Natalie Davis, *Society and Culture in Early Modern France* (Palo Alto, Calif.: Stanford University Press, 1965), 130.

11. Stephen Greenblatt, "Invisible Bullets," in J. Dollimore and A. Sinfield, eds., *Political Shakespeare* (Manchester, N.H.: Manchester University Press, 1985), 40.

12. Terry Eagleton, *Walter Benjamin: Towards a Revolutionary Criticism* (London: Verso Press, 1981), 148.

13. See the argument by Peter Stallybrass and Allon White in their *The Politics and Poetics of Transgression* (Ithaca, N.Y.: Cornell University Press, 1986).

14. See Rosalind O'Hanlon, "Recovering the Subject: Subaltern Studies and Histories of resistance in Colonial South Asia," *Modern Asian Studies* 22, no. 1 (1988).

15. James Scott, *Weapons of the Weak* (New Haven: Yale University Press, 1986).

16. Ludtke has written that protests should be "regarded as occasional manifestations of a wide complex of structured processes and situations" and that "research into traces of suppressed needs should not be confined to manifest expressions of dissatisfaction, opposition, and resistance." Alf Ludtke, "Everyday Life, the Articulation of Needs and 'Proletarian Consciousness'—Some Remarks on Concepts" (unpublished manuscript, n.d.), 4. See also Ludtke, "Organizational Order or Eigensinn? Workers' Privacy and Workers' Politics in Imperial Germany," in Sean Wilentz, ed., *Rites of Power: Symbolism, Ritual, and Politics since the Middle Ages* (Philadelphia: University of Pennsylvania Press, 1985).

17. Jean Comaroff, *Body of Power, Spirit of Resistance* (Chicago: University of Chicago Press, 1985), 196.

18. Ibid.

19. See Nicholas B. Dirks, *The Hollow Crown: Ethnohistory of an Indian Kingdom* (Cambridge: Cambridge University Press, 1987).

20. Louis Dumont, "A Structural Definition of a Folk Deity," *Contributions to Indian Sociology* 3 (1959).

21. Arjun Appadurai and Carol Breckenridge, "The South Indian Temple: Authority, Honour, and Redistribution," *Contributions to Indian Sociology*, n.s., 10, no. 2 (1976).

22. Kathleen Gough, "The Social Structure of a Tanjore Village," in McKim Marriott, ed., *Village India* (Chicago: University of Chicago Press, 1955).

23. Arthur Van Gennep, *The Rites of Passage* (Chicago: University of Chicago Press, 1960).

24. Victor Turner, *The Ritual Process* (Chicago: Aldine Press, 1969).

25. Greenblatt, *Shakespearean Negotiations*, 119.

26. Christopher Fuller, "The Hindu Pantheon and the Legitimation of Hierarchy," *Man*, n.s., 23 (1987).

27. Ibid., p. 37.

28. Ibid.

29. Ibid.

30. Ibid.

31. See Michel de Certeau, *The Practice of Everyday Life* (Berkeley: University of California Press, 1984).

32. Michel Foucault, *The History of Sexuality*, vol. 1 (New York: Vintage, 1980), pp. 94–97.

The Circulation of Social Energy

STEPHEN GREENBLATT

I BEGAN with the desire to speak with the dead.

This desire is a familiar, if unvoiced, motive in literary studies, a motive organized, professionalized, buried beneath thick layers of bureaucratic decorum: literature professors are salaried, middle-class shamans. If I never believed that the dead could hear me, and if I knew that the dead could not speak, I was nonetheless certain that I could recreate a conversation with them. Even when I came to understand that in my most intense moments of straining to listen all I could hear was my own voice, even then I did not abandon my desire. It was true that I could hear only my own voice, but my own voice was the voice of the dead, for the dead had contrived to leave textual traces of themselves, and those traces make themselves heard in the voices of the living. Many of the traces have little resonance, though every one, even the most trivial or tedious, contains some fragment of lost life; others seem uncannily full of the will to be heard. It is paradoxical, of course, to seek the living will of the dead in fictions, in places where there was no live bodily being to begin with. But those who love literature tend to find more intensity in simulations—in the formal, self-conscious miming of life—than in any of the other textual traces left by the dead, for simulations are undertaken in full awareness of the absence of the life they contrive to represent, and hence they may skillfully anticipate and compensate for the vanishing of the actual life that has empowered them. Conventional in my tastes, I found the most satisfying intensity of all in Shakespeare.

I wanted to know how Shakespeare managed to achieve such intensity, for I thought that the more I understood this achievement, the more I could hear and understand the speech of the dead.

The question then was how did so much life get into the textual traces? Shakespeare's plays, it seemed, had precipitated out of a sublime confrontation between a total artist and a totalizing society. By a total artist I mean one who, through training, resourcefulness, and talent, is at the moment of creation complete unto himself; by a totalizing society I mean one that posits an occult network linking all human, natural, and cosmic powers and that claims on behalf of its ruling elite a privileged place in this network. Such a society generates vivid dreams of access to the linked powers and vests control of this access in a religious and state bureaucracy at whose pinnacle is the symbolic figure of the monarch. The result of this confrontation between total artist and totalizing society was a set of unique, inexhaustible, and supremely powerful works of art.

In the book I have written something of this initial conception survives, but it has been complicated by several turns in my thinking that I had not foreseen. I can summarize those turns by remarking that I came to have doubts about two things: "total artist" and "totalizing society."

I did not, to be sure, doubt that the plays attributed to Shakespeare were in large part written by the supremely gifted alumnus of the Stratford grammar school. Nor did I cease to believe that Renaissance society was totalizing in intention. But I grew increasingly uneasy with the monolithic entities that my work had posited. No individual, not even the most brilliant, seemed complete unto himself—my own study of Renaissance self-fashioning had already persuaded me of this—and Elizabethan and Jacobean visions of hidden unity seemed like anxious rhetorical attempts to conceal cracks, conflict, and disarray. I had tried to organize the mixed motives of Tudor and Stuart culture under the rubric *power*, but that term implied a structural unity and stability of command belied by much of what I actually knew about the exercise of authority and force in the period.

If it was important to speak of power in relation to Renaissance literature— not only as the object but as the enabling condition of representation itself—it was equally important to resist the integration of all images and expressions into a single master discourse. For if Renaissance writers themselves often echoed the desire of princes and prelates for just such a discourse, brilliant critical and theoretical work in recent years by a large and diverse group of scholars had demonstrated that this desire was itself constructed out of conflicting and ill-sorted motives. Even those literary texts that sought most ardently to speak for a monolithic power could be shown to be the sites of institutional and ideological contestation.

But what does it mean to pull back from a notion of artistic completeness, on the one hand, and totalizing power, on the other? It can mean a return to the text itself as the central object of our attention. To speak of such a return has a salutary ring—there are days when I long to recover the close-grained formalism of my own literary training—but the referent of the phrase "the text itself" is by no means clear. Indeed, in the case of Shakespeare (and of the drama more generally), there has probably never been a time since the early eighteenth century when there was less confidence in the "text." Not only has a new generation of textual historians undermined the notion that a skilled editorial weaving of folio and quarto readings will give us an authentic record of Shakespeare's original intentions, but theater historians have challenged the whole notion of the text as the central, stable locus of theatrical meaning. There are textual traces—a bewildering mass of them—but it is impossible to take the "text itself" as the perfect, unsubstitutable, freestanding container of all of its meanings.

The textual analyses I was trained to do had as their goal the identification and celebration of a numinous literary authority, whether that authority was ultimately located in the mysterious genius of an artist or in the mysterious perfection of a text whose intuitions and concepts can never be expressed in other terms.[1] The great attraction of this authority is that it appears to bind and fix the energies we prize, to identify a stable and permanent source of literary power, to offer an escape from shared contingency.

This project, endlessly repeated, repeatedly fails for one reason: there is no escape from contingency.

All the same, we do experience unmistakable pleasure and interest in the literary traces of the dead, and I return to the question of how it is possible for those traces to convey lost life. Over the past several generations this question has been addressed principally by close reading of the textual traces, and I believe that sustained scrupulous attention to formal and linguistic design will remain at the center of literary teaching and study. But in the essays that follow I propose something different: to look less at the presumed center of the literary domain than at its borders, to try to track what can only be glimpsed, as it were, at the margins of the text. The cost of this shift in attention will be the satisfying illusion of a "whole reading," the impression conveyed by powerful critics that had they but world enough and time, they could illuminate every corner of the text and knit together into a unified interpretive vision all of their discrete perceptions. My vision is necessarily more fragmentary, but I hope to offer a compensatory satisfaction: insight into the half-hidden cultural transactions through which great works of art are empowered.

I propose that we begin by taking seriously the collective production of literary pleasure and interest. We know that this production is collective since language itself, which is at the heart of literary power, is the supreme instance of a collective creation. But this knowledge has for the most part remained inert, either cordoned off in prefatory acknowledgments or diffused in textual analyses that convey almost nothing of the social dimension of literature's power. Instead, the work seems to stand only for the skill and effort of the individual artist, as if whole cultures possessed their shared emotions, stories, and dreams only because a professional caste invented them and parceled them out. In literary criticism, Renaissance artists function like Renaissance monarchs: at some level we know perfectly well that the power of the prince is largely a collective invention, the symbolic embodiment of the desire, pleasure, and violence of thousands of subjects, the instrumental expression of complex networks of dependency and fear, the agent rather than the maker of the social will. Yet we can scarcely write of prince or poet without accepting the fiction that power directly emanates from him and that society draws upon this power.[2]

The attempt to locate the power of art in a permanently novel, untranslatable formal perfection will always end in a blind alley, but the frustration is particularly intense in the study of the Shakespearean theater for two reasons. First, the theater is manifestly the product of collective intentions. There may be a moment in which a solitary individual puts words on a page, but it is by no means clear that this moment is the heart of the mystery and that everything else is to be stripped away and discarded. Moreover, the moment of inscription, on closer analysis, is itself a social moment. This is particularly clear with Shakespeare, who does not conceal his indebtedness to literary sources, but it is also true for less obviously collaborative authors, all of whom depend upon collective genres, narrative patterns, and linguistic conventions.[3] Second, the theater manifestly addresses its audience as a collectivity. The model is not, as with the nineteenth-century novel, the individual reader who withdraws from the public world of affairs to the privacy of the hearth but the crowd that gathers together in a public play space.[4] The Shakespearean theater depends upon a felt community: there is no dimming of lights, no attempt to isolate and awaken the sensibilities of each individual member of the audience, no sense of the disappearance of the crowd.

If the textual traces in which we take interest and pleasure are not sources of numinous authority, if they are the signs of contingent social practices, then the questions we ask of them cannot profitably center on a search for their untranslatable essence. Instead we can ask how collective beliefs and experiences were shaped, moved from one medium to another, concentrated in manageable aesthetic form, offered for consumption. We can examine how the boundaries were marked between cultural practices understood to be art forms and other, contiguous, forms of expression. We can attempt to determine how these specially demarcated zones were invested with the power to confer pleasure or excite interest or generate anxiety. The idea is not to strip away and discard the enchanted impression of aesthetic autonomy but to inquire into the objective conditions of this enchantment, to discover how the traces of social circulation are effaced.

I have termed this general enterprise—study of the collective making of distinct cultural practices and inquiry into the relations among these practices—a poetics of culture. For me the inquiry is bound up with a specific interest in Renaissance modes of aesthetic empowerment: I want to know how cultural objects, expressions, and practices—here, principally, plays by Shakespeare and the stage on which they first appeared—acquired compelling force. English literary theorists in the period needed a new word for that force, a word to describe the ability of language, in Puttenham's phrase, to cause "a stir to the mind"; drawing on the Greek rhetorical tradition, they called it *energia*.[5] This is the origin in our language of the term "energy," a term I propose we use, provided we understand that its origins lie in rhetoric rather than physics and that its significance is social and historical. We experience that energy within ourselves, but its contemporary existence depends upon an irregular chain of historical transactions that leads back to the late sixteenth and early seventeenth centuries.[6] Does this mean that the aesthetic power of a play like *King Lear* is a direct transmission from Shakespeare's time to our own? Certainly not. That play and the circumstances in which it was originally embedded have been continuously, often radically, refigured. But these refigurations do not cancel history, locking us into a perpetual present; on the contrary, they are signs of the inescapability of a historical process, a structured negotiation and exchange, already evident in the initial moments of empowerment. That there is no direct, unmediated link between ourselves and Shakespeare's plays does not mean that there is no link at all. The "life" that literary works seem to possess long after both the death of the author and the death of the culture for which the author wrote is the historical consequence, however transformed and refashioned, of the social energy initially encoded in those works.

But what is "social energy"? The term implies something measurable, yet I cannot provide a convenient and reliable formula for isolating a single, stable quantum for examination. We identify *energia* only indirectly, by its effects: it is manifested in the capacity of certain verbal, aural, and visual traces to produce, shape, and organize collective physical and mental experiences. Hence it is associated with repeatable forms of pleasure and interest, with the capacity to arouse disquiet, pain, fear, the beating of the heart, pity, laughter, tension, relief, wonder. In its aesthetic modes, social energy must have a minimal predictability—enough to make simple repetitions possible—and a minimal range: enough to reach out beyond a single creator or consumer to some community, however constricted. Occasionally, and we are generally interested in these occasions, the predictability and range will be far greater: large numbers of men and women of different social classes and divergent beliefs will be induced to explode with laughter or weep or experience a complex blend of anxiety and exaltation. Moreover, the aesthetic forms of social energy are usually characterized by a minimal adaptability—enough to enable them to survive at least some of the constant changes in social circumstance and cultural value that make ordinary utterances evanescent. Whereas most collective expressions moved from their original setting to a new place or time are dead on arrival, the social energy encoded in certain works of art continues to generate the illusion of life for centuries. I want to understand the negotiations through which works of art obtain and amplify such powerful energy.

If one longs, as I do, to reconstruct these negotiations, one dreams of finding an originary moment, a moment in which the master hand shapes the concentrated social energy into the sublime aesthetic object. But the quest is fruitless, for there is no originary moment, no pure act of untrammeled creation. In place of a blazing genesis, one begins to glimpse something that seems at first far less spectacular: a subtle, elusive set of exchanges, a network of trades and trade-offs, a jostling of competing representations, a negotiation between joint-stock companies. Gradually, these complex, ceaseless borrowings and lendings have come to seem to me more important, more poignant even, than the epiphany for which I had hoped.

The textual traces that have survived from the Renaissance and that are at the center of our literary interest in Shakespeare are the products of extended borrowings, collective exchanges, and mutual enchantments. They were made by moving certain things—principally ordinary language but also metaphors, ceremonies, dances, emblems, items of clothing, well-worn stories, and so forth—from one culturally demarcated zone to another. We need to understand not only the construction of these zones but also the process of movement across the shifting boundaries between them. Who decides which materials can be moved and which must remain in place? How are cultural materials prepared for exchange? What happens to them when they are moved?

But why are we obliged to speak of movement at all? Except in the most material instances—items of clothing, stage properties, the bodies of actors— nothing is literally moved onto the stage. Rather, the theater achieves its representations by gesture and language, that is, by signifiers that seem to leave the signifieds completely untouched. Renaissance writers would seem to have endorsed this intangibility by returning again and again to the image of the mirror; the purpose of playing, in Hamlet's conventional words, is "to hold as 'twere the mirror up to nature: to show virtue her feature, scorn her own image, and the very age and body of the time his form and pressure" (3.2.21–24). The mirror is the emblem of instantaneous and accurate reproduction; it takes nothing from what it reflects and adds nothing except self-knowledge.

Perhaps this is what the players actually thought they were doing, but it is worth considering how convenient and self-protective the image of the mirror must have seemed. Artists in a time of censorship and repression had ample reason to claim that they had taken nothing from the world they represented, that they had never dreamed of violating the distance demanded by their superiors, that their representations only reflected faithfully the world's own form. Yet even in Hamlet's familiar account, the word *pressure*—that is, impression, as with a seal or signet ring—should signal to us that for the Renaissance more is at stake in mirrors than an abstract and bodiless reflection. Both optics and mirror lore in the period suggested that something was actively passing back and forth in the production of mirror images, that accurate representation depended upon material emanation and exchange.[7] Only if we reinvest the mirror image with a sense of pressure as well as form can it convey something of its original strangeness and magic. And only with the recovery of this strangeness can we glimpse a whole spectrum of representational exchanges where we had once seen simple reflection alone. In some exchanges the object or practice mimed onstage seems relatively untouched by the representation; in others, the object or practice is intensified, diminished, or even completely evacuated by its encounter with the theater; in still others, it is marked as a prize—something "up for grabs"—in an unresolved struggle between competing representational discourses. The mistake is to imagine that there is a single, fixed, mode of exchange; in reality, there are many modes, their character is determined historically, and they are continually renegotiated.

. . . [I]t might be useful to note some of the more common types [of these modes]:

1. *Appropriation.* There seems to be little or no payment or reciprocal understanding or quid pro quo. Objects appear to be in the public domain, hence in the category of "things indifferent" (adiaphora): there for the taking. Or, alternatively, objects appear to be vulnerable and defenseless, hence graspable without punishment or retaliation.

The prime example of adiaphora is ordinary language: for literary art this is the single greatest cultural creation that may be appropriated without payment. One of the simplest and most sublime instances is Lear's anguished "Never, never, never, never, never." But once we pass beyond the most conventional and familiar expressions, we come upon instances of language use that are charged with potential dangers, powerful social charms that cannot be simply appropriated. And under certain circumstances even ordinary language may be surprisingly contested.

The prime example of the vulnerable is the lower classes, who may at most times be represented almost without restraint.

2. *Purchase.* Here something, most often money, is paid by the theater company for an object (or practice or story) that is staged. The clearest instances are properties and costumes. The inventories that have survived suggest that theater companies were prepared to pay a high price for objects with a high symbolic valence: "Item, 1 popes miter"; "Item, 3 Imperial crowns; 1 plain crown"; "Bought a doublet of white satin laid thick with gold lace, and pair of round paned hose of cloth of silver, the panes laid with gold lace £7.00."[8] Some of the costumes were made directly for the players; others came via transactions that reveal the circuitous channels through which social energy could be circulated: suits were given by gentlemen to their servants in lieu of cash payment (or in addition to such payment); the servants sold the clothes to the players; the players appeared onstage in clothes that might actually have belonged to members of the audience.

The companies did not pay for "rights" to stories, so far as I know—at least not in the modern sense—but the playwright or company did pay for the books used as sources (for example, Holinshed or Marguerite of Navarre or Giraldi Cinthio), and the playwright himself was paid.

3. *Symbolic Acquisition.* Here a social practice or other mode of social energy is transferred to the stage by means of representation. No cash payment is made, but the object acquired is not in the realm of things indifferent, and something is implicitly or explicitly given in return for it. The transferring agency has its purposes, which may be more or less overt; the theater picks up what it can get and gives in return what it must (for example, public celebration or humiliation). . . . [Sometimes] the charismatic religious practice of exorcism, under attack by the official church, is brought onto the stage, where its power is at once exploited and marked out as a fraud: "Five fiends have been in poor Tom at once: of lust, as Obidicut; Hobbididence, prince of dumbness; Mahu, of stealing; Modo, of murder; Flibbertigibbet, of mopping and mowing, who since possesses chambermaids and waiting-women."

We can further distinguish three types of symbolic acquisition:

a. *Acquisition through Simulation.* The actor simulates what is already understood to be a theatrical representation. The most extreme instance is the theater's own self-representations—that is, simulations of actors performing plays, as in *The Spanish Tragedy, Hamlet, The Knight of the Burning Pestle,* or *The Roman Actor*—but many of the most resonant instances involve more complex simulations of the histrionic elements in public ceremonials and rituals. For example, . . . the spectacular royal pardons that were understood by observers to be theatrical occasions were staged as theatrical occasions in plays such as *Measure for Measure.*

b. *Metaphorical Acquisition.* Here a practice (or a set of social energies) is acquired indirectly. For example, after 1606 players were forbidden to take the name of the Lord in vain—that is, every use of the words "God" or "Christ Jesus" or "Holy Ghost" or "Trinity" onstage, even in wholly pious contexts, would be subject to a £10 fine.[9] The regulation threatened to remove from the performances not simply a set of names but a whole range of powerful energies, rituals, and experiences. The players' simple and effective response, sanctioned by a long tradition, was to substitute for the interdicted words names like Jove and Jupiter, each a miniature metaphor for the Christian God. To take a slightly more complex example, when the fairies in *A Midsummer Night's Dream* "consecrate" the marriage beds with field-dew, they are, in a mode at once natural and magical, enacting (and appropriating to the stage) the Catholic practice of anointing the marriage bed with holy water.[10]

Metaphorical acquisition works by teasing out latent homologies, similitudes, systems of likeness, but it depends equally upon a deliberate distancing or distortion that precedes the disclosure of likeness. Hence a play will insist upon the difference between its representation and the "real," only to draw out the analogy or proportion linking them. The chorus in *Henry V* urgently calls attention to the difference between the theater's power to command the imagination of the audience and the prince's power to command his subjects, but as the play unfolds, those powers become revealingly confounded. Or again, the strategies of the theater and the family, seemingly far removed, are revealed by King Lear to be mirrors of each other.[11]

c. *Acquisition through Synecdoche or Metonymy.* Here the theater acquires cultural energy by isolating and performing one part or attribute of a practice, which then stands for the whole (often a whole that cannot be represented). For example, . . . verbal chaffing becomes in Shakespeare's comedies not only a sign but a vital instance of an encompassing erotic heat otherwise impossible to stage in the public theater.

Inquiries into the relation between Renaissance theater and society have been situated most often at the level of reflection: images of the monarchy, the lower classes, the legal profession, the church, and so forth. Such studies are essential, but they rarely engage questions of dynamic exchange. They tend instead to posit two separate, autonomous systems and then try to gauge how accurately or effectively the one represents the other. But crucial questions typically remain outside the range of this critical practice: How is it determined what may be staged? To what extent is the object of theatrical representation itself already a representation? What governs the degree of displacement or distortion in theatrical representation? Whose interests are served by the staging? What is the effect of representation on the object or practice represented? Above all, how is the social energy inherent in a cultural practice negotiated and exchanged?

If we are to attempt an answer to these questions, it would be well to begin with certain abjurations:

1 There can be no appeals to genius as the sole origin of the energies of great art.

2. There can be no motiveless creation.

3. There can be no transcendent or timeless or unchanging representation.

4. There can be no autonomous artifacts.

5. There can be no expression without an origin and an object, a *from* and a *for*.

6. There can be no art without social energy.

7. There can be no spontaneous generation of social energy.

Bound up with these negations are certain generative principles:

1. Mimesis is always accompanied by—indeed, is always produced by—negotiation and exchange.

2. The exchanges to which art is a party may involve money, but they may involve other currencies as well. Money is only one kind of cultural capital.

3. The agents of exchange may appear to be individuals (most often, an isolated artist is imagined in relation to a faceless, amorphous entity designated society or culture), but individuals are themselves the products of collective exchange. In the Renaissance theater this collective nature is intensified by the artists' own participation in versions of joint-stock companies. In such companies individual venturers have their own sharply defined identities and interests (and their own initial capital), but to succeed they pool their resources, and they own essential properties in common.

If there is no expressive essence that can be located in an aesthetic object complete unto itself, uncontaminated by interpretation, beyond translation or substitution—if there is no mimesis without exchange—then we need to analyze the collective dynamic circulation of pleasures, anxieties, and interests.[12] This circulation depends upon a separation of artistic practices from other social practices, a separation produced by a sustained ideological labor, a consensual classification. That is, art does not simply exist in all cultures; it is made up along with other products, practices, discourses of a given culture. (In practice, "made up" means inherted, transmitted, altered, modified, reproduced far more than it means invented: as a rule, there is very little pure invention in culture.) Now, the demarcation is rarely, if ever, absolute or complete, nor can we account for it by a single theoretical formulation. We can think up various metaphors to describe the process: the building of a set of walls or fences to separate one territory from adjacent territories; the erection of a gate through which some people and objects will be allowed to pass and others prohibited; the posting of a sign detailing the acceptable code of behavior within the walled territory; the development of a class of functionaries who specialize in the customs of the demarcated zone; the establishment, as in a children's game, of ritualized formulas that can be endlessly repeated. In the case of the public theater of the late sixteenth and early seventeenth centuries, these metaphors were literalized: there was the actual construction of a building, the charging of admission to cross the threshold, the set of regulations governing what could and could not be presented on the stage, a set of tacit understandings (for example, no one was actually to be killed or tortured, no one was to have sex on stage, no one was really cursing or praying or conjuring, and so forth), the writing of scripts that could be screened ahead of time by the censors, rehearsals, the relative nonparticipation of the audience, the existence of theater companies of professional actors.

This literalization and institutionalization of the place of art makes the Renaissance theater particularly useful for an analysis of the cultural circulation of social energy, and the stakes of the analysis are heightened by the direct integration of Shakespeare's plays—easily the most powerful, successful, and enduring artistic expressions in the English language— with this particular mode of artistic production and consumption. We are not, that is, dealing with texts written outside the institution and subsequently attached to it or with encysted productions staged in a long-established and ideologically dormant setting but with literary creations designed in intimate and living relation to an emergent commercial practice. For the most part these creations seem intended at once to enhance the power of the theater as an institution and to draw upon the power this institution has already accumulated. The desire to enhance the general practice of which any particular work is an instance is close to the center of all artistic production, but in the drama this desire is present in a direct, even coarse, sense because of the overwhelming importance and immediacy of material interests. Shakespeare the shareholder was presumably interested not simply in a good return on an individual play but in the health and success of his entire company as it related both to those who helped regulate it and to its audience. Each individual play may be said to make a small contribution to the general store of social energy possessed by the theater and hence to the sustained claim that the theater can make on its real and potential audience.

If each play is bound up with the theater's long-term institutional strategy, it is nonetheless important to avoid the assumption that the relation between mode and individual performance is always harmonious. It is possible for a playwright to be in tension with his own medium, hostile to its presuppositions and conditions, eager to siphon off its powers and attack its pleasures. Ben Jonson's career makes this tension manifest, and one can even glimpse it at moments in Shakespeare's. We can say, perhaps, that an individual play

mediates between the mode of the theater, understood in its historical specificity, and elements of the society out of which that theater has been differentiated. Through its representational means, each play carries charges of social
energy onto the stage; the stage in its turn revises that energy and returns it to
the audience.

Despite the wooden walls and the official regulations, the boundaries between the theater and the world were not fixed, nor did they constitute a logically coherent set; rather they were a sustained collective improvisation. At
any given time, the distinction between the theater and the world might be
reasonably clear and the boundaries might assume the quality of self-evidence, so that the very cataloging of distinctions might seem absurd: for example, *of course* the theater audience could not intervene in the action on
stage, *of course* the violence could only be mimed. But one can think of theaters that swept away every one of the supposedly self-evident distinctions,
and more important for our purposes, Renaissance players and audiences
could think of such counter-examples.

In consequence, the ratio between the theater and the world, even at its
most stable and unchallenged moments, was never directly taken for granted,
that is, experienced as something wholly natural and self-evident. Forces
both within and without the theater were constantly calling attention to
theatrical practices that violated the established conventions of the English
playhouse. When Protestant polemicists characterized the Catholic Mass as
theater, the attack conjured up a theater in which (1) the playhouse disguised
itself as a holy place; (2) the audience did not think of itself as an audience
but as a community of believers; (3) the theatrical performance—with its
elaborate costumes and rituals—not only refused to concede that it was an
illusion but claimed to be the highest truth; (4) the actors did not fully grasp
that they were actors but actually believed in the roles they played and in the
symbolic actions they mimed; and (5) the spectacle demanded of the audience not a few pennies and the pleasant wasting of several hours but a life-
long commitment to the institution that staged the show. Similarly, the playwrights themselves frequently called attention in the midst of their plays
to alternative theatrical practices. Thus, for example, the denouement of
Massinger's *Roman Actor* (like that of Kyd's *Spanish Tragedy*) turns upon
the staging of a mode of theater in which princes and nobles take part in plays
and in which the killing turns out to be real. It required no major act of imagination for a Renaissance audience to conceive of either of these alternatives
to the conventions of the public playhouse: Both were fully operative in the
period itself, in the form of masques and courtly entertainments, on the one
hand, and public maimings and executions, on the other.

Thus the conventional distinction between the theater and the world, however firmly grasped at a given moment, was not one that went without saying;
on the contrary, it was constantly said. This "saying" did not necessarily subvert the distinction; often, in fact, it had the opposite effect, shoring up and

insisting upon the boundaries within which the public theater existed. Nor did recognizing alternatives necessarily make these boundaries seem "merely" arbitrary; attacks on illegitimate forms of theater tended to moralize the existing practice. But the consciousness in the sixteenth century, as now, of other ways to construe the relation between the theater and the world heightened awareness of the theater as a contingent practice, with a set of institutional interests, motives, and constraints and with the concomitant possibility of inadvertently or deliberately violating these very interests. This possibility, even if never put into practice, affected the relation of the theater both to social and political authorities and to its own sense of itself: even the theater's moments of docile self-regulation, the instances of its willingness to remain well within conventional limits, were marked out as strategies, institutional decisions taken to secure the material well-being of the playing company.

The sustained cultural representation of alternative theatrical practices was probably sufficient by itself to call attention to the specific interests, vulnerabilities, and objective social conditions of the public stage. Even without transgression or persecution, the theater would have been denied the luxury at times granted to privileged cultural institutions, particularly those that perform public rites and preserve cultural memory: the luxury of forgetting that its representatives have a concrete, material interest in the rituals they perform and the boundaries they observe. But in fact the theater in the sixteenth and seventeenth centuries constantly violated its interests and transgressed its boundaries. Indeed these boundaries were defined in relation to transgressions that were fully understood as such only after the fact, and the interests of the theater could be clearly understood only when they had been violated. The Tudor and Stuart regulations governing the public stage were confused, inconsistent, and haphazard, the products neither of a traditional, collective understanding nor of a coherent, rational attempt to regularize and define a new cultural practice. They were instead a jumble of traditional rules and offices designed to govern older, very different theatrical practices and a set of ordinances drawn up hastily in response to particular and local pressures. As a result, even the relatively peaceful and prosperous moments in the troubled life of a theater company had an air of improvisation rather than of established and settled fact.[13]

This institutional improvisation frames the local improvisations of individual playwrights. Hence Shakespeare's representational equipment included not only the ideological constraints within which the theater functioned as an institution but also a set of received stories and generic expectations, including, as his career progressed, those established by his own earlier plays. And though in many of his materials he worked within fairly well-defined boundaries—he could not, for example, have Prince Hal lose the battle of Agincourt—Shakespeare actually had at every point a surprising range of movement. The choices he made were not purely subjective or individual or disinterested, but they were choices: there are dozens of tellings of the Lear story—it is part of the ideology of the family in the late Middle Ages and Renaissance—yet in none of them, so far as I know, does Cordelia die in Lear's arms.

But if we grant the Elizabethan theater this provisional character, should we not say that its air of improvisatory freedom is countered by a still greater insistence on the contained and scripted nature of the represented actions? After all, theatrical performance is distinct from most other social practices precisely insofar as its character is predetermined and enclosed, as it forces its audience to grant that retrospective necessity was prospective: the formal necessity disclosed when one looks back on events that have already occurred was in fact the necessity disclosed in the existence, before the performance itself, of the script.[14] Life outside the theater is full of confusion, schemes imperfectly realized, arbitrary interference, unexpected and unpredictable resistances from the body. On the stage this confusion is at once mimed and revealed to be only scripted. Of course, we may say that even on stage there is no certainty: the actors may forget their lines or blurt them out before their cue or altogether refuse to perform, the clown may decide to improvise, individuals in the audience may abandon the voluntary submission expected of them and intervene in the performance, the scaffolding may collapse and force the cancellation of the show. But this absurd, almost entirely theoretical contingency only gives the touch of freedom that seasons that disclosure of necessity.

We could argue further that one of the ideological functions of the theater was precisely to create in its audience the sense that what seemed spontaneous or accidental was in fact fully plotted ahead of time by a playwright carefully calculating his effects, that behind experienced uncertainty there was design, whether the design of the human patriarchs—the fathers and rulers who unceasingly watched over the errant courses of their subjects—or the overarching design of the divine patriarch. The theater then would confirm the structure of human experience as proclaimed by those on top and would urge us to reconfirm this structure in our pleasure.

But if the improvisational provisionality of the theater is not necessarily subversive ideologically, neither is the hidden order of scripted performance necessarily orthodox. Not only can the audience withhold its confirmation of that order and refuse to applaud, but the order itself is marked out as theatrical and to that extent unreal. In applauding, the audience need only be confirming its own practical interests in the playhouse.

Can we speak, however, of "practical interests" in this context? Should we not say that the theater escapes from the network of practices that governs the circulation of social energy? The public theater would seem to be of no use to the audience at all in providing material or symbolic strategic advantage: the events depicted on the stage do not impinge directly on the practical arrangements of the members of the audience, and via the script an abstractness, an atemporality, is concealed behind the powerful illusion of unfolding life. These special conditions, though important, do not constitute the theater as a place radically detached from the realm of social practice. In the first place, the theater does have obvious use-value for several classes of people: those who act, write for it, regulate it, provide costumes, build and maintain the playhouses, ferry customers across the river, pick pockets or pick up tricks during the performance, provide refreshment, sweep up after the crowd, and so forth. Only one group—the audience—appears to be excluded from practical activity, and an activity cannot become nonpractical because it excludes a social group, for then virtually all activities would become nonpractical. Second, the audience's pleasure is in some important senses useful. The Renaissance had theories, as we do, arguing on both physiological and psychological grounds for the practical necessity of recreation, and these were supplemented by explicitly political theories. An audience watching a play, Nashe suggested, would not be hatching a rebellion. Third, the practical usefulness of the theater depends largely on the illusion of its distance from ordinary social practice. The triumphant cunning of the theater is to make its spectators forget that they are participating in a practical activity, to invent a sphere that seems far removed from the manipulations of the everyday. Shakespeare's theater is powerful and effective precisely to the extent that the audience believes it to be nonuseful and hence nonpractical.[15] And this belief gives the theater an unusually broad license to conduct its negotiations and exchanges with surrounding institutions, authorities, discourses, and practices.

These negotiations were defined by the unequivocal *exclusion* of relatively little from the privileged space of the playhouse, even though virtually everything represented on the stage was at least potentially dangerous and hence could be scrutinized and censored. The Elizabethan theater could, within limits, represent the sacred as well as the profane, contemporary as well as ancient times, stories set in England as well as as those set in distant lands. Allusions to the reigning monarch, and even to highly controversial issues in the reign, were not necessarily forbidden (though the company had to tread cautiously); the outlawed practices and agents of the Catholic faith could be represented with considerable sympathy, along with Turks, Jews, witches, demons, fairies, wild men, ghosts. Above all—and the enabling agent of this range of representational resource—the language of the theater was astonishingly open: the most solemn formulas of the church and state could find their way onto the stage and mingle with the language of the marketplace, just as elevated verse could alternate in the same play with the homeliest of prose. The theater is marked off from the "outside world" and licensed to operate as a distinct domain, but its boundaries are remarkably permeable.

For the circulation of social energy by and through the stage was not part of a single coherent, totalizing system. Rather it was partial, fragmentary, conflictual; elements were crossed, torn apart, recombined, set against each other; particular social practices were magnified by the stage, others diminished, exalted, evacuated. What then is the social energy that is being circulated? Power, charisma, sexual excitement, collective dreams, wonder, desire, anxiety, religious awe, free-floating intensities of experience. In a sense the question is absurd, for everything produced by the society can circulate unless it is deliberately excluded from circulation. Under such circumstances, there can be no single method, no overall picture, no exhaustive and definitive cultural poetics.

· · · · · · · · · ·

I had dreamed of speaking with the dead, and even now I do not abandon this dream. But the mistake was to imagine that I would hear a single voice, the voice of the other. If I wanted to hear one, I had to hear the many voices of the dead. And if I wanted to hear the voice of the other, I had to hear my own voice. The speech of the dead, like my own speech, is not private property.

NOTES

First appeared in 1988.

1. The classic formulation by W. K. Wimsatt, Jr.: "In each poem there is something (an individual intuition—or a concept) which can never be expressed in other terms" ("The Structure of the 'Concrete Universal' in Literature," in *Criticism: The Foundations of Modern Literary Judgment*, ed. Mark Schorer, Josephine Miles, and Gordon McKenzie, rev. ed. [New York: Harcourt, Brace, and World, 1958], p. 403).

2. To be sure, a wide range of literary studies have implicitly, and on occasion explicitly, addressed the collective experience of theatre: E. K. Chambers's encyclopedic studies of the theatrical institutions in the Middle Ages and the Renaissance, Glynne Wickham's volumes on early English stages, Robert Weimann's analysis of Shakespeare and the popular tradition, C. L. Barber's discussion of Shakespeare and folk rituals, a large number of books and articles on the rhetorical materials with which Shakespeare worked, and so forth. The present study is an attempt to supplement these volumes by exploring the poetics of Renaissance culture.

3. We may posit (and feel) the presence of a powerful and highly individuated creative intelligence, but that creativity does not lead us back to a moment of pure sublime invention, nor does it secure a formal textual autonomy.

4. Novels may have been read aloud to members of the household, but the differentiation of the domestic group is alien to the organization of the theatrical audience.

5. George Puttenham, *The Arte of English Poesie*, in *Elizabethan Critical Essays*, ed. G. Gregory Smith, 2 vols. (London: Oxford University Press, 1904), 2:148. See, likewise, Sir Philip Sidney, *An Apologie for Poetrie*, in Smith, 1:201. The term derives ultimately from Aristotle's *Rhetoric* (33.2.2), as interpreted especially by Quintilian (*Institutio* 8.3.89) and Scaliger (*Poetices* 3.27).

6. And back before the late sixteenth and early seventeenth centuries as well, since the transactions that enable the creation of Shakespeare's plays are possible only because of prior transactions. Theoretically, at least, the chain has no end, though any inquiry has practical limits and, moreover, certain movements seem more important than others.

7. Jurgis Baltrusaitis, *Le Miroir: Essai sur une légende scientifique: Révélations, science fiction, et fallacies* (Paris: Elmayan, 1978).

8. These items are from the inventory of the Lord Admiral's Men in *Henslowe's Diary*, ed. R. A. Foakes and R. T. Rickert (Cambridge: Cambridge University Press, 1961), app. 2, pp. 320–25.

9. For the terms of "An Acte to Restraine Abuses of Prayers," see E. K. Chambers, *The Elizabethan Stage*, 4 vols. (Oxford: Clarendon, 1923), 4:338–9. It is not clear how strictly this regulation was enforced.

10. These maneuvers were not always successful. In 1639 it was reported that "Thursday last the players of the Fortune were fined 1000£ for setting up an altar, a bason, and two candlesticks, and bowing down before it upon the stage, and although they allege that it was an old play revived, and an altar to the heathen gods, yet it was apparent that this play was revived on purpose in contempt of the ceremonies of the Church" (quoted in Gerald Eades Bentley, *The Jacobean and Caroline Stage*, 7 vols. [Oxford: Clarendon, 1941–68], 1:277). Bentley expresses some reservations about the accuracy of this account.

11. Stephen Greenblatt, "The Cultivation of Anxiety: King Lear and His Heirs," *Raritan* 2 (1982): 92–124. I should add that members of joint stock companies in the early modern period customarily referred to each other in familial terms.

12. "Dynamic circulation" is Michel Foucault's phrase (*L'Usage des plasirs*, vol. 2 of *Histoire de la sexualité* [Paris: Gallimard, 1984], pp. 52–53).

13. Glynnc Wickham, who has argued that the Elizabethan regulations were somewhat more methodical than I have allowed, emphasizes the players' creative flexibility in response: "It is this freedom from rigidly doctrinaire approach to play writing and play production, coupled with the will to adapt and improvise creatively within the limits of existing opportunities, which ultimately explains the triumph of Jacobean and Caroline actors in bringing this drama successfully to birth despite the determined efforts of the clergy, town-councillors and Chambers of Commerce to suppress it" (*Early English Stage, 1300–1660*, vol. 2, part 2: 1576–1660 [London: Routledge and Kegan Paul, 1972], p. 208). But wc might add—as Wickham himself recognizes—that some of the most severe regulations, such as those suppressing the great mystery cycles and prohibiting unlicensed playing troupes, very much helped the major Elizabethan and Jacobean companies.

14. For reflections on this distinction between retrospective and prospective identity, see Pierre Bourdieu, *Outline of a Theory of Practice*, trans. Richard Nice (Cambridge: Cambridge University Press, 1977). I have found Bourdieu's book extremely suggestive.

15. In this regard, we may invoke what Bourdieu calls "a restricted definition of economic interest" that is the historical product of capitalism:

> The constitution of relatively autonomous areas of practice is accompanied by a process through which symbolic interests (often described as "spiritual" or "cultural") come to be set up in opposition to strictly economic interests as defined in the field of economic transactions by the fundamental tautology "business is business"; strictly "cultural" or "aesthetic" interest, disinterested interest, is the paradoxical product of the ideological labour in which writers and artists, those most directly interested, have played an important part and in the course of which symbolic interests become autonomous by being opposed by material interests, i.e., by being symbolically nullified as interests. (p. 177)

Cultural Studies: Two Paradigms

STUART HALL

IN SERIOUS, critical intellectual work, there are no "absolute beginnings" and few unbroken continuities. Neither the endless unwinding of "tradition," so beloved on the History of Ideas, nor the absolutism of the "epistemological rupture," punctuating Thought into its "false" and "correct" parts, once favored by the Althusserans, will do. What we find, instead, is an untidy but characteristic unevenness of development. What is important are the significant *breaks*—where old lines of thought are disrupted, older constellations displaced, and elements, old and new, are regrouped around a different set of premises and themes. Changes in a problematic do significantly transform the nature of the questions asked, the forms in which they are proposed, and the manner in which they can be adequately answered. Such shifts in perspective reflect not only the results of an internal intellectual labor, but the manner in which real historical developments and transformations are appropriated in thought, and provide Thought, not with its guarantee of "correctness" but with its fundamental orientations, its conditions of existence. It is because of this complex articulation between thinking and historical reality, reflected in the social categories of thought, and the continuous dialectic between "knowledge" and "power," that the breaks are worth recording.

Cultural Studies, as a distinctive problematic, emerges from one such moment, in the mid-1950s. It was certainly not the first time that its characteristic questions had been put on the table. Quite the contrary. The two books which helped to stake out the new terrain—Hoggart's *Use of Literacy* and Williams's *Culture and Society*—were both, in different ways, works (in part) of recovery. Hoggart's book took its reference form the "cultural debate," long sustained in the arguments around "mass society" and in the tradition of work identified with Leavis and *Scrutiny*. *Culture and Society* reconstructed a long tradition which Williams defined as consisting, in sum, of "a record of a number of important and continuing reactions to . . . changes in our social, economic and political life" and offering "a special kind of map by means of which the nature of the changes can be explored" (p. 16). The books looked, at first, simply like updating of these earlier concerns, with reference to the post-war world. Retrospectively, their "breaks" with the traditions of thinking in which they were situated seem as important, if not more so, than their continuity with them. The *Uses of Literacy* did set out—much in the spirit of "practical criticism"—to "read" working-class culture for the values and meanings embodied in its patterns and arrangements: as if they were certain kinds of "texts." But the application of this method to a living culture, and the rejection of the terms of the "cultural debate" (polarized around the high/low culture distinction) was a thoroughgoing departure. *Culture and Society*—in one and the same movement—constituted a tradition (*the* "culture-and-society" tradition), defined its "unity" (not in terms of common positions but in its characteristic concerns and the idiom of its inquiry), itself made a distinctive modern contribution to it—*and* wrote its epitaph. The Williams book which succeeded it—*The Long Revolution*—clearly indicated that the "culture-and-society" mode of reflection could only be completed and developed by moving somewhere else—to a significantly different kind of analysis. The very difficulty of some of the writing in *The Long Revolution*—with its attempt to "theorize" on the back of a tradition resolutely empirical and particularist in its idiom of thought, the experiential "thickness" of its concepts, and the generalizing movement of argument in it—stems, in part, from this determination to *move on* (Williams's work, right through to the most recent *Politics and Letters*, is exemplary precisely in its sustained developmentalism). The "good" and the "bad" parts of *The Long Revolution* both arise from its status as a work "of the break." The same could be said of E. P. Thompson's *Making of the English Working Class*, which belongs decisively to this "moment," even though, chronologically it appeared somewhat later. It, too, had been "thought" within certain distinctive historical traditions: English Marxist historiography, economic and "labor" history. But in its foregrounding of the questions of culture consciousness and experience, and its accent on agency, it also made a decisive break: with a certain kind of technological evolutionism, with a reductive economism and an organizational determinism. Between them, these three books constituted the caesura out of which—among other things—"Cultural Studies" emerged.

They were, of course, seminal and formative texts. They were not, in any sense, "textbooks" for the founding of a new academic subdiscipline: nothing could have been further from their intrinsic impulse. Whether historical or contemporary in focus, they were, themselves, focused *by*, organized through and constituted responses to, the immediate pressures of the time and society in which they were written. They not only took "culture" seriously—as a dimension without which historical transformations, past and present, simply could not adequately be thought. They were, themselves, "cultural" in the *Culture and Society* sense. They forced on their readers' attention the proposition that "concentrated in the word *culture* are questions directly raised by the great historical changes which the changes in industry, democracy, and class, in their own way, represent, and to which the changes in art are a closely related response" (p. 16). This was a question for the 1960s and 70s, as well as the 1860s and 70s. And this is perhaps the point to note that this line of thinking was roughly coterminous with what has been called the "agenda" of the early New Left, to which these writers, in one sense or another, belonged, and whose texts these were. This connection placed the "politics of intellectual work" squarely at the center of Cultural Studies from the beginning—a concern from which, fortunately, it has never been, and can never be, freed. In a deep sense, the "settling of accounts" in *Culture and Society*, the first part of *The Long Revolution*, Hoggart's densely particular, concrete study of some aspects of working-class culture and Thompson's historical reconstruction of the formation of a class culture and popular traditions in the 1790–1830 period formed, between them, the break, and defined the space from which a new area of study and practice opened. In terms of intellectual bearings and emphases, this was—if ever such a thing can be found—Cultural Studies' moment of "re-founding." The institutionalization of Cultural Studies—first, in the Centre at Birmingham, and then in courses and publications from a variety of sources and places—with its characteristic gains and losses, belongs to the 1960s and later.

"Culture" was the site of the convergence. But what definitions of this core concept emerged from this body of work? And, since this line of thinking has decisively shaped Cultural Studies, and represents the most formative *indigenous* or "native" tradition, around what space were its concerns and concepts unified? The fact is that no single, unproblematic definition of "culture" is to be found here. The concept remains a complex one—a site of convergent interests, rather than a logically or conceptually clarified idea. This "richness" is an area of continuing tension and difficulty in the field. It might be useful, therefore, briefly to resume the characteristic stresses and emphases through which the concept has arrived at its present state of (in)-determinacy. (The characterizations which follow are, necessarily crude and over-simplified, synthesizing rather than carefully analytic.) Two main problematics only are discussed. Two rather different ways of conceptualizing "culture" can be drawn out of the many suggestive formulations in Raymond Williams's *Long Revolution*. The first relates "culture" to the sum of the available descriptions through which societies make sense of and reflect their common experiences. This definition takes up the earlier stress on "ideas," but subjects it to a thorough reworking. The conception of "culture" is itself democratized and socialized. It no longer consists of the sum of the "best that has been thought and said," regarded as the summits of an achieved civilization—that ideal of perfection to which, in earlier usage, all aspired. Even "art"—assigned in the earlier framework a privileged position, as touchstone of the highest values of civilization—is now redefined as only one, special form of a general social process: the giving and taking of meanings, and the slow development of "common" meanings—a common culture: "culture," in this special sense, "is ordinary" (to borrow the title of one of Williams's earlier attempts to make his general position more widely accessible). If even the highest, most refined of descriptions offered in works of literature are also "part of the general process which creates conventions and institutions, through which the meanings that are valued by the community are shared and made active" (p. 55), then there is no way in which this process can be hived off or distinguished or set apart from the other practices of the historical process: "Since our way of seeing things is literally our way of living, the process of communication is in fact the process of community: the sharing of common meanings, and thence common activities and purposes; the offering, reception and comparison of new meanings, leading to tensions and achievements of growth and change" (p. 55). Accordingly, there is no way in which the communication of descriptions, understood in this way, can be set aside and compared externally with other things. "If the art is part of society, there is no solid whole, outside it, to which, by the form of our question, we concede priority. The art is there, as an activity, with the production, the trading, the politics, the raising of families. To study the relations adequately we must study them actively, seeing all activities as particular and contemporary forms of human energy."

If this first emphasis takes up and reworks the connotation of the term "culture" with the domain of "ideas," the second emphasis is more deliberately anthropological, and emphasizes that aspect of "culture" which refers to social *practices*. It is from this second emphasis that the somewhat simplified definition—"culture is a whole way of life"—has been rather too neatly abstracted. Williams did relate this aspect of the concept to the more "documentary"—that is, descriptive, even ethnographic—usage of the term. But the earlier definition seems to me the more central one, into which "way of life" is integrated. The important point in the argument rests on the active and indissoluble relationships between elements or social practices normally separated out. It is in *this* context that the "theory of culture" is defined as "the study of relationships between elements in a whole way of life." "Culture" is not *a* practice; nor is it simply the descriptive sum of the "mores and folkways" of societies—as it tended to become in certain kinds of anthropology. It is threaded through *all* social practices, and is the sum of their interrelationship. The question of what, then, is studied, and how, resolves itself. The "culture" is those patterns of organization, those characteristic forms of human energy which can be discovered as revealing themselves—in "unexpected identities and correspondences" as well as in "discontinuities of an unexpected kind" (p. 63)—within or underlying *all* social practices. The analysis of culture is, then, "the attempt to discover the nature of the organization which is the complex of these relationships." It begins with "the discovery of patterns of a characteristic kind." One will discover them, not in the art, production, trading, politics, the raising of families, treated as separate activities, but through "studying a general organization in a particular example" (p. 61). Analytically, one must study "the relationships between these patterns." The purpose of the analysis is to grasp how the interactions between all these practices and patterns are lived and experienced as a whole, in any particular period. This is its "structure of feeling."

It is easier to see what Williams was getting at, and why he was pushed along this path, if we understand what were the problems he addressed, and what pitfalls he was trying to avoid. This is particularly necessary because *The Long Revolution* (like much of Williams's work) carries on a submerged, almost "silent" dialogue with alternative positions, which are not always as clearly identified as one would wish. There is a clear engagement with the "idealist" and "civilizing" definitions of culture—both the equation of "culture" with *ideas*, in the idealist tradition; and the assimilation of culture to an *ideal*, prevalent in the elitist terms of the "cultural debate." But there is also a more extended engagement with certain kinds of Marxism, against which Williams's definitions are consciously pitched. He is arguing against the literal operations of the base-superstructure metaphor, which in classical Marxism ascribed the domain of ideas and of meanings to the "superstructures," themselves conceived as merely reflective of and determined in some simple fashion by "the base," without a social effectivity of their own. That is to say, his argument is constructed against a vulgar materialism and an economic determinism. He offers, instead, a radical interactionism: in effect, the interaction of all practices in and with one another, skirting the problem of determinacy. The distinctions between practices is overcome by seeing them all as variant forms of *praxis*—of a general human activity and energy. The underlying patterns which distinguish the complex of practices in any specific society at any specific time are the characteristic "forms of its organization" which underlie them all, and which can therefore be traced in each.

There have been several, radical revisions of this early position: and each has contributed much to the redefinition of what Cultural Studies is and should be. We have acknowledged already the exemplary nature of Williams's project, in constantly rethinking and revising older arguments—in going on thinking. Nevertheless, one is struck by a marked line of continuity through these seminal revisions. One such moment is the occasion of his recognition of Lucien Goldmann's work, and through him, of the array of Marxist thinkers who had given particular attention to superstructural forms and whose work began, for the first time, to appear in English translation in the mid-1960s. The contrast between the alternative Marxist traditions which sustained writers like Goldmann and Lukacs, as compared with Williams's isolated position and the impoverished Marxist tradition he had to draw on, is sharply delineated. But the points of convergence—both what they are against, and what they are about—are identified in ways which are not altogether out of line with his earlier arguments. Here is the negative, which he sees as linking his work to Goldmann's: "I came to believe that I had to give up, or at least to leave aside, what I knew as the Marxist tradition: to attempt to develop a theory of social totality; to see the study of culture as the study of relations between elements in a whole way of life; to find ways of studying structure . . . which could stay in touch with and illuminate particular artworks and forms, but also forms and relations of more general social life; to replace the formula of base and superstructure with the more active idea of a field of mutually if also unevenly determining forces" (*NLR* 67, May–June 1971). And here is the positive—the point where the convergence is marked between Williams's "structure of feeling" and Goldmann's "genetic structuralism": "I found in my own work that I had to develop the idea of a structure of feeling. . . . But then I found Goldmann beginning . . . from a concept of structure which contained, in itself, a relation between social and literary facts. This relation, he insisted, was not a matter of content, but of mental structures: 'categories which simultaneously organize the empirical consciousness of a particular social group, and the imaginative world created by the writer.' By definition, these structures are not individually but collectively created." The stress there on the interactivity of practices and on the underlying totalities, and the homologies between them, is characteristic and significant. "A correspondence of content between a writer and his world is less significant than this correspondence of organization, of structure."

A second such "moment" is the point where Williams really takes on board E. P. Thompson's critique of *The Long Revolution* (cf. the review in *NLR* 9 and 10)—that no "whole way of life" is without its dimension of struggle and confrontation between opposed *ways* of life—and attempts to rethink the key issues of determination and domination via Gramsci's concept of "hegemony." This essay ("Base and Superstructure," *NLR* 82, 1973) is a seminal one, especially in its elaboration of dominant, residual and emergent cultural practices, and its return to the problematic of determinacy as "limits and pressures." Nonetheless, the earlier emphases recur, with force: "we cannot separate literature and art from other kinds of social practice, in such a way as to make them subject to quite special and distinct laws." And, "no mode of production, and therefore no dominant society or order of society, and therefore no dominant culture, in reality exhausts human practice, human energy, human intention." And this note is carried forward—indeed, it is radically accented—in Williams's most sustained and succinct recent statement of his position: the masterly condensations of *Marxism and Literature*. Against the structuralist emphasis on the specificity and "autonomy" of practices, and their analytic separation of societies into their discrete instances, Williams's stress is on "constitutive activity" in general, on "sensuous human activity, as practice," from Marx's first "thesis" on Feuerbach; on different practices conceived as a "whole indissoluble practice"; on totality. "Thus, contrary to one development in Marxism, it is not 'the base' and 'the superstructure' that need to be studied, but specific and indissoluble real processes, within which the decisive relationship, from a Marxist point of view, is that expressed by the complex idea of 'determination'" (*M & L*, pp. 30–31, 82).

At one level, Williams's and Thompson's work can only be said to converge around the terms of the same problematic through the operation of a violent and schematically dichotomous theorization. The organizing terrain of Thompson's work—classes as relations, popular struggle, and historical forms of consciousness, class cultures in their historical particularity—is foreign to the more reflective and "generalizing" mode in which Williams typically works. And the dialogue between them begins with a very sharp encounter. The review of *The Long Revolution*, which Thompson undertook, took Williams sharply to task for the evolutionary way in which culture as a "whole way of life" had been conceptualized; for his tendency to absorb conflicts between class cultures into the terms of an extended "conversation"; for his impersonal tone—above the contending classes, as it were; and for the imperializing sweep of his concept of "culture" (which, heterogeneously, swept everything into its orbit because it was the study of the interrelationships between the forms of energy and organization underlying *all* practices. But wasn't this—Thompson asked—where History came in?) Progressively, we can see how Williams has persistently rethought the terms of his original paradigm to take these criticisms into account—though this is accomplished (as it so frequently is in Williams) obliquely: via a particular appropriation of Gramsci, rather than in a more direct modification.

Thompson also operates with a more "classical" distinction than Williams, between "social being" and "social consciousness" (the terms he infinitely prefers, from Marx, to the more fashionable "base and superstructure"). Thus, where Williams insists on the absorption of all practices into the totality of "real, indissoluble practice," Thompson does deploy an older distinction between what is "culture" and what is "not culture." "Any theory of culture must include the concept of the dialectical interaction between culture and something that is *not* culture." Yet the definition of culture is not, after all, so far removed from Williams's: "We must suppose the raw material of life experience to be at one pole, and all the infinitely complex human disciplines and systems, articulate and inarticulate, formalized in institutions or dispersed in the least formal ways, which 'handle,' transmit or distort this raw material to be at the other." Similarly, with respect to the commonality of "practice" which underlies all the distinct practices: "It is the active process—which is at the same time the process through which men make their history—that I am insisting upon" (*NLR* 9, p. 33, 1961). And the two positions come close together around—again—certain distinctive negatives and positives. Negatively, against the "base/superstructure" metaphor, and a reductionist or "economistic" definition of determinacy. On the first: "The dialectical intercourse between social being and social consciousness—or between "culture" and intercourse between social being and social consciousness—or between "culture" and "*not* culture"—is at the heart of any comprehension of the historical process within the Marxist tradition. . . . The tradition inherits a dialectic that is right, but the particular mechanical metaphor through which it is expressed is wrong. This metaphor from constructional engineering . . . must in any case be inadequate to describe the flux of conflict, the dialectic of a changing social process. . . . All the metaphors which are commonly offered have a tendency to lead the mind into schematic modes and away from the interaction of being-consciousness." And on "reductionism": "Reductionism is a lapse in historical logic by which political or cultural events are 'explained' in terms of the class affiliations of the actors. . . . But the mediation between 'interest' and 'belief' was not through Nairn's 'complex of superstructures' but through the people themselves" ("Peculiarities of the English," *Social Register,* 1965, pp. 351–352). And, more positively—a simple statement which may be taken as defining virtually the whole of Thompson's historical work, from *The Making* to *Whigs and Hunt-*

ers, *The Poverty of Theory* and beyond—"capitalist society was founded upon forms of exploitation which are simultaneously economic, moral and cultural. Take up the essential defining productive relationship . . . and turn it round, and it reveals itself now in one aspect (wage-labor), now in another (an acquisitive ethos), and now in another (the alienation of such intellectual faculties as are not required by the worker in his productive role)" (ibid., p. 356).

Here, then, despite the many significant differences, is the outline of one significant line of thinking in Cultural Studies—some would say, *the* dominant paradigm. It stands opposed to the residual and merely reflective role assigned to "the cultural." In its different ways, it conceptualizes culture as interwoven with all social practices; and those practices, in turn, as a common form of human activity: sensuous human praxis, the activity through which men and women make history. It is opposed to the base-superstructure way of formulating the relationship between ideal and material forces, especially where the "base" is defined as the determination by "the economic" in any simple sense. It prefers the wider formulation—the dialectic between social being and social consciousness: neither separable into its distinct poles (in some alternative formulations, the dialectic between "culture" and "non-culture"). It defines "culture" as *both* the meanings and values which arise amongst distinctive social groups and classes, on the basis of their given historical conditions and relationships, through which they "handle" and respond to the conditions of existence; *and* as the lived traditions and practices through which those "understandings" are expressed and in which they are embodied. Williams brings together these two aspects—definitions and ways of life—around the concept of "culture" itself. Thompson brings the two elements—consciousness and conditions—around the concept of "experience." Both positions entail certain difficult fluctuations around these key terms. Williams so totally absorbs "definitions of experience" into our "ways of living," and both into an indissoluble real material practice-in-general, as to obviate any distinction between "culture" and "not-culture." Thompson sometimes uses "experience" in the more usual sense of consciousness, as the collective ways in which men "handle, transmit or distort" their given conditions, the raw materials of life; sometimes as the domain of the "lived," the mid-term *between* "conditions" and "culture"; and sometimes as the objective conditions themselves—against which particular modes of consciousness are counterposed. But, whatever the terms, both positions tend to read structures of relations in terms of how they are "lived" and "experienced." Williams's "structure of feeling"—with its deliberate condensation of apparently incompatible elements—is characteristic. But the same is true of Thompson, despite his far fuller historical grasp of the "given-ness" or structuredness of the relations and conditions into which men and women necessarily and involuntarily enter, and his clearer attention to the determinacy of productive and exploitative relations under capitalism. This is a consequence of giving culture-consciousness and experience so pivotal a place in analysis.

The *experiential pull* in this paradigm, and the emphasis on the creative and on historical agency, constitutes the two key elements in the *humanism* of the position outlined. Each consequently accords "experience" an authenticating position in any cultural analysis. It is, ultimately, where and how people experience their conditions of life, define them and respond to them, which, for Thompson defines why every mode of production is also a culture, and every struggle between classes is always also a struggle between cultural modalities; and which, for Williams, is what a "cultural analysis," in the final instance, should deliver. In "experience," all the different practices intersect; within "culture" the different practices interact—even if on an uneven and mutually determining basis. This sense of cultural totality—of *the whole* historical process—overrides any effort to keep the instances and elements distinct. Their real interconnection, under given historical conditions, must be matched by a totalizing movement "in thought," in the analysis. It establishes for both the strongest protocols against any form of analytic abstraction which distinguishes practices, or which sets out to test the "actual historical movement" in all its intertwined complexity and particularity by any more sustained logical or analytical operation. These positions, especially in their more concrete historical rendering (*The Making, The Country and the City*) are the very opposite of a Hegelian search for underlying Essences. Yet, in their tendency to reduce practices to *praxis* and to find common and homologous "forms" underlying the most apparently differentiated areas, their movement is "essentializing." They have a particular way of understanding the totality—though it is with a small "t," concrete and historically determinate, uneven in its correspondences. They understand it "expressively." And since they constantly inflect the more traditional analysis towards the experiential level, or read the other structures and relations downwards from the vantage point of how they are "lived," they are properly (even if not adequately or fully) characterized as "culturalist" in their emphasis: even when all the caveats and qualifications against a too rapid "dichotomous theorizing" have been entered. (Cf. for "culturalism," Richard Johnson's two seminal articles on the operation of the paradigm: in "Histories of Culture/Theories of Ideology," *Ideology and Cultural Production*, eds. M. Barrett, P. Corrigan *et al.*, Croom Helm, 1979; and "Three Problematics" in *Working Class Culture:* Clarke, Critcher and Johnson, Hutchinsons and CCCS, 1979. For the dangers in "dichotomous theorizing," cf. the Introduction, "Representation and Cultural Production," to Barrett, Corrigan *et al.*)

The "culturalist" strand in Cultural Studies was interrupted by the arrival on the intellectual scene of the "structuralisms." These, possibly more varied than the "culturalisms," nevertheless shared certain positions and orientations in common which makes their designation under a single title not altogether misleading. It has been remarked that whereas the "culturalist" paradigm can be defined without requiring a conceptual reference to the term "ideology" (the *word*, of course, does appear: but it is not a key concept), the "structuralist" interventions have been largely articulated around the concept of "ideology": in keeping with its more impeccably Marxist lineage, "culture" does not figure so prominently. Whilst this may be true of the Marxist structuralists, it is at best less than half the truth about the structuralist enterprise as such. But it is now a common error to condense the latter exclusively around the impact of Althusser and all that has followed in the wake of his interventions—where "ideology" has played a seminal, but modulated role: and to omit the significance of Lévi-Strauss. Yet, in strict historical terms, it was Lévi-Strauss, and the early semiotics, which made the first break. And though the Marxist structuralisms have superseded the latter, they owed, and continue to owe, an immense theoretical debt (often fended off or downgraded into footnotes, in the search for a retrospective orthodoxy) to his work. It was Lévi-Strauss's structuralism which, in its appropriation of the linguistic paradigm, after Saussure, offered the promise to the "human sciences of culture" of a paradigm capable of rendering them scientific and rigorous in a thoroughly new way. And when, in Althusser's work, the more classical Marxist themes were recovered, it remained the case that Marx was "read"—and reconstituted—through the terms of the linguistic paradigm. In *Reading Capital*, for example, the case is made that the mode of production—to coin a phrase—could best be understood as if "structured like a language" (through the selective combination of invariant elements). The a-historical and synchronic stress, against the historical emphases of "culturalism," derived from a similar source. So did a preoccupation with "the social, *sui generis*"—used not adjectivally but substantively: a usage Lévi-Strauss derived, not from Marx, but from Durkheim (the Durkheim who analyzed the social categories of thought—e.g. in *Primitive Classification*—rather than the Durkheim of *The Division of Labour*, who became the founding father of American structural-functionalism).

Lévi-Strauss did, on occasion, toy with certain Marxist formulations. Thus, "Marxism, if not Marx himself, has too commonly reasoned as though practices followed directly from praxis. Without questioning the undoubted primacy of infrastructures, I believe that there is always a mediator between praxis and practices, namely, the conceptual scheme by the operation of which matter and form, neither with any independent existence, are realized as structures, that is as entities which are both empirical and intelligible." But this—to coin another phrase—was largely "gestural." This structuralism shared with culturalism a radical break with the terms of the base/superstructure metaphor, as derived from the simpler parts of the *German Ideology*. And, though "It is to this theory of the superstructures, scarcely touched on by Marx" to which Lévi-Strauss aspired to contribute, his contribution was such as to break in a radical way with [all its] terms of reference, as finally and irrevocably as the "culturalists" did. Here—and we must include Althusser in this characterization—culturalists and structuralists alike ascribed to the domains hitherto defined as "superstructural" a specificity and effectivity, a constitutive primacy, which pushed them beyond the terms of reference of "base" and "superstructure." Lévi-Strauss and Althusser, too, were anti-reductionist and anti-economist in their very cast of thought, and critically attacked that transitive causality which, for so long, had passed itself off as "classical Marxism."

Lévi-Strauss worked consistently with the term "culture." He regarded "ideologies" as of much lesser importance: mere "secondary rationalizations." Like Williams and Goldmann, he worked, not at the level of correspondences between the *content* of a practice, but at the level of their forms and structures. But the manner in which these were conceptualized were altogether at variance with either the "culturalism" of Williams or Goldmann's "genetic structuralism." This divergence can be identified in three distinct ways. First, he conceptualized "culture" as the categories and frameworks in thought and language through which different societies classified out their conditions of existence—above all (since Lévi-Strauss was an anthropologist), the relations between the human and the natural worlds. Second, he thought of the manner and practice through which these categories and mental frameworks were produced and transformed, largely on an analogy with the ways in which language itself—the principal medium of "culture"—operated. He identified what was specific to them and their operation as the "production of meaning": they were, above all, *signifying* practices. Third, after some early flirtations with Durkheim and Mauss's social categories of thought, he largely gave up the question of the relation *between* signifying and non-signifying practices—between "culture" and "not-culture," to use other terms—for the sake of concentrating on the *internal* relations within signifying practices by means of which the categories of meaning were produced. This left the question of determinacy, of totality, largely in abeyance. This causal logic of determinacy was abandoned in favor of a structuralist causality—a logic of *arrangement*, of internal relations, of articulation of parts within a structure. Each of these aspects is also positively present in Althusser's work and that of the Marxist structuralists, even when the terms of reference had been regrounded in Marx's "immense theoretical revolution." In one of Althusser's seminal formulations about ideology—defined as the themes, concepts and representations through which men and women "live," in an imaginary relation, their relation to their real conditions of existence—we can see the skeleton outline of Lévi-Strauss's "conceptual schemes between praxis and practices." "Ideologies" are here being conceptualized, not as the contents and surface forms of ideas, but as the unconscious categories through which conditions are represented and lived. We have already commented on the active presence in Althusser's thinking of the linguistic paradigm—the second element identified above. And though, in the concept of "over-determination"—one of his most seminal and fruitful contributions—Althusser did return to the problems of the relations *between* practices and the question of determinacy (proposing, incidentally, a thoroughly novel and highly suggestive reformulation, which has received far too little subsequent attention), he did tend to reinforce the "relative autonomy" of different practices, and their internal specificities, conditions and effects at the expense of an "expressive" conception of the totality, with its typical homologies and correspondences.

Aside from the wholly distinct intellectual and conceptual universes within which these alternative paradigms developed, there were certain points where, despite their apparent overlaps, culturalism and structuralism were starkly counterposed. We can identify this counterposition at one of its sharpest points precisely around the concept of "experience," and the role the term played in each perspective. Whereas, in "culturalism," experience was the ground—the terrain of "the lived"—where consciousness and conditions intersected, structuralism insisted that "experience" could not, by definition, be the ground of anything, since one could only "live" and experience one's conditions *in and through* the categories, classifications and frameworks of the culture. These categories, however, did not arise from or in experience: rather, experience was their "effect." The culturalists had defined the forms of consciousness and culture as collective. But they had stopped far short of the radical proposition that, in culture and in language, the subject was "spoken by" the categories of culture in which he/she thought, rather than individual productions: they were *unconscious* structures. That is why, though Lévi-Strauss spoke only of "Culture," his concept provided the basis for an easy translation, by Althusser, into the conceptual framework of ideology: "Ideology is indeed a system of 'representations,' but in the majority of these cases these representations have nothing to do with 'consciousness': . . . it is above all as structures that they impose on the vast majority of men, not via their 'consciousness' . . . it is within this ideological unconsciousness that men succeed in altering the 'lived' relation between them and the world and acquiring that new form of specific unconsciousness called 'consciousness'" (*For Marx*, p. 233). It was, in this sense, that "experience" was conceived, not as an authenticating source but as an effect: not as a reflection of the real but as an "imaginary relation." It was only a short step—the one which separates *For Marx* from the "Ideological State Apparatuses" essay—to the development of an account of how this "imaginary relation" served, not simply the dominance of a ruling class over a dominated one, but (through the reproduction of the relations of production, and the constitution of labor-power in a form fit for capitalist exploitation) the expanded reproduction of the mode of production itself. Many of the other lines of divergence between the two paradigms flow from this point: the conception of "men" as bearers of the structures that speak and place them, rather than as active agents in the making of their own history; the emphasis on a structural rather than a historical "logic"; the preoccupation with the constitution—in "theory"—of a nonideological, scientific discourse; and hence the privileging of conceptual work and of Theory as guaranteed; the recasting of history as a march of the structures (cf. passim, *The Poverty of Theory*): the structuralist "machine" . . .

There is no space in which to follow through the many ramifications which have followed from the development of one or [an]other of these "master paradigms" in Cultural Studies. Though they by no means account for all, or even nearly all, of the many strategies adopted, it is fair to say that, between them, they have defined the principal lines of development in the field. The seminal debates have been polarized around their thematics; some of the best concrete work has flowed from the efforts to set one or [an]other of these paradigms to work on particular problems and materials. Characteristically—the sectarian and self-righteous climate of critical intellectual work in England being what it is, and its dependency being so marked—the arguments and debates have most frequently been over-polarized into their extremes. At these extremities, they frequently appear only as mirror-reflections or inversions of one another. Here, the broad typologies we have been working with—for the sake of convenient exposition—become the prison-house of thought.

Without suggesting that there can be any easy synthesis between them, it might usefully be said at this point that neither "culturalism" nor "structuralism" is, in its present manifestation, adequate to the task of constructing the study of culture as a conceptually clarified and theoretically informed domain of study. Nevertheless, something fundamental to it emerges from a rough comparison of their respective strengths and limitations.

The great strength of the structuralisms is their stress on "determinate conditions." They remind us that, unless the dialectic really can be held, in any particular analysis, between both halves of the proposition—that "men make history . . . on the basis of conditions which are not of their making"—the result will inevitably be a naive humanism, with its necessary consequence: a voluntarist and populist political practice. The fact that "men" can become conscious of their conditions, organize to struggle against them and in fact transform them—without which no active politics can even be conceived, let alone practiced—must not be allowed to override the awareness of the fact that, in capitalist relations, men and women are placed and positioned in relations which constitute them as agents. "Pessimism of the intellect, optimism of the will" is a better starting point than a simple heroic affirmation. Structuralism does enable us to begin to think—as Marx insisted—of the *relations* of a structure on the basis of something other than their reduction to relationships between "people." This was Marx's privileged level of abstraction: that which enabled him to break with the obvious but incorrect starting point of "political economy"—bare individuals.

But this connects with a second strength: the recognition by structuralism not only of the necessity of abstraction as the instrument of thought through which "real relations" are appropriated, but also of the presence, in Marx's work, of a continuous and complex movement *between different levels of abstraction*. It is, of course, the case—as "culturalism" argues—that, in historical reality, practices do not appear neatly distinguished out into their respective instances. However, to think about or to analyze the complexity of the real, the act or practice of thinking is required; and this necessitates the use of the power of abstraction and analysis, the formation of concepts with which to cut into the complexity of the real, in order precisely to reveal and bring to light relationships and structures which cannot be visible to the naive naked eye, and which can neither present nor authenticate themselves: "In the analysis of economic forms, neither microscopes nor chemical reagents are of assistance. The power of abstraction must replace both." Of course, structuralism has frequently taken this proposition to its extreme. Because thought is impossible without "the power of abstraction," it has confused this with giving an absolute primacy to the level of the formation of concepts—and at the highest, most abstract level of abstraction only: Theory with a capital "T" then becomes judge and jury. But this is precisely to lose the insight just won from Marx's own practice. For it is clear in, for example, *Capital,* that the *method*—whilst, of course, taking place "in thought" (as Marx asked in the 1857 Introduction, where else?)—rests, not on the simple exercise of abstraction but on the movement and relations which the argument is constantly establishing between *different levels* of abstraction: at each, the premises in play must be distinguished from those which—for the sake of the argument— have to be held constant. The movement to another level of magnification (to deploy the microscope metaphor) requires the specifying of further conditions of existence not supplied at a previous, more abstract level: in this way, by successive abstractions of different magnitudes, to *move towards* the constitution, the *reproduction,* of "the concrete in thought" as an effect of a certain kind of thinking. This method is adequately represented in *neither* the absolutism of Theoretical Practice, in structuralism, nor in the anti-abstraction "Poverty of Theory" position into which, in reaction, culturalism appears to have been driven or driven itself. Nevertheless it is intrinsically *theoretical*, and must be. Here, structuralism's insistence that thought does not reflect reality, but is articulated on and appropriates it, is a necessary starting point. An adequate *working through* of the consequences of this argument might begin to produce a method which takes us outside the permanent oscillations between abstraction/anti-abstraction and the false dichotomies of Theoreticism *vs.* Empiricism which have both marked and disfigured the structuralism-culturalism encounter to date.

Structuralism has another strength, in its conception of "the whole." There is a sense in which, though culturalism constantly insists on the radical particularity of its practices, its mode of conceptualizing the "totality" has something of the complex simplicity of an expressive totality behind it. Its complexity is constituted by the fluidity with which practices move into and out of one another: but this complexity is reducible, conceptually, to the "simplicity" of praxis—human activity, as such—in which the same contradictions constantly appear, homologously reflected in each. Structuralism goes too far in erecting the machine of a "Structure," with its self-generating propensities (a "Spinozean eternity," whose function is only the sum of its effects: a truly structura*list* deviation), equipped with its distinctive instances. Yet it represents an advance over culturalism in the conception it has of the necessary *complexity* of the unity of a structure (over-determination being a more successful way of thinking this complexity than the combinatory invariance of structuralist causality). Moreover, it has the conceptual ability to think of a unity which is constructed through the *differences* between, rather than the homology of, practices. Here, again, it has won a critical insight about Marx's method: one thinks of the complex passages of the 1857 Introduction to the *Grundrisse* where Marx demonstrates how it is possible to think of the "unity" of a social formation as constructed, not out of identity but out of *difference*. Of course, the stress on difference can—and has—led the structuralisms into a fundamental conceptual heterogeneity, in which all sense of structure and totality is lost. Foucault and other post-Althussereans have taken this devious path into the absolute, not the relative, autonomy of practices, via their necessary heterogeneity and "necessary non-correspondence." But the emphasis on unity-in-difference, on complex unity—Marx's concrete as the "unity of many determinations"—can be worked in another, and ultimately more fruitful, direction: towards the problematic of relative autonomy and "over-determination," and the study of *articulation*. Again, articulation contains the danger of a high formalism. But it also has the considerable advantage of enabling us to think of how specific practices (articulated around contradictions which do not all arise in the same way, at the same point, in the same moment), can nevertheless be thought *together*. The structuralist paradigm thus does—if properly developed—enable us to begin really to *conceptualize* the specificity of different practices (analytically distinguished, abstracted out), without losing its grip on the ensemble which they constitute. Culturalism constantly affirms the specificity of different practices—"culture" must not be absorbed into "the economic": but it lacks an adequate way of establishing this specificity theoretically.

The third strength which structuralism exhibits lies in its decentering of "experience" and its seminal work in elaborating the neglected category of "ideology." It is difficult to conceive of a Cultural Studies thought within a Marxist paradigm which is innocent of the category of "ideology." Of course, culturalism constantly makes reference to this concept: but it does not in fact lie at the center of its conceptual universe. The authenticating power and reference of "experience" imposes a barrier between culturalism and a proper conception of "ideology." Yet, without it, the effectivity of "culture" for the reproduction of a particular mode of production cannot be grasped. It is true that there is a marked tendency in the more recent structuralist conceptualizations of "ideology" to give it a functionalist reading—as the necessary cement of the social formation. From this position, it is indeed impossible—as culturalism would correctly argue—to conceive either of ideologies which are not, by definition, "dominant": or of the concept of struggle (the latter's appearance in Althusser's famous ISA's article being—to coin yet another phrase—largely "gestural"). Nevertheless, work is already being done which suggests ways in which the field of ideology may be adequately conceptualized as a terrain of struggle (through the work of Gramsci, and more recently, of Laclau), and these have structuralist rather than culturalist bearings.

Culturalism's strengths can almost be derived from the weaknesses of the structuralism position already noted, and from the latter's strategic absences and silences. It has insisted, correctly, on the affirmative moment of the development of conscious struggle and organization as a necessary element in the analysis of history, ideology and consciousness: against its persistent downgrading in the structuralist paradigm. Here, again, it is largely Gramsci who has provided us with a set of more refined terms through which to link the largely "unconscious" and given cultural categories of "common sense" with the formation of more active and organic ideologies, which have the capacity to intervene in the ground of common sense and popular traditions and, through such interventions, to organize masses of men and women. In this sense, culturalism *properly* restores the dialectic between the unconsciousness of cultural categories and the moment of conscious organization: even if, in its characteristic movement, it has tended to match structuralism's over-emphasis on "conditions" with an altogether too-inclusive emphasis on "consciousness." It therefore not only recovers—as the necessary moment of any analysis—the process by means of which classes-in-themselves, defined primarily by the way in which economic relations position "men" as agents— become active historical and political forces—for themselves: it also— against its own anti-theoretical good sense—*requires* that, when properly developed, each moment must be understood in terms of the level of abstraction at which the analysis is operating. Again, Gramsci has begun to point a way through this false polarization in his discussion of "the passage between the structure and the sphere of the complex superstructures," and its distinct forms and moments.

We have concentrated in this argument largely on a characterization of what seem to us to be the two seminal paradigms at work in Cultural Studies. Of course, they are by no means the only active ones. New developments and lines of thinking are by no means adequately netted with reference to them. Nevertheless, these paradigms can, in a sense, be deployed to measure what appear to us to be the radical weaknesses or inadequacies of those which offer themselves as alternative rallying-points. Here, briefly, we identify three.

The first is that which follows on from Lévi-Strauss, early semiotics and the terms of the linguistic paradigm, and the centering on "signifying practices," moving by way of psychoanalytic concepts and Lacan to a radical re-centering of virtually the whole terrain of Cultural Studies around the terms "discourse" and "the subject." One way of understanding this line of thinking is to see it as an attempt to fill that empty space in early structuralism (of both the Marxist and non-Marxist varieties) where, in earlier discourses, "the subject" and subjectivity might have been expected to appear but did not. This is, of course, precisely one of the key points where culturalism brings its pointed criticisms to bear on structuralism's "process without a subject." The difference is that, whereas culturalism would correct for the hyper-structuralism of earlier models by restoring the unified subject (collective or individual) of consciousness at the center of "the Structure," discourse theory, by way of the Freudian concepts of the unconscious and the Lacanian concepts of how subjects are constituted in language (through the entry into the Symbolic and the Law of Culture), restores the *decentered* subject, the contradictory subject, as a set of positions in language and knowledge, from which culture can appear to be enunciated. This approach clearly identifies a gap, not only in structuralism but in Marxism itself. The problem is that the manner in which this "subject" of culture is conceptualized is of a transhistorical and "universal" character: it addresses the subject-in-general, not historically determinate social subjects, or socially determinate particular languages. Thus it is incapable, so far, of moving its in-general propositions to the level of concrete historical analysis. The second difficulty is that the processes of contradiction and struggle—lodged by early structuralism wholly at the level of "the structure"—are now, by one of those persistent mirror-inversions, lodged exclusively at the level of the unconscious processes of the subject. It may be, as culturalism often argues, that the "subjective" is a necessary moment of any such analysis. But this is a very different proposition from dismantling the whole of the social processes of particular modes of production and social formations, and reconstituting them exclusively at the level of unconscious psychoanalytic processes. Though important work has been done, both within this paradigm and to define and develop it, its claims to have replaced *all* the terms of the earlier paradigms with a more adequate set of concepts seems wildly over-ambitious. Its claims to have integrated Marxism into a more adequate materialism is, largely, a semantic rather than a conceptual claim.

A second development is the attempt to return to the terms of a moral classical "political economy" of culture. This position argues that the concentration on the cultural and ideological aspects has been wildly overdone. It would restore the older terms of "base/superstructure," finding, in the last-instance determination of the cultural-ideological by the economic, that hierarchy of determinations which both alternatives appear to lack. This position insists that the economic processes and structures of cultural production are more significant than their cultural-ideological aspect; and that these are quite adequately caught in the more classical terminology of profit, exploitation, surplus-value and the analysis of culture as commodity. It retains a notion of ideology as "false consciousness."

There is, of course, some strength to the claim that both structuralism and culturalism, in their different ways, have neglected the economic analysis of cultural and ideological production. All the same, with the return to this more "classical" terrain, many of the problems which originally beset it also reappear. The specificity of the effect of the cultural and ideological dimension once more tends to disappear. It tends to conceive the economic level as not only a "necessary" but a "sufficient" explanation of cultural and ideological effects. Its focus on the analysis of the commodity form, similarly, blurs all the carefully established distinctions between different practices, since it is the most *generic* aspects of the commodity-form which attract attention. Its deductions are therefore, largely, confined to an epochal level of abstraction: the generalizations about the commodity-form hold true throughout the capitalist epoch as a whole. Very little by way of concrete and conjunctural analysis can be derived at this high-level "logic of capital" form of abstraction. It also tends to its own kind of functionalism—a functionalism of "logic" rather than of "structure" or history. This approach, too, has insights which are well worth following through. But it sacrifices too much of what has been painfully secured, without a compensating gain in explanatory power.

The third position is closely related to the structuralist enterprise, but has followed the path of "difference" through into a radical heterogeneity. Foucault's work—currently enjoying another of those uncritical periods of discipleship through which British intellectuals reproduce today their dependency on yesterday's French ideas—has had an exceedingly positive effect: above all because in suspending the nearly-insoluble problems of determination Foucault has made possible a welcome return to the concrete analysis of particular ideological and discursive formations, and the sites of their elaboration. Foucault and Gramsci between them account for much of the most productive work on *concrete analysis* now being undertaken in the field: thereby reinforcing and—paradoxically—supporting the sense of the concrete historical instance which has always been one of culturalism's principal strengths. But, again, Foucault's example is positive only if his general epistemological position is not swallowed whole. For in fact Foucault so resolutely suspends judgment, and adopts so thoroughgoing a skepticism about any determinacy or relationship between practices, other than the largely contingent, that we are entitled to see him, not as an agnostic on these questions but as deeply committed to the necessary non-correspondence of all practices to one another. From such a position neither a social formation, nor the State can be adequately thought. And indeed Foucault is constantly falling into the pit which he has dug for himself. For when—against his well-defended epistemological positions—he stumbles across certain "correspondences" (for example, the simple fact that all the major moments of transition he has traced in each of his studies—on the prison, sexuality, medicine, the asylum, language and political economy—all appear to converge around exactly that point where industrial capitalism and the bourgeoisie make their fateful, historical rendezvous), he lapses into a vulgar reductionism, which thoroughly belies the sophisticated positions he has elsewhere advanced.[1]

I have said enough to indicate that, in my view, the line in Cultural Studies which has attempted to *think forward* from the best elements in the structuralist and culturalist enterprises, by way of some of the concepts elaborated in Gramsci's work, comes closest to meeting the requirements of the field of study. And the reason for that should by now also be obvious. Though neither structuralism nor culturalism will do, as self-sufficient paradigms of study, they have a centrality to the field which all the other contenders lack because, between them (in their divergences as well as their convergences) they address what must be the *core problem* of Cultural Studies. They constantly return us to the terrain marked out by those strongly coupled but not mutually exclusive concepts culture/ideology. They pose, together, the problems consequent on trying to think *both* the specificity of different practices and the forms of the articulated unity they constitute. They make a constant, if flawed, return to the base/superstructure metaphor. They are correct in insisting that this question—which resumes all the problems of a nonreductive determinacy—is the heart of the matter: and that, on the solution of this problem will turn the capacity of Cultural Studies to supersede the endless oscillations between idealism and reductionism. They confront—even if in radically opposed ways—the dialectic between conditions and consciousness. At another level, they pose the question of the relation between the logic of thinking and the "logic" of historical process. They continue to hold out the promise of a properly materialist theory of culture. In their sustained and mutually reinforcing antagonisms they hold out no promise of an easy synthesis. But, between them, they define where, if at all, is the space, and what are the limits, within which such a synthesis might be constituted. In Cultural Studies, theirs are the "names of the game."

NOTE

First appeared in 1980.

1. He is quite capable of wheeling in through the back door the classes he recently expelled from the front.

The Born-Again Telescandals

SUSAN HARDING

THE STORY of modernity in America—or rather the version of the story that equates modernity with secularity—emerged out of late 19th and early 20th century debates over the validity of Biblical literalism and the public worthiness of its defenders, orthodox Protestants who came ultimately to be known as "fundamentalists." The contests—which were scattered across the country in universities, public schools, seminaries, denominations, legislatures, courts, elections, the press, and local and national literatures—had unstable and contradictory outcomes. But, according to virtually every narrative (insider as well as outsider) of the struggle, after the Scopes trial in 1925, fundamentalists "separated out." That is, they accepted their designation as unfit for "modernity" and for "modern" political discourse, which henceforth were understood to be intrinsically secular and off-limits to Biblical literalists. The definition of orthodox Protestants as "pre-modern" and their exclusion from public life were thus founding acts of this, the secularizing, version of the modernity narrative, providing both its essential binary opposition (fundamentalist and modern) and its telos (the march of modernity toward ever more secularity).

Over the next fifty years, orthodox Protestants, and even those who proudly proclaimed themselves militant anti-modernist fundamentalists, did not entirely vacate public life, but the modernity narrative that would so exclude them held together as a story, as grounds for their incomplete political and cultural segregation, and as a source of modern subjectivity. After the mid-1970s, orthodox Protestants, in particular, outspoken Biblical literalists, began to break separatist taboos and with escalating success deployed their interpretive practices to an ever expanding range of worldly targets. In 1979, fundamentalists broke the ultimate barrier and plunged en masse into the national political arena, most strikingly through the organization of the Moral Majority under the Reverend Jerry Falwell. Over the next decade, Falwell and other major televangelical preachers fashioned their fundamentalist, conservative charismatic, and evangelical followings into a national born-again constituency that left in its wake what has come to be known as "the Christian perspective on moral issues." In this context, the discursive events of the last decade constitute a rupture in the history of fundamentalism as it was constructed by the modernity narrative. Let us call it "the revolt of the excluded fundamentalist other."

The fact that fundamentalists continued to exist in the late 20th century was something of an anomaly within the modernity paradigm, but their sudden rise to public prominence was shocking from the "modern" point of view. They not only proliferated aggressive counter-discourses—anti-worldly polemics, story genres and public rituals attacking and subverting secular liberal discourses—but also launched a more literal "de-separation" (desegregation) process, as militant Bible believers began to colonize middle and upper echelons of mainstream political, economic, social and cultural institutions. The events of the 1980s were utterly unexpected and unintelligible in terms of the story of modernity, and indeed, I think, must be understood, in part, as a protest against and dramatic disruption of that story. In word and deed, fundamentalists contested the elemental narrative frames of modernity, at least temporarily dislocating the boundary between fundamentalist and modern, destabilizing both subject positions, and desecularizing the public arena.

This essay discusses what appears to be the concluding episode of the revolt: the born-again telescandals of 1987 and 1988, a long year of media events launched in March of 1987 by Oral Roberts' plea for $8 million lest God take him home, taking off with the exfoliating revelations of the misdeeds of Jim and Tammy Faye Bakker and their skirmishes with Jerry Falwell, and, finally, after a lull, coming to a dramatic conclusion with Jimmy Swaggart's fall from grace.

At first blush, the scandals seem to be the "modern" dream come true: pompous misplaced preachers brought down by their own greed, lust and hypocrisy, a moment of predicably grotesque narrative closure on a pesky little chapter in the unfolding subtext of modernity marching on. I would like to bracket this reading of the scandals by shifting the focus from the preachers' misdeeds to the representation of those misdeeds on TV and in the newspapers, a shift which brings into view the scandalized as well as the scandalizers and suggests that the scandals (or rather the telescandals) were a continuation of the 1980s revolt against the modernity narrative rather than a confirmation of it.

Indeed, the telescandals were the moment in which the revolt reached its most fevered pitch, fragmenting the illusion of the fundamentalist whole, accentuating the similarities between fundamentalist and modern, and stripping away modernity's storied ploys, the ones that would hide it as a story and present it instead as history, as objective reportage, as "what's really going on." The outcome of these representational movements was more like a spectacle than a story—a narrative free zone in which history, fiction, and the Bible were equivalent sources of narrative figures and frames, and the boundaries between religious and secular, fictional and factual, authors and characters, participants and observers were called into question, interrogated, crisscrossed, suspended, relocated and multiplied. In other words—I am suggesting there was something distinctly postmodern about the telescandals and, more generally, about the eruption of these ostensibly pre-modern others onto the public stage.

Let me briefly illustrate what I mean: Ted Koppel represented the voice of modernity for millions of Americans throughout the born-again telescandals, which yielded sixteen blockbuster Nightline programs. In May of 1988, he aired an hour-long prime time special report intended to settle once and for all, as he put it, "what this has got to do with." None of the scandalizers (Roberts, the Bakkers, or Swaggart) were present, nor were the scandalous events reviewed in any descriptive way. This particular episode in the telescandals was for exegesis, commentary and midrash by and for the scandalized.

The title of the show, "The Billion Dollar Pie," its opening collage of talking heads, and Koppel's initial sally of remarks all had the same vector: to "unmask" televangelism, to reveal its real and vulgar business nature, rendering not just the scandalizers but all its preachers false prophets, worthy only of satire and shunning. In fact, what Koppel produced was a bald caricature of social scientific explanation, one that undermined his own ostensible detachment, that inspired a cascade of mixed metaphors, wild intertextualities and backtalk from his guests, and began to erase the very distinction between him and "them" which he had to establish in order to have any authority at all.

In . . . the opening collage, Ted Koppel laid out the show's thesis while images flashed across—proliferating TV ministries, a pie with money-colored filling, the birthrate declining across the century. Then Jack Sims vividly narrated another version of the thesis, punctuated midway by a checkerboard of talking heads from the PTL telescandal:

TED KOPPEL (voiceover): In all, there are 1600 television ministers. Sixteen hundred. And of the $1.5 billion grossed annually by television ministries, just three of them—Pat Robertson's, Jimmy Swaggert's and Jim Bakker's—took in close to $500 million. It's a big pie, but the slices are anything but evenly divided. And because the birthrate in this country dipped sharply in the 1930s, there are fewer people in their 50s replacing those among the big givers who are dying off. The donor base is shrinking. And for televangelism, rocked by scandals, it couldn't have come at a worse time.

JACK SIMS, Religious Market Analyst: Last March, it was as if the aging evangelicals were like dinosaurs that walked onto an iceberg. The end of March, when Oral announced that he was being kidnapped by God and held for ransom, the iceberg broke off and began to float south. Atop the iceberg, the aging evangelical dinosaurs began to fight.

MAN [John Ankerberg]: The Reverend Bakker has been involved in episodes with prostitutes, and he has also been involved in homosexual incidents.

REV. JIM BAKKER, Televangelist: If anyone has these charges against me, I want them to come forward publicly with this proof.

REV. JIMMY SWAGGERT, Televangelist: I don't appreciate preachers that get mixed up in adultery and every other type of sin that one can imagine, and them blaming Jimmy Swaggert for it.

MAN, Bakker's Lawyer [Norman Gruttman]: There is smellier laundry in his hamper than the laundry that he thought was in Reverend Bakker's.

REV. BAKKER: There was a plot to hostilely take over the PTL by Jimmy Swaggert.

REV. JERRY FALWELL, Televangelist: If he decides he wants to come back, he'll preside over a funeral. The funeral of his ministry.

MRS. BAKKER: I wake up every morning wishing that they had killed me.

REV. FALWELL: Their own clandestine behavior brought this terrible thing upon them.

MR. SIMS: But the real story of American religion is not the dinosaurs, it's the iceberg. It's floating south and melting, and all the aging evangelical electronic dinosaurs are going to die.

Jack Sims, himself a queer crossbreed—"religious market analyst"—mixed up Darwin, Disney and the Book of Revelation in his tale of electronic evangelical dinosaurs in a way that foreshadowed the hybrid scene setting and boundary blurring that ensued. Koppel greeted his TV audience from a huge, plush, packed Memphis church and introduced his guest preachers: Jack Wimber, Jerry Falwell, E. V. Hill, James Kennedy, Jack Hayford, James Robison, and, via satellite, on a TV screen, Robert Schuller. Everyone (Koppel, the celebrity preachers, the satin-robed choir, and the brimming congregation) seemed at home in this pastiche of the religious and the secular, news and entertainment, postmodern electronics and a premodern God, but it was hardly a propitious setting for a "serious discussion" of the complex conditions that brought about the televangelical scandals. Koppel, leaving poor Jack Sims out in the cold, abruptly shifted metaphoric gear and called his guests "hogs at the trough" in his opening punch. Within minutes he was caught in a quagmire of pious backtalk—Falwell essentially retorted to Koppel, "So are you," then Hill and Hayford mystified all by wrestling over the sinfulness of sex.

KOPPEL (on camera): I must tell you that over the past couple of years, as many of you know, we have done a great many programs on Nightline on some of these problems that televangelists have been having, particularly the Bakkers and Jimmy Swaggert. You know what the sources of our information are? Not private detectives, not our own great reportorial skills. Other preachers. You guys. Other preachers. I conclude from this that what's going on here is a battle royale in the business world. This has got nothing to do with saving souls. This has got nothing to do with evangelical Christianity. What this has got to do with is a huge billion-dollar pie. (Applause.) Or to put it in a somewhat different sense, we've got a bunch of hogs at the trough here. And they see that one way of elbowing the other hog away from the trough is this business of sexual infidelity.

REV. FALWELL: That's true. And of course that's going on today, as you well know, in the journalism world, the business world and every vocation under the heavens, which in no way vindicates or justifies this happening in the religious world.

REV. E. V. HILL, Mount Zion Baptist Church: This is reducing sin to sex. And so when you say, "I've sinned," everybody wants to know, "Who'd you have?"

Jerry Falwell appears on Nightline. © 1988 Copyright Capital Cities/ABC, Inc.
Photo Courtesy Capital Cities/ABC, Inc.

But I submit that there are—and you're dealing with it—I submit that there are some sins here in Proverbs 6:16. The last one closes out with, "He that soweth discord among the brotherhood." And here are the sins that God hates the most, so he wrote, and sex ain't in it. (Applause, laughter.) Sex ain't in it.

KOPPEL: See, you're, you're missing—

REV. HILL: Wait a minute, let me just say it.

KOPPEL: Reverend Hill—

REV. HILL: ". . . a lying tongue—

KOPPEL (motions "time out" with hands):—Hold it, hold it.

REV. HILL:—". . . innocent blood (applause, laughter . . .), wicked imagination, running into mischief, and sowing discord." He hates these the most, and sex ain't on the list. And we have towns and churches torn apart because of lying lips and sowing discord, as you said, among the ministry.

KOPPEL: Yeah, Now, what I—

REV. JACK HAYFORD, Church on the Way: I don't doubt the validity of that list, that's scriptural, but I would recall to you, dear brother, there's another list I read somewhere of 10, and sex is on it.

KOPPEL: What I'm trying to get at here is money. We're not just talking about sins. We're talking about people who are competing for millions and tens of millions of dollars. (Applause.)

And so the show went on, the metaphors slipping and sliding, the preachers resisting and disrupting Koppel's withering story line as they drew from a spellbinding panoply of theological voices crafted through the ages to thwart each other and to astound and stupefy unbelievers. The show dissolved first into a mishmash of arguments among the preachers over fine points of Scripture, doctrine and ecclessiology, and then into a kind of staged populist inquisition as members of the audience stood and leveled "Biblically based" charges against the TV preachers, who in turn spoke back in a splendid jumble of artfully humble voices.

Koppel never lost his composure, but he certainly lost control of the discussion as well as his privileged position as the man who would unmask these bandits once and for all. Surely, "TV production values" interrupted Koppel's effort to "get a grip on the reality" behind the scandals—that is, he himself, Mr. Modern Secularity, was torn between story and spectacle. But the spectacularizing forces destablizing the modernity metanarrative—on Koppel's show, in the telescandals, and throughout the recent decade of born-again rhetorical eruptions—were much bigger than TV. I will shortly explore some of those forces at work specifically in the PTL telescandals—but first I would like to contextualize them, in my own way talking back to the illusion of the fundamentalist whole and the image of the televangelical empires as premodern anachronisms destined for extinction. They will emerge instead as often quarrelsome, always proliferating discursive vanguards, first, of a hitherto hidden born-again world which has become a kind of frontier zone in which premodern, modern and even postmodern cultural forms are intermingling and reproducing wildly, and, second, of a born-again diaspora, a movement into the unborn-again world that would blur so many of the boundaries between the two worlds that it might seem only a miracle—or a lot of money—could resurrect the myth of modernity.

LIFTING MODERNITY'S VEIL

According to a 1982 Gallup poll, 35% of adult Americans said they were "born-again" (that is, had experienced a turning point in their lives when they committed themselves to Jesus Christ), and 37% held a "literal view of the Bible" (that is, considered the Bible to be the actual Word of God and [said that it] is to be taken literally, word for word). By either criterion there are some 50 million adult Americans whom we might call "orthodox Christians."[1] The majority are affiliated with historic evangelical denominations, Black denominations, and mainline Protestant denominations. In recent decades the social and economic profile of orthodox Christians as a whole has increasingly approximated that of other Americans. They continue to be more concentrated in the South than other parts of the country and more conservative politically and morally—however, they are not nearly as homogenous in this latter regard as is imagined by most outsiders.[2]

A minority of orthodox Christians—perhaps 10–15 million adults—are affiliated with Pentecostal and (self-described) fundamentalist denominations and pastoral networks, and it is they who come to mind when "fundamentalism" is used in the sense of "not modern." It is they who characterize the face of orthodox Christians for most outsiders. As a whole, they do tend to be somewhat poorer and less educated—as well as still more Southern (and Southwestern) and conservative than other Americans—but it is the better-off and more educated among them who have been most politically visible and vocal in recent years, as we shall see shortly.

Fundamentalist and Pentecostal groups emerged more or less independently out of late 19th and early 20th century Bible conferences and revivals, and both movements engendered new forms in the 1940s and 50s. Billy Graham and his nonmilitant fundamentalist allies, relabeling themselves "evangelicals" in the late 1950s, consciously sought to engage in what they called "American culture" as they joined more mainline denominations, built substantial churches, sophisticated media ministries, well-credentialed colleges and seminaries, and a certain, rather dignified, political presence, most strikingly in Billy Graham's Presidential friendships. Meanwhile, Oral Roberts and his Pentecostal brethren were elaborating their own novel forms. One morning in 1947 (to paraphrase Roberts), God led Oral to a passage in the Bible (John 3:2) that revealed to him that God wanted his people to prosper and be healthy in this life, that "God is a good God," not a God of suffering and toil and sacrifice, but a God of well-being, comfort and rewards in this life. So began "health and wealth theology" among Pentecostals, which became the touchstone of their emerging faith enterprises and one of the wedges that opened up the "charismatic movement"—the spread of Pentecostal ideas and practices into the mainline denominations during the 1960s and 1970s.

Both Graham and Roberts were pioneers in the use of TV for evangelism and faith healing, and most of the current electronic churches also had their origins in the 1940s and 1950s in relatively modest local churches and ministries. By the 1970s, hundreds of entrepreneurial pastors had parlayed their local operations into literal corporations, extending their reach far beyond church walls via radio, TV, music and publishing operations. Until the PTL crisis, the dozen biggest electronic empires (all located in the South and California) took in over a billion a year, employed over 1000 men and women each, and paid out many millions of dollars in payroll every month. They hired ad agencies, market consultants and corporate lawyers, and their bosses justified their six-figure salaries by saying they were paid no more than the CEOs of other major corporations.

The TV empires, then, are as much businesses as they are churches—indeed the electronic churches are anomalous, mercurial, protean creatures, at once religious, economic and political. Far from being pre-modern relics, atavisms of an earlier age, the televangelists are a late capitalist cross-breed intertwining symbolic production, consumption and social reproduction. They are harbingers of an emerging political economic order in which the stakes are as much collective identities, cultural ideas and symbols as they are profits, markets, political power, and lost souls.

Most of the second generation of TV preachers are charismatics or Pentecostals, and many of them, most notably Pat Robertson and Jimmy Swaggart, also mix in selected fundamentalist forms of faith, revival, activism in the world. Jerry Falwell and Jim Bakker, on the other hand, kept the fundamentalist and Pentecostal forms separate and, more than any of the TV preachers, exaggerated their distinguishing features—Falwell is Mr. Modern Fundamentalism, and Bakker is Mr. Postmodern Pentecostalism.[3]

JERRY FALWELL'S EMPIRE

Jerry Falwell's world in Lynchburg, Virginia, is a very serious, solid, industrious kind of place. The language, architecture, ceremonies, and rites of daily life of Thomas Road Baptist Church communicate its singular commitment to "reach out to a world of lost and dying men and to win their souls to Christ." What distinguished Falwell from his fellow fundamentalists from the beginning was his superhuman entrepreneurial zeal. Falwell, who comes from a family of small businessmen, got into the business of producing Christians on a whale of a scale. In 1971, Elmer Towns, Falwell's top theologian and "church-growth scientist," paraphrased Falwell's strategy in this way:

> Falwell pointed out that big shopping centers, big corporations, and big business have provided jobs and prosperity for our nation. . . . Business is usually on the cutting edge of innovation and change because of its quest for finances. . . . Therefore the church would be wise to look at business for a prediction of future innovation. The greatest innovation in the last 20 years is the development of the giant shopping centers. . . . A combination of services . . . two large companies with small supporting stores has been the secret of the success of shopping centers. The Thomas Road Baptist Church believes that the combined ministries of several agencies in one church can not only attract the masses to the gospel, but can better minister to each individual who comes.[4]

During the 1960s and 1970s, Thomas Road added one ministry after another; Falwell's church grew and grew. He built a 5000 seat sanctuary, a school, college and university. He turned his regional media ministry into a national enterprise with a following in the multimillions, and gradually, beginning in 1976, he came to distinguish himself as the leader of the movement organized by born-again TV empires and churches that plunged their constituents into the national political arena during the 1980 Presidential campaign and carried out what I have called the revolt of the fundamentalist other.

Like everything else, Jerry Falwell took TV literally. He used it to broadcast his church services exactly as they were performed. Later, he upscaled the services somewhat with light pop gospel tunes and select Christian celebrity singers, but he never really formatted his shows for TV; he never used TV to generate its own realities. Likewise, although his message opened up to more "current events" and "moral issues," it never strayed too far from its fundamentalist gospel core. Above all, Falwell used TV to spread the Word, the linear story of Christ's death, burial and resurrection, which offered irreversible transformation to all who would accept it. Ignoring TV's built-in preference for visually dramatic performance, Falwell seemed to be all story and no spectacle.

Through it all, Jerry Falwell and his fundamentalist allies were engaged in the business of making a distinct Christian conservative middle class counterculture and using higher education, the national news and national politics to chip away at the cultural hegemony of its opposite number, the alleged secular, liberal middle class. This was very serious business. Jerry Falwell, his empire and his allies stand for production, hard work, restraint, sacrifice, delayed gratification, steady growth, contained crises, hierarchy, male dominance, sexual repression, obedience to Godly others, the word, narrative structure and authority, fixed identity, place, authenticity, depth and centeredness.

JIM AND TAMMY FAYE BAKKER'S EMPIRE

Meanwhile, another entrepreneurial movement was emerging in Pentecostal Christendom during the 1950s, 1960s and 1970s, one that turned all those serious fundamental terms upside down. This movement, drawing from somewhat lower class factions than Falwell's movement, reached its apogee in Jim and Tammy Faye Bakker's Heritage USA, a kind of postmodern Pentecostal mecca. Their "inspirational theme park" conspicuously celebrated consumption, play, excess, indulgence, immediate gratification, wild swings of growth and crisis, anti-hierarchy, feminization, polymorphous sexuality, the godly powers of ordinary men and women, visual images, spectacle and narrative fragmentation, disposable identities, movement, artifice, surfaces, and decenteredness.

The cultural and theological reversals at Heritage USA were not accidental. The significant "cultural other" against which prosperity pentecostals fashioned their discourse and practice was not "the world" defined by the liberal, secular middle class, but the world defined by fundamentalism. The early healing evangelists of the 1940s and 1950s had themselves worked against the grain of the more fundamental voices of Pentecostal church pastors, but in the late 1970s, Jim and Tammy Faye Bakker set out to build a little world in the image of their version of the "positive gospel." Jim Bakker liked to compare his kingdom to the camp meetings of his youth, and the $100 book promoting Heritage USA describes its origins in this way:

During boyhood summers in Michigan, Jim Bakker attended campmeetings where he had his most moving spiritual experiences in an old tabernacle with a sawdust floor. Even then, looking beyond the stuffy cabins with lumpy mattresses, looking beyond the muddy swimming holes and "outdoor plumbing" he dreamed of a day when God's people could come together in beautiful, pleasant surroundings. Aware that lifestyle was changing in 20th Century America, Jim knew that drab, outmoded campgrounds would no longer appeal to Christians. . . . God impressed on Jim . . . the need to carry the spirit of the campmeeting movement into the 21st Century, and the concept of Heritage USA came into being.[5]

And so, in Fort Mills, South Carolina, Heritage USA was built, a place, a language and a practice that performed a ceaseless if implicit critique of fundamentalism's restraint, its sacrificial logic, its obsession with authority, hierarchy and rules. Heritage USA was an ensemble of replicas, relics, facades, imitations, simulations, props and sets drawn from Biblical Jerusalem, the Old West, small-town America, Hollywood, modern suburbs and tourist resorts. Nothing was simply itself; everything was palpably a production, a reproduction, or a performance.

Just inside the entrance to Heritage USA, you could visit Billy Graham's "actual" boyhood home. In the study, on the wall, a series of photographs depict Billy's home being dismantled, brick by brick, and rebuilt on the edge of Heritage USA property, the displacement and appropriation of Graham's home having become part of its significance. Heritage's centerpiece was [an artificial] "water park" with a 3-story waterslide. Nearby was the Grand Hotel and Main Street shopping mall, a hodgepodge of pastel-colored Victorian and colonial surfaces, and down the road, past the water park, and the tennis courts, condos and campgrounds, healing and prayer were available 24 hours a day in the Upper Room, an "exact replica" of the building where Jesus and his disciples had their last supper, except that this one looked like a replica. Across the road was another self-proclaiming replica, an "ancient amphitheater" where several nights a week the Passion Play was performed, complete with special effects, new characters (mainly, Satan incarnate), and new episodes, all intended to "heighten the dramatic tension" of Christ's final days.

Church services and camp meetings at Heritage were held in the TV studio and an adjacent auditorium which in no respect resembled a church. The Bakkers never used TV to represent the traditional rituals; instead, their TV realities, including their TV personalities, broke through the screen and expanded in the empirical world. The accent was always on performance, visuals, excess, spectacle, not on words, or the Word, at least not as fundamentalists understood the Word. The linear, irreversibly life-changing story of Christ's death, burial and resurrection, of suffering and of sacrifice, gave way to a cornucopia of miracle stories of God's healing, restoration, infinite love and bountiful gifts.

From the beginning, Heritage troubled many Christians who noticed the internal counter-cultural message—its suppression of sacrifice theology—but few guessed how far the Bakkers had gone in the direction of antinomian heresy, of rejecting all earthly restraints. At the time of their demise, the Bakkers not only promised their partners material abundance and well-being, but were refining a gospel of infinite forgiveness, a folk theology that seemed almost to sanction sinning by guaranteeing God's perpetual forgiveness in advance.

It is not so surprising then that the two discursive traditions represented by Falwell and [the] Bakkers' televangelical empires cast the born-again scandals in dramatically different terms. The fact that this conflict assumed center stage in the PTL crisis, however, virtually undermined the possibility that the voice of the third discursive tradition weighing into the fray, that of secular modernity, would ever get a solid grip on the telescandals.

THE PTL TELESCANDALS

The PTL scandals of 1987 and 1988 spread two grand dramas across [U.S.] TV screens. One [was] composed of the sensational misdeeds of Jim and Tammy Faye Bakker—his night with Jessica Hahn, her blackmailing him, more sexual improprieties, gross financial misconduct, tax fraud, bankruptcy, million dollar spending sprees, and so on. The other drama was born when Jerry Falwell's friendly takeover of PTL turned into a hostile one and launched a gaudy series of media skirmishes (known as the "Holy War") between the two professed Christian camps during which Falwell's forces and the press successively revealed, and endlessly reiterated, interrogated and dissected the Bakkers' misdeeds before a national audience.

Roland Barthes might have said the PTL scandal was a boxing match that kept dissolving into a TV wrestling match. An orderly bout, based on the demonstration of excellence and directed, like a story, toward an outcome (the definitive downfall of the Bakkers), kept evolving into a more chaotic bout in which each moment was immediately intelligible as spectacle and the most natural outcome was baroque confusion. As Barthes put it, "Some fights, among the most successful kind, are crowned by a final charivari, a sort of unrestrained fantasia where the rules, the laws of the genre, the referee's censuring and the limits of the ring are abolished, swept away by a triumphant disorder which overflows into the hall and carries off pell-mell wrestlers, seconds, referee and spectators."[6]

Perhaps the essence of spectacle is the loss of a unitary authorial point of view, a proliferation of points of view such that stories pile up fantastically, realities clash and mingle indiscriminately, and the total effect of everyone vying for narrative control is an irrepressible sense of events-out-of-control, of confusion, disorder, and a constant instablity of genres, borders, roles, rules. The disordering forces at work in the PTL telescandal that kept it from settling into a singular storied tradition were: First, the unholy and profoundly unstable authorial alliance between the fundamentalist and journalistic points of view; second, the spectacularizing desires of the narrators themselves—their allusory excesses, feuds and histrionics; third, the . . . anarchic words and deeds of the scandalizers; and fourth, a fistful of competing sideshows, of secular scandals grabbing for public attention. Such forces spectacularize—in this instance, specifically disrupting efforts to narrate the scandals from a "modern" point of view—by destabilizing the boundary between fundamentalist and modern, by foregrounding the processes of fabrication (fabulation), and by constantly juxtaposing contradictory points of view.

Take, for example, the profusion of allusions. In measured doses, literary and historical allusions help "make sense" of events by suggesting narrative frames that, in effect, interpret characters, plots, subplots, motives, climaxes, tragic flaws and moral meanings. In excess, they produce "a sort of unrestrained fantasia." During the PTL crisis, the Bakkers, for their part, were figured, among others, as Elmer Gantry, the Marcoses, Adam and Eve, David and Bathsheba, Ivan Boesky, Catholics buying and selling indulgences, and Gary Hart. Falwell, meanwhile, was figured (usually, he figured himself) as, among others, Protestant Reformers, Lee Iaacoca, Nathan, the SEC, God in the Garden after the Fall, and Christ cleaning out the moneychangers. The scandal as a whole was compared to [the novel] The Scarlet Letter, the sinking of the Titanic, the Book of Revelation, [the television program] Dynasty, and the war between Iran and Iraq. Such hyperfiguration spectacularized by calling attention to the narrative process, to the narrators as "telling stories" and therefore "having a point of view," which helped break whatever spell of "truth" they might have cast.

The major narrators also kept bringing each other into focus as narrators by calling attention to their "motives," "interests," and "biases." Journalists made several attempts to "unmask" Jerry Falwell, to find evidence of his plotting to take over PTL, and constantly speculated about his "real motives" (for example, he wanted to appropriate the PTL TV network, or the PTL audience, or simply the free prime time exposure). Falwell, of course, argued back that, at least when reporters turned on him, they were displaying their "secular liberal bias." In the process, the press lost some of its pretense of standing outside the fray, detached, disinterested, objective, reporting events. At the same time, Falwell's pose as a selfless man of God was compromised.

Nor were the press and Falwell above all histrionics. Ted Koppel and his Nightline crew orchestrated the most frenetically embroiling episode of the telescandals, a three-night series of shows in late May of 1987. The series opened with a full, heated, but indecisive, airing of the charges against Falwell. The second show was the first live interview with Jim and Tammy Faye Bakker since the scandal broke, and it was pure spectacle. Twenty-three million people watched the Bakkers be themselves, with a touch of remorse and lots of "love." The series concluded, inconclusively, with a "prognosis" on televangelism featuring, of all people, Jerry Falwell.

Falwell produced his own fireworks on the morning of the third day of the Nightline series by calling a press conference to display evidence that the Bakkers were not truly repentent. He waved a letter from the Bakkers asking

Jerry Falwell takes the plunge down Heritage Island's Typhoon waterslide.
Photo courtesy Lynn Hey.

for money, homes, cars, benefits, guards and a full-time maid, and he told a new version of that night in the Clearwater motel, exactly what Jim and his confederates, John Wesley Fletcher and an unnamed "third man," did to Jessica. As performances go, it was still rather rhetorical, but nonetheless stunning—spectacular in a way—to hear the sordid details spill from Falwell's lips. [Bakker's] role as chief of Heritage USA also inspired some performances from the usually stiff Falwell, reaching a peak when [Falwell] finally, on September 10, 1987, slid down Heritage Island's 3-story Typhoon waterslide. After posing with (a person dressed up as) "Allie the Alligator" atop the slide, Falwell "took the plunge," arms crossed at his chest and dressed in a business suit, looking [as though he were] about to be baptized . . . or buried.

The scandalizers—those about whom the narrators narrated—were another spectacularizing force, as they kept resisting and disrupting narrative frames, characterizations, plottings and climatic moments. After every barrage of charges leveled [at] the Bakkers, they were still standing when the smoke cleared, smiling and chatting about God's love and forgiveness. They refused to be shamed into oblivion, escaped narrative grips and talked back, irrepressibly, from their own point of view. They would not simply die and go away. Indeed, lingering in the wings is a potential narrative frame, which if only they could slip it into place, would produce the greatest of all spectacles. If only Jim and Tammy Faye could fashion themselves as innocent victims, slain by the forces of evil . . . they might rise again.

Finally, compounding the sense of spectacle was a backdrop of secular telescandals (Irangate, the Hart affair, the Marine spy case, Ivan Boesky, Wall Street drug raids), a whole host of lesser televangelists, hungry, waiting for the titans to fall, and the unshakable sense that we, the audiences, were inside the telescandal too—that it had caught us up, variously, and put us down somewhere else, changed imperceptibly perhaps—that just possibly, for instance, the line between the modern and the archetype of premodernity, the fundamentalist, moved in some way that made us all "different."

Of course, the story is not over. The spectacularizing forces of the telescandals did not abolish the myth of modernity; confused and confounded it, yes, but modern subjectivity actually "needs" . . . an occasional feast of fundamentalists, for it emerges out of the contradictory processes of internalizing and expelling fundamentalist otherness. Just as surely as Ted Koppel orchestrated "The Billion Dollar Pie" as a spectacle in which his "hogs at the trough" thesis was lost in a cascading melee of excited criticism, proof texting and posturing, he also in the end did his best to pull his modern point of view out of the fire.

Once again let me illustrate what I mean: Koppel's evening in the Memphis church concluded with thousands of people standing up and cheering Jerry Falwell's assertion, "I do believe the Bible is the infallible Word of God." This moment, of course, bore no apparent relationship to the scandals or to televangelism; as a biting retort to a hostile question from a fellow Baptist in the audience, it further fractured the fundamentalist whole; the sight of thousands cheering the literal Bible was spectacular from any point of view; and insofar as it was "great TV," it confirmed Falwell's innuendo that Koppel was also a hog at the trough. But it was also the moment which, from the modern point of view, most categorically distinguished Koppel from Falwell, Koppel's otherwise disconcertingly cool, reasonable and remarkably well regarded co-author during the telescandals, by stigmatizing Falwell as an unrepentent Biblical literalist.

AUDIENCE MEMBER: I have heard at least five of you on the tube, and when I hear you, you've got all the answers. I'm surprised and amazed at your humility. You know exactly how we're supposed to understand the Bible, you won't consider any other view, you know exactly who's going to be saved and who's not going to be saved. I believe that at least you, Mr. Falwell, and Mr. Robison [both are Baptist preachers] believe that the Bible is the totally inspired word of God, without any admixture of any kind of error. Genesis 17:7 and 8 says that God made an eternal covenant with Israel. Eternal covenant. And yet it is my understanding that both you gentlemen somehow must think he has abrogated this covenant, because you think it is your Christian duty to convert Jews. I believe there's a contradiction in this, and I'd like you to explain it.

REV. FALWELL: All right. First of all, let me ask you this. Which Baptist church are you a member of?

AUDIENCE MEMBER: Prescott Memorial. (Laughter and some boos.)

KOPPEL: Wait, does that have some meaning?

AUDIENCE MEMBER: What difference does that make?

KOPPEL: Does that have some meaning? Well, I'm not sure I'd like to know. Does it make any difference?

REV. FALWELL: Well, most Baptists believe in the inerrancy of the Bible. Do you?

AUDIENCE MEMBER: No, I don't.

REV. FALWELL: All right. Fine. I just wanted to know where you were. Now, the fact is I do believe the Bible is the infallible word of God. I do—

(Over half the audience, the choir, the arrayed preachers, stand up, applaud, cheer and shout "Amen.")

AUDIENCE MEMBER: May I respond? May I respond to that?

REV. FALWELL: You've had your time; be quiet for a moment.

AUDIENCE MEMBER: The ovation means they agree with you; that doesn't necessarily mean you're right.

REV. FALWELL: Hush! Let me tell you something. Now, the Bible—because we do believe the Bible is the inerrant word of God, and because that Bible says Jesus is the way, the truth, the life, and no man cometh under the Father but by me, Jesus doing the talking, I don't have a plan of salvation, God does, and I believe that Jews, gentiles, Moslems, blacks, white, rich, poor, all come the same way, through the death burial, resurrection of Christ, whom we learn about in an inerrant Bible.

Shortly [after this], Koppel said goodnight to his church guests, and then tacked on a clip for his TV audience that would be his last grasp at the modernity narrative, by way of pastor John Sherfey, a "really real" premodern preacher in a little Virginia church whom Koppel had introduced in his opening collage. With a country gospel tune in the background, we pan in on Sherfey's church from above and find ourselves sitting in the pews with Ted and John, dressed in flannel shirts and looking a little like distant cousins.

SINGER: Oh, I love to walk with Jesus like the publicans of old / When he gathered them about him and the blessed tidings told.

KOPPEL: John, I want to end where we began, right here in the pews of your church. Is there a lesson in all this that you can draw for us?

REV. SHERFEY: Yes, I think so. I think a lot of times, Ted, what I tell my people here is, don't get their eyes fastened on man. Look to God. Because man'll let you down. Of course, I do want to be a pattern, as I go in and out of this church. As I go up and down these rows, as I walk the streets of Stanley, wherever I'm at. I want to live so that I'd be a pattern for them to follow. But I still don't want them to get their eyes fastened on me, and take them off Jesus. See. Set your mind and your fixings on things above, and not on this earth.

(Short clip of Rev. Sherfey shaking hands of his people as they leave church and saying, "Bless you, Brother, and praise the Lord.")

SINGER: I will follow / All the way, Lord / I will follow Jesus all the way / Oh I love to walk with Jesus like the man of long ago—

A touching scene, and a bit of a spectacle—Koppel and his TV crew in a little church in the hills of Virginia, concocting the image of a "good preacher" (read pre-entrepreneurial, prepolitical, premodern, prepostmodern) who told us the lesson of all this is that we must keep our eyes on God, not man. But visually, musically and idiomatically, Koppel had nonetheless reconstituted the quaint premodern fundamental other and rather unceremoniously dumped him into the Southern countryside where we may presume Koppel is telling us such folk belong.

Of course, Koppel and his co-reporters are not working alone to save the modern point of view. The meeting of the Society for the Scientific Study of Religion in November, 1988, was bristling with papers tinkering away at theories of modernity, trying to patch up the holes the fundamentalists had run through. And the MacArthur Foundation has recently awarded millions of dollars to projects which would restore and globalize the binary opposition between "fundamentalism" and "modernity" and reconfirm upon the latter a studied, if ruffled, moral superiority.

Much money and many raconteurs can do wonders, but it seems doubtful that the secularizing version of the story of modernity can ever be put back together again. That version proposes that, when we look upon the TV preachers and their electronic escapades, we see figures and scenes from the past. In fact, it may make more sense to say we are gazing into the future.

In retrospect, Jack Sims provided the perfect prefatory fable to the Koppel show. With respect to the fate of the big TV preachers, he may or may not have accurately fabulated "reality," but his language, the manner of his fabulation, was indubitably precise. His wild imagery vividly conveyed the exquisite unexpectedness and improbability of the characters and events that composed the telescandals. Aging evangelical electronic dinosaurs, crawling onto an iceberg, fighting tooth and nail, as the iceberg floats south, melting, to the inevitable doom of all. The tale speaks ending, but the language, its cyborg creatures and mixed metaphors and mythic time and space, speaks beginning . . . the opening up of a new world composed of preposterous categorical hodgepodges and antic crisscrossings of social boundaries. Religious mingles with secular, churches become businesses, Christ dispenses grace and miracles on TV, preachers call themselves CEOs and run for President, faith healers build ultramodern hospitals, AT&T hires New Age consultants and churches hire religious market analysts, creationists call themselves scientists, and scientists discover the ineffable. If something is ending, perhaps it is the world in which the things forming these zany amalgamations were kept apart, separated, in their place, properly ordered and moving progressively toward some end.

NOTES

An earlier version of this paper first appeared in 1988 as "The World of the Born-Again Telescandals."

1. *The Gallup Report*, 1982, 31–2. Gallup produced a stricter definition of "evangelicals" by calculating how many Americans met both criteria (born-again and Biblical literalist) and had ever witnessed or (encouraged someone to believe in) Christ. Seventeen percent (about 27 million adults) met all three criteria.

2. *Sojourner* magazine, for example, advocates liberal and even some relatively radical positions on issues of war and poverty. Billy Graham is viewed by most non-evangelicals as very conservative, but he has made some remarkably liberal proposals in recent years regarding disarmament, Soviet relations and world poverty; see his *Approaching Hoofbeats*. Nor do all orthodox Christians even agree that abortion and homosexuality are immoral. James Davidson Hunter, *Evangelicalism: The Coming Generation*, documents the range of evangelical political and moral views.

3. Falwell does not "typify" fundamentalism, nor the Bakkers Pentecostalism. Rather, their communities have exaggerated certain features of the cultural trappings of their religious traditions in ways that seem to parallel the dialectic between modern and postmodern cultural forms in secular architecture, literature and popular culture.

4. Towns and Falwell, *Church Aflame*, pp. 40–41.

5. Bakker and Bakker, *Heritage Village Church*, p. 91.

6. Barthes, *Mythologies*, p. 23.

BIBLIOGRAPHY

Bakker, Jim and Tammy Faye Bakker. *Heritage Village Church: The Story of People That Love*. Toronto: Boulton Publishing Services. 1986.

Barthes, Roland. *Mythologies*. New York: Hill and Wang. 1972.

"The Billion Dollar Pie," Ted Koppel Special Report, aired May 12, 1988.

The Gallup Report, "Religion in America," Report Nos. 201–202. June–July, 1982.

Graham, Billy. *Approaching Hoofbeats: The Four Horsemen of the Apocalypse*. Waco, Texas: Word Books. 1983.

Harrell, David Edward, Jr. All Things Are Possible: *The Healing and Charismatic Revivals in Modern America*. Bloomington: Indiana University Press. 1975.

———. *Oral Roberts: An American Life*. San Francisco: Harper & Row. 1985.

Hunter, James Davidson. *Evangelicalism: The Coming Generation*. Chicago: University of Chicago Press. 1987.

Lash, Scott and John Urry. *The End of Organized Capitalism*. Cambridge: Polity Press. 1987.

Marsden, George M. *Fundamentalism and American Culture: The Shaping of Twentieth-Century Evangelicalism, 1870–1925*. New York: Oxford University Press. 1980.

———. *Reforming Fundamentalism: Fuller Seminary and the New Evangelicalism*. Grand Rapids: William B. Eerdmans Publishing Company. 1987.

Towns, Elmer and Jerry Falwell. *Church Aflame*. Nashville: Impact Books. 1971.

Secrets of Success in Postmodern Society

ELIZABETH G. TRAUBE

One could argue that . . . films bear an intricate and woefully
unanalyzed relationship to their society.
—I. C. Jarvie, *Seeing through Movies*

FROM THE Gilded Age on, the American fiction of the self-made man or success hero has been used to reformulate an older republican dream of individual freedom in the context of an increasingly organized, consumption-oriented, corporate capitalist society. My concern in this article is with one such
reformulation. From an analysis of four unabashedly minor Hollywood films,
I will abstract a certain ideological pattern that came into circulation during
the Reagan era.

The films were released between 1984 and 1987, at the height of that era.
They are: *All the Right Moves* (1984), starring Tom Cruise; *Ferris Buehler's
Day Off* (1986; subsequently referred to as *Ferris Buehler*), starring Matthew
Broderick; *Nothing in Common* (1986), starring Tom Hanks and Jackie Gleason; and *The Secret of My Success* (1987; subsequently referred to as *Secret*),
starring Michael J. Fox. These films form a cycle, defined by overlapping
similarities in story, theme, and locale. All four are concerned with individual
mobility and success, as achieved in high school *(All the Right Moves, Ferris
Buehler)* or in the corporate workplace *(Nothing in Common, Secret)*. At a
more abstract level, all have plot structures based on an opposition between
youth and age, to which other oppositions are made to correspond as the plots
unfold.

With the exception of *Nothing in Common*, the films star teen idols and
were intended for today's biggest ticket-buyers, the 12- to 19-year-old movie
audience. Hanks, whose main appeal is to young adults, resembles Cruise,
Broderick, and Fox in an important respect. He and the younger stars specialize in conveying a cool, breezy, highly verbal, yet distinctly boyish style of
rebellious independence.[1] In *All the Right Moves*, however, Cruise is cast
against this type. The film was a box office flop. By contrast, both *Nothing in
Common* and *Secret* did moderately well in their respective seasons, and *Ferris Buehler*, with its ultra-ironist hero, was the smash hit of the summer of
1986.

In this article I try to contextualize the relative box office popularity of cinematic images of success. My thesis, in brief, is that a fantasy embedded in the commercially successful success stories in my cycle appeals primarily to the young corporate employees of today and tomorrow. In short, I interpret the films as part of the making of the new middle classes.

Before I develop this thesis, its theoretical foundations require definition. An anthropology of commercial film or other mass-mediated forms of culture must be adjusted to the particular conditions of cultural production in modern capitalist society. In a system where many forms of culture are produced as commodities by the few for the many, the relationship of cultural forms to collective experience is singularly complex. What, if anything, connects the implicit meanings that mass cultural forms may embody to the lived culture of receiving audiences? Assuming there is a connection, what is its nature and how is it established? Do the patterns of significance in mass cultural texts that analysis may uncover originate in the imaginative needs of "audience subcultures" (Gans 1974), as a neo-Durkheimian reflectionist theory of mass culture would have it? Or is the content of mass culture entirely determined by its elite producers, the corporate owners and media professionals who control what manipulationist theory knows as the "culture industry" (Horkheimer and Adorno 1972)?

In a lucid article on theories of modern culture, Richard Johnson (1986–87) argues that what requires study is a total process, a circuit of production, circulation, and consumption of cultural forms. But existing theories, he suggests, express only particular moments or stages of the process. He asks,

> What if they are all true, but only as far as they go, true for those parts of the process which they have most clearly in view? What if they are all false or incomplete, liable to mislead, in that they are only partial, and therefore cannot grasp the process as a whole? What if attempts to "stretch" this competence (without modifying the theory) lead to really gross and dangerous (ideological?) conclusions? (1986–87:45–46)

Reflectionist theory takes the viewpoint of the receiving audience, whose broadly shared values supposedly find expression in what these theorists tend to call "popular" culture. Among the limits of this viewpoint is its neglect of the culture industry, and a resultant tendency to misrepresent the process of production as governed exclusively by market forces, or, as the saying goes, as "giving the audience what it wants." But audience preferences are only one of many factors that influence production decisions. Producers also shape their works to conform to dominant sensibilities and values, including those of the producing community itself. Indeed, as Richard Slotkin notes (1984:412), among the most important audiences in film production is the "audience of fellow producers."

Moreover, the preferences of the mass audience can only influence production insofar as they are known, and the culture industry's favored instruments of knowledge (market research techniques, ideas about public opinion circulating in the mass media) are notoriously unreliable (Gitlin 1983). Film audiences, in particular, went singularly underresearched for many years, perhaps, I. C. Jarvie suggests (1970:108), because a complacent film industry had grown accustomed to a seller's market.

Thus, producers respond to an obscurely informed interpretation of audience needs, "a myth," as Slotkin calls it (1984:412) "about who the audience is and what it wants." As part of the raw material for cultural production, such a "myth of the audience" is eventually incorporated into cultural products and returned to consumers. What returns along this circuit is not a reflection but a highly selective version of collective sentiment, the culture industry's ideologically structured image of popular desires and fears. Active mass participation in the circuit begins at this point, with the reception of cultural goods by social groups. Once again to cite Slotkin (1984:413), "The mass audience does not make what it sees, but receives and reacts to what is produced by others."

Manipulationist views of mass culture as indoctrination never lose sight of the industry's activities. They are limited, however, by what Johnson calls "productivism" (1986–87:55), a tendency to reduce the process of reception to that of production. The unwarranted assumption here is that whatever messages mass-media elites put into their texts are automatically realized in the consciousness of the receiving "masses." Reception, in this account, is no more than the passive, uncontextualized assimilation of ruling ideas by subordinate classes.

Ironically, in neglecting to account for how mass cultural forms are subjectively interpreted and situationally used, the older manipulation theory is unable to explain the power that it attributes to cultural forms (Ohmann 1981). For if audiences could not *re*-cognize their ideals, beliefs, desires, or fears among the images circulated by the culture industry, why would they find those images compelling? The manufactured consent that neo-Gramscians call hegemony, ideological domination, is manufactured from the debris of common sense and recycled in a never-ending array of mass-mediated versions of the world (Hall 1982). For a given version to penetrate everyday thought and practice and so perform its hegemonic function, audiences must be able to relate it to their socially conditioned imaginative needs.

At this critical conjunction between the textualized goods of the culture industry and the private, everyday lives of their consumers, at least two modes of analysis would ideally converge. We need both systematic analyses of texts and cultural accounts of text-reception, studies of the structural properties of mass cultural forms and ethnographies of their social uses. Such a Janus-faced study would explore the interactions between the public production of culture and cultural creativity in everyday life.

Janice Radway's work on romances and their readers (1984) is an important contribution to this project. Radway begins with the social situation of actual readers and incorporates their insights into a highly original analysis of the narrative texts. But the passage may also be made in the other direction, from narrative texts to their readers. An ethnographer who took this latter route could search for correspondences between patterns embodied in mass cultural narratives and the more loosely structured stories that people tell about their lives, their narrative constructions of personal and collective identity. In the process, of course, the ethnographer would probably come to revise the original textual analysis. On the other hand, I suspect that preunderstandings of mass entertainment culture would help to elucidate the fictions through which people live their lives.[2]

Although the analysis that follows focuses on films as texts and not on actual processes of production and reception, it is informed by the model of the cultural circuit. Its framing questions are: what brings particular story forms into circulation and makes them compelling to audiences at certain moments, and what potential implications does their hegemonic status have for social relations? To answer these questions fully would require different forms of inquiry, supplementary studies of producing and receiving communities. But the assumption common to the present study and to those I have yet to undertake is that the answers lie outside of texts themselves, in their social and historical conditions of production and use.

Vicissitudes of the Success Hero

The idea of the self-made man has done yeoman and postyeoman service in American culture. From Benjamin Franklin to presidential candidate Michael Dukakis's immigrant father, tokens of the type are celebrated as incarnations of the American dream, the dream of an open, mobile society where individuals rise through talent and achievement. Conversely, the disappearance of the self-made man is a recurrent theme in 20th-century literature, used to signify the negation of the dream.

Whatever his fate in social reality (where his presence has been greatly exaggerated), it is unlikely that the self-made man will disappear as an ideological figure. For success ideology has never been static, as its historians have demonstrated (Cawelti 1965; Wyllie 1954). It has existed in multiple versions, and these have changed over time, registering and responding to historically engendered cultural tensions.

In all its versions, success ideology has appealed primarily to the middle classes. Thus, its history is embedded in the massive transformation of the American middle classes that began in the Gilded Age. Between 1870 and 1940, the development of corporate capitalism led to the displacement of the older propertied, entrepreneurial middle classes by the new salaried middle classes of white-collar employees. These latter have steadily expanded with the proliferation of the large organizations on which they depend.

The making of the new middle classes was a cultural as well as an institutional process. In its cultural dimension, it involved a partial rejection of inherited ideas and values. What has unfolded over the last hundred years has been represented as a clash of cultures, a conflict, in Warren Sussman's expressive if slightly overcondensed phrase, between "an older culture, often loosely labeled Puritan-republican, producer-capitalist culture, and a newly emerging culture of abundance" (1984:xx).

Although the crucial battles were not fought until the 1920s and 1930s, the conflict took shape in the Gilded Age. According to inherited middle-class morality, success depended on the disciplinary virtues of the Protestant ethic, industry, thrift, sobriety, self-restraint, and was of less importance than the "character-building" effects of work itself. Success manuals and dime novelists such as Horatio Alger did their best to perpetuate this tradition under new conditions. But, as American industry grew ever larger and more concentrated in the three decades after the Civil War, its very productivity weakened the Protestant ethic.

Under this pressure, Alan Trachtenberg observes (1982:81), the image of success "accumulated its ambiguities." Successful businessmen who claimed status as traditional self-made men contributed to a secularized ethic of entrepreneurial success. For however attractive the image of the sober, industrious Businessman Hero might have been to new economic elites in pursuit of legitimacy, it failed to exhaust popular attitudes toward the business world. What more and more impressed the public was the aggressive competitiveness of the robber barons, as well as the material wealth such men enjoyed. These attitudes are refracted in another traditional success hero popularized in humorous literature, a shrewd, enterprising, upwardly mobile rogue, who succeeds by cunning and trickery, and who is more concerned with material success than with self-improvement (Cawelti 1965:63–73).

Industrious workers and materialistic men on the make have one thing in common. Both types of success hero are radical individualists; they transform themselves and their social situation through personal initiative. In their spirit of independence and self-reliance, success heroes exhibit their kinship with the frontiersman, that archetypal individualist of American myth, whose self-transformation takes the form of mastering the savage in the name of civilization (Slotkin 1986:86–87). While big business has often sought to exploit the affinity and represent the entrepreneur as the preserver of frontier individualism, critics of the new corporate society have used the same frontier imagery to attack it (Sussman 1984:32).

For incorporation in its early stages engendered what Alan Trachtenberg calls a "cultural paradox" (1982:84), a tension between individualism and organization that has persisted into the present. The tension bears most heavily upon the new white-collar middle classes, whose common characteristic is their dependence on bureaucratic organizations.

With the proliferation of bureaucracies in business, government, and the professions, the organization of work underwent a radical transformation that C. Wright Mills (1953) named the "managerial demiurge." Mills isolated the centralization of knowledge and of control over labor processes as a fundamental feature of the white-collar world. The development of modern management entailed the appropriation of individual initiative and skills—what Harry Braverman (1974) called the separation of conception from execution. From this process, which reduces much of white-collar work to a form of manual labor, follows the increasingly hierarchical organization of the white-collar world. At the bottom are the deskilled white-collar masses of office workers and service personnel. Above them are the hierarchically ranked managers and professionals who comprise a new professional-managerial class (PMC).[3] Between managed and managers, a widening gap intervenes, maintained in part through the substitution of educational certification for practical experience as the means of mobility (Lash and Urry 1987:73–74).

Within the ranks of the PMC, bureaucratization also affects criteria for advancement. In bureaucratic organizations such as large corporations, work is a necessary but not sufficient condition for promotion up the managerial hierarchy, a theme that success manuals and middle-class magazines began to articulate soon after the turn of the century. Thus, image or appearance became a central concern of the new success literature, displacing the entrepreneurial values of self-reliance, effort, and achievement. Increasingly, young men were advised to develop self-confidence, willpower, magnetism, charm, qualities designed to attract, please, and impress other people. These virtues are condensed in what became an obsession of the new middle classes, the widely circulated concept of "personality," as opposed to "character" (Sussman 1984:274–284).

Two tendencies of modern life intertwine in the preoccupation with personality. On the one hand, personality has been represented and received as a strategy for success in the corporate workplace, a key feature of what sociologists call the "bureaucratic ethic." Since the 1950s, sociologists have generally agreed that corporate life was eroding the entrepreneurial ethic. They have differed, however, with regard to the content of the new elite and of the "structure of feeling" typical of the professional-managerial class.

With the partial exception of Mills, sociologists in the 1950s singled out the bureaucratic emphasis on adjustment, harmony, and deference, as an index of the "other-directedness" of the PMC. In this view, articulated by David Riesman (1950) and developed by William Whyte (1956), organizational life promoted cooperation and conformism at the expense of individualism and self-reliance. The new managerial type, his critics argued, was an overintegrated, compulsive team player, the faceless Organization Man whom the culture industry has more often vilified than heroized.

In the 1970s, however, academics shifted the terms of the attack. Individualism, they argued, was not disappearing among the PMC but assuming a degraded form. Thus Daniel Bell (1976) held the consumerist values of late capitalism responsible for a new "hedonism," while Christopher Lasch (1979) detected a rising "narcissism," which he attributed to the interplay of consumerism and bureaucratic dependence.

Whereas Lasch offered a largely impressionistic account of the corporate workplace, sociologists of the professional-managerial class have pursued a more empirically based mode of analysis (see Bensman 1967; Bensman and Vidich 1971; Jackall 1983). In the process they have refined Mills's model of the "bureaucratic entrepreneur" (1950:118–146). Like Mills, they interpret "other-directedness" as a self-consciously adopted mask, a strategic style assumed in the corporate struggle for power. For in a world where achievement does not in itself confer success, what is essential is the ability to mask and dissimulate, to project the well-staged image at the well-timed moment. Self-control persists as a virtue, but it takes the form of self-manipulation, as in Mannheim's model of the "self-rationalized man" (Bensman and Vidich 1971:49–50; Jackall 1983:124–125). Here we seem to have at least one factor in the emergence of a "postmodern" self, a self who resides in the shifting surfaces of a carefully staged personality.

Viewed from another angle, however, personality is not something to control but to release. The notion of self implied here is not a set of instrumental masks but rather an end or goal, an essence to develop, cultivate, get in touch with, realize, and above all, fulfill. Like the idealized performing self of the bureaucratic ethic, the version of success as self-fulfillment has been primarily addressed to the new middle classes. Embodied in New Thought and an array of therapies of release, in the whole cult of leisure and relaxation that promises compensation for the degradation of work, the self-fulfillment ideal is fundamental to the consumption ethic of modern capitalism.[4] Its roots are in 19th-century self-culture and, more distantly, in Franklin and Jefferson's vision of a natural elite who would create a just society by realizing their personal talents. Since the turn of the century, however, the idea of success as personal fulfillment has been privatized and commodified.

What Elisabeth Long (1985:63–90) calls the "corporate suburban" pattern of success gives narrative expression to the modern ideal. Crystallizing in the 1950s, the pattern defined success as the product of a partial retreat from the world of work into a familial world of leisure. Its initiating work was the 1955 novel *The Man in the Grey Flannel Suit* (subsequently made into a movie starring Gregory Peck), in which the hero voluntarily limits his ambitions and trades career advancement for the emotional fulfillment of a rich family life.

William Whyte interpreted the novel as a legitimation of the bureaucratic ethic. Such fictions, he claimed in *The Organization Man*, work to reconcile the middle class to the limited opportunities for independence in corporate society. But as Long argues in her analysis of success literature, there is also an oppositional content. In its nostalgic, mystified way, the image of the home as a refuge from a competitive, masculine workplace does provide a vantage point for critical reflection on capitalist society.

Long goes on to argue that the quest for a univocal, monolithic middle-class consciousness is misdirected (1985:181). In other words, as in Todd Gitlin's recent rumination (1986:159–160), there may be no single structure of feeling out there in middle-class society. Instead, there would seem to be a number of interrelated currents, which the culture industry partially absorbs, packages, and returns to the public in various configurations. Let us turn now to certain images of success that were projected in the mid-1980s.

CAREER TRAINING

All the Right Moves is an old-fashioned success story, set in a Pennsylvania mill town. Its decent, honest, industrious boy hero, Steph (Tom Cruise), is the son of an equally decent, honest, industrious steelworker. Steph, the star of the high school football team, espouses an unromantic version of the mobility ideology. He sees sport as it sometimes appears to working-class students, as a means of admission to college. In Steph's carefully devised plan, his athletic abilities will bring him multiple football scholarships, from which he will select the one offered by the college with the best engineering program. His long-term goal is to convert manual ability into certification for a white-collar career.

The film contrasts Steph's rational, calculating drive toward self-improvement to the impulsive conduct of his best friend, Brian, who conforms to a Hollywood stereotype of the sensual but moral working-class youth. Brian winds up engaged to his pregnant girlfriend and obliged to forgo his scholarship for wage labor in the mill. In thus restricting his life chances, Brian performs the ideological function of the success hero's friend, which is to portray class difference as a product of differential individual abilities, characters, and choices.

But Steph is not the unique author of his destiny. He is well on the way to becoming a self-made man, in his own modest terms, when a brief lapse of self-control threatens to rob him of all that he has worked to achieve. Steph's fortunes are reversed by the very event that would have foreshadowed his anticipated mobility and brought the plot of a more romantic success story to a climax, the Big Game against an upper-middle-class high school. Situated halfway through the film, this Big Game is lost and initiates the hero's decline.

In the locker room after the game, Steph, who played tolerably well himself, protests against the coach's unjust abuse of a teammate. For this impulsive display of solidarity, Steph is dropped from the team. He then gives in to a less noble impulse and joins an angry crowd in defacing the coach's house. The coach sees him and retaliates by blackballing him among college admissions officers.

His once bright future abruptly blocked through the older man's enmity, Steph must enter the mill and resign himself to a life of manual labor. He is saved from this fate through the intervention of his girlfriend and the coach's wife. The women prevail upon the coach to put aside his anger, and when the coach's own hopes of mobility are fulfilled in the form of a position at Cal Poly Tech, he arranges to take Steph along. This happy news is conveyed to

Steph in the yard of the mill, the symbolic boundary between blue-collar and white-collar worlds.

If Cruise's earnest Steph is reminiscent of earlier days, Matthew Broderick's Ferris Buehler may well be the first thoroughly postmodern hero of a teen comedy, the 1986 hit film *Ferris Buehler's Day Off*. The film was directed by John Hughes, the impresario of the teen comedy genre, whose credits include *Sixteen Candles*, *The Breakfast Club*, and *Pretty in Pink*. But *Ferris Buehler* stands slightly apart from the rest of the Hughes oeuvre. Whereas teen comedies may be generically constrained to subvert or in some way question whatever versions of adult values they present, in *Ferris Buehler* the antiauthoritarian impulse is carried to an extreme, leaving no space for any form of reconciliation between the generations. *Ferris Buehler* also contrasts with other Hughes films in its intentionally open, fragmented story line, repeatedly interrupted by Ferris's asides to the audience. With its self-conscious, ironic attitude toward the events it narrates, the film reflects a tendency of contemporary mass culture to appropriate "high" cultural forms.

Ferris is an appropriate inhabitant of this postmodern narrative universe. He is a creature composed entirely of surfaces, the product of the multiple masks he assumes. When the film ends, we know little more about him than we did at the beginning, or rather, we know him only through his artful stagings of self.

The film's setting is a prosperous, upper-middle-class Chicago suburb, at the other end of the class spectrum from *All the Right Moves*. It is similar, however, to the setting of Cruise's earlier film, *Risky Business*, in which the teenage hero goes briefly into business as a pimp in order to pay for damage he has done to his father's car. By contrast, Ferris Buehler's project is not work but play; destruction of a paternal car is not the motivation but the resolution of the plot; and the entrepreneurial virtues displayed in *Risky Business* are replaced by skills of another sort. In the person of Ferris Buehler, Tom Sawyer meets late monopoly capitalism, and "play" constitutes training for success in a bureaucratized, corporatized, high-tech society.

The plot, such as it is, turns around Ferris's desire to play hooky from school, in the company of his best friend, Cameron, and his girlfriend, Sloane. In the first part of the film, Ferris overcomes a series of obstacles to his desire. First, he feigns illness to his oversolicitous parents; then he coerces the reluctant Cameron into joining him and persuades him to borrow his father's cherished Ferrari; lastly, he and Cameron execute an intricate scheme to get Sloane out of school. This last maneuver involves them in a contest of wits with Rooney, the persecutory, none too bright school principal. Rooney's dogged pursuit of Ferris throughout the film contrasts with the permissive style of Ferris's careerist parents. But he is not effective in controlling the truant, a computer whiz kid, who sets up a dense electronic screen of fake messages that anticipate and thwart Rooney's every move.

Rooney's avowed purpose is "to catch this kid and put a helluva dent in his future." Supposedly, what makes this particular exploit so risky is that it is Ferris's ninth sick day and, if caught, he will be held back for a year. In fact, however, that risk is eliminated early in the film, when Ferris breaks into the high school computer system and adjusts his absentee record, even as the outraged Rooney scans the monitor.[5] Such pleasure as the movie provides derives not from any suspenseful pursuit, but rather from the escalating demonstrations of Ferris's omnipotence, which guarantees that all interfering adults will be made fools of, at best, and utterly humiliated, at worst.

The middle segments of the film chronicle the stolen day of leisure. In the film's most outrageously narcissistic fantasy, Ferris becomes the central attraction in a German-American parade. Standing on a float, surrounded by buxom blondes in peasant blouses, he delivers a rendition of *Twist and Shout*, accompanied by a crowd of admiring blacks. Apparently, the blacks recognize the white boy's superior talent, a motif that is fast becoming a convention in the suburban-kids-in-the-city genre.[6]

The blacks are not alone in their admiration for Ferris. For reasons that the film never bothers to make clear, everyone adores him, with the partial exception of his resentful sister, Jean, and the ambivalent Cameron. Through Cameron, in particular, the film recognizes ambivalent feelings that its viewers may have toward Ferris. A middle-class Huck Finn, pressed into adventure by his bolder friend, Cameron's misgivings are compounded by doubts that viewers may well share regarding the authenticity of Ferris's friendship. Cameron's manifest singleness of purpose contrasts with Ferris's doubleness. Single-minded adults like Rooney are fair game for Ferris's trickery, but his manipulation of the loyal Cameron is potentially more disturbing. Nor is the tension alleviated when Ferris presents himself to the audience as a therapist-surrogate, who only compelled Cameron to take the Ferrari in order to help overcome his fear of his father. Ferris assumes this role only to deny it by confiding that he also loves to drive the Ferrari.

In teen comedies the destiny of a paternal car is fixed from the moment that a son borrows it. What is interesting is the way in which auto destruction operates in *Ferris Buehler*. When Cameron accidentally sends the driverless car over a cliff, Ferris is (almost) visibly distraught and offers to take the blame. Cameron refuses, claiming that if he hadn't wanted to provoke a confrontation with his father, he would never have taken the car at all. Thus Ferris's "diagnosis" becomes Cameron's psychological truth. Through Ferris's agency, Cameron is able to cast off his repressions and get in touch with the Oedipal anger that he had been directing against himself. For Cameron, the day amounts to a session of assertiveness therapy, whereas Jean learns the inverse lesson, appropriate to her gender, and comes to understand her anger toward her brother as a defense against her own sexuality.

I do not mean to dignify the film's psychologizing, but rather to underscore the asymmetric organization of emotional development. Only the lesser characters have inner feelings, which are supposedly elucidated through their transferential relationships to Ferris. If Ferris operates at one level as a therapist-surrogate, that role in turn symbolizes a condition of impenetrability, autonomy, and control, the celebrated "blankness" of pop postmodernism. To be the object and not the subject of transference; to know and never be known; to be needed and never to need; to manipulate the emotions of others without ever revealing an inner self; such is the condition of the success hero in this film.

Both *All the Right Moves* and *Ferris Buehler* derive from the boy hero tradition, which links the achievement of success to an opposition between youth and age. Since success ideology began to shift in the late 19th century, that tradition has been distributed between two poles. At one pole, ambitious, industrious youths achieve success as a reward for toil, self-denial, and obedience to authority. Clustered at the other pole is an ever-expanding assortment of more romantic, roguish heroes, boys who prefer play to work, who succeed through tricks or daring deeds, like the adult men-on-the-make of humorous literature, and who routinely subvert established conventions and repressive authority. Over the course of the 20th century, this latter type has come to predominate in success stories. Mark Twain, and not Horatio Alger, had sensed the direction of history.[7]

From the perspective of 1980s success stories as well as that of the larger boy hero tradition, *All the Right Moves* appears to have made all the wrong moves. Firstly, the film's vision of success seems overly modest in the light of a tendency to replace the scaled-down dreams of 1970s success stories with more extravagant fantasies. It might have sufficed for Rocky Balboa to "go the distance" in the first *Rocky* film, and for Tony Manero simply to *get* to Manhattan in *Saturday Night Fever*, but the 1980s sequels to these films have transformed Rocky into a world-class champion and Tony into a Broadway superstar. By contrast, college admission, although it was a satisfactory resolution to the film *Breaking Away*, may now seem as mundane to middle-class audiences as it does to Ferris.

But a more serious problem has to do with the *way* that success is achieved in *All the Right Moves*, specifically, with the hero's radical lack of autonomy. Steph's powerlessness contrasts most sharply with Ferris's omnipotence. It also distinguishes *All the Right Moves* from the moderately successful 1987 release, *Hoosiers*, a second-chance story with affinities to the early *Rocky* cycle. *Hoosiers* also deals with high school sports and mobility. Its youthful characters are undisciplined farm boys who must learn the traditional values of strenuous effort, loyalty, and unquestioning obedience to the coach (played by Gene Hackman). But that move is completed in the first part of the film; the remainder concentrates on a string of victories over increasingly difficult opponents, culminating with the primarily black team of an Indianapolis high school. Thus, submission to paternal authority empowers the boys, and the pleasure of the film derives from the vision of the underdog triumphant. As in the first *Rocky* films, moreover, albeit more subtly, an association of blacks with the superior social group plays upon white middle-class status anxieties and racist resentment.

All the Right Moves, in contrast, is a liberal film. Although it romanticizes the white, ethnic working-class world it depicts, Steph's desire to escape into the middle class is positively represented, and the liberal view of education as a path to social mobility is not called into question. Had Steph's lack of autonomy been attributed to structural conditions, the message of the film would have gravitated to the left. Instead, both the cause and the solution of his predicament is an insufficiently bureaucratized educational system that is overly susceptible to personal influence. Not social conditions but the emotionally motivated acts of individuals—Steph's impulsive defiance of authority, the coach's vengeance and subsequent repentance—are what determine success and failure. But in projecting this liberal image of a society open to talent, the film diminishes its boy hero, to a degree that audiences apparently found unacceptable. It is not the theme of patronage per se that is problematic (as we will see shortly), but the drastic restriction of Steph's ability to take control over his life. Even Alger's obedient heroes were rewarded for service freely rendered to powerful men, whereas Steph must passively await his benefactor's change of heart. In terms of the larger boy hero tradition, the film reverses the antiauthoritarian drift in 20th-century fictions. With its vision of limited opportunities and its almost willful refusal to gratify fantasies of individual empowerment, the film runs counter to a dominant ideological tendency in the Reagan era of optimism.

In contrast to the paternalistic resolution of *All the Right Moves, Ferris Buehler* projects a prolonged and exaggerated fantasy of total freedom from supraindividual authority. In humiliating Rooney, "killing" the paternal Ferrari, and resisting the pangs of conscience and remorse, the teenage heroes rebel against all forms of repressive control, whether external or internalized. Disrespect for adult authority in the film entails a willful rejection of the Protestant ethic of self-improvement through work. For Steph, that ethic is necessary but insufficient. In *Ferris Buehler* the work ethic is a thing of the past, rendered obsolete by the bureaucratized, denaturalized school environment, and by the nearby city of pleasure and consumption that beckons to Ferris so seductively. Right conduct is defined in uncompromisingly remissive terms, as self-gratification, excess, indulgence, release, the playful overcoming of every obstacle to desire.[8]

Ferris himself exemplifies the psychological type adapted to a world of commodified leisure and bureaucratized work. In Ferris the renunciative self of the old ethic is superseded by a self that is opaque, decentered, volatile, defined by a play of shifting surfaces as opposed to a fixed and stable inner core. His cool rebelliousness is not an expression of inner needs or a sign of some emotional struggle, but a highly crafted and effective strategy for dominating others.

As a condensed expression of the double assault on the work ethic, *Ferris Buehler* provides a narrative charter for the consumption ethic and a lesson in the qualities required for a successful bureaucratic career. The film is an example of what Richard Ohmann calls class instruction for elites, a narrative pedagogy that celebrates a socially useful, seductively antiauthoritarian style. Ferris is a particularly uncompromising version of a new type of ironist hero, whose seeming rebelliousness is in fact what qualifies him for success in the corporate world. His adult equivalent is Gordon Gekko, the ruthless, amoral corporate takeover artist in Oliver Stone's *Wall Street* (1987), with the difference that Ferris had a director bold enough to cast him as the hero.

Well, sort of a hero. The film hedges its bet, appealing through Cameron to the cult of feeling that also characterizes middle-class culture. The inclusion adds a twist to the underlying libidinal structure of the narrative. Even as the film plays upon a fantasy of the rebelliously independent self, it also appeals to longings for a benevolent authority. Thus Ferris, who is rebel to negligent parents and repressive principals, a pleasure ego breaking free of controls, is himself the omnipotent patriarch to Sloane, Cameron, and Jean. What is missing from this image of a restored surrogate family is any sense of tension with the corporate world of work. Is not the message that the corporate force embodied in Ferris will sustain us all?

FINDING FULFILLMENT IN ADVERTISING

David Bosner, the hero of *Nothing in Common*, is well versed in the manipulation of images. As played by Tom Hanks, David is the young, upwardly mobile creative director of a Chicago-based advertising agency. His job is to turn consumer goods into carriers of meaning, and his profession has historically promoted a consumption ethic for capitalist society. Since the 1920s, advertisers have stimulated demand by selling "satisfactions" rather than goods themselves (Marchand 1985). Consumer goods and services, in other words, are packaged as solutions to social dilemmas, vehicles of self-identity, means to self-fulfillment. In its daily practice advertising exemplifies the postmodern separation of substance from image.

Nothing in Common weaves advertising into a story of success and succession. David's father, Max, is a clothing salesman for a retail company. Played by Jackie Gleason, Max personifies an earlier stage in the corporate expansion of sales, when formerly independent agents were proletarianized by large corporations (Edwards 1979:85–87). Like the door-to-door aluminum salesman in *Tin Men* (1987), Max belongs to the past. His profession is being displaced by more modern marketing techniques, including advertising, and his individual career is winding down, while David's star is on the rise. In contrast to *The Color of Money* (1987), where Paul Newman as the Old Pro transmits his expertise to Tom Cruise, the Kid Successor, Max has nothing to pass on to David. The father operates in this film as a negative model for the son. As the plot unfolds, Max's constrictive machismo is contrasted to David's cultivation of a culturally feminine sensitivity-to-the-needs-of-others. Conversely, in the world of work, David recovers precisely what the proletarianized Max has lost, a symbolically masculinizing sense of independence.

When we meet him, David has come to a critical juncture in his career. Having just been promoted to an office with a window, he now aspires to a partnership. According to Charley, his boss and benevolent patron, creativity alone will not advance him that far. To become a partner, Charley advises him, he will have to "hustle clients." Thus begins a new stage in David's career as a professional seducer.

According to sociologist Joseph Bensman (1983), client-agency relationships in advertising resemble the relationship of king-and-courtier, although the agencies' self-representation of their compulsive deference as "client prostitution" might suggest "courtesan" as the appropriate image. In their pursuit of accounts agency personnel must influence clients by attraction rather than coercion, seducing them with dazzling ideas and a pleasing, ingratiating manner. Under these conditions, insincerity becomes a culturally valued style.

David assumes the seducer's mask in his first encounter with a coveted client, an airline industrialist by the name of Woolrich. What keeps David amusing and attractive in these scenes is Hanks's ability to convey the essential doubleness of the character's conduct. With his breezy, ironic style, Hanks is able to make us admire David's skillful performance in pandering to a client. Yet even as the film solicits our admiration, it also insists on the feminizing implications of David's bureaucratic virtuosity, by having him be picked up by Woolrich's executive daughter, Cheryl Ann.

Complicating David's work life is the collapse of his parents' marriage. After thirty years, his mother, Lorraine, has left the vulgar, uncommunicative Max and is trying to make a life of her own. Although Lorraine's abdication of the caretaker role is presented with some degree of sympathy, the film is structured by anxieties over the provision of maternal nurturance. Her attempt to create a life of her own is juxtaposed to the film's two opposed models of independent women. At one pole is the humorless, ambitious, masculinized Cheryl Ann. Her counterpart is David's high school girlfriend Donna. A college drama teacher and director of experimental theater, Donna represents the moderately independent, nonthreatening woman, whose commitment to her work still leaves her abundant time to give David emotional support.

As a stubbornly noncommercial avant-garde artist (whose work is made to appear somewhat silly in our one glimpse of it), Donna also forms the third term in a ternary system of elite careers. Despite the film's self-presentation as a story about the conflicting claims of work and family, its main concern is with divisions within the public world of work. Donna represents a precapitalist form of artistic production, the conventionally feminine world of cultural creativity that stands opposed to the masculine world of corporate business. A second opposition internal to the business world distinguishes the newer, consumption-oriented, professional elites, represented by Charley and David, from the older, production-oriented industrial elites, represented by Woolrich and Cheryl Ann. A particularly elaborate scheme of oppositions defines this relationship and expresses the ambiguous character of advertising. The ambiguity is the product of the taxonomy, which situates the commercial artistry of advertising between the purely expressive, feminine art world and the purely utilitarian, masculine world of commerce. Like the mediating categories in ritual systems, advertising participates in opposed poles.

From one perspective, advertising is feminized, associated with the seductive labor it involves, but also with more maternal images of nurturance and repose. This latter representation of the advertising profession as an indulgent, nurturing mother is conveyed through a series of scenes between David and Charley, which take place in the agency's private health club and alternate with David's pursuit of the Woolrich account. The club is a circular, dome-covered rooftop paradise, centered around an immense swimming pool, of which only a small portion is used for lap-swimming. The club's atmosphere of quiet and relaxation has therapeutic overtones and evokes a cult of emotional release. Thus yoga and tai chi are practiced in the club, whereas such ascetic forms of fitness culture as body-building or grueling workouts are apparently excluded. The overall image is of an "abundance therapy" that channels and releases untapped psychic energy.

Juxtaposed to the oceanic health club is the rugged outdoors, where Woolrich summons the reluctant David for a combination duck shoot and business meeting. For Woolrich, sport is a masculine, purposeful, productive activity, not a restful regression but a utilitarian extension of work life. David, who is appalled by this compulsive production, is heard protesting off-camera that he doesn't *want* to lug dead ducks onto the plane. As he appears on screen, of course, he is profusely thanking Woolrich for his share in the spoils of the hunt.

In opposition to the ethic of work and self-denial represented by Woolrich, advertising participates in the consumption ethic of self-indulgence and fulfillment that the profession has helped to promote. But the advertising profession has had an ambivalent attitude toward the consumption ethic, and also toward the Consumer, that figure whom it invested with the culturally feminine traits of impulsiveness and emotionality (Marchand 1985:168). Advertisers themselves are producers, after all, of images and, ideally, consumer desires. Within the process of production, identification with consumers is a manipulative technique, a means to an end, and this encourages an ironic, sometimes contemptuous sense of distance from consumers.

In the film this process is positively represented. Scenes of David and his staff at work depict the creation of ads as a form of boyish play. It is play with a practical purpose, but nevertheless a basically pleasurable, outrageous activity, something that, as David's director reminds him, they would do "only as long as it was fun." On this axis of opposition, advertising stands for a sphere of youthful freedom and creativity, poised against a repressive industrial authority.

To be more precise, the advertising profession appears as a realm where the principle of paternal succession operates in a liberatory manner, in contrast to the oppressive paternalism of the industrial elites. Cheryl Ann, the daughter whose father "raised her to be a corporate executive . . . to be a man," is a mere extension of the Father's authority. Someday, as David tells her at their parting, she will "make some corporation a hell of a CEO." But this, of course, is precisely what Woolrich intends for her. Although the masculinized woman will succeed in the corporate workplace, she is denied the possibility of achieving autonomous selfhood by her patriarchal father.

David, the feminized advertising man, finally rebels against Woolrich's authority, in the name of familial ties. When Woolrich insists that David make a presentation in New York on the day that Max is scheduled to undergo surgery, David casts off the pressures for deference, strips off his mask, and explodes at Woolrich, man-to-man. Within the terms of the bureaucratic ethic, such a loss of self-control is a fatal error, and indeed, Woolrich has David fired by Cheryl Ann. But David's defiant choice of family over career is soon rendered inconsequential, thanks to Charley's intervention.

Charley pacifies Woolrich, saves the account, and instructs David to attend to his relationship with Max. After Max's operation, when David announces that he is taking an indefinite leave in order to get to know his father, Charley conveys his warm support and promises to keep the office with the window waiting for David's return. Charley appears in his final scene without any of the toupees that he had vainly experimented with earlier in the film. His bald, uncovered head expresses his acceptance of age, and signifies that the principle of succession will operate properly within the agency.

Under these ideal conditions, David quickly resolves the various issues in his personal life. He makes a commitment to Donna and bids an affectionate farewell to his mother. Lorraine has decided that she must go away to find herself, and she leaves her son with full responsibility for the care of his crippled, convalescent father. The final image is of David in his new role as maternal caretaker. He is wheeling Max out of the hospital and beaming with satisfaction, perhaps in anticipation of the quality time they two will share together.

Yet it is Charley who makes it possible for David to find fulfillment in his private life, without any costs to his career. The fantasy of overthrowing bureaucratic controls, reasserting masculine independence within a feminized workplace, and then combining career and family life is embedded in a fantasy of having an omnipotent professional protector who averts all harm. As the strong and caring patron who is both father and mother, Charley's function undercuts the very tension between work and family on which the film is manifestly based.

Despite surface similarities to earlier stories of success as personal fulfillment, *Nothing in Common* transforms the message of the pattern it reproduces. The plot of *Man in the Grey Flannel Suit* may have encouraged accommodation to restricted career opportunities. Nevertheless, the hero's choice of family over work also conveyed an oppositional theme, a critique, however partial and implicit, of the degradation of labor in the bureaucratized white-collar workplace. In contrast, *Nothing in Common* projects a fantasy of unlimited possibilities, at least, for the young, white, male professional class.

The professional workplace of the film's imagination is open to talent, rewards independence, and encourages personal fulfillment. Its form is that of family in which men are both father and mother.

STRUGGLING UPWARD

If *Nothing in Common* reformulates the work versus family plot of the personal fulfillment tradition, *The Secret of My Success* identifies itself with the Horatio Alger boys' tales of individual mobility through work, ambition, character, and (the element that Alger never managed to eliminate) luck. Brantley Foster, the hero of *Secret*, played by Michael J. Fox, is a poor but enterprising Kansas farm boy who goes to New York to become a self-made man. By the end, he has far outstripped the Alger heroes, who rise to moderate security and middle-class respectability. Brantley's rise knows no such limits and is effected by a combination of means that would have shocked Horatio Alger.

Secret opens with glimpses of the humble farm where Brantley was raised, intercut with shots of his arrival in New York. Brantley, who has already demonstrated his initiative by earning a college degree, recalls his farewell to his parents and looks forward to his new life in New York City as the opening credits roll.

The imagery of the prologue evokes the 19th-century self-improvement literature directed to aspiring small-town boys and farm boys. Brantley's rural origins (conveyed in a few shots of barns and barnyards) bespeak the traditional disciplinary virtues of industry, perseverance, honesty, abstinence, and thrift. His personal attributes are also implied in a special sense of obligation to his mother, the figure who typically molds character in the 19th-century inspirational literature (Wyllie 1954:29–30). An iron that his mother insists on giving him ("You don't want to be wrinkled in New York") condenses the middle-class habits of neatness and order and may perhaps be read as an icon of the Protestant ethic. Brantley accepts his mother's iron reluctantly, although he will have exceptional use for it later on. In the dream that he playfully shares with her, self-discipline may be a means but affluence is the end, measured in jacuzzis, penthouses, and expensive women. Although his background links him to the old moralistic literature of work, the content of his dream evokes the consumption-oriented definition of success.

The dream is put on hold when Brantley arrives in New York and takes up residence in a slum apartment. The city is presented to us as a sharply divided world. Brantley's and our first impressions are of a colorful, volatile underclass, composed of ethnic and youth subcultures, and featuring a variety of hookers with whom he seems to feel a certain affinity. Yet a little later, when his own prospects have dimmed, the streets take on a menacing character. In what will be practically our last glimpse of the ghetto, it manifests itself to an unemployed Brantley as a place where violent crime is controlled by police surveillance, a separate world of transgression and repression. The poor function in the film as they do in the larger ideology of consumption, as the negative self-image of the consumer (Bauman 1987:186). Their situation is the threat that gives meaning to Brantley's upward struggle.

Opposed to the motley world of the streets is the high-rising, streamlined business world, with its ultra-modern, glassy architecture and regimented flow of disciplined businessmen, whose ranks Brantley had hoped to join. But he soon discovers that he has come into an economy of scarcity. New York is no longer the mythical city of opportunity and free competition, where individuals rise and fall according to their merits. Once a testing ground for heroes, the city has become the site for a ruthless competition among giant corporations. To his horror, Brantley discovers that the company which had offered him employment has fallen victim to a hostile takeover, and that his position has been cut in the ensuing shakeup.

Brantley has other unpleasant surprises in store for him. Personnel officers demand "practical experience," and display a negative attitude toward his educational qualifications more characteristic of the prebureaucratic work culture of the 19th century than of the corporate world that these officers represent. Brantley, however, is adaptable. On the model of Ferris Buehler, he promptly falsifies his résumé to stress the school of experience, only to be stymied by another obstacle. He had no ready answer to the last personnel officer's question: "Can you be a minority woman?"

Adversity, which first fanned his spirit of self-reliance, now dampens but cannot quench it. However, after a glimpse of the streets in their violent manifestation, he modifies his initial resolve to make it entirely on his own. His mother has given him the telephone number of a distant relative. This "Uncle Howard" turns out to be the forbidding Howard Prescott, CEO of the giant Pemrose corporation, "a multinational conglomerate with 27 different divisions, with products ranging from dog food to missile guidance systems." Despite his reluctance to trade on a kin tie, Brantley presents himself at Pemrose as the boss's nephew, and so gains admission to see Prescott.

Apparently impressed by Brantley's self-confidence, Prescott gives the young man a job in the mailroom. Starting at the bottom is no stigma for an aspiring self-made man. The problem is the limited structure of opportunity. Passage from the lower to the upper strata of the corporate hierarchy is almost as difficult as from the streets into the business world. As Brantley is told by his coworker, Melrose: "You can't get paroled out of the mailroom!"

Melrose depicts Pemrose as a semifeudal society of status and privilege, governed by a strict hierarchical code. The white-collar masses of mailroom workers, clerks, and secretaries who make up the lower rank are not to "consort" with the upper rank of managerial elites, whom Melrose refers to as "suits." All this hierarchy, however, has produced chaos rather than order. In Melrose's prophetic words: "This place is a zoo. Nobody knows what anyone else is doing."

"Nobody" includes Rattigan, the dictatorial supervisor of the mailroom, who takes an instant dislike to Brantley and hounds him in a manner reminiscent of Rooney, the school principal in *Ferris Buehler*. The Irish names of these comic blocking characters are probably intended as references to police authority, and the ease with which the heroes evade their surveillance is a sign that such repressive control belongs to the past. And indeed, within the world of large organizations, personal domination is rendered obsolete by bureaucratic control systems.

The film's representation of Pemrose draws upon notions of bureaucracy as a multiple threat, to entrepreneurial values, to the possibility of finding personal satisfaction in work, and to the traditional ideal of a fully meritocratic social hierarchy. Melrose embodies the potential consequences of bureaucratic control at the lower echelons of the system, where narrowly defined tasks and limited mobility produce apathy (Blau and Meyer 1971:61–71). Melrose's function in the film, however, is less to illustrate the negative impact of bureaucratization on worker motivation than to serve as a foil for Brantley's virtues. Cast from the same mold as a traditional Alger type, Melrose is the loyal friend who lacks the hero's courage and initiative, but who stands by him and ultimately benefits from his success. Thus Melrose's limited ambition and his ironically deferential acceptance of the bureaucratic hierarchy underscore Brantley's identification with the self-made man of the old entrepreneurial ideology.

Brantley learns from Melrose that while the mailroom may be a prison, it is one in which the inmates do the surveillance. Mailroom workers, Melrose explains, have special access to the flow of information, and Brantley proceeds to take advantage of that position. Like Melrose, he can complete his rounds in a fraction of the time allotted, but the industrious Brantley puts his spare time to productive use. He pores over stacks of interoffice memos and research reports obtained from the corporate reference center. This intellectual activity, we are led to believe, reverses the effects of bureaucratization on work. Unwilling to be a cog in any machine, whether rusty or well oiled, Brantley triumphs over the managerial demiurge. In a bureaucratized workplace, where knowledge is centralized and appropriated from above by management, Brantley reappropriates intellectual control over the work process.

In a hierarchical social universe, however, the efficacy of knowledge depends on the status of the knower. Although Brantley has theoretically overcome the separation of conception from execution, he remains restricted in practice. His problem is how to enter the ranks of the decision-making managerial elite in a system that has broken the connection between merit and mobility. Brantley's New York experiences have taught him to be skeptical of the optimistic work-and-win ideology of the old middle classes. He turns instead to image making.

Whereas the artful Ferris Buehler impersonated various figures of authority, Brantley goes one better. He simply invents an executive persona out of whole cloth, or more precisely, out of the corporate signs of status—an office, a nameplate, a secretary, and personalized stationery. In his capacity as mailroom worker, Brantley requisitions these status symbols on behalf of one "Carlton Whitfield," which is the name of a cousin who, according to Brantley's father in the prologue, had returned to Kansas "with his head shaved and an earring stuck in his cheek." The real Carlton failed to make it up from the streets, but Brantley's creation is a rising executive, whose identity he assumes by the simple device of donning a suit. Clothes, as Melrose suspected, really do make the man.

Brantley's solution to his mobility problem is a fine parody of the bureaucratic ethic. For Brantley, however, self-manipulation is only a device to gain entry to the upper echelons of management. Once arrived, our hero boldly speaks his mind, albeit in Carlton's name. Whereas *Nothing in Common* contrasts David's old self to the new one, *Secret* works by contrasting Brantley's forthright, candid style to the submissive deference of Prescott's bureaucratic chieftains. With his creative intelligence and refusal to be controlled, Brantley bears a resemblance to Mills's bureaucratic entrepreneur. His displays of independence in the boardroom arouse anxiety laced with envy among Prescott's craven executive yes-men.

There is one yes-woman, as well, Christie Wills, an elite, Harvard-educated prodigy, who is also Prescott's mistress. Her presence in the pack serves as a warning of the feminizing effects of deference on men and, conversely, the masculinizing effects of ambition on women. Like Cheryl Ann, Christie is a mere extension of her powerful father-lover. She submits to Prescott both sexually and professionally, not, the film suggests, out of calculated self-interest, but under the influence of erotic attraction to authority. For women, submission in the workplace appears as a sublimated expression of the female Oedipus complex, a displaced version of what would be appropriate in the conjugal family.

Christie, however, will be liberated from her dependency by Brantley, who falls madly in love with her at first sight. She appears in his fantasy as the soft, feminine creature who she really is, her compliant nature revealed in its proper, romantic form. Although Brantley does not know of her affair with Prescott, he observes her deference to the boss, and the first stage in his reeducation of Christie is to convince her of the superior rationality of his own economic policies.

We of course know that Brantley is Pemrose's future, but the content of that future is somewhat elusive. On the surface, Brantley is the bearer of the entrepreneurial ethic, who will reinfuse an increasingly dysfunctional bureaucracy with the traditional middle-class virtues. In this code, the boy hero from Kansas embodies the frontier spirit of independence. Under the influence of this spirit, as Brantley himself demonstrates, routinized and degraded bureaucratic work can be redeemed, made into an opportunity for self-creation and for the amelioration of society, as in the old entrepreneurial ideology. To this end, the decadent bureaucratic authoritarianism that rewards deference over initiative must give way to the spirit of Jeffersonian and Jacksonian democracy condensed in Brantley's agrarian background. The promise is that a heroic individual from the producing class of small farmers will transform the static corporate hierarchy into a true meritocracy.

If, however, we follow the film's own cues and read gender into the scheme, the symbolic value of this transformation becomes ambiguous. Prescott's conflict with Brantley/Carlton develops around the question of how to respond to an imminent hostile takeover of Pemrose. Prescott's strategy for dealing with the threat is to institute drastic cutbacks in all departments, supposedly to amass capital for the company's defense. Christie and the others obediently set to work, earmarking departments and midwestern distribution centers for elimination, while Brantley/Carlton argues for a diametrically opposed approach. His strategy is not to contract but to expand, specifically, to expand distribution in the midwestern zone.

In case we have any doubts about the sexual significance of Prescott's defensive strategy, there are repeated references to the necessity to "cut hard and deep," and a free-standing phallic statue outside Prescott's office enforces the theme of castration. But if Prescott's timorous policy threatens to emasculate the company, it is less certain that Brantley's expansive solution is remasculinizing at a symbolic level. Let us note that the opposition is between a production-oriented economics of scarcity and a consumption-oriented economics of abundance. For Prescott, who sees the problem in terms of overproduction, the solution is to reduce distribution, whereas Brantley reads the problem as one of underconsumption and hence sees expanded distribution as the solution. Whatever vague reference is being made here, whether to supply-side economics or even to New Dealism, is less persuasive, I think, than the internal reference to intersignifying oppositions. The contrastive economic strategies refer us back to Prescott's style of fitness culture, on the one hand, and to Brantley's affair with Prescott's wife, on the other.

As in *Nothing in Common* images of fitness culture have symbolic meaning, but the style of fitness favored by Prescott is at the other pole from the feminine cult of relaxation and release. The patriarch of Pemrose is a devotee of a masculine cult of strenuosity. The routines that he practices include jogging and running on a treadmill, both evocative of compulsive work and self-denial. He imposes these tastes on his subordinates, who are visibly infantilized by his strict discipline. Prescott's recommendations for the company merely translate this ascetic code into economics. Brantley's rural roots notwithstanding, it is Prescott who stands for the old Puritan ethic. And in this film too, the Puritan must die.

Brantley's real education does not take place at a desk. It is inaugurated in a swimming pool and a boudoir belonging to his "Aunt Vera," Prescott's beautiful, sensual, frustrated wife. Vera seduces a reluctant Brantley before she knows his identity. When he is revealed as her "nephew," the mildly incestuous aspect of the affair only increases her delight. Brantley's fear of

Vera is treated playfully and is never projected onto her. "Just when I thought it was safe to go back in the water!" he cries, as she attacks him in the pool, to the leitmotif from *Jaws*. Later, still fixated on oral imagery, he tells Melrose that being chased by a dog with "a mouth as big as my head" was the best thing that happened to him, while the worst thing was "getting laid." "Brantley," says Melrose for all of us, "I'm not sure you've got your priorities straight."

Brantley's priorities are what the film is all about. He thinks that he needs to take control of sexual relations, and to a point, the film solicits our agreement. We are expected to approve of his reeducation of Christie, and at least to appreciate his virtuosity in conducting the noisy lovemaking of his next-door neighbors to a phallocentric climax. But his increasingly frenzied attempts to exert control over Vera's sensuality indicate that the real problem is the release of his own. Before Brantley makes it to the top he is purged of his residual Puritanism. His drive for perfection has to be detached from the compulsive resistance to pleasure, for which Vera repeatedly rebukes him. What comes naturally to Ferris and David must be taught to their country cousin. It falls to Vera to take the farm out of the boy by giving Brantley the truly practical education of a courtesan.

Brantley has more in common with Sister Carrie than with any upstanding Alger hero. His covert identification with the hookers in the prologue resurfaces in the affair with Vera. Repeated attempts to deny the identification only affirm it. Thus Brantley, trying to discourage Vera, pleads, "I'm not free anymore!" "What!" cries Vera, "you mean you're going to charge me?" Or again, when Vera, about to introduce him to the rich and powerful, tells him to "do to them what you did to me," his automatic retort is, "I can't do that, Vera!"

But this remains to be seen. What Vera meant, she explains, is for him to use his "irresistible boyish charm" on her influential friends. To this, he acquiesces. What goes overlooked is that Brantley had initially refused Vera's offers of patronage, with their connotation of a reward for sexual favors. These scruples apparently forgotten, Brantley embraces the role of the courtesan.

The testing of the courtesan takes place at a party at Prescott's estate. Included among the guests are three important bankers, members of the old upper class, to which Vera also belongs. Her father, we have learned, was the self-made founder of Pemrose, a true captain of industry who, while not exactly Met 400, would have conferred membership in upper society on his daughter.

Where *Nothing in Common* opposed a crass, philistine industrialist to cosmopolitan professional elites, the image of the class system projected in *Secret* has a nostalgic appeal. In the party segment, the status difference between the old and the new upper classes is visually underlined and slanted in favor of the older class fraction. Contrasted to Vera's self-confident, relaxed and cultivated guests, Prescott and his executives appear compulsive, insecure, and common. This contrast is communicated through rock video techniques. Using music and images to tell the story, the scene shifts back and forth between two social groupings, an emergency business conference led by Prescott, and a more leisurely company made up of Brantley, Vera, and the three financial magnates, who retire to a gazebo. With Vera looking on, Brantley delivers a speech which we do not hear, but from the approving smiles of the audience, it is clear that they recognize the speaker as one of their own.

The visual structuring of this segment is important to the narrative, for it gives a new inflection to the content of Brantley's contribution to Pemrose. He is no longer the repressed midwestern farm boy, but a "natural aristocrat," perfectly at ease among the business aristocrats of the Eastern seaboard. It is as if he has taken on what Pierre Bourdieu (1984:170, 172) would call a new "habitus," a structured and structuring system of dispositions, expressed through the very orientation of the body, and also through the array of taste preferences that make up a "life-style." In a few hours, he seems to have acquired the system of bodily movements, gestures, expressions, and consumption habits that distinguish the upper social class from the merely rich. We may justifiably suspect that what bureaucracy needs from Brantley is something other than the rural middle-class virtues.

Following the party, the film moves rapidly to a conclusion. Brantley/Carlton is exposed and loses both his positions at Pemrose. In the process, Brantley and Christie are estranged and reconciled, each having learned of the other's affair. Despite a suggestion that the affairs cancel each other out, the effects of the reconciliation are not symmetric. In exchanging Prescott for Brantley, Christie does not transcend patriarchal love. She merely trades a crass, coercive master for one who is charming and considerate. For Brantley, however, loving Christie means a double recovery of control. Firstly, he has converted her from his rival to an admiring subordinate in the workplace. Secondly, through her he escapes the disruptive, uncontrollable attraction to the seductive mother.

The reconciliation of the lovers paves the way for a carnivalesque resolution to the success story. On the very day that Pemrose is about to be taken over by Davenport, a corporate raider who would destroy the company for profits, Brantley bursts into the conference room. Flanked by Christie, Melrose, and his ex-secretary, Jean, Brantley announces to the startled executives that the tables are turned. Pemrose is going to take over Davenport's company, with its strong distribution capacities, and thus realize Brantley's consumption-oriented plan. All this has been made possible by Vera, who has secured stock control of Pemrose and has persuaded her banker friends to finance the Davenport takeover for Brantley. Wearing a blouse that resembles a Matisse print, Vera glides regally into the boardroom, preceded by Brantley's new "financial advisers." With this array of patrician patrons behind him, Brantley wrests control of Pemrose away from Prescott.

It is a festive fantasy. As a vision of the redemption of the community, what is striking is the combination of egalitarian with hierarchical ideals. Brantley effects an alliance between the lowest and the highest social strata, the white-collar working class from the mailroom and the secretarial pool and the old upper class. He acts as a cross between a populist leader from the plains and a young pretender to the throne. The film's epilogue suggests that the latter self-image prevails. Our last glimpse of Brantley finds him securely ensconced in a world of aristocratic consumption, which he shares with Christie, Melrose, and Vera. He has risen from the barnyard to the penthouse of his dreams, but his tastes have been upgraded along the way, perhaps by his elite women, and the jacuzzi is replaced by a formal night at the opera.

The final scene alludes to the contrast between old and new upper classes and conveys a contrast between two ideas of the businessman. An opera-going Brantley evokes what Richard Hoffstadter (1962:244–254) calls the American tradition of the cosmopolitan merchant, the civilized and civilizing businessman who was interested in and supportive of high culture. This mercantile ideal of gentlemanly leisure and cultivation as well as work was displaced in the 19th century by the ideal of the self-made man, a type viewed by the old elites much as *Secret* views its managerial villains, as vulgar and/or overascetic parvenus.

Admittedly, the opera scene in *Secret* is directly modeled on the Hollywood notion of "class" projected in countless movies, and not on a historical social type. But what needs appreciation is that the film projects its negative image of the PMC from above, not from below. Despite the overt populist overtones, its critique of the corporate bureaucracy is from the perspective of the highest social class. In short, it is the capitalists who will redeem capitalism.

At a psychosexual level, there is a similar blurring of perspectives. Brantley's usurpation of Prescott's position is an almost manifest Oedipal rebellion against a jealous father who had hoarded all the available women, like some primal leader out of Freud's *Totem and Taboo*. Yet, like the fantasy of social rebellion with which it is condensed, the Oedipal rebellion is embedded in a fantasy of authority. According to the family romance implicit in the film, the secret of Brantley's success is that he is really of noble birth, the child of Vera and the three bankers, and thus the true heir to Pemrose. Prescott, in this fantasy, is neither Brantley's relative (recall his real mother's vagueness about their connection) nor Vera's husband (an alliance which she in fact severs).

Thus *Secret* confronts us with the same ambivalence that we encountered in *Nothing in Common* and *Ferris Buehler*, but not in *All the Right Moves*. Brantley, David, and Cameron are idols of consumption. They rebel against overdisciplinary, controlling males who still adhere to Puritan values of work, abstinence, and frugality (reduced in the case of Cameron's father to keeping an expensive car that he never drives). In each case, the rebellion is presented as the central event in the narrative; less emphasis is placed on the condition of its possibility, that is, the enabling presence of an omnipotent, protective authority, Vera and the bankers, Charley, and Ferris himself. Organization, it would appear, has become the guarantor of individual freedom.

Conclusions

Tension between individualism and organization is a persistent feature of 20th-century American life. It was heightened, however, during the Reagan era. Following the lead of an undeniably popular President, political and economic elites joined in celebrating the entrepreneurial hero as the preserver of the old frontier spirit. With one eye on its potential audiences, the culture industry followed more cautiously. This latest burst of enthusiasm for the entrepreneur came at a time when entrepreneurialism was receding as a reality. For the culture industry's coveted young, middle-class audience, in particular, the bureaucratic corporation is the most likely destination, and is the locus of anxieties that the industry has long known how to market.

Among the most ubiquitous themes of mass culture since the 1960s is the subversion of our mobility, freedom, and humanity by an overorganized society. Our fictional defender against the bureaucratic threat is the Professional, an intergeneric figure who appears in action films as well as comedies and drama. His constant resource is his professional expertise and skill, which are his resources in the contest against the forces of Organization. That contest can be inflected in various ways. A convention of many films, for example, is to contrast the insidious doubleness of bureaucratic authority to heroic singleness of purpose. Speech, the quintessential instrument of duplicity, may then take on a negative value, in which case the hero will tend to avoid it and communicate through concrete deeds. Sylvester Stallone's Rambo character is an extreme form of this tendency and embodies a mystified critique of capitalism's abstract character (Traube 1986).

In contrast, what is striking about the comic antibureaucrats analyzed in this article is that they possess the properties valued by the world they appear to oppose. Well-educated, highly verbal, seductive, ironic, and adept at shape-changing, they revel in the gap between image and reality, exploiting it to their own advantage. Conversely, their opponents, who are notably deficient in the seductive virtues, only appear to represent established systems of control. Rooney, Woolrich, Rattigan, and Prescott personify the repressive ethic of compulsive work and self-denial that is now outmoded.

In a postindustrial society, where the reproduction of capital depends more on consumption than on production, seduction replaces repression as a mode of social control. This point has been made persuasively by Pierre Bourdieu (1984:154), among others. What should not be overlooked here is the role played by the culture industry in shaping the consumption ethic on which it depends. Moreover, one suspects that the producing community's own self-image may have contributed to the latest version of the Professional hero. Who, after all, is more skilled at image-manipulation than the original dream-makers, the professional elites of the culture industry? *Nothing in Common*'s idealized advertising world is an almost transparent substitute for the film industry, and there may be more than a little self-flattery in the whole fantasy of a prebureaucratic community restored by a young professional.

But if the fantasy referred solely to the producers' self-image, it would not appeal to audiences. These films, I have argued, address the hopes and anxieties of middle-class youth regarding the corporate work world that they have joined or are about to join. In the midst of the rhetorical Reaganite insistence on recovering the past and its frontier values, these films urge us to reconcile ourselves to the present, to live, in short, according to the standards of the corporate world of bureaucratic organizations. That world's potential dangers are selectively recognized in the films, and the emphasis is placed on the maintenance of gendered identities. Between the Scylla of dependence that threatens men and the Charybdis of ambition awaiting women, the films steer a course toward the comic resolution. Without any of the fanfare that attends the killing of the puritanical father, the permissive, corporate father is quietly reinstated, and young men and women take their places as his sons and daughters. Our moment of freedom, embodied in the hero's rebellion, leads us into a benign state of dependency.

NOTES

First appeared in 1989.

Acknowledgments. A draft of this article was presented at the Little Three Conference on "Work and Play," held at Wesleyan University's Center for the Humanities, January 14–16, 1988. I am grateful to the conference organizers, especially Richard Vann and the CFH staff, and to the participants; in particular, I thank Jan Dizard for his thoughtful commentary. Marylin Arthur and Bruce Greenwald shared my sense that *Secret* would repay close scrutiny, contributed their insights, and encouraged me in this project. Sally Banes and Nöel Carroll helped from start to finish, as companions at the movies, and as editors and critics of earlier versions of this article. For this final version, I am also grateful to the other members of the Wesleyan Cultural Studies organizing group, Hazel Carby, Richard Ohmann, Richard Stamelman, and Khachig Tölölyan.

1. Mark Crispin Miller (1986) also discusses the ideological implications of this general character type in a paper that has many points in common with this one, although I was well into the analysis when I read it. Foster Johnson, a student in my seminar on mass culture, first called the character type to my attention and speculated on the social sources of its popularity. In retrospect, I think his comments were a point of departure for this article. I hope he will feel they have been put to good use.

2. I have in mind Paul Willis's (1981) ethnography of working-class youths. Willis's primary concern in this important study is with the creativity of working-class culture, and specifically, with everyday forms of resistance to dominant values. Yet the resemblances between the narrative he elicits from the lads' discourse on work bears such strong resemblances to the romantic adventurism of mass media fictions that the connection warrants analytical attention.

3. The term "service class" is also used to refer to this class fraction (Lash and Urry 1987).

4. The larger phenomenon of consumption culture has roots in therapeutic culture, which is now one of its several strands. On therapeutic culture, see Philip Rieff (1966) and T. J. Jackson Lears (1981, 1983).

5. The hero of *War Games*, also played by Matthew Broderick, performs a similar prank, only to suffer pangs of remorse. Ferris's casual rule-breaking indicates how far advanced he is along the path away from the older selfhood.

6. See, for example, *Adventures in Baby-Sitting* (1987).

7. Daniel Rodgers (1978:140–142) detects the split in children's literature within Alger's stories themselves. Thus, even the self-avowed defender of the Protestant ethic included elements that undercut the old morality, by making his heroes' success depend on luck as well as on industry. In a recurrent pattern, the Alger heroes perform impulsive acts of kindness or courage for strangers, who turn out to be rich and powerful and subsequently become their benefactors.

8. The term "remissive" derives from Rieff's concept of an ethic of release. It is used by John Carroll (1987) in a critique of the psychological type promoted by the consumption ethic.

References Cited

Bauman, Zygmunt. 1987. Legislators and Interpreters. Ithaca: Cornell University Press.

Bell, Daniel. 1976. The Cultural Contradictions of Capitalism. New York: Basic Books.

Bensman, Joseph. 1983. Dollars and Sense: Ideology, Ethics and the Meaning of Work in Profit and Nonprofit Organizations. New York: Schocken Books.

Bensman, Joseph, and Arthur Vidich. 1971. The New American Society. Chicago: Quadrangle Books.

Blau, Peter, and Marshall Meyer. 1971. Bureaucracy in Modern Society. New York: Random House.

Bourdieu, Pierre. 1984. Distinction: A Social Critique of the Judgement of Taste. Richard Nice, trans. Cambridge: Harvard University Press.

Braverman, Harry. 1974. Labor and Monopoly Capitalism. New York: Monthly Review Press.

Carroll, John. 1987. Puritan, Paranoid, Remissive: A Sociology of Modern Culture. London: Routledge & Kegan Paul.

Cawelti, John. 1965. Apostles of the Self-Made Man: Changing Concepts of Success in America. Chicago: University of Chicago Press.

Edward, Richard. 1979. Contested Terrain: The Transformation of the Work Place in the Twentieth Century. New York: Basic Books.

Gans, Herbert. 1974. Popular Culture and High Culture: An Analysis and Evaluation of Taste. New York: Basic Books.

Gitlin, Todd. 1983. Inside Prime Time. New York: Pantheon Books.

———. 1986. We Build Excitement. In Watching Television. Todd Gitlin, ed. Pp. 136–161. New York: Pantheon Books.

Hall, Stuart. 1982. The Rediscovery of "Ideology": Return of the Repressed in Media Studies. In Culture, Society and the Media. M. Gurevitch et al., eds. Pp. 56–90. London: Methuen.

Hoffstadter, Richard. 1962. Anti-Intellectualism in American Life. New York: Vintage Books.

Horkheimer, Max, and Theodor Adorno. 1972. The Culture Industry: Enlightenment as Mass Deception. In The Dialectic of Enlightenment. Pp. 120–167. New York: Herder & Herder.

Jackall, Robert. 1983. Moral Mazes: Bureaucracy and Managerial Work. Harvard Business Review 16(5):118–130.

Jarvie, I. C. 1970. Movies and Society. New York: Basic Books.

Johnson, Richard. 1986–87. What Is Cultural Studies Anyway? Social Text 16:38–80.

Lasch, Christopher. 1979. The Culture of Narcissism. New York: Warner Books.

Lash, Scott, and John Urry. 1987. The End of Organized Capitalism. Madison: University of Wisconsin Press.

Lears, T. J. Jackson. 1981. No Place of Grace: Antimodernism and the Transformation of American Culture. New York: Pantheon Books.

———. 1983. From Salvation to Self-Realization: Advertising and the Therapeutic Roots of the Consumer Culture. *In* The Culture of Consumption. Richard Fox and T. J. Jackson Lears, eds. Pp. 2–38. New York: Pantheon Books.

Long, Elisabeth. 1985. The American Dream and the Popular Novel. Boston: Routledge & Kegan Paul.

Marchand, Roland. 1985. Advertising the American Dream. Berkeley: University of California Press.

Miller, Mark Crispin. 1986. Deride and Conquer. *In* Watching Television. Todd Gitlin, ed. Pp. 183–228. New York: Pantheon Books.

Mills, C. Wright. 1950. The Power Elite. New York: Oxford University Press.

———. 1953. White Collar. New York: Oxford University Press.

Ohmann, Richard. 1981. Where Did Mass Culture Come From? The Case of Magazines. Berkshire Review 16:85–101.

Radway, Janice. 1984. Reading the Romance: Women, Patriarchy and Popular Literature. Chapel Hill: University of North Carolina Press.

Rieff, Philip. 1966. The Triumph of the Therapeutic: Uses of Faith after Freud. New York: Harper & Row.

Riesman, David. 1950. The Lonely Crowd: A Study of the Changing American Character. New Haven: Yale University Press.

Rodgers, Daniel. 1978. The Work Ethic in Industrial America. Chicago: University of Chicago Press.

Slotkin, Richard. 1984. Prologue to a Study of Myth and Genre in American Movies. Prospects 9:407–432.

———. 1986. The Fatal Environment: The Myth of the Frontier in the Age of Industrialization. Middletown, Conn.: Wesleyan University.

Sussman, Warren. 1984[1974]. Culture as History: The Transformation of American Society in the Twentieth Century. New York: Pantheon Books.

Trachtenberg, Alan. 1982. The Incorporation of America: Culture and Society in the Gilded Age. New York: Hill & Wang.

Traube, Elizabeth. 1986. Redeeming Images: The Wild Man Comes Home. Persistence of Vision 3/4:71–94.

Whyte, William. 1956. The Organization Man. New York: Simon & Schuster.

Willis, Paul. 1981[1977]. Learning to Labor: How Working Class Kids get Working Class Jobs. New York: Columbia University Press.

Wyllie, Irvin. 1954. The Self-Made Man in America. New Brunswick: Rutgers University Press.

Selections from *Marxism and Literature*

RAYMOND WILLIAMS

BASE AND SUPERSTRUCTURE

Any modern approach to a Marxist theory of culture must begin by considering the proposition of a determining base and a determined superstructure. From a strictly theoretical point of view this is not, in fact, where we might choose to begin. It would be in many ways preferable if we could begin from a proposition which originally was equally central, equally authentic: namely the proposition that social being determines consciousness. It is not that the two propositions necessarily deny each other or are in contradiction. But the proposition of base and superstructure, with its figurative element and with its suggestion of a fixed and definite spatial relationship, constitutes, at least in certain hands, a very specialized and at times unacceptable version of the other proposition. Yet in the transition from Marx to Marxism, and in the development of mainstream Marxism itself, the proposition of the determining base and the determined superstructure has been commonly held to be the key to Marxist cultural analysis.

The source of this proposition is commonly taken to be a well-known passage in Marx's 1859 Preface to *A Contribution to the Critique of Political Economy*:

> In the social production of their life, men enter into definite relations that are indispensable and independent of their will, relations of production which correspond to a definite stage of development of their material productive forces. The sum total of these relations of production constitutes the economic structure of society, the real foundation, on which rises a legal and political superstructure and to which correspond definite forms of social consciousness. The mode of production of material life conditions the social, political and intellectual life process in general. It is not the consciousness of men that determines their being, but, on the contrary, their social being that determines their consciousness. At a certain stage of their development, the material productive forces of society come in conflict with the existing relations of production or—what is but a legal expression for the same thing—with the property relations within which they have been at work hitherto. From forms of development of the productive forces these relations turn into their fetters. Then begins an epoch of social revolution. With the change of the economic foundation the entire immense superstructure is more or less rapidly transformed. In considering such transformations a distinction

should always be made between the material transformation of the economic conditions of production, which can be determined with the precision of natural science. and the legal, political, religious, aesthetic or philosophic—in short, ideological—forms in which men become conscious of this conflict and fight it out. (*Selected Works* [London, 1962], 1:362–4)

This is hardly an obvious starting-point for any cultural theory. It is part of an exposition of historical materialist method in the understanding of legal relations and forms of state. The first use of the term "superstructure" is explicitly qualified as "legal and political." (It should incidentally be noted that the English translation in most common use has a plural—"legal and political superstructures"—for Marx's singular "juristicher und politischer Überbau.") "Definite forms of social consciousness" are further said to "correspond" to it (*entsprechen*). Transformation of the "entire immense superstructure," in the social revolution which begins from the altered relations of productive forces and relations of production, is a process in which "men become conscious of this conflict and fight it out" in "ideological forms" which now include the "religious, aesthetic, or philosophic" as well as the legal and political. Much has been deduced from this formulation, but the real context is inevitably limited. Thus it would be possible, simply from this passage, to define "cultural" ("religious, aesthetic or philosophic") forms in which "men become conscious of this conflict," without necessarily supposing that these specific forms are the whole of "cultural" activity.

There is at least one earlier use, by Marx, of the term "superstructure." It is in *The Eighteenth Brumaire of Louis Napoleon*, 1851–2:

Upon the several forms of property, upon the social conditions of existence, a whole superstructure is reared of various and peculiarly shaped feelings [*empfindungen*], illusions, habits of thought and conceptions of life. The whole class produces and shapes these out of its material foundation and out of the corresponding social conditions. The individual unit to whom they flow through tradition and education may fancy that they constitute the true reasons for and premises of his conduct. (*Selected Works* [London, 1962], 1:272–3)

This is an evidently different use. The "superstructure" is here the whole "ideology" of the class: its "form of consciousness"; its constitutive ways of seeing itself in the world. It would be possible, from this and the later use, to see three senses of "superstructure" emerging: (a) legal and political forms which express existing real relations of production; (b) forms of consciousness which express a particular class view of the world; (c) a process in which, over a whole range of activities, men become conscious of a fundamental economic conflict and fight it out. These three senses would direct our attention, respectively, to (a) institutions; (b) forms of consciousness; (c) political and cultural practices.

It is clear that these three areas are related and must, in analysis, be interrelated. But on just this crucial question of interrelation the term itself is of little assistance, just because it is variably applied to each area in turn. Nor is this at all surprising, since the use is not primarily conceptual, in any precise way, but metaphorical. What it primarily expresses is the important sense of a visible and formal "superstructure" which might be analyzed on its own but which cannot be understood without seeing that it rests on a "foundation." The same point must be made of the corresponding metaphorical term. In the use of 1851–2 it is absent, and the origins of a particular form of class consciousness are specified as "forms of property" and "social conditions of existence." In the use of 1859 it appears in almost conscious metaphor: "the economic structure of society—the real foundation [*die reale Basis*], on which rises [*erhebt*] a legal and political superstructure [*Überbau*]." It is replaced, later in the argument, by "the economic foundation" (*ökonomische Grundlage*). The continuity of meaning is relatively clear, but the variation of terms for one part of the relationship ("forms of property, social conditions of existence"; "economic structure of society"; "real basis"; "real foundation"; *Basis; Grundlage*) is not matched by explicit variation of the other term of the relationship, though the actual signification of this term (*Überbau*; superstructure) is, as we have seen, variable. It is part of the complexity of the subsequent argument that the term rendered in English explication (probably first by Engels) as "base" is rendered in other languages in significant variations (in French usually as *infrastructure*, in Italian as *struttura*, and so on, with some complicating effects on the substance of the argument).

In the transition from Marx to Marxism, and then in the development of expository and didactic formulations, the words used in the original arguments were projected, first, as if they were precise concepts, and second, as if they were descriptive terms for observable "areas" of social life. The main sense of the words in the original arguments had been relational, but the popularity of the terms tended to indicate either (a) relatively enclosed categories or (b) relatively enclosed areas of activity. These were then correlated either temporally (first material production, then consciousness, then politics and culture) or in effect, forcing the metaphor, spatially (visible and distinguishable "levels" or "layers"—politics and culture, then forms of consciousness, and so on down to "the base"). The serious practical problems of method, which the original words had indicated, were then usually in effect bypassed by methods derived from a confidence, rooted in the popularity of the terms, in the relative enclosure of categories or areas expressed as "the base," "the superstructure."

It is then ironic to remember that the force of Marx's original criticism had been mainly directed against the separation of "areas" of thought and activity (as in the separation of consciousness from material production) and against the related evacuation of specific content—real human activities—by the imposition of abstract categories. The common abstraction of "the base" and "the superstructure" is thus a radical persistence of the modes of thought which he attacked. That in the course of other arguments he gave some warrant for this, within the intrinsic difficulties of any such formulation, is certainly true. But it is significant that when he came to any sustained analysis, or to a realization of the need for such analysis, he was at once specific and flexible in his use of his own terms. He had already observed, in the formulation of 1859, a distinction between analyzing "the economic conditions of production, which can be determined with the precision of natural science" and the analysis of "ideological forms," for which methods were evidently less precise. In 1857 he had noted:

> As regards art, it is well known that some of its peaks by no means correspond to the general development of society; nor do they therefore to the material substructure, the skeleton as it were of its organization.

His solution of the problem he then discusses, that of Greek art, is hardly convincing, but the "by no means correspond" is a characteristic practical recognition of the complexity of real relations. Engels, in his essay *Feuerbach and the End of Classical German Philosophy*, still argued specifically, showing how the "economic basis" of a political struggle could be dulled in unconsciousness or altogether lost sight of, and how a legal system could be projected as independent of its economic content, in the course of its professional development. Then:

> Still higher ideologies, that is, such as are still further removed from the material, economic basis, take the form of philosophy and religion. Hence the interconnection between conceptions and their material conditions of existence becomes more and more complicated, more and more obscured by intermediate links. But the interconnection exists.

This relational emphasis, including not only complexity but recognition of the ways in which some connections are lost to consciousness, is of course very far from the abstract categories (though it supports the implication of separate areas) of "superstructure" and "base."

In all serious Marxist analysis the categories are of course not used abstractly. But they may have their effect none the less. It is significant that the first phase of the recognition of practical complexities stressed what are really quantitative relations. By the end of the nineteenth century it was common to recognize what can best be described as disturbances, or special difficulties, of an otherwise regular relationship. This is true of the idea of "lags" in time, which had been developed from Marx's observation that some of the "peaks" of art "by no means correspond to the general development of society." This could be expressed (though Marx's own "solution" to this problem had not been of this kind) as a matter of *temporal* "delay" or "unevenness." The same basic model is evident in Engels's notion of the relative distance ("still further removed") of the "higher ideologies." Or consider Engels's letter to Bloch of September 1890:

> According to the materialist conception of history, the *ultimately* determining element in history is the production and reproduction of real life. More than this

neither Marx nor I have ever asserted. Hence if somebody twists this into saying that the economic element is the only determining one, he transforms that proposition into a meaningless, abstract, senseless phrase. The economic situation is the basis, but the various elements of the superstructure—political forms of the class struggle and its results, to wit: constitutions established by the victorious class after a successful battle, etc., juridical forms, and even the reflexes of all these actual struggles in the brains of the participants. Political, juristic, philosophical theories, religious views and their further development into systems of dogma—also exercise their influence upon the course of the historical struggles and in many cases preponderate in determining their *form*. There is an interaction of all these elements in which, amid all the endless host of accidents (that is, of things and events whose inner interconnection is so remote or so impossible of proof that we can regard it as non-existent, as negligible), the economic movement finally asserts itself as necessary. Otherwise the application of the theory to any period of history would be easier than the solution of a simple equation of the first degree.

This is a vital acknowledgement of real and methodological complexities. It is particularly relevant to the idea of "determination," which will be separately discussed, and to the decisive problem of consciousness as "reflexes" or "reflection." But within the vigor of his contrast between real history and a "meaningless, abstract, senseless phrase," and alongside his recognition of a new (and theoretically significant) exception—"the endless host of accidents"—Engels does not so much revise the enclosed categories—"the basis" ("the economic element," "the economic situation," "the economic movement") and "the various elements" (political, juridical, theoretical) of "the superstructure"—as reiterate the categories and instance certain exceptions, indirectnesses, and irregularities which obscure their otherwise regular relation. What is fundamentally lacking, in the theoretical formulations of this important period, is any adequate recognition of the indissoluble connections between material production, political and cultural institutions and activity, and consciousness. The classic summary of "the relationship between the base and the superstructure" is Plekhanov's distinction of "five sequential elements: (i) the state of productive forces; (ii) the economic conditions; (iii) the socio-political regime; (iv) the psyche of social man; (v) various ideologies reflecting the properties of this psyche" (*Fundamental Problems of Marxism*, Moscow, 1922, 76). This is better than the bare projection of "a base" and "a superstructure," which has been so common. But what is wrong with it is its description of these "elements" as "sequential," when they are in practice indissoluble: not in the sense that they cannot be distinguished for purposes of analysis, but in the decisive sense that these are not separate "areas" or "elements" but the whole, specific activities and products of real men. That is to say, the analytic categories, as so often in idealist thought, have, almost unnoticed, become substantive descriptions, which then take habitual priority over the whole social process to which, as analytic categories, they are attempting to speak. Orthodox analysts began to think of "the base" and "the superstructure" as if they were separable concrete entities. In doing so they lost sight of the very processes—not abstract relations but constitutive processes—which it should have been the special function of historical materialism to emphasize. I shall be discussing later the major theoretical response to this loss: the attempt to reconstitute such processes by the idea of "mediation."

A persistent dissatisfaction, within Marxism, about the proposition of "base and superstructure," has been most often expressed by an attempted refinement and revaluation of "the superstructure." Apologists have emphasized its complexity, substance, and "autonomy" or autonomous value. Yet most of the difficulty still lies in the original extension of metaphorical terms for a relationship into abstract categories or concrete areas between which connections are looked for and complexities or relative autonomies emphasized. It is actually more important to observe the character of this extension in the case of "the base" than in the case of the always more varied and variable "superstructure." By extension and by habit, "the base" has come to be considered virtually as an object (a particular and reductive version of "material existence"). Or, in specification, "the base" is given very general and apparently uniform properties. "The base" is the real social existence of man. "The base" is the real relations of production corresponding to a stage of the development of material productive forces. "The base" is a mode of production at a particular stage of its development. Of course these are, in practice, different propositions. Yet each is also very different from Marx's central emphasis on productive *activities*. He had himself made the point against reduction of "the base" to a category:

> In order to study the connection between intellectual and material production it is above all essential to conceive the latter in its determined historical form and not as a general category. For example, there corresponds to the capitalist mode of production a type of intellectual production quite different from that which corresponded to the medieval mode of production. Unless material production itself is understood in its specific historical form, it is impossible to grasp the characteristics of the intellectual production which corresponds to it or the reciprocal action between the two. (*Theorien Über den Mehrwert*, cit. Bottomore and Rubel, 96–7)

We can add that while a particular stage of "real social existence," or of "relations of production," or of a "mode of production," can be discovered and made precise by analysis, it is never, as a body of activities, either uniform or static. It is one of the central propositions of Marx's sense of history, for example, that in actual development there are deep contradictions in the relationships of production and in the consequent social relationships. There is therefore the continual possibility of the dynamic variation of these forces. The "variations" of the superstructure might be deduced from this fact alone, were it not that the "objective" implications of "the base" reduce all such variations to secondary consequences. It is only when we realize that "the base," to which it is habitual to *refer* variations, is itself a dynamic and internally contradictory process—the specific activities and modes of activity, over a range from association to antagonism, of real men and classes of men—that we can begin to free ourselves from the notion of an "area" or a "category" with certain fixed properties for deduction to the variable processes of a "superstructure." The physical fixity of the terms exerts a constant pressure against just this realization.

Thus, contrary to a development in Marxism, it is not "the base" and "the superstructure" that need to be studied, but specific and indissoluble real processes, within which the decisive relationship, from a Marxist point of view, is that expressed by the complex idea of "determination."

.   .   .   .

FROM REFLECTION TO MEDIATION

The usual consequence of the base-superstructure formula, with its specialized and limited interpretations of productive forces and of the process of determination, is a description— even at times a theory—of art and thought as "reflection." The metaphor of "reflection" has a long history in the analysis of art and ideas. Yet the physical process and relationship that it implies have proved compatible with several radically different theories. Thus art can be said to "reflect the real world," holding "the mirror up to nature," but every term of such a definition has been in protracted and necessary dispute. Art can be seen as reflecting not "mere appearances" but the "reality" behind these: the "inner nature" of the world, or its "constitutive forms." Or art is seen as reflecting not the "lifeless world," but the world as seen in the mind of the artist. The elaboration and sophistication of arguments of these kinds are remarkable.

Materialism appears to constitute a fundamental challenge to them. If the real world is material, it can indeed be seen in its constitutive forms, but these will not be metaphysical, and reflection will be necessarily of a material reality. This can lead to the concept of "false" or "distorted" reflection, in which something (metaphysics, "ideology") prevents true reflection. Similarly, the "mind of the artist" can be seen as itself materially conditioned; its reflection is then not independent but itself a material function.

Two versions of this materialism became dominant in Marxist thinking. First, there was the interpretation of consciousness as mere "reflexes, echoes, phantoms, and sublimates"; this was discussed in relation to one of the concepts of ideology. But as a necessary complement to this reductive account, an alternative interpretation of consciousness as "scientific truth," based on real knowledge of the material world, was strongly emphasized. This alternative could be extended relatively easily to include accounts of "knowledge" and "thought," but for obvious reasons it left "art" relatively neglected and exposed. Within this version the most common account of art was then a positivist theory, in which the metaphor of "reflection" played a central role. The true function of art was defined in terms of "realism" or less often "naturalism"—both nineteenth-century terms themselves much affected by related concepts of science. Art reflected reality; if it did not it was false or unimportant. And what was reality? The "production and reproduction of real life," now commonly described as "the base," with art part of its "superstructure." The ambiguity is then obvious. A doctrine about the real world expressed in the materialism of objects leads to one kind of theory of art: showing the objects (including human actions as objects) "as they really are." But this can be maintained, in its simplest form, only by knowing "the base" as an object: the development already discussed. To know the "base" as a process at once complicates the object-reflection model which had appeared so powerful.

This complication was fought out in rival definitions of "realism" and "naturalism." Each term had begun as a secular and radical emphasis on human social knowledge. Naturalism was an alternative to supernaturalism; realism to a deliberately falsifying ("romanticizing," "mythmaking," "prettifying") art. Yet the enclosure of each concept within a special doctrine of "the object as it really is" reduced their radical challenge. The making of art was incorporated into a static, objectivist doctrine, within which "reality," "the real world," "the base," could be *separately* known, by the criteria of scientific truth, and their "reflections" in art then judged by their conformity or lack of conformity with them: in fact with their positivist versions.

It was at this point that a different materialist theory became necessary. For it was only in very simple cases that the object-reflection model could be actually illustrated or verified. Moreover, there was already a crucial distinction between "mechanical materialism"—seeing the world as objects and excluding activity—and "historical materialism"—seeing the material life process as human activity. The simplest theories of "reflection" were based on a mechanical materialism. But a different account appeared possible if "the real world," instead of being isolated as an object, was grasped as a material social process, with certain inherent qualities and tendencies. As earlier in idealism, but now with altered specification, art could be seen as reflecting not separated objects and superficial events but the essential forces and movements underlying them. This was in turn made the basis for distinction between "realism" (dynamic) and "naturalism" (static).

Yet it is quickly evident that this is radically incompatible with any doctrine of "reflection," except in one special and influential adaptation. The movement from abstract objectivism to this sense of objectified process was decisive. But the sense of objectified process can be almost at once rendered back to its original abstract and objectivist condition, by a definition of the already known (scientifically discovered and attested) "laws" of this process. Art can then be defined as "reflecting" these laws. What is already *and otherwise* known as the basic reality of the material social process is reflected, of course in its own ways, by art. If it is not (and the test is available, by comparison of this given knowledge of reality with any actual art produced), then it is a case of distortion, falsification, or superficiality: not art but ideology.

Rash extensions were then possible to new categorical distinctions: not progressive art but reactionary art; not socialist art but bourgeois or capitalist art; not art but mass culture; and so on almost indefinitely. The decisive theory of art as reflection, not now of objects but of real and verifiable social and historical processes, was thus extensively maintained and elaborated. The theory became at once a cultural program and a critical school.

It has of course been heavily attacked from older and often more substantial positions. It has been widely identified as a damaging consequence of a materialist outlook. But once again, what is wrong with the theory is that it is not materialist enough. The most damaging consequence of any theory of art as reflection is that, through its persuasive physical metaphor (in which a reflection simply occurs, within the physical properties of light, when an object or movement is brought into relation with a reflective surface—the mirror and then the mind), it succeeds in suppressing the actual work on material—in a final sense, the material social process—which is the making of any art work. By projecting and alienating this material process to "*reflection*," the social and material character of artistic activity—of that art-work which is at once "material" and "imaginative"—was suppressed. It was at this point that the idea of reflection was challenged by the idea of "mediation."

"Mediation" was intended to describe an active process. Its predominant general sense had been an act of intercession, reconciliation, or interpretation between adversaries or strangers. In idealist philosophy it had been a concept of reconciliation between opposites, within a totality. A more neutral sense had also developed, for interaction between separate forces. The distinction between "mediate" and "immediate" had been developed to emphasize "mediation" as an indirect connection or agency between separate kinds of acts.

It is then easy to see the attraction of "mediation" as a term to describe the process of relationship between "society" and "art," or between "the base" and "the superstructure." We should not expect to find (or always to find) directly "reflected" social realities in art, since these (often or always) pass through a process of "mediation" in which their original content is changed. This general proposition, however, can be understood in several different ways. The change involved in mediation can be simply a matter of indirect expression: the social realities are "projected" or "disguised," and to recover them is a process of working back through the mediation to their original forms. Relying mainly on the concept of "ideology" as (class-based) distortion, this kind of reductive analysis, and of "stripping," "laying bare" or "unmasking," has been common in Marxist work. If we remove the elements of mediation, an area of reality, and then also of the ideological elements which distorted its perception or which determined its presentation, will become clear. (In our own time this sense of mediation has been especially applied to "the media," which are assumed to distort and present "reality" in ideological ways.)

Yet this negative sense of "mediation," which has been heavily supported by psychoanalytical concepts such as "repression" and "sublimation," and by "rationalization" in a sense close to the negative sense of "ideology," has

coexisted with a sense which offers to be positive. This is especially the contribution of the Frankfurt School. Here the change involved in "mediation" is
not necessarily seen as distortion or disguise. Rather, all active relations between different kinds of being and consciousness are inevitably mediated,
and this process is not a separable agency—a "medium"—but intrinsic to the
properties of the related kinds. "Mediation is in the object itself, not something between the object and that to which it is brought."[1] Thus mediation is
a positive process in social reality, rather than a process added to it by way of
projection, disguise, or interpretation.

It is difficult to be sure how much is gained by substituting the metaphor of
"mediation" for the metaphor of "reflection." On the one hand it goes beyond
the passivity of reflection theory; it indicates an active process, of some kind.
On the other hand, in almost all cases, it perpetuates a basic dualism. Art does
not reflect social reality, the superstructure does not reflect the base, *directly*;
culture is a mediation of society. But it is virtually impossible to sustain the
metaphor of "mediation" (*Vermittlung*) without some sense of separate and
pre-existent areas or orders of reality, between which the mediating process
occurs whether independently or as determined by their prior natures. Within
the inheritance of idealist philosophy the process is usually, in practice, seen
as a mediation between categories, which have been assumed to be distinct.
Mediation, in this range of use, then seems little more than a sophistication of
reflection.

Yet the underlying problem is obvious. If "reality" and "speaking about
reality" (the "material social process" and "language") are taken as categorically distinct, concepts such as "reflection" and "mediation" are inevitable.
The same pressure can be observed in attempts to interpret the Marxist phrase
"the production and reproduction of real life" as if production were the primary social (economic) process and "reproduction" its "symbolic" or "signifying" or "cultural" counterpart. Such attempts are either alternatives to the
Marxist emphasis on an inherent and constitutive "practical consciousness,"
or, at their best, ways of specifying its actual operations. The problem is different, from the beginning, if we see language and signification as indissoluble elements of the material social process itself, involved all the time both in
production and reproduction. The terms of actual displacement and alienation
experienced in class societies have led to recurrent concepts of isolated relations between "separate" orders: "reflection" from idealist thought through
naturalism to a positivist kind of Marxism; "mediation" from religious
thought through idealist philosophy to Hegelian variants of Marxism. To the
extent that it indicates an active and substantial process, "mediation" is always the less alienated concept. In its modern development it approaches the
sense of inherent constitutive consciousness, and is in any case important as
an alternative to simple reductionism, in which every real act or work is me-
thodically rendered back to an assumed primary category, usually specified
(self-specified) as "concrete reality." But when the process of mediation is
seen as positive and substantial, as a necessary process of the making of

meanings and values, in the necessary form of the general social process of signification and communication, it is really only a hindrance to describe it as "mediation" at all. For the metaphor takes us back to the very concept of the "intermediary" which, at its best, this constitutive and constituting sense rejects.

. . . .

HEGEMONY

The traditional definition of "hegemony" is political rule or domination, especially in relations between states. Marxism extended the definition of rule or domination to relations between social classes, and especially to definitions of a *ruling class*. "Hegemony" then acquired a further significant sense in the work of Antonio Gramsci, carried out under great difficulties in a Fascist prison between 1927 and 1935. Much is still uncertain in Gramsci's use of the concept, but his work is one of the major turning-points in Marxist cultural theory.

Gramsci made a distinction between "rule" (*dominio*) and "hegemony." "Rule" is expressed in directly political forms and in times of crisis by direct or effective coercion. But the more normal situation is a complex interlocking of political, social, and cultural forces, and "hegemony," according to different interpretations, is either this or the active social and cultural forces which are its necessary elements. Whatever the implications of the concept for Marxist political theory (which has still to recognize many kinds of direct political control, social class control, and economic control, as well as this more general formation), the effects on cultural theory are immediate. For "hegemony" is a concept which at once includes and goes beyond two powerful earlier concepts: that of "culture" as a "whole social process," in which men define and shape their whole lives; and that of "ideology," in any of its Marxist senses, in which a system of meanings and values is the expression or projection of a particular class interest.

"Hegemony" goes beyond "culture," as previously defined, in its insistence on relating the "whole social process" to specific distributions of power and influence. To say that "men" define and shape their whole lives is true only in abstraction. In any actual society there are specific inequalities in means and therefore in capacity to realize this process. In a class society these are primarily inequalities between classes. Gramsci therefore introduced the necessary recognition of dominance and subordination in what has still, however, to be recognized as a whole process.

It is in just this recognition of the *wholeness* of the process that the concept of "hegemony" goes beyond "ideology." What is decisive is not only the conscious system of ideas and beliefs, but the whole lived social process as practically organized by specific and dominant meanings and values. Ideology, in its normal senses, is a relatively formal and articulated system of meanings, values, and beliefs, of a kind that can be abstracted as a "worldview" or a "class outlook." This explains its popularity as a concept in retrospective analysis (in base-superstructure models or in homology), since a *system* of ideas can be abstracted from that once living social process and represented, usually by the selection of "leading" or typical "ideologists" or "ideological features," as the decisive form in which consciousness was at once expressed and controlled (or, as in Althusser, was in effect unconscious, as an imposed structure). The relatively mixed, confused, incomplete, or inarticulate consciousness of actual men in that period and society is thus overridden in the name of this decisive generalized system, and indeed in structural homology is procedurally excluded as peripheral or ephemeral. It is the fully articulate and systematic forms which are recognizable as ideology, and there is a corresponding tendency in the analysis of art to look only for similarly fully articulate and systematic expressions of this ideology in the content (base-superstructure) or form (homology) of actual works. In less selective procedures, less dependent on the inherent classicism of the definition of form as fully articulate and systematic, the tendency is to consider works as variants of, or as variably affected by, the decisive abstracted ideology.

More generally, this sense of "an ideology" is applied in abstract ways to the actual consciousness of both dominant and subordinated classes. A dominant class "has" this ideology in relatively pure and simple forms. A subordinate class has, in one version, *nothing but* this ideology as its consciousness (since the production of all ideas is, by axiomatic definition, in the hands of those who control the primary means of production) or, in another version, has this ideology imposed on its otherwise different consciousness, which it must struggle to sustain or develop against "ruling-class ideology."

The concept of hegemony often, in practice, resembles these definitions, but it is distinct in its refusal to equate consciousness with the articulate formal system which can be and ordinarily is abstracted as "ideology." It of course does not exclude the articulate and formal meanings, values, and beliefs which a dominant class develops and propagates. But it does not equate these with consciousness, or rather it does not reduce consciousness to them. Instead it sees the relations of domination and subordination, in their forms as practical consciousness, as in effect a saturation of the whole process of living—not only of political and economic activity, nor only of manifest social activity, but of the whole substance of lived identities and relationships, to such a depth that the pressures and limits of what can ultimately be seen as a specific economic, political, and cultural system seem to most of us the pressures and limits of simple experience and common sense. Hegemony is then not only the articulate upper level of "ideology," nor are its forms of control only those ordinarily seen as "manipulation" or "indoctrination." It is a whole body of practices and expectations, over the whole of living: our senses and assignments of energy, our shaping perceptions of ourselves and our world. It is a lived system of meanings and values—constitutive and constituting—which as they are experienced as practices appear as reciprocally confirming.

It thus constitutes a sense of reality for most people in the society, a sense of absolute because experienced reality beyond which it is very difficult for most members of the society to move, in most areas of their lives. It is, that is to say, in the strongest sense a "culture," but a culture which has also to be seen as the lived dominance and subordination of particular classes.

There are two immediate advantages in this concept of hegemony. First, its forms of domination and subordination correspond much more closely to the normal processes of social organization and control in developed societies than the more familiar projections from the idea of a ruling class, which are usually based on much earlier and simpler historical phases. It can speak, for example, to the realities of electoral democracy, and to the significant modern areas of "leisure" and "private life," more specifically and more actively than older ideas of domination, with their trivializing explanations of simple "manipulation," "corruption," and "betrayal." If the pressures and limits of a given form of domination are to this extent experienced *and in practice internalized*, the whole question of class rule, and of opposition to it, is transformed. Gramsci's emphasis on the creation of an alternative hegemony, by the practical connection of many different forms of struggle, including those not easily recognizable as and indeed not primarily "political" and "economic," thus leads to a much more profound and more active sense of revolutionary activity in a highly developed society than the persistently abstract models derived from very different historical situations. The sources of any alternative hegemony are indeed difficult to define. For Gramsci they spring from the working class, but not this class as an ideal or abstract construction. What he sees, rather, is a working people which has, precisely, to become a class, and a potentially hegemonic class, against the pressures and limits of an existing and powerful hegemony.

Second, and more immediately in this context, there is a whole different way of seeing cultural activity, both as tradition and as practice. Cultural work and activity are not now, in any ordinary sense, a superstructure: not only because of the depth and thoroughness at which any cultural hegemony is lived, but because cultural tradition and practice are seen as much more than superstructural expressions—reflections, mediations, or typifications—of a formed social and economic structure. On the contrary, they are among the basic processes of the formation itself and, further, related to a much wider area of reality than the abstractions of "social" and "economic" experience. People seeing themselves and each other in directly personal relationships; people seeing the natural world and themselves in it; people using their physical and material resources for what one kind of society specializes to "leisure" and "entertainment" and "art": all these active experiences and practices, which make up so much of the reality of a culture and its cultural production, can be seen as they are, without reduction to other categories of content, and without the characteristic straining to fit them (directly as reflection, indirectly as mediation or typification or analogy) to other and determining manifest economic and political relationships. Yet they can still be seen as elements of a hegemony: an inclusive social and cultural formation which indeed to be effective has to extend to and include, indeed to form and be formed from, this whole area of lived experience.

Many difficulties then arise, both theoretically and practically, but it is important to recognize how many blind alleys we may now be saved from entering. If any lived culture is necessarily so extensive, the problems of domination and subordination on the one hand, and of the extraordinary complexity of any actual cultural tradition and practice on the other, can at last be directly approached.

There is of course the difficulty that domination and subordination, as effective descriptions of cultural formation, will, by many, be refused; that the alternative language of co-operative shaping, of common contribution, which the traditional concept of "culture" so notably expressed, will be found preferable. In this fundamental choice there is no alternative, from any socialist position, to recognition and emphasis of the massive historical and immediate experience of class domination and subordination, in all their different forms. This becomes, very quickly, a matter of specific experience and argument. But there is a closely related problem within the concept of "hegemony" itself. In some uses, though not I think in Gramsci, the totalizing tendency of the concept, which is significant and indeed crucial, is converted into an abstract totalization, and in this form it is readily compatible with sophisticated senses of "the superstructure" or even "ideology." The hegemony, that is, can be seen as more uniform, more static, and more abstract than in practice, if it is really understood, it can ever actually be. Like any other Marxist concept it is particularly susceptible to epochal as distinct from historical definition, and to categorical as distinct from substantial description. Any isolation of its "organizing principles," or of its "determining features," which have indeed to be grasped in experience and by analysis, can lead very quickly to a totalizing abstraction. And then the problems of the reality of domination and subordination, and of their relations to co-operative shaping and common contribution, can be quite falsely posed.

A lived hegemony is always a process. It is not, except analytically, a system or a structure. It is a realized complex of experiences, relationships, and activities, with specific and changing pressures and limits. In practice, that is, hegemony can never be singular. Its internal structures are highly complex, as can readily be seen in any concrete analysis. Moreover (and this is crucial, reminding us of the necessary thrust of the concept), it does not just passively exist as a form of dominance. It has continually to be renewed, recreated, defended, and modified. It is also continually resisted, limited, altered, challenged by pressures not at all its own. We have then to add to the concept of hegemony the concepts of counter-hegemony and alternative hegemony, which are real and persistent elements of practice.

One way of expressing the necessary distinction between practical and abstract senses within the concept is to speak of "the hegemonic" rather than the "hegemony," and of "the dominant" rather than simple "domination." The reality of any hegemony, in the extended political and cultural sense, is that, while by definition it is always dominant, it is never either total or exclusive. At any time, forms of alternative or directly oppositional politics and culture exist as significant elements in the society. We shall need to explore their conditions and their limits, but their active presence is decisive, not only because they have to be included in any historical (as distinct from epochal) analysis, but as forms which have had significant effect on the hegemonic process itself. That is to say, alternative political and cultural emphases, and the many forms of opposition and struggle, are important not only in themselves but as indicative features of what the hegemonic process has in practice had to work to control. A static hegemony, of the kind which is indicated by abstract totalizing definitions of a dominant "ideology" or "worldview," can ignore or isolate such alternatives and opposition, but to the extent that they are significant the decisive hegemonic function is to control or transform or even incorporate them. In this active process the hegemonic has to be seen as more than the simple transmission of an (unchanging) dominance. On the contrary, any hegemonic process must be especially alert and responsive to the alternatives and opposition which question or threaten its dominance. The reality of cultural process must then always include the efforts and contributions of those who are in one way or another outside or at the edge of the terms of the specific hegemony.

Thus it is misleading, as a general method, to reduce all political and cultural initiatives and contributions to the terms of the hegemony. That is the reductive consequence of the radically different concept of "superstructure." The specific functions of "the hegemonic," "the dominant," have always to be stressed, but not in ways which suggest any *a priori* totality. The most interesting and difficult part of any cultural analysis, in complex societies, is that which seeks to grasp the hegemonic in its active and formative but also its transformational processes. Works of art, by their substantial and general character, are often especially important as sources of this complex evidence.

The major theoretical problem, with immediate effect on methods of analysis, is to distinguish between alternative and oppositional initiatives and contributions which are made within or against a specific hegemony (which then sets certain limits to them or which can succeed in neutralizing, changing, or actually incorporating them) and other kinds of initiative and contribution which are irreducible to the terms of the original or the adaptive hegemony, and are in that sense independent. It can be persuasively argued that all or nearly all initiatives and contributions, even when they take on manifestly alternative or oppositional forms, are in practice tied to the hegemonic: that the dominant culture, so to say, at once produces and limits its own forms of counter-culture. There is more evidence for this view (for example in the case of the Romantic critique of industrial civilization) than we usually admit. But there is evident variation in specific kinds of social order and in the character of the consequent alternative and oppositional formations. It would be wrong to overlook the importance of works and ideas which while clearly affected by hegemonic limits and pressures, are at least in part significant breaks beyond them, which may again in part be neutralized, reduced, or incorporated, but which in their most active elements nevertheless come through as independent and original.

Thus cultural process must not be assumed to be merely adaptive, extensive, and incorporative. Authentic breaks within and beyond it, in specific social conditions which can vary from extreme isolation to pre-revolutionary breakdowns and actual revolutionary activity, have often in fact occurred. And we are better able to see this, alongside more general recognition of the insistent pressures and limits of the hegemonic, if we develop modes of analysis which instead of reducing works to finished products, and activities to fixed positions, are capable of discerning, in good faith, the finite but significant openness of many actual initiatives and contributions. The finite but significant openness of many works of art, as signifying forms making possible but also requiring persistent and variable signifying responses, is then especially relevant.

TRADITIONS, INSTITUTIONS, AND FORMATIONS

Hegemony is always an active process, but this does not mean that it is simply a complex of dominant features and elements. On the contrary, it is always a more or less adequate organization and interconnection of otherwise separated and even disparate meanings, values, and practices, which it specifically incorporates in a significant culture and an effective social order. These are themselves living resolutions—in the broadest sense, political resolutions—of specific economic realities. This process of incorporation is of major cultural importance. To understand it, but also to understand the material on which it must work, we need to distinguish three aspects of any cultural process, which we can call traditions, institutions, and formations.

The concept of tradition has been radically neglected in Marxist cultural thought. It is usually seen as at best a secondary factor, which may at most modify other and more decisive historical processes. This is not only because it is ordinarily diagnosed as superstructure, but also because "tradition" has been commonly understood as a relatively inert, historicized segment of a social structure: tradition as the surviving past. But this version of tradition is weak at the very point where the incorporating sense of tradition is strong: where it is seen, in fact, as an actively shaping force. For tradition is in practice the most evident expression of the dominant and hegemonic pressures and limits. It is always more than an inert historicized segment; indeed it is the most powerful practical means of incorporation. What we have to see is not just "a tradition" but a selective *tradition*: an intentionally selective version of a shaping past and a pre-shaped present, which is then powerfully operative in the process of social and cultural definition and identification.

It is usually not difficult to show this empirically. Most versions of "tradition" can be quickly shown to be radically selective. From a whole possible area of past and present, in a particular culture, certain meanings and practices are selected for emphasis and certain other meanings and practices are neglected or excluded. Yet, within a particular hegemony, and as one of its decisive processes, this selection is presented and usually successfully passed off as "the tradition," "the significant past." What has then to be said about any tradition is that it is in this sense an aspect of *contemporary* social and cultural organization, in the interest of the dominance of a specific class. It is a version of the past which is intended to connect with and ratify the present. What it offers in practice is a sense of *predisposed continuity*.

There are, it is true, weaker senses of "tradition," in explicit contrast to "innovation" and "the contemporary." These are often points of retreat for groups in the society which have been left stranded by some particular hegemonic development. All that is now left to them is the retrospective affirmation of "traditional values." Or, from an opposite position, "traditional habits" are isolated, by some current hegemonic development, as elements of the past which have now to be discarded. Much of the overt argument about tradition is conducted between representatives of these two positions. But at a deeper level the hegemonic sense of tradition is always the most active: a deliberately selective and connecting process which offers a historical and cultural ratification of a contemporary order.

It is a very powerful process, since it is tied to many practical continuities—families, places, institutions, a language—which are indeed directly experienced. It is also, at any time, a vulnerable process, since it has in practice to discard whole areas of significance, or reinterpret or dilute them, or convert them into forms which support or at least do not contradict the really important elements of the current hegemony. It is significant that much of the most accessible and influential work of the counter-hegemony is historical: the recovery of discarded areas, or the redress of selective and reductive interpretations. But this in turn has little effect unless the lines to the present, in the actual process of the selective tradition, are clearly and actively traced. Otherwise any recovery can be simply residual or marginal. It is at the vital points of *connection*, where a version of the past is used to ratify the present and to indicate directions for the future, that a selective tradition is at once powerful and vulnerable. Powerful because it is so skilled in making active selective connections, dismissing those it does not want as "out of date" or "nostalgic," attacking those it cannot incorporate as "unprecedented" or "alien." Vulnerable because the real record is effectively recoverable, and many of the alternative or opposing practical continuities are still available. Vulnerable also because the selective version of "a living tradition" is always tied, though often in complex and hidden ways, to explicit contemporary pressures and limits. Its practical inclusions and exclusions are selectively encouraged or discouraged, often so effectively that the deliberate selection is made to verify itself in practice. Yet its selective privileges and interests, material in substance but often ideal in form, including complex elements of style and tone and of basic method, can still be recognized, demonstrated, and broken. This struggle for and against selective traditions is understandably a major part of all contemporary cultural activity.

It is true that the effective establishment of a selective tradition can be said to depend on identifiable institutions. But it is an underestimate of the process to suppose that it depends on institutions alone. The relations between cultural, political, and economic institutions are themselves very complex, and the substance of these relations is a direct indication of the character of the culture in the wider sense. But it is never only a question of formally identifiable institutions. It is also a question of *formations*; those effective movements and tendencies, in intellectual and artistic life, which have significant and sometimes decisive influence on the active development of a culture, and which have a variable and often oblique relation to formal institutions.

Formal institutions, evidently, have a profound influence on the active social process. What is abstracted in orthodox sociology as "socialization" is in practice, in any actual society, a specific kind of incorporation. Its description as "socialization," the universal abstract process on which all human beings can be said to depend, is a way of avoiding or hiding this specific content and intention. Any process of socialization of course includes things that all human beings have to learn, but any specific process ties this necessary learning to a selected range of meanings, values, and practices which, in the very closeness of their association with necessary learning, constitute the real foundations of the hegemonic. In a family, children are cared for and taught to care for themselves, but within this necessary process fundamental and selective attitudes to self, to others, to a social order, and to the material world are both consciously and unconsciously taught. Education transmits necessary knowledge and skills, but always by a particular selection from the whole available range, and with intrinsic attitudes, both to learning and social relations, which are in practice virtually inextricable. Institutions such as churches are explicitly incorporative. Specific communities and specific places of work, exerting powerful and immediate pressures on the conditions of living and of making a living, teach, confirm, and in most cases finally enforce selected meanings, values, and activities. To describe the effect of all institutions of these kinds is to arrive at an important but still incomplete understanding of incorporation. In modern societies we have to add the major communications systems. These materialize selected news and opinion, and a wide range of selected perceptions and attitudes.

Yet it can still not be supposed that the sum of all these institutions is an organic hegemony. On the contrary, just because it is not "socialization" but a specific and complex hegemonic process, it is in practice full of contradictions and of unresolved conflicts. This is why it must not be reduced to the activities of an "ideological state apparatus." Such apparatus exists, although variably, but the whole process is much wider, and is in some important respects self-generating. By selection it is possible to identify common features in family, school, community, work, and communications, and these are important. But just because they are specific processes, with variable particular purposes, and with variable but always effective relations with what must in any case, in the short term, be done, the practical consequence is as often confusion and conflict between what are experienced as different purposes and different values, as it is crude incorporation of a theoretical kind. An effective incorporation is usually in practice achieved; indeed to establish and maintain a class society it must be achieved. But no mere training or pressure is truly hegemonic. The true condition of hegemony is effective *self-identification* with the hegemonic forms: a specific and internalized "socialization" which is expected to be positive but which, if that is not possible, will rest on a (resigned) recognition of the inevitable and the necessary. An effective culture, in this sense, is always more than the sum of its institutions: not only because these can be seen, in analysis, to derive much of their character from it, but mainly because it is at the level of a whole culture that the crucial *interrelations*, including confusions and conflicts, are really negotiated.

This is why, in any analysis, we have also to include *formations*. These are most recognizable as conscious movements and tendencies (literary, artistic, philosophical or scientific) which can usually be readily discerned after their formative productions. Often, when we look further, we find that these are articulations of much wider effective formations, which can by no means be wholly identified with formal institutions, or their formal meanings and values, and which can sometimes even be positively contrasted with them. This factor is of the greatest importance for the understanding of what is habitually specialized as intellectual and artistic life. In this fundamental relation between the institutions and formations of a culture there is great historical variability, but it is generally characteristic of developed complex societies that formations, as distinct from institutions, play an increasingly important role. Moreover, since such formations relate, inevitably, to real social structures, and yet have highly variable and often oblique relations with formally discernible social institutions, any social and cultural analysis of them requires procedures radically different from those developed for institutions. What is really being analyzed, in each case, is a mode of specialized practice. Moreover, within an apparent hegemony, which can be readily described in generalizing ways, there are not only alternative and oppositional formations (some of them, at certain historical stages, having become or in the process of becoming alternative and oppositional institutions) but, within what can be recognized as the dominant, effectively varying formations which resist any simple reduction to some generalized hegemonic function.

It is at this point, normally, that many of those in real contact with such formations and their work retreat to an indifferent emphasis on the complexity of cultural activity. Others altogether deny (even theoretically) the relation of such formations and such work to the social process and especially the material social process. Others again, when the historical reality of the formations is grasped, render this back to ideal constructions—national traditions, literary and artistic traditions, histories of ideas, psychological types, spiritual archetypes—which indeed acknowledge and define formations, often much more substantially than the usual generalizing accounts of explicit social derivation or superstructural function, but only by radically displacing them from the immediate cultural process. As a result of this displacement, the formations and their work are not seen as the active social and cultural substance that they quite invariably are. In our own culture, this form of displacement, made temporarily or comparatively convincing by the failures of derivative and superstructural interpretation, is itself, and quite centrally, hegemonic.

DOMINANT, RESIDUAL, AND EMERGENT

The complexity of culture is to be found not only in its variable processes and their social definitions—traditions, institutions, and formations—but also in the dynamic interrelations, at every point in the process, of historically varied and variable elements. In what I have called "epochal" analysis, a cultural process is seized as a cultural system, with determinate dominant features: feudal culture or bourgeois culture or a transition from one to the other. This emphasis on dominant and definitive lineaments and features is important and often, in practice, effective. But it then often happens that its methodology is preserved for the very different function of historical analysis, in which a sense of movement within what is ordinarily abstracted as a system is crucially necessary, especially if it is to connect with the future as well as with the past. In authentic historical analysis it is necessary at every point to recognize the complex interrelations between movements and tendencies both within and beyond a specific and effective dominance. It is necessary to examine how these relate to the whole cultural process rather than only to the selected and abstracted dominant system. Thus "bourgeois culture" is a significant generalizing description and hypothesis, expressed within epochal analysis by fundamental comparisons with "feudal culture" or "socialist culture." However, as a description of cultural process, over four or five centuries and in scores of different societies, it requires immediate historical and internally comparative differentiation. Moreover, even if this is acknowledged or practically carried out, the "epochal" definition can exert its pressure as a static type against which all real cultural process is measured, either to show "stages" or "variations" of the type (which is still historical analysis) or, at its worst, to select supporting and exclude "marginal" or "incidental" or "secondary" evidence.

Such errors are avoidable if, while retaining the epochal hypothesis, we can find terms which recognize not only "stages" and "variations" but the internal dynamic relations of any actual process. We have certainly still to speak of the "dominant" and the "effective," and in these senses of the hegemonic. But we find that we have also to speak, and indeed with further differentiation of each, of the "residual" and the "emergent," which in any real process, and at any moment in the process, are significant both in themselves and in what they reveal of the characteristics of the "dominant."

By "residual" I mean something different from the "archaic," though in practice these are often very difficult to distinguish. Any culture includes available elements of its past, but their place in the contemporary cultural process is profoundly variable. I would call the "archaic" that which is wholly recognized as an element of the past, to be observed, to be examined, or even on occasion to be consciously "revived," in a deliberately specializing way. What I mean by the "residual" is very different. The residual, by definition, has been effectively formed in the past, but it is still active in the cultural process, not only and often not at all as an element of the past, but as an effective element of the present. Thus certain experiences, meanings, and values which cannot be expressed or substantially verified in terms of the dominant culture are nevertheless lived and practiced on the basis of the residue—cultural as well as social—of some previous social and cultural institution or formation. It is crucial to distinguish this aspect of the residual, which may have an alternative or even oppositional relation to the dominant culture, from that active manifestation of the residual (this being its distinction from the archaic) which has been wholly or largely incorporated into the dominant culture. In three characteristic cases in contemporary English culture this distinction can become a precise term of analysis. Thus, organized religion is predominantly residual, but within this there is a significant difference between some practically alternative and oppositional meanings and values (absolute brotherhood, service to others without reward) and a larger body of incorporated meanings and values (official morality, or the social order of which the other-worldly is a separated neutralizing or ratifying component). Again, the idea of rural community is predominantly residual, but is in some limited respects alternative or oppositional to urban industrial capitalism, though for the most part it is incorporated, as idealization or fantasy, or as an exotic—residential or escape—leisure function of the dominant order itself. Again, in monarchy, there is virtually nothing that is actively residual (alternative or oppositional), but, with a heavy and deliberate additional use of the archaic, a residual function has been wholly incorporated as a specific political and cultural function—marking the limits as well as the methods—of a form of capitalist democracy.

A residual cultural element is usually at some distance from the effective dominant culture, but some part of it, some version of it—and especially if the residue is from some major area of the past—will in most cases have had to be incorporated if the effective dominant culture is to make sense in these areas. Moreover, at certain points the dominant culture cannot allow too much residual experience and practice outside itself, at least [not] without risk. It is in the incorporation of the actively residual—by reinterpretation, dilution, projection, discriminating inclusion and exclusion—that the work of the selective tradition is especially evident. This is very notable in the case of versions of "the literary tradition," passing through selective versions of the character of literature to connecting and incorporated definitions of what literature now is and should be. This is one among several crucial areas, since it is in some alternative or even oppositional versions of what literature is (has been) and what literary experience (and in one common derivation, other significant experience) is and must be, that, against the pressures of incorporation, actively residual meanings and values are sustained.

By "emergent" I mean, first, that new meanings and values, new practices, new relationships and kinds of relationship are continually being created. But it is exceptionally difficult to distinguish between those which are really elements of some new phase of the dominant culture (and in this sense "species specific") and those which are substantially alternative or oppositional to it: emergent in the strict sense, rather than merely novel. Since we are always considering relations within a cultural process, definitions of the emergent, as of the residual, can be made only in relation to a full sense of the dominant. Yet the social location of the residual is always easier to understand, since a large part of it (though not all) relates to earlier social formations and phases of the cultural process, in which certain real meanings and values were generated. In the subsequent default of a particular phase of a dominant culture there is then a reaching back to those meanings and values which were created in actual societies and actual situations in the past, and which still seem to have significance because they represent areas of human experience, aspiration, and achievement which the dominant culture neglects, undervalues, opposes, represses, or even cannot recognize.

The case of the emergent is radically different. It is true that in the structure of any actual society, and especially in its class structure, there is always a social basis for elements of the cultural process that are alternative or oppositional to the dominant elements. One kind of basis has been valuably described in the central body of Marxist theory: the formation of a new class, the coming to consciousness of a new class, and within this, in actual process, the (often uneven) emergence of elements of a new cultural formation. Thus the emergence of the working class as a class was immediately evident (for example, in nineteenth-century England) in the cultural process. But there was extreme unevenness of contribution in different parts of the process. The making of new social values and institutions far outpaced the making of strictly cultural institutions, while specific cultural contributions, though significant, were less vigorous and autonomous than either general or institutional innovation. A new class is always a source of emergent cultural practice, but while it is still, as a class, relatively subordinate, this is always likely to be uneven and is certain to be incomplete. For new practice is not, of course, an isolated process. To the degree that it emerges, and especially to the degree that it is oppositional rather than alternative, the process of attempted incorporation significantly begins. This can be seen, in the same period in England, in the emergence and then the effective incorporation of a radical popular press. It can be seen in the emergence and incorporation of working-class writing, where the fundamental problem of emergence is clearly revealed, since the basis of incorporation, in such cases, is the effective predominance of received literary forms—an incorporation, so to say, which already conditions and limits the emergence. But the development is always uneven. Straight incorporation is most directly attempted against the visibly alternative and oppositional class elements: trade unions, working-class political parties, working-class life styles (as incorporated into "popular" journalism, advertising, and commercial entertainment). The process of emergence, in such conditions, is then a constantly repeated, an always renewable, move beyond a phase of practical incorporation: usually made much more difficult by the fact that much incorporation looks like recognition, acknowledgement, and thus a form of acceptance. In this complex process there is indeed regular confusion between the locally residual (as a form of resistance to incorporation) and the generally emergent.

Cultural emergence in relation to the emergence and growing strength of a class is then always of major importance, and always complex. But we have also to see that it is not the only kind of emergence. This recognition is very difficult, theoretically, though the practical evidence is abundant. What has really to be said, as a way of defining important elements of both the residual and the emergent, and as a way of understanding the character of the dominant, is that *no mode of production and therefore no dominant social order and therefore no dominant culture ever in reality includes or exhausts all human practice, human energy, and human intention.* This is not merely a negative proposition, allowing us to account for significant things which happen outside or against the dominant mode. On the contrary it is a fact about the modes of domination, that they select from and consequently exclude the full range of human practice. What they exclude may often be seen as the personal or the private, or as the natural or even the metaphysical. Indeed it is usually in one or other of these terms that the excluded area is expressed, since what the dominant has effectively seized is indeed the ruling definition of the social.

It is this seizure that has especially to be resisted. For there is always, though in varying degrees, practical consciousness, in specific relationships, specific skills, specific perceptions, that is unquestionably social and that a specifically dominant social order neglects, excludes, represses, or simply fails to recognize. A distinctive and comparative feature of any dominant social order is how far it reaches into the whole range of practices and experiences in an attempt at incorporation. There can be areas of experience it is willing to ignore or dispense with: to assign as private or to specialize as aesthetic or to generalize as natural. Moreover, as a social order changes, in terms of its own developing needs, these relations are variable. Thus in advanced capitalism, because of changes in the social character of labor, in the social character of communications, and in the social character of decision-making, the dominant culture reaches much further than ever before in capitalist society into hitherto "reserved" or "resigned" areas of experience and practice and meaning. The area of effective penetration of the dominant order into the whole social and cultural process is thus now significantly greater. This in turn makes the problem of emergence especially acute, and narrows the gap between alternative and oppositional elements. The alternative, especially in areas that impinge on significant areas of the dominant, is often seen as oppositional and, by pressure, often converted into it. Yet even here there can be spheres of practice and meaning which, almost by definition from its own limited character, or in its profound deformation, the dominant culture is unable in any real terms to recognize. Elements of emergence may indeed be incorporated, but just as often the incorporated forms are merely facsimiles of the genuinely emergent cultural practice. Any significant emergence, beyond or against a dominant mode, is very difficult under these conditions; in itself and in its repeated confusion with the facsimiles and novelties of the incorporated phase. Yet, in our own period as in others, the fact of emergent cultural practice is still undeniable, and together with the fact of actively residual practice is a necessary complication of the would-be dominant culture.

This complex process can still in part be described in class terms. But there is always other social being and consciousness which is neglected and excluded: alternative perceptions of others, in immediate relationships; new perceptions and practices of the material world. In practice these are different in quality from the developing and articulated interests of a rising class. The relations between these two sources of the emergent—the class and the excluded social (human) area—are by no means necessarily contradictory. At times they can be very close and on the relations between them much in political practice depends. But culturally, and as a matter of theory, the areas can be seen as distinct.

What matters, finally, in understanding emergent culture, as distinct from both the dominant and the residual, is that it is never only a matter of immediate practice; indeed it depends crucially on finding new forms or adaptations of form. Again and again what we have to observe is in effect a pre-emergence, active and pressing but not yet fully articulated, rather than the evident emergence which could be more confidently named. It is to understand more closely this condition of pre-emergence, as well as the more evident forms of the emergent, the residual, and the dominant, that we need to explore the concept of structures of feeling.

NOTES

First appeared in 1977.

1. T. W. Adorno, "Thesen zur Kunstsoziologie," Kolner Zeitschrift fur Soziologie und Soziopsychologie, xix, 1 (March 1967).

LINDA ALCOFF is professor of philosophy at Syracuse University.

SALLY ALEXANDER teaches cultural studies at the University of East London. She has written on feminism and women's work in nineteenth- and twentieth-century Britain. She is an editor of *History Workshop Journal*.

TONY BENNETT is dean in the Division of Humanities at Griffith University, where he was also the founding director of the Institute for Cultural Policy Studies. He is the author of *Formalism and Marxism* (Routledge, 1979), *Bond and Beyond: The Political Hero of a Popular Hero* (with Janet Wollacott) (Routledge, 1986), and *Outside Literature* (Routledge, 1990). He is presently completing a study of museums, to be published under the title *Show and Tell: The Museum, the Fair and the Exhibition*.

PIERRE BOURDIEU is professor of sociology at the Collège de France, Paris, and director of studies at L'Ecole des hautes étudies. His books include *Outline of a Theory of Practice* (Cambridge University Press, 1977), *Homo Academicus* (Stanford University Press, 1987), *Distinctions* (Harvard University Press, 1984), *Language and Symbolic Power* (Harvard University Press, 1991), and *Toward a Reflexive Sociology* (with Loic Wacquant) (University of Chicago Press, 1992).

NICHOLAS DIRKS is professor of history and anthropology at the University of Michigan. He is the author of *The Hollow Crown* (Cambridge University Press, 1987) and the editor of *Colonialism and Culture* (University of Michigan Press, 1992). He is currently working on a study of colonial discourse and postcolonial political culture in India.

GEOFF ELEY is professor of history at the University of Michigan. He is the author of *From Unification to Nazism: Reinterpreting the German Past* (Unwin Hyman, 1986) and *Reshaping the German Right: Radical Nationalism and Political Change after Bismarck* (Yale University Press, 1980). He is finishing a book on the European Left from the mid-nineteenth century to the present.

MICHEL FOUCAULT was professor of the history of systems of ideas at the Collège de France until his death in 1984. His books include *Madness and Civilization* (1988), *The Order of Things* (1973), *The Archaeology of Knowledge* (1972), *The Birth of the Clinic* (1974), *Discipline and Punish* (1979), and *The History of Sexuality* (1980).

HENRY LOUIS GATES, JR., is director of African American studies and professor of English at Harvard University. He is the author of *Signifying Monkey: A Theory of Afro-American Literary Criticism* (Oxford University Press, 1989) and *Figures in Black: Words, Signs, and the Racial "Self"* (Oxford University Press, 1989).

STEPHEN GREENBLATT is professor of English at the University of California, Berkeley. He is the author of *Shakespearean Negotiations* (University of California Press, 1989) and, most recently, of *Marvelous Possessions: The Wonder of the New World* (University of Chicago Press, 1991).

RANAJIT GUHA is senior research fellow at the Australian National University. He is the author of *Elementary Aspects of Peasant Insurgency in Colonial India* (Oxford,

1983) and *A Rule of Property for Bengal: An Essay on the Idea of Permanent Settlement* (Longman, 1982).

STUART HALL is professor of sociology at the Open University. He is the author of *Drifting into a Law and Order Society* (NCCL UK, 1988) and *The Hard Road to Renewal: Thatcherism and the Crisis of the Left* (Verso, 1988) and the editor of *New Times: The Changing Face of Politics in the 1990s* (Routledge, 1991).

DONNA HARAWAY is a professor in the History of Consciousness program at the University of California, Santa Cruz, where she teaches feminist theory, technoscience studies, and women's studies. She is the author of *Crystals, Fabrics, and Fields: Metaphors of Organicism in Twentieth-Century Developmental Biology* (Yale University Press, 1976), *Primate Visions: Gender, Race, and Nature in the World of Modern Science* (Routledge, 1989), and *Simians, Cyborgs, and Women: The Reinvention of Nature* (Routledge and Free Association Books, 1991).

SUSAN HARDING is professor of anthropology at the University of California, Santa Cruz. She is the author of *Remaking Ibieca* (University of North Carolina Press, 1984) and is currently completing a book on the born-again community of Liberty Baptist Church in Lynchburg, Va.

DICK HEBDIGE is dean of critical studies at the California Institute of the Arts. He is the author of *Subculture: The Meaning of Style* (Methuen, 1979), *Cut 'n' Mix: Culture, Identity, and Caribbean Music* (Routledge, 1987), and *Hiding in the Light: On Images and Things* (Routledge, 1988).

SUSAN MCCLARY is professor of musicology at McGill University in Montreal. She is the author of *Feminine Endings: Music, Gender, and Sexuality* (University of Minnesota Press, 1991) and *George Bizet's Carmen* (Cambridge University Press, 1992). She is currently working on a book entitled *Power and Desire in Seventeenth-Century Music*.

SHERRY B. ORTNER is professor of anthropology at the University of Michigan. She is the author of *Sherpas through their Rituals* (Cambridge University Press, 1978) and *High Religion: A Cultural and Political History of Sherpa Buddhism* (Princeton University Press, 1989) and the coeditor (with Harriet Whitehead) of *Sexual Meanings* (Cambridge University Press, 1988). She is working on a study of class and culture in the contemporary United States.

MARSHALL SAHLINS is professor of anthropology at the University of Chicago. He is the author of, among other books, *Islands of History* (University of Chicago Press, 1976) and *Culture and Practical Reason* (University of Chicago Press, 1985).

ELIZABETH G. TRAUBE is professor of anthropology at Wesleyan University. She has studied ritual and society in East Timor and is presently researching the production and reception of mass cultural narratives in the United States. She is the author of *Cosmology and Social Life: Ritual Exchange among the Mambi of East Timor* (University of Chicago Press, 1987) and *Dreaming Identities: Class, Gender, and Generation in 1980s Hollywood Movies* (Westview, 1992).

RAYMOND WILLIAMS was professor of drama and fellow of Jesus College, Cambridge, until his death in 1988. He is the author of *Marxism and Literature* (Oxford University Press, 1977), *Culture and Society* (Columbia University Press, 1983), *The Country and the City* (Oxford University Press, 1975), and *Keywords* (Oxford University Press, 1976).

JUDITH WILLIAMSON is the author of *Consuming Passions: Politics and Images of Popular Culture* (Marion Boyars, 1985) and *Decoding Advertisements: Ideology and Meaning in Advertisement* (Marion Boyars, 1984).